William Buell Sprague

Annals of the American Associate, Associate Reformed, and Reformed Presbyterian Pulpit

Or, commemorative notices of distinguished clergymen of these denominations in the United States

William Buell Sprague

Annals of the American Associate, Associate Reformed, and Reformed Presbyterian Pulpit
Or, commemorative notices of distinguished clergymen of these denominations in the United States

ISBN/EAN: 9783337295547

Printed in Europe, USA, Canada, Australia, Japan

Cover: Foto ©ninafisch / pixelio.de

More available books at **www.hansebooks.com**

ANNALS

OF THE

AMERICAN ASSOCIATE, ASSOCIATE REFORMED,

AND

REFORMED PRESBYTERIAN PULPIT;

OR,

COMMEMORATIVE NOTICES

OF

DISTINGUISHED CLERGYMEN

OF THESE

DENOMINATIONS IN THE UNITED STATES,

FROM THEIR COMMENCEMENT TO THE CLOSE OF THE YEAR EIGHTEEN HUNDRED AND FIFTY-FIVE.

WITH HISTORICAL INTRODUCTIONS.

BY WILLIAM B. SPRAGUE, D. D.

NEW YORK:
ROBERT CARTER & BROTHERS,
530 BROADWAY.
1869.

Cambridge: Presswork by John Wilson and Son.

ASSOCIATE.

PREFATORY NOTE

In writing the following sketches, I have made free use of a volume, published in 1839, by the Rev. James P. Miller, entitled "Biographical Sketches and Sermons of Some of the First Ministers of the Associate Church in America; to which is prefixed an Historical Introduction," &c. I am also indebted to the lamented author of this volume for the use of some other valuable biographical material, which had not been embodied in his printed work. Dr. Beveridge, than whom I believe there is no better authority, has responded to my numerous applications with the utmost promptness and cordiality. From Drs. Alexander and Peter Bullions, both of whom are now among the lamented dead, I have received very important aid; as also from Rev. Dr. McElwee, the Rev. Dr. J. T. Cooper, and my much esteemed neighbour, the Rev. Mr. Morrow. To the Rev. Dr. Thomas Goodwillie I am under great obligation for large quantities of manuscript, containing the results of his researches through his father's voluminous correspondence, and shedding much light on the history of many of the earlier ministers. What my obligations are, and what those of the Christian public are, to the Rev. Dr. McClelland, those who read his letter upon Dr. Anderson, will be able to judge. And finally, I must mention, with special gratitude, Mr. John McAllister, of Philadelphia, who, though not, for many years past, connected with the Associate Church, had his early training and associations there, and has been in relations, more or less intimate, with many of its more distinguished ministers. He has met all my requests in the most satisfactory manner, and with a graceful readiness equally creditable to the kindness of his heart, and his hereditary veneration for the Church of his fathers. The sketches themselves will reveal the names of many others, who have been important helpers to me in this enterprise, and to each of whom I beg now to offer my hearty thanks.

W. B. S.

HISTORICAL INTRODUCTION.*

The Associate Church in North America had its origin in a petition of some individuals, who had migrated hither from Scotland and Ireland, to the Anti-burgher Associate Synod of Scotland, that they would send them some ministers, whose views of truth and duty were in accordance with those in which they had themselves been educated. In answer to this petition, Messrs. Alexander Gellatly and Andrew Arnot were sent to Pennsylvania in the year 1753; the former, with a view of settling permanently in this country, the latter to remain for only two years. Agreeably to instructions which they had received from the parent Synod, they proceeded, in November of the year in which they arrived, to constitute themselves a Presbytery, under the name of the Associate Presbytery of Pennsylvania. Their labours, though attended, in the beginning, by many adverse circumstances, were yet, in a good degree, successful; and it was not long before applications were made for their services from different parts of Pennsylvania, and from New York, Delaware, Virginia and North Carolina.

Mr. Arnot returned to Scotland at the end of two years, and Mr. Gellatly died after being in the country seven years; but others came in their places, and, at the commencement of the Revolutionary War, the number had increased to thirteen. On the 20th of May, 1776, the Presbytery was divided,—the Ministers and Congregations in New York and farther East constituting what was called the Presbytery of New York, while those in Pennsylvania and farther South remained under the original designation,—the Presbytery of Pennsylvania.

There were, at this time, in the Province of Pennsylvania, three ministers belonging to that Body of dissenters from the Church of Scotland, known as "Reformed Presbyterians." It was proposed to form a union between these Ministers and the Associate Presbytery of Pennsylvania; and this was finally accomplished on the 13th of June, 1782, but not without great opposition, and only by the casting vote of the Moderator. The United Body denominated themselves the Associate Reformed Synod; but the portion of the Associate Presbytery that disapproved the measure continued their organization.

In consequence of this union, the Presbytery of Pennsylvania was reduced to two Ministers, with their Elders; and, as the Presbytery of

* Sketch of the Assoc. Ch. by Rev. Messrs. W. J. Cleland and J. P. Miller.—Hist. Introd. to Miller's Sketches and Sermons.—Church Memorial.

New York joined the union, these constituted the entire Associate Body in North America. The Ministers referred to were William Marshall of Philadelphia and James Clarkson of York County, Pa. The Synod of Scotland, however, soon sent over others to their assistance, and, ultimately, two of those who had at first joined the union abandoned it, and returned to the Presbytery of Pennsylvania.

In 1794, the Rev. John Anderson, D.D., of Beaver County, Pa., was appointed Professor of Theology, and continued to hold this office until 1819, when he resigned on account of the infirmities of age. In 1820 it was agreed to establish two Seminaries; one at Philadelphia, of which Dr. Banks was chosen Professor; and the other at Cannonsburg, of which Dr. Ramsay was chosen Professor the ensuing year. The death of Dr. Banks in 1826 terminated the Eastern Seminary, or rather the Eastern was united at that time with the Western, and Dr. Ramsay was afterwards chosen to the Professorship in the united institution. The duties of this office he discharged alone until 1835, when a second Professor was elected. At this time the average number of students was about twenty, though it afterwards increased to nearly double of that number.

Numerous applications for preaching being made to the Presbytery of Pennsylvania from Kentucky and Tennessee, the Presbytery recommended to the applicants to refer their request for missionaries immediately to the Synod of Scotland; and, having done so, two missionaries (the Rev. Messrs. Robert Armstrong and Andrew Fulton) were sent to Kentucky, with authority to constitute themselves into a Presbytery. These missionaries arrived in Kentucky in the spring of 1798, and, in November following, formed themselves, with Ruling Elders, into a Presbytery, by the name of the Presbytery of Kentucky.' This accession of strength enabled these Presbyteries to form themselves into a Synod; and, accordingly, the Synod, or Court of Review, designated as the Associate Synod of North America, had its first meeting at Philadelphia in May, 1801. The Synod consisted of seventeen Ministers, who were divided into four Presbyteries,—namely, of Philadelphia, of Chartiers, of Kentucky, and of Cambridge. Appeals might be taken from this Synod to that of Scotland until the year 1818; but at that time the General Associate Synod of Scotland declared it a co-ordinate Synod.

As early as the year 1800 the Associate Presbytery of Kentucky sent up a request to the Presbytery of Pennsylvania that there might be some public authoritative deliverance against the practice of slave-holding. The Presbytery complied with the request, declaring slave-holding to be a moral evil, and altogether incapable of justification; at the same time urging the duty of endeavouring to enlighten the public mind in respect to it. But as the brethren in Kentucky found their efforts in relation to this object, for the most part, unavailing, they resolved to relieve their consciences by leaving the State; and, accordingly, in 1804, they removed, with their congregations, to the adjoining free States of Ohio and Indiana.

As, however, there were Associate congregations in the States of Virginia, North Carolina, South Carolina and Tennessee, some of whose members were already becoming slave-holders, a petition was presented to the Synod, in 1808, by some of the emigrants from Kentucky to Ohio, that all persons of this description should be excluded from the communion of the Church. This led to the adoption of an Act by the Synod, in 1811, declaring it to be a moral evil to hold negroes in bondage, directing the members of the Church under their care to set them at liberty; or if this were, from any cause, impracticable, to treat them as if they were free in respect to food, clothing, instruction and wages; and those who refused to heed these directions they declared unworthy of the fellowship of the Church. It seems, however, that this Act never went extensively into effect; the consequence of which was that the Synod, in 1831, passed a yet more stringent Act, by which all slave-holders were, from that time, forbidden to approach the Lord's table. In 1840 a Letter was addressed by the Synod to the people in their connection living in the Carolinas, which had the effect of removing the last vestige of slave-holding from the Associate Church, and of leaving no trace of that Church throughout that entire region, with the exception of one or two churches in East Tennessee. The Synod, having had no very definite rules of Discipline, had an overture prepared, and sent down to the Presbyteries, which was enacted as a Book of Discipline, in 1817; but, being subsequently found defective, a substitute for it was adopted by the Synod in 1843.

About the year 1820 a union was attempted between the Associate Presbyterian Church and the Associate Reformed Synod of the West, who had separated from what was, at that time, the General Associate Reformed Synod, on account of the alleged latitudinarian principles of the latter; but, after considerable correspondence, which, for a time, seemed to indicate a favourable result, the attempt was abandoned.

In 1825 the Synod, apprehending that Hopkinsianism and Unitarianism, then known to be extensively prevalent in New England, might spread into other parts of the country, published a Warning against these systems, especially the former, which they regarded as a reproduction of the system of Pelagius.

The Associate Church engaged, at an early period, in the work of Missions; though her efforts were, for a long time, confined necessarily to the domestic field. Missionaries were very early sent to the Carolinas, who were instrumental in forming a Presbytery in that region. In 1822 two were sent to Canada West, who laboured for a short time in the region now occupied by the Presbytery of Stamford. In 1825 commenced a series of missions to Missouri and the Far West, the result of which has been the rapid and extensive growth of the Associate Church throughout that whole region. These missions have been sustained at an annual expense of six or seven thousand dollars, raised chiefly by contributions.

HISTORICAL INTRODUCTION.

In 1842 the Synod first moved in the work of Foreign Missions. Two missionaries (Messrs. Banks and Gordon) were appointed to labour in Trinidad; but Mr. Gordon soon died; and, though two or three other ministers, and some private members of the Church, went to labour in the same field, yet, in consequence of the unhealthfulness of the climate, the American missionaries all withdrew, leaving the work in the hands of a missionary of the United Presbyterian Church of Scotland, to whose support the Synod made a liberal contribution. They have since had a missionary in California, and two or three in Oregon; besides a Presbytery, consisting of three ministers, with their families, in Sialkot, Hindoostan.

About 1832 two ministers in the South,—one in Virginia, the other in South Carolina,—were subjected to discipline on account of their connection with Slavery, and, after retaining an independent position for several years, united with the Associate Reformed Synod of the South. A minister of the Presbytery of Miami also joined with a suspended member of the same Presbytery, and formed what they denominate the "Free Associate Presbytery of Miami." Between 1836 and 1840, certain difficulties agitated the Presbyteries of Cambridge, Albany and Vermont, which resulted in a division of the two former, and the withdrawment of all the members of the Presbytery of Vermont. These constituted themselves into a Synod, claiming to be the True Associate Synod of North America. A correspondence with a view to a re-union was opened in 1850, and continued till 1854, when the object was effected. In 1851 the brethren of the Reformed Dissenting Presbytery made overtures for a union with the Associate Church; and, after the requisite negotiation, the union was formed, a single member of the Presbytery only dissenting from the measure.

At this time the Associate Church consisted of 21 Presbyteries, 147 ordained Ministers, 274 Congregations, and 20,617 Communicants. In 1858, when the union with the General Synod of the Associate Reformed Church took place, there were 21 Presbyteries, 198 ordained ministers, 293 congregations and 23,505 communicants. The amount contributed to benevolent objects during the year was $12,588.93.

At the time of the union between the Associate and Associate Reformed Churches, there were in the Associate Church the following periodical publications:—The Evangelical Repository, Monthly, published at Philadelphia; The Presbyterian Witness, a Weekly newspaper, published at Cincinnati; and the Westminster Herald, a Weekly newspaper, published at New Wilmington, Lawrence County, Pa. The Herald was the continuation of the Friend of Missions, a small Weekly, published at Pittsburg.

The Associate Presbyterian Church of North America, being a branch of the Church of Scotland, has always held the doctrines of the Reformation as embodied in the standards of the Westminster Assembly. The Form of Presbyterial Church Government, and the Directory for Public Worship and for Family Worship, have also been recognized as authoritative by this Body. The twenty-third chapter of the Confession of Faith, respecting the relation of the Civil Magistrate to the Church, is received with some explanations, which are given in the Declaration and Testimony adopted and published by the Church. These explanations deny to the Civil Magistrate any right of control in the Church, as it respects either her doctrine or her discipline. This Church has always adhered, as a matter of principle, to the use of a literal poetic version of the Book of Psalms, in singing the praises of God. The "Declaration and Testimony," above referred to, contains an explanation and defence of some of the doctrines of the Confession of Faith, and states the prevailing errors against which the Church considers herself called upon to testify. To this Declaration and Testimony is prefixed a narrative of the leading facts in her history, and the reasons of her restricting her communion within her own bounds.

CHRONOLOGICAL INDEX.

[On the left hand of the page are the names of those who form the subjects of the work—the figures immediately preceding denote the period, as nearly as can be ascertained, when each began his ministry. On the right hand are the names of those who have rendered their testimony or their opinion in regard to the several characters.]

SUBJECTS.	WRITERS.	PAGE.
1753. Alexander Gellatly		1
1758. Matthew Henderson	Thomas Beveridge, D.D.	2
1763. William Marshall	Rev. James P. Miller / John McAllister, Esq.	7
1772. James Clarkson	Thomas Beveridge, D.D. / Rev. James P. Miller	15
1783. John Anderson, D.D.	Thomas Beveridge, D.D. / Alexander McClelland, D.D.	17
1784. Thomas Beveridge	Thomas Beveridge, D.D.	31
1788. David Goodwillie	Thomas Goodwillie, D.D. / Peter Bullions, D.D.	40
1788. Archibald Whyte	Thomas Goodwillie, D.D. / Peter Bullions, D.D.	47
1796. John Banks, D.D.	Alexander Bullions, D.D. / James M. Mathews, D.D.	52
1797. Andrew Fulton	Andrew Heron, D.D.	56
1798. Robert Armstrong	James Morrow, Esq. / Thomas Beveridge, D.D. / Andrew Heron, D.D.	58
1799. Francis Pringle	Thomas Goodwillie, D.D. / Hon. William B. McClure	64
1800. Thomas Allison	Rev. James P. Miller / Rev. John T. Brownlee	71
1801. Thomas Hamilton	James M. Mathews, D.D.	75
1803. James Ramsay, D.D.	Thomas Beveridge, D.D. / Rev. David G. Bullions / Rev. S. F. Morrow	77
1805. Joseph Shaw, LL.D.	Peter Bullions, D.D. / Hon. Archibald McIntyre	85
1806. Robert Bruce, D.D.	John Black, D.D. / Alexander Bullions, D.D. / Rev. Andrew Bower	90
1809. John Walker	Thomas Beveridge, D.D. / Rev. D. G. Bullions	95
1820. Andrew Stark, LL.D	Peter Bullions, D.D. / Rev. D. G. Bullions	101
1821. Abraham Anderson, D.D	William M. McElwee, D.D. / Robert Baird, D.D.	107
1822. James Martin, D.D.	Thomas Beveridge, D.D / Rev. S. F. Morrow	112
1823. David Carson	William M. McElwee, D.D.	117
1824. James Whyte	Hugh Mair, D.D. / Rev. D. G Bullions	121
1825. James Patterson Miller	Thomas Hanna, D.D. / Joseph T. Cooper, D.D / Rev. S. F. Morrow	126
1848. Thomas Beveridge Hanna	Rev. S. F. Morrow	132

ALEXANDER GELLATLY.*
1753—1761.

ALEXANDER GELLATLY was a native of Perth, Scotland, and was born about the year 1720. We know nothing of his history until the year 1752, when we find him a student of Theology in connection with the Antiburgher Synod of Scotland. That Synod had been urgently requested, by some of the inhabitants of the Eastern Counties of Pennsylvania, chiefly emigrants from Scotland and Ireland, to send missionaries among them, that they might enjoy Christian institutions in the same form to which they had been accustomed in their native country. With a view to meet this exigency, Mr. Gellatly was licensed to preach, and, as he was the first Missionary of the Associate Church to this country, he is justly entitled to the name of the Father of the Secession in the United States. He was accompanied hither by the Rev. Andrew Arnot, minister at Midholm, who, however, had leave to return, and actually did return, at the end of a year. They embarked early in the summer of 1753, and arrived here sometime before the close of the year.

Shortly after their arrival, agreeably to their instructions, they constituted themselves into a Presbytery, under the name of the Associate Presbytery of Pennsylvania, subordinate to the Associate Antiburgher Synod; and, after a division of the Synod into General and Provincial Synods, subordinate to the Associate Synod of Edinburgh. They soon became obnoxious to some of their brethren, who had occupied their field of labour before them, and the Presbytery of Newcastle, subordinate to the Synod of New York and Philadelphia, published a Warning against them, representing them in the light of schismatics and errorists. They also, at the same time, republished at Lancaster, Pa., a book by a Mr. Delap, which had appeared not long before in Ireland, in which he attacks the Associate Synod in respect to their religious covenant bond. These publications were answered by the Seceders, within a little more than a year after their arrival, in a work published at Lancaster, and entitled "A Detection of Injurious Reasonings and Unjust Representations." It consists of two parts. The first part is by Mr. Gellatly, "wherein," according to the title, "the injury done to truth, and the unjust representation of, and reflections upon, the conduct of the Associate Presbytery, by the Rev. Mr. Delap, in his remarks upon some of the articles mentioned in their confession of sins, and on the act of Presbytery concerning their terms of communion, are discovered." The second part was begun by Mr. Arnot before his return to Scotland, and finished by Mr. Gellatly. It purports to contain "a discovery of farther injury to the truth by the Presbytery of Newcastle, in their Judicial Warning and Appendix, and their unjust representation of the principles and practices of the Seceders." The whole work extends to two hundred and forty pages. An Answer to this soon appeared, by Messrs. R. Smith and S. Finley, entitled "The Detection Detected." This again was replied to in 1758, by Mr. Gellatly, in a volume of more than two hundred pages, under the following title:—"Some Observations upon a late piece entitled 'The Detection Detected, or a Vindication, etc.,' containing a discovery of the manner how the Rev. Messrs. S. Finley and

* The Church Memorial.—Miller's Sketches.

R. Smith, the authors of said piece, handle the Obligations of the National and Solemn League, the Nature of Faith, the Gospel Offer, and some other points; and showing that the Detection is not detected in the manner they pretend." There is a slight tinge of severity in Mr. Gellatly's writings, but they show considerable learning and ability.

Mr. Gellatly was settled at Middle Octorora, in Lancaster County, and Oxford, in Chester County, Pa. Here he laboured with great diligence during the remainder of his life. He died on the 12th of March, 1761, in the forty-second year of his age, and the eighth after his arrival in America. He left a widow and an infant daughter, neither of whom long survived him.

Mr. Gellatly was a man of vigorous intellect, of great wit, and of a gentle and amiable spirit. He never wavered in his adherence to what he belived to be truth, and never shrunk from any effort or sacrifice necessary to its defence. In the expression of his countenance, especially in the pulpit, there was a mingled mildness and majesty, that gave great effect to his evangelical utterances. He was an earnest, faithful, able minister of the Gospel.

MATTHEW HENDERSON.
1758—1795.
FROM THE REV. THOMAS BEVERIDGE, D.D.

CANNONSBURG, August 1, 1855.

Rev. and dear Brother:—I at length fulfill my promise to furnish you some account of the life and character of the Rev. Matthew Henderson. As it is now sixty years since his death, his contemporaries have nearly all passed away; but I have endeavoured to avail myself of the most authentic information concerning him within my reach. He is worthy of being commemorated in a more extended Memoir than it is possible should be written at this day.

MATTHEW HENDERSON was one of the earliest Missionaries of the Associate or Secession Church of Scotland to the United States, and was the pioneer of that Church in what was then regarded as the Western wilderness, embracing the Western part of Pennsylvania and the unknown region beyond. He was born in Fifeshire, Scotland, in the year 1735, and, according to the testimony of some members of his family, received his classical education at Glasgow College. He entered at an early period of life upon the study of Theology under the Rev. Alexander Moncreiff, one of the four first Seceders,—a man whose own theological course had been pursued under the celebrated John Mark, of Leyden, who was himself eminent in his day for learning, piety, courage and generosity. Mr. Moncrieff was called "the Lion" among the fathers of the Secession, and his pupil, Mr. Henderson, appears, in this respect, to have imbibed the spirit of his Preceptor. He was licensed at the early age of twenty-one; and was ordained two years afterwards, in the summer of 1758, by the Presbytery of Perth and Dunfermline, and was immediately sent across the Atlantic to strengthen the hands of the brethren who were labouring in Pennsylvania.

He was the third permanent Missionary, sent by the Associate Church to these then British Colonies; his predecessors having been Messrs. Alexander Gellatly and James Proudfit. His acceptance of this missionary appointment speaks highly in favour of his zeal and self denial in the cause of Christ. At this time a missionary appointment to the wilds of America was regarded as nearly equivalent to a banishment to Botany Bay. It was with the utmost difficulty that one or two, out of a large number appointed, could be prevailed on to accept of such a mission. The most rigorous measures were frequently employed, and even deposition from the ministry threatened, but all in vain. There is, however, no account of any reluctance on the part of Mr. Henderson, or any resort to coercive measures. He appears to have been willing to engage in the work assigned him, and to have possessed the adventurous, fearless, and hardy spirit which fitted him so peculiarly for a pioneer of the Gospel in the wilderness.

It was probably soon after his arrival in America that Mr. Henderson was settled at Oxford, Lancaster County, Pa., where he appears to have laboured upwards of twenty years. It is also probable that he had the pastoral care of at least one other place; as about one third or fourth of his manuscript sermons, written between the years 1777 and 1779, and preserved by his children, are marked "*Pen*," which is evidently a contraction for the name of a place, but what it was has not been ascertained. About three years after his coming to America, the Rev. Alexander Gellatly, the father of the Secession in the United States, died in the forty-second year of his age, having exercised his ministry eight years in Middle Octorora, not far from Oxford. By this event, which took place in 1761, Mr. Henderson was left with only two associates in the ministry,—Mr. James Proudfit, of Pequea, and Mr. Mason, the father of Dr. John M. Mason, of New York. These three, at this time, constituted the Presbytery of Pennsylvania, the only Court of the Associate Church then in this country.

Mr. Henderson appears to have continued in the pastoral charge of Oxford till about the year 1781. In the mean time he was married to Miss Mary Faris, and became the father of several children. His name appears, up to about this time, in meetings held with a view to the union of the Associate and Reformed Presbyteries. In the measures adopted to effect this union he took a decided part with Messrs. Marshall and Clarkson against what he considered the loose and ambiguous terms in which the union was at last consummated. And it is not unlikely that, had he been present when the union was effected, he would have joined the brethren in refusing to accede to it. But he had, in the mean time, been removed to a great distance, where he had not full opportunity of knowing the true state of things, and he, with his people, acceded for a time to the union. This event took place in 1782; and in 1789, having become dissatisfied with the newly organized Church, he made application to his former brethren of the Associate Presbytery of Pennsylvania, acknowledging his error in having withdrawn from their fellowship, and, agreeably to his request, he was restored. The proceedings on this occasion were published, and they evince a candid and ingenuous spirit on the part of Mr. Henderson, and a spirit of tenderness and faithfulness on the part of his brethren.

Mr. Henderson was, at this time, Pastor of the Associate Congregations of Chartiers and Buffalo, Washington County, Pa. To these places he removed, in compliance with a call, in 1782; though he appears to have visited this region as early as 1779. It is probable that he commenced the removal of his family to the West in the year 1781, or it may be 1782. After proceeding some distance, reports of the disturbances caused by the Indians reached them, and excited such an alarm that he left his family at Conegocheaque, and proceeded alone to his new charge. The family remained here about a year, in a very uncomfortable situation, having no better dwelling than a rude cabin. Nor was their condition in this respect greatly improved, when they were once more united by their removal to the scene of Mr. Henderson's labours.

For several years after Mr. Henderson's settlement in Chartiers, in 1782, he was the only Minister of the Associate Church West of the Mountains. In consequence of this he had the care of not only his own widely extended flock, but of several vacancies in the neighbourhood. Among these were Mingo and Mill Creek, to which congregations the Presbytery addressed letters, as well as to his own proper charge, at the time of his restoration to their fellowship.

His life was evidently one of much labour, as well as hardship. He was accustomed to write his sermons, at least partially, though not in a hand easily legible. The inscription on his tombstone bears witness that he never for once disappointed his people on the Sabbath. He attended diligently to the duties of catechising and visiting from house to house. And as he abounded in labours, so an evident blessing attended them. And, though the generation which enjoyed his ministrations have nearly all passed away, the continued flourishing state of the congregations in which he finished his labours, has, no doubt, been owing, in a great measure, to the character which his ministry had impressed upon them.

His voice was remarkable for its distinctness and power. In the summer season he usually preached in a tent, at the foot of a hill, which is now occupied as the grave-yard of the congregation. From the bottom to the top of the hill is about fifty rods, and yet not only the sound of his voice, but his words, could be heard distinctly at that distance. He, neither in conversation nor in the pulpit, laid aside the broad vernacular of his country. His manner of addressing his people was also, according to the custom of his native land, plain and familiar. He called them all simply by their proper names, like a father addressing his children. His reproofs of vanity or ill-behaviour, especially in the sanctuary, were sometimes plain, and even scathing, but not ill-natured. It has been related that, on one occasion, when a young female had made her appearance at church with a new dress, and had arisen several times to change her seat, or go out of the assembly, Mr. Henderson had noticed her movements, and, at last, having observed her rising once more, he said to her very calmly,—"That is the fourth time, my lass, that you have changed your seat. You can sit down now; we have a seen your braw new gown." The lass, to be sure, did not wait for a second invitation to be seated.

In his appearance Mr. Henderson was of a very swarthy complexion. He had a keen black eye, was of large size and very erect figure, and possessed great muscular power. An anecdote has been related of him, and sometimes erroneously attributed to others, which illustrates his great physical strength, and also the treatment to which even Ministers of the Gospel were exposed in those early times. On one occasion, when travelling over the Mountains to meet with his brethren in Presbytery, he happened to lodge at a tavern, where two men took the liberty of treating him with great rudeness. This he endured with much patience. His patience, however, was mistaken for timidity, and only encouraged their impertinence, till at last nothing would do but he must fight. This, of course, he was disposed to decline; but, whether he would or not, they were determined upon an assault. Seeing, at last, that he could not evade them, he arose, and deliberately stripping off his black coat, laid it aside, saying,—" Lie there, the Rev. Mr. Henderson, and now Matthew, defend yourself." So saying, he seized one of the men, and dashed him out through an open window; and was preparing to send the other by the same road to keep him in company. But this one, seeing the kind of man they had to deal with, was in no hurry to put himself in the way of such rough usage. Mr. Henderson, having thus taught them somewhat after the manner of Gideon's teaching the men of Succoth with the thorns and briars of the wilderness, passed the rest of the night in peace and quietness.

Mr. Henderson appears to have been peculiarly affectionate towards his family, and in all his intercourse with society. His numerous and scattered sheep rendered it necessary for him to be often absent from home, and frequently for a week or more at a time. But he would surmount almost any difficulty rather than cause uneasiness to his family by an absence beyond the appointed time. He expected a like punctuality on their part; and if the return of any absent member were delayed, he would ride ten miles or more to ascertain whether any accident had happened. The day before his death, he had been disappointed by the continued absence of Mrs. Henderson, and two of his daughters, who had been detained while on a visit to some friends at a distance. One of his daughters, however, returned during the day. He appeared to be much gratified at meeting her, and, having walked out with her to the place where he was killed the next morning, he gave her repeated charges, in case of his death, to be kind to her mother. This and some other occurrences seemed almost to indicate a presentiment that his end was at hand.

At the age of sixty he had become somewhat infirm, but not to such a degree as to interfere with his labours. His infirmities were no doubt occasioned by the hardships to which he had been exposed, and from which he took but little pains to protect himself. An aged member of the church who heard him once in his youth, when preaching in a tent during a shower, recollects that when some one was so kind as to hold an umbrella over his head, he respectfully declined the proffered favour, and proceeded in the services of the day, regardless of the rain. But, though fearless of other evils, he had been long troubled much with the fear of death—not so much with the fear of leaving the world as of the pains of dying; and it pleased a kind Providence to take him away in such a manner that he was exempted from the evils which he greatly feared. He was killed by the falling of a tree on the 2d of October, 1795, aged sixty years, and in the thirty-seventh year of his ministry, reckoning from the time of his Ordination.

The circumstances of his death, as related by the daughter who was with him at the time, are as follows:—On the evening of October 1st he had expressed to his children a wish that they would fell a bee-tree, which had been discovered on his farm; and preparations were accordingly made to proceed to it early in the morning. He had acquainted his daughter *Elizabeth*, then a child of ten years of age, of their purpose, and told her that, if she could get up in the morning without awaking her younger sister, *Jane*, she might go with him. Accordingly, the next morning, he went quietly to her bed, and touched her gently, to awake her without disturbing her sister. She was soon up and dressed for the expedition. Supposing her father to be also ready and waiting for her, she hastened forthwith to his room, but found him on his knees engaged in secret prayer, and immediately withdrew. After a little she observed him going down to the spring with a basin and towel to wash himself, as was his custom in the morning. Some time after he returned, she again ventured into his room, and again found him engaged in prayer. Soon afterwards he came out, and, taking her by the hand, led her to the place, where two of his sons had been for some time engaged in felling the tree. The tree stood upon a bank, and it was supposed would fall down the side of it. Mr. Henderson and his daughter approached towards it on the higher ground, where it was thought there was no danger. Here they stood, for a little time, at some distance from the tree, awaiting its fall. It proved to be decayed in the center, and fell much sooner than was anticipated, and in an opposite direction also. Mr. Henderson, notwithstanding repeated cautions given to him, would always, when a tree began to fall, run from it in a direction opposite to that in which he supposed it to be falling. On this occasion, as usual, he ran, but in the same direction with the falling of the tree. His daughter followed his example, but varied somewhat in her course, and escaped injury. Her father had run to such a distance that it was only the branches that reached him, and his body was but little mutilated. Only a slight flesh wound was found upon his head, yet he appeared to have died instantly, not having been observed to move or breathe by his sons who were immediately beside him.

Mr. Henderson was an earnest friend of education, and had an important agency in those incipient measures which finally resulted in the establishment of Jefferson College.

Mr. Henderson was blessed with a numerous family—in all, fourteen children. Of these, four died in infancy. The others lived to maturity, and a number of them to a great age. *Matthew*, his eldest son, was a very respectable minister of the Associate Reformed Church, and was for many years Pastor of a Congregation in the forks of Yough. *Ebenezer*,* his third son, was a minister of the Associate Church, and was about to be settled in Philadelphia when he died. He had given promise of much eminence in the ministry, and died much lamented. Two of Mr. Henderson's daughters and one son are still living.

I am very truly yours,
THOMAS BEVERIDGE.

---

* The Rev. Thomas Goodwillie has furnished the following additional particulars concerning Mr. EBENEZER HENDERSON:—"He was taken on trial for license to preach, May 25, 1799; and on trials for Ordination, May 12, 1800. In June, 1802, he accepted a call from Pittsburgh and Turtle Creek, and was settled over these churches in July following, and about the same time was married to a Miss Noble, of Octorora. According to appointment, he went on a mission to the Carolinas. He took a fever, and, being anxious to get home, continued to ride on horseback till he came to an inn in Staunton, Va., where he was so very ill and delirious that he could proceed no farther; and here he died among strangers. My brother and myself, in going on a mission to the Carolinas, stopped at the same inn in Staunton, in the beginning of May, 1824. An old lady in the inn recollected his death, and related to us the circumstances. In my journal I find I have written,—'Here we visited the grave of the Rev. Ebenezer Henderson, in the Presbyterian church yard. At the head of the grave there is a sand stone with this inscription:—' Here lies the body of the Rev. Ebenezer Henderson, a native of Pennsylvania, who departed this life September 17, 1804.' He had two children, a son and a daughter.'"

WILLIAM MARSHALL.
1763—1802.
FROM THE REV. JAMES P. MILLER.

SOUTH ARGYLE, N. Y., April 12, 1850.

Rev. and dear Sir; You ask me for a sketch of the late Rev. William Marshall of Philadelphia. I am quite willing to comply with your request, though, in doing so, I must be indebted chiefly to some notices of Mr. Marshall written shortly after his death by Mr. David Hogan, one of his intimate friends, and a Ruling Elder in his congregation in Philadelphia, during the whole period of his connection with it. I think it probable that this is now the only source of any extended information concerning him that can be relied on. A number of years ago, I made diligent inquiry among the members of the congregation to which he formerly ministered, for reminiscences concerning him; but I found only a solitary individual,—a very aged lady, who had any recollections of him; and those were so general as not to be worthy of special consideration.

WILLIAM MARSHALL was born about the year 1740, near Abernethy, in the County of Fife, Scotland. His father was a respectable farmer, and for many years an Elder in the Associate congregation, under the pastoral care of the Rev. Alexander Moncrieff, one of the four ministers who first seceded from the Church of Scotland.

Having gone through his preparatory studies, he was admitted into the Divinity Hall, under the inspection of Mr. Moncrieff, of whom he always spoke with affectionate regard. After attending the usual course of Lectures, he was taken under the care of the Associate Presbytery of Perth, with a view to his being licensed to preach the Gospel, and with the particular design of his being sent to America. His several discourses delivered before the Presbytery having been approved, he was in due time licensed to preach, and was immediately sent on a mission to Pennsylvania.

He landed in Philadelphia in August, 1763. In October, 1764, the congregation at Deep Run, Buck's County, gave him a call to become their Minister. The Congregations of Octorora and Muddy Creek also made out calls for him soon afterwards. These three calls were presented to the Presbytery that met, on the 1st of November, 1764, at Octorora. The Presbytery having referred it to Mr. Marshall to make his own selection, he accepted the call from Deep Run, giving, as reasons for doing so, the unanimity of the people, their having been formerly disappointed, and the fact that their local situation rendered it difficult for the Presbytery to supply them with preaching. He was, accordingly, ordained at Deep Run, on the 30th of August, 1765, the Sermon on the occasion being preached from John iii, 10, by the Rev. John Mason.

Petitions for supply of preaching being sent to the Presbytery from Philadelphia, Mr. Marshall preached there; and, in 1768, a call for him was presented to the Presbytery from the Congregation in Philadelphia, with reasons for his removal. After considerable delay, the Presbytery loosed him from his charge at Deep Run, on the 19th of April, 1769, and presented to him the call from Philadelphia, which he accepted with this limitation,—"that his installment be delayed till the Lord grant him further light about it." This was agreed to.

For two years after, he preached mostly in Philadelphia, and on the 30th of April, 1771, the pastoral relation between him and the congregation was fixed. Mr. Annan preached on the occasion from Isaiah liii, 11.

Mr. Marshall was the first of the Associate Presbytery that officiated in Philadelphia. The number of the people was small, and, as they had no place of worship, he preached in a vendue store. A small farm-house was afterwards occupied in Shippen street; but this being limited by deed to a congregation in connection with the Burghers, and a contest about the property being likely to ensue, it was resolved to build another place of worship. A lot of ground was purchased in Spruce Street, and the church erected in 1771. But the expense of the building far exceeded the ability of the people; and, notwithstanding the vigorous efforts of Mr. Marshall in collecting money, a heavy and embarrassing debt remained on the congregation for many years.

In the contest between Great Britain and her Colonies, Mr. Marshall was decidedly in favour of the latter. When the British took possession of Philadelphia in 1777, he was obliged to take refuge in the country, and for some time preached to the people of his former charge at Deep Run. His Congregation at Philadelphia suffered much at this time from the evils of War. The church was converted into a hospital for the Hessians; the pews were torn down and destroyed, and the windows nearly all broken; the people were scattered through the various parts of the country, and several of them never returned. A good deal of Mr. Marshall's furniture was carried off; so that, when the British left the city in 1778, he and the congregation had to begin the world anew; and it was some time before the church was fully repaired.

No transaction in which Mr. Marshall was ever engaged, was followed with so important consequences to himself, and to the Church with which he was connected in America, as the opposition he made to a union with the Reformed Presbytery, or, as they are commonly called, Covenanters.

From the commencement of the American Revolution, the ministers of the Associate Presbytery were unanimously in favour of it; and the ministers of the Reformed Presbytery took the same side. One difference between the two Bodies seemed thus to be done away; and a union was, accordingly, proposed. A conference on the subject was held in Lancaster County in 1777. Mr. Marshall, however, was opposed to this union from the beginning, on any plan but that of the Reformed Presbytery's giving an explicit approbation of the principles of the Associate Presbytery. He was against any compromise, or the drawing up of articles of union in terms of doubtful construction.

On the 13th of June, 1782, the union with the Reformed Presbytery was agreed upon by the casting vote of the moderator, Mr. Proudfit. The minority protested and appealed to the Synod in Scotland. This appeal being refused, Mr. Marshall read another protest,—taking the ground that the powers of the Associate Presbytery were vested in those who adhered to its true principles and constitution; and he, as Clerk, took up the minutes and papers of the Presbytery, and, with the minority, retired to the Session House, chose a new Moderator, and, having done some business, adjourned.

Mr. Marshall had the satisfaction to find the part he had taken approved by the Associate Synod, and the number of his adherents constantly increased. His situation in his own congregation, however, was not agreeable—some of his people, among whom were four or five Elders, leaned towards the union; and, though they attended his ministry, mutual jealousies arose, which finally issued in an open rupture.

In the beginning of 1786 a petition was produced at a meeting of Trustees, several of whom were Elders, to the Assembly of the State, to annul that clause in the Deed of Trust for the church which confined it to a congregation in subordination to the Associate Synod in Scotland; urging that this was improper on the ground that the Colonies were independent. The petition was carried through the congregation, and signed by a number of its members, and was afterwards presented to the Assembly. Mr. Marshall drew up a remonstrance against altering the Deed of Trust, which was also signed by his friends, and given in to the Assembly. Both parties were heard before a Committee of that Body. At length a bill was brought in which annulled the subordination to the Synod, and, besides, added a clause whereby church officers were obliged to take the oath of allegiance to the State. The Assembly threw out this last section; and, as was the mode at that time, postponed the third reading of the bill till their next session.

Matters were hastening to a crisis in the congregation. The Elders were cited to appear before their Presbytery, which met in Philadelphia on the 31st of May, 1786. Their conduct was voted censurable; but, before they proceeded to any censure, a paper was read, signed by four of the Elders, signifying that they neither were nor had been in connection with the Presbytery since 1782, but belonged to another denomination. After reading this paper, the Presbytery, on motion of Mr. Marshall, immediately proceeded to censure. They deposed four of the Elders, suspended one, and excluded all five from the fellowship of the church.

The excommunication, according to the Deed of Trust, deprived the Elders of their office as Trustees also; but they, in retaliation, resolved to hold their offices by force, and to expel Mr. Marshall. Accordingly, in a day or two, they sent him a written notice, forbidding him to enter the church. They barricaded the door and windows, and kept guard around the building. On the next Sabbath morning, Mr. Marshall, acting by legal advice, went to the church to demand entrance. He was met by the armed Elders and their adherents, and forbidden to enter; upon which he retired and preached in an adjoining building. The next Sabbath, the Elders procured a minister belonging to the Associate Reformed Synod, to preach in the church; they keeping guard as on the preceding Sabbath. Mr. Marshall went to the church for admittance, but was again met by the armed men. On being refused entrance, he read a paper protesting against any person occupying his pulpit, to which he had not forfeited his right. He then retired and preached as before.

Mr. Annan, within a few Sabbaths after Mr. Marshall had been thus violently kept out of his meeting-house, came on from Boston, and was employed to preach in it, under circumstances that induced the suspicion, on the part of Mr. Marshall and his friends, that the course which had been adopted might have been the result of collusion between him and the Elders. He was afterwards installed as Pastor in that meeting-house, and by the authority of Synod; but, as the effort to gather a congregation was less successful than had been expected, he left it, and removed from the city only a few weeks before Mr. Marshall's decease.

In consequence of these violent proceedings, Mr. Marshall instituted a suit for the recovery of his meeting-house. In the mean time, the Trustees of the

College unanimously granted him their Hall to preach in, until the case was determined. Here he continued about five years, until his new church was finished.

At the session of the Legislature in the fall of 1786, the Bill for breaking the Deed of Trust was again taken up; and a renewed opposition made to it by Mr. Marshall, principally on the ground that the contest was at issue in the Supreme Court. The Bill, however, passed into a law; but not without considerable opposition from several of the members of Assembly, who even entered a protest against it.

Able lawyers were employed on both sides in the trial before the Supreme Court. A mandamus was issued, ordering the Trustees to restore the pulpit to Mr. Marshall, or show cause why they would not. Their answer to the order in substance was, "that Mr. Marshall, being in a minority in the vote about closing the Union, schismatically separated from the Presbytery, and appealed to a Foreign Synod, to which Americans are not subject; that the Presbytery, in consequence of this conduct, by their warning, dismissed him from his pastoral charge; and that, therefore, he had no right to the pulpit; and therefore could not be restored." To this plea Mr. Marshall put in a replication that "the church was for the use of the congregation, under the inspection of the Associate Presbytery, as said Presbytery is subordinate to the Associate Synod of Edinburgh; and that he was not dismissed from the pastoral care of the congregation in June, 1782, nor deposed according to the form of discipline in use among Presbyterians.'

The plea and reply came before a Jury, in January, 1789. Clergymen of various denominations were brought before the Court, or their depositions read, in order to give information about various ecclesiastical matters that occurred in the cause. The Court, in the charge to the Jury, said it was a new case in law and fact, and that they must decide according to the first principles of reason. No decision was given at this trial, as the Jury was equally divided. The case was again brought up in July, 1790. The pleadings of the lawyers were able and eloquent. Judges McKean and Rush, who were on the bench, gave opposite charges to the Jury. The verdict was against Mr. Marshall.

This was a period in Mr. Marshall's life, in which he suffered much reproach, vexation and loss. He had always had a very slender income,—not quite two hundred and twenty dollars; but, notwithstanding his own poverty, and that of his congregation, and though he was in the decline of life and without a place for public worship, yet he does not seem to have been at all discouraged, but to have borne his adversities with firmness and resolution.

The congregation resolved immediately to erect a new house for the worship of God, purchased a lot in a central situation, and finished the edifice within about a year. It was opened for the first time, July 31, 1791. Mr. Marshall's first discourse was from Haggai ii, 7, 8, 9. "And I will fill this house with glory, saith the Lord of Hosts. The silver and the gold is mine. The glory of this latter house shall be greater than the glory of the former; and in this house will I give peace, saith the Lord of Hosts."

After having been long in the fire of contention, it was grateful to Mr. Marshall and his people to settle down in peace. The temporal affairs of the church were also prosperous.

About the year 1795 Mr. Marshall, as Moderator of the Presbytery, licensed the first Preacher, belonging to his denomination, who had been educated in

America. Others were afterwards licensed, and by some accessions the Presbytery increased so as to divide into four Presbyteries, and erect itself into a Synod. The first Associate Synod met in Philadelphia, on the 21st of May, 1801, and was opened with a Sermon by Mr. Marshall, who was the first Moderator. A friend said to him, a little before the meeting,—" If you live to preach the Synodical Sermon and to constitute the Synod, you may almost say, with old Simeon,—' Now let me depart in peace!'" He cheerfully replied,—" You think I may then sing my *nunc dimittas*."

His public services were now nearly at an end, as he only lived to see the second meeting of Synod, in May, 1802. He was, shortly after this, attacked with a disease of the liver, which was aggravated and hastened to a fatal termination by his going, in the course of the summer, to New York to assist in ordaining Mr. Hamilton, and to Carlisle, to install Mr. Pringle. He died on the 17th of November, 1802, in the sixty-second year of his age and the thirty-eighth of his ministry. On the Sabbath but one before his decease, he preached, sitting in his chair, from Psalm cxix, 75,—" I know, O Lord, that thy judgments are right, and that thou in faithfulness hast afflicted me." The inscription upon his tombstone contains the original Hebrew of the passage,—" I know that my Redeemer liveth."

Mr. Marshall published a Sermon on Psalmody, preached before the Associate Presbytery in 1773, designed to show that the Psalms of David only are to be sung in worship, and that Watts' Psalms and all other Hymns are unlawful to be used in the Church. He afterwards published a Catechism for Youth, to which was annexed an explanation of religious names and sects. In conjunction with Mr. Beveridge, he wrote a Catechism for Children. Between him and Mr. Beveridge a very intimate friendship subsisted; and after the death of the latter, Mr. Marshall wrote " Some remarkable Passages of his Life." He also wrote a Vindication of the Associate Presbytery in answer to an attack upon it by Mr. Annan, in 1791. A Theological Tract on the Propriety of removing from places where the Yellow Fever prevails, was addressed by him to the Serious People in Philadelphia and New York, some of whom had scruples about this matter. An Act of the Associate Presbytery against Occasional Hearing, being printed, he accompanied it with a review of the different religious denominations in the United States, in order to illustrate the propriety of the Act.

I may mention, in connection with the last named but one of Mr. Marshall's publications, an anecdote illustrative of the facility with which he could make an apt retort. As he was leaving Philadelphia, at one time, on account of the Yellow Fever, a man on the other side of the street accosted him, saying,— " The wicked flee when no man pursueth, but the righteous are as bold as a lion." To which Mr. Marshall replied,—"A prudent man foreseeth the evil and hideth himself, but the simple pass on and are punished."

Mr. Marshall was esteemed by the whole Body of Christians with which he was connected, as well as by others, for his usefulness and his good conduct as a citizen. As an evidence of the high estimation in which he was held, his Funeral was attended by the Governor and Chief Justice of the State and a large number of most respectable citizens.

Mr. Marshall, in person, was of the largest size. He was some two or three inches over six feet high, and withal quite fleshy. I remember hearing the following anecdote told of him in Pennsylvania. In the primitive churches in that

State, especially in the German Counties, the pulpits were very small. They resembled a deep flour barrel placed upon its end, much more than a modern pulpit. And the opening for the door was in proportion to the size of the enclosure. Mr. Marshall being called to preach in one of those pulpits, the door of which was too small to allow him to pass into it, he, without anticipating any difficulty of this kind, walked up the steps and attempted to enter, when he found his ingress most unexpectedly arrested. He saw at once that he had no way of entering the pulpit but by raising his body above the top of it. He effected his purpose by placing his hands on the upper edge on each side of the door, and then raising his body so high that he could draw his legs in through the opening. Of course such a circumstance could not occur without producing a visible smile in the congregation. Mr. Marshall immediately commenced his worship by reading the common metre version of the 100th Psalm, in which occur the following lines:—

"Know ye the Lord that He is God;
Not we, but *He us* made."

The following extract of a letter from John Adams, the second President of the United States, to his daughter, dated Philadelphia, March 30, 1777, bears a rather singular testimony to the patriotism of Mr. Marshall, as well as of his people, in reference to the great struggle which issued in our Independence:—

"I have been this afternoon to a place of worship which I never attended before. It is the church of Scotch Seceders. They have a tolerable building, but not yet finished. The congregation is not large and the people are not very genteel. The Clergyman who officiates here is a Mr. Marshall, a native of Scotland, whose speech is yet thick and broad, although he has officiated in this place near ten years. By his prayer and several passages in his sermon, he appears to be a warm American; from whence I conclude that most of his congregation are so too; because I generally suppose that the Minister will, in a short time, bring his people to his way of thinking, or they will bring him to theirs, or else there will be a separation.

"After service, the Minister read a long paper, which he called an Act of the Presbytery of Pennsylvania, appointing a Fast, which is to be kept next Thursday. It is as orthodox in politics, as it is pious and zealous in point of religion."

Mr. Marshall was married, it is believed, in or about the year 1774, to a Mrs. Marshall, the widow of a sea-captain. They had four children,—only one of whom, *William*, lived to mature years. Mrs. Marshall died at the house of Mrs. Walker, her oldest daughter by the first marriage, (who had previously been the second wife of Dr. Witherspoon, President of Princeton College,) near Carlisle, July 14, 1804. For many years previous to her death she had been helpless from palsy.

If the above sketch of one of the Fathers of that branch of the Church with which I am connected will answer your purpose, I shall feel gratified in having placed it at your disposal.

With much respect yours truly,
JAMES P. MILLER.

FROM JOHN McALLISTER, ESQ.

PHILADELPHIA, February 28, 1853.

Dear Sir: Mr. Marshall, concerning whom you inquire, was the first minister of whom I had any knowledge. My father was an Elder of his church. He baptized me, and I was accustomed to sit under his preaching till I was sixteen years old,—the period of his death. He was a frequent visitor at my father's house, and I often saw him at his own.

Mr. Marshall was a tall man, of a large frame, and held himself very erect. He had a commanding intellectual forehead. Before the period from which I can recollect him distinctly, he had been afflicted with something like a cancerous affection, which had eaten off a part of one side of his nose; but I presume that, previous to that, he had been rather a handsome man. The members of his family severally were, I think, very large, well-formed people. I remember to have seen it stated in an obituary of his brother, Dr. Andrew Marshall, of London, that he once fought a duel with a Dr. Walsh, who was small and thin, and who, when he had taken his station, placed himself so as to present the smallest surface to his antagonist; and Dr. Marshall regarded this as cowardly, and turned "the whole of his large front" towards Walsh, contemptuously desiring him to take good aim.

Mr. Marshall's manner was always dignified—he seemed like one who had been accustomed to move in good society, and to be treated with deference and respect. He always walked with a cane, which, at every step, he struck heavily on the ground or pavement, but without inclining his body. He was very much attached to Dr. Anderson, the first Professor of Divinity in his denomination. Dr. Anderson was very small of stature and allowed his head to droop forward. When he visited this city, he was always Mr. Marshall's guest; and I can remember how much I used to be struck with the contrast when they were walking in company;—Mr. Marshall's height seemed to be towering, and the contrast was the greater for Mr. Marshall's holding himself erect, while Dr. Anderson bent forward.

Mr. Marshall made himself very generally acceptable in the ordinary intercourse of society. He was a cheerful and agreeable companion, had a large fund of anecdotes at command, and knew how to relate them very effectively. His wife, previous to her being married to him, was a widow lady, who kept a genteel boarding house; and, as her husband's salary, from his small congregation, was not adequate to the support of a family, they still continued to take boarders. As the Old Congress generally sat in Philadelphia, some of the members always boarded at Mr. Marshall's; as did also some of the members of the Convention of '87, which formed the Constitution of the United States. I have often heard my father speak of the very pleasant evenings which he spent at Mr. Marshall's in those days, in listening to the remarks of himself and his boarders.

Of Mr. Marshall, as a Preacher, I am not able to say much from my own recollection; but I believe his general ability in the pulpit was never questioned. He always "prefaced" the Psalm at the beginning of the morning services. His discourses in the morning were generally from two, three or more verses; and this was called "Lecturing." He was strongly in favour of continuing the Scotch practice of "lining" the Psalm in singing. My father generally performed the duties of "Precentor" even to the last; and he would fain have changed to reading two lines at a time, or even dispensing with the reading altogether; but Mr. Marshall could never consent to such an innovation.

He was very strenuous on the subject of keeping up all the services on Sacramental occasions, namely,—the observance of a Fast on the Thursday previous and a total abstinence on that day from business; a Sermon on Saturday afternoon, after which the tokens were distributed; and two Sermons on the Monday morning succeeding. He very much regretted the "defection" in the Associate Reformed Body in relation to the Fast Day, as he did also the publication of Dr. Mason's book bearing on that subject. The services on the morning, when the Sacrament was dispensed, were very long; the Action Sermon, fencing the tables, etc., occupied so much time that, although we began precisely at ten o'clock, it was about two o'clock before the communicants were seated at the first table. Then his addresses at the table were very long; and I believe we did not get away until from four to half-past four in the afternoon. While he was distributing the tokens on Saturday afternoon, he would repeat the Song of Solomon in what I suppose would be called "Intoning."

I am aware that Mr. Marshall was thought to be irritable. I do not recollect to have ever witnessed any demonstrations of that temper; and I am quite sure that, in his treatment of children at least, he was remarkably kind and affectionate. His amusement was the cultivation of a small piece of ground, in the rear of his dwelling, as a flower-garden. His little study adjoining his parlour opened into this garden. I often spent an afternoon there with him. After passing some time in the garden, he would ask me into his study, when he would address me on the subject of religion. On one occasion, a few days after I had proposed to my father to let me leave the Grammar School of the University and prepare myself for some active business, Mr. Marshall introduced the subject, and, in a most affectionate manner, urged me to continue at my studies with a view to the Ministry. He then asked me to kneel beside him, and he poured forth a most fervent prayer that the Lord would incline my heart to his service in the Ministry of the Gospel. The whole scene is fresh in my recollection.

Mr. Marshall was extensively known and very highly esteemed in Philadelphia; and that too by our most respectable citizens. He and Dr. Rush were intimately acquainted. Dr. Rush's great medical practice prevented his attending church very regularly; but I can remember his coming occasionally to hear Mr. Marshall. They were in the habit of conversing familiarly on religious subjects; and Dr. Rush would sometimes borrow of Mr. Marshall volumes of sermons by some of the old Scottish divines. When the Spruce Street Church was built, in 1770, Mr. Marshall wished to call on the citizens for contributions, and it was necessary to procure the permission of the Governor. The Brief was obtained through the influence of Dr. Rush; as Mr. Marshall states in a manuscript which is in my possession. The Brief itself is now before me, with the bold, strong signature of John Penn, and of his Secretary, Joseph Shippen, "By his Honour's command." It authorizes Mr. Marshall and the Elders and Deacons to apply, "in a decent and becoming manner," for contributions to an amount not exceeding one thousand pounds, and limiting them to twelve months from the date, March 25, 1771. Mr. Marshall says, in the manuscript referred to,—"Such was my assiduity that I was known in the city as 'the sturdy beggar.' My salary then was only £80 per annum."

On the 4th of July, 1780, the honorary degree of A. M. was conferred upon Mr. Marshall by the University of Pennsylvania—at the same time it was conferred upon six other clerical gentlemen, and on one person not clerical, who was no other than Thomas Paine. There is a full account of that Commencement in Dunlap's paper. It was the first after Dr. Ewing became Provost, and his Address is published *in extenso*. There seems to have been some "flourish" on the occasion. Chevalier Luzerne, Minister from France, and other distinguished characters are named as being present; and we may imagine that as many of the Reverend gentlemen who were to be honoured with the A. M. as could be got together, would be ranged before the audience, and in the midst of them "Mr. Thomas Paine," as Dunlap styles him.

About the time that Mr. and Mrs. Marshall ceased taking boarders, probably about 1791, the Vicomte De Noailles arrived here, driven from France by the fury of the Revolution. He rented from Mr. Marshall his dwelling house, and Mr. M. withdrew to a small building which he had rented in the rear, reserving the privilege of passing through the entry of the main building. De Noailles was a fine looking, gentlemanly man. He had many conversations with Mr. Marshall, who was much entertained by his society. While residing in that house, he would hear, from time to time, of some member of his family perishing by the guillotine; and Mr. Marshall would of course sympathize with him in these afflictions. The Duke of Orleans, with his two brothers, Duc de Montpensier and Duc de Penthievre, made their home with Vicomte de Noailles for some time after their arrival in Philadelphia. When Mr. Cass was Minister to France, Louis Philippe related to him the adventures of himself and brothers in America; and Mr. Cass understood him to say that, while in Philadelphia, he occupied the lower part of a house belonging to the Rev. Mr. Marshall in Walnut Street, above Fourth Street. There is some slight error here—Mr. Marshall's dwelling was in Spruce Street above Third, but his church was in Walnut above Fourth.

Mr. Marshall's congregation was never large. They were almost all very plain people,—old country folks,—Scotch with a considerable sprinkling of Irish.

With sentiments of respect,
I am sincerely yours,
JOHN McALLISTER.

JAMES CLARKSON.*
1772—1811.

JAMES CLARKSON was born, and educated, and became a Minister of the Gospel, in Scotland, but of the details of his early history, it is believed there is, in this country at least, no record. He migrated to America about 1772, soon after the arrival of the first ministers sent hither by the General Associate Synod of Scotland. Shortly after he came, (in 1773,) he was ordained to the work of the ministry, and was settled as Pastor of the Associate Church in Guinston, York County, Pa. He took an active part in the discussions which terminated in the formation of the Associate Reformed Church, by the union of the Associate and Reformed Presbyterian Bodies, in 1782; and distinguished himself particularly by being one of the only two ministers (William Marshall being the other) who finally held out against the union. He was chosen Moderator of the Associate Synod in 1802. His congregation was in that part of York County called "the Barrens," where the land is proverbially poor, and the people in those days were as poor as the land; the consequence of which was that his salary never much exceeded two hundred dollars per annum; but with this, and the proceeds of a small farm, he was enabled to support his family. He continued in the diligent discharge of his pastoral duties, till within a few years of

---

*Miller's Sketches.—MSS. from Rev. Dr. Beveridge, and Rev. Thomas Goodwillie.

his death, when, on account of increasing infirmity, he was obliged to withdraw from active labour and resign his charge. He died in the year 1811.

Mr. Clarkson was twice married. His first wife died in 1798, the mother of six children,—three sons and three daughters. By the second marriage he had only one child,—a son. The youngest son by the first marriage, *Thomas Beveridge*, was born about the year 1794. He had finished his Theological course, under Dr. Anderson, in the spring of 1819, but, owing to imperfect health, was not licensed till about a year afterwards. His health, however, improved very much during his travels through the Church as a Missionary. He was ordained on the 13th of August, 1822; accepted a call from Mercersburgh and McConnelsburgh, on the 30th of October following, and, on the 8th of October, 1823, was settled as Pastor of these congregations. Here he laboured very acceptably and successfully for about ten years, when his health failed him and he resigned his charge. He died in the early part of the year 1836. He was a man of fine personal appearance, and of remarkably graceful and attractive manners. So much of natural vivacity had he, and withal so much of Christian principle and feeling, that it seemed as if no disease or trouble, or even the near approach of death, could have any effect upon his spirits. He left a widow and three children. The only son, a pious and promising youth, died ere he had reached manhood. One of his daughters is the wife of the Rev. James G. Carson.

The Rev. Dr. Beveridge writes me concerning Mr. Clarkson as follows:

"I never saw Mr. James Clarkson, and could add nothing of consequence to what his son Thomas has communicated to Mr. Miller for his Sketches. I remember having heard Dr. Ramsay speak of a very singular effect produced upon him by a thunder-storm. He was riding with Mr. Clarkson when they were overtaken by a thunder-storm, and, had it not been for his knowledge of Mr. C.'s strictly temperate habits, he would have supposed him to be intoxicated. It would appear that the electricity had some peculiar influence over his nerves, for which I am not physiologist enough to account. Mr. James Martin, a very aged elder of Chartiers, once gave me an account of his admission to the Associate Church at Guinston, which showed that, though Mr. Clarkson was firmly attached to his profession, he had more liberality than some would be disposed to give him credit for. Mr. Martin, at the time, had in view a removal to the West, and stated this as a difficulty in the way of his uniting with the Associate Church, that he might be placed where he could not have access to ordinances dispensed in that Society, and might then consider it his duty to resort to them elsewhere. 'James,' said Mr. Clarkson, 'your business is to inquire about present duty. As to the future, it will be time to inquire about your duty, when Providence places you in circumstances calling for it.' I would infer, from the manners of Mr. Clarkson's children, with most of whom I had a slight, and with one of them a very intimate, acquaintance, that the father had been a man of more than ordinary refinement,—a true Gentleman as well as a true Christian."

The following is the testimony of Mr. Miller, as recorded in his Sketches:—

"Although Mr. Clarkson was naturally hasty in his temper, yet, in his Session and also with others, he was persuasive, mild and patient, and, at no time, had he any unhappy jangling. He never had an ear for tattlers, but always endeavoured to turn their attention to themselves—this generally cut the tale short, and kept him in ignorance of every thing in the congregation but what would come before the session in a regular way.

"In admitting members to the Communion he was exceedingly particular. This he used to think was one of the most difficult duties he had to perform as a minister, and it gave him the greatest anxiety. His manner was to request those who made application and were admitted to attend on the next Communion, to converse with him, in order to see whether they had made any attainments in knowledge, and that he might have another opportunity of instructing them as to the nature of the ordinance, and of recommending books for their perusal: accordingly, before a Communion, in appointing a day for young people to converse with him, a day was mentioned for all those to come who had been admitted at the last Communion. This was no doubt one way in which his people were well instructed in Secession principles.

"With regard to his preaching, he pursued the old and the best plan of expounding the Psalms, and lecturing in the forenoon. He might be called a systematic and doctrinal Preacher generally. Though he could not be called an elegant speaker, yet he was an interesting Preacher; and had an impressive earnestness in his manner well calculated to draw attention. His enunciation was clear, manly and distinct; and though he sometimes hesitated, he would frequently speak with fluency.

"All his talents were of the useful rather than the brilliant kind. As a man, he was cheerful and affable; at the same time he possessed a native dignity of which he could not easily divest himself,—undeviatingly adhering to what he conceived to be right, regardless of consequences. Mr Clarkson was a zealous, faithful and conscientious supporter of the Secession Testimony in America; and his labours seem to have been blessed with unusual success. The Secession Church has now upwards of one hundred and eighty congregations in America, the great majority of which lie in the United States, West of the Alleghany Mountains, and it has been remarked by those who have opportunities of personal acquaintance in most of those congregations, that there is scarcely one known in which some of those who were members in Guinston congregation are not to be found. And in many cases they formed the nucleus of the congregation."

JOHN ANDERSON, D.D.
1783—1830.
FROM THE REV. THOMAS BEVERIDGE, D.D.

CANNONSBURG, Sept. 19, 1848.

Rev. and dear Sir:—I received yours of 13th ult., and, instead of thinking it any trouble to prepare such an article as you desire, respecting the late Dr. Anderson, I am obliged to you for the honour of assigning to me such a task.

JOHN ANDERSON was born in England, near the Scotch border, about the year 1748. He was the only child of his parents, and, at an early period of his life, was deprived of his father. After completing the usual course of studies, he was licensed in connection with the Associate or Secession Church of Scotland; but, labouring under the two fold disadvantage of a weak voice and a hesitating manner, his services in the pulpit were so little valued that, for some years, he desisted from the exercise of the ministry, and was employed as a corrector of the press. In the year 1783 he migrated to the United States. He went with his aged mother from Scotland to Belfast, Ireland, and thence sailed in June of that year for Philadelphia, where he arrived some time in August. His voyage was, in several respects, a disastrous one. His library and other effects were put on board of a different ship from the one in which he sailed, and the vessel, being unseaworthy, was lost, and, as there was no insurance, this proved the entire loss of all his earthly property. But what affected him much more was the death of his aged and widowed mother, who was coming with him to a land of strangers, and whom, notwithstanding all his entreaties to have her preserved for burial on the shore, he was obliged to commit to the deep.* After his arrival in the United States, he spent some years in preaching in the South, in the State of New York, and the Eastern part of Pennsylvania. In the summer of 1788 he went West of the Alleghany Mountains, and preached at two places in Beaver

---

* Another authority has it that his mother died while the vessel was aground, nine miles below Newcastle, Del., and was buried on an island in the river near that place.

County, about eight miles apart,—the one then known as Mill Creek and the other as Harman's Creek, now Service and Frankfort. Returning to the East side of the Mountains, he was, after the requisite trial, ordained by the Associate Presbytery of Pennsylvania, in the Hall of the University of Pennsylvania, at Philadelphia, October 31, 1788,—the Rev. William Marshall presiding and preaching the Ordination Sermon. Having preached for a while in Eastern Pennsylvania, he returned, in the spring of 1789, to Western Pennsylvania, where he preached till the latter part of summer, and in August went to Philadelphia and New York. He attended the meeting of Presbytery at Cambridge, N. Y., on the 10th of September, on occasion of the Installation of my father. In the spring of 1790 he went to preach in Rockbridge County, Va., but returned again to Western Pennsylvania, and received a call from Mill Creek and Harman's Creek, which he accepted at a meeting of the Presbytery in New York, in the autumn of 1792.

Not long after his settlement here he was married to Miss Elizabeth Ingles, who made him an excellent and devoted wife. She survived him many years, and died at Service, aged upwards of ninety, having lost both her sight and hearing, so that the only intelligence which could be conveyed to her was by the sense of touch.

The country in which he settled was then new, and continued till the time of his decease to be but thinly inhabited. His salary was small, not more than two hundred dollars, which, together with a hundred dollars per annum for his services as Professor of Theology, constituted all the means of his earthly support. As, however, he was married to a prudent woman, and as they lived in the most economical manner and had no children to provide for, he not only managed to subsist upon his small income, but even spared something occasionally out of it to aid some of the more necessitous of his students, by boarding them without charge and giving them money.

I have referred to the fact that he was Professor of Theology—he was elected to that office in the year 1792; and received the degree of Doctor of Divinity from Jefferson College, in 1808. A small two story log building was erected upon the farm on which he lived, for the accommodation of his theological students. A library was also collected, consisting of about a thousand volumes of rare and valuable works, most of which were donations from brethren of the Associate Church in Scotland. In his office as Professor he continued till the spring of 1819, when, owing to the infirmities of age, he resigned. He still attended to the duties of his pastoral office, till April 6, 1830, when, during his attendance upon a meeting of his Presbytery, he was suddenly called to his rest, in the eighty-second year of his age. The number of students under his care was never large—it probably never exceeded ten, and was generally not more than five or six. His chief employment as a Professor was in reading Lectures on Marck's "*Medulla Theologiæ.*" These he enlarged, on each repetition of them, until they became so voluminous that, although he read each day of the week except Monday and Saturday, from the middle of the day till from three to five o'clock, during the four months of the session, he was not able, with his last class, to finish the whole system during the four years of their attendance. The Lectures were full of sound and valuable instruction, but would likely have been more useful had they been more brief. He occasionally attended to the Exegetical reading of the New Testament, and taught Hebrew, but, owing to the time occupied in

Didactic Theology, these branches were attended to but imperfectly. No instruction was given in Biblical Literature or Ecclesiastical History, separate from such incidental notices of these things as came in the way in his Lectures on Theology.

He was a man whom all his pupils venerated, and although they sometimes indulged in complaints respecting the uncultivated region where the Seminary had been established, and the tedious manner of their Teacher, yet they all, without exception, cherish his memory with the most singular regard. His acquirements in literature in general were uncommon, and especially in Theology, to which his attention was drawn, not only by his office as a Minister and Professor, but by his devoted attachment to Divine truth. It was the remark of his intimate friend, Dr. Nisbet, when he heard of his coming to this country, that "Such a Body of Divinity had never before crossed the Atlantic." His habits of study were such as few men could endure for a year, though he persevered in them from youth to extreme old age. It is doubtful whether he ever purposely made a social visit, and, as to exercise of body, he appeared to have tried it so little as not even to have any tolerable idea of his own physical strength. He has, for instance, been known to attempt lifting a log which would have been a tolerable draught for two horses. He attended to the duties of visiting ministerially the families and sick of his congregation with exemplary fidelity, and was punctual also in attending Ecclesiastical Courts, even at a great distance, so long as he was able; and, on these occasions, when thrown into the society of friends, he showed himself not destitute of some degree of sociability; but, unless called out by some such occasions, he rarely left his study from the beginning to the end of the year. In consequence of this diligence, accompanied with a sound judgment and retentive memory, he became one of the most profound of theologians. He had also a most correct and discriminating mind; and his writings show that he was not only familiar with the sentiments of others, but able to enter into fields of controversy, scarcely, if at all, occupied before, and to investigate them in such a manner as to leave little or nothing to be gleaned by those who came after him.

Perhaps nothing in his character was so singular as his abstraction of mind and entire ignorance of the common affairs of life. He was, in this respect, a mere child. A few incidents will afford the best illustration of this trait in his character. During his stay at Philadelphia, in the house of a friend who was extensively engaged in business, and had a large family daily at his table, the Doctor, who could never be made to attend at the ringing of the bell, had been forgotten at breakfast, and, being once out of mind, he was the more readily forgotten a second time at dinner. He, however, persevered in his studies, unmindful of this neglect, till the craving for food in his naturally vigorous constitution overcame his relish for books, and towards the usual hour for tea, he came down to the lady of the house, rubbing his hands, as was his custom when embarrassed or agitated, and observed, in his usual hesitating manner,—" I think, Mrs. Y——, I feel a little hungry." On the same or another occasion, when about leaving the city for the West, the gentleman with whom he lodged, knowing that he had no money, furnished him enough to bear the expenses of the journey; but, knowing also his thoughtless habits, he soon followed him after he had left his house, and, calling at a book-store to which the Doctor often resorted, he found him expending the last of his money in the purchase of books. As to missing his way, and meeting with strange adventures in his travels, when not in company with some other person,—these things were almost matters of course. His custom was, when setting out on a journey, to put a book into his pocket—this he would soon begin to read, and become altogether unmindful of every thing else. The horse, being well acquainted with his master's habits, would take advantage of this abstraction, and, while the rider was regaling himself with this food for the mind, would very quietly betake himself to such food as he found by the wayside. In this posture they would continue perhaps for an hour, the Doctor reading and the horse feeding, till, by some means, he would be aroused from his reverie, when he would bestir himself to get the horse once more set in motion. Again the book would be resumed, and again the horse, neither much injured nor alarmed by the blows he had received, would resume his feeding. Thus they would proceed, the horse also not unfrequently choosing the direction in which it best pleased him to travel, till the Doctor would be quite bewildered. On one occasion, having set out from home upon a cold day in the winter, with a view to attend a distant meeting of Presbytery, he indulged himself for a while in his usual practice of reading till the severity of the weather compelled him to desist. He now found himself in a place which he could not recognize, and began to urge his horse forward with unwonted activity, but, having ridden all day without discovering any habitation, or meeting any person from whom he could obtain directions, when the evening came, as a last resort, he gave the reins to the horse, thinking he might lead him to some shelter for the night. The horse, thus left to himself, soon brought him to an opening in the woods, and made directly for a habitation at a little distance. When arrived at the house, the Doctor knocked at the door, which was opened by an aged lady of respectable appearance, of whom, while he was shivering with the cold, he inquired, in a supplicating tone, whether he could get lodgings for the night. To his great surprise the lady accosted him by name, saying, "Dear me, is this you, Mr. Anderson?" Finding that it was his own wife, he enquired, with great astonishment,—" And how did *you* come here?" It was his own house, around which, at the distance of a mile or two, he had been travelling all day. It was no uncommon thing for him, when on a journey, to bring home nothing of a large supply of linen, except what was on his back. He has been known, after preaching, to mount another person's horse, and ride away with it, simply because its colour was grey like that of his own. He knew nothing of the times of sowing and reaping, nor had he the least idea of the management of any business of a worldly nature, not even so much as to know whether the horns of a lady's saddle should be before or behind, or that such saddles should have horns at all. It is said that, having once attempted to put on a saddle for his wife, and having put it on with the horns behind, when told of his error, he expressed his astonishment that *saddles* should have *horns*.

He was, in temper, somewhat irascible, and, although distinguished for meekness and humility, he was also impatient of contradiction, so far as related to matters of principle. This appears to have been partly owing to his ardent love of truth, and partly to his slowness and difficulty in expressing his mind, which, it may be observed, frequently produce this impatience. Although it was evident to all his acquaintances that he struggled much against the influence of his natural temper, yet it would sometimes gain a momentary ascendancy. This did not often happen, but when it did, he would immediately afterwards manifest the deepest humiliation and penitence, soliciting, again and again, the pardon of those against whom he had spoken with severity, and confessing, with the greatest grief, this infirmity of his nature. Perhaps in nothing did the power of Divine grace more clearly manifest itself than in its contests with this corruption. It was often exceedingly painful to his friends to witness his humiliation on these occasions. The inward anguish of his spirit betrayed itself even in the death-like paleness of his face. In his case, those Psalms which represent the spiritual troubles of the believer as dimming the eye, wasting the flesh, and otherwise deeply affecting the body, were no mere figures of speech. As a proof that anger, though sometimes prevailing, was one of those things which he allowed not. it may be mentioned that nothing of this infirmity betrays itself in his writings. Though engaged repeatedly in controversies, and sometimes treated with rudeness, he always replies with the utmost moderation and calmness, and even with great respect for the person of his opponent.

Although it might not be anticipated, from some of the preceding remarks, yet all his acquaintances considered him as very much of a gentleman, in the best sense of the term. He was remarkable for his modesty, kindness and deference to others. In these respects, and even in his external carriage, he bore a striking resemblance to the Hon. John Q. Adams. Strange as it may seem that such a similarity should exist between persons in such different spheres of life, and who probably never saw each other,—yet such as have had some acquaintance with both have often noticed it.

But the trait of character for which Dr. Anderson was most eminent, and which made him seem like one not belonging to the age in which he lived, was his extraordinary piety. Few, if any, in modern times, have lived so near Heaven as did this venerable man. A large portion of his time, both evening and morning, he spent in secret prayer, and with Mrs. A. in reading the Scriptures, and in spiritual conversation. It was their custom also, many times during the year, to observe family fasts,—the greater portion of the day being employed by them and their domestics in alternate prayers in the family and closet. He was eminently distinguished by his love of the truth, and zeal for promoting it. He was equally eminent for a strict and conscientious conformity to the law of God in his practice. Perhaps few men ever illustrated better, by their example, the power of settled principles in religion. He had no enthusiasm,—was carried away by no excitement—both in the pulpit and out of it, his usual manner was perfectly calm. All classes esteemed him as a man to whom few, if any, might be compared for sincere and devoted love to the Lord Jesus.

As a Preacher, Dr. Anderson was never regarded as having any claim to popularity, as this term is generally understood. He was so slow in speaking that some of his students could even, without the use of stenography, write his sermons in full as he delivered them. But though not an animated speaker, both the matter of his discourses and the spirit in which he spoke, showed him to be in great earnest. Such also was his deep insight into the mysteries of the Gospel, his acquaintance with the work of the Spirit of God, and his skill in applying the word to the cases of his hearers, that his ministry was held in the highest esteem among persons eminent for godliness. He was remarkable for his correctness in method and language. His hesitating manner appeared indeed to arise, in a great degree, from his unwillingness to say anything which was not, both in sentiment and language, the very thing which he intended. His hesitation, also, was not attended with coughing, stammering or any of its usual accompaniments in others. He would stand perfectly still, and apparently at ease, till he could settle in his mind what he was to say; so that, when persons became familiar with his manner, as it appeared to give no pain to himself, it caused no uneasiness to them. As an illustration of the esteem in which his ministry was held by godly persons, I may mention the following anecdote. On a certain occasion the venerable Dr. McM———, of the Presbyterian Church, together with a younger brother, attended upon his preaching. The young man listened with great impatience, and, after the services were concluded, began to speak of the sermon in terms of positive contempt. The aged and eminently pious father replied,—" It is well for us, my dear brother, that God has not given to that man the gift of utterance,—else there would soon be none left to hear you and me."

In person Dr. Anderson was of very low stature, but of a robust appearance for so small a man. His countenance was mild, his eye dark and piercing,—and of such power that, even in old age, he could see better than most persons in their youth. He never had occasion to make use of glasses.

As an Author, the small number of the society to which he belonged, and the unpopularity of most of the principles which he defended, have prevented his attaining that celebrity to which the intrinsic value of his works entitles him. He excels in the accurate arrangement of his thoughts, the precision with which they are expressed, and the clearness and force of his reasoning. He is one of those controvertists whom it is difficult to find off their guard. He appears to anticipate the cavils and objections which might be raised against him, and so expresses himself as to cut off all just occasion of this kind. His style is correct and chaste, but without ornament. In several respects, his writings resemble those of President Edwards, whom he much admired, and whose Theological creed, with few exceptions, was the same with his own.

Besides some sermons and smaller works in pamphlet form, he published, at different times, the following,—" Essays on Various Subjects, Relative to the present State of Religion," Glasgow, 1782; "A Discourse on the Divine Ordinance of Singing Praise," Philadelphia, 1791; and a Vindication of this Discourse, Philadelphia, 1793. These two Discourses were followed by a larger work on the same subject, entitled, " *Vindiciæ Cantus Dominici*," Philadelphia, 1800. In these works he defends the use of the inspired Psalms in the public and solemn worship of God, and opposes the introduction of other compositions in their place. He also published, in 1793, a small book entitled " The Scripture Doctrine of the Appropriation, which is in the Nature of Saving Faith, Stated and Illustrated." This work has been among the most acceptable and useful of his writings. An edition of it having been published in Scotland, some of the views defended in it were opposed by the Rev. Andrew Fuller, in his " Gospel worthy of all acceptation." While in the Southern States Dr. Anderson also published a Series of Letters, addressed to the Rev. Mr. Hemphill, of the Associate Reformed Church. These relate to a union which had been effected between a portion of the Associate and the Reformed Presbyterians. In 1806 he published a book entitled " Precious Truth." This is a defence of some doctrines of the Gospel, and of the writings of Messrs. Marshall, Hervey and others, from charges brought against them by Dr. Bellamy. His last publication was a " Series of Dialogues on Church Communion." This is partly a reply to the Plea of Dr. John M. Mason for Catholic Communion, and partly a defence of the Communion maintained in the Secession Church. It was published at Pittsburg in 1820, and is at the same time the largest and most elaborate of all his works. He was employed also by Mr. Cramer, of Pittsburg, to prepare notes to an edition of Brown's Dictionary of the Bible, published in 1807. These notes are regarded by such as possess this edition of that work, as adding much to its value. The manuscripts left by Dr. Anderson were very numerous, but not intended for publication. He had thoughts of committing them to the flames before his death, but this was prevented by the sudden manner of his departure. It is not, however, likely that his wishes in respect to their publication will be disregarded.

That your present undertaking, and all your labours for advancing the cause of our common Lord, may be abundantly blessed, is the sincere desire of
Yours very respectfully,
THOMAS BEVERIDGE.

FROM THE REV. ALEXANDER McCLELLAND, D.D.

NEW BRUNSWICK, March 8, 1848.

Rev. and dear Sir: Your request that I should communicate to you some of my recollections and impressions concerning my venerated Teacher, Dr. John Anderson, comes to me, on various accounts, with all the force of a command. Yet it finds me in such a state of health, and so occupied with professional engagements, that you must be content with a very hurried and imperfect discharge of the duty. Agreeably to your expressed wish, which entirely coincides with my own feelings, I shall confine myself to *personal* reminiscences,—saying nothing, or at least very little, which did not fall under my actual observation. Nor do I fear that the lapse of years has so blurred the picture that I shall expose myself to the charge of not holding the mirror true to nature. The impression made on my mind was like an inscription chiselled in marble, and will last while memory holds her seat.

I became acquainted with the Doctor thirty-five years ago,—the first time I saw him being at a meeting of his Presbytery in Pittsburg, when I received admission into the Theological Seminary of which he was Professor. When the roll was called, and a small mouse-like voice answered to his name, I looked to the quarter from which it proceeded with no little curiosity and considerable disappointment. It was quite evident that his greatness did not lie in externals. He was remarkably small; his stature not much exceeding five feet, with a large head enveloped in a forest of thick, tangled hair, which, spreading itself over his head and back, gave him the appearance of that odd South American animal called the Gnu. Nature, in setting him up, had forgotten to supply the convenience of a neck, and there seemed to have been a great lack of muscle where it ought to have been, as his head was constantly inclined to his breast at an angle of forty-five degrees. His voice was low, though not unmusical, and he spoke with much hesitation and embarrassment. Indeed, he seemed to shrink from the labour of speaking at all,—sitting in a retired corner of the room like one in a dream on whom surrounding objects made no impression, except when startled by a remark addressed to him personally. With one feature the most fastidious disciple of Lavater would have been satisfied,—a pair of brilliant black eyes,—though it was not easy to get a sight of them,—being generally fixed in earnest contemplation on the waistband of his indispensables.

Such was the casket. Let us now, as appearances are often deceiving, take a *look within*. His learning was solid, various and accurate, proving that, in his youth, he must have been a vigorous student. I doubt whether, at that time, he had quite his equal in the country West of the Alleghanies. He was thoroughly versed in the Old Theology, an excellent Latin scholar, and in Greek highly respectable. Of his Hebrew attainments I know nothing, but suspect that he was here deficient. He was well versed in the old Logic and Metaphysics, and took great delight in works of that kind. From remarks that casually dropped from him, I infer that he must have picked up considerable information in Physiology and Natural History; so that it would have been rather hazardous for a stranger, in conversing with him, to assume that he was quite ignorant on any subject. Few were able to appreciate his acquirements, on account of his singular inability to start topics of discourse, and to give out his thoughts when they were started by others. A slight allusion to a classic story, or fact in science, or philosophical opinion, would often betray the existence of a rich fountain below the surface; but every drop was to be obtained by *hard pumping*, and few had the patience for this or the necessary skill. Accordingly, his friends generally observed his best wine came last. At the first mention of a subject, he appeared to know nothing; but, under a judicious course of *vellication*, by questioning, objecting and occasional assault on some of his intellectual hobbies, he would begin to show signs of life, and surprise his hearers as well by the vivacity as the richness of his illustrations.

As a Theological Lecturer, he was extremely methodical, confining himself closely to his text book, which was the Medulla and Compend of John Mark. This divine was a special favourite with him; his obscure and crabbed diction being considered the beau ideal of elegant Latinity. The minute and endless divisions in which he abounds proved a great stumbling block to our worthy Professor, as it was an affair of conscience with him to follow them, and thus he engaged himself in tedious details when he should have been exhibiting the great and commanding principles of his subject. I must confess that he sometimes made me weary. His manner was embarrassed and hesitating,—resembling that of one who reads to himself a manuscript hard to decipher, and he seldom let us off with less than three hours. A great fault in our course was its being entirely confined to Didactic and Polemic Theology. We never recited a lesson in Ecclesiastical History, nor translated a single chapter in the Old or New Testaments. Doubtless he would have pleaded that they did not belong to his department; but, as he was the only Professor to whom the Church entirely looked for the instruction of her sons, the neglect was inexcusable. We should remember, however, that this was nearly forty years ago, when the "System" was acknowledged sole monarch in the domain of Theology almost universally,—having not only over-topped its rivals, but, like Aaron's rod, swallowed them up.

Truth requires me to state that there was an exercise held every Saturday morning, which we called "Biblical," and which really deserved the name. A Committee had reported, at a previous meeting, various difficulties or apparent contradictions in Scripture, which it was made the duty of another Committee to explain and harmonize. The occasion was full of interest and instruction, though our young critics complained oftentimes that sufficient latitude was not allowed them, and that they were pinned down too closely to the old traditional exegesis. The student who, in explaining a passage, did not "go out by the footsteps of the flock," or quoted, in any case whatever, a Limborch and Whitby, against a Calvin and John Owen, always felt that he was on perilous ground. A peculiar jerking of the chair, and repeated enunciations of that famous Hebrew guttural, which a Dutch grammarian defines "*vox porculi clamantis ad matrem*," had warned the gallant youth to mix with his valour a little discretion. Some instances of the *crash* which saluted an unfortunate genius when he neglected these "premonitory symptoms," were so excessively ludicrous that I sometimes call one up to relieve a fit of *tic doloreux*. After all, the surest test of merit in a teacher is the result of his labours; and whatever were the defects of his course, (faults of the age rather than the man,) it is generally admitted that he sent forth excellent Preachers. I do not, of course, rank myself in the number, but I am pretty confident that nowhere else would I have been subjected to the same mental discipline, or obtained the same amount of preparation for the ministerial work.

His Preaching had the same general characteristics with his Theological Lectures, but it differed in two respects, which were striking to the most careless observer. The first was its plain and practical cast. The moment he entered the pulpit, he seemed to forget that there was such a thing as controversial divinity in existence, but dwelt on the simplest truths of the Gospel in the most simple manner possible,—like a father charging and exhorting his children, or a nurse cherishing her babes. We were sometimes desirous of hearing him discuss a subject argumentatively, and sometimes he indulged us; but instances were rare. It was quite plain the old man thought he had other business on hand than drilling eight students in theological dialectics. The matter of his discourses was intensely evangelical. The fulness of Christ as a Saviour, his perfect righteousness, the obligation of the Holy Law as administered by the great Mediator, the grace of the sanctifying Spirit, the blessedness of reconciliation to God, the full and free offers of the Gospel,—these were the themes on which he always expatiated with an artlessness and sweet simplicity of thought and expression that never failed to interest even those who "cared for none of these things."

The other peculiarity was the surprising animation which he occasionally displayed. I have already observed that his elocution was generally feeble and ineffective; but not unfrequently a thought, or whole train of thought, would break in upon him, that seemed to stir up his soul from its lowest depths. The change that came over him, at such times, was astonishing. The tongue of the stammerer now spoke plainly—his form would dilate, his voice roll like thunder, and his little black eyes would sparkle like two burning torches. He was often so pungent and overpowering on these occasions that I confess myself to have felt ill at ease, and that I was glad to see a collapse, which usually took place after a few minutes.

But his personal qualities as a Man and a Christian were those which made the strongest impression on my young mind. In this respect I had opportunities of appreciating him not enjoyed by my fellow students. Our theological session continued only during the winter season—early in the spring, they all dispersed to their respective homes, and a re-union did not take place till late in the following autumn. But my case was different. Having come from the State of New York, where all my kindred resided, I found myself in the midst of strangers; and this circumstance, with others not deserving mention, determined me to continue with the old gentleman during the whole summer. The locality of his residence was somewhat peculiar and worth a brief description.

The mansion, a small cabin, having a single story and constructed of rough logs, was situated in a narrow gorge between two hills of such respectable altitude, that, in many parts of the country, they would be called mountains. The valley was less than a quarter of a mile wide, and divided by a pleasant brook which made sweet music, as it merrily passed along by the side of a rich natural meadow, covered by noble sugar-maples, and extending up to the house. Egress from the place was impossible, except by taking a long circuit through the woods, or climbing one of the hilly ramparts that invested it on all sides. Our nearest neighbour was a mile and a half distant, unless a dark solitary man might be called such, who lived a mile higher up the creek, but who, not professing "Secession Principles," and moreover labouring under a strong suspicion of being a Yankee, was considered a little worse than *nobody*. In fact, we were as much shut out from the great world, as the monks of St. Bernard in their Alpine pass, besides having a much smaller family,—our whole establishment consisting of the Doctor and his wife, two girls, whom, in the want of children, they had taken to bring up, myself, and an old grey horse, whom I reckon with the humanities on account of his wonderful sagacity and the care he took of his master. It need scarcely be said that there were few signs of cultivation in our vicinity. All around us for miles was "vast wilderness and boundless contiguity of shade," such as would have fully satisfied the amiable Cowper, when sighing after a retreat from the follies of the world. Reading one day his beautiful lines,—"Oh, for a lodge," &c., to Mrs. Anderson, that excellent lady was so affected with his want of suitable accommodations that we conversed repeatedly, (not knowing that he had been dead some years,) on the subject of inviting him to come over and "lodge" with us, at the usual student's rate of five shillings a week.

In this lonely spot Dr. Anderson passed the greater part of his life. Here, after serving God faithfully in his day and generation, he died, and here I, a volatile boy of fifteen, was shut up, by a wise and gracious Providence, for three years, to learn, by the contemplation of a living example, what Christian holiness is, and what high degrees of it a poor, miserable worm of earth can attain with the aid of heavenly grace.

How far he was indebted to his retired and isolated situation, removing him from the temptations incident to a public life, I will not decide. To detect the nice proportions in which nature, grace and external influences combine to the formation of character,—that, for instance, of a Leighton, or Blaise Pascal, is an operation of the *higher chemistry*, the secret of which is with Him who made us. But we can appreciate with considerable accuracy the *fact*,—the actual *result* which this combined agency produces; and, applying this principle to the subject of my remarks, I say, with confidence, that he was no common man. From the first day of my acquaintance with him, it struck me that his piety was something quite unearthly, and not to be explained by any of the "laws of mind" laid down in Brown and Stewart. To say that he was animated by a profound reverence for the Supreme Being, never named Him without making a perceptible pause in his discourse, paid marked regard to the Divine laws and institutions, was a strict observer of the Lord's day, &c., &c., would be to talk quite prettily and appropriately of some persons; but, applied to John Anderson, of Service Creek, would be ridiculous bathos. God was his *life*, his *soul*, his *all in all!* In God his whole moral man *lived* and *moved* and had its *being!* He walked with Him constantly, as a personal friend; and I doubt whether there was a moment when He was not present to him as a distinct object of thought. Very soon this fact struck me so forcibly that I determined to make the old man my particular study; and began to play the spy on him to a greater extent than, under other circumstances, would have been dignified or proper. Ten times a day have I gone to his study door, and peered through the key-hole to see what he was doing; and eight times out of the ten I found him on his knees. My little sleeping apartment was next to his, and often, long after our old wooden clock had commenced striking the small hours, I heard the low breathings of one in earnest devotion. Seeking an explanation, I was told, by the old lady, after some cross-questioning, that, being extremely subject to nervous wakefulness, he found nothing better to do than rise and spend a half hour in prayer. This mode of composing unquiet nerves appeared to me a strange business, and I resolved to know more about it. Searching carefully the partition, I found a large cranny, to which I applied my ear with such good effect that I was able to catch much of what he said—and such praying I never heard before, nor expect to hear again. It was not prayer in the common acceptation of the term, but an *outgush* of holy, child-like confidence in a Father with whom he was in familiar colloquy; sometimes taking the form of a confession of unworthiness, sometimes that of an humble interrogatory, then passing over into a sort of argumentative pleading, in which he would remind his Heavenly Friend of his engagements in the everlasting covenant, of some gracious promise in the Word, of the blood-shedding on Mount Calvary, of his past providential dealings, and all this with such deep feelings of love, gratitude, self-abasement and triumphant hope, that I was absolutely astounded and tore myself away, aghast at the presumption with which I had been violating the sanctity of a place, holy as Heaven itself; stealing, like a vile thief and eaves-dropper, into the nuptial chamber, where the Lord was communing with his mystic spouse. To my mind there was something awful in the thought of a mortal creature holding such close correspondence with the invisible world;—nestling itself, if I may so speak, in the very bosom of God. Many a night it robbed me of sleep, and when, on the following morning, the little man joined our family circle, in his usual quiet and unobtrusive way, I would gaze at him as if I *saw a spirit!*

Much of this temper he carried into his religious exercises in the family, though I have heard it questioned,—only, however, by persons not favourably situated for judging. He was undoubtedly dull oftentimes; but this proceeded from his extreme timidity; for, with all his excellencies, he was as bashful as a child. Odd as the remark may seem, it is strictly true, that the presence of a pair of lubberly students would weigh him down to the earth; and, accordingly, I always observed that our vernal migration produced the happiest effect upon him. He seemed to feel that he was alone with God, and the little flock committed to his guardianship, of which my extreme youth allowed him to consider me a part. It was now his spirit became emancipated, bounded at once into the empyrean, and there soared and swam like the eagle in its native element. Happy old man! Death must have been comparatively a very trifling change to him; for the hallowed employments and pleasures on which he entered, were those which formed the whole happiness of his earthly existence.

Much of that almost infantile ignorance of the world for which he was remarkable, may be traced to this absorption of the mind in higher objects. His natural shrewdness was considerable, and the only reason of its imperfect development in relation to common occurrences must have been the small degree of interest he felt in them. They passed by, as the successive parts of a landscape pass by the traveller in a rail-car, while engaged in animated conversation. They were seen, but that was all. The faculty of attention did not act on them; consequently they never lodged deep enough to fructify into maxims and rules of conduct. Thus he was known to miss the road to his own church (never with old grey) after travelling it every second Sabbath for twenty years. It is extremely doubtful whether he could discriminate between a dish of pork and of mutton, calling each by its proper name. On one occasion he exchanged a valuable horse, which a designing knave persuaded him was lame, for one that was stone blind and in the last stage of the glanders. There was nothing allied to stupidity in this, for I have not the smallest doubt that if he had felt it to be his duty to study *horse-flesh*, he would, in less than six months, have made himself the best farrier in the district.

In the same way may be explained another peculiarity in his character, on which I have often reflected. There were few or none of his acquaintance with whom he had close and confidential intercourse. Loved by all, and in turn loving all, (for his heart was tender to a fault), he knew little of the pains and pleasures of human friendship. At least, I never heard him speak of more than two persons, the Rev. Messrs. Marshall and Beveridge, (both of them deceased,) in such a way as to suggest that they were any more to him than others possessing equal intrinsic worth. The truth is that one great object preoccupied his mind—the Lord Jesus was so sensibly and ever present that his heart had no room for any other, except as " beloved for Christ's sake." In this absolute independence of created sources of enjoyment, even the most innocent, there was a wonderful contrast between him and the pious Dr. Doddridge, with an equally striking likeness to Leighton and Payson. The former could scarcely live, except when basking in a friend's smile. His correspondents were numerous, and his peace of mind seems to have been entirely at their mercy. Witness the following paragraph from one of his letters, which, coming from such a man; must excite not only pity but astonishment. "Your reflections on the love of God, and the vanity of creature love, are just, and I enter into the spirit of them. I have a few darling friends ; yet from them I meet with frequent disappointments. You, in particular, are always friendly and kind ; yet, though I have some of the most delightful enjoyments of friendship with you, pain of parting, and the impatience of absence, embitter even these. My present happiness lies so much in my friends that they frequently discompose me. Every thing like a slight or neglect from them touches to the quick, and when I imagine them out of humour I am so far from being cheerful that I cannot be goodnatured. If they look upon me *a little more coldly than ordinary,* while they express their affection for another, I am uneasy, and a thousand minute occurrences, which others take no notice of, are to me some of the most solid afflictions of my life. They unfit me for pleasure and business. May God forgive me, they unfit me for devotion too."

Poor dear Philip ! as brave old Luther would exclaim when he received communications, not unlike this of our good Doctor, from his namesake and prototype, the amiable Melancthon. Well might he add in the following paragraph,—" Let us learn to place supreme affection upon our Creator, for it is that alone which can afford us lasting satisfaction." His bark would have enjoyed a much more quiet berth in the chopping seas and cross currents of life, had he not so unwisely attached to it so many miserable *hedgers*, instead of holding on with calm and undivided reliance to the great sheet anchor within the vail. Dr. Anderson could not possibly have used such language under any circumstances. There was but one friend whose absence or frown could give him serious discomposure, and that friend never "*looked coldly on him.*"

Accordingly, he was always cheerful and happy. Though quiet and silent above most men, and generally looking downward, as if occupied with something he did not care to speak of, yet those who caught the expression of his eye, saw that he was conversing with serene and pleasant thoughts. When suddenly addressed, he would start as if from a dream, and ask the speaker to repeat his remark. He had evidently been in the land of Beulah, discoursing with " the shining ones who walk there, because it is on the borders of Heaven." Earth had little that could annoy such a spirit. I never knew him, during my three years' daily intercourse, to utter a fretful word concerning his secular concerns, or express a wish for something not at hand, or betray a secret thought that his earthly condition could in any way be bettered. His salary was about two hundred and eighty dollars a year, half of which his people paid in provisions. These were not always the best of their kind ;— a fact that often ruffled the good humour of his worthy partner ;—but never was there a bosom more unfit than that of her liege lord to be the depository of her griefs. She never could ascertain even whether he *heard* her. This want of sympathy on so tender a point was positively the only drop of bitterness in her cup of domestic felicity;—from which may be inferred, without much violence, that, on the whole, the current of life ran pretty smooth in our little valley.

Another feature of character was his extraordinary humility. Dr. Anderson was a writer of considerable distinction. Few divines of the day were his superiors. Moreover, a respectable and growing denomination of Christians looked upon him, if not as their Moses and spiritual founder, at least as their ecclesiastical Joshua, who, by his prowess in the theological battle-field, had given them deliverance from their enemies round about. The manifestation of a little self-complacency, at times, would, under such circumstances, have been quite pardonable. A certain composed dignity, which seems to say in the most delicate manner possible that they and their company are not precisely on an equal footing, is supposed to sit very gracefully on distinguished persons. But it was a gracefulness which he never reached. It always appeared to me that, living, as he did, in constant communion with God, he could not rise from the prostration of soul belonging to his habitual employment so as to assert his proper place among men; accustomed to lie low in the dust before the "Excellent Glory," he crouched and shrunk before the most insignificant mortal. Examples without number could be given.

His deportment at meetings of the clergy has been already noticed. We always observed, on such occasions, that, if there was a corner of the room particularly dark and retired, he was sure to occupy it. Scarcely ever would he rise to speak, even on subjects of importance, unless compelled by circumstances or a call of the Moderator. I have repeatedly seen attempts made, by his brethren in the ministry, to pay him a compliment—but it was never undertaken twice by the same person. The old man would turn red in the face, as if struck with apoplexy, groan forth, with many repetitions, his favourite Hebrew guttural, and jerk his chair from right to left with surprising agility. He seemed to think that the speaker could not be in earnest, but was laughing at him. Few things annoyed him more, in the intercourse of society, than being addressed as Doctor of Divinity—not that he felt (as far as I could learn) any scruples of conscience on the subject, but because he could not bear to be distinguished from his brethren. I have heard and read of a similar antipathy expressed by certain divines since that time, but, in most cases, have indulged in a little skepticism as to its reality. Somehow, above all the din of their noisy protestation *"nolo doctorari,"* the small voice has made itself heard, whispering that, *at heart*, they like to bear the cross rather better than their quiet neighbours! But no such suspicion could possibly be harboured against Dr. Anderson. A more artless, simple-minded being never existed. He could no more appear what he was not, or conceal what he was, than an infant at the breast.

Perhaps the most striking exemplification of his humble and subdued spirit was the readiness with which he acknowledged his faults to those whom, by some heat of temper, he had offended. I will not deny the fact that he had his share of what Buchanan calls the *"perfervidum ingenium Scotorum,"*—in other words, that he was sometimes a little vehement, only, however, in matters of controversy, and when he thought important principles at stake. When raised to such a point that he became distinctly conscious of it, he would retire from his parlour into his sanctum, where he would remain a few minutes; then return, "calm as a summer morning," and, with a meek apology, resume the argument. I, myself, at the early age of sixteen, have had the honour of receiving his *amende honorable*—when the wonder was, not that he had been irritated, but that he did not attempt to cool my polemic ardour by some vigorous application of the *argumentum a posteriori*. I am glad to say that, on such occasions, I had grace to be greatly humiliated and grieved.

The usual subject of dispute was the War which had just commenced between our country and Great Britain. The old gentleman was a violent Democrat, —principally on religious grounds; as he considered the British Government to be a great Anti-Christian power, which, by its usurpation of headship over the Church, and its hostility to a "covenanted reformation," had entailed upon itself all the woes written in the Apocalypse. The younger belligerent was a thorough-going Federalist, full of fire and fury against the "unnatural contest" with our amiable mother. On the whole we were not badly matched. My adversary understood his subject, and had Grotius on the Rights of Neutrals at his fingers' ends. Unfortunately for him, I had something at my *tongue's* end, which *he* had not,—a prodigious quantity of words; and once, I so completely overwhelmed him with my nonsense that he lost all patience, —actually calling, without any attempt at circumlocution, the only son of my respected father a—*magpie!* His manner was violent, and his voice trembled with excitement. Scarcely had the unlucky word escaped him, when he turned pale with horror, and rushed into his little closet, where he remained half an hour. But, oh, the transformation that had taken place in that brief period! It could be compared to nothing but the change wrought in the tumultuous sea of Tiberias, when it heard the voice of its God, saying, in tones that penetrated to its deepest caverns, "Peace! Be still!" The scene that ensued is as fresh before my mind as if it occurred yesterday. There stands the strong man, bowing himself before a petulant child! Suffocated with emotion,—the tears streaming down his aged cheeks, and every limb trembling as if in a paroxysm of fever, he seizes my hand convulsively, and pours out his confession of the wrong he has done me, with a fervour and contrition of soul, that could not have been more deep or heartfelt, had he plunged a knife into my bosom!

I merely give this as a specimen of the man. In view of his whole character, it must be granted that his qualities were not the stuff which *heroes* are made of—such, at least, as stand for heroes in the world's vocabulary; but his record is on high; and he has long since gone to a place where I apprehend few of these gentlemen will bear him company.

I shall conclude my sketch with a brief notice of his worthy lady, to whom I have already more than once alluded. The old adage that marriages are made in Heaven, but so strangely jumbled, in their voyage downward, that few have the happiness of lighting on their proper mates, was signally refuted in the case of this truly primitive couple. Their manner of coming together was characteristic. The Doctor, having arrived at the shady side of forty,—his good people, sympathizing with his lonely and helpless condition, felt a great desire to see him married. But how to bring it about, in a country where the good old patriarchal mode of settling preliminaries by some judicious Eliezer of Damascus had gone into disuse, was a riddle which no Sphynx among them could expound. Providence, however, took the affair into his own hands, and accomplished it in the most quiet way imaginable,—providing him with a most excellent Eve, in a certain sense from his very side. On a pleasant winter night, while chatting with the honest Scotch farmer at whose house he lodged, the latter, encouraged by certain favourable appearances, introduced the subject of matrimony. The Doctor, having a distinct perception that this kind of covenant imperatively required a female, (differing here from the old "solemn league and covenant," which acknowledged, as parties contracting, only "noblemen, knights, burgesses, citizens and ministers of the Gospel,") was asking, in a tone of utter bewilderment and hopelessness, where on earth she could be obtained, when the door opened suddenly; and in entered the farmer's sister-in-law, a huge, antique maiden of forty-five, who resided with him in the capacity of deputy house-keeper. She was no Venus, nor exactly the lady who stood before the glowing fancy of Milton when he sang,

"Grace was in all her steps, Heaven in her eye,
In every gesture, dignity and love."

But she was a pious and discreet Christian damsel, well skilled in the mystery of preparing the Doctor's favourite broth, and who could lilt Ralph Erskine's "Gospel Sonnets" like a nightingale. Struck with a sudden thought, James replied, "Atweel, Minister, What's to hinder thee from buckling with oor Lizzy here"? The good minister was electrified, seized the idea at once, wondering that it had never occurred before; and Lizzy, nothing loth, was, in a short time, installed mistress of the manse.

Their union was a "crowning mercy" to both, especially to the husband. She proved, in every respect, the very thing he needed—a Sarah, to guide his house with discretion (though she never gave him an Isaac); an Aaron to speak for him before the Pharaohs of the world, when it was needful to commune with them in the way of secular business; and a Miriam to refresh him in his hours of weariness with a Psalm of David; while, in his own proper domain, she was proud and happy to acknowledge his immeasurable superiority. Indeed, it was quite evident that, though comparing them physically, one might, without any great stretch of fancy, conceive of his creeping into her pocket, she thought him the greatest specimen of a man (the "two Erskines" perhaps excepted) that had lived since the days of the Apostles! She was never seriously offended with me but once—by my proposing that she should sing to him Burns' famous song, "John Anderson, my joe." Other delinquencies met with a ready forgiveness—my felonious visits, for instance, to her honey jar and hens' nests; the revengeful pranks on her two maidens for informing against me; and even my schismatical proceedings "anent the War"; but that I should advise her to address *Mr. Anderson* with the profane familiarity of an old tinker's wife, threw the good soul into a terrible consternation. She was really angry, and nothing but pity on my youth restrained her from calling me outright a "Doeg, the Edomite"—nay, a very "Rabshakeh"! She did not survive him long, and is lying, as I suppose, at his side, in the little burial yard, not far from their dwelling. With my knowledge of the locality, I almost fancy that I could point out the very spot. Wherever it be, the ground is holy; for it contains precious dust; and were the question, what part of our great mother's bosom shall be our final resting place, worth one moment's thought, I would ask no higher honour than that of lying at their feet.

Yours with sincere regard and in Christian bonds,
ALEXANDER McCLELLAND.

THOMAS BEVERIDGE.*

1784—1798.

THOMAS BEVERIDGE was born in the year 1749, of respectable parents, at Eastside, Parish of Fossoway, Fifeshire, Scotland. He was brought up under the ministry of the Rev. William Mair, of Muckart, author of Lectures on the first three chapters of Matthew's Gospel; which Lectures are introduced with a preface from Mr. Beveridge's pen. Having gone through his preparatory course, he became a student of Theology under the direction of the Rev. William Moncrieff, of Alloa.

* Brief Memoir by Rev. William Marshall.—Miller's Sketches.—MS. from his son, Rev. Thomas Beveridge, D.D.

Not long after he was licensed to preach, he was appointed Assistant to the Rev. Adam Gib, an aged minister of Edinburgh, with whom he laboured to great acceptance, for some time, as a son with a father. In the year 1783 the Associate Presbytery of Pennsylvania having sent to Scotland for aid, the General Associate Synod appointed Mr. Beveridge to come to America; and, accordingly, after being ordained by the Associate Presbytery of Edinburgh, he came to this country in the spring of 1784. Shortly after his arrival, he took his seat in the Associate Presbytery of Pennsylvania, convened at Philadelphia.

Scarcely had he become a member of the Body, when they found occasion to put his abilities in requisition for a very important service. It was thought expedient to draw up a "Testimony for the Doctrine and Order of the Church of Christ," accommodated, in some respects, to the peculiar state of things in this country; and Mr. Beveridge was appointed to frame the instrument. This work he performed in the course of the ensuing summer; and in August of that year it was approved and adopted by the Presbytery. A request having been preferred to the Presbytery, by several respectable inhabitants of Cambridge, N. Y., that a minister might be sent to them, who should dispense the ordinances according to the received principles of the said Presbytery, Mr. Beveridge was sent, in the course of the autumn, to labour in that place; and, after he had remained there a few months, the people were so well satisfied with him as to wish to secure his permanent services.

In the spring of 1785 he visited the city of New York, and was instrumental in planting a church of his own communion there; and, though he was never afterwards directly connected with it, he seemed always to regard it with an almost parental affection.

Having received and accepted a call from Cambridge, he was inducted to his pastoral charge by the appropriate solemnities, on the 10th of September, 1789. The Sermon on the occasion was preached by the Rev. (afterwards Dr.) John Anderson.

Here Mr. Beveridge continued to labour with the most exemplary zeal and fidelity during the rest of his life. Though he was eminently devoted to the interests of his immediate charge, yet he by no means confined his labours to them, but went abroad, especially into the neighbouring towns, as occasion or opportunity offered, in aid of the great purposes of his ministry. In 1788 he presided at the Ordination of the Rev. David Goodwillie, in the Hall of the University of Pennsylvania, Philadelphia, and, in 1792, at the Ordination of the Rev. John Cree,* in the city of New York, and preached on both occasions.

In June, 1798, he set out for Barnet, Vt., with a view to assist one of his brethren, the Rev. David Goodwillie, in the administration of the Lord's Supper. In passing through the town of Ryegate, he took a draught of bad water, which brought on a violent dysentery that issued in his death. Notwithstanding he was quite ill when he reached Barnet, he preached on Saturday; and, after assisting in the administration of the ordinance, (though so feeble that he was obliged to do it in a sitting posture,) he preached again on Sabbath evening. This was his last effort in public; and it was characterized by an indescribable fervour

---

* JOHN CREE was an emigrant from Scotland, and was settled in the city of New York in 1791,—shortly after his arrival in this country. He was obliged to leave his congregation on account of an inadequate support, and afterwards settled in Ligonier Valley, about fifty miles East from Pittsburg, where he laboured but a few years before his decease. He left a widow and several daughters.

of spirit, which seemed to say that he was conscious of standing near the portals of Heaven. His death occurred three weeks after this; and the interval he occupied almost entirely in exercises of devotion, or in testifying to those around him concerning his experience of the power and excellence of the Gospel.

When the news of his illness reached his congregation, two of his Elders were immediately sent to ascertain his condition, and render him all needed aid; and, as they did not return at the expected time, so great was the impatience of his flock to hear from him, that two others were dispatched on the same errand; but they were too late in their arrival at Barnet even to look upon his corpse, as it had just been committed to the grave.

The disease by which Mr. Beveridge was affected, unhappily proved contagious, and was communicated to several members of the family of Mr. Goodwillie. Two of Mr. G.'s children died of it, and were buried in the same grave, previous to the death of Mr. B; and Mr. G. himself was so ill that his recovery was well-nigh despaired of. The Sabbath found them in these affecting circumstances; and when Mr. B. saw that a number of people had come together from sympathy for the afflicted family,—notwithstanding the earnest entreaties of his friends, he raised himself up in the bed, and, after prayer and praise, delivered a pertinent and excellent discourse on Psalm xxxi, 23: "O love the Lord, all ye his saints." The Church at Barnet was at that time in a divided state; and he made a most pathetic application of his subject to their peculiar circumstances, and solemnly declared that, if they persevered in their contentions, he would be a witness against them in the judgment. His sermon was an hour long; and the effort, as might have been expected, proved too much for him. In the course of the night following, the intensity of his disease greatly increased, and both himself and his friends relinquished every hope of his recovery. Just at the dawn of day he sat up in his bed, and said,—"I am a dying man, and am dying fast; but as to bodily pain, I am free from it. I feel no more of this than you do, nor is there a man in Barnet who is more at ease than I am. Did you ever witness any thing similar to this? Are you not also persuaded I am dying?" Upon being answered by one of them,—"yes," "It is well," said he, "I am not afraid to die." Mr. G. and his family having now come into the room, Mr. Beveridge remarked that he would pray with them once more before he departed; and immediately he stretched forth his hands, and commended to God, with an audible voice, the Church of Christ in general, the Secession Body in particular, his own congregation at Cambridge, especially the younger portion of it, his brethren in the ministry, Mr. Marshall in Philadelphia, and Mr. Goodwillie, by name, praying that they might be sustained under their severe afflictions; and, finally, he prayed for those who had so faithfully ministered to him in his illness; and, having committed his own soul into his Redeemer's hands, he concluded, in allusion, no doubt, to what David says in the close of the seventy-second Psalm, with these words:—"*The prayers of Thomas Beveridge are now ended.*" After this, he addressed words of exhortation to those who were about him, accommodating himself with great felicity to their different characters and circumstances. In the afternoon he called for Mr. Goodwillie, and asked him if he knew what time the Son of Man would come; and he replied that he thought it would be about ten o'clock the ensuing night, or at latest about cock-crowing; and the answer proved prophetic; for, at just about ten, he expired without a struggle.

His body lies in the burial place at Barnet, and in the part of it appropriated to the use of Mr. Goodwillie's family, by the side of his two children who died of the same disease with himself. A suitable monument has been built over his grave.

Mr. Beveridge was married, shortly after his settlement in Cambridge, in 1789, to Jeanet Frothingham, who had come, with her widowed mother, from Scotland to this country about the commencement of the War of the Revolution. She died November 8, 1820, having lived a widow twenty-two years. They had five children, three sons and two daughters. The youngest son, and fourth child, is the Rev. *Thomas Beveridge*, D.D., now (1863) Professor of Theology at Xenia, O.

THOMAS HANNA BEVERIDGE, a grandson of the subject of this sketch, and a son of the Rev. Thomas Beveridge, D.D., was the eldest child of his parents, and was born in Philadelphia, March 31, 1830. His early intellectual developments were somewhat remarkable. At the age of ten or eleven—his father having meanwhile removed to Cannonsburgh—he commenced the study of Latin, and, in 1842, when he was only twelve, entered the Freshman class of Jefferson College. He graduated in 1847, having been kept at home for a year before entering the Junior class. His religious character was developed silently and gradually, without any sudden and marked change at any particular time. In the fall of 1847 he commenced the study of Theology under the instruction of the Rev. Abraham Anderson, D.D. and his father. After passing through the usual course of study and the usual trials, he was licensed to preach by the Presbytery of Chartiers in the summer of 1851; but, as he was then only twenty-one years of age, it was with the understanding that he should be permitted to continue his theological studies during the ensuing winter. He, accordingly, attended the Seminary a fifth session, preaching occasionally in the neighbourhood. During part of the year 1851 he was engaged in preparing for the press an account of the life of the Rev. T. B. Hanna, and a selection of his sermons, which was published shortly after. After suffering severely from ill health, and visiting various places, he went to Philadelphia in the early part of 1853, and in June of that year commenced his labours in what was then called the Mission Church, now the Sixth United Presbyterian Church of Philadelphia. He was ordained in October following. On the 13th of June, 1854, he was married to Mary Kerr McBride, of Philadelphia, by whom he had two children, both sons. In August, 1860, agreeably to a request from the congregation in Kishacoquillas, in Mifflin County, Pa., he consented to supply their pulpit for two Sabbaths. He was accompanied by his wife and children, and he enjoyed the journey exceedingly. The morning after their arrival at the house of the friend with whom they stopped, (Wednesday,) he was seized with a violent illness, which proved to be congestion of the brain, and terminated his life in the afternoon of the same day. His remains were removed to Philadelphia, and his Funeral, the next Monday, was attended with every demonstration of affectionate respect. He possessed a vigorous and highly cultivated intellect, with the most kindly and benignant spirit, and adorned every relation that he sustained. A writer in Forney's Philadelphia Press presents the following outline of his labours:—

"The life of Mr. Beveridge was a busy and brief one. He was born in March, 1830, and died on the threshold of his thirty-first year. And yet the catalogue of his labours, even though his field was in the unostentatious sphere of the ministry,—a department requiring more labour, and exhibiting fewer immediate results, than any other human profession, is a record of unceasing toil, assiduity and attention. Let us briefly recapitulate. At twenty-one he had passed through College and the Theological Seminary. At twenty-two, he publishes a volume biographical of Rev. T. B. Hanna, (a young divine whose career much resembled his own,)—a work highly creditable to his head and heart; at twenty-three, he assumes the charge of a congregation in this city; at twenty-four, he becomes a Presbyter of the Associate Synod, and is ordained to the holy work of the Ministry; at twenty-six, he edits and transcribes for the press ' Anderson's Lectures on Theology,"—a task of wonderful magnitude; at twenty-eight, he assumes the editorship of the Evangelical Repository, the magazine of his denomination; at twenty-nine, he is chosen Clerk of the United Presbyterian General Assembly; at thirty, he is elected a member of the Assembly's Mission Board; and, in his thirty-first year, he suddenly leaves the scene of his labours for that of labour's reward."

FROM THE REV. THOMAS BEVERIDGE, D.D.

CANNONSBURG, January 16, 1848.

Reverend and dear Sir: As nearly all those who have personal recollections of my father have passed away, I will not decline your request that I should furnish you with some general estimate of his character, though I do it under the full consciousness of the great delicacy of bearing testimony concerning one to whom I sustain so near and tender a relation.

In respect to his early history I can add nothing of interest to the materials already within your reach, except perhaps in one particular. This relates to the opposition which he made to the principle of Ecclesiastical Establishments. He has been much blamed by some, and much commended by others, for contributing to a revolution of sentiment on this subject, both in Britain and America. At the time when the first Seceders withdrew from the prevailing party in the Established Church of Scotland, in 1733, although they complained of many corruptions in the Church as established, and in the Establishment itself, yet they made no complaint against the *principle* of Establishments. They were opposed to what they considered great corruptions in some of the laws regulating the settlement of ministers, yet they were themselves settled according to these laws, and received their salaries from the Government, the same as others. But very soon after their secession, the faults of the Establishment began to appear to some of the Seceders to be inseparable from its very nature. As Mr. Barnes says of the *abuses* of slavery, they appear to belong to the very essence of the thing. Hence they began to entertain doubts on the general question of Establishments. These were avowed first and most prominently among the members of the General Synod or Anti-Burgher division of the Secession. Some of their young men, when on trials for license, hesitated to give an unqualified assent to those articles of the Westminster Confession, which are generally considered as favouring the Civil Establishment of religion, and as giving to the Magistrate some control over the Church in matters purely religious. At first these scruples were so far removed that the Confession was received without any express limitation. My father entertained these scruples, in common with some others, and was the first one ordained with an explicit allowance of objections against the Confession on this point. Immediately after his Ordination, he sailed for the United States, and was appointed, together with Dr. Anderson, to prepare an exhibition of the principles of the Associate Church, suited to their circumstances in this country. Into this exhibition, or Testimony as it is generally called, he introduced his views of the Magistrate's power, and a limitation of the approbation of the Confession on this subject. For doing this he was much blamed by those of his brethren in Scotland who still continued to advocate Civil Establishments of Religion. He was also severely handled by some other Presbyterian denominations in the United States, whose views of the separation of Church and State did not extend so far as his own. This exhibition of the principles of the Associate Church was republished in Scotland, and strengthened very much the hands of those who have of late years been called Voluntaries. It was made the model of a new exhibition of the principles of the General Synod, which, after several years' consideration, was enacted in 1804. This new testimony not only follows the form of the American, but embraces nearly the same principles on the subject of the Magistrate's power. It was on this ground strenuously opposed by a few eminent men, who, in consequence of its adoption, were separated from their brethren. With the exception, however, of these men, the voluntary principle, favoured by this Testimony, has become nearly universal among the Seceders in Scotland, and appears to be extending itself rapidly throughout Britain and the other Protestant nations of Europe. It is likely that, in effecting this revolution, there were many whose influence was greater than that of my father. Yet whatever influence he had, it was exerted zealously upon this side. He, however, complained that some of his brethren had carried their opposition to Establishments to such an extreme that he could not follow them; and he is, by no means, to be identified with all the views defended at present under the name of *Voluntaryism*. He even expressed an entire willingness, so far as related to himself, that some of the expressions in the American Testimony on this subject should be altered to obviate the exceptions which had been urged against them, and particularly the expression respecting the Magistrate,—that "his whole duty as a Magistrate respects men, not as Christians, but as members of civil society." *

Although my father did not come to the United States till after the Revolution, he was a warm advocate of the cause of the Colonies in their struggle with Great Britain for their Independence; and when appointed as a Missionary to the United States, in 1783, he consented without hesitation. At this time ministers in Scotland had almost the same horror of a mission to America as if it had been a banishment to Botany Bay. The petitions sent to the General Synod from various parts of the States were frequent and urgent, and the Synod entered upon the subject of missions with commendable zeal. Both ministers and people contributed money to bear the expenses of the missionaries, and collected libraries for them, with great liberality, yet this reluctance could not be overcome. The Synod appointed some with the liberty of returning, after a fixed time, if they were not satisfied. Such as consented to go on this condition returned at the expiration of the time appointed. Many utterly refused a mission on any terms. The Synod at last proceeded so far in their zeal that they required every young man at his license to go, so that a willingness to accept of a mission to the United States was somewhat uncommon. However, the interest which my father had felt in the cause of the Colonies, as well as his zeal for the promotion of the Kingdom of Christ in the world, made him welcome this field of labour, when assigned to him. Nor did his readiness in this case proceed from any weak and transient impulse —it was the result of principles which fortified him against the difficulties and discouragements attending his mission to a new country, and to a small society, labouring under a general odium for refusing to consent to a union which they regarded as a defection from their principles, and also for maintaining their connection with a Church in Britain, at a time when the hostile feeling to that country was still at its height. On his arrival, he was far from expressing any disappointment. In a letter written to Professor Bruce, about ten months afterwards, he gives his first impressions in terms very favourable both to the country and to the people,—and

---

* McKerrow's Hist. Secession, Chapt XI, pp. 378, *et seq.* Edition, 1841. Bruce's Review, pp. 118, 222, 350, &c. Ass. Test., Part I, Sec. 15.

makes candid allowances for what he felt obliged to condemn. This will appear the more worthy of notice when it is added that, during all, or at least the most, of this time, he had been subjected to considerable expenses, and yet had received no compensation for his ministerial services, his funds being thus reduced so far that he began to meditate upon selling some of his books, of which he had brought over about five or six hundred volumes. This letter was published in the Christian Magazine, Edinburgh, 1799, and is re-published in Mr. Miller's Sketches, pp. 487-90. Mr. M. regards it as "a striking specimen of the quickness and accuracy of his discernment, the correctness of his observation, and the candour of his remarks." Had he been aware of all the circumstances under which it was written, it is probable he would have added that it affords equally striking proof of a disregard to the things of the world, faith in the Providence of God, and great cheerfulness of spirit. In the last paragraph of the letter, he banters Professor Bruce about coming to America, on the ground that his wife and family would not stand in his way. This would hardly be understood, as it was intended, unless the reader were apprized that the Professor lived and died a bachelor.

In this letter he expresses his opposition to ministers occupying themselves in farming, yet, soon after his settlement in Cambridge, in September, 1789, having married a lady who derived a small inheritance from her parents, he was persuaded by her to invest it in a farm, which proved a happy circumstance for her and her family of five little children, when, in less than nine years after her marriage, she was left a widow. His salary was small and the family was left destitute of any means of support, except what was derived from this farm. But though, against his own inclination, settled upon a farm, he paid little or no attention to it, so that it never diverted him from his studies or other ministerial duties.

Those who best remember his ministry all unite in testifying that he did not excel as an Orator. He retained his Scotch pronunciation, and, although of a mild disposition, it is said that, in his public speaking, his manner was somewhat severe and stern. Sometimes persons not familiar with the Scotch dialect were not able fully to understand him, and occasionally even ludicrous blunders resulted from this circumstance. At one time he had chosen for his text Rom. iii, 27 : " Where is boasting then," etc. ? In the course of his sermon he found occasion to say a good deal, according to his way of pronouncing it, against *bosten*. A simple-hearted hearer afterwards expressed his surprise that Mr. Beveridge should have taken occasion to deal so sharply with good old Thomas Boston. It is evident, however, that, in more important things, his qualifications for the ministry were beyond the ordinary standard; and his ministerial labours, both in the pulpit and out of it, were held in much esteem.

He has been sometimes spoken of as excelling in the appropriateness of his texts to different seasons and occasions. An instance of this has been mentioned to me, as occurring soon after his arrival in America. The War being just closed, he took occasion to address the congregation to which he was preaching from the words of the prophet Jeremiah xxxi, 2 : " The people who were left of the sword found grace in the wilderness." I have seen an account, in some History of the Revolution, of this text being used by some minister of the Gospel at the close of the War. Whether the reference was to my father, or whether he and some other had been led to select the same text, I am not able to say ; but of the fact of his preaching from it on this occasion I have no reason to doubt.

He was also very plain and pointed in his manner of preaching. As an instance of this, I have heard mentioned the case of one of his Elders, in all respects among the most prominent men in the congregation, who had been charged with an aggravated offence, for which he was, after due process, deposed and excommunicated. On the first Sabbath after the affair came to light, my father took for his text the words of Christ respecting Judas,—John vi, 70: "Have not I chosen you twelve, and one of you is a devil?" It is said that the guilty person was repeatedly heard to groan with anguish during the discourse, yet he was so far from resenting it that he still continued to attend on my father's ministrations, and was one of those who undertook a journey of a hundred and fifty miles to see him, when on his death-bed at Barnet. He always cherished his memory with the greatest regard, and often spoke of him with tears. It may not be uninteresting to add that this Elder never ceased to attend upon the ordinances of religion, and, before his death, which happened a few years ago, he was restored as a penitent to the communion of the church.

But though my father appears to have been somewhat severe and pointed in his manner as a Preacher, he was of a pacific and affectionate disposition. This is evident, not only from the testimony of his acquaintances, but from various incidents in his life. It would hardly be possible for any one who had not a kind and friendly disposition to have acquired such an interest in the affections of others as was acquired by him. One of the friends of his youth, the late Mr. Barlass,* of New York, formerly a Minister in Scotland, travelled with him, when he was setting out for this country, to a certain point where it had been agreed that they would part. During the whole journey of some miles, such was their grief that neither of them was able to speak; and when they came to the appointed place, they parted without uttering a word. This minister, having been, by a mysterious Providence, laid aside from his office, immediately set out with a view to spend the rest of his days with his old friend in America; but, to his great grief, heard of his death as soon as he landed at New York. The affection subsisting between my father and Mr. Marshall, of Philadelphia, was more like that of brothers of the same family than of common friends. Perhaps it might be more justly said that it was far beyond any affection founded merely on consanguinity. He also lived on terms of the greatest intimacy with all his brethren, both in Scotland and the United States. Such also was the regard of the members of his congregation and others in the neighbourhood among whom he had laboured, that, long after his death, they could hardly speak of him without tears.

His pacific disposition, and also his disregard of worldly things, appear from the course which he pursued in reference to his own temporal affairs and those of his congregation. He was the first Minister of any Presbyterian denomination settled in the township of New Cambridge, as it was then called, and as such he became entitled to the possession or use of some land, agreeably to certain provisions made by the original proprietors of the township; but, as this claim was in some way disputed, he quietly yielded it rather than go to law. In like manner, after the union constituting the Associate

---

* WILLIAM BARLASS was born in the Parish of Fowlis, about eight miles from Perth, Scotland, and was settled for some years at Whitehill, where he continued till 1797. He was a man of uncommonly fine personal appearance. In his old age one of his eyes was destroyed by a cancer, but the other was peculiarly brilliant and piercing. He was said by his countrymen to have been in the foremost rank of popular preachers. A grave charge, however, was brought against him, the truth of which he always denied, even till within a few moments of his death; and I learn from the best authority that there is good reason to believe that it had its origin in malice. Still there was so much credit given to it that he desisted wholly from the exercise of his ministry. He came to New York in August, 1798, and, for two years after his arrival, was engaged in teaching the classics. He then became a bookseller, and was very useful as an importer of rare and valuable foreign works. He remained in this business till the close of life. He died on the 7th of January, 1817. The next year a volume of his Sermons was published, to which was appended the correspondence of the author with the Rev. John Newton.

Reformed Church had taken place, he was forcibly deprived of his place of worship by a few of the friends of that union; but he persuaded his congregation, who generally adhered to him and their profession, to give up, for the sake of peace, what they all regarded as their just rights. They, accordingly, went to work, and soon erected a new and much superior church, and prospered not the less, either in their temporal or spiritual affairs, for having submitted to what they felt to be a wrong.

He was generally considered quick in discovering the true characters of men, and in foreseeing the turn which events were likely to take. Something of this talent appears in his letter to Prof. Bruce, referred to above. He appeared also to have attained, in some cases, a foresight of things, not like the extraordinary gift of prophecy, and yet beyond what could be the result of mere common prudence. Instances of this kind have occurred in the lives of good men, which can hardly be denied to be extraordinary, and they may perhaps be best accounted for as intimations which they have received in answer to prayer. He is spoken of by Mr. Marshall as eminent in prayer, and having intimate communion with God; and it is likely that, in this way, he was led to certain anticipations which appeared to be beyond what natural reason, without any such aid, could suggest. As an instance of this, may be mentioned his having told a very intimate friend that his youngest was the only one of his three sons who would succeed him in his office. The event in this case corresponded to his anticipations, although it must have appeared, at the time, no way probable. The health of the two older brothers was much more vigorous than that of the youngest, yet both of them died in their youth. There appeared to be many hindrances in the way of the youngest, particularly after the decease of the others, yet it pleased Providence to bring him forward to the Ministry. In directing his attention this way, his father's saying could have had no influence, as he had no knowledge of it till after he was engaged in preaching. That he also had some presentiment of his approaching death, before leaving his family and congregation for the place where he was attacked by a mortal disease, was generally supposed at the time. The last sermon which he preached to his people before his departure was on the words of Christ, John xvii, 11,—"And now I am no more in the world, but these are in the world; and I come to thee." This sermon he appears to have repeated at Barnet, after he was seized with the disorder which terminated in his death. His letter to Mr. Marshall, published in the Memoir of his life, appears very suitable to the condition of a person writing under the impression that the time of his departure was at hand. His wife also noticed something uncommon in the particular manner in which he bade farewell to her and his little children, when leaving them. Such things, indeed, are often noticed after an event occurs, which would not at all be regarded but for that event; yet it is sometimes difficult to resist the impression that people have been acting under some presentiments of approaching events.

My father, as I have been informed by several persons, and as I am also told is stated in the Minutes of the Associate Presbytery of Pennsylvania, was elected by that Presbytery Professor of Theology, but declined an acceptance of this post, in consequence of which, Dr. Anderson was elected. In some branches of theological learning it is likely that he would have been found well qualified for this station, but he may have regarded the qualifications of Dr. Anderson as, in other respects, superior to his own, and declined the office in order that Dr. A. might be chosen to fill it.

From an early period of his life, he had devoted much of his attention to the study of Church History, and had collected a number of rare books in this department. It was generally supposed that he was occupied, in his leisure moments, in preparing for publication something either on the General History of the Church, or of some portion of it. Whether he had actually written any thing of the kind I am not able to say. His hand-writing was remarkably illegible; and it being supposed, at the time of his death, that nothing could be made of his manuscripts, no care was taken of them, and they were soon destroyed. If, however, his attention to this department of literature resulted in no permanent benefit to the public from his own labours, it was of some service in giving direction to the studies and labours of another, who afterwards became both useful and eminent as an Historian. The late Dr. McCrie, in a letter addressed to myself, states that it was the report of my father's attainments in Church History which first directed his attention to the subject.

Very few of my father's writings have been published, and those which have been are all brief articles; chiefly letters and sermons. The most important work of this kind in which he engaged was the Testimony of the Associate Church in the United States. This was chiefly penned by him, as it is evidently much more in his style than that of Dr. Anderson, the other member of the Committee appointed to prepare it. He wrote with great facility, and was considered in Church Courts as much more at home in drafting papers than in making speeches. His style excels in ease and simplicity, but sometimes exhibits signs of negligence, especially in some of his private letters, the publication of which was probably not anticipated by him.

I am, my dear Sir, truly yours,

THOMAS BEVERIDGE.

DAVID GOODWILLIE.*
1788—1830.

DAVID GOODWILLIE, a son of James and Mary (Davidson) Goodwillie, was born December 26, 1749, in Tanshall, in the Parish of Kinglassie, about fifteen miles North of Edinburgh, and was baptized by the Rev. John Erskine, son of the celebrated Ralph Erskine. His father was a member of the Established Church of Scotland, and a Ruling Elder in the Parish of Kinglassie, whose minister, Mr. Currie, at first publicly favoured the Erskines and others who seceded from the Established Church of Scotland in 1733; but when, by his writings, he came to oppose the Secession or Associate Church, his Ruling Elder, espousing their cause as the cause of God, joined that Church, and became a member of the Congregation of Abernethy, twelve miles distant. When the Associate Congregation of Leslie was organized, he became a member and an Elder, and continued so till his death, which occurred in January, 1782.

The subject of this sketch is supposed to have been employed in manual labour until he was about eighteen years of age, when he began to study with a view to the ministry of the Gospel. He commenced his academical course at Alloa, and finished it at the University of Edinburgh. He studied Theology under the direction of Professor Moncreiff, at Alloa, where the Theological Seminary of the Associate Church was established. After his Theological course was completed, the Associate Synod recommended that he should be licensed to

---

*MS. from his son, Rev. Dr. Thomas Goodwillie, and Communication from Rev. Dr Alexander Bullions.

preach; and, accordingly, having gone through the preparatory trials with acceptance, he *was* licensed, by the Presbytery of Kirkcaldy, early in October, 1778. The next month, by appointment of the Synod, he went to Ireland, where he remained nearly a year, preaching to the vacant congregations of the Associate Church; after which he returned to Scotland. In September, 1785, he went, by appointment of Synod, to England, and was engaged for the greater part of a year preaching in Kendal, in Westmoreland County, and Whitehaven, in Cumberland County. The rest of the time between his licensure and his mission to America he was employed in fulfilling appointments in preaching to the vacant congregations of the Associate Church in different parts of Scotland.

In consequence of an application from the Associate Presbytery of Pennsylvania to the Associate Synod of Scotland for preachers to be sent to America, and of a petition from the Church and town of Barnet, Vt., to that Synod to send them an ordained minister, the Synod recommended to Mr. Goodwillie to go to America, in response to these applications. He acceded to the proposal; and, having taken leave of his relatives and friends, he sailed from Greenock for New York, in company with the Rev. Archibald Whyte, on the 15th of May, 1788. He arrived at New York on the 5th of May following, and preached there on the three succeeding Sabbaths, after which he went to Philadelphia, where he was received by the Associate Presbytery of Pennsylvania, on the 28th of the same month. The Presbytery, with a view to his greater usefulness, resolved to ordain him at an early period, and assigned him subjects of trials for Ordination.

According to appointment of Presbytery, he preached in Oxford and Rocky Creek, Pa., in June and July; in Rockbridge, Va., in August; in Mill Creek, Franklin, Rocky Creek, and other places in the same region in Pennsylvania, in September and October. He attended the meeting at Pequea, October 1, 1788, and, his trials for Ordination having been sustained, he was ordained to the office of the Holy Ministry, in the Hall of the University of Pennsylvania, on the 31st of the same month,—the Rev. Thomas Beveridge preaching the Ordination Sermon, and delivering the Charge, both of which were afterwards published.

About the close of November Mr. Goodwillie reached Cambridge, Washington County, N. Y., where he laboured during the next winter, occasionally preaching also in Argyle and Saratoga. In April, 1789, he returned to Philadelphia, where he attended the meeting of the Presbytery, and then went to Carlisle, Pa., and laboured there and thereabouts during the months of May and June. During the remainder of the summer he was occupied chiefly in preaching in the city of New York, but in September went again to Cambridge, and presided at the Installation of the Rev. Thomas Beveridge, as Pastor of the Congregation in that place.

The towns of Barnet and Ryegate, lying on the Connecticut River, in the State of Vermont, were settled by companies from Scotland before the Revolutionary War, who, during that period, associated with a view to obtain preachers according to their own faith. It has already been stated that the Congregation of Barnet had requested the Associate Synod of Scotland to send them a minister; and in May, 1789, a communication was received, directing them to apply to the Associate Presbytery of Pennsylvania, to which the Synod had sent, as missionaries, Mr. Goodwillie and Mr. Whyte. Accordingly, in June following, the town petitioned that Presbytery that they would supply them with preaching, intimating, at the same time, a preference for the services of Mr. Goodwillie. The Presbytery responded favourably to their application, and, accordingly, Mr.

G. came to Barnet in November, 1789, and laboured there till the end of February, 1790, occasionly preaching also in Ryegate. On the 5th of July, 1790, the congregation gave him a unanimous call to become their minister. This call he accepted, and, after all the requisite preliminaries had been attended to, he was installed as Pastor of that congregation on the 8th of February, 1791,—Mr. Beveridge presiding, and the Rev. Dr. Anderson preaching the Sermon, from Acts xxvi. 22. When the call from Barnet was executed, twelve members of the congregation of Ryegate attended and signed a paper of adherence to the call, expecting to receive a portion of his labours. On petition to the church and town of Barnet, the congregation of Ryegate were allowed one-sixth part of Mr. Goodwillie's labours, beginning with his settlement in Barnet, and continuing till the autumn of 1822, when they obtained a settled minister. Mr. Goodwillie was the first Presbyterian minister settled in the State of Vermont, and, for nine years, the first settled minister of any denomination in the County of Caledonia.

On the 7th of May, 1790, Mr. Goodwillie was married to Beatrice, daughter of David and Margaret (Gardner) Henderson, by their friend, the Rev. William Marshall, in his own house in Philadelphia. Mrs. Goodwillie was a native of Kirkcaldy, Scotland, and came to this country with Mr. Goodwillie in 1788, and resided two years with her brother in Fredericksburg, Va. She was a lady of the finest intellectual and moral qualities, and proved in every respect a helpmeet to her husband, and a benefactress to the congregation over which he presided.

For twelve or fifteen years after his settlement in Barnet, Mr. Goodwillie suffered not a little from the privations and discomforts incident to a newly settled country, and still more from the dissensions of a few individuals, and from two difficult and doubtful cases of discipline. But, even during this period, the church was always in a flourishing state, the number of its members being regularly on the increase.

In answer to petitions from Canada for preaching, he left home, by appointment of Presbytery, in January, 1798, and travelled upwards of a hundred and fifty miles beyond Montreal, and returned towards the close of February, having performed a journey of more than six hundred miles through the woods, amidst the frosts and snows of winter.

In the year 1804 Mr. Goodwillie was subjected to some annoyance by certain attacks that were made upon him outside of his own communion, but he met them with great Christian forbearance and dignity, and they never injured him further than to produce a temporary disquietude. His congregation continued to prosper, in respect to both numbers and spirituality. It appears from the Church Record that, during his ministry, more than four hundred persons were enrolled on the list of communicants at Barnet, and it is supposed that nearly two hundred made an open profession of their faith at Ryegate, making the whole number whom he admitted to Church fellowship, during a ministry of forty years, about six hundred.

In 1826 Mr. Goodwillie was relieved, in a measure, from the cares and labours of his office, by the settlement of his son *Thomas* as his colleague. The Ordination and Installation took place on the 27th of September, on which occasion the Charge to the youthful Co-pastor was delivered by his venerable father.

On the 4th of February, 1827, Mrs. Goodwillie died in the sixty-sixth year of her age, in the triumphs of faith, and with the words,—" O Lord Jesus, come quickly,"—upon her lips. Her aged husband, though bowed under the rod, was enabled to say, as she lingered on the borders of the invisible world,—" I resign you to the Lord, from whom I received you."

The last time Mr. Goodwillie dispensed the Lord's Supper to his church was on the 27th of June, 1830. Two days after this, he delivered the Charge to the Rev. William Pringle,* at his ordination at Ryegate, ten miles from his residence. On the 18th of July he preached his last sermon to his congregation, from the text,—" There remaineth, therefore, a rest for the people of God : Let us, therefore, labour to enter into that rest." The discourse was one of uncommon power, and deeply affected his audience. On Thursday following he seemed overcome by the excessive heat of the weather, and this exhaustion was quickly followed by congestion of the lungs, attended with cough and raising of blood. His sickness continued twelve days, during the greater part of which time he was delirious; but, in the near approach of death, he recovered the use of his reason, and rendered the most abundant testimony to the all sustaining power of Christian faith. He died on the 2d of August, 1830, in the eighty-first year of his age, and the fifty-second of his ministry. His Funeral was attended by an immense concourse; and on the next Sabbath an excellent Funeral Discourse was delivered by the Rev. William Pringle, from Psalm cxlii, 5. His death was greatly lamented, not only throughout the region in which he lived, but wherever he was known.

Mr. Goodwillie participated in some degree in civil affairs. In 1805 the town of Barnet elected him a member of the Legislature of the State, which held its session that year at Danville, seven miles from his residence. He always returned home on Saturday and preached to his people on the Sabbath. In 1807 he was chosen Town Clerk, and afterwards Town Treasurer, and was annually re-elected to these offices till 1827, when he declined a re-election. He was appointed the first Postmaster of Barnet in 1808, and held the office till 1818. He had a very extensive correspondence, especially with eminent clergymen, both in this country and in Scotland.

Mr. Goodwillie was the father of eight children,—four sons and as many daughters. Two of his children, a son and daughter, died in early youth, in 1798, of an epidemic, on the same day and under peculiarly afflictive circumstances. Two of his sons, *Thomas* and *David*, were graduated at Dartmouth College in 1820, studied Theology under Dr. Banks at the Eastern Theological Seminary of the Associate Church in Philadelphia, and were licensed to preach by the Associate Presbytery of Cambridge, September 29, 1823, their venerable

---

*The Rev. WILLIAM PRINGLE was born in Perth, Scotland, in 1790. His father was the Rev. Alexander Pringle, D.D., who, for more than sixty years, was minister of the Associate Congregation of Perth. After being, for some time, a student at the University of Edinburgh, he studied Medicine, and was admitted to practice, and shortly after migrated to Canada. He soon determined, however, not to practise Medicine, and returned to Scotland and prosecuted the study of Theology under the Rev. John Dick, D.D., of Glasgow. He was licensed by the Associate Presbytery of Perth, April 15, 1823, and immediately entered upon his labours as a probationer. Having preached, for some time, in Scotland, he again left his native country, and came to the United States, in the autumn of 1827, and soon after joined the Associate Presbytery of Cambridge. He received a call from the Associate Congregation of Ryegate, Vt., and was ordained, and installed Pastor, by the Presbytery of Cambridge, June 29, 1830. Here he laboured faithfully until his health failed, in consequence of which he resigned his charge on the 21st of June, 1852. He died suddenly, of an organic disease of the heart, December 14, 1858. He was engaged, during the last years of his life, upon a work entitled "The Cosmography of Scripture," and was just finishing it when he died, the last sentence being left incomplete. He was an excellent Scholar, an able Preacher, and was highly respected in all his relations.

father being the Moderator of the Presbytery. *Thomas*, as has already been stated became a colleague with his father. *David* accepted a call from the congregation, of Deer Creek, Poland and Liberty, on the line running between Pennsylvania and Ohio, and was ordained and installed by the Associate Presbytery of Ohio, on the 26th of April, 1826. Two of his daughters were married to clergymen,—the one to the Rev. Alexander Bullions, D.D.,* the other to the Rev. John Donaldson.

FROM THE REV. THOMAS GOODWILLIE.

BARNET, VT., August 15, 1862.

My dear Sir: I will not refuse the request you make of me, though a compliance with it must subject me to the somewhat delicate task of speaking of my own much loved and venerated father. I shall endeavour, however, to

---

* ALEXANDER BULLIONS, a son of William and Isabella (Malcolm) Bullions, was born in Auchtergaven, Scotland, in February, 1779. His father was a farmer, and both his parents were exemplary members of the Church of Scotland, in the bosom of which he was himself born and baptized. His mother taught him to read, and he never attended school more than a month until he was seven years old, there having been no school in the neighbourhood in which his father lived. The family having now changed their residence, he was accustomed to attend school in the winter, and to work on his father's farm in the summer, till he had reached his sixteenth year. The first thing of which he had any recollection was a resolution to be a Preacher; and the reason was that he thought all ministers were good men, and that this would be a sure way to get to Heaven. He subsequently formed the purpose to be a Missionary, in connection with a conversation that his sister had with him about the judgment day. His mind was, from his earliest years, much turned towards serious things, and for six years after he made a profession of religion he thought he had unbroken communion with God. When he joined the Church, which was not far from the age of sixteen, he joined the Associate, and not the Established, Church, to which his parents belonged. He fitted for College at two parochial schools, and at an excellent Academy in Perth. He entered the University of Edinburgh in 1798, having previously read the greater part of the Latin and Greek Classics. He remained at the University four years; and then studied Theology for about five years under the Rev. Archibald Bruce, of Whitburn. On the 20th of May, 1806, he was licensed to preach by the Associate Presbytery of Perth. He had regular appointments for only four Sabbaths previous to his leaving Scotland. It was his wish to go to India as a Missionary; but no British vessel at that time would carry out a missionary, because it was thought that any attempt to introduce Christianity there would lead to Revolution. He sailed for New York on the 4th of October, 1806, and landed on the 8th of December following. He remained in New York till after the first Sabbath in January, and then went to Albany and passed a Sabbath, and thence to Cambridge, and took charge of the congregation with which he continued till the close of his life. He was married in September, 1810, to Mary Goodwillie, who died in 1830. They had six children, all of whom lived to become members of the Church. Two of his sons have been graduated at Union College,—*David Goodwillie*, in 1835, who became a clergyman, and was for some time settled as a colleague with his father, but is now (1863) in the Old School Presbyterian Church, and settled as Pastor at West Milton; and *William*, in 1844, who became a Physician, settled in Argyle, and died in 1851. His eldest daughter, *Margaret*, was married to the Rev. William Pringle. Dr. Bullions was married about two years after the death of his first wife, to Mary, daughter of William McClellan, of Hebron, who died without issue in April, 1855. He received the degree of Doctor of Divinity from the Western University in Pennsylvania about 1830. In the course of his ministry he performed a great amount of missionary labour at different periods. In 1824 he spent fourteen weeks labouring in Upper Canada. In 1846 he spent nearly the entire year in travelling in the capacity of a missionary in the States of Ohio, Virginia, Missouri and Iowa. Dr. Bullions, with two or three others of his brethren, fell under censure of the Associate Synod many years ago, and were suspended and deposed the same day, with their congregations. They continued a separate organization until the meeting of Synod in Albany, in 1854, when a reunion was effected. Dr. Bullions published a Tract entitled "Marah's Waters Sweetened, or Afflictions and Consolations of the Righteous"; another on Repentance; and another on Pardon, which has been republished by the Presbyterian Board of Publication; besides various contributions to periodicals. He died at Cambridge, June 26, 1857, in the eightieth year of his age. He was a man of great intellectual power, of extensive acquirements, of boundless good humour, of unswerving integrity, of a most genial spirit, of earnest devotion to his work, and of a commanding and far reaching influence.

say nothing concerning him which any body who knew him well would regard as even doubtful.

I may say, without the fear of contradiction, that my father was an eminently devoted and successful Minister. During his whole ministry, even to old age, he was not only diligent in performing the public services of the Sabbath and visiting the sick, but he paid, annually, a Pastoral visit to each family in the congregations of Barnet and Ryegate, and catechised parents and children in public meetings in different parts of the two towns. On one occasion the female head of a family, which he called to visit, refused to receive him as a Minister. As he was about leaving, he turned round at the door of her house, and, wiping his feet on the floor, said to her,—" Christ commanded them whom He sent to preach the Gospel in every house or city to shake off the very dust of their feet as a testimony against them who would not receive them nor hear their words, and to depart, saying,—' Be ye sure of this—the Kingdom of God is come near unto you.' " But the truth and grace of God soon prevailed, for what he said and did on this occasion had such an effect upon the woman that she soon professed her faith in Christ, and he baptized both herself and her children.

He brought from Scotland a large library, chiefly theological, though many of the books were much damaged by the exposure to which they were subjected in their transportation up the Connecticut River. When at home, he kept closely confined to his study-room, adjoining his library, and, even till near the close of life, he was in the habit of continuing his studies till midnight. His manuscript sermons and lectures show that they were prepared with great care and labour. On Sabbath forenoon he was accustomed to expound the Scriptures; and he expounded most of the Books of the Old Testament as well as the New, not only bringing out the great truths contained in them, but exhibiting them in their practical bearings. His sermons were systematic, logical and highly evangelical. He was eminent in the gift of prayer. The whole tenor of his ministrations was adapted to advance the knowledge, faith and Christian activity of his people.

My father's mental endowments were well suited to his calling and condition, and his ministrations were, to the end of life, acceptable and profitable to the people among whom he laboured. He was a man of close observation, of profound common sense, of a thorough knowledge of human nature, and of such general information on most subjects of interest that his presence was felt to be an element of pleasure and improvement in almost any circle. He was candid and charitable in his judgment of others, and was a wise Counsellor, and a faithful and affectionate Friend. His people consulted him in respect to their temporal as well as spiritual matters; and they never had reason to regret having followed his advice. He was withal a very good Physician; and he often had occasion, especially while the country was new, to unite medical with pastoral attentions. He was social and affable, and had many humorous anecdotes at command, which he always related in the proper place and at the right time. He had great shrewdness and promptness, which enabled him sometimes to meet a difficult case in a most felicitous manner. He was called to marry a couple in Cambridge in 1789, and, just as he was commencing the ceremony, a young man in the company arose and said,— " I object to this marriage because the bride has promised to marry me." He immediately took the bride, bridegroom and objector into a room by themselves, where the bride confessed that she had promised to marry the objector, and said that she was *willing and ready to fulfil that engagement!* He advised the bridegroom, as the bride had treated him so disingenuously, to have nothing more to do with her—and he readily took the advice. All then returned to the room where the marriage was to be celebrated, and he actually married the lady to the gentleman who had raised the objection. He then sat down to comfort the disappointed bridegroom; and, in the presence of the whole company, he exhorted him not to be discouraged, as there were young women in abundance who would make good wives. "Here," said he, "is a pretty black-eyed lass—what would you think of making suit to her?" The young man took advantage of the hint, and the black-eyed beauty soon became his wife, and the wisdom of the advice was manifest in the fact that it turned out that he got the better wife of the two. When my father was Moderator of the Associate Synod in 1803, after the motion for final adjournment was carried, one of the members, Mr. B———, rose and very improperly introduced some of his own personal grievances in reference to certain other members. Several immediately rose to reply, when the Moderator said,—"The Synod has agreed to final adjournment. Mr. B. is out of order. He has disburdened his conscience. Let us pray;" and, immediately after prayer, adjourned the Synod till the next year—and thus the affair was happily ended. When a member of the Legislature of Vermont in 1805, his reply to the arguments of an opponent was so forcible and facetious that the whole house was convulsed with laughter; and his opponent, though he knew it was at his expense, had the magnanimity not to resent it.

He was a great friend of learning, and laboured publicly and privately till an Academy was established at Peacham, five miles from his residence, and several years before any other clergyman was settled in this region. He was one of the Board of Trustees from its origin in 1795 to 1827, and during this time attended all the annual meetings of the Board, and was for many years its President. When the Semi-Centennial Anniversary of the Institution was celebrated, several very eminent men took part in the exercises, and the good and faithful offices of this early benefactor were not forgotten.

I think I may safely say that he left behind him a name which is still fragrant throughout this region.

Believe me very truly yours,
THOMAS GOODWILLIE.

FROM THE REV. PETER BULLIONS, D.D.

Troy, February 26, 1863.

My dear Sir: My first meeting with the Rev. David Goodwillie was in Cambridge, in 1818, the year after I came to the United States. I accompanied him, by his request, to Barnet, the place of his residence, to assist him in the administration of the Lord's Supper. From that time we were always friends, and my meetings with him were sufficiently frequent, and my relations with him sufficiently intimate, to supply me with the requisite material for the communication you ask for.

Mr. Goodwillie had the advantage of a fine personal appearance. He had a large frame, though he was not corpulent, and a full face, beaming with intelligence and good humour. His movements were easy and rapid, and his general air indicated a wakeful mind and a habit of industry. He had a vigorous and well-trained intellect, and withal more than commonly versatile—for there was scarcely any thing to which he did not find it easy to turn his hand. He was one of the most amiable and benevolent of men, and his genial and kindly spirit attracted every body. And yet no man was truer than he to his own convictions. When his judgment was once matured upon any subject, it must be an argument of extraordinary force that could ever reverse it. At the same time he was not intolerant towards those who differed from him, but lived in the kindest relations with all with whom he had any intercourse. The right which he claimed of judging for himself in respect to all subjects, he cheerfully accorded to others. In all the intercourse of private life he was a most agreeable companion—while his conversation was never trifling or undignified, it was lively, racy, intelligent, sometimes sparkling with wit, and always breathing a most benevolent spirit.

I have not often heard Mr. Goodwillie preach, but I believe I have a tolerably correct idea of what he was in the pulpit. He may have been accustomed, for the most part, to write his sermons fully; but my impression is that, in his later years, a portion at least of his preparation for the pulpit was merely mental and spiritual—he used to sit in his chair and muse, and then go forth and deliver his Master's message. I remember to have heard that, on one occasion, he arose in the pulpit, and stood for some time in perfect silence; and afterwards, when asked for an explanation, he said,—"I was just casting about for a bright thought to launch forth with." His voice was pleasant, without being very loud; his enunciation distinct, and his manner considerably animated, without much gesture. His sermons, in respect to both matter and construction, were what you might expect from his having been educated in Scotland, and among the Seceders—they were intensely evangelical, and were divided and subdivided with most systematic exactness. They were, I think, especially adapted to instruct and edify.

But one of the most striking peculiarities of Mr. Goodwillie's character was his remarkable facility at adaptation. While he preached the Gospel faithfully and attended well to all the interests of his flock, he was put in requisition for various civil and secular services, all of which he performed as acceptably as if his training had been in civil life; though he never even seemed to put off the character of a Christian Minister even while he was immediately engaged as a servant of the State. On one occasion, when he was a member of the Vermont Legislature, there was a good deal of infidel influence in the house, and one of these sceptical gentry took it into his head to move that they should, perhaps on account of a pressure of business, continue their sittings on the Sabbath. The eyes of the members were generally directed towards Mr. Goodwillie, and one person who was sitting near him called to him to second the motion. He immediately rose, in great dignity, and said,—"I second the motion, Sir; not because I approve of it, but because I should like to know who are the persons in this house that are willing thus to profane God's holy day. I call for the ayes and nays, Sir." The motion was instantly withdrawn. He never forgot that he was a Minister of the Gospel, and never allowed others to forget it.

I am, Reverend and Dear Brother,
Yours Faithfully,
P. BULLIONS.

ARCHIBALD WHYTE.

1788—1849.

FROM THE REV. THOMAS GOODWILLIE, D.D.

BARNET, VT., January 1, 1863.

Dear Sir: Agreeably to your request, I send you a brief sketch of the life of the Rev. Archibald Whyte, drawn chiefly from information obtained from his son, and from my father's somewhat extensive correspondence with him; and also a statement of my own impressions of his character, derived from an intimate acquaintance with him of more than thirty years.

ARCHIBALD WHYTE was born December 25, 1755, on Westlock farm, in the Parish of Eddleston, Peebleshire, Scotland. His father was Thomas Whyte, a farmer possessing considerable property, and the maiden name of his mother was Dalziel. He is supposed to have laboured on his father's farm till he was about twenty years of age. Having prosecuted his preparatory studies under Alexander Tweedie, of Temple, he entered the University of Edinburgh in 1777, and remained till 1781. His certificate of membership in the Associate Congregation of Howgate is dated February, 1777. From 1781 to 1786 he studied Theology under Professor Moncrieff, in the Theological Seminary of the Associate Synod of Scotland, at Alloa. He was licensed to preach in August, 1786, probably by the Associate Presbytery of Edinburgh, and preached his first sermon in Kilwinning immediately after. He continued for twenty months to preach, according to his appointments, in the congregations of the Associate Church in different parts of Scotland. In response to a petition from the Associate Presbytery of Pennsylvania to the Associate Synod of Scotland, in 1787, that Synod appointed Mr. Whyte and my father to come to America; and, in fulfilment of that appointment, they crossed the ocean, and landed in New York on the 5th of May, 1788. On the Sabbath succeeding their arrival, Mr. Whyte preached in New York, and immediately after directed his course North to Washington County, where he preached—at Cambridge and Argyle—until about the middle of September. In the mean time, his credentials were presented to the Associate Presbytery of Pennsylvania, in Philadelphia, and he was regularly received by that Presbytery. From that time till 1796 he itinerated and preached, by appointment of Presbytery, in the States of New York, Pennsylvania and Virginia, and twice visited the Carolinas, where he was very kindly received; and one of their congregations gave him a call, offering £70 sterling as a salary; but he declined it, chiefly, it would seem, from his opposition to Slavery. During the same period he preached in the Western parts of Pennsylvania, beyond the Allegheny Mountains. After having preached a year in America, he was ordained by the Associate Presbytery of Pennsylvania, May 26, 1789, at Muddy Creek, (now Guinston,) York County, Pa., the Rev. Thomas Clarkson presiding at his Ordination, and preaching from I. Cor. iv, 2.

After having been in America two years, he was married, May 27, 1790, to Margaret Kerr, of Marsh Creek, Adams County, Pa. For a few years his wife accompanied him, as he travelled about preaching in different and distant parts of the country. The Presbytery of Pennsylvania had many vacant congregations to supply, scattered through all the immense region from Barnet, Vt., on the North, to South Carolina on the South, and as far West as the parts of Pennsylvania adjacent to the Ohio River. As the preachers under the care of the Presbytery were few, Mr. Whyte had many long and difficult journeys to make, North, South and West, in fulfilling his appointments. These journeys he made on horseback; and, not having been accustomed to this mode of travelling in his youth, he never became an expert horseman. As his wife, who was a better equestrian than himself, accompanied him on these journeys, it is said that she used to ride on before him through the deep waters to be forded, and the difficult and dangerous places to be passed, and then gave him directions how to follow. In a few years after their marriage, when their children began to multiply, it became necessary to provide a permanent place of abode. After travelling together through the Carolinas in 1792, they came to Cambridge, N. Y., the greater portion of his labours being required in that part of the Associate Church. Here he obtained for his family temporary accommodations in the house of his friend, the Rev. Thomas Beveridge, who was Pastor of the Associate congregation in that place. In 1792 he received a considerable sum of money, as patrimony, from Scotland, with which he purchased three hundred and twenty acres of land in Argyle, Washington County, N. Y., part of which he improved, and built the house upon it in which he lived and died. Notwithstanding his home was in Argyle, he continued, for many years, to fulfil, with great punctuality, the appointments of Synod and Presbytery to preach in the vacant congregations in different parts of the country, though, in doing so, he was often obliged to take long and tedious journeys, and sometimes to be absent from home for several months. In 1812, after preaching for some time in the Eastern parts of Pennsylvania, he crossed the Allegheny Mountains again; and, in 1813, he laboured in the Western parts of that State near the Ohio River. Between 1796 and 1822 he was eight times in this place, then the place of my father's residence, assisting him at the dispensation of the Lord's Supper; and, as late as the winter of 1831–32, he preached here six months during the Pastor's absence on account of his health. The last time he preached was at North Argyle, a few miles from his residence, on Sabbath, October 5, 1845, in the forenoon, from Matt. v, 16, and in the afternoon from John viii, 36. He was now near the close of his ninetieth year, and had been a Preacher for more than fifty-nine years. The disease of which he died was of but four days' continuance, although, for a month or two previous to its commencement, a slight decline of the vital power had been observed. On the Wednesday immediately preceding his death, he became deeply lethargic; and nothing could arouse him for any length of time except religious exercises, in which he would still devoutly engage. He died in Argyle, which had been his home forty-nine years, on the 6th of January, 1849, twelve days after he had completed his ninety-third year. At his Funeral, which was very numerously attended, the Rev. Alexander Bullions, D.D., long his kind and faithful friend, delivered an appropriate Discourse, and Messrs. Miller and Mairs engaged in prayer.

Mr. Whyte was extremely methodical in all his habits. He kept memoranda of almost every thing pertaining to his ministry. From his Diary it appears that he had preached eighteen hundred and forty times, in a hundred and twenty-eight different places;—namely, one hundred times in fifty-four places in Scotland, and seventeen hundred and forty times in seventy-four places in America.

Mr. Whyte was a valuable member of Church Courts. He was Moderator of the Associate Synod, which met at Pittsburg, Pa., in 1813, and was for many years Clerk of the Associate Presbytery of Cambridge. He always cherished a strong attachment to the religious principles and usages of the Church of which he lived and died a member and a Minister.

He was a man of deep devotion and active piety. His trials were numerous and various, and some of them peculiarly severe; but his meekness, patience and resignation were most exemplary. He was modest and humble, upright and honourable, careful and conscientious in the discharge of his duties to God and man. He had a cheerful, contented and social disposition, that threw sunshine into every circle where he might happen to be.

He brought from Scotland a large and valuable Theological library, with which he had made himself very familiar. As he possessed superior talents and learning, and was especially well versed in Theology, his sermons were rich in evangelical truth, well digested and arranged, and were eminently adapted to edify the intelligent and pious part of his congregation. He was never a popular Preacher, but it was the fault of his hearers if he was not always, in a high degree, a useful one.

Mr. Whyte was fond of hearing and telling a good anecdote. He had many such at his command, and knew well how to suit them to company, times and circumstances. I remember the following, having some reference to himself, which he used sometimes to relate with great zest. Not long after he began to preach, and before he left Scotland, he called, on one occasion, on the Rev. David Somerville,* a venerable but rather eccentric man, who afterwards came to this country. He was conducted into the room where Mr. Somerville had just commenced family worship. He was very particular in praying for his wife, children and servants, each by name. Mr. Whyte was waiting for his turn, when the excellent minister mentioned "the lad who came in at the 'oor o' prayer;" and earnestly prayed that "his five bit loaves, and few sma fishes, with which he fed the people, might be greatly blessed and multiplied to them." "Sma, sma enough, indeed, thought I," added this humble modest man, when he related the anecdote.

Mrs. Whyte died on the 1st of January, 1819, aged fifty-four years. They had six children,—four sons and two daughters. The eldest son enlisted in the War of 1812-15, and died in the army. The youngest, *Archibald*, born August 3, 1800, was graduated at Union College in 1822; studied Theology under Dr. Banks in the Eastern Theological Hall of the Associate Church; was licensed to preach by the Associate Presbytery of Cambridge, June 19, 1826; was ordained and settled as Pastor of the Associate Congregation of Baltimore, Md., December 5, 1827; and, in 1833, removed thence to one of the Carolinas.

Wishing you great success in the important work in which you are engaged,

I remain, with high esteem,

Yours very truly,

THOMAS GOODWILLIE.

FROM THE REV. PETER BULLIONS, D.D.

TROY, February 25, 1863.

My dear Sir: It was not more than a week or two after my arrival in this country, in 1817, that I made the acquaintance of the Rev. Archibald Whyte, and from that time till his death I had the pleasure, not only of being intimately acquainted with him, but of reckoning him among my most valued friends.

---

* DAVID SOMERVILLE was born in Scotland, West of Edinburgh, and, after passing through the usual preparatory studies in the country, entered the University of Edinburgh. Having completed the usual academical course, he studied Theology under the Rev. Professor Moncrieff, of the Associate Synod of Scotland. After being licensed to preach, he laboured chiefly within the bounds of the Presbytery of Glasgow; and, having received a call from the Associate congregation at Strathaven, he was ordained and installed there about the year 1769 or 1770. He laboured there with much success for nearly twenty years, when, in consequence of a great loss of blood from the nose, he became so much enfeebled that he felt obliged to resign his charge. After making a short visit in Ireland, he came with his family to this country, being attracted hither especially by the fact that he had a brother settled as a merchant in Baltimore. He arrived here in the year 1790 or '91, and shortly after became a member of the Associate Presbytery, and, as his health permitted, preached in the vacancies in Pennsylvania and Virginia. He died in Rockbridge County, Va., about the year 1793. He is represented as having been an earnest, devoted minister, very active and useful in Church Courts, and, before the loss of blood in Scotland already referred to, very popular as a public speaker. He published a Sermon preached at Paisley, Scotland, on a day of Humiliation, in 1776; and it has been republished in Mr. Miller's volume of Biographical Sketches and Sermons.

We were accustomed to visit frequently at each other's houses, and to indulge in the fullest and freest interchange of thought and feeling; and it is not unlikely that our relations were the more intimate from the fact that we were both natives of the same country, and had, to some extent, common recollections and associations.

In stature Mr. Whyte was rather below the medium, with about the usual amount of flesh—he had a high and capacious forehead, and a long face, the lower part of which was more than ordinarily thin. The general expression of his countenance was highly benignant, and it indicated also what he really possessed,—a sound and well balanced intellect. His heart was as full of kindness as that of any other man you would meet; and no one knew better than he the luxury of serving a friend, or of doing good even to the most undeserving. And while he was so generous and benevolent, he was no less discreet and thoughtful, and never by inadvertence placed himself in any equivocal attitude, or put in jeopardy the interests, or wounded the feelings, of others. His mind had nothing of what would commonly be called brilliancy, but it was clear and logical, and generally worked out results which it would not be easy to gainsay. And it was not a mind that was prone to keep in a beaten track—there was often a richness, freshness and beauty in his thoughts, which would have done no dishonour to many a man of wider fame and higher pretensions.

And this leads me to speak of him as a Preacher—and here I am obliged to acknowledge that he had not a single attribute of a popular speaker. His sermons were excellent—they were fully written out, and in respect to spirit, sentiment, and I may add style, were all that could be desired—indeed he possessed rare skill in evolving the meaning of a passage—while every thing was so simple as to be adapted to the humblest intellect, there would often be an air of originality about it that the most cultivated mind would greatly admire. But these excellent sermons were—shall I say murdered in the delivery. It was a great burden to him to commit to memory; and when he had done his best, he could not be sure that his memory would not fail him; and hence his delivery was laboured, embarrassed, and often exceedingly painful to his hearers. Though his sermons were always replete with excellent matter, and were well worthy of the attention of any audience, it was only that portion of his hearers who could overlook a crude and most unattractive manner, who could suitably estimate the privilege of sitting under his preaching. I heard him preach a sermon on Saturday before a Communion at Cambridge, which both myself and Dr. Alexander Bullions were so much pleased with that we asked him if he would favour us with the perusal of the manuscript. He did so, and the first the old gentleman knew of it, it appeared as an article in a Magazine of which I was at that time editor, signed *Lukos* (White.) I knew that he would not be offended by the liberty; and he *was* not, but laughed heartily when the fact was made known to him.

In Ecclesiastical Bodies his voice was not often heard, but when he did speak, he was sure to command attention by an exhibition of good sense and sound judgment. Every thing that he said and did was according to rule, and was dictated by temperate and enlightened views of the subject under consideration. His opinions always derived great weight from his acknowledged clearsightedness, sobriety, integrity and impartiality. A stranger to all show and pretension, he was a mass of solid excellence.

I am, Reverend and Dear Brother,
Yours respectfully,
P. BULLIONS.

JOHN BANKS, D.D.*
1796—1826.

JOHN BANKS was born in Stirling, Scotland, about the year 1763. He received his education, both classical and theological, in his native country. He was settled, for some time, as a Minister, in the Presbytery of Edinburgh, and, just before he left Scotland, was an Assistant to the Rev. Adam Gib; but he resigned his charge and crossed the ocean in 1796, with a view to find a home and a permanent field of labour in this country. During the winter of 1796-97, he was engaged in preaching to the Associate Congregation in the city of New York, and received a call to become their Pastor, which, however, he declined in 1798. Shortly after this he received another call from the Associate Congregation of Cambridge, N. Y.: this he accepted, and was installed in his pastoral charge in September, 1799. Here he remained till June, 1802, when he was "loosed" from his charge and accepted the Pastorship of the Church in Florida, N. Y. During the fourteen years that he continued here, he united with the office of a Minister of the Gospel that of a Teacher, receiving into his family and under his instruction, not only boys with a view to their being fitted for College, but young men who wished to prosecute the study of Hebrew as part of their preparation for entering the ministry.

In 1808 the degree of Doctor of Divinity was conferred upon him by Union College.

In December, 1815, it was resolved, at a congregational meeting of the Associate Church in Philadelphia, to invite Dr. Banks, with the approbation of Presbytery, to labour among them as a permanent supply. The proposed measure having received the sanction of Presbytery, he accepted the invitation, being "loosed" from the pastoral charge of the congregation at Florida, on account of insufficient salary, in February, 1816. He arrived, with his family, in Philadelphia, in May following, and commenced his labours in his new field, and, at the same time, opened a Select School for instruction in Greek and Latin; and afterwards he took charge of the Grammar School connected with the University, and had also quite a number of pupils in Hebrew, among whom were several clergymen of the city. After having served the congregation, as a permanent supply, for about two years, they gave him a unanimous call, in May, 1818, to become their Pastor. He accepted the call, and was installed the next month, the Sermon on the occasion being preached by the Rev. Thomas Hamilton, and the Charge to the Pastor and the People given by the Rev. Thomas Smith.† In 1818, he was Moderator of the Associate Synod.

In May, 1820, the Associate Synod elected him Professor of Theology in the Eastern Theological Seminary, situated at Philadelphia. In accepting the office, he made the following communication to the Synod:—"My present engagements in the University are necessary to the support of my family. The revenue from the University amounts to $1,000 per annum. But, on account of the superior

---

* MSS. from Rev. Drs. A. Bullions and Thomas Goodwillie, and J. McAllister, Esq.

† THOMAS SMITH was an emigrant from Scotland. He was appointed as a missionary to this country by the Associate Synod in 1790, but declined the appointment. Some time afterwards, however, he came hither, and travelled for many years without receiving any calls. He was at last settled at Huntington, Pa., and died in August, 1825.

excellence of the studies connected with the teaching of Theology, I should resign my situation in the University for $500 per annum, and, had it been in my power, I should have been glad to teach Theology without any pecuniary remuneration at all." The Minute of the Synod in relation to this proposal is as follows:—
" After considering, at some length, Dr. Banks' proposal, the Synod cannot but acknowledge his generosity in offering to make such a sacrifice by resigning his place in the University, &c.; but they cannot at present engage to pay the sum of $500 per annum, and would not think themselves justified in desiring him to relinquish his place in the University." It appears, however, that, by some subsequent arrangement, the sum of five hundred dollars was actually paid to him.

Dr. Banks retained his relation both to the Church and to the Seminary, discharging his duties to each with great fidelity, till the close of his life. On the 9th of April, 1826, he went through all the services of the Sabbath with unaccustomed energy and solemnity. The next morning, about nine o'clock, he was struck with apoplexy, and expired almost immediately, without a struggle or a groan, in the sixty-third year of his age.

Dr. Banks published a Sermon, on the " Unsearchable Riches of Christ," preached at the Ordination of the Rev. Thomas Hamilton, in 1802.

In 1799 he was married to Mary Miller, of Octorora, Lancaster County, Pa., by whom he had five children,—all sons. His second son, *John*, and his fourth son, *William*, became Physicians. His third son, *Joseph*, was a Minister of the Associate Church. He was born at Florida, N. Y., July 27, 1806; was graduated at the University of Pennsylvania in 1823; and was a student of Theology under his father at the time of his death in 1826. He was licensed by the Associate Presbytery of Philadelphia, October 1, 1828, and shortly after went South, and was ordained October 15, 1831, by the Associate Presbytery of Carolina, as Pastor of Bethany and Sardis Churches, S. C., and Pisgah and Nob Creek, N. C. He subsequently settled in the congregations of Northfield, Stow and Springfield, O.; but, in consequence of feeble health, resigned his charge, and accepted an appointment as Chaplain in the Western Penitentiary of Pennsylvania, at Allegheny City. He was appointed a Missionary to the Island of Trinidad, July 27, 1843, and, for eight years, laboured earnestly in that capacity. On his return, in 1851, he established a semi-monthly paper, styled "The Friend of Missions." He was, for many years, a sufferer from consumption, of which he died at his residence in Mercer, Pa., April 8, 1859. He was an accomplished Scholar and well read Theologian. On the 2d of June, 1831, he was married to a Miss Roseburgh, of Pittsburg, who died on the 31st of July, 1840. On the 22d of January, 1852, he was married to Mrs. Elizabeth W. Walker, widow of the Rev. W. Houston Walker,* of Ohio, who survived him. Mrs. Dr. Banks remained some years in Philadelphia after the death of her husband, and then returned to Florida, where he had been settled, and died in 1833.

* W. HOUSTON WALKER is believed to have been a native of Mercer County, Pa. He graduated at Franklin College, O., and was licensed to preach in the summer of 1838. He was married to a Miss Whitten, of Pittsburg. Soon after his licensure he was settled at Scottsville, a small village about twenty miles below Pittsburg, and near the Ohio River. His health failed within less than two years from his settlement, and he died at the house of his relative, the Rev. John Walker, June 23, 1841. He was an earnest preacher, and exceedingly zealous against Slavery. When asked why he introduced the subject into every sermon, his answer was that he could find no text which did not lead to it.

FROM THE REV. ALEXANDER BULLIONS. D.D.

CAMBRIDGE, N. Y., October 21, 1852.

Dear Sir: My first meeting with Dr. Banks was in this place, early in the year 1807. He had been, for several years, settled over the congregation of which I have since been Pastor; but he was, at that time, in charge of a church in Florida, Montgomery County. I cannot say that my relations with him were ever very intimate; and yet we often met as co-presbyters and otherwise; and probably I knew enough of him, especially as his character was a somewhat striking one, to justify me in attempting to comply with your request.

Dr. Banks had the advantage of a good personal appearance. He was a portly, well-made man, with a complexion uncommonly ruddy, owing, as I have reason to believe, to a strong tendency of blood to his head. His countenance was expressive of a susceptibility to strong emotion. His manners were unstudied, but not ordinarily lacking in dignity. He dealt much in anecdote, and enjoyed a hearty laugh, though he was not particularly fond of being himself the subject of it. In what is commonly called a knowledge of the world he was a mere child; and there are innumerable traditions, many of them of the most laughable kind, illustrating this trait in his character. Though he had some excellent talents, he was so guileless that he was ill-prepared to encounter the trick and artifice of the world. He was naturally of a most excitable temperament; and I doubt not that this was connected with the tendency of blood to the head, to which I have already referred.

As a Preacher, Dr. Banks' manner was in a high degree monotonous. His voice was melodious, and not at all lacking in power; but he had trained it to such perfect uniformity that its legitimate effect upon an audience was by no means secured. He wrote his sermons, I think, pretty fully, and committed them to memory; though I do not know but that he may have occasionally resorted to other modes of preaching. His sermons had in them a large amount of good, solid divinity, but they were not characterized by a graceful or particularly correct style, and were, especially in the early parts of his ministry, deficient in pointed application. I have heard many men *preach*, whom I should rank much above Dr. Banks, but as a *Lecturer*, I do not remember to have heard more than two individuals whom I regarded his superiors. The reason of his excellence in this department was that he had a memory that retained nearly every thing; and he had not only read all the best critics and commentators on the Scriptures, but had thoroughly digested them; and they were always entirely at his command, and he generally used them with excellent judgment. I have often, in private, and for my own edification, set him to talking upon the Prophecies, and other obscure portions of Scripture, and I generally found that he had an opinion considerately formed, and that he had arguments at hand with which to defend it.

Dr. Banks had little or no imagination, but his judgment seemed to be good in regard to all matters that were not immediately of a worldly kind. He was one of the most diligent students that I ever knew. If he left home on business, he would be pretty likely to take along with him some musty folio, with which to occupy any leisure that he might have on the way. Vitringa and Owen were among his favourite authors; and his familiarity with these and other kindred writers can hardly be imagined. He was a most thorough Latin, Greek, and Hebrew scholar. So intimately acquainted was he with the Hebrew Bible, that I greatly doubt whether you could have read to him a verse from any part of the English Bible, but that he would have instantly given you the corresponding Hebrew. He could also write Hebrew with great ease. He was a capital teacher, and made many excellent scholars; but I have understood that he was a fearful disciplinarian.

Dr. Banks was, so far as I know, an acceptable Pastor, though his people were aware of his uncommon excitability, and it is doubtful whether they had that love for him that cast out all fear. It is probable that this constitutional feature modified somewhat his religious character; but I think all who knew him must have felt satisfied that he was sincerely devoted to the honour of his Master and the best interests of his fellow-men.

I am truly yours,
ALEXANDER BULLIONS.

FROM THE REV. J. M. MATHEWS, D.D.

NEW YORK, January 8, 1858.

My dear Sir: I cannot hesitate a moment about complying with your request for my recollections of my venerable friend and former teacher, the Rev. Dr. Banks. He was settled as a minister at Cambridge, a few miles from my native place, when I was graduated at College, and, as my mind was directed to the study of Theology, and I knew that he had a great name as a Hebrew scholar, I determined to avail myself of the benefit of his instruction in the Hebrew language. I accordingly placed myself under his care, and remained with him long enough to enable me to form a pretty good estimate of his character and his remarkable acquirements.

Dr. Banks had naturally a strong, vigorous mind, but was remarkably deficient in imagination. Beyond most men whom I have known, he carried his heart in his hand. He had great strength of feeling; and when he was excited, his feelings would sweep along with the impetuosity of a whirlwind. In his extreme frankness he would often offend against the dictates of prudence, and say and do things which his sober judgment would not justify. He had also, in an eminent degree, the gift of believing,—believing things which to most other persons would have seemed incredible. But he had noble and generous qualities, and it was no difficult thing to pacify him, even when he was under the strongest excitement.

But what constituted Dr. Banks' chief distinction was his remarkable familiarity with the Hebrew language. To this the whole energy of his mind seemed to be directed. He lived and moved and seemed to find a great part of his enjoyment among Hebrew roots. As an instructor, I should unhesitatingly assign to him the very first rank: he was not only never at a loss, but I always felt that what he imparted was only a drop to an ocean, compared with what he possessed. Sometimes after I had gone through my recitation, he would refer to some difficult passage in the lesson, and would say,—" Come, here is one glorious dark place that we have passed over—let us look at it a little;" and then he would give me the various renderings of which it was susceptible, and finally would give the one which he thought the best. He seemed literally to revel over such passages, and he never failed to pour a flood of light upon them.

As a Preacher there was nothing about Dr. Banks that could be considered attractive. Of course he never showed a manuscript in the pulpit; and I do not know whether he ever wrote his sermons—certainly I had no evidence that he did. His delivery was entirely monotonous and without animation, and withal was pretty strongly marked with the Scotch accent. His discourses, however, were always sensible, and contained much of Bible truth, given out after the Scotch manner. His love of Hebrew discovered itself strongly even in the pulpit; insomuch that he rarely used the common translation of the Bible, but evidently translated the Hebrew for himself as he went along. To a student of Hebrew he was a most instructive preacher, but to one who was altogether ignorant of the language, a good deal in his sermons would be of little account.

I remember a striking incident illustrative of his love of Hebrew that once occurred in his administration of the Lord's Supper. He had occasion to quote the passage in the Prophecy of Isaiah—" Surely He hath borne our griefs and carried our sorrows." And having quoted it in English, he gave the Hebrew word for " hath borne," which sounds as if it were written *Nansan*. There was an honest old Scotchman sitting next to me, who supposed that the Doctor had said, with his usual Scotch accent, " Not so," and he instantly said to himself, in so loud a whisper that I heard it,—" And how is it then ?" By this time the Doctor went on to explain *Nansan* and relieved the old gentleman by saying that the meaning of the word was " He lifted up and carried away " our griefs and sorrows.

I do not think that Dr. Banks had ever much to do with his people, except from the pulpit; but still he was greatly respected by them, as well as by the community at large.

Yours as ever,
J. M. MATHEWS.

ANDREW FULTON.*
1797—1818.

ANDREW FULTON was born and educated in Scotland, but I am able to learn nothing concerning his early history. He was licensed to preach the Gospel, by the Associate Presbytery of Kilmarnock, on the 17th of December, 1793. After being employed about three years and a half—part of the time in Ireland—as a probationer, he was taken on trial for Ordination, with a view to being sent on a mission to the State of Kentucky, in response to an application that had been made, by several individuals residing in that State, to the General Associate Synod of Scotland. On the 28th of June, 1797, he, with another licentiate,—Mr. Robert Armstrong, was solemnly ordained, at Craigend, near Perth, by the Associate Presbytery of Perth,—the Rev. Alexander Pringle presiding on the occasion, and preaching from Mark xvi, 15.

Mr. Fulton, with his missionary companion, sailed for America on the 8th of August, following their Ordination, and arrived in New York on the 13th of October. They proceeded immediately towards their missionary field. There being, at that day, no regular public conveyance across the Alleghany Mountains, they travelled on foot from Carlisle, Pa., to Pittsburg. As they arrived at Pittsburg just at the opening of winter, it was thought inexpedient that they should attempt to descend the Ohio River before the next spring. They, therefore, remained in the neighbourhood of Pittsburg during the winter of 1797-98, and were employed in preaching to different congregations, as there was occasion or opportunity.

Early in the spring they resumed their journey to Kentucky. They descended the Ohio River to Limestone, now Maysville, Ky., in one of the ordinary rude boats, then the only vessel known upon those Western waters. Kentucky being,

*Miller's Sketches.

at that time, the great point in the West towards which the tide of emigration was flowing, these missionaries readily found others preparing for the same destination; and they actually joined with one or two families of emigrants in fitting out a boat for the voyage, and also performed their part of the labour in managing it.

In November, 1798, after their arrival in Kentucky, they proceeded, agreeably to their instructions, to constitute themselves a Presbytery, under the name of the Associate Presbytery of Kentucky. They found here a wide field open before them, and frequent applications from different parts of the State were made for their services. Mr. Fulton accepted a call from the congregation of Drennon's Creek, in Henry County, where he laboured with great diligence and success for seventeen years. The greater part of his congregation, however, from a conscientious opposition to Slavery, had, meanwhile, removed to the State of Indiana and settled near Madison, Jefferson County. In November, 1815, Mr. Fulton, by the authority of Presbytery, followed them, and they again came under his pastoral charge. Here also his labours were attended by a manifest blessing, and his congregations were rapidly upon the increase. But within less than three years from the time of his arrival there, his labours and his life were both at an end. He died of a fever, on the 10th of September, 1818, in the sixty-third year of his age. He left a widow and three children,—two daughters and a son, the latter of whom was born but a few hours before his father's death. Mrs. Fulton was subsequently married to Colonel James Morrow, of South Hanover, Ind.; and one of the daughters became the wife of the Rev. James Adams, of Massie's Creek, O.

FROM THE REV. ANDREW HERON, D.D.

CEDARVILLE, O., March 16, 1863.

Rev. and dear Brother: In your highly respectable list of deceased Fathers of the Associate Presbyterian Church, I know of none more worthy of commemoration than Andrew Fulton. From the reminiscences and associations of my early boyhood I had formed a high estimate of his character before I ever saw him; and personal acquaintance in after life, instead of diminishing, enhanced, the estimate. This acquaintance, it is true, was formed only a few years before his death; and, owing to the distance of our locations from each other, our intercourse was necessarily infrequent. But it was amply sufficient to enable me to form a correct opinion of the man—for he was one of those transparent beings whose characters are so unobscured by any veil, that you can see through them at a single glance.

Mr. Fulton's personal appearance was much in his favour. He was of about the middle height, a little inclined to be stout, of rather a florid complexion, and a countenance in which intelligence and benignity were so beautifully blended that it was difficult to say which had the preponderance. His manners were as simple as childhood itself, and his manners were a faithful index to his heart. Indeed if I were to search among all my acquaintances of former days to find the most perfect specimen of true Christian simplicity, I believe I should settle upon Andrew Fulton. He was emphatically a Nathaniel,—"an Israelite in whom was no guile." He was cheerful and social in his disposition, and yet had the gravity and dignity becoming a minister of the Gospel. He was most laborious in his calling,—ever watchful for opportunities of doing good, and cheerfully sacrificing any personal interest for the promotion of his Master's cause. And while he was firm in his adherence to his own well-matured convictions, one of the most conspicuous traits of his character was the gentleness and mildness which he manifested in his treatment of others. He was no Esau to "over drive," but, like Jacob, his manner was to "lead on softly."

Such being the spirit of the man, his labours were highly esteemed and greatly blessed. He made no pretensions to splendid oratory, and scrupulously avoided every thing like parade or ostentation. But his discourses were always framed with good judgment and logical correctness; were full of evangelical truth luminously presented, and faithfully applied to the hearts and consciences of his hearers; and were delivered with his characteristic directness and simplicity. And the results of his labours are, to this day, a standing testimony to the fidelity and diligence that characterized his ministry. It has been my privilege, more than once, to pass some time in the congregation of Carmel, Ind., where he finished his course, and where the Rev. Moses Arnott is now the esteemed Pastor; and rarely have I found a people so much distinguished by an intelligent acquaintance with Gospel truth, and exhibiting such evidence of vital and practical godliness as that congregation. The Lord grant that many more "Carmels" may "blossom as the rose," to the glory and praise of the great Husbandman.

I remain your brother in Christ,
ANDREW HERON.

ROBERT ARMSTRONG.*

1798—1821.

ROBERT ARMSTRONG was a native of Midholm, Roxboroughshire, Scotland; but little is known of his parentage, except that it was very humble. Neither his tomb-stone, nor any other record, so far as is known, reveals the year of his birth. He was brought up under the ministry of the Rev. Andrew Arnot. He received his classical education at the University of Edinburgh, and afterwards studied Theology at Whitburn, under the Rev. Archibald Bruce, at that time the Professor of the General Associate Synod. The certificate of his Ordination to the Ministry is dated June 15, 1797. He had been licensed to preach, sometime in the winter preceding, by the Associate Presbytery of Kelso.

From his early youth he was thrown almost entirely on his own resources; but, by his energy and perseverance, he effectually overcame all the obstacles that he found in his way. He taught a country school, or acted as private tutor in the families of gentlemen; and, by this means, was enabled to make extensive acquirements in literature and science, as well as in Theology.

He was licensed and ordained with a view to his coming to America. In the year 1796 an application was made to the General Associate Synod of Scotland, by some members who lived near Lexington, Ky., for a minister of their own communion to be sent to them; and the petition was answered by sending two ministers instead of one,—namely, Mr. Armstrong and Mr. Andrew Fulton. At the time the request was received by the Synod, Mr. Armstrong had not yet finished his course of study preparatory to the ministry; and the fact that he

* Miller's Sketches.—Evangelical Repository, 1858.

was thus prospectively selected by the Synod, would seem to indicate that they regarded him as possessing special qualifications for the contemplated mission.

The two persons above named were commissioned by the Synod to constitute themselves, on their arrival at the place of their destination, into a Court, by the name of the Associate Presbytery of Kentucky. Having spent the preceding winter in Pennsylvania, they arrived in Kentucky in the summer of 1798, and, on the 28th of November following, in obedience to the Synodical instructions, they constituted the Court. Mr. Armstrong now received a unanimous call to act as Pastor to the United Congregations of Davis' Fork, Miller's Run and Cane Run; and he was installed in this charge on the 23d of April, 1799. Here he continued to labour with acceptance and success till the autumn of 1804.

In the course of this year the members of Mr. Armstrong's three congregations, having become tired of living in a region in which Slavery existed, and having come to the conclusion that it was hostile to the cultivation of religion, (their Pastor also sympathizing deeply in their convictions and feelings on the subject,) formed a purpose of migrating, almost *en masse*, to the State of Ohio. They forthwith accomplished their purpose, and removed to Greene County, O., confidently expecting that their Minister would soon be re-settled among them. They were quickly organized under the name of the United Congregation of Massie's Creek and Sugar Creek; and, on the 2d of September of the same year, he was ordered by Presbytery to rejoin his charge. The state of things about him was exceedingly rude—he sometimes preached in a cabin, and sometimes under the shade of a tree, until they got up a log meeting house; which, after a while, gave place to a more commodious and comfortable church edifice.

Here Mr. Armstrong laboured with great self-denial, and not without pleasing success, for seventeen years. Shortly after this, his charge was divided, and another minister was settled over one-half of it. His labours, from this time, were confined to Massie's Creek Congregation, until the 9th of January, 1821, when, from causes which in no degree reflected upon his good name, he demitted his charge about ten months before his decease.

A short time previous to his death, he went to Flat Rock in the State of Indiana, intending also to remove his family thither. He returned on the 27th of September, and, on the succeeding night, was taken very ill. He was satisfied that his end was near; but he had no anxious fear in the prospect of his departure. To a young minister, who visited him at this time, he expressed his full confidence of the truth of the doctrines he had preached, and spoke of them as the ground of his immortal hopes. He died on Sabbath morning, the 14th of October, 1821. His Funeral Sermon was preached by the Rev. James Adams, from Daniel xii. 2.

He was married to a Miss Andrews, daughter of one of the members of his congregation, who, with two daughters, survived him. His widow was subsequently married to the Rev. Mr. Neil, at that time a minister of the Reformed Dissenting Presbytery, and one of the daughters also was married to a clergyman.

The only productions of Mr. Armstrong's pen that are known to have been published are a few letters addressed to his friends in Scotland, and after his decease, a Sermon on Romans viii. 32, and a Charge delivered to the Rev William Hume, at his Ordination.

FROM JAMES MORROW, ESQ.

GREENE COUNTY, O., December 13, 1849.

Rev. and dear Sir: My opportunities for knowing the Rev. Robert Armstrong concerning whom you inquire, have probably been better than those of almost anybody now living. I was for a time under his ministry in Kentucky, and was among those who called him to Ohio, in the year 1804. I was a member of his congregation, and on terms of friendship with him, for more than seventeen years.

Mr. Armstrong was small of stature, but had a commanding expression of countenance. He was not of a robust constitution; yet zeal in his Master's cause prompted him to perform a great amount of labour, and led him to endure hardness as a good soldier of Jesus Christ. Though sociable, he still maintained his dignity; though faithful, he was not censorious; though cheerful, he was far from levity. In his intercourse with the world the golden rule was his guide. He was free to speak about worldly things, and seemed desirous to render himself useful in every relation; in respect to the present as well as the future. In his living he was economical without being penurious, and practised a degree of hospitality which was honourable to him alike as a man and a minister. He had treasured up a great many interesting anecdotes, especially respecting remarkable providences, which he could introduce to good purpose, in accommodation to the company in which he happened to find himself. He brought with him from the old country some notions of rank that were not exactly in harmony with the spirit of our republican institutions; but he prudently suppressed them, and very happily conformed to the habits of the people among whom his lot was cast.

You can hardly conceive the difficulties which he had to encounter, growing out of the fact that the country was then, to a great extent, a wilderness. His journeys, taking him over bad roads and across deep waters, were attended with not only fatigue but danger; yet, with all these difficulties, he would travel South, on horseback, about two hundred miles, to attend a meeting of Presbytery in Tennessee, and then again, about three times that distance East, to attend a meeting of Synod in Pennsylvania. The houses being literally few and far between, it was necessary to carry both " purse and scrip," and this he did without a murmur. I speak on this subject knowingly, for sometimes I had the pleasure of travelling with him.

He was exemplary in the duty of attending Ecclesiastical Courts, and had a due share of influence in all of them. I have been informed that, for some time after his arrival in Kentucky, his preparation for the pulpit cost him considerable study; but his discourses were uniformly well composed and appropriate. He often administered the Lord's Supper without assistance, attending to all the duties not only of the immediate occasion but of the days observed in connection with it. He was evidently sometimes greatly fatigued; and yet he never seemed to falter in his work.

His manner of preaching was solemn and impressive; and though his delivery was somewhat slow, it was far from being wearisome. The great theme of his public ministrations was Jesus Christ and Him crucified. He would sometimes exhibit the terrors of the law for the conviction of sin, but always in connection with the gracious provisions of the Gospel. He would rebuke with all authority, sometimes by a look, sometimes by words, growing sharper as the case seemed to require. On one occasion he was preaching to a large assembly; and before the tent (a platform seated under the shade of a tree) were several young people laughing and talking and eating. He at first reproved them mildly, but without effect. Then, with a stern countenance, he quoted the proverb,—"Though thou shouldst bray a fool in a mortar among wheat with a pestle, yet will not his foolishness depart from him." This, with a few additional remarks, silenced the frivolity of the young people, and made them thoroughly ashamed. I may safely say that he was a conscientious, devoted and able Minister of the New Testament.

Very respectfully,

JAMES MORROW.

FROM THE REV. THOMAS BEVERIDGE, D.D.

CANNONSBURG, October 18, 1859.

My dear Sir: My acquaintance with the Rev. Robert Armstrong was not for a long period, but it was quite intimate. In the autumn of 1819 I was sent as a probationer to what was then called the Presbytery of Kentucky, (now Miami,) of which Mr. Armstrong was a member. I was chiefly occupied in preaching at Xenia, Greene County, O., only four miles from the church in which he ministered, and much of the time was spent either at his house, or elsewhere in his company. Being settled at Xenia the next year, and a virtual separation having taken place between Mr. Armstrong and his congregation about the same time, he was frequently one of my hearers, and spent a good deal of time with me as a visitor.

One of the first things which would strike the attention, in forming an acquaintance with Mr. Armstrong, was the singular disproportion between his physical and his intellectual and moral nature. He was not only of low stature and slender frame but absolutely dwarfish. He would never wear any article of dress closely fitting his body, nor even a pair of boots fitted to the size of his extremely delicate feet. By this means, and also by his grave and dignified behaviour, he, in a great measure, counteracted the impression which his personal appearance was fitted to make. The late Major James Galloway, who had been for many years under his ministry, and assisted in preparing his body for burial, remarked that he had never before had any idea of the smallness of his body;—that it was more like the body of a child than of a man. One of his eyes was also turned outward, and seemed always to be looking sideways, even when he was looking straight before him. This frequently occasioned mistakes,—persons on one side of him supposing that he was addressing them, when he was speaking to some one immediately in front. On one occasion, having reproved a hearer for some disorder, an individual on the side of the eye which was always looking sideways, finding that eye fixed upon him, spoke out in the congregation, denying that he had been making any disturbance. Mr. Armstrong forthwith turned around to him and said,—"Sir, I was not meaning you, but a guilty conscience needs no accuser." Although, in these respects, his appearance was somewhat to his disadvantage, yet his face was well formed, and indicative of refinement, firmness, intelligence and kind affections. There was also such a propriety and natural dignity in his behaviour that few persons commanded more general or more deserved respect. He was not a man with whom either strangers or friends would feel disposed to trifle.

He was fond of company, and quite ready, entertaining and instructive in conversation. Frequently, when a literary or religious topic was introduced, he would become quite animated, and give something like a continuous lecture upon it. Yet, though, at such times, in a great measure engrossing the conversation, there was nothing like egotism or vanity in his remarks, and he was as ready to be the listener as the lecturer.

Mr. Armstrong was, by no means, lacking in moral courage. He never hesitated to express his opinion on any suitable occasion, or to administer a reproof where he believed it was merited. Being at the house of a friend, where another guest was very forward in conversation, he availed himself of an opportunity to make him acquainted with his mind in a way not to be mistaken. This individual was about to propose a question to him, and prefaced it with many expressions of modesty and confessions of ignorance. "Mr. Armstrong," said he, "when we poor ignorant people are in company with you learned men, we wish to get from you all the information we can— so I hope you will excuse me for proposing a question to you which has caused me some study." Mr. Armstrong did not wait to hear the question, but immediately replied,—"Sir, when I hear persons making such professions of ignorance, I always conclude that they wish to be considered as possessed of more than common information." At another time, being present in a house during family worship, and observing a Quaker sitting with his hat on, he arose very deliberately and removed it. Having travelled a journey of a hundred and fifty miles, to preach in a vacant congregation and dispense the ordinance of the Supper, when about to return home, a member of the congregation came to him, and offered him as compensation for his service between two and three dollars, making some apologies for the smallness of the sum. Mr. Armstrong refused to accept the money. "Sir," said he, "there is not one of you who would consent to go to Massie's Creek, bear the expenses of the journey thither and home again, spend between two and three weeks in attending to my affairs, and then accept of such a sum as a remuneration for your services. No, you must either do better, or I will accept of nothing. I don't care for myself—I am able to live independently of any compensation for my ministerial labours; but if I submit to such imposition, you will be ready to practise it upon young men, and others not able to live without compensation." The good effect of this lesson was not only apparent at the time, in a more liberal contribution, but there is reason to believe that it has not even yet been forgotten by the members of that congregation.

It must not be inferred, however, from these incidents, that there was ordinarily any thing like severity in Mr. Armstrong's manner. This was never the case except when he had to do with affectation, injustice, meanness, or something fitted to excite indignation, or meriting sharp reproof. In his intercourse with persons whom he respected he perhaps even erred in the opposite direction—in being too indirect in pointing out their faults. He was accustomed, when he saw any thing amiss in his friends, to relate some anecdote, or throw out some general remarks, calculated to set them right, without making any direct personal application. As he frequently spoke of this as a commendable method of conveying an admonition, and was known to be in the habit of availing himself of it, the very natural consequence was to keep his friends always on the watch, and to lead them frequently, in conversing with him, to put to themselves the question—" Does he mean me? or is he not endeavouring to bring some fault of mine to my notice?"

Mr. Armstrong's attainments in Theology and general literature were very respectable. He laboured under some disadvantages in his youth, which, however, proved to him, as they have done to many others, advantages in the end. His mind was disciplined by the very hardships attending his early education. In the field of his ministerial labour his leisure and opportunities for study were limited. But he had a vigorous mind, a good literary taste, quite a large and valuable library, and, so far as his opportunities permitted, he was a diligent student. Such were his acquirements, and such his standing among his brethren, that when Dr. Ramsay was elected Professor of Theology in 1821, Mr. Armstrong was the only opposing candidate, and received a respectable vote, though left in a minority.

As a Preacher, Mr. Armstrong was far from being brilliant, or in the common acceptation of the word, highly popular. His discourses were chiefly of the didactic type, and had somewhat the character of theological treatises; but they were marked by such comprehensiveness and vigour of thought, and delivered with such marked propriety and calm earnestness, that he was usually listened to with close attention. His voice, considering especially his diminutive size, was remarkable for its power and compass. He spoke with great deliberation, distinctness and readiness. He was a successful labourer in his Lord's vineyard, and his name deserves to be held in everlasting remembrance. I am very sincerely yours,

THOMAS BEVERIDGE.

FROM THE REV. ANDREW HERON, D.D.

CEDARVILLE, GREENE COUNTY, O., March 2, 1863.

Rev. and dear Sir: The name of the Rev. Robert Armstrong, concerning whom you inquire, is associated with some of my earliest recollections. When I was a mere boy, in Scotland, my native country, a deep and indelible impression was made upon my mind by reading in the Scottish Magazines letters from the Rev. Messrs. Armstrong and Fulton, Missionaries from the General Associate Synod of Scotland, containing details of their journeyings and labours through the wilderness of Kentucky. At that time I had not the remotest thought of ever being associated in the same work with these brethren, on this side of the Atlantic. But the early impression retained its place, and when, after my licensure in 1813, I became personally acquainted with them, I found it more than realized.

My opportunities of personal acquaintance with Mr. Armstrong were comparatively slight, being, in a great measure, limited to our meetings, from year to year, in the Associate Synod. He and his congregation had, on account of Slavery, removed from Kentucky to Greene County, O., where he died, while my location was in the valley of Virginia. Our acquaintance was, however, sufficient to enable me to form a pretty accurate estimate of his character and worth.

With a corporeal frame much below an average size, Mr. Armstrong possessed a vigorous and capacious mind,—remarkable rather for promptitude of conception, power of comprehension and solidity of judgment, than for any of the more brilliant and startling qualities. Neither in the pulpit or out of it was he ever known to make any effort at display. In conversation he was always solid, instructive, and yet lively. Perfectly natural and unaffected in his manners and behaviour, he commanded the universal confidence and esteem of all with whom he associated. His sermons were always thoroughly digested, logically arranged, and faithfully applied to the consciences of his hearers. I am assured by many of his former parishioners, whom I knew intimately, that he was perseveringly faithful and assiduous in the discharge of his more private pastoral duties, teaching not only "publicly but from house to house," ever aiming to be instrumental in bringing sinners to Christ, and "in building up saints in their most holy faith."

As a member of a Church Court he had few equals. He was emphatically a man of business. It was always a pleasure to serve on a Committee with him. Clear headed, prompt and systematic, it was seldom that a Report that came from either his lips or his pen, had to encounter much opposition.

One of his most prominent and attractive characteristics was his truly catholic spirit. While he was sincerely attached to the distinctive principles of the Church with which he was connected, and ever ready to defend them, he embraced, in the ardour of his affection, all who gave evidence of being the followers of the Lamb. He was no Ultraist or Sectarian.

In a word, Robert Armstrong was one of the strong men of his denomination during the period in which he lived, and his memory will be long revered, and the results of his labours gratefully acknowledged, throughout the whole region where he exercised his ministry.

I remain, Reverend Sir, yours fraternally,
ANDREW HERON.

FRANCIS PRINGLE.
1799—1833.
FROM THE REV. THOMAS GOODWILLIE, D.D.

BARNET, VT., September 3, 1862

Dear Sir: I am happy to send you, in compliance with your request, a sketch of the life of the Rev. Francis Pringle. The material for the sketch has been partly furnished by his son, a most respectable gentleman of the city of New York, and partly drawn from my father's correspondence with Mr. Pringle, and other early ministers of the Associate Church. I think you may rely upon the authenticity of every part of it.

FRANCIS PRINGLE was born in Path-Head, a suburb of Kirkcaldy, Fifeshire, Scotland, in the year 1747. His parents were worthy and intelligent members of the Associate Congregation of Path-Head, and were very careful in the religious education of their children. His father was a manufacturer of linen-ticking, in moderate worldly circumstances.

Francis, the third of nine children, naturally grave and quiet, early manifested a desire for a liberal education, which his parents encouraged by sending him to a Grammar School in Kirkcaldy to study the classics. In his fifteenth year he became a member of the Associate Congregation of Path-Head, and thenceforward prosecuted his studies with a view to the Holy Ministry; though he did not take a regular college course. In his eighteenth year he began the study of Theology at Alloa, under the Rev. Professor Moncrieff, in the Theological Hall of the Associate Synod. Having completed the prescribed theological course, he was, after the usual trials, licensed to preach the Gospel by the Associate Presbytery of Kirkcaldy, when he was in the twenty-first year of his age. A few months after he began to preach, he was sent to Ireland to supply the vacant Congregation of Gilnahirk, near Belfast. Though the congregation was not large, nor the situation in other respects very inviting, he commenced his work there with great zeal, and some of the good fruits of it began quickly to appear. So acceptable were his services that the congregation, at no distant period, gave him a call to become their Pastor. After due deliberation, he accepted the call, and was ordained, and installed as Pastor of the Associate Congregation of Gilnahirk, by the Associate Presbytery of Belfast, on the 25th of August, 1772.

On the 13th of September, 1775, he was married to Margaret, daughter of Henry Black, a merchant of Kirkcaldy, Scotland, a godly man, and an Elder of the Associate Church in that place.

Mr. Pringle's ministrations in this field of labour were evidently attended with the Divine blessing. For twenty-six years he laboured here with great fidelity, and with a good degree of success. But, in 1798, the "Irish Rebellion" broke asunder the endeared relation between him and his people. The "United Irish men's oath" to throw off the Government of Great Britain had been secretly administered to many Protestants as well as Roman Catholics. Several young men belonging to Mr. Pringle's congregation had taken that oath, and were known to be engaged in conspiracy against the Government; and some of the members of the congregation openly favoured the treasonable project. This was a painful state of things for their Pastor to contemplate. Parties in disguise ranged through the country at night in quest of fire-arms. Such a party came to his house one Sabbath night, and very civilly asked for his gun. He told them that he had no gun; that he had no need of one; that he was a man of peace, and determined to follow peace, and that the weapons of his warfare were spiritual. "Allow me," he proceeded, "to tell you that you are engaged in rebellion against a legitimate Government, which is a great crime, and deserves the severest punishment. I entreat you to desist from your wicked course, which will end in disappointment and disgrace, and bring you to the gallows. I shudder at your crime and its consequences." They thanked him for his well-meant advice, and proceeded on their march in quest of fire-arms. Subsequently, the Government enforced the oath of allegiance on many who had taken the United Irishmen's oath. Some of his congregation had taken both of these oaths, but insisted that, as the oath of allegiance was forced upon them, it was not binding. Mr. Pringle considered such persons as guilty of perjury, and thought that it was his duty to utter the unwelcome truth. He soon found that there was a portion of his congregation to whom his ministrations would not be any longer acceptable. To purge the church by discipline, at such a time and in such circumstances, seemed impossible. To remain neutral he deemed neither safe nor proper. He could not know who were friends or who were foes. He became anxious also for his sons, some of whom were approaching manhood, and thought it dangerous for them to remain among a people tainted with treason. Accordingly, after prayerful deliberation, he came to the conclusion that it was every way desirable that he should remove his family from Ireland. He proceeded forthwith to take the necessary steps to a proper dissolution of the Pastoral relation and the winding up of his family affairs, and then took a sorrowful farewell of many endeared members of his congregation and other acquaintances, and, with his wife and five sons, left Gilnahirk in the autumn of 1798, leaving behind their eldest and only surviving daughter, then lately married. Having determined to migrate to America, they paid a visit to their relatives in Kirkcaldy and Path-Head, who persuaded them to remain there till the next summer. He immediately engaged in preaching in the vacant congregations of the Associate Church in Scotland, and became acquainted with the Rev. Doctors McCrie and Paxton, and some other Ministers of the Associate Synod, with whom he corresponded after his removal to America.

But he was anxious to be engaged in his Master's work on this side of the ocean. Leaving his eldest son to attend the University of Edinburgh, he, with his wife and four sons, having taken an affectionate leave of their many relatives and friends in Kirkcaldy, embarked, on the 8th of August, 1799, for New York. After a boisterous passage of seven weeks, during which he maintained family worship every day, and preached on three of the included Sabbaths, they arrived safely in New York, on the 26th of September, where they received a cordial welcome from the members of the Associate Congregation of that city. It appears that it was his design, according to the recommendation of the General Associate Synod of Scotland, to go on a mission to Nova Scotia; but, not finding a vessel in Scotland sailing directly for that Province, he took one for New York, intending to go thence to Nova Scotia by the earliest opportunity. But, when he arrived in New York, he ascertained that, on account of the prevalence of the Yellow Fever, no vessel would sail for Nova Scotia during that season. This seemed a providential indication in favour of his accepting an invitation from the Associate Presbytery to remain and preach in their vacancies. He supplied the vacant Congregation in New York until the next spring, to their very general acceptance. He was formally received as a member of the Associate Presbytery of Pennsylvania, on the 12th of May, 1800. According to the appointment of Presbytery, he preached in the vacant congregations in the Eastern part of Pennsylvania, and received a call to the Associate Congregation of Carlisle, where he was installed by that Presbytery, August 27, 1802, it being understood that the small neighbouring congregation of Dickinson should receive a portion of his pastoral labours.

Mr. Pringle, during his long life, not only performed a vast amount of labour, but was "in afflictions oft," enduring them with a patient and submissive spirit. He had thirteen children, all of whom died before their parents, except two, who still survive, and are the only members of the family who were married. Seven of the children died when young—the rest lived to maturity, and were an honour to their excellent parents. Four of their sons received a liberal education, and two of them became settled ministers of the Gospel. The eldest and only surviving daughter, who was married in Ireland, is yet living there at an advanced age. His eldest son, who still survives, finished his education at the University of Edinburgh, and was, for forty years, engaged in various duties in the old Bank of New York. Some years after Mr. Pringle came to this country, he experienced a grevious trial in the death of his third son, who became partially deranged, and was drowned when absent from home. He was a man of superior talents and excellent education, having graduated at Dickinson College. The news of the heart-rending event reached his excellent father just as he was about to enter the pulpit on Sabbath morning. With ready submission to the will of God and the most calm self-control, he went through all the public services of the day; and yet, for many years after, he could not allude to the subject without manifest emotion.

His two youngest sons, *James* and *Francis*, were both graduated at Dickinson College in 1808; both studied Theology under the Rev. Dr. John Anderson, at that time Professor in the Theological Seminary of the Associate Church; and both were licensed to preach, by the Associate Presbytery of Philadelphia, in October, 1812.

JAMES PRINGLE was distinguished for great originality, a vivid imagination, and ardent feelings; and he was withal a very diligent and successful student. He became a very acceptable Preacher, and received a call from the Associate Congregation of Steel Creek, N. C., where he was ordained and settled in April, 1814. He was chosen Moderator of the Synod in 1818.

FRANCIS PRINGLE, JR., was a man of superior intellect, of great good judgment and high culture, and so devoted to his studies that he frequently continued them through nearly the whole night. He received a call from Ryegate, Vt., and one from Xenia and Sugar Creek, O. The latter he accepted, and was ordained and installed by the Associate Presbytery of Chartiers in November, 1811. Here he laboured with great diligence and fidelity until 1817, when, being of a delicate constitution, his health failed, in consequence of which he made a journey to North Carolina, to visit his brother James, where he died of consumption, March 15, 1818, in the twenty-ninth year of his age. His brother, who was a man of vigorous constitution, continued to preach the Gospel to the bond and the free until the following autumn, when he was seized with a lung fever, of which he died on the 28th of October, in the thirtieth year of his age. These two brothers, who were strongly attached to each other in life, were scarcely divided in death—they died in the same house, the same room, and the same bed; they were laid in the same grave; and the same monument records their excellence and their end. The bereaved father, though he felt the rod in these dispensations most keenly, was still able to recognize, with a truly filial and submissive spirit, the hand that wielded it.

But Mr. Pringle's afflictions were not yet at an end. She who, for fifty years, had been the companion of his pilgrimage, and the sharer of his joys and sorrows, and, for some years, the only remaining member of his family, died on the 15th of February, 1826, in the seventy-eighth year of her age. He felt the loss most deeply, as she was a woman of superior discernment, of great Christian excellence, of extensive religious knowledge, and had been in every way a helpmeet to him. Being now left alone, so far as wife and children were concerned, he had a comfortable home offered to him in a family belonging to his congregation, where his wants were kindly ministered to as long as he remained in Carlisle. In consequence of the increasing infirmities of age, he resigned his pastoral charge, and preached his Farewell Sermon on the 14th of May, 1832,—the occasion being, both to him and his people, one of most tender interest. He now accepted the kind and oft-repeated invitation of his only surviving son to take up his residence with him in the city of New York. Though he had reached the age of fourscore and four years, he was still able and ready to do some work in his Lord's vineyard. He preached, by invitation, in Troy, Cambridge, Salem, Hebron, and other places in the same region. He returned to the city and spent the following winter, preaching occasionally, reading and visiting, and in various ways rendering himself useful. In the spring of 1833 he visited Newark, N. J., where he preached, spending the Sabbath at the house of a friend. As he was dressing himself the next morning, his foot caught in a fold of the carpet, in consequence of which he fell, and fractured his thigh near the hip-joint. He was unable to rise, but a call soon brought the family to his assistance. He was carried home to his son's in a litter. The most skilful surgeons pronounced the case incurable. He suffered little pain, and became able to move himself from one room to another in a wheeled chair. He endured the affliction with most exemplary patience, and calmly anticipated his approaching departure. In a few months the fractured limb became dropsical, and his health gradually declined, till, with an unwavering faith in his gracious God and Redeemer, he died on the 2d of November, 1833, in the eighty-fifth year of his age, and the sixty-fourth of his ministry.

Mr. Pringle preached a Sermon on the Qualifications and Duties of the Ministers of Christ, before the Associate Synod of Ireland, at its opening Session in Belfast, July 12, 1793, which was published by request of the Synod, and has since been republished in this country. Soon after his decease, a Sermon on "Prayer for the Prosperity of Zion" was published in the Religious Monitor, which he had sent to the editor for publication, and was supposed to have been written by him a short time before his death. Both these productions are highly creditable at once to his ability and his faithfulness.

Mr. Pringle was a remarkable textuary. You might recite any part of the Bible, and he could at once give you the book, chapter and verse; or if you were yourself to mention these, he could quote the passage. He studied the Bible more than all other books; and hence his wonderful facility at quoting it. His excellent lectures and sermons were admirably illustrated by a long life of singular purity and goodness. He had a rare gift of teaching the young and the old, both in public and in private, and he had a mild, yet effectual, way of reproving and rebuking, as well as teaching, admonishing and exhorting.

Mr. Pringle never had a robust constitution, but, by a very regular and temperate manner of living, he uniformly enjoyed good health. One of the prominent traits of his character was his great promptitude and punctuality in fulfilling all his appointments, and performing all his work in due season, and in an exact and orderly manner. His observance of Divine Providence was close and constant, and his submission to his Heavenly Father's will, under great trials, was cheerful and unqualified. His profound reverence for God, his solemnity in all sacred services, his evident spiritual-mindedness, his daily meditations on the Divine works and word, his meekness, zeal and humility,—all proved him a man of God, with a pure heart, a good conscience and faith unfeigned.

He was devoted to the interests of the Church within whose bosom Providence had cast his lot, and the Church in turn manifested, in various ways, her appreciation of his extraordinary worth. In 1804 he was chosen Moderator of the Associate Synod, and, about the same time, Stated Clerk of Synod, which office he held till 1827, when he resigned, and the Synod voted him "thanks for his long and faithful services." In 1828 he was again chosen Moderator. After the death of Messrs. Marshall and Clarkson, he was chiefly instrumental in keeping alive the Associate Presbytery of Philadelphia; for, though the only minister left in it, he occasionally visited all the vacant congregations and cherished them with paternal care. By the appointment of the Associate Synod, he was one of the annual examiners of the Theological Seminary established at Philadelphia, and he faithfully fulfilled the office.

He possessed that godliness which, with contentment, is great gain. So economically did he manage his temporal affairs that, with a salary of less than three hundred dollars, and occasional donations from benevolent individuals and other sources, he creditably supported his family, gave four of his sons a collegiate education, performed journeys every year to the Presbytery and Synod, and yet contributed quite liberally to various objects of benevolence. By his last will, he gave the greater part of his library to the Theological Seminary of the Associate Church in Philadelphia. He was a burning and shining light, an eminent example both to ministers and to people.

With high esteem yours truly,
THOMAS GOODWILLIE.

FROM THE HON. WILLIAM B. McCLURE.

PITTSBURG, October 12, 1857.

My dear Sir: The Rev. Francis Pringle, concerning whom you ask for my recollections, I remember with intense affection and gratitude. My impressions of his character were received in early childhood, and my acquaintance with him began as far back as my memory can go, and continued without intermission for many years. My opportunities of observation were favourable, so far as I had capacity to observe. He was the Gamaliel at whose feet I was brought up.

His family had, at that time, grown up to manhood, and gone forth into the world; and he and his aged wife lived alone. Being the beloved Pastor of our family, and his presence as well as that of his wife always welcome, this aged couple made frequent visits to our house, a pleasant rural residence about a mile distant from the town of Carlisle, where they always were at home, and where they oftentimes remained for days and weeks together. These friendly and welcome visits continued without interruption for a long period.

Mr. Pringle's parish, though not large in point of numbers, covered a wide extent of territory, and the duty of pastoral visitation became proportionally arduous; but he performed this duty regularly and punctually, regardless of roads and of weather. If any of his flock were absent from the services of the Sanctuary, this watchful shepherd inquired at once into the reason, and, in case of sickness, he was at their side within less than twenty-four hours. I suppose there was not a man, woman or child, under his pastoral care, with whose whole character, mental, moral and physical, he was not conversant. He understood them about as well as a parent understands the temper and disposition of his children; and he bestowed on each little less than a paternal regard. This gave him the advantage which a physician has, who is familiar with the constitutions and habits of his patients. He inspired fear of a peculiar sort,—the fear of doing any thing to distress him.

The personal appearance of Mr. Pringle, it is easy to remember, but difficult to describe. In stature I should think he might have been rather below the medium. He was erect in his person, lithe and active, and even in old age sat handsomely upon a horse, and was no mean pedestrian. His features were neither delicate nor coarse, but strong, well defined and expressive. His high and venerable head was crowned with a profuse and healthy suit of fine, silvery hair. His eyes were serene and blue as the sky, and the general expression of his countenance was a beautiful embodiment of his whole character. His dress was always neat, but plain, and not fitted, in any way, to attract attention.

His manners were, or seemed to be, the natural result of his moral and physical organization. They were frank, simple, cordial, and brimful of benevolence. That they were not otherwise than attractive is evident from the fact that young and old, ignorant and educated, merry and sad, were sure to be attracted by his company. While he always breathed a cheerful spirit, he never lost sight of the appropriate dignity of his calling.

Mr. Pringle was in the habit of retiring early and rising early. He took a great deal of exercise daily. He never missed his walk when the weather permitted. I have seen him, on a rainy day, walk backward and forward, with great energy and rapidity, in the parlour, for an hour at a time. I remember, on one occasion, when the snow had fallen a foot deep upon the ground, he went to work and shovelled a path through it for a considerable distance. There was no necessity whatever for his doing this; but he said he must take his exercise; and this was the mode of taking it which he preferred.

His love of truth amounted almost to a passion. In the statement of facts he could not endure artificial embellishments or exaggerations. His own habit of never deviating a particle from sober verity is pretty well illustrated by the following anecdote:—A man (no parishioner of his or of any body else) whose habit of frequent intoxication caused many feuds at home, would, after his frolic was over, voluntarily come to Mr. Pringle to express his penitence and promise reformation. On one occasion when this individual was leaving Mr.

Pringle's house, he remarked,—" This unfortunate man has been to see me on the same errand forty times." A person, who happened to be present when the remark was made, said to him,—" Mr. Pringle, why do you speak so much at random? You say forty times—you might as well have said fifty or a hundred—is this mode of speaking quite in accordance with your own precepts?" "Oh, yes," he replied, " it is fully so;" and, leaving the room, came back in a moment with a little blank-book and a pencil in his hand. " Now, said he, " here you may count thirty-nine marks, each one of which denotes a visit similar to the last; and this one makes forty. Indeed," he continued, " several of his calls were omitted; for the idea did not strike me until the frequency of his visits suggested it; and my intention is, when they reach fifty, to show him these entries, hoping it may have some effect to shame him into sobriety or an attempt at reformation; for I do not suppose that he has any correct idea of the frequency of his transgressions, or the violations of his promises of amendment." He added,—" You see now that in this I have spoken the truth, and have not dealt in figures of speech, but in figures of arithmetic."

When he felt himself called upon to administer reproof, it was done after the fashion of the Old Prophets—there was no circumlocution, or indirectness or excessively delicate handling; but the rebuke was just as personal and pointed as if he had said, in so many words,—" Thou art the man." But his manner, after all, was so mild and his look so benevolent, that, instead of giving offence, he usually made himself the object of deeper reverence. His manner of rebuking a profane swearer was something like this—said he, " Instead of taking your Maker's name in vain, substitute some harmless and indifferent words for these terrible expletives—say, for example, tree, pot, kettle, horse—try this, and it will seem to you absurd; and so it is absurd and nothing more. But your way of swearing is equally absurd, with profaneness superadded. This vice gratifies no appetite as some vices do : he is a silly fish that swallows a hook that has no bait upon it. My young friend, God is the hearer of prayer; and when a man calls upon his Maker daily to damn his soul, it would be surely no wonder if He should take him at his word."

One of his sons, the Rev. James Pringle, who was stationed, if I mistake not, in one of the Carolinas, and who, like Demetrius, had a good report of all men, died very suddenly. A casual visitor was present when the letter was received, announcing the sad intelligence. Neither parent betrayed any violent emotion. In a calm voice, Mr. Pringle said to his wife,—" Peggy, James never cost us a tear until now. 'The Lord gave and the Lord hath taken away, blessed be the name of the Lord.' Let us retire and pray that we may obtain strength to bear with Christian fortitude our terrible bereavement."

He once married a couple, whose mutual infirmities of temper sometimes marred, to some extent, their domestic harmony. Some time after, he made a journey to the neighbourhood, and, calling upon them, was received most cordially. He asked leave to invite some company to meet him at their house the next evening, which was cheerfully granted. Having assembled several of those who had been guests at the wedding, he requested his host and hostess to stand up on the floor, which they did; and then, in a manner the most impressive, he married them over again. After the ceremony was ended, he, in the most artless and affectionate way, said that he wished to remind them of some mutual promises they had made before, in presence of himself and those witnesses—and he had taken this method of doing it. The evening passed off pleasantly, and his intrepid conduct, instead of giving offence, increased affection; and this sensible pair were in the habit, ever after, of sending him valuable presents as long as they lived.

Some of his rural parishioners, whose week-day employments were in the open field, being unused to a sedentary habit, would occasionally fall asleep during the sermon. For this offence his manner of reproof was somewhat original. After patiently permitting them to enjoy their nap for about ten minutes, or for such length of time as he deemed sufficient to refresh them, without saying one word, or for a moment losing the calm, benevolent expression of his countenance, or making the least pause in his discourse, he would bring down a volume of David's Psalms on the big Bible that lay closed before him, with such prodigious force that the crack resembled the report of a musket, and in an instant "murdered sleep." The silence in church was always profound, and equally so in the street; and this gave to these explosions a fearful distinctness, that made them as appalling as they were irresistible.

Mr. Pringle was remarkable for self control. I never saw him at any time, or under any circumstances, exhibit the least sign of impatience or discontent, or give utterance to a hasty expression. The great equableness of his spirit, and the uniform consistency of his life, left a powerful impression in favour not only of his own character, but of the cause to which he was so earnestly devoted. As a couple of men were working on the Baltimore turnpike road, near Carlisle, Mr. Pringle happened to be passing along on foot, and one said to the other, "There goes Mr. Pringle; he looks thinner than usual." "Yes," replied the other, "but he is all in Heaven, except what you see of him."

Few men of his day, or of any day, have been the subjects of more heartfelt respect and affection than Mr. Pringle. He was constantly receiving presents, not merely from his parishioners, but often from those of different denominational connection from his own. His name was a household word in town and country. At a party or a wedding, the young and gay would cluster around him. On the street, men of the roughest nature and most careless life always spoke to him, and of him, in most emphatic tones of good will and cordial regard. His character was an institution in the sphere in which he moved. He scattered cheerfulness, and love, and light, wherever he went. We looked at him as a star whose light was borrowed from a source beyond the sun.

Very truly,
Your friend and obedient servant,
WILLIAM B. McCLURE.

THOMAS ALLISON.*

1800—1840.

The parents of THOMAS ALLISON were natives of Scotland, and members there of the Anti-Burgher branch of the Secession Church. The father, John Allison, was a man distinguished not only for piety, but also for intelligence and mental activity. The mother, Jane (Brownlee) Allison, not less distinguished for the same qualities, belonged to a numerous family, now scattered through Scotland and the United States, including among its members the Rev. —— Brownlee, many years Pastor of the Secession Church in Falkirk, Scotland; his brother, the Rev. William C. Brownlee, D.D., of the Reformed Dutch Church in the city of New York, etc. They migrated to this country at an early period, and lived for some time in Eastern Pennsylvania, where—

* MS. from Rev. J. T. Brownlee.

probably in the County of York—their seventh son, *Thomas*, was born, on the 3d of June, 1771. His parents, however, removed, in his early childhood, to Chartiers, Washington County, in the Western part of the State. There he passed his youthful days, but in what manner is not certainly known, though the presumption is that he was engaged principally in agricultural pursuits. The known character of his parents for intelligence, piety and unflinching adherence to the religious truths they professed, is the only evidence furnished in respect to the character of the early religious training he received.

He did not enter upon his classical studies till he was somewhat advanced,—probably not till he had attained his majority; and then he pursued them chiefly at Cannonsburg Academy, now Jefferson College. He prosecuted his theological studies under the direction of the Rev. Dr. John Anderson, the first regularly appointed Theological Professor in connection with the Associate Presbyterian Church in the United States. Having gone through the regular course of four years, he was licensed to preach about the beginning of the year 1800. The branch of the Church to which he belonged being then comparatively small, and many of the congregations connected with it being already supplied with Pastors, most of whom were missionaries sent over by the parent Church in Scotland, his ministrations as a licentiate were confined to a few congregations, though these were widely scattered.

From the beginning, he was well received as a Preacher, in evidence of which is the fact that calls were soon made for his pastoral services by the United Congregations of Mount Hope and Cross Creek, the former in Washington County, Pa., the latter in Brooke County, Va., and by the congregation in Cambridge, Washington County, N. Y. He accepted the call from the first mentioned congregation, and was ordained, and installed as their Pastor, by the Presbytery of Chartiers, in the year 1801. The relations thus constituted between him and these congregations continued till a short time before his death, when, on account of age and infirmity, and at his own request, the Presbytery dissolved it.

Mr. Allison's physical constitution was robust, and his general health, at least during the greater part of his life, good,—in testimony of which is the fact that he was prevented from preaching, by illness, but a very few Sabbaths during his whole ministry, and those few were chiefly during the last years of his life, when he was subject to occasional violent attacks of sick headache. For several days previous to his death, he had been slightly indisposed; but it was only two days before, that he was seized with congestion of the stomach and bowels, which, after subjecting him to severe suffering, terminated his life. He died in April, 1840. His remains were followed to the grave by a large concourse of people, including not only his own congregation, but the greater part of the community in which he lived; but, though several of his brethren in the ministry were present, no Funeral Sermon was preached, it being, at that time, a custom in the Associate Church and some other branches of the Church in that part of the country, to bury their dead without ceremony, on the ground that silence best becomes such a solemnity.

In the year 1800,—some time before his settlement in the ministry,—he was united in marriage with Anne, daughter of the Rev. Matthew Henderson, for some years Pastor of the Associate Congregation of Chartiers at Cannonsburg, Pa. Having survived her husband more than thirteen years, she was removed by death on the 4th of October, 1853. They had twelve children, eight daughters and four sons; some of whom are deceased, while others still remain, (1855) in the different walks of public or private usefulness.

FROM THE REV. JAMES P. MILLER.

South Argyle, April 13, 1850.

My dear Sir: I cheerfully comply with your request for some brief account of the late Rev. Thomas Allison. My early years were passed in a congregation adjoining that of which he was Pastor; and for three or four years after I left College I was accustomed constantly to sit under his ministry. I therefore knew him intimately, and am in little danger of mistaking in regard to the prominent features of his character.

In his person he was about five feet ten inches high, of a sandy complexion, rather florid, and somewhat inclined to corpulency. His manners were bland and gentlemanly, so that he was never otherwise than at home in the most polished society; and yet this seemed to be rather the product of nature than of culture.

He possessed a mind distinguished at once for vigour and discrimination. He was capable of grappling successfully with abstruse and difficult questions, either in Morals or Theology, and would not unfrequently present a striking and original view of a subject as soon as it was proposed to him. He thought with much accuracy and precision, and expressed his thoughts with great ease, in corresponding language. He was remarkable for strong common sense, and an intimate knowledge of the human heart. His views of men and things were equally minute and correct, and betokened a habit of close observation.

Mr. Allison was not naturally a man of active physical habits. This, I have no doubt, interfered somewhat with the popularity, if not the success, of his ministry. His preaching was rather practical than doctrinal. His voice was feeble and incapable of any great compass. He had a fine command of language in the pulpit as well as elsewhere, and his matter also was uniformly good, but he loved a careless, half-lounging posture, and perhaps his general manner indicated less interest in his subject than was desirable to secure the highest degree of attention. Still, however, there was so much well-digested thought in his discourses, and such uncommon felicity of expression, that he was always listened to with interest, and the greater, in proportion to the intelligence of his hearers. In the application of his discourse, without any alteration of his voice, he would sometimes be exceedingly impressive. I ought to add that his aversion to physical effort never kept him from the faithful discharge of his pastoral duties. I never heard it intimated that he was lacking in due attention to the interests of his flock. He was fond of reading, and kept himself well informed of the general progress of things in the world.

In the ordinary intercourse of society he was affable and agreeable, and abounded in pleasant anecdotes. His powers of conversation I have not often known surpassed. He was, however, capable of the keenest sarcasm, and showed great impartiality in the use of it, dealing it out alike upon friends and foes. It may be that he did not always wield this dangerous weapon with the utmost discretion.

Mr. Allison was exceedingly averse to going from home, or to receiving appointments to be fulfilled at a distance. He was, however, a good member of a Public Body, and his opinion was always listened to with respectful deference. He was perhaps distinguished rather for sustaining and forwarding important measures than for originating them.

I am, Reverend and dear Sir, with respect, yours truly,
JAMES P. MILLER.

FROM THE REV. JOHN T. BROWNLEE.

WEST MIDDLETOWN, Pa.. January 22, 1855.

Dear Sir: I have a distinct remembrance of the Rev. Mr. Allison, concerning whom you inquire, having passed several of my earliest years under his ministry, but his death occurred when I was too young to enable me to write much concerning him from personal knowledge. I am obliged, therefore, in complying with your request, to rely, for the most part, upon the testimony of others; but his character has always been so familiar to me that I believe I may venture to speak of it with some degree of confidence.

Mr. Allison's mental abilities were regarded by all who knew him and were capable of judging, as very far above mediocrity. His scholarship was both extensive and accurate. As a Preacher, though not distinguished for that commanding eloquence which sometimes holds an auditory entranced, he was yet possessed of a free elocution, and his sermons were, in the estimation of all enlightened and cultivated minds, of a high order. They were generally prepared with great care and many of them written out fully; but, whether fully written or preached from an outline, so correct was his analysis of his subject, so full and clear and logical the division, so precise and 'pointed the discussion, that not only was criticism for the most part disarmed, but often the enthusiastic admiration of the most critical hearer elicited. His habit of full and careful preparation he followed up as long as he continued to preach; and it is worthy of note that so impressed was he with a sense of the importance not only of full but of fresh preparation for the pulpit, that he seldom, if ever, made use of the notes of a former discourse without subjecting them to a careful revision. A few of the notes of his sermons in the earlier years of his ministry I have had an opportunity to examine; and I can truly say that they all seemed to me to bear the stamp of intellectual greatness; and not only so, but were verbally and literally, and even in their punctuation, correct; and yet so distrustful was he of any former preparations, that his revision of them for after use was always made with pen in hand.

But great as were Mr. Allison's abilities, and the consequent influence which he exerted in the pulpit, perhaps he made himself still more powerfully felt in the Church Courts. The windy eloquence that sometimes takes the attention of a popular auditory, if indulged in at all in a Church Court, passes only for wind; while real talent and acquirements, coupled, as they were in the case of Mr. Allison, with a fervid and vigilant zeal for the welfare of Christ's cause, cannot fail to exert a commanding influence. During the last few years of his life, his hearing was so impaired that—much to the regret of his brethren in Church Courts—he was, to a great extent, disqualified for taking an active part in their proceedings. Previous to this, his position was always that of a leading member; and, possessed as he was of a strong mind, a sound judgment, and an ardent zeal for the purity of God's truth and the prosperity of his cause in the world, he exerted not only a powerful, but generally a highly salutary, influence. It should, however, perhaps, be stated, in this connection, that he had one quality of mind that, in some circumstances, tended rather to neutralize his otherwise good influence. Though, in most cases, he was abundantly able to expose the fallacious or defective reasoning of an opponent, without resorting to any such means, he sometimes, under circumstances of special provocation, employed a caustic severity of retort, that made him rather an object of dread than of respect with some who differed from him in judgment.

His publications were few and inconsiderable. He always felt an aversion to authorship. The only printed productions he left were some which he could not well avoid, principally Reports which he wrote as Chairman of various important Committees, (a post which he often occupied,) and which were published in the Minutes of Synod, and frequently in separate pamphlets. These were all characterized by marked ability, but they were generally on subjects of temporary or local interest, and they have passed away with the occasions which originated them.

I remain, with high respect, very truly yours,
JOHN T. BROWNLEE.

THOMAS HAMILTON.*
1801—1818.

THOMAS HAMILTON was born near the borough of Washington, Washington County, Pa., about the year 1776. His father was a highly respectable citizen, and, for some time, held the office of High Sheriff of the County. His early religious impressions are supposed to have been received through the influence of a godly mother. While he was yet quite young, his mind had taken a decidedly religious direction, and he expressed a wish to devote himself to the Ministry of the Gospel; and this desire was cordially responded to by his friends. He received the rudiments of his education at the Grammar School at Cannonsburg, Pa., which has since become Jefferson College; and was afterwards connected, as a student, with Dickinson College, though the absence of his name from the College Catalogue would seem to imply that he did not graduate.

After completing his literary course, he entered the Theological School of the Associate Church, under Dr. Anderson, and was a member of the first or second class that passed through that institution. In due time he was taken on trial for licensure, and was actually licensed (it is believed) in the year 1801.

After he had preached for some time in different vacancies of the Associate Church, he was sent to supply a Congregation in the city of New York, which had been organized by the Rev. Thomas Beveridge, in the spring of 1785. Notwithstanding this congregation numbered among its members some influential and prominent families, they had not—owing, as is supposed, to the small number of Associate Ministers then in the country—up to this time ever had a settled Pastor. After Mr. Hamilton had preached to them a few Sabbaths, they gave him a call, which he accepted; and, on the 10th of June, 1802, he was ordained to the sacred office, and installed as Pastor of that Congregation. In connection with these services was the administration of the ordinance of the Lord's Supper. Dr. Banks preached the Ordination and Installation Sermon, and Mr. Marshall presided at the dispensation of the Sacrament.

Mr. Hamilton continued in the faithful discharge of his ministerial duties for about sixteen years, when he was suddenly arrested by the malady that terminated his life. After a somewhat lingering illness, he died at New York, on the 23d of August, 1818, at the age (as is believed) of about forty-one or forty-two.

The only production of Mr. Hamilton's pen, known to have been published, is a Sermon appended to the brief sketch of his life by Mr. Miller, and another in the fifteenth volume of the Religious Monitor.

* Miller's Sketches.—MS. from John McAllister, Esq.

Mr. Hamilton was married on the 26th of May, 1827, at Rockland, Del., to Margaretta Marshall, daughter of William Young. They had four children at the time of his death,—three sons and one daughter. The eldest son, *William Young*, was graduated at Jefferson College in 1833, studied Theology at the Seminary at Cannonsburg, was licensed to preach, and had actually supplied for a time some vacant congregations, by appointment of Synod, but, in consequence of some mental disorder, was taken off from his labours for several years, and, though he partially recovered, he never afterwards resumed them. He died in or about 1860. Mrs. Hamilton removed to Philadelphia with her family immediately after her husband's death, and remained there till her own death, which occurred on the 5th of April, 1827.

FROM THE REV. JAMES M. MATHEWS, D.D.

NEW YORK, April 7, 1863.

My dear Dr. Sprague: When I came to New York to reside in 1804, the Rev. Thomas Hamilton was settled here as Pastor of the Associate Church, and I very soon made his acquaintance, and continued in pleasant relations with him to the close of his ministry and life. Though we belonged to different denominations, and were therefore not ecclesiastically thrown together, yet we occasionally visited each other, and often met in the ordinary intercourse of society, so that I had a good opportunity of judging of his more prominent characteristics. Though upwards of forty years have passed since our last meeting, my recollections of him are sufficiently distinct to justify me in attempting to comply with your request.

Mr. Hamilton was a man of a sound, well-balanced mind, and of a highly respectable degree of cultivation. He never said brilliant or startling things, but he impressed you at once as a man of calm, reflective habit, who always reached his conclusions deliberately, and who rarely had occasion to abandon them. He was naturally kind and amiable, but was resolute in his adherence to his convictions of right, and would never yield them for the sake of accommodating a friend, or from any considerations of personal convenience. His habits were rather the opposite of demonstrative, especially in general society, though he always seemed to enjoy familiar intercourse with his friends. My impression is that he never mingled much in public concerns, and had but little acquaintance outside of his own congregation or immediate circle; though this was not the result of any illiberal views or feelings, but of a somewhat delicate temperament that naturally courted retirement. In person he was tall and slender, and of a prepossessing countenance. He was a sensible rather than an impressive Preacher—his sermons were carefully written, and delivered memoriter; and though his preaching did not captivate the multitude, it edified the thoughtful and intelligent. He was very diligent and conscientious in all his pastoral duties, availing himself of every opportunity to direct the thoughts and regards of his people to their higher interests. Both in the pulpit and out of it there was an all pervading seriousness about him, which marked him as a man of God. His whole air and manner kept you mindful of his high vocation.

Mr. Hamilton was strongly attached to the Associate Church, and always ready to promote its interests by every means in his power. At the same time I never saw in him the least indication of a sectarian spirit, and I doubt not that he was a cordial well-wisher to the prosperity of every evangelical denomination. I well remember that he stood high in the regards of Dr. Mason for his great probity, consistency and Christian worth.

Your ever affectionate friend, J. M. MATHEWS.

JAMES RAMSAY, D.D.*
1803—1855.

JAMES RAMSAY was born in Lancaster County, Pa., on the 23d of March, 1771. His parents, Robert and Mary Ramsay, belonged, at the time of his birth, to the Reformed Presbyterian Church, or Covenanters, and were always much respected for their intelligence and piety. James was the first-born of fifteen children, the larger number of whom he survived. About two years after his birth, his parents removed from Lancaster County to what was then known as the Western Wilderness, and resided about two years at Williamsport, on the Monongahela River. The settlements in that region were few and scattered, and were constantly exposed to the hostile incursions of the surrounding Indians. It was amidst such scenes of danger, and those of the Revolution which immediately followed, that James first formed his acquaintance with the world; and to this no doubt was to be attributed, in some degree, the remarkable energy of character which he exhibited in after life.

At the end of two years the family removed from Williamsport to Pigeon Creek, then within the bounds of the Congregation of the venerable Dr. McMillan, one of the most distinguished of the fathers of the Presbyterian Church. With this church the parents connected themselves, as did their son James also, at a very early period of his life.

At the age of twenty-one he made a joint purchase of a farm, two miles from the village of Frankfort, Beaver County, Pa., and went with one of his brothers to reside there. This was within the bounds of the Presbyterian Congregation of Mill-Creek. Here, after some time, he was induced to change his ecclesiastical relations. He was led to this chiefly in consequence of the substitution, then becoming quite common in the West, of Watts' Hymns for David's Psalms in the public worship of God. Being fully convinced that this usage was unscriptural and adverse to the legitimate ends of devotion, he felt himself constrained by conscience to join a communion whose practice on this subject was in accordance with his own convictions. He, accordingly, united with the Associate Congregations of Service and King's Creek, then and for many years afterwards under the pastoral care of the Rev. Dr. Anderson, Professor of Theology in the Associate Church. His change of ecclesiastical connection was attended with no unkind feeling either on his own part, or on the part of the brethren from whom he felt obliged to separate.

It is not known at what period of his life his thoughts were first directed towards the Ministry, though he seems to have meditated such a purpose previous to his connection with the Associate Church. It is supposed that he commenced his classical studies under his minister, Dr. Anderson, when he was about twenty-five years of age. He afterwards studied at the Jefferson Academy, since incorporated as Jefferson College. In the year 1805 he received from this institution the degree of Master of Arts. After completing his classical studies, he pursued the study of Theology under Dr. Anderson—this was between the years 1800 and 1803.

* Evangelical Repository, 1855.—MS. from Rev. Dr. Beveridge.

Mr. Ramsay was licensed at Buffalo, by the Presbytery of Chartiers, on the 14th of December, 1803, when he was within a few months of completing his thirty-third year. He laboured for some six weeks after his licensure in the Presbytery of Chartiers, and then, during the greater part of the remainder of the year 1804, in the Presbyteries of Cambridge and Philadelphia. At the close of this year, he returned to Chartiers, and laboured within the bounds of that Presbytery till his settlement. He received an urgent invitation to take charge of the Associate Congregation of Cambridge, N. Y., then vacant by the removal of Dr. Banks; but he thought it his duty to decline it. At a meeting of the Presbytery of Chartiers, April 17, 1805, four calls were put into his hands from as many different congregations; and the one which he finally accepted was from the Congregation of Chartiers. Here he was ordained and installed on the 4th of September following, the Sermon on the occasion being preached by the Rev. Thomas Allison.

He addressed himself now to the various duties of the pastoral office with the utmost faithfulness and assiduity. In the sixteenth year of his ministry, he was called to a post of increased responsibility. Dr. Anderson having, in 1819, resigned the Professorship of Theology, the Synod, at their next meeting, in 1820, resolved to establish two Seminaries, to be called the Eastern and Western. In 1821 Mr. Ramsay was chosen Professor in the Western Seminary; and, in the ensuing winter, entered upon the duties of his new office, being at this time fifty years of age. This post, in connection with his pastoral duties in a large congregation, rendered his subsequent life very laborious. To his other offices was added the Professorship of Hebrew in Jefferson College, to which, however, he devoted but a small part of his time. He resided on a farm about a mile from Cannonsburg, and read Lectures to his students at his own house. Most of them boarded in his house; but, as the number increased, and the boarding of so many became inconvenient, he removed from his farm into Cannonsburg, where he was relieved from the necessity of taking more than suited the convenience of his family. After the death of Dr. Banks, Professor of the Eastern Seminary, which occurred in 1826, the Synod agreed, in 1828, to unite the two Seminaries; and, in 1830, they fixed upon Cannonsburg as the place, and the next year elected Dr. Ramsay (for he had received the degree of Doctor of Divinity from Jefferson College in 1824) Professor in the united institution. He continued to attend to the duties of his Professorship till the meeting of the Synod at Washington, in 1841, when he gave notice of his intention to resign. This was in conformity with a resolution, adopted by him a long time before, that he would not hold his office after reaching the age of seventy. His resignation was tendered at the meeting of Synod at Xenia, in 1842, and was accepted with warm expressions of respect for his character and gratitude for his services.

He still continued in his pastoral relation, and was able for several years more to attend to all his ministerial duties. In June, 1849, he felt it necessary to urge the resignation of his pastoral charge, which had been previously offered, but the consideration of which had been delayed by the Presbytery, in compliance with a petition from the congregation. He was, accordingly, released from his charge, after having held it upwards of forty-four years.

Some time after resigning his Professorship, Dr. Ramsay returned to the farm which he had left for the sake of the students, and continued his residence there till about eighteen months before his death, when he removed with his wife to Frankfort, and resided with their son-in-law, the Rev. Dr. M'Elwee. He still continued, though in his eighty-fourth year, to preach occasionally in his son-in-law's pulpit; and, though feeble in body, was cheerful and even lively in conversation. Three weeks before his death, he was seized with cholera-morbus, from which he recovered, only, however, to sink under another disease to which he had been subject for many years. He died on the 6th of March, 1855, within a few days of having completed his eighty-fourth year.

In the summer of 1805 he was married to Margaret, daughter of James Paxton, who resided in the neighbourhood of Chambersburg, Pa. They became the parents of two children,—a son and a daughter. The son, *James P.*, was graduated at Jefferson College in 1827; studied Theology under his father for five consecutive years; was licensed to preach, by the Presbytery of Chartiers, August 27, 1833; after itinerating a short time, accepted a call, in November, 1834, from the Congregation of Deer Creek, New Bedford, Lawrence County, Pa.; and was ordained and installed in that charge, July 31, 1835, by the Associate Presbytery of Ohio. Here he continued to labour with great fidelity for about twenty years, when he was obliged, on account of long continued and increasing indisposition, to demit his pastoral charge. He subsequently took up his residence in New Wilmington, and, occasionally, for a time, exercised his ministry when his health permitted. He died in great peace on the 30th of January, 1862. He was a man of highly respectable powers, and of an amiable and gentle spirit; was an instructive and impressive Preacher, and an attentive and faithful Pastor. The daughter *Maria*, became the wife of the Rev. William M'Elwee, D.D., Pastor of the Associate Congregation of Frankfort, Beaver County, Pa.—Mrs. Ramsay still (1864) survives, being now in her eighty-fourth year.

Dr. Ramsay never published any thing more extended than a Presbyterial Report; but, after his death, there appeared, in connection with a brief "Memorial" of him, the outlines of nineteen sermons, several of which had been taken down at the time of their delivery.

FROM THE REV. THOMAS BEVERIDGE, D.D.

CANNONSBURG, May 10, 1855.

Rev. and dear Brother: My first acquaintance with the Rev. Dr. Ramsay was formed, when I was in the ninth year of my age, at which time he preached as a probationer in Cambridge, N. Y. It was continued by occasional visits, and our frequently being together at Synodical meetings, till the year 1835, when we became associated as Professors in the Theological Seminary at Cannonsburg. This relation brought us into habits of almost daily intercourse, and our intimacy continued till the time of his removal to Frankfort, in 1853, so that my opportunities of judging of his character were very abundant.

Dr. Ramsay was quite tall and slender, and not altogether graceful in his movements, but it is rarely that a countenance meets our view in which are indicated with such distinctness, and in such agreeable harmony, quickness of discernment, mildness of temper, affectionateness of disposition and contentment of mind. Little children, of whom he was very fond, were attracted to him at once by the kindness and cheerfulness so apparent in the expression of his countenance, in his conversation and whole deportment. There were also blended with these indications such seriousness and gravity as ensured respect and gave force to his ministry.

In his intercourse with society he always showed himself, as to all the substantial qualities of that character, to be a true Gentleman. Few could be compared to him in the talent for entertaining and instructive conversation. His mind was not only well stored with religious truth, but well informed on almost every subject of importance. He was not disposed to engross the conversation, or direct attention to himself, but, in his own modest way, could express his mind freely and appropriately on all common topics. He was not rude, dogmatical, or over-bearing, but remarkably affectionate, and ever ready to yield all due deference to others. While he abhorred duplicity and flattery he was yet careful not causelessly to wound the feelings of any; but rather to say things which would be agreeable and useful. His friendships were warm, almost unbounded, and though he was capable of dislike, he knew how to treat even an enemy with decent courtesy. The consequence of this was that he was always a most welcome guest in the houses of his acquaintances; he was usually the centre of attraction in the social circles with which he mingled, and his society was courted equally by young and old, rich and poor.

Perhaps no trait in his character was more prominent, more universally admitted and admired, than his strict unbending integrity. In this respect, it would be hard to find his equal, and it is believed it would be impossible to find his superior. Such was his reputation for honesty and integrity, that, not long before his death, a gentleman of the highest standing in the County remarked in reference to a question affecting his character for veracity, that, if Dr. Ramsay was convicted of falsehood, he could never again believe himself. His honesty in his dealings was such that persons who could not comprehend his conscientiousness were ready to accuse him of simplicity. Few could be as watchful to take the advantage of others in a bargain as he was to avoid it. He has been often known, at auctions, to bid up articles where there was no competition, through an unwillingness to obtain them under their true value. A gentleman who had sold or traded away a horse for the Doctor, came to him and boasted that he had gained for him an advantage of ten dollars, supposing that this would be highly gratifying. The Doctor never signified whether he was pleased or not, but, upon the first opportunity, quietly handed over ten dollars to the person supposed to be the loser in the bargain.

In connection with this may be noticed his disregard of wealth; his indifference in this respect, if not indulged even to a fault in himself, was certainly, in some cases, the occasion of faults in others. It encouraged imposition. He was far from being ignorant of worldly things. He knew even better than the most of men what was just and proper in worldly transactions; he knew as well as others when he was defrauded, but would rather submit to injustice than contend—hence, unprincipled persons often took advantage of him in their dealings, presuming that it might be done with impunity. In a few, and but very few, instances, his indignation against the meanness of individuals in their extortion prompted a resistance to which the love of money could never have moved him. In the early part of his ministry, he had some difficulties to contend with in providing for his family, but the blessing annexed to liberality attended him, and, for the remainder of his life, though not what would generally be regarded as a rich man, he had not only a competence but an abundance.

Dr. Ramsay was very celebrated for a peculiar kind of wit, which derived much of its power from his gravity, and was so far from detracting from his ministerial character and usefulness that it rather added to both. His wit was altogether remote from levity; neither was he addicted to malicious or biting sarcasm; but he abounded in a species of wit of the most innocent and inoffensive character. His remarks were often so unexpected, uttered with so much apparent seriousness, and exhibited things in such a ridiculous light, that their power in provoking laughter was altogether irresistible. Something of this often appeared in the pulpit, but so restrained and connected with his seriousness, that it seldom, if ever, had any tendency to produce a smile, but often smote upon the conscience with great power. As an example of this may be mentioned a remark made in a sermon preached not many years before his decease. He had heard, as was thought, an unfavourable report respecting some young people whose parents were members of the Church, and took occasion, without any allusion to individuals, to describe in a very striking manner their course of conduct and its consequences. He closed by observing that such young persons were in the broad way that leadeth to destruction; "Yes," said he, "going to the pit as fast as their feet can carry them; unless," he added, as if correcting himself, "they take Judas' road." He often introduced observations of this kind in a manner so unexpected and yet so appropriate, that the hearers were at the same time agreeably surprised and powerfully impressed. He seldom preached without saying something which, either in itself, or in the peculiar and pointed way in which he uttered it, was calculated to take a firm hold of the conscience, and excite serious reflections. To borrow one of his own expressions, sometimes used respecting the performances of others—" His sermons had teeth."

As a Preacher, the Doctor would not be ranked among the most popular by a certain class, though, by some of the best judges, he was considered as one of the greatest orators. He undoubtedly possessed many and great excellencies. His general acceptability, when commencing his ministry, is evident not only from the number of the calls which he received, but from the respectable character of the congregations giving them. Three of these, at least, were, at this time, among the largest, most intelligent and pious congregations of the Associate Church. As he advanced in years, his application to study, and the increase of his religious experience, rendered his ministerial labours still more valuable. The first impression with strangers was seldom favourable. He spoke slowly, though without any painful embarrassment. His style was plain, and his manner not altogether graceful. But, after a little familiarity with his manner, the hearer not only became reconciled to it, but it seemed even to add to the effect of his preaching. It was obvious to every one that he had no thought of what he was doing with his hands or feet, or how he appeared in the eyes of the people,—that his whole soul was engaged in his Master's work. Though slow, and not at all boisterous in speaking, he was always earnest, sometimes burning with zeal. The method of his sermons was clear and logical. His subjects were remarkably appropriate to the occasion. His illustrations were scriptural, and often exceedingly pertinent and striking. He generally comprehended much in a few words, so that those who looked more to the thoughts than the volubility of the speaker, had no cause for weariness. He would weary intelligent people less by a sermon of an hour and a half than many rapid speakers would in half an hour. Looking merely at the thoughts, he would say more in a few minutes than many would say in a whole day, or perhaps in all their lifetime.

He had a just perception of things, and a lively imagination, and hence excelled particularly in description. He made a frequent and unusually happy use of the figure called *Personification*. His example was once quoted, by the Professor of Rhetoric in Jefferson College, to illustrate this figure; with the observation that a distinguished member of Congress, who happened to hear him, in passing through the village, had spoken of him as one of the few pulpit *orators* he had ever heard. Some of his descriptions, though they could not now be given in his own words, or accompanied with his manner, will be long remembered by the hearers. Such, for instance, is his account of the descent of Moses from the Mount, to which he, on one occasion referred, at the close of the dispensation of the Supper, expressing to the people his fear that, like Israel at that time, some of them would soon be found singing and dancing about the golden calf, applying his remarks to the sin of inordinately seeking after wealth.

Another peculiarity in his preaching was the method which he often employed to gain and fix the attention of his hearers. He would, without any appearance of having studied this as an art, begin with some remarks, the particular object of which the hearers would not readily perceive. After he had excited their curiosity as to his design, fixed their attention and prepared the way, he would make the application to the purpose intended so unexpectedly and so appropriately that they were taken by surprise, and convinced almost before they were aware of it. He seemed in this to have copied the spirit, without following the form, of some of our Saviour's parables.

Upon a Sabbath which happened to be the first day of the year, the Doctor read for his text, John iii, 16 : " For God so loved the world that He gave his only begotten Son," &c.; and, after looking around for a little upon the congregation, as his habit was, he began by observing that this was New Year's day, and then enlarged upon the practice of making it a time for offering gifts. After keeping the minds of the people, for some time, in suspense, as to the connection of such remarks with the solemn work of the ministry, he added that the text revealed to us the greatest and best of all gifts,— God's gift of his only begotten Son.

All the Doctor's acquaintances agree in opinion that in no part of his ministerial duty did he excel more than in prayer. His manner in this exercise, like that in his preaching, was slow and deliberate, almost hesitating, yet few could be compared to him for appropriateness, propriety and fervency. His theological students often remarked how apposite his prayers were to the subjects under discussion. The afflicted and dying appeared generally to regard one of his prayers as the greatest of all services which could be rendered to them in this world. He seemed not only to have a peculiar power to carry his fellow-worshippers with him to a Throne of Grace, but to bring away something for their profit and consolation. He was often sent for in cases of sickness, not only by the members of his congregation but by strangers, and even by such as had previously professed but little regard for his ministry. There was no one whose conversation and prayers were more valued than his in cases of this kind.

Though noted for his strict adherence to his religious profession, he was far from being uncharitable towards those whose creeds differed from his. He loved the image of Christ wherever he could find any traces of it; he rejoiced in the prosperity of all parts of his Kingdom, and spoke of the satisfaction which was sometimes manifested by the members of one denomination in hearing of some evil befalling another, as one of the surest indications of the want, or at least the weakness, of grace. In his private intercourse with his brethren of other churches, while faithful to his own profession, he was not forward to enter into controversy, or say offensive things; and, in his public ministrations, when his subjects led him to speak of opinions and usages which he condemned, he did so in such a spirit that no reasonable person could be displeased. He was accustomed to inculcate upon students and young preachers a respectful treatment of such as differed from them, observing that there was little prospect of convincing men by causelessly wounding their feelings and insulting their judgments. As the consequence of this course of conduct, he secured the favourable regards of all good men, and even the respect of bad men. No Minister of the Associate Church had a better reputation either in it or out of it. Every one was ready to rise up in his defence, and to repel indignantly any attack made upon his character.

As a Professor of Theology, his department was Didactic Theology and Hebrew. In teaching Theology his custom was, on alternate days, to read a short Lecture and catechise the students on the subject of it. The latter of these exercises was what he chiefly depended on for informing their minds. He had no ambition to make to himself a name by an affectation of originality, or the introduction of novelties. With excellent powers of judgment and discrimination, with an imagination and ingenuity sufficient to have raised him to a high rank among those having the reputation of original thinkers, he was content to travel in the old and safe way in which others had gone before him. He was firmly attached to the system of doctrine derived from the Bible by the first Reformers and their immediate successors. He was thoroughly familiar with it, and very capable of teaching it in a clear and comprehensive manner. In the Hebrew he was in a great measure self-taught, never having proceeded much, if at all, beyond the first principles of the language, till his election as Professor. But, considering his age at this time, and the multiplicity of his labours, it was rather remarkable that he made such progress in this branch of study as he did. So far as is known, there were no complaints of his incompetency in teaching it. He excelled as a critic upon the performances of the students, having a quick discernment of any thing amiss in the doctrines advanced, the plans of their sermons, their style and general character as speakers. Still he had not an eye merely for their faults, but could see and commend what was worthy of praise. In pointing out faults, he was not usually severe, but sometimes could not refrain from the indulgence of his wit, and raising a laugh at the expense of the young men. Yet, in doing this, there was evidently no intention to give offence, and generally none was taken. The standing of those ministers who prosecuted their studies under him is generally such as to reflect no discredit upon their Teacher.

That which constituted his greatest excellence was his sincere and ardent piety. No man was less disposed to make a parade of his religion—no man less needed to do it. His piety shone forth so clearly in his whole life that it could not be hid—it was a piety not in word but in deed and in truth. Like all members of the human family, he had his infirmities, but they were neither numerous nor glaring. It has been said of some that even their faults lean to virtue's side. It might be said of Dr. Ramsay that his chief faults consisted in the excess of his virtues. His modesty, his indifference to the world, his forbearance and his friendships, were sometimes carried to an extreme.

Yours sincerely and respectfully,
THOMAS BEVERIDGE.

FROM THE REV. DAVID G. BULLIONS.

WEST MILTON, N. Y., February 9, 1863.

My dear Sir: All that I knew personally concerning Dr. Ramsay fell within the period of my theological education. I was his pupil for four years, and was accustomed to recite to him or hear his Lectures five days in the week. I knew him not only as an Instructor but as a Preacher, and occasionally met him also in private, so that I had a tolerably good opportunity of forming a judgment of his general character.

Dr. Ramsay had a highly intellectual expression of countenance. He was a tall, lean, rather gaunt looking man, with thin high cheek bones, high forehead, a small but piercing eye. He was social and pleasant in private intercourse, and could bear his part to advantage in conversation on almost any subject that might come up. There was nothing arrogant or assuming about him, but yet he had great self-control, and was little likely to be awed by the force of circumstances, no matter what they might be.

As a Teacher, he was very systematic and perspicuous, and adhered with great tenacity and exactness to the accredited standards of orthodoxy in his Church. He evidently had the interests of his pupils greatly at heart, and was always ready to confer favours upon them whenever it was in his power.

His style of preaching was somewhat peculiar. I presume he never wrote his sermons, at least when I was accustomed to hear him, beyond the merest outline. He had a sharp, shrill voice, and a clear and ready utterance; and though, at the beginning of his discourse, he usually manifested little emotion, as he advanced his mind would often fire up, and he would deliver himself with great energy, and very considerable effect. When his mind was in a more passive attitude, he would generally stand with his two hands in the pockets of his pantaloons; but when he was aroused, he would lift his pocket Bible, with his right hand, above his head, and the gesture, if not the most graceful, really had great power in it. His sermons were richly stored with Gospel truth, and were highly prized by those who welcome the truth in its simplicity.

Dr. Ramsay was undoubtedly one of the leading spirits of the Associate Church in his day. He had great control in Deliberative Bodies, and was honoured alike for his integrity, good judgment and firmness of purpose. His name is still fragrant in the circles in which he was known.

Fraternally yours,
D. G. BULLIONS.

FROM THE REV. S. F. MORROW.

ALBANY, July 8, 1862

My dear Sir: When I entered the Theological Seminary at Cannonsburg, Dr. Ramsay had just resigned his Professorship, but he still had his home there, and I had frequent opportunities of seeing him. I had seen him indeed at my father's house, while I was yet a mere child; but my first acquaintance with him, and my earliest intelligent observation of his character, were at the time to which I have referred. Notwithstanding his connection with the Seminary had ceased, he still took a deep interest in its prosperity, and was ready to do any thing in his power that was likely to minister to it. He would sometimes be present at our exercises in preaching, and his criticisms upon our performances were generally very just and pertinent, though occasionally seasoned by a slight dash of sarcasm. The Doctor's weakest point, perhaps, in connection with the pulpit, was a rather awkward and uncultivated pronunciation. On one occasion, when he was present at one of our exercises, a student made such fearful havoc with even the plainest rules of orthœpy, that one of his fellow-students who was called upon to criticise the performance read off a list of this kind of offences that seemed truly appalling, but, by way of comforting his brother, added that *he pronounced a good many words correctly.* The Doctor, taking the full force of the joke, and withal being quite aware that his own greatest strength did not lie in that direction, quietly remarked that there were no words in the sermon but what *he* could understand, and added that the criticism which had been made, reminded him of another which a young man made upon a performance of his fellow-student, namely, that "his pronoonciation" (*a* pronounced as if it were *ah*) "was very *absoord.*"

Dr. Ramsay was tall and slender, and altogether of no gainly appearance. His manners were exceedingly plain, though their simplicity and kindliness made you easily forget what seemed to be the want of early culture. But he was a man of capacious mind and of highly liberal attainments. He was profoundly read in Theology, and was never at a loss for arguments wherewith to defend any of the articles of his faith. He had performed excellent service as a Professor, and had retired amidst the benedictions and grateful remembrances of the whole Church. He was a logical and highly instructive Preacher, but his manner was ordinarily too deliberate to suit the multitude, though he sometimes would get an impulse that would render his utterance both fluent and fervent. In the early part of his ministry, he wrote his sermons, then fell into the habit of preaching from mere premeditation, but, in his later years, returned, as I have been informed, to his early practice of writing. He had a very strong hold of the affections of his people, and indeed he enjoyed, in a high degree, the respect and confidence of all who knew him. He exerted great influence in the Church, not only by his general character as an able, learned and eminently godly man, but by the prudent and vigorous control which he exercised in her various Deliberative Bodies. When I knew him, he had become, to some extent, disabled by infirmity; but, as long as he lived, his presence was felt to be an element of power.

Dr. Ramsay was so conscientious that his scruples in respect to small matters would sometimes excite a smile. For instance, I remember to have heard that, on one occasion, his wife went out and purchased some article at what she considered a very reasonable rate, and, on her return, spoke rather exultingly of her good bargain. The Doctor inquired of her what the ordinary price of the article was, and, on being told, went straight off, without saying a word, and made up the full price. If there was a doubt at any time in regard to what justice permitted or required, he never gave himself the benefit of it.

Yours truly,
S. F. MORROW.

JOSEPH SHAW, LL.D.*
1805—1824.

JOSEPH SHAW, a son of James and Ann (Patterson) Shaw, was born in the Parish of Rattray, Aberdeenshire, Scotland, and was baptized on the 6th of December, 1778. His parents were respectable, pious persons, but in rather moderate worldly circumstances. He spent his early years in his native village, where he had the advantages of good schools and of good society. Here he acquired not only a common education, but the necessary preparation for entering College. He became a member of the University of Edinburgh a little before he had completed his thirteenth year. He never ceased to regret commencing his collegiate course at so early a period, before his faculties were sufficiently developed to enable him to take the full advantage of all the instruction which he there enjoyed; and he was accustomed, in view of his own experience, to caution parents against committing a similar mistake in respect to their children. The expenses of his college life were met principally by his father, but partly also by his own efforts in teaching a school during his vacations. His course at the University was at a period when nearly every Professorship was identified with some illustrious name,—such as Robertson, Blair, Playfair, Daelzel, Dugald Stewart, &c. He graduated in the year 1794.

* Memoir by Rev. A. Whyte, jr.—MS. from Rev. Dr. A. Bullions.

From his earliest years he had manifested a serious turn of mind, and while he was yet quite young had become a member of the Associate Church. He had also, from the commencement of his academical studies, had in view the Ministry of the Gospel as his profession; and, accordingly, immediately after leaving the University, he entered the Associate Divinity Hall at Whitburn, thereby placing himself under the instruction of the venerable Professor Bruce. Here he remained nearly the whole of five years, and at the close of his theological course, in 1799, was licensed to preach the Gospel. The winter previous to his licensure he spent in Edinburgh, reviewing some of his former studies, and prosecuting others that did not belong to the ordinary course. He was a member of an Association that met weekly for purposes of literary, moral and religious improvement, and was here greatly respected by all his associates. At this time his style of writing was rather dry and frigid, but characterized by great neatness and precision. And, as this was the kind of style that marked his preaching as a probationer, he did not succeed well in catching the popular ear, and, so far as is known, received no call from any congregation to settle among them. By the ministers, however, his services seem to have been more highly appreciated; and hence, when the Associate Church in Walnut Street, Philadelphia, became vacant by the death of the venerable William Marshall, application being made to the General Associate Synod of Scotland for a successor, they unanimously appointed Mr. Shaw to the place.

He accepted the appointment, and, in the autumn of the year 1805, arrived in Philadelphia, and commenced his labours in the congregation to which he had been designated. In due time he received and accepted a call to become their Pastor, and was installed shortly afterwards. His services were highly acceptable, and his prospects of usefulness altogether promising.

In the year 1809 Mr. Shaw went to Guinston, about seventy miles from Philadelphia, to dispense the Lord's Supper; and, during his absence, was seized with the then prevailing influenza. In consequence of not taking suitable care of himself, his lungs became seriously affected, so that he was confined to his room and even to his bed for several months, and no less than fifteen blisters were successively applied for his relief. By the blessing of God attending the skilful and faithful treatment of Dr. Rush, he gradually recovered in some degree, but he was able to preach but little for several years, and never subsequently enjoyed perfect health. Under these circumstances he judged it proper to terminate his ministry at Philadelphia—and so he did in 1810; but this result was not reached without considerable disquietude and dissatisfaction. His sufferings, in connection with both his severe illness and the separation from his charge, were believed to have been spiritually beneficial to him; and from that time it was remarked that the tone of his Christian and Ministerial character was much more elevated than it had been at any preceding period.

He spent a portion of the summer after his removal from Philadelphia in making a voyage to Nova Scotia for the improvement of his health, preaching occasionally as he found himself able. The next winter he spent in Cambridge, N. Y., with his friend Dr. Alexander Bullions, endeavouring, by gentle exercise and a cautious use of medicine, to improve his physical condition; and he partially succeeded. During this visit he delivered to the congregation to which Dr. Bullions ministered a series of discourses which were listened to with great interest, and, as an expression of their gratitude and sympathy, they presented him with a handsome sum of money. With his characteristic liberality, however, he applied this donation to the founding of a ministerial library among them, which has since become the most valuable library of its kind in the whole region.

In 1813 Mr. Shaw received and accepted an invitation to become Professor of Languages in Dickinson College. Here he continued, labouring with great zeal and fidelity, until 1815, a short time before the operations of the College were suspended. In that year the Trustees of the Albany Academy called him to the same Professorship in their institution which he had previously held at Carlisle. Here also he taught with great success, and was equally admired for his talents and accomplishments and esteemed for his private virtues. Under him and his able associates the institution took a higher stand than it had at any preceding period. In 1821 he was honoured with the degree of Doctor of Laws from Union College.

Dr. Shaw had, for many years, been subject to a periodical illness, during the month of August, resembling the influenza from which he had suffered so seriously in 1809. In August, 1824, soon after the commencement of the summer vacation in the Academy, he left Albany for Philadelphia; and, on his arrival there, was seized with a violent cold, from which, however, he had partly recovered before the close of the week. He was engaged to preach on the following Sabbath; and though, on the morning of that day, he was threatened with serious illness, yet, being unwilling to disappoint the congregation who had expected his services, he went through the regular exercises of the forenoon. His disease almost immediately developed itself in a raging fever; but in three or four days it had apparently spent itself, and every thing seemed to indicate a speedy recovery. Scarcely had the favourable change begun to be realized before there was a fearful relapse, in which was recognized very soon the harbinger of approaching death. In a few hours his spirit had fled. His disease proved to be an inflammation of the stomach, and was pronounced by his medical attendants to be one of the most deceptive and malignant cases which had ever come within their observation.

Dr. Shaw published a Sermon preached before the Albany Bible Society, in 1820. The last sermon that he ever preached, entitled "The Gospel Call," was published, shortly after his death, in connection with a brief biographical notice of the author. Several of his discourses appeared at a still later period in the Religious Monitor—also a series of Dissertations on the Sanctification of the Church, and the Gospel Ministry.

FROM THE REV. PETER BULLIONS, D.D.

TROY, March 14, 1854.

Dear Sir: My friend and countryman, Dr. Shaw, concerning whom you ask for my personal recollections, was in several respects a superior, even a remarkable, man.

I cannot say that his personal appearance was particularly prepossessing. He was short and thick, firmly built, and always neat in his appearance. His face was full and square, his eye dark and penetrating, and the whole expression of his countenance, though not specially benignant, was deeply intellectual. His manners in general society were far from being free; and he would doubtless have been more generally popular, if he had been more communicative; but those who knew him well and were admitted to his confidence, knew that he was capable of warm and generous feelings.

His mind, in its general character, was rather solid than brilliant. Without any high degree of imagination, he possessed a sound, discriminating judgment, good logical powers, and an exact and delicate taste. While he was at the University of Edinburgh, I have been informed that his written productions underwent so careful a pruning by his own hand, that there was sometimes a sacrifice of spirit and interest to rigid correctness; but this fault gradually disappeared; and, though his writing was always so correct as well-nigh to bid defiance to criticism, his sermons at least came to exhibit a very good degree of evangelical unction.

And this leads me to speak of him as a Preacher. His manner in the pulpit was more than commonly quiet and unpretending, and I cannot say that it was very impressive. But his discourses were sure to be highly relished by the more intelligent and reflecting class. They were written fully out, even to the application, but his manuscript was never seen in the delivery. And they were not only written, but evidently written with remarkable care, in respect to both sentiment and style. He never went into the pulpit half prepared, and could never tolerate any thing there but beaten oil.

Dr. Shaw's naturally retiring and taciturn manner disqualified him for the highest degree of usefulness in private religious intercourse. He had not a facility at introducing serious conversation, especially in regard to one's personal state; but he was nevertheless a truly devout man, and had no communion with the spirit of worldliness and levity. Indeed the temper which he manifested was eminently a Christian temper; and his general deportment in the world reflected honour on his profession as a Minister of Christ.

I should not do him justice if I were not to add that he was more than commonly charitable and public spirited. He imparted liberally of his substance to those who were in need. He was the friend of those great institutions designed to aid in spreading the Gospel through the world, only the infancy of which, however, he lived to witness—he fully sympathized with the spirit in which they originated, and contributed to them according to his ability.

He possessed not only a highly vigorous, but highly cultivated, mind, as might have been expected from the fact that his course at the University of Edinburgh was during one of the most brilliant periods in the history of that Institution—while Robertson, the Historian, was its Principal, and Blair, Finlayson, Playfair and Dugald Stewart were among its Professors. With a mind thus thoroughly furnished in the various departments of knowledge, and especially in the classics, and with a happy talent at rendering himself intelligible to every capacity, he was a most thorough and efficient teacher. In his discipline he was exact,—probably severe—at any rate such was the opinion of some of his pupils who were able to testify from a pretty large experience; but this was only the acting out of his natural temperament in connection with a controlling desire to do most and best for those who were committed to his care.

I had no acquaintance with Dr. Shaw in Scotland, and never saw him until I came to this country in 1817, when I found him a Professor in the Albany Academy; but from that time till his death, I knew him well, and reckoned him among my intimate friends. I am happy thus to bear testimony to his high intellectual, moral and Christian worth.

Yours truly,
PETER BULLIONS.

FROM THE HON. ARCHIBALD McINTYRE.

ALBANY, March 24, 1849.

My dear Sir; From the time that Dr. Shaw removed to this city, and became Professor of Languages in the Albany Academy, he was very intimate in my family, and spent many of his leisure hours with us. It was seldom that a day passed, whilst we remained in Albany, that he did not call; and although the heads of the family might be out, he would spend what time he had to spare with the children, to whom he was warmly attached.

After the removal of my family to Philadelphia, Dr. Shaw spent his summer vacations with us; and there he departed this life, deeply lamented by all who knew him. I can truly say that I never knew a man of more incorruptible integrity, or more disinterested benevolence, than he possessed. So firmly did he stand to his own convictions of what was true and right that I verily believe he would have suffered martyrdom rather than depart, in the slightest degree, from what he regarded as the strict line of Christian duty. His charity to the poor was limited only by his means. He was in the habit of placing a sum of money in Mrs. McIntyre's hands, at the commencement of winter, to be appropriated by her to the relief of the suffering poor. He dressed neatly but plainly, and was remarkably temperate in both eating and drinking. He was strictly economical, never spending any thing needlessly, while yet he was more indifferent to worldly gains than almost any person I have ever known. On one occasion, he placed in my hands a thousand dollars, with a request that I would invest it for him according to my own judgment. I bought State stock with the money, and handed him the certificate for it. Some two years afterwards, I was informed, by the Cashier of the State Bank, that, although this stock stood on his books, no interest thereon had been paid or called for. I spoke to Dr. Shaw on the subject, and found that he had forgotten that he had any such certificate in his possession, though, upon examination, he quickly found it among his papers.

Dr. Shaw was modest and unassuming in his manners, and in general society was somewhat inclined to be taciturn, so that only those who were intimate with him could fully appreciate his extraordinary worth. Though always ready to converse on religious subjects, he was free from sanctimonious airs, and did not forget the wise saying of Solomon, that "every thing is beautiful in its place." Notwithstanding his retired habits, he was a diligent student of human nature, and few men knew better what was going on in the world than he. He possessed great meekness and equanimity of temper, and, though not insensible to injuries, never indulged in a spirit of retaliation.

I cannot say that Dr. Shaw, as a Preacher, was especially attractive to the multitude, but his discourses were full of excellent thought, and were marked by decided ability. Every thing that came from his pen indicated a careful and thoughtful habit of mind. He had the reputation of being a very superior scholar, and I have no doubt that he possessed one of the most cultivated minds of his day, in this country.

I am, my dear Sir,
With sincere respect and esteem,
Your most obedient servant,
A. McINTYRE.

ROBERT BRUCE, D.D.*
1806—1846.

ROBERT BRUCE was born in the parish of Scone, County of Perth, Scotland, in 1776. He was descended from a highly respectable family, which traced their ancestry back to Robert Bruce, the famous King of Scotland. Having gone through the preparatory course of study, he entered the University of Edinburgh in 1798, being then in his twenty-second year. During his College life he was a most diligent student, having not only an intense love of books, but an iron constitution also, which enabled him to gratify this passion with impunity to the largest extent. In 1801 he was admitted as a student of Divinity, after an examination by the Associate Presbytery of Perth, and for five years prosecuted his theological studies under the venerable Professor A. Bruce. Here, as in his college course, he devoted himself most assiduously to his studies, with corresponding rapidity of improvement; and, by his exemplary and winning deportment, rendered himself a favourite, not only with his Professor, but with all his fellow students.

He was licensed to preach by the Associate Presbytery of Perth, in 1806; and was immediately after selected, by the Scottish Synod, to come as a Missionary to the United States. In fulfilment of this appointment, he reached this country before the close of that year. After travelling some two or three years, as a Missionary, chiefly in the Carolinas, he found his way to Fort Pitt, (now Pittsburg,) and became the Pastor of the Associate Congregation in that place. In 1820, when the Western University was founded, he was chosen its President; a position for which his high character and liberal attainments eminently qualified him. In this capacity he served, with great acceptance and usefulness, until 1843, when he tendered the resignation of his office. After this he had an important agency in establishing another institution, (Du Quesne College,) of which he became Provost, and held the place till the close of his life. This, however, was for only a brief period, as he died on the 14th of June, 1846, in the seventieth year of his age. The last sermon he ever preached was from John xiv, 2. "In my Father's house are many mansions." The whole period of his residence in this country was forty years. He exercised his ministry in Pittsburg thirty-six years; presided over the Western University twenty-three years; and was Provost of Du Quesne College two years.

He was honoured with the degree of Doctor of Divinity, by Jefferson College, in 1824.

Dr. Bruce published an Address delivered before the Pittsburg Philosophical Society, 1828, and a small volume of Discourses on various points of Christian Doctrine and Practice, 1829.

In 1810 he was married to Margaret, daughter of George and Joanna Gosman, of the city of New York. They had a large family of children,—sons and daughters. Mrs. Bruce died at Pittsburg, on the 24th of April, 1851.

* Obituary Notices.—Communication from John McAllister, Esq.

FROM THE REV. JOHN BLACK, D.D.

PITTSBURG, May 18, 1848.

My dear Sir: I am willing to do any thing in my power towards erecting a suitable monument in honour of my much valued and deeply lamented friend, Dr. Bruce. I was for many years in most intimate relations with him, and had as good an opportunity of understanding his peculiar traits of character as I have ever had in respect to almost any other man. For upwards of ten years I was Professor in the Western University of Pennsylvania, of which he was at the same time Principal; and we were in habits not only of constant intercourse but of most intimate friendship. He was constituted with rare attractions of character, and the nearer you came to him the more irresistible you found them.

Dr. Bruce was, in the best sense, a Christian Gentleman. His manners, though without any thing like studied refinement, were what you might expect as the natural product of a noble mind and a generous heart, developed under the influence of good society. While he was a model of fairness and frankness in all his intercourse, and was incapable of any thing approaching unworthy concealment, he was yet perfectly discreet, and never gave offence or inflicted a wound unnecessarily. His naturally fine feelings were sanctified and elevated by the living power of Christianity; and you will rarely find an instance in which nature and grace have co-operated more effectually to form a character that every body delighted to honour.

Dr. Bruce was eminent as a scholar. His knowledge of the Greek language particularly was very exact and extensive. In the University of Edinburgh, where he was educated, the Greek language was, and, for aught I know, still is, taught with extreme accuracy; and, having a decided taste for this study, he pursued it to a great extent, and made corresponding attainments. But he did not pursue this branch to the exclusion of others—he was an excellent mathematician also, and was well skilled in mental and moral science. Indeed his education was uncommonly complete—it was not easy to introduce any subject connected with literature or general science, upon which he had not bestowed much thought, and was not ready to express an intelligent opinion.

As a Divine, Dr. Bruce occupied a high place among the more eminent of his contemporaries. He had long been a diligent and vigorous student of Theology, and had investigated every part of that sublime science with the most scrutinizing care. The result of his inquiries ultimately placed him very firmly on Calvinistic ground; and I do not suppose that, at least from the time he came to this country, he departed a hair's breadth from the doctrines contained in the Westminster Confession of Faith, as it was received by the General Assembly of the Church of Scotland. This system of doctrine gave the general complexion to his preaching; a very good specimen of which you will find in his published Sermons. He was highly acceptable in the pulpit, and rarely, if ever, carried thither an offering that cost him nothing. His discourses were well prepared, and were rich in evangelical truth, presented in a form well fitted to secure to it a lodgment in the mind, and an influence over the heart.

Dr. Bruce exerted a wide and important influence during the whole period of his ministry. He was ready to every good work. There are many living witnesses to the purity of his example, the benevolence of his spirit, the elevation of his whole character.

I am very truly yours,
JOHN BLACK.

FROM THE REV. ALEXANDER BULLIONS, D. D.

CAMBRIDGE, N. Y., October 21, 1852.

Dear Sir: I cannot decline your request for my recollections of my early, honoured and deeply lamented friend, the late Rev. Dr. Bruce. I first became acquainted with him in the year 1798, when we were students together at the High School in Perth. We were afterwards associated in our studies, and in habits of most familiar intercourse, for three years, at the University of Edinburgh. We subsequently spent five years together in the study of Theology, under the Rev. Archibald Bruce, of Whitburn. We were both licensed the same year, by the same Presbytery. In short, we lived, slept and studied together pretty much for eight years. We migrated together to the United States, and though, after our arrival here, we resided at a considerable distance from each other, we usually met at least once a year, and, in addition to this, kept up a pretty constant correspondence. I mention these circumstances to show you that if I do not give you a correct idea of Dr. Bruce's character, it will not be for the want of sufficient opportunities to become acquainted with it.

Dr. Bruce's personal appearance was fine and commanding. He was, I should suppose, a little less than six feet in height; portly and symmetrical in his form; with a face rather full, and marked with an open and intelligent expression. His physical constitution was uncommonly firm, and his health almost uniformly vigorous. While his manners were free from any thing like parade or ostentation, they were still sufficiently cultivated to enable him to mingle with ease in the best society. The characteristic feature of his mind was a clear and solid judgment. Along with this was associated a good deal of imagination, which, in his earlier years particularly, he was rather fond of indulging; but it was never his most prominent characteristic. His moral qualities were of a high order. His integrity was like granite—what he believed to be true and right he adhered to, no matter what sacrifice it might cost him. At the same time, he had much of a benevolent and considerate spirit, and never needlessly offended the prejudices or wounded the feelings of any body. He was above all trick and artifice; was a fervent lover of truth; and was ambitious to excel in every thing good. In his intercourse with general society he was discreet and cautious, and yet, on account of his intelligence, generosity, and fine social qualities, he was always felt to be a most agreeable companion. He was never otherwise than a devout and exemplary Christian, though truth constrains me to say that the religious feeling seemed to me to have been more vigorous in him in the early part of his course than it ever was afterwards. I always thought that the study of Philosophy in College, and his literary pursuits in after life, proved unfavourable to the development of his religious affections.

As a Preacher, Dr. Bruce was always acceptable,—I may say even popular, from first to last. His manner in the pulpit was dignified and manly; his utterance distinct, unembarrassed and sufficiently rapid; and his voice clear and sonorous, and loud enough to fill any church. When he began to preach, he had forty or fifty discourses carefully written out; but though, for a while, he preached memoriter, he subsequently preached, I think, for the most part, from short notes; and his sermons were generally rich in strong, well digested thought. I remember a circumstance, somewhat mortifying to himself at the time, which showed that he had some difficulties to overcome in forming the habit of extemporaneous speaking. When we were at College, in Edinburgh, we were both members of a Society, to which Dr. Dick, "the Christian Philosopher," and some other eminent men, then belonged, designed for moral and religious improvement. Bruce had been urged to try his hand in some of the discussions, and at length resolved that he would do so. He rose, on one occasion, with a smile upon his countenance, that seemed to be the harbinger of some very pleasant remarks; but he stood and stood, in unbroken silence, until the smile gradually passed off, and gave way to a look of disappointment and mortification; and he actually sat down without delivering himself of a single word. He said afterwards that he had got an idea by the tail, but it escaped him before he had got full possession of it. He was not, however, discouraged by this unsuccessful effort, but subsequently tried again and again, with increasing success, until, after a while, he became a fluent and effective extemporaneous speaker. It was a fault in his early compositions, and even in his prayers, that his language was not always sufficiently simple. I remember an instance in which he was offering a morning prayer in my mother's family, and, in referring to the fallen angels, he spoke of them as having been "detruded into Tartarus." I mentioned it to him afterwards, and told him that he had been upon stilts; but he said he had not used a word but that every body knew the meaning of. I proposed to appeal to my mother to see what would be her definition of the words "detruded" and "Tartarus," but he did not seem willing to hazard the experiment.

In his Theological views Dr. Bruce was at last thoroughly Calvinistic; though he did not reach that point until he had encountered serious difficulties. So far as I know, these difficulties commenced, or at any rate were greatly increased, by his hearing Dugald Stewart's lectures on Philosophy. We were both so much troubled by the vexed question of Divine Decrees and Moral Agency that, on one occasion, we left our room at about nine o'clock in the evening, and walked a mile and a half to converse with a student of Theology of the Established Church, with a view to obtain some aid in settling our minds on this mysterious subject. We remained with him until after twelve o'clock; and though we found him a Calvinist, and went with an honest desire to be relieved of our difficulties, we undoubtedly left him an Arminian, and such I have reason to believe he continued to the end of his ministry. After we had retired that night, I well remember that Bruce remarked, with no small concern, that he did not see how he should ever be able to subscribe to the Confession of Faith preparatory to entering the Ministry. This apprehension, however, was not realized, as his difficulties yielded to more mature enquiry, and he reposed at last in the Calvinistic system, I believe, with undoubting confidence.

Dr. Bruce was, through his whole life, a vigorous and untiring student. During the three years that we lived together at Edinburgh, he rarely went to bed before one or two o'clock in the morning, and never found time for any thing that was not designed to aid, either directly or indirectly, in the enlargement of his knowledge or the culture of his intellectual or moral faculties. And the same remark substantially applies to the period during which he was a student of Theology. After he became President of Du Quesne College, his devotion to science and literature was most intense; and I am inclined to think that his zeal in acquiring and communicating this kind of knowledge may have interfered somewhat with his preparations for the pulpit, and perhaps with the general efficiency of his ministry. He was, however, always an able Preacher, as well as a diligent student and a learned man.

Yours faithfully,
ALEXANDER BULLIONS.

FROM THE REV. ANDREW BOWER.

PHILADELPHIA, August 14, 1850.

Reverend and dear Sir: You have asked for my recollections of the late venerable Dr. Bruce, Minister of the Associate Presbyterian Church in Pittsburg. I knew him well, and have no other than the most grateful recollections of him. He was long an inmate of the family of my grandparents; and this, in connection with my relation to him as a student of the University and a member of his congregation, gave me an opportunity of understanding very thoroughly his character and habits. Nevertheless, I cannot undertake to be very particular, but shall only attempt to give you a general portrait of the man, as he still lives in my affectionate remembrances.

As a Preacher, he was decidedly popular and successful. In his earlier years he was accustomed to make the most careful and mature preparation for the pulpit; writing his sermons out most elaborately, and then delivering them memoriter: his manner, however, was free and earnest, as if he had been speaking extempore. In after life, when much of his time was necessarily devoted to the College over which he presided, his pulpit preparations cost him much less labour; and yet he continued to the last to be an acceptable Preacher.

In private life he was universally and most deservedly esteemed. With a remarkably bland and amiable temper, he combined good powers of conversation, and uncommonly dignified manners; which rendered him a favourite in every circle where he was well known. He was particularly careful, in all his intercourse, to avoid giving needless occasion of offence; and he was one of the last men with whose feelings any one would be willing to trifle. At the same time he was always true to his convictions of duty, and counted no sacrifice dear which he was satisfied that duty required of him.

As President of the College, he discharged his duties with great ability and fidelity. He had cultivated his powers in early life with great care, and he brought to this responsible station the fruits of long continued intellectual labour in a thoroughly furnished mind. A large number whom he has been instrumental of training to honourable usefulness, and who are now occupying various respectable stations in society, would cheerfully bear testimony to the salutary influence he exerted in cultivating their minds and moulding their characters.

It was sometimes thought, by some of his friends, that many people, while he lived, scarcely did him justice, in the opinion they formed of him. He was naturally so retiring and unostentatious that it was really necessary to know him well, in order to fully estimate his merits; but so amiable and attractive were his qualities that the more one knew, the more he wished to know, of him. It has been said that he was related to the Royal family of Scotland: however that may be, I am sure that he was, in the best sense, a royal man; possessing a great intellect and a great heart, and accomplishing great good for his generation and for posterity.

Dr. Bruce was intimately associated with several eminent men, particularly with the late Rev. Doctors Kerr and Black, the latter of whom has but lately deceased; and in his intercourse with them, he, at once, received and imparted high intellectual and spiritual benefit. He enjoyed, in a very unusual degree, not only the confidence and esteem, but the veneration, of the mass of the community in which his lot was cast; and when he died, the great and universal demonstrations of sorrow showed that, then at least, there was a due appreciation of his uncommon worth, and of the loss that was sustained by his departure.

Your friend and brother,
ANDREW BOWER.

JOHN WALKER.
1809—1845.

FROM THE REV. THOMAS BEVERIDGE, D.D.

XENIA, O., March 12, 1863.

Dear Sir: In compliance with your request, I will now give you some account of the Rev. John Walker.

JOHN WALKER was born some time in the year 1787, in Washington County, Pa. His parents, with whom I was well acquainted, and in whose house I was a boarder for a year, were remarkable for their piety. As, however, is often the case in the work of the Spirit, their piety, though equally sincere, was manifested with some diversity. The father was distinguished for his gravity, the mother for her life and energy. The son inherited the prominent traits of the mother's character much more than the father's. After completing his classical studies at Jefferson College, in his native County, he studied Theology under the venerable Dr. Anderson, and was licensed in 1809, when he was in the twenty-second year of his age. He was soon afterwards settled in Mercer County, Pa. But, after struggling for three years with the hardships of poverty, he resigned his charge, preaching his Farewell Sermon on those words so appropriate to his own circumstances,—Acts xx, 31: "Therefore watch, and remember that, by the space of three years, I ceased not to warn every one, night and day, with tears." He was next settled in 1814, in Harrison County, O., where he continued to labour till his death, which occurred in 1845.

My first acquaintance with Mr. Walker was formed in 1815, at a meeting of the Associate Presbytery of Chartiers, of which he was at that time a member. As the members of the Presbytery began to collect, I noticed one man coming in, who I had not the remotest suspicion was either a Minister or an Elder. He was of middle height, very sandy in complexion, his features sharp, his eyes light coloured, quick and piercing, his hair rough, curled and matted, his dress neither very neat nor clerical. His countenance indicated unusual life, energy and good-humour. His motions were rapid and incessant. A seat appeared to be to him a place of confinement rather than of rest. He seldom sat more than a few minutes at a time, and then was continually shifting his position. One would have much more readily supposed him to be a person engaged in some roving business than a Preacher. I was not, however, left a long time in perplexity. The gentleman, who had attracted my attention, having somehow ascertained that I was a young student of Theology arrived from a distant part of the country, came to me, and with as much frankness and kindness as if we had been old acquaintances. shook hands with me, and told me that his name was *Walker*. He inquired about my affairs, and took as much interest in them as if I had been a near relative. By his free and friendly manner he won his way at once to my heart, and he never lost his place in it. How great is the mistake of many in maintaining a respectful distance toward strangers, and especially young strangers, instead of meeting them with familiarity and affection! Mr. Walker had no formality or stiffness in his manner, calculated to repel either young or old, acquaintances or strangers, but was every where and with all classes free, and even forward, though not impertinent. He had the happy art, when travelling, and, on all occasions, when thrown into the company of strangers, to form an acquaintance with them without exposing himself to the charge of being an intruder. The secret of this art was that he evidently sought this acquaintance, not for the mere gratification of curiosity, or for any selfish ends, but to promote the pleasure and profit of the company. He seldom, if ever, failed, when travelling, to secure attention to religious exercises, morning and evening, at public houses and on board of steam or canal boats, and he managed to introduce them in such a way that often the irreligious, instead of being displeased, appeared to be gratified.

At the time of the interview above mentioned, Mr. Walker was the Pastor of the Associate Congregations of Unity, Cadiz, Mt. Pleasant and Piney Fork, Harrison County, O. He had a charge like an Episcopal Diocese in extent, and yet these congregations formed but a small part of the scene of his labours. He was, for several years, the only minister of the Associate Church in all the Northern part of Ohio, with the exception of one or two whose charges were near the Pennsylvania line. Throughout this region there were numerous small settlements of families, whose main dependence was upon him for supply, and who all looked to him as a common father. Indeed, his popularity and influence among them were almost boundless. A large portion of his time was spent in travelling among these people, preaching and exhorting from house to house. He had a horse about equally remarkable for his unsightly appearance and his speed in travelling. He would mount Ball, as he called him, and set out on his missionary tours, riding at the rate of fifty or sixty miles a day over the then new and rough roads of Ohio. On his way from home he would call at different places, and make appointments for preaching at his return. Having proceeded to the extreme limit of his journey, and perhaps spent the Sabbath there, he would commence his journey homewards, preaching according to his previous engagements, probably at three or four places during the day. He was not accustomed to write any thing more than a brief outline of his sermons, and often he wrote nothing at all. On one occasion, when returning home, he came to a place where he found the people assembled for sermon, according to an appointment he had made, but forgotten. The hour had arrived, and he had not so much as thought of a text. His own situation, however, soon suggested one, and he preached an excellent sermon from the words of Peter to the cripple,—Acts iii, 6: "Silver and gold have I none, but such as I have give I thee." If the sermon were not silver and gold, there is reason to believe that it proved to the hearers, like the healing of the cripple, immensely more valuable.

Mr. Walker was not a profound scholar, nor a man of uncommon strength of intellect, but was remarkable, beyond most men, for the readiness and sprightliness of his thoughts. Hence he excelled in debate, and was frequently engaged in public disputations. He had a public debate on Baptism with Alexander Campbell, the leader of the sect which bears his name. A report of this was published, and though the book was miserably executed, it was not discreditable to Mr. W.'s abilities as a disputant. He was also engaged at different times in public disputes on other subjects, and rather courted than shunned such opportunities of defending what he believed to be the truth. In such contests he was remarkable not only for his readiness, but for his self-possession and good-nature.

He never became confused, ruffled in temper, or abusive in language, though he sometimes made his opponent writhe under the shafts of his wit. As a specimen of his readiness in retort may be mentioned his reply to Mr. Campbell, who, in his debate with Mr. W., accused him of having burnt one of his (Mr. C.'s) books. Mr. Walker observed that his opponent was under a mistake; "The book," said he, "was my own; I bought it and paid for it."

As Mr. Walker made but little preparation for the pulpit, his sermons were not finished compositions, if one might call by that name what had never been properly composed at all. Yet his life and energy made him generally acceptable as a Preacher, and few men have been more useful in building up the Church. His free and friendly manner, his indefatigable zeal and faithfulness, together with his plain and impressive way of exhibiting the truths of the Gospel, fitted him, in an eminent degree, for the field of his labour in the new settlements. In a few years his charge increased so as to support three ministers instead of one; a large Presbytery was gathered around him, and some time before his death this Presbytery was divided into two, of both which he might be considered the spiritual father. His manner as a public speaker was not in all things according to rule, but his evident sincerity and earnestness more than made amends for any faults of this kind, and his preaching was much relished not only by plain people, but by such persons of good taste as had a love to the Gospel. He was usually interesting, and sometimes truly eloquent; and, though unsparing in his attacks upon whatever he regarded as sinful, he was a general favourite. Baptists, Methodists, Quakers, and others whose peculiar views he was ever ready to oppose, when an opportunity offered, yet always held him in the highest estimation. They had the fullest confidence in his honesty, piety and good-will. He blended together, as few have been able to do, the utmost zeal against what he believed to be error, with the kindest feelings toward those who held it.

He was distinguished for his hospitality to friends and strangers. His house was more like a tavern than a private dwelling. His generosity in this and in other respects extended far beyond his means, which were never abundant. He had little tact for the management of worldly affairs, and was always embarrassed, yet never allowed his embarrassments to impair the generosity of his disposition. Having met with repeated losses by the burning of his house with nearly all its contents, by the failure of such as he had trusted, and by his own mismanagement of his affairs, in his later years he united the practice of Medicine to his labours as a Pastor. Indeed, having studied Medicine in his youth, he had before this acted to some extent as a Physician, though without compensation. Now, however, he commenced the business as a regular practitioner; but between gratuitous services to the poor, moderate charges where he made any, and the neglect of his patients to pay, his medical practice did but little to relieve him.

At the time when Mr. Walker first settled in Ohio, he purchased a small farm on which he resided. But as no literary institution existed at that time in the neighbourhood, he soon formed the design of having one established; and, finding the citizens of the nearest villages not forward to move in this business, he, in connection with a neighbour, laid out a town on the adjacent portions of their farms, with a view to the establishment of such an institution. The town was called New Athens; and, while a large portion of it was still covered with trees instead of houses, a classical school was commenced. Mr. W. several times visited the Legislature at Columbus, and exerted himself for years, amidst much opposition, to obtain a Charter for an Academy, and, though repeatedly defeated, he never desisted till he had obtained a Charter, not for an Academy, but for Franklin College. This institution he always cherished with parental fondness, and, though never holding the office of a Teacher, or having any personal interest in it, he was ready to make almost any sacrifice for its sake. It has sometimes been in a flourishing state, but at present, owing to the removal of some of its ablest Professors, it is in a somewhat precarious condition. It was no inconsiderable proof of Mr. W.'s zeal in the cause of literature, that, under discouragements which would quite have disheartened almost any other man, both before and after obtaining a Charter for his College, he still persevered till the close of his life in his hopes, his labours and sacrifices for this institution. His zeal, however, was not for literature in the abstract, but as a handmaid to religion. His chief concern was to furnish facilities for the classical education of young men preparing for the ministry, and nothing gratified him more than the fact that so large a proportion of the youth educated at this College had devoted themselves to the ministry, chiefly in the various branches of the Presbyterian Church.

He was of a very lively, sanguine temperament, ever ready to look upon the bright side of things. It was this turn of mind which occasioned his worldly embarrassments. He made his calculations in the anticipation that all things were to work favourably, and without taking into the account any mishaps or losses. Consequently, his hopes were seldom realized; yet, when one scheme failed, he was ever ready with another, designed to extricate him from the last embarrassment, but he still entered upon it with the same want of caution. Thus he kept on, struggling and hoping, but never rising above his difficulties. His peculiar turn of mind rendered him one of the most agreeable and entertaining companions. Wherever he was, he still proved the life of the company with which he mingled. It seemed as if nothing could either ruffle his temper or exhaust his good-humour.

Yet, though his conversation might sometimes even border on levity, he was a man of the most sincere piety and ardent zeal in the cause of Christ. Nothing like levity was to be seen in his behaviour when engaged in religious duties, nor was there the least disposition, when in the pulpit, to indulge in that wit which, at other times, appeared like an exhaustless and irrepressible fountain. His seriousness and earnestness were such as would soon banish from the mind all thoughts of jesting and all remembrance of his jests. He was a most zealous advocate of Temperance, even to Total Abstinence, long before the formation of Temperance Societies, and when the cause was by no means so popular as at present. He was also a most decided opponent of Free Masonry and all kindred Institutions. But, above all, his zeal against Slave-holding was boundless. He carried his opposition so far as to refuse giving pecuniary aid to emancipate slaves, conceiving that this would be a recognition of the master's right to them as property.

His kindness of disposition, his love of peace, and his readiness of mind, made him particularly useful in reconciling parties who were at variance; and few cases of this kind came before his Presbytery, or the Associate Synod, in which he was not employed as a mediator. Sometimes he was sent hundreds of miles to attend to affairs of this kind, and he seldom failed in his efforts to restore peace. One of his enemies, (for he did not altogether escape enmity,) in allusion to these labours of love, was pleased to call him "The Synod's Scavenger." Happy would it be for Zion if her streets abounded more in scavengers of the same kind.

Mr. Walker died on the 8th of March, 1845. The disease which, in a few days, closed his active and useful life, was erysipelas in the throat. This disease had been prevailing extensively in the neighbourhood, and had been treated by him, in numerous cases, with much success. But when attacked by it himself, with an unaccountable obstinacy he refused to employ the same means which had proved so successful in his treatment of others. Owing to the nature of the disease, he was unable to converse without much difficulty and pain; but none who knew his life could need his dying testimony to satisfy them that his end was peace.

Mr. Walker was twice married. His first wife was Miss Rachel Scroggs, a sister of the Rev. Joseph Scroggs, D.D., of Ligonier Valley, Pa. By this marriage he had six children,—four sons and two daughters. The third son, T. B. Walker, studied Theology, and was licensed to preach, but did not continue long in the ministry. His second wife was a Miss Morrow of Philadelphia, who survived him, and is married to a Mr. Nash, a respectable gentleman of Iowa. One or two of her children by Mr. Walker are still living.

Yours sincerely,
THOMAS BEVERIDGE.

FROM THE REV. D. G. BULLIONS.

WEST MILTON, February 10, 1868.

My dear Sir: I believe I knew the Rev. John Walker well enough to feel justified in attempting a compliance with your request for some brief notices of his character. I met him first at Cannonsburg, in 1837, when I went there as a student of Theology, and, as he was a member of our Board of Examiners, I saw him regularly at every examination during my four years' course in the Seminary. In addition to this, I was for six months engaged in teaching a school within the limits of his congregation, and, during that time, was a regular attendant on his ministry, and a frequent visitor at his house, so that I had the opportunity of seeing him under a variety of circumstances. I have seen him also at my father's house, and, on one occasion, I remember to have heard him preach, with great animation and earnestness, in my father's pulpit, on the text,—" Our feet shall stand within thy gates, O Zion."

Mr. Walker had an expression of countenance indicative of quickness of thought and general strength and earnestness of character. His motions were rapid and energetic rather than graceful—and the remark applies as well to the movements of his mind as his body—he was characteristically earnest and active in every thing that he undertook, while he asked no other question in regard to the means of accomplishing his object than simply whether they were right. He was a man of generous and kindly feelings, and yet, under the intensity of his convictions, he would sometimes say and do things which a different spirit would have modified or perhaps avoided altogether.

As a Preacher, Mr. Walker enjoyed a high reputation, and was in some respects quite peculiar. His general appearance in the pulpit was bold and commanding. His voice was loud and strong, but inclined to be harsh; and, as he waxed warm under the influence of his subject, he sometimes swept along with almost the force of a tempest. His utterance was very rapid, and he rarely, if ever, hesitated for a thought or a word—and yet he was, more strictly perhaps than any clergyman I have ever known, an extemporaneous preacher. He lived about three-quarters of a mile from his church; and I remember his once telling me that his habit was to make his morning sermon on the first half of his way to church, and, when he had reached a certain stump, to begin upon the afternoon sermon, and both were finished by the time he had reached the church door. The consequence of this was that his sermons were characterized more by bold and striking appeals than by any very close logical processes; though he really showed himself possessed of very good powers of argumentation, whenever he was pleased to bring them into exercise. In his sermons, as they were so purely extemporaneous, he was very apt to make episodes with reference to any passing events that might occur to him; and sometimes he would give a sarcastic thrust at the prevailing errors or questionable habits of the times, that would come like a streak of lightning. The tone of his ministrations was decidedly evangelical, and yet it was highly denominational also, as no man could be more conscientiously and earnestly, not to say exclusively, devoted than he was to the interests of his own Communion. As he was a Physician as well as a Minister of the Gospel, the duties of the two professions often came near running into each other— that is, he would frequently go from the pulpit to the sick bed, and not less frequently from the sick bed to the pulpit; and yet his duties in each case were performed as faithfully, and, for aught I know, as successfully, as if he had been exclusively a Minister or exclusively a Doctor.

Mr. Walker, I think, excelled as a Pastor. He was much among his people, always labouring for their spiritual interests, and especially ready to mingle as a comforter with the afflicted. His disinterested regard for their welfare, as well as his naturally genial and generous spirit, made him a general favourite among them.

He was an active and influential member of Church Courts and other Deliberative Bodies. He comprehended readily every subject that came up for discussion, and it cost him no effort to present his views of it in detail, or, if need be, to enforce them by argument. His natural constitution well qualified him to be a controlling spirit.

For nothing was Mr. Walker more distinguished than his hatred of Slavery —I think I may safely say that he was distinguished even among the brethren of his own denomination, who, as a Body, have always been proverbially hostile to that institution. It seemed to be ever uppermost in his thoughts, and his deprecation of it became as natural to him as his breath. Often as I have heard him preach, and perform other religious services, I do not remember a single instance in which he failed to give expression, in some way, to his deep feeling on this subject. On one occasion I was present at a Communion in his church, including the preparatory services, and those which followed it, and I noticed that in every one of the exercises the sin of slaveholding was prominently introduced.

Such, in general, are my recollections of Mr. Walker, and I shall be glad if you find them, in any degree, serviceable to you.

Fraternally yours,
D. G. BULLIONS.

ANDREW STARK, LL.D.*
1820—1849.

ANDREW STARK, son of David and Margaret (Hay) Stark, was born at Sheilknows, in the Parish of Slamannan and County of Sterling, Scotland, in the year 1790. His father was a farmer in easy circumstances, and both his parents were persons of excellent character, and educated their children to fear God and reverence religion. His mother particularly was distinguished for both intelligence and piety. They had a large family of children, eight of whom lived to mature age.

Andrew, having discovered at an early age much more than an ordinary degree of aptness to learn, was favoured in his opportunities for improvement above the rest of the children. His first instructions in Latin he received at the Parish School in Slamannan, but he was soon transferred to the Grammar School at Falkirk, and subsequently to a school at Loanhead of Denny, which he attended for about six months, living at home, and walking to the school, a distance of about four miles, every day.

At the close of this period, in the beginning of 1805, he entered the University of Glasgow, which he attended for six successive winters. During two or three of the summer vacations, after his second session at College, he was occupied in teaching a small country school in the neighbourhood of his father's residence.

In the autumn of 1809 he commenced a school in Glasgow, in the hope of being able thus to procure the means of support while he prosecuted his studies at the University. Here he continued till the close of the Session of College, in April, 1811, when he took the Degree of Master of Arts. As his school at Glasgow did not answer his expectations, he removed to the Parish of Bethkennar, near Falkirk, where he taught a public school, with great success, for upwards of two years.

Previously to his leaving Glasgow he had entered on the study of Divinity. The Theological Seminary of the denomination with which he was connected was then under the superintendence of Professor Paxton, in Edinburgh; and the time of attendance was in the months of September and October. Mr. Stark's attendance commenced in September, 1810, and was continued, though not without some interruption, during the three following sessions.

In the autumn of 1813, upon leaving the Divinity Hall, he went to London, (Chelsea,) where he engaged as a classical teacher. But, finding that his knowledge of Latin Prosody was not adequate to the place which he occupied, he retired, for a short time, to a situation in Guilford, in the County of Surrey, where less was required of him, and where he could devote a considerable part of his time to the study of Prosody. After being absent nearly a year, he returned to Chelsea, where he continued, till the time of his entering on trials for licensure as Classical Teacher, in a boarding school, under the Rev. Weeden Butler, a clergyman of the Church of England. In the autumn of 1816 he spent a few weeks at Edinburgh to complete his course at the Divinity Hall, and immediately after returned to Chelsea.

* MSS. from the Rev. Dr. Peter Bullions and Rev. Andrew Shiland.

At one period of his life, probably while prosecuting his philosophical studies, his mind became perplexed with doubts in respect to the Divine authority of the Sacred Scriptures. He, however, instituted a most thorough inquiry on the subject, and the result was that all his doubts were put to flight, insomuch that he declared himself as fully convinced of the truth of Revealed Religion as he was of his own existence.

After his return to Chelsea in 1816, he seems to have been not a little perplexed as to the question whether it was, on the whole, his duty to enter the ministry. His hesitation did not arise from any doubts of the truth and importance of what he would be expected to preach, but from the idea that perhaps he was better adapted to some other employment, and could be more useful in it. In the summer of 1817, after having suffered a severe illness of several weeks, he returned to Scotland, and spent two or three months with his parents, and, having, in the mean time, been relieved of his perplexity in regard to the course of duty, he was taken on trials for licensure, and in due time was actually licensed to preach the Gospel as a probationer, by the Associate Presbytery of Edinburgh. His first sermon was preached in the pulpit of his cousin, the Rev. Dr. Stark, of Denny Loanhead, on the 26th of October, 1817. Having preached in several vacant congregations, he was sent to the Congregation of South Shields, which had then recently become vacant; and, after preaching there for a month, he received a call to become their Pastor. He accepted the call, and was ordained and installed on the 16th of September, 1818. The connexion thus formed, however, was not of long continuance. The Presbytery, at their very next meeting, received a communication from him, purporting to be the demission of his charge; and, at a subsequent meeting, in January, 1819, he strenuously urged its acceptance; assigning as a reason that the moral and religious state of the congregation was such that he could not continue to be their Pastor, and, according to his own views, be faithful. The Presbytery deemed the ground of his demission insufficient, and declined accepting it; but it was subsequently referred to the Synod, and ultimately the Presbytery, in accordance with the Synod's instructions, dissolved the pastoral relation. This occurred on the 14th of June, 1819.

Immediately after the meeting of Presbytery in January, he went to London with a view to obtain employment again as a Teacher. In a short time he was introduced to a gentleman of large fortune, who employed him to give private lessons to his son; and also introduced him to Sir Frederick Vane, who put his services in requisition in a similar way. In June of that year he entered into a new engagement with Sir Frederick, in the fulfilment of which he went to reside with him at his country seat on the Cumberland Lakes, where he continued for a year, amidst many advantages for improvement and enjoyment. On the termination of this engagement, he resolved on migrating to the United States; and, accordingly, in the month of June, 1820, he returned to Scotland, and made a farewell visit to his parents. He then proceeded once more to London, and, some time before the close of August, embarked for New York, where he arrived on the 6th of October. He came to this country without any fixed purpose in regard to his employment, willing to devote himself either to preaching or teaching as the Providence of God might seem to direct.

For a year after his arrival in the country, he preached occasionally, and superintended the studies of two or three boys,—the sons of wealthy gentlemen in the city of New York; and, in the mean time, was looking out for some place where he might be permanently engaged as a Teacher. Dr. Mason, who was then President of Dickinson College, Carlisle, proposed to him to become a Professor in that institution; and he was not disinclined to listen to the proposal; but, just at that time, circumstances occurred which gave a different direction to his mind, and finally determined him to devote himself wholly to the ministry. The Grand Street Church, in the Associate connection, in the city of New York, had then recently become vacant by the death of their Pastor, the Rev. Thomas Hamilton, and Mr. Stark had, by request, occasionally supplied their pulpit; and so acceptable were his services that they sent an urgent request to the Presbytery to secure him as their stated supply for several months. The result was that he received a unanimous call to become their Pastor, which, after considerable hesitation, he accepted, and was installed in the early part of May, 1822.

Mr. Stark's settlement over the Grand Street Church proved highly favourable to its prosperity. Divisions, which had previously existed, were quickly healed, and the church grew, by gradual and healthful accessions, and became distinguished for its stability and efficiency. He was honoured with the degree of Doctor of Laws, by the University of London, about the year 1844 or '45.

Dr. Stark had naturally a good constitution, but it had been greatly impaired by a violent fever in London, before he came to this country. But though his health, after his arrival here, was always delicate, he rarely suffered his infirmities to interfere with the regular discharge of his pastoral duties, except when he was actually confined to his bed. During one whole summer, he preached with mustard applications or blisters upon his breast, though his congregation, and in some instances even his own family, were not allowed to know it.

At length, however, he became so enfeebled that his physician advised strongly to a temporary cessation from labour, and recommended to him to make a visit to his native country. He fell in with the proposal, and embarked for England on the 3d of July, 1849, having taken leave of his people the preceding Sabbath, in the full expectation of returning to them again after a few months. He was able to preach twice on the passage; but, soon after his arrival in Scotland, his symptoms became much more unfavourable, and the little strength that remained to him seemed to be rapidly wasting. Subsequently to this, however, there was an apparently favourable change; and both he and his friends had strong hopes that it would prove the harbinger of a complete restoration. In this state of hopeful convalescence, he retired to his bed, and fell into an apparently quiet slumber, in which he continued until death had done its work. He had, for some time previous, evinced a high state of spirituality, and only a few hours before, had offered a prayer in the family, so remarkable for pertinence and copiousness and elevation, that all who were present listened to it not only with deep interest, but with devout admiration. He died on the 18th of September, 1849, at Denny Loanhead, Scotland, at the house of his cousin, the Rev. Dr. Stark. His remains were sent to this country, and are entombed in the Greenwood Cemetery. His Funeral Sermon was preached in Scotland, by his cousin, and in New York, by the Rev. Dr. Peter Bullions.

Dr. Stark was married on the 8th of May, 1823, to Ellen, daughter of John and Mary McKie, of New York. They had five children,—three sons and two daughters. The eldest, *John M.*, was graduated at Union College in 1849, became a Physician, settled in the city of New York, and has now (1863) the position of Surgeon, under the Government, at Fort Schuyler. One of the daughters is married to the Rev. Andrew Shiland.

The following is a list of Dr. Stark's publications:—

A Sermon entitled "Charitable Exertions an Evidence of a Gracious State;" a Sermon preached at the Ordination of Mr. Irvine, at Hebron; [Published in the second volume of the Religious Monitor;] a Metrical Version of the Church of Scotland Defended; Biography of the Rev. James Whyte, prefixed to his Sermons; a Lecture on Marriage; Remarks on a Pamphlet, by the Associate Presbytery of Albany, in a Letter to the Associate Congregation of Grand Street.

He wrote also a History of the Secession, in a series of papers, published first in the Religious Monitor, and afterwards in the Associate Presbyterian Magazine. To the latter publication he contributed largely.

FROM THE REV. PETER BULLIONS, D.D.

TROY, March 18, 1854.

Dear Sir: When I went to College at Edinburgh in the year 1810, I found Mr. (afterwards Dr.) Stark there, as a student of Divinity, under the Rev. Professor Paxton. I formed a very pleasant, though not especially intimate, acquaintance with him at that time, and knew that he had a high standing in his class, both as a scholar and a friendly and honourable man. I had but little intercourse with him during the period that intervened between the close of his theological course and my coming to this country; and it was not till he came hither himself, in the year 1820, that my relations with him became in any degree intimate. From that time till his death, we were on terms of uninterrupted and confiding intimacy.

There was nothing very strongly marked in Dr. Stark's personal appearance. He was rather below the medium height, was not unusually thin, nor yet inclined to corpulency; had regular features, a dark complexion, and a dark piercing eye; and altogether his face might be said to be of a highly intellectual cast; and to the careful observer it revealed the true character of his mind. His perceptions were both quick and clear; and his judgments of character, though generally formed with great rapidity, seemed almost infallible. His manner would be thought by a stranger to be somewhat distant and reserved; but when one became intimate with him, and had gained his confidence, (and indeed no one *could* be intimate with him till he had done this,) his reserve gave place to frankness and cordiality. He was remarkable for never even seeming to profess what he did not feel—he abhorred hypocrisy in every form, and few men, perhaps, have ever been more free from it.

Dr. Stark deservedly ranked high as a Preacher. His sermons were carefully written out, and were full of excellent evangelical instruction. It was evident, from the large amount of well-digested, well-arranged and well-expressed thought which they contained, that they had been elaborated with devout care. They were delivered memoriter, without any extraordinary animation, with little gesture, and with no attempt at any thing like pulpit oratory; and yet there was a simplicity, dignity and fitness about his manner,— a solemnity and earnestness so impressive that he could hardly be otherwise than acceptable to any audience. He was particularly felicitous in expository preaching or lecturing. His intimate knowledge of the original languages, as well as of biblical literature and criticism, with his remarkably logical and precise habits of thought, gave him an advantage here which I think few have possessed. His preaching was far less exciting than instructive—it was eminently fitted to make enlightened and thorough Christians. His public prayers were simple, evangelical and appropriate. One peculiarity of manner in prayer, and occasionally in preaching, attracted the attention of a stranger rather painfully, but ceased to be noticed by his stated hearers—I refer to a rapid movement or quivering of the eyelids, which I always supposed was a nervous affection.

In the pastoral visitation of the people of his charge he was regular and assiduous—in visiting the sick and dying, conscientious and diligent. The dwellings of the poor were even more familiar to him than the mansions of the rich. He valued men not for their wealth or rank, but for their worth, and especially for their piety; and his intercourse with all was respectful, friendly and profitable.

In a Deliberative Assembly Dr. Stark had great influence,—and justly. He was a ready extemporaneous speaker, but he rarely spoke on these occasions, except in cases of importance, and then it was always manifest that he had something to say. His clear, safe, vigorous mind was sure to be awake and in exercise where the perplexity of the case demanded penetration and forecast. But unless some such exigency occurred, a whole session of a Presbytery or Synod might pass and his voice be scarcely heard.

In religious matters he was tolerant and liberal, but decided and firm in his own views, and honestly and devotedly attached to the principles of the Associate Presbyterian Church. In private, he was a truly devout man, carrying the influence of religious principle into every department of social life. It was his habit to rise early, and the first business of the day was to gather his family around him for domestic worship. After praise and reading, not a chapter merely, but a large portion of Scripture in course, in which each member of the family took a part, the prayer which followed was such a model of simple, earnest, familiar pleading for all present, for absent friends, his people, the poor, afflicted, tempted, dying,—for the whole Church, for all men, as to impress even the thoughtless, and make the reflecting feel that it was good to be there—and then, when the business of the day was over, early in the evening, the same services were repeated.

Besides this, his rule was to spend the hour immediately after breakfast, or early in the forenoon, in private meditation and devotion; and he adhered to this when at home, under every variety of circumstances, with scrupulous punctuality. In his family, too, he was a fine model of Christian dignity, propriety and faithfulness. He was particularly attentive to the spiritual interests of his children, showing them, by both example and precept, what true religion is, and endeavouring to impress them with its obligations.

Exactness and punctuality in all matters were ever with Dr. Stark a part of religion. His engagements were never made thoughtlessly, and when made they were ever held sacred, and he was perhaps never known to fail of fulfilling them. He was economical in all his habits, but never mean; though his salary was very moderate and even inadequate, he never complained, and he had always at hand the means of rendering assistance where it was necessary. And these means were bestowed with a promptness and liberality as generous as they were unostentatious. Such confidence had those who knew him in his judicious application of means for the relief of the poor, that several of the wealthy men in his congregation, and among his acquaintances, frequently made him their almoner in this duty, and his applications for means to relieve special cases of suffering and distress were always successful.

Dr. Stark's acquisitions were such as might have been expected from his fine intellectual powers. As a classical and English scholar, he may be said to have belonged to the first class. He had also a great amount of general knowledge, and kept himself thoroughly posted in regard to passing events, whether political, moral or religious. There was almost nothing he did not know, and, in the circles of private friendship, his conversation was as instructive and profitable as it was social and cheerful. Though he never published much, what he did publish is highly creditable to both his intellect and his heart. He had great power of condensing, and though his style was perfectly clear, he never troubled his readers with any waste words. His Biography of the Rev. James Whyte, introducing a volume of Mr. Whyte's Sermons, and his History of the Secession Church, published in the Presbyterian Magazine, show that he was capable of high excellence in different kinds of writing.

Ever truly yours, PETER BULLIONS.

FROM THE REV. D. G. BULLIONS.

WEST MILTON, January 19, 1863.

My dear Sir: My recollections of Dr. Stark date back to my childhood. I used to see him at my father's house when I was a small boy, and he came to assist my father at the Communion; and I knew him all along until I had entered the ministry, and was associated with him in the services of *his* Communion. Indeed I knew him quite intimately till the close of his life.

Dr. Stark was very much favoured in respect to his personal appearance. He was rather short and stout, had a round face and florid complexion, indicating a fine constitution, and had a bright piercing look that would prevent any body from asking the question whether or not he was an intellectual man. His mind had been subjected to the highest degree of culture that the most thorough Scotch education could secure. As a classical scholar, I believe he had few equals in this country. Such was his familiarity with Homer's Iliad that I have heard him say that if the last copy of it were lost from the world, he thought he could, without much difficulty, reproduce it. As might be expected, he had a high reputation as a Teacher, associating, as he did, with the maturest scholarship, those other qualities of mind and heart which gave him easy control over the young.

Dr. Stark's discourses were admirable specimens of sound logic. They were carefully and accurately written, his style being so correct as to defy criticism, and so perfectly clear that his meaning was never rendered doubtful even to the humblest capacity in his congregation. His thoughts were always legitimately drawn from his text, and never betrayed a disposition to be wise above what is written. He never wandered away out of the range of evangelical themes for the sake of administering to any body's capricious taste; he felt—and he conscientiously acted upon the conviction—that the instrumentality for doing his work had been supplied to him by God's Word, and that he had no right to look beyond it. His voice was not loud, but it was distinct, and easily filled almost any church. He had but little gesture, but what he had was simple and natural. There was a subdued fervour and unction in his manner, that helped greatly to give his sermons their effect, while yet there was nothing that approached the appearance of artificial excitement. I think he rarely preached without mature preparation, though this was evidently rather a matter of principle than necessity, as he had no difficulty in extemporizing in Church Courts, and on other occasions where the exigency demanded it. I may say here that he was a highly influential member of the Synod, and though not disposed to put himself forward, his opinions were always received with that marked respect and deference to which they were so justly entitled.

Dr. Stark was one of the most generous and magnanimous of men. He was incapable of taking any undue advantage, or placing himself in any equivocal attitude, for the sake of accomplishing any selfish object. I regard him as having been a fine specimen of both intellectual and moral nobility.

raternally yours, D. G. BULLIONS.

ABRAHAM ANDERSON, D.D.*
1821—1855.

ABRAHAM ANDERSON was born near Neuville, in Cumberland County, Pa., on the 7th of December, 1789. He was a son of Abraham and Elizabeth Anderson, both of whom emigrated from the North of Ireland, a few months before his birth. His mother originally belonged to the Associate Church, and his father to the Presbyterian Church of Ireland; though, previous to his leaving Ireland, he had transferred his relation to the Associate Body. He (the son) remained at home, labouring upon his father's farm, until he had reached early manhood. During the war of 1812 he was called out with the militia under General Harrison; and, while thus engaged, he not only gained credit as a soldier, but uniformly exhibited the most exemplary deportment. His Sabbaths were spent in reading his Bible and some other religious books which he had taken with him; and that copy of the Bible he always kept and cherished with most reverential care. On his return home from his tour of military duty, in 1813, he immediately commenced his preparation for the ministry. Without any previous course of study, he entered Jefferson College, where they were accustomed, at that time, to receive students before they had yet begun the study of the Classics. He remained there four years, and graduated in 1817, having been distinguished through his whole course for diligent application and excellent scholarship.

Immediately after leaving College he commenced the study of Theology under the Rev. Dr. John Anderson, who was at that time the Theological Professor in the Associate Church. He continued with him one session, (five months,) and then studied under the general direction of the Presbytery three years; at the same time prosecuting a course of medical study under the direction of Dr. Letherman, one of the most eminent physicians in that part of the country. He was chosen Professor of Languages in Jefferson College in 1818, and accepted the office and retained it until 1821. In October, 1821, he was licensed to preach; and, after itinerating, about two months, in Pennsylvania and the Eastern part of Ohio, he went, by appointment of Synod, into the Southern States, and was very soon settled over the Congregations of Steele Creek and Bethany, Mecklenberg County, N. C. After remaining here about ten years, during which time he exerted a highly beneficial influence, not only upon his own immediate congregations, but throughout the whole extent of the Presbytery,—his health had suffered so much, from the effect of the climate, that he found it necessary to seek a Northern residence; though he resolved to remain until a suitable person could be found to succeed him. In 1831 an Act was passed in the Synod of the Associate Church, requiring the excommunication of all slaveholders; which, whatever might have been his views of the subject, he knew he should be unable to carry out. Having received an appointment from the Synod to visit certain churches at the North, he visited Hebron, Washington County, N. Y.; and, as he did not think it prudent to return immediately, on account of the prevalence of the cholera, he remained and preached at Hebron for some time. After he returned to the South, in the

---

* Communication from himself.—Evangelical Repository, 1856.

autumn of 1832, the congregation at Hebron sent a call after him; and the fact of a person's having been found to succeed him, in connection with the embarrassment occasioned by the Synodical Act on Slavery, led him to accept it. He, accordingly, returned to Hebron in the summer of 1833, and settled there. He held the Pastoral relation to that church fourteen years and a half. In the autumn of 1847 he was elected Professor in the Theological Seminary of the Associate Church at Cannonsburg, as successor to the Rev. Dr. Martin. This post, in connection with the Professorship Extraordinary of Hebrew in Jefferson College, and the collegiate charge of the Congregation of Miller's Run, he held till the close of life.

The disease, which terminated his life, was an inward inflammation, which had troubled him for many years. It was not, however, till within a few months of his death that it began seriously to interfere with his stated labours. In December, 1854, he found it necessary to cease from the exercise of his ministry, in the Congregation of Miller's Run, and to devolve the whole care of it on his colleague, the Rev. Dr. Beveridge. He still attended, though often with much pain, to his duties in the Seminary, and preached frequently on Sabbath evening. His condition for many weeks had seemed alternately more and less hopeful, until the 29th of April, 1855, when there was a decisive change that indicated that the time of his departure could not be distant. His sufferings in his last days were intense, insomuch that he was prevented from engaging much in conversation; but his mind was evidently in a tranquil and trusting state, and those who saw him die were fully persuaded that he felt nothing of death's sting or death's terrors. He died on the 9th of May, and was buried the next day at Chartiers, beside the graves of his parents.

The degree of Doctor of Divinity was conferred upon him by Franklin College, Ohio, in the autumn of 1846.

He was married at Salem, Washington County, N. Y., on the 9th of October, 1832, to Mary, daughter of John and Eliza Law. They had one child only, a daughter, who is married.

Dr. Anderson's publications are

A Circular to the Churches in the Carolinas, about 1824; a Sermon on Covenanting, published in the Philadelphia Repository; and a Criticism on a Decision in a Church Case, given by a Judge in Vermont.

I had the pleasure of a slight acquaintance with Dr. Anderson, having met him during a meeting of the Associate Synod in Albany a few years before his death. I was impressed by his grave and dignified appearance, and by the evidence he gave, in all his conversation, of a sound, well balanced and well cultivated mind. He seemed especially at home in talking about the distinguished men in his denomination who had passed away, and evidently cherished their memories with great reverence. He also kindly communicated to me an account of the leading events of his own life, of which I preserved written memoranda that I have availed myself of in writing the present sketch.

FROM THE REV. W. M. McELWEE. D.D.

FRANKFORT SPRINGS, BROWN COUNTY, Pa., April 4, 1859.

Rev. and dear Brother: My acquaintance with Dr. Abraham Anderson commenced in September, 1822, while he was delivering his Ordination trials before the Presbytery of the Carolinas, and was afterwards cultivated in long journeyings with him to and from several meetings of the Associate Synod; in many meetings of the Carolina Presbytery; in many meetings to dispense the Lord's Supper; in several meetings as delegates to the Convention of Reformed Churches; in many meetings of the Theological Board; in almost numberless meetings in our respective habitations, both in the South and in the North; and by a somewhat extended friendly correspondence. The acquaintance for which Providence afforded such ample opportunity soon ripened into the most intimate and cordial friendship,—a friendship which never suffered the least interruption or abatement during his lifetime, and in which I confidently expect that we shall mutually rejoice amidst the scenes beyond the vail.

Dr. Anderson's exterior was large, massive and comely; and though large bodies and little souls are often conjoined, in his case the glory within was equal or superior to the expectations inspired by the outward form. He was able to accomplish much in a little time. What time he usually employed in preparing for the Sabbath I know not; but, if an emergency required it, he could collect and arrange the materials of a sermon in a very brief period. He was not so remarkable, however, for the activity of his mental operations as for the compass and extent of his mental vision. Whatever subject he had occasion to handle, he seemed to rise above it, and to view all its different sides at once, with all the objections which might be brought against the view which he maintained. An elderly man in the South, connected with the Old School Presbyterian General Assembly, heard Dr. Anderson occasionally, and compared him to a great ploughshare, which makes a wide furrow and buries all the weeds out of sight.

To a strong, well balanced mind were added, in the case of Dr. Anderson, a habit of great diligence, and the art of gathering up fragments of time and bits of opportunity and turning them to some good account. It does not appear that he kept a Diary; but he kept a note book in which he recorded, with some remarks, any text by which his mind was impressed in reading; and when his reflections did not lead him to fix on any particular subject for the Sabbath, he had recourse to this storehouse for assistance.

To an industrious spirit was added the love of order. His books and papers were kept in their proper places. The different parts of his apparel were properly disposed, and his expenditures were not suffered to flow out at random. He noted in a little book the incomes and outlays of the year; and, at the end of the year, marked the paper and laid it by, and began anew. Indeed, the love of order was conspicuous in every thing about him—in his garden, yard and stable, as well as in his dwelling.

The result of his well directed industry was a large store of varied information. He could read a Latin system of Divinity almost as freely as he could read English. He was so familiar with the Greek of the New Testament that, in family worship, he was accustomed to read the chapter directly from the original. He had a good acquaintance with the Hebrew of the Old Testament, and with Ancient and Modern History, and with the principles of our Republican Government and of the Common Law. He was a good Physician, in all ordinary cases, and not ignorant of Chemistry, nor of Agriculture or Architecture. He was a man of excellent common sense, and was much at home amidst the details of practical life.

He was distinguished for humility and patience. He thought it no degradation to leave his seat in College, and ride through the country, preaching the Gospel to the poor and ignorant; and, when settled in a pastoral charge, he was not above preaching from house to house or of ministering to the humblest child of sorrow. He was full of zeal and full of kindness. When, in the commencement of my ministry, I told him of any difficulty, or discouragement, or cause of perplexity, however trifling the thing was, he never made light of it, but listened with fixed attention; and, when he had comprehended the case, he set himself to render me the desired assistance as promptly and as earnestly as if I had been his own son. When I first saw him, his lofty head and stern countenance led me to doubt whether there was much of tenderness in his nature; but an intimate acquaintance with him revealed to me a heart full of the most generous and kindly sympathy.

He was remarkable for sincerity and magnanimity. If he had proposed a measure to the Presbytery or Synod, and a brother proposed something better, he would abandon his own proposal and urge the substitute. He did nothing through strife or vain glory. He never spoke that others might hear how well he could speak, nor continued to harangue and reason for the sake of victory. I never witnessed the semblance of envy or jealousy in any thing that he said or did, either in public or private.

Dr. Anderson was as far as possible from any thing like levity. He was cheerful and affable, and would sometimes laugh heartily, but his ordinary habit of mind was grave. I remember to have heard him relate but one really laughable story, and that was somewhat at his own expense.

He was a highly acceptable and useful Preacher. Though he was a large and strong man, such was his bodily organization that he could speak only in a conversational tone; but, as his pronunciation was very distinct, he could still be heard with ease by a large assembly. It must be stated further that he had this mental peculiarity—while his memory readily grasped and retained ideas, he had less ability than the generality of men to remember and repeat sentences. At the beginning of his ministry, he wrote his sermons at full length, as young ministers of the Associate Church generally do; but it took him a whole week to commit a sermon, and, after so much labour, he was hampered in the delivery. He concluded, after a few trials, that if he could preach only in this way, it would be necessary for him to abandon the ministry. The plan which he finally adopted was that of writing the heads and particular divisions, with a few sentences under each division, indicating the course of thought to be pursued; and, in this way, he very soon came to preach with ease and comfort. The matter of his discourses was solid and rich, but the language and style of delivery were plain and simple. The body of his sermon was usually argumentative, but in the close he almost uniformly made an impressive appeal to the conscience.

He was, I think, even more distinguished on the floor of Synod than in the pulpit. In a time of excitement, his calm, dignified mien and gentle voice were as oil on the troubled waters. When darkness brooded over the Assembly, and many were unable to see the point at issue, his cool, luminous statement of the matter in question would often dissipate the darkness, and give to the discussion a new and better direction. He was eminently fitted for the chair of Didactic and Polemic Theology. His great intellectual ability and solid learning, his dignified appearance and admirable propriety of conduct, his condescending kindness and unfailing patience, made him all that could be desired in that important post.

Yours with great respect and sincere affection,
W. M. McELWEE.

FROM THE REV. ROBERT BAIRD, D.D.

NEW YORK, January 3, 1863.

My dear Dr. Sprague: am sure you will find it easy to obtain a more satisfactory account of the late Dr. Abraham Anderson than I am able to give you, and yet my recollections of him are very distinct, and my opportunities for forming a judgment of his character were not inconsiderable. I knew him first as Professor in Jefferson College, during the latter part of my course in that institution; and, though he was appointed to the Professorship immediately after he was graduated, it was universally conceded that he was well fitted for the place, and acquitted himself in it with high honour. I knew him at a later period, when he had returned to Cannonsburg as Professor in the Theological Seminary; for, though I did not myself, at that time, reside there, I was there as an occasional visitor, and took care never to lose an opportunity of visiting Dr. Anderson. What he was as a Professor in the Seminary I had no means of knowing, except from report; but the uniform testimony, so far as I know, was, that he possessed high qualifications for his department, and was eminently acceptable and useful.

Dr. Anderson's mind was calm, reflective, discriminating, logical, rather than highly imaginative. No matter what might be the subject that occupied him, he held it to his mind till he had made himself master of it in its different bearings and proportions. His intellectual powers were marked by great sobriety and harmony—he did not view things in an exaggerated form—as the simple truth, so far as it came within the range of his faculties, was the object at which he aimed, so he generally attained it by the simplest and most natural process. As his mind was one of great activity, and his habits were essentially industrious, it was to be expected that he would have large mental acquisitions; and no one could be well acquainted with him without perceiving that this expectation was fully realized. He seemed almost equally at home in the Languages, the Mathematics, Intellectual Philosophy and Logic; and though he made no show of his attainments, they were all at his command, as so much well adjusted intellectual furniture.

Dr. Anderson was a man of a kindly and benevolent spirit, and always ready to confer a favour whenever it was in his power, though he was perhaps the opposite of demonstrative. He never said or did any thing merely for effect. In the ordinary intercourse of society, he was rather inclined to be reserved, though, with his intimate friends, he was delightfully free and communicative. His religious character was pure, elevated, consistent, without the least approach to any thing that savoured of enthusiasm. I do not remember ever to have heard him preach; but his reputation as a Preacher was just what you would expect from the general character which I have ascribed to him—his sermons were sensible, logical, and highly evangelical, and better fitted, in respect to both matter and manner, to interest and edify the thoughtful and intelligent hearer than to powerfully impress and bear away the multitude. He had great influence in Church Courts, not only from his general weight of character, but from his familiarity with the usages of such Bodies, and his facility at public business. He had, throughout the whole community, the reputation of a wise, learned, unostentatious, excellent man. His death was felt to be a calamity far beyond the limits of his own denomination.

I am, my dear Dr. Sprague,
Ever yours most truly,
R. BAIRD.

JAMES MARTIN, D.D.*
1822—1846.

JAMES MARTIN, a son of William Martin, was born in Albany, N. Y., May 12, 1796,—his parents having emigrated from Ireland to this country a short time before. While he was yet a child, the family removed to the town of Argyle, Washington County, N. Y. His parents had been members of the Associate Presbyterian Church in their native country, and their desire to enjoy religious privileges in the same ecclesiastical connection was a principal reason of their removal to Argyle. James worked upon his father's farm until he was seventeen or eighteen years of age, when he expressed the desire, and formed the purpose, of obtaining a collegiate education. He commenced his preparation for College at a private school in the village of Argyle, and afterwards became a member of the Washington Academy at Cambridge, where he remained until he was fitted to enter College at an advanced standing. He entered the Junior class in Union College, Schenectady, in 1817, and, having held a very high rank as a scholar throughout his whole course, graduated in 1819.

Mr. Martin had the benefit of a strictly religious education, and was always exemplary in his external deportment, but did not make a public profession of his faith till he was approaching the close of his academical course. He was accustomed to scrutinize closely every doctrine that he received, and at one time the whole system of Christianity appeared to him so great a mystery that he found himself inclined to pause on the borders of skepticism. He, however, ultimately reposed, with the fullest conviction, in the entire system of evangelical doctrine, and gave abundant proof of its power in his daily life.

At a meeting of the Associate Synod at Pittsburg, in May, 1819, the Rev. Dr. Anderson, on account of his advanced age, tendered his resignation as Professor of Theology,—agreeably to an intimation given the preceding year,—which was now accepted. A change of the location of the Theological Seminary being necessary, before the appointment of another Professor could with propriety be made, a Resolution was adopted, deferring that appointment, and committing the education of the students to the respective Presbyteries within whose bounds they resided. Mr. Martin, in consequence of this Resolution, commenced his theological studies under the care of the Presbytery of Cambridge; but when a Theological Seminary was established at Philadelphia, and Dr. Banks elected to the Professorship, Mr. Martin, with several other students, became connected with this new institution.

At the meeting of Synod at Philadelphia, in May, 1822, he was appointed to be taken on trial for licensure by the Presbytery of Cambridge; and, in pursuance of that appointment, was actually licensed to preach the Gospel, on the 2d of September following.

The Associate Congregation of Albany, almost immediately after he was licensed, petitioned the Presbytery that they might be allowed to have his services for one year; and their request was granted. But, after he had been preaching for some time to this congregation, he became strongly impressed with the idea

* Evangelical Repository, VI.—Communication from his family.

that it was very desirable that he should spend another term at the Seminary; and, accordingly, having obtained permission from the Presbytery, he passed the greater part of the winter term of 1822–23 in again attending on the instructions of Dr. Banks. In the spring of 1823 he returned to Albany, where he continued to labour so acceptably to the people, that, in the course of the year, he received a unanimous call to become their Pastor. This call having been accepted, he was ordained, and installed Pastor of that congregation, on the 19th of May, 1824. The Sermon on the occasion was preached by the Rev. Mr. Campbell, and the Charge to the Minister and the people was given by the Rev. Dr. Shaw.

In 1833 Mr. Martin became connected, editorially, with the Religious Monitor,—a periodical publication which had been commenced some time before, but had had no responsible editor. He did not, at first, allow his name to appear on the title page, though he had the exclusive editorial control of the work; but, in 1836, he became its proprietor as well as editor, and, from that time, his connection with it, in both capacities, was distinctly announced. This connection continued until the close of the fifteenth volume; and the work, in his hands, acquired a high character, even beyond the limits of his denomination.

In May, 1840, Mr. Martin attended the meeting of the Synod, in Philadelphia, in his usual health, as he supposed, with the exception of a slight cold. At that meeting it was found necessary to send a Commission to Barnet, Vt., to settle some difficulties that had arisen in the Presbytery of Vermont. Mr. Martin was one of the Commissioners, and, being chosen Moderator, it devolved on him to open the meeting with a Sermon. The Commission was to meet in Barnet, about two hundred miles from Albany, on the 10th of July. When the time arrived for setting out on this journey, Mr. Martin was still suffering severely from his cold, though there was nothing to occasion him any alarm. As he proceeded, with his brethren, on the journey, travelling by private conveyance, he became increasingly ill, having a very severe cough, attended with considerable fever. The day before they were to meet in Barnet, and when they were within a short distance of the village of Bradford, on the Connecticut River, he was seized with a violent hemorrhage from the lungs. They hastened on to Bradford; and when Mr. Martin got out of the carriage, at the hotel, and sat down on the steps of the piazza, the first resting place at hand, the blood was flowing freely from his mouth. After obtaining medical aid, the hemorrhage was stopped, and they proceeded on their journey. But, shortly after reaching Barnet, the hemorrhage returned with increased violence, and it was repeated for several successive days. The disease, with the depletion that was judged necessary to arrest it, so reduced his strength that he was obliged to remain in Barnet several weeks before he was able to return home; and, indeed, so great was his prostration that his system never afterwards fully recovered its former tone.

During the whole of that year he scarcely attempted to speak in public at all; but, the next year, his health was so far improved that he was able to appear quite frequently in his pulpit. At the meeting of the Synod in 1842, in consequence of Dr. Ramsay's resignation of the Professorship of Didactic Theology and Hebrew in the Theological Seminary, it became necessary to elect a successor to him in that office; and the person chosen was Mr. Martin. He accepted the place, and immediately resigned his pastoral charge at Albany, after an acceptable and useful ministry there of eighteen years.

In the summer of 1842 Mr. Martin removed, with his family, to Cannonsburg, Pa., where the Theological Seminary was located, and entered on the duties of his new appointment, at the opening of the term in the fall of that year.

In 1843 Mr. Martin was honoured with the degree of Doctor of Divinity from Jefferson College.

Dr. Martin proved himself a very competent and acceptable Professor. He preached occasionally for his brethren, and in vacant churches in the neighbourhood, but his strength was nearly all given to the immediate duties of his Professorship. The last time he attempted to preach was at a place called Peter's Creek, where he went to assist in the administration of the Lord's Supper. The effort was too much for him, and the next day the hemorrhage, by which he had been so often afflicted, returned upon him, and he resolved not to hazard again an effort at public speaking. He, however, soon recovered from this attack, and his improved condition awakened the hope that his life and usefulness might be prolonged through a series of years; but this hope proved sadly delusive. On the evening of the 24th of April, 1846, after a day of more than usual exercise and comfort, he experienced a return of hemorrhage so violent that he was never afterwards able to leave his bed for more than a few minutes at a time. He lingered, in great patience and in the full exercise of all his faculties, until the 15th of June, when he quietly passed away.

Dr. Martin was married, in 1825, to Rebecca, daughter of Matthew and Elizabeth (Given) White, of Albany. By this marriage there were four children, two of whom died in infancy. Mrs. Martin died in 1835. In May, 1836, he was married to Jane, daughter of John Watson, of Cannonsburg, Pa., who became the mother of five children,—all daughters.

Besides the liberal contributions which Dr. Martin made to the Religious Monitor, he published a duodecimo volume, (the substance of which, however, originally appeared in the Monitor,) entitled "An Essay on the Imputation of Adam's First Sin to his Posterity," 1834; and a Sermon entitled "The Duty of Submission to Church Rulers Explained and Defended," 1841. This was the Discourse which he had prepared to preach at Barnet, when he was prevented by an attack of illness from fulfilling the appointment.

FROM THE REV. THOMAS BEVERIDGE, D.D.

CANNONSBURG, May 14, 1854.

Dear Sir: I am not at all disposed to decline your request for my recollections of the late Dr. Martin, as he was a valued and intimate friend whose memory I delight to honour.

Though I had occasionally seen him at an earlier period, I may say that my acquaintance with him commenced while I was residing at Cambridge, N. Y., and a short time previous to his settlement in Albany. From that time till the close of his life I knew him intimately. While I had a Pastoral charge in Philadelphia, he often assisted me on Communion occasions, and I sometimes went to Albany to render him similar aid. During the last four years of his life we were associated as Professors in the same Theological Institution, and, of course, were in habits of constant and familiar intercourse.

There was nothing in Dr. Martin's personal appearance that would be likely particularly to attract you. He was rather below the middle size, with dark complexion, dark hair and light eyes, and a face bearing strong marks of intellect. He had an uncommonly well-shaped and expressive forehead. His movements were characterized by deliberation and dignity.

In his manners he was gentlemanly, though in general society somewhat reserved. When you knew him intimately, however, his reserve disappeared, and he became a highly agreeable companion. Though he was far removed from every thing like levity, he would occasionally unbend in the confidence of private intercourse, and would sometimes participate in lively and even jocose conversation. His habit, however, was to be grave; and the departure from it formed the exception,—not the rule. He was generous and honourable in all his relations. His hospitality scarcely had a limit; and I have understood that so many were willing to avail themselves of it, that, with a moderate salary, he found it somewhat difficult to meet his current expenses.

Of the character of Dr. Martin's intellect I need not speak particularly, as it will be sufficiently manifest from what I shall say of him in his different relations. As a Preacher, he always had a high rank in his denomination—indeed, his popularity, so far as I know, was universal. His voice, though not one of extraordinary power, was clear, melodious and impressive; and it was sufficiently loud to fill with ease our largest places of worship. His enunciation was remarkably distinct, so that every word fell upon your ear in all its fulness. There was no great variety in his intonation, neither could his delivery be considered in any degree monotonous. He had no exuberance of gesture, but what he had was appropriate, and fitted to render his utterances more impressive. His manner was energetic and effective, but not highly impassioned—you saw the workings of a vigorous and earnest intellect, but little of that warm glow that indicates deep and powerful emotion. His sermons were far from being imaginative or beautiful; but they were full of well digested thought, were arranged with logical accuracy, and while they were so plain that the common mind could not fail readily to apprehend them, they showed so much intellectual vigour and such careful elaboration, that the most profound and cultivated minds were arrested by them. He often wrote out his discourses at length, and often preached from a full outline; and sometimes, I believe, without much premeditation; but never, so far as I know, had even notes before him in the pulpit.

No where were Dr. Martin's powers brought out to better purpose than in Church Courts. There his quick perceptions, his sound judgment, his admirable self-possession, his perfect familiarity with every thing pertaining to ecclesiastical procedure, gave him an influence which few ministers ever acquire. I remember an instance in which he had taken an active part in a process that resulted in the suspension of an old Scotch Elder; and however the Elder might have been dissatisfied with the result, he afterwards expressed his admiration of Dr. Martin's perfect coolness and dignity in the management of the case.

Dr. Martin was a good general scholar, and acquired knowledge with great ease; and he knew how to turn his knowledge to the best account. I think, however, that he was more indebted for his acquisitions to his facility at acquiring than to any remarkable degree of application. He was somewhat averse to bodily exercise; and this probably reacted, to some extent, upon his mental habits. I do not mean to intimate that he was not a student, but only that he was not in this respect greatly distinguished. I ought to add that, during the last few years of his life, his health was so much impaired as to disqualify him for severe or protracted mental effort.

As a Professor, Dr. Martin was very competent, conscientious, diligent and acceptable. His attainments in his department were highly respectable, and he had a more than common facility at communicating his own knowledge to the minds of others. He was a remarkably good critic; and though he sometimes perhaps approached severity, yet so just were his remarks, and so manifestly dictated by a desire to benefit the students, that they were generally little disposed to complain. I ought to add that he was uncommonly faithful in respect to their spiritual interests; availing himself of every opportunity to urge upon them the paramount importance of cultivating practical godliness. I well remember that, on occasion of one of their meetings, he inquired of them whether if there was one traitor among the twelve who constituted our Lord's immediate family, there was not reason to fear that there was more than one among *them*, as they were double the number. He evidently lived, during the whole period of his Professorship, under a deep impression that his time for serving his Master and the Church on earth was short, and this, no doubt, gave a complexion, in some degree, to his inter course with the students.

Yours very respectfully,
THOMAS BEVERIDGE.

FROM THE REV. S. F. MORROW.

ALBANY, July 7, 1862.

My dear Sir: I met the Rev. Dr. Martin, concerning whom you ask for my recollections, for the first time, at the meeting of the Associate Synod, in Xenia, O., in 1842,—the same year that he was appointed Professor of Theology and Hebrew in our Theological Seminary. The next time I saw him was in the fall of the same year, when he entered on the duties of his Professorship, and I became a student under him. I had the benefit of his instruction during my whole course in the institution, and his connection with it, as a Professor, continued but a single session after mine, as a student, closed. It was chiefly in his relation as Professor that I knew him, though I met him occasionally in private, and perhaps had sufficient means of forming a correct idea of his character.

Dr. Martin could hardly fail to impress you, at first sight, as a thoughtful, earnest, resolute man. His manner was in a high degree dignified, and at first he seemed not very accessible; but, as you came to know him better, you found him familiar and affable, and manifesting quite a genial spirit. There was very little reserve in his intercourse, even with the students, after he became well acquainted with them; and he generally secured, in a high degree, both their respect and good-will. He was susceptible of very strong feeling, but he exercised great self-control, and was very rarely betrayed into any hasty or indiscreet utterances which he had occasion to regret.

Dr. Martin was a good general scholar, and, in the department of Theology particularly, his views were exceedingly clear and well digested. He had a well defined system of faith, and though he did not regard all its parts of equal importance, there was no point of what he believed to be Scripture doctrine that he held lightly. As an Instructor, he had a happy faculty at bringing his own mind in contact with the minds of his pupils, and putting them in possession of the exact shade of thought which he wished to convey. We always felt, when we were listening to him, that we were getting the results of mature and profound reflection.

As a Preacher, Dr. Martin was rather didactic than hortatory, edifying than highly popular. He was always perfectly self-possessed, and uttered himself with a dignified calmness, that evinced his high estimate of the truth he was delivering, and predisposed his audience, especially the more intelligent portion of them, to give him their fixed attention. He was not profuse in his gesture, though the little that he had was unstudied and appropriate, and evidently the prompting of the thought which he was developing. An air of simplicity and naturalness pervaded his whole manner. His thoughts were clearly conceived and clearly expressed, and the tone of his preaching was eminently doctrinal and evangelical. It was impossible to listen to him attentively without either gaining some clearer views of Divine truth, or becoming more deeply impressed with its importance.

Dr. Martin had great control in a Deliberative Body. With strong common sense and a deep insight into the human character, and an intimate acquaintance with the details of public business, he was always recognized as *a* master spirit, if not *the* master spirit, of any Deliberative Assembly to which he happened to belong. He was regarded by many as rigid in his views of ecclesiastical discipline, but his course in this respect, whatever it might be, was evidently only the following out of his conscientious convictions.

In general, Dr. Martin was at the greatest remove from every thing that had in it the semblance of trifling; but he would now and then say something that would reveal a vein of quiet humour. One instance of this now occurs to me. The mania for cultivating whiskers had not then been introduced into this country; but one of our students had nevertheless ventured so far upon making himself singular as to suffer his beard to grow much beyond what the usage of that day would justify. It so happened that this student, in a sermon that he delivered as an exercise in the Seminary, used the expression, "beard the lion in his den;" and when the Doctor came to criticise him, he remarked, in substance, that he did not like that expression; that, though he had not his spectacles, and did not see very distinctly, he thought he recognized something on his face that might have suggested it; but he added that, for his part, he did not like whiskers, and the only man whom he ever knew wear them in the pulpit, he believed had no piety.

Very truly yours,
S. F. MORROW.

DAVID CARSON.*
1823—1834.

DAVID CARSON, a son of David and Jane (Oliver) Carson, was born in Greencastle, Franklin County, Pa., on the 25th of October, 1799. His parents, who were of Scotch ancestry, though natives of the North of Ireland, migrated to the United States in 1798, and took up their abode in Greencastle, where they placed themselves under the ministry of the Rev. John Young, of the Associate Reformed Church. Mr. Young was succeeded by the Rev. John Lind, under whose pastoral care the son passed his early years. It was through Mr. Lind's influence that his attention was first permanently directed to his immortal interests, and that, at a later period, he formed the purpose of devoting himself to the Christian Ministry; and it was under his instruction also that he went through the course of study preparatory to entering College. In due time he entered Jefferson College, where he maintained a high rank as a scholar, and graduated in 1819. It was during his college life—it is believed in 1818—that he made a public profession of his faith in connection with the Associate Reformed Church.

It was about this time that that Church was so deeply agitated with the controversy on the subject of Communion, which resulted in the union of a large portion of it, under the lead of Dr. Mason, with the General Assembly Presbyterian Church. The rupture thus made in the Church to which Mr. Carson belonged,

---

* MSS. from his son, Rev. D. W. Carson, and Rev. Dr. Beveridge.

in connection with the bitter contests which attended it, occasioned him great perplexity and distress. He shrank from the prospect of entering the ministry at such an inauspicious period; and, having finished his collegiate course, he endeavoured to find a situation in which he might be advantageously employed as a Teacher. Providence seemed to baffle every attempt which he made in this direction; and, finding, at last, that there was no other door open to him, he entered on a course of Theological study in the Seminary of the Associate Reformed Church in the city of New York. He was there during the winters of 1820–'21, and of 1821–'22; but the winter of 1822–'23 he spent at Philadelphia, pursuing his studies under the Rev. Dr. Banks, Professor in the Theological Seminary of the Associate Presbyterian Church, chiefly with a view of perfecting himself in a knowledge of the Hebrew,—Dr. Banks being, at that time, esteemed one of the most eminent Hebrew scholars in America. It was some time during this year that he decided, after long and severe mental conflict, to connect himself with the Associate Presbyterian Church; and, accordingly, after passing the usual trials, he was licensed to preach the Gospel, by the Associate Presbytery of Philadelphia, on the 8th of October, 1823.

By the rules of the Associate Church, licentiates on probation for the office of the ministry were required to itinerate within the bounds of the Church, for at least one year, as missionaries under the appointment of the Synod. This service Mr. Carson seems to have performed to great and universal acceptance. He received calls from the Congregations of Octorora, &c., in the Presbytery of Philadelphia; from Poland, in the State of Ohio; from the Congregations of Big Spring, Pistol Creek and Munroe, in East Tennessee; and from several other places. He accepted the call from the Congregations in Tennessee, on the ground that they were in more unpromising circumstances, and, owing to their isolated position, less likely to obtain a Pastor, than the others. He was, accordingly, ordained to the work of the Ministry, and installed as Pastor of these congregations in October, 1824.

In this large and widely scattered charge he laboured for about ten years. In October, 1833, he was elected Professor of Hebrew, Biblical Antiquities, Chronology and Church History in the Associate Presbyterian Seminary, then at Cannonsburg. Having signified his acceptance of this appointment, he resigned his pastoral charge, and removed with his family to his expected field of labour in the spring of 1834; and shortly after his arrival there, he received and accepted a call from the congregation of Washington, Pa., to labour among them as their Pastor. The journey of upwards of six hundred miles, which brought him to Cannonsburg, he performed in a private conveyance, reaching his destination in the month of June. But he did not live to enter on the duties of his Professorship. His constitution, though naturally vigorous, had been somewhat enfeebled by excessive labour. His journey, too, had been attended with great fatigue, as, besides removing his family, he brought with him a number of negroes, who had been manumitted by their master, and sent, under his care, to be settled in the Free States. A few weeks after his arrival in Cannonsburg, he was prostrated by a disease from which he had previously been a sufferer, and to the removal of which—now that it had settled upon his lungs—medical skill proved unavailing. He died, after a confinement of four or five weeks, on the 25th of September, 1834. During his last illness, his mind was in a state of perfect tranquillity, and was occupied chiefly upon subjects pertaining to the

Kingdom of Christ. His death was every way worthy of the devoted Christian life which had preceded it.

Mr. Carson's only publications were occasional articles which appeared in some of the periodicals of the day, the longest of which was a Review of the Hopkinsian system,—the prevailing system of doctrine in the region in which he lived. This was published in the County paper at Maryville.

Mr. Carson was married, in October, 1827, to Jane, daughter of James and Eleanor (Cowan) Gellespy—the family was one of great respectability, and was connected with one of his congregations. They had three children, two of whom are now (1863) ministers of the Gospel, in connection with the United Presbyterian Church. Mrs. Carson still survives.

FROM THE REV. WILLIAM M. McELWEE, D.D.

FRANKFORT, BEAVER COUNTY, PA., December 3, 1863.

Rev. and dear Brother: I have been somewhat tardy in answering your letter asking for some estimate of the character of the Rev. David Carson, partly because I supposed the matter did not require haste, but chiefly because I had to wait for certain papers which, I calculated, would enable me to do greater justice to the subject.

I had not the happiness of much intercourse with Mr. Carson. Our first meeting was in the city of Steubenville, Ohio, in the summer of 1824. At that time we lodged together in the house of a common friend two or three days, and I heard him preach a single sermon. Our next meeting was in the city of Baltimore, where we assisted the Rev. A. Whyte in administering the Lord's Supper. This was in the spring of 1830. From Baltimore we travelled together by steamboat to Philadelphia; and in the latter city attended the meeting of the Associate Synod for eight or ten days, boarding, however, at different houses. When the Synod had adjourned, we returned to Baltimore, lodged with a common friend, and preached together on the Sabbath. There was a meeting of the Associate Synod at Cannonsburg, in October, 1833. Mr. Carson and myself were in attendance. In the course of that meeting he was chosen Professor of Ecclesiastical History and Hebrew Antiquities, in the Theological Seminary at Cannonsburg, and, accepting the appointment, he moved thither with his family, in June, 1834. Having come to Cannonsburg about the middle of the week, and learning from Dr. Ramsay that I had the Sacrament of the Lord's Supper on hand, and would probably be alone, he was so kind as to take his horse and come to my assistance. When the Sacrament was over he returned with me to my house; and the next morning we rode over to Robinson, seven miles, and attended a meeting of the Associate Presbytery of Chartiers. These interviews were so few and distant from each other that, had no other means of knowing Mr. Carson been thrown in my way, I should hardly feel warranted to claim any thing more than a superficial acquaintance with him. But, boarding with Dr. Ramsay's family from the fall of 1822 till the spring of 1825, with whom Mr. Carson had boarded during his collegiate course, I was made very familiar with his name and character before I had seen his face. In the fall of 1825 I supplied his pulpit in Blount County, Tenn., for two months, the Synod having sent him on a mission to the State of Missouri. He was very often spoken of by the people of his charge during those months, and, though it is long since his death, my familiarity with him has been kept up by constant friendly intercourse with Mrs. Carson and her two sons who have entered the ministry.

Mr. Carson was somewhat beneath the ordinary stature, being five feet and four or five inches in height. He was. however, a strong, sturdy man, broad in the shoulders and well compacted. His forehead was lofty and broad, his cheeks well rounded and having a fresh, rosy tint. Being short-sighted, he wore spectacles, both in and out of the pulpit.

In respect of mental and moral qualities, Mr. Carson was distinguished among his associates at College, and among his brethren in the Ministry. But that which arrested the attention and secured the approval of others was not a single excellence shining in him with transcendent brightness, but a happy combination of many excellencies, possessed by others indeed, but not often in the same degree or the same variety.

Mr. Carson's intellectual endowments were of a high order. His ideas were clear and manly, his language was appropriate, direct and forcible, not combined with puerile platitudes or tawdry ornaments. And the gifts which his Maker had bestowed upon him he cultivated with diligence. He applied himself closely to his studies at College, and at the Theological Seminary, and through life, as he found opportunity. He was indeed so moulded and attempered that whatever he did, he did it with his might. When in his youth he engaged in play, he was among the foremost in the play. When he entered into conversation with others, he brought all his powers into exercise, and did not speak of one matter, while his thoughts wandered after another —when he laughed, he did not laugh with a sort of reluctance, but cordially, with such lively ringing tones that it was refreshing to hear him. I am reminded, in this connection, of an anecdote that was told of him, in Dr. Ramsay's family, in the winter of 1823. There had been a religious awakening in Jefferson College, in the spring of 1818 or '19. All the students were impressed more or less. A young man by the name of Trimble, rooming with Mr. Carson, was deeply impressed. In solemn seriousness, bordering on melancholy, he took it into his head that it was a sin to laugh. He informed Mr. Carson of the conclusion to which he had come. Mr. C. could not agree with him. The matter was debated for some time; and, as neither was able to convince the other, they agreed to ask the opinion of Dr. Ramsay. This was done the next morning at the breakfast table. "Dr. Ramsay," inquired Mr. C.—, "What is your opinion about laughing—is it a sin to laugh?" Dr. R., looking around the table, and observing that all were composed and waiting for his answer, said, with a dry humour, for which he was remarkable,— "It is just as sinful to laugh as it is to sneeze." Mr. C., unable to maintain his gravity, burst into so hearty a laugh, that even Mr. Trimble was obliged to participate in it.

Mr. Carson was distinguished for his fervent piety. Like Elijah he was very zealous for the Lord God of hosts. Like the beloved John, he was a sincere lover of Christ and of all the things of Christ. He was remarkable for tenderness of conscience, deep humility and a lively concern about the salvation of his brethren according to the flesh. These and various other distinctive traits of Christian character came out in his daily life, and they are strikingly manifest in many of his letters which have been preserved and have been submitted to my inspection.

In his public ministrations Mr. Carson displayed decided ability, but his manner was so simple, and his utterances so plain and so well filled up with corresponding feelings, that perhaps no hearer ever suspected that he was trying to exhibit himself. His delivery was not rapid but distinct and emphatic. Very often his eyes were suffused and the tears flowed freely; yet there was no trembling of the voice nor distortion of the countenance. When he assisted me at the Sacramental service in 1834, he introduced the exercises of the Sabbath by reading and expounding the 63d Psalm. In offering the expository remarks his feelings rose at once. He went on for thirty-five or forty minutes, the tears flowing continually; but those who sat at a distance only observed a singular solemnity and earnestness.

Being sincere, earnest and hearty in the Lord's cause, he did not smother his convictions, but cherished them, and acted in accordance with them. Embracing in 1818 Dr. Mason's scheme of Catholic Communion, he received the Lord's Supper, for the first time, at the hands of Dr. McMillan, a minister of the General Assembly, though he still regarded the Associate Reformed Church as his proper home. Being convinced, in 1822, that Promiscuous Communion is injurious to the cause of truth, and subversive of wholesome discipline, he renounced it, withdrew from those that favoured it, with whom he had been accustomed to go, and attached himself to the brethren of the Associate Church, who regarded that form of communion as a very dangerous kind of latitudinarianism. Believing Slavery to be a moral evil, he assailed it even in Tennessee, and did all he could to purge the Church and the land of it. He likewise testified against Freemasonry, and the use of songs of human composition in the solemn worship of God. When, in Divine providence, he was called to minister among strangers, he seems not to have considered very much whether the hearers would receive his testimony or not. He was so faithful to his convictions that he did not blink the truth, or shun a plain, open testimony in its behalf, under any circumstances.

In addition to what I have already said of the character of Mr. Carson's ministrations, I may say that he had a noble voice, strong and clear, but not harsh, which he had the power of modulating according to his own will. He could lower it to a whisper audible throughout the church, however large, and in a moment raise it up to thunder tones. I distinctly remember having myself been startled, when, after many petitions uttered in a moderate tone, he called out, with a loud, ringing tone,—" Awake, awake, put on thy strength, Oh Arm of the Lord, awake as in ancient days, in the generations of old."

I will only notice one other feature in Mr. Carson's character,—namely, his strong faith in the testimony of God. He believed the doctrinal teachings of the Word to be the most sure and certain truth. He believed the laws of God to be the dictates of Divine wisdom and goodness, working out the right and good way. He believed the ordinances of God's appointment to be the only means of acceptable worship. He believed the threatenings and trembled, the promises and rejoiced. He so realized the being, presence and power of the Master as to be in a great measure regardless of the approval or scorn of men. "By faith the Elders obtained a good report," and our Elder obtained his good report in the same way. Animated by this heavenly principle, he read and studied, prayed, and preached and walked, " choosing rather to suffer affliction with the people of God than to enjoy the pleasures of sin for a season."

Yours with sincere respect,
WILLIAM M. McELWEE

JAMES WHYTE.*
1824—1827.

JAMES WHYTE, a son of James and Helen Whyte, was born in Muthill, in Perthshire, Scotland, in the year 1794. His father cultivated a small farm, from the profits of which he was able to maintain his family in a creditable manner.

* Memoir prefixed to his Sermons.—MS. from Mrs. Whyte.

Both of his parents were professors of religion, attached to the Secession Church, and, for a long period, members of the Associate Congregation of Kinkel, under the pastoral care of the Rev. Mr. Muckersie, an eminently godly minister and author of a well known Catechism. They were particularly careful in the religious training of their children; and to their good influence, under God, this son gratefully ascribed his preservation from many youthful follies and gross sins. While he was yet very young he showed a great fondness for study, and this led his parents to resolve on giving him the advantages of a collegiate education. Having fitted for College in his native place, he entered at Glasgow in the year 1810; and about the same time both his parents were removed by death. During his whole College course he was diligent in study and exemplary in deportment, and showed himself possessed of talents that gave promise of distinguished usefulness. In 1815, about the time that he left College, his mind was first seriously and earnestly directed to the subject of religion as a personal matter; and, after several months of ineffectual striving in the spirit of the Law, he was brought to a cordial compliance with the terms of the Gospel and became a cheerful and active Christian. Shortly after this he commenced the study of Theology in the Divinity Hall at Edinburgh, under the direction of the Rev. Mr. Paxton, at that time Professor of Divinity to the General Associate Synod. In consequence of the death of his parents, he had been left, in a great measure, dependent upon his own exertions for the means of defraying the expenses of his education; but this he was enabled to do by teaching a school, first in the neighbourhood of Dunblane, and afterwards at Menstrie, near Stirling, during his vacations. Having completed his course of theological study preparatory to licensure, and having gone through the usual exercises for trials before the Presbytery, he was licensed to preach the Gospel by the Presbytery of Stirling, in connection with the Antiburgher Church, in the spring of 1819. He commenced his labours in the Orkney Islands, and was invited to a settlement there, which, however, he declined.

The same year, and not far from the time that he was licensed to preach, he was married to Jane, daughter of Alexander and Ellen (Ford) Whyte, of Limekilns, in Fifeshire.

Mr. Whyte, from his very first appearance in the pulpit, attracted unusual attention, and his services were put in requisition by some of the most respectable congregations within the limits of the Body with which he was connected. After the two Bodies, Anti-Burghers and Burghers, were merged in the United Associate Church, he continued to preach, with great acceptance, within the new organization, and several highly important vacancies were at his command, if he would have accepted them. As, however, he was not entirely satisfied with the principles of Union, and took exceptions to some of the early measures adopted by the Body with which he was now in connection, he withdrew from that communion in 1824, and joined with a few others in protesting against it. And now, in fulfilment of a purpose which had even preceded his entrance on the ministry, he resolved to cross the Atlantic and seek a field of labour in the United States; and, accordingly, he arrived with his family in New York, in October, 1824. Shortly after his arrival, he joined the Associate Church, and, wherever he preached, was listened to with the deepest interest. Two calls,—one from Argyle, and another from Salem, were presented to him at the same time; and, having accepted the latter, he was ordained, and installed over that congregation, on the 6th of July, 1825.

It was a striking illustration of Mr. Whyte's unassuming and unambitious spirit that he was disposed to accept this very retired sphere of labour, when his talents would have entitled him to look for one of the most prominent pulpits in the country. Here, however, he continued to labour, with great satisfaction and efficiency, until he was dismissed to his reward. His last illness was an inflammation of the lungs, terminating on the brain. He had gone to Argyle to preach; and, after going through the accustomed labours at the church, on the Sabbath, he was expected to preach at the poor-house in the evening, but was too unwell to fulfil the appointment, and, instead of attempting it, returned home. In the latter stage of his illness, his mind was so far unstrung that he took no note of any thing that was passing around him. Just before his death he seemed to fall asleep for a few moments; and, on opening his eyes, was asked whether he had been asleep; and his reply was, "Yes, blessed be his holy name;" and, shortly after, fell into his last slumber. He died, after an illness of about ten days, on the 13th of December, 1827. His Funeral Sermon was preached by the Rev. Dr. Alexander Bullions, of Cambridge.

Mr. Whyte was the father of five children,—four daughters and one son. Of these only one daughter, with the mother, still (1862) survives.

Some time after Mr. Whyte's death, a volume of his Sermons was published in this country, and afterwards republished in Scotland. The Scottish edition included also a sketch of his life.

FROM THE REV. HUGH MAIR, D.D.

FERGUS, CANADA WEST, October 18, 1848.

Rev. and dear Sir: Your request that I should furnish you with some of my recollections of the Rev. James Whyte it gives me pleasure to comply with. My acquaintance with him was quite intimate, and my attachment to him devoted; but our personal intercourse was confined almost entirely to the period of his curriculum as a theological student, and scarcely extended at all to his ministerial course. I will give you freely my idea of his character, resulting not merely from my own intimacy with him, but from what I know of his general reputation.

As a Man, he was amiable, unassuming and benevolent. In his conduct in the various relations of life he was uniformly correct, prudent and dignified. Towards those whom he deemed his superiors he was always deferential in his bearing; while towards his inferiors he exhibited the most graceful and winning condescension. As a Friend, he was devoted and constant; full of that warm and generous sympathy that makes a friend so welcome in the hour of need. In short, his private character presented a rare assemblage of excellencies, which might very well justify the application of those lines of the Roman poet:—

"Incorrupta fides, undique veritas,
Quando illum inveniet parem."

As a Christian, he was at once humble and fervent. His uncommon devotedness to God appeared in almost all his movements. No one who saw him could doubt that his grand aim was to attain to the highest measure of Christian holiness. It was emphatically true of him that he had his conversation in Heaven. Whatsoever things were true, honest, just, lovely and of good report,—these things he ever cultivated and pursued. From his boyhood till near the period of his dissolution, he was wont to keep a Diary, wherein he uniformly noted the dispensations of Providence toward himself, the Church and the world; and studied so to improve these, through grace, as to render them constantly subservient to his sanctification. In his devotional exercises he had great enjoyment; nor were his prayers confined to stated periods; for while he was conscientious and regular in the performance of secret and family worship, he was much given to ejaculatory prayer,—thus exemplifying the Apostolic precept,—" Pray without ceasing." Religion with him was far enough from being a matter of mere expediency, or a subject of mere mental speculation. It was a matter of the highest personal and practical concern,— that filled his whole soul and regulated his whole life.

As a Preacher of the Gospel, he was gifted in no common degree. So far as impression or popular effect was concerned, it is not too much to say that he stood in the first rank. He had a remarkable power of seizing and enchaining the attention of an audience. His preaching was far enough from being mere declamation; while his discourses were marked with great simplicity and classical accuracy of expression, and at the same time indicated a glowing and highly poetical fancy, they were replete with evangelical sentiment, and possessed an unction that bespoke a deep and strong current of religious feeling,—an all absorbing interest in the topic which he had in hand. He had a marked predilection for the descriptive kind of preaching; and here he showed himself to possess remarkable graphic power. His descriptions were those of a master painter; for he infused into his characters so much life, and often threw around them such an incomparable charm, that the effect upon his audience was prodigious. The minutest circumstances connected with character, (circumstances which would have been by ordinary minds entirely over-looked,) he would seize upon and exhibit with surprising effect. He was full of earnest and impassioned appeals to the heart and conscience; and it was not easy for any one who heard him to resist the impression that the one commanding object that he had in view was to promote the glory of his Master in the salvation of his fellow-creatures. He was a scribe well instructed in the mysteries of the Kingdom, a workman that needed not to be ashamed.

And while he was a most faithful and earnest Preacher of the Gospel, his labours were eminently acceptable,—not merely in his own denomination, but among Christians of other communions. He was, indeed, a magnet of universal attraction. But it was not merely or chiefly the blaze of genius, or the glow of imagination, but the holy kindlings of a heart actuated by an intense desire for the salvation of a dying world, through the power of the Cross, that rendered his public ministrations so irresistible. You may judge something of his popularity in Scotland from the fact that he received from various congregations no less than thirteen calls, to settle with them in the ministry,—a circumstance quite unprecedented, at least in the Secession Church. But his popularity never injured him. He continued to the close of life the same humble, unostentatious, self-distrustful person as he was at the commencement of his career. By a mysterious dispensation of Providence he was called early to his rest and his reward; but there are many, on both sides of the Atlantic, who will never forget the charm of his example or the power of his ministrations.

I am, with sincere and affectionate regard, truly yours,
HUGH MAIR.

FROM THE REV. D. G. BULLIONS

WEST MILTON, February 6, 1863

My dear Sir: My acquaintance with the Rev. James Whyte was comparatively brief, though it covered the whole period of his residence in this country. As he was settled in the immediate neighbourhood of my father's charge and of my own home, he very soon became intimate in our family, and so continued till he went to take possession of one of the Heavenly mansions.

Though I was myself quite young, he made a strong impression upon me, and my recollections of him have scarcely faded at all with the lapse of years.

He was rather a short, thick-set man, with light complexion and light hair, and an expression of countenance blending finely the intellectual with the graceful and the amiable. His general appearance betokened rather feeble health; and this I believe to have been a true index to his actual condition. His manners were exceedingly quiet and gentle, indicating an utter unconsciousness of his fine intellectual powers and of the almost unprecedented popularity which had attended him as a Preacher prior to his coming to this country. He was deliberate in his movements and quiet in his whole bearing. Though there was no approach to any thing like a distant or unsocial manner, I should say that he was rather sedate than cheerful. This might have been partly the result of natural temperament, but I doubt not that his deep sense of the solemnity and responsibility of the work in which he was engaged had also much to do with it. But you could not fail to discover at once that he was one of the most benevolent of men. His heart was always going out in strong desires for the happiness of all whom his influence could reach; and these desires were evidently the working of not only a naturally amiable but deeply Christian spirit.

The several traits of character which I have attributed to Mr. Whyte came out very impressively in his ministrations in the pulpit. I cannot say that he was a bold, startling, or especially striking Preacher; but he was pre-eminently tender, gentle and attractive—his sermons were written with great care, and in a style of uncommon grace and beauty, and were of a deeply evangelical type; and they were delivered in that simple, earnest, even beseeching manner, that drew his audience to him by an irresistible influence. He certainly had uncommon power as a Preacher; and the secret of it lay, to a great extent, in his utter self-forgetfulness, and his manifest deep concern that his message might take effect upon the hearts and consciences of those whom he was addressing. He would pour out his bright and beautiful thoughts with such inimitable fervour and pathos that he must have been singularly constituted who could listen to his simple and glowing utterances without being impressed by them. I heard him preach the sermon, which has since been published, on that touching incident in our Saviour's history,—the raising of the Widow's son in the city of Nain; and his tones of deep pathos, conveying sentiments such as his subject would naturally suggest to such a mind, almost vibrate on my ear to this day.

In his pastoral duties Mr. Whyte was most diligent and faithful. He was especially at home amidst scenes of sorrow, and knew as well as any other man how to bind up the bleeding heart. As a natural consequence, he possessed, in a very uncommon degree, the affection of his people, and, when he died, they became literally a congregation of mourners.

I think he had little to do with the more general concerns of the Church, especially as they were connected with Ecclesiastical Bodies. All his tastes and habits were adverse to every thing of a controversial bearing, and I think also he had not much executive talent—his forte undoubtedly lay in the easy and effective discharge of the immediate duties of a Preacher and a Pastor.

Fraternally yours,
D. G. BULLIONS.

JAMES PATTERSON MILLER.*
1825—1854.

JAMES PATTERSON MILLER, a son of Hugh and Mary (Patterson) Miller, was born at King's Creek, Beaver County, Pa., on the 1st of August, 1792. His father, though not directly involved in the famous Whiskey Insurrection in Western Pennsylvania, did not refuse to permit his house to become an asylum to some who were implicated in it. The son, James P., though then only a few years old, distinctly remembered having seen two men at his father's house, who, when visitors were known to be approaching, would retreat to the garret, drawing after them the ladder by which they had ascended. His mother, who was an earnestly religious woman, devoted this son, in her own solemn desire and purpose, from his very birth, to the Ministry of the Gospel. It is believed that his knowledge of this fact had no small influence in enabling him to resist the temptations to which he was afterwards subjected to seek preferment in political life.

He commenced the study of Latin, under the instruction of the Rev. George Scott, a Presbyterian minister, near Hookstown, in the year 1809. In due time he entered Jefferson College, and it is believed that his attendance there terminated in 1814, though, for some reason, he did not receive the degree of Bachelor of Arts until 1818. While he was a student in College, his mother died suddenly of dysentery, and both himself and a younger brother were brought to the borders of the grave by the same disease. In subsequently giving an account of the state of his mind in the near prospect of dissolution, he said,—" My physical powers were utterly prostrated, so that I was unable to speak, yet my mental faculties seemed unimpaired. I heard the physician say that I would probably not live an hour. I remembered my mother's prayers in the family, when my father was occasionally absent, which had always made a strong impression on my mind. My firm belief that she was a true Christian, and that her prayers for me would be heard, gave me great consolation, and I could say with hope,—'I am thy servant, the son of thine hand-maid.'"

Shortly after leaving College, he took charge of an Academy in Winchester, Va. Here he proved himself an excellent disciplinarian as well as very competent teacher; and he secured, in a high degree, the confidence and good-will of both his employers and pupils. During his residence here he mingled chiefly with Episcopalians, and had much pleasant intercourse with them, and was not a little edified by the Episcopal Ministry (that of the late Bishop Meade) under which he sat; but his attachment to the Church of his fathers, in respect to both doctrine and polity, remained undiminished.

After a residence in Virginia of between one and two years, he returned to Pennsylvania, and commenced the study of Theology in the Theological Seminary, under the Rev. John Anderson, D.D., in the autumn of 1815. He attended the Seminary two sessions, and then took charge of a Classical School in Cadiz, O., where he remained, it is believed, a year or two. In 1820 he was married to Elizabeth, daughter of John Roberts, of Cannonsburg, and, shortly after this,

* MSS. from Mrs. Miller and Rev. Dr. Hanna.

removed to Steubenville, O., where he became the Principal of another Academy. He was taken on trials for licensure in the spring of 1821, but was not actually licensed till the spring of 1825. Some have supposed that this delay on his part was occasioned by a somewhat serious impediment in his speech, which he was apprehensive would disqualify him, in a great measure, for the labours of the pulpit; while others, and perhaps with better reason, have conjectured that it was attributable to some lingering aspirations for political life. The latter supposition is rendered more probable from the fact that it was not till after he had suffered a sore bereavement that he resumed his original purpose of preaching the Gospel.

Notwithstanding Mr. Miller was indefatigable in his labours as a Teacher, yet his active mind sought additional employment, and his predilection for political life prompted him to become the editor, for some time, of a political newspaper. He is said to have been the first person in the State of Ohio, who publicly urged the claims of General Jackson to the Presidency of the United States. At this time there was every thing to indicate that he would quickly become absorbed in politics; but that Infinitely Wise Providence that often disappoints our hopes in the ordering of our lot, had another path marked out for him. Mr. Miller's wife, who was a highly estimable lady, and had never been satisfied with his having failed to carry out his original purpose to preach the Gospel, was seized with erysipelas, and died, after a short illness, in December, 1824, leaving two young children. This event, as appears from a private record of it, made, at the time, by his own hand, was the means of giving a new direction to his course of life, and leading him solemnly to renew his purpose to enter on the Gospel Ministry. But, before receiving license, he spent a few months, chiefly with a view to obtain a better knowledge of Hebrew, with Dr. Ramsay, at that time Professor in the Theological Seminary at Cannonsburg. The first year of his ministry he spent chiefly in itinerating in the West; and the next year he was sent, by the Synod, with the Rev. John Walker, Pastor of a Church at New Athens, O., to visit various places in Indiana, Illinois and Missouri, which were destitute of religious ordinances. The winter of 1827–28 was signalized by the prevalence of heavy rains and desolating floods throughout that region, by means of which the hardship and fatigue attendant on his mission were greatly increased.

He was ordained at Unity, in the Presbytery of Muskingum, on the 6th of September, 1827. In 1828 he received another appointment, by the Presbytery, as a Home Missionary, in connection with Mr. John Kendall.* The year following he received a call from Madison, Ind., and one from Argyle, Washington County, N. Y.; the latter of which he accepted. On the 3d of May, 1829, he was married to Amanda Davidson, daughter of a Physician, of Xenia, O.; who became the mother of three children; and, in October of the same year, he was installed Pastor of the church to which he had been previously called. Here he exercised his ministry with exemplary diligence during a period of twenty-two years. The congregation over which he was placed was divided, in 1830, into North and South Argyle, on account of the large area over which it

---

* JOHN KENDALL was a native of Greene County, O. He studied Theology under Dr. John Anderson, and was appointed to be taken on trials for licensure in 1815, but for some unknown reason he declined. He then went to Xenia, O., and became editor of a secular newspaper, in which business he continued ten or twelve years. He, however, subsequently changed his purpose, and in the summer of 1827 was licensed to preach. He itinerated for a few years through the churches, but was at length attacked by catalepsy, which very materially impaired his intellect. After living for some years in a secluded state he died

was scattered. The Church of South Argyle, to which his labours were confined after the division, was, during his whole ministry, not only blessed with peace, but with a gradual and almost constant increase of intelligent and exemplary members. Several congregations in Indiana and Illinois were composed, to a great extent, of persons who had emigrated from South Argyle.

Mr. Miller had, during his whole ministry, taken a deep interest in Missions, not only to the Heathen, but also to destitute places in our own country, and had contributed pecuniary aid to this cause up to the full measure of his ability. He often expressed his regret that he was too far advanced in life to devote himself to the work of Foreign Missions. Several times he visited Canada on short missionary excursions, and, in 1844, spent a few months in itinerating among the destitute in the Far West. In 1850 the Associate Presbyterian Church determined to send missionaries to the Territory of Oregon. Mr. Miller, believing that his prosperous Church in South Argyle would have no difficulty in supplying itself with a Pastor, offered his own services as a Missionary to Oregon, provided a person better suited to the enterprise could not be found. His offer was cordially accepted; and, accordingly, in the year 1851, he, with Mr. Samuel Irvine, a son of an old fellow-student of Mr. Miller, set out for this new and arduous field of labour. The parting with his congregation and friends was most sad and tender, and his Farewell Sermon, which was preached on the 2d of March, was addressed to a weeping audience. He embarked at New York for San Francisco on the 15th of April, and arrived on the 28th of May; thence, on the 4th of June, he sailed for Oregon, and arrived at the mouth of the Columbia River on the 8th. Here, in a small village, where religious services had never been performed, and the Sabbath never recognized as a day of rest, he planted himself in the spirit of a true missionary, and, in a course of untiring self-sacrifice and devotion to his work, spent the remainder of his days.

During the three years of his ministry here, Mr. Miller enjoyed excellent health, insomuch that he was never taken off from his labours by indisposition for a single day. In September, 1853, he organized a congregation, and his public services, considering the new country and the small population, were well attended. He was mainly instrumental in uniting the members of the Associate and the Associate Reformed Presbyterian Churches in Oregon into one Body, under the name of the United Presbyterian Church of Oregon. His prospects of usefulness were never brighter than when God, in his infinite wisdom, was pleased to bring both his services and his life to a close.

Mr. Miller had often expressed the hope that he might be permitted to be engaged in active duty while he lived, and had remarked that he could never join in the petition of the Litany to be delivered from sudden death, believing that, if he were prepared, as a Christian ought always to be, sudden death was much to be preferred to a lingering fatal malady. And this desire of his heart was signally granted. He preached his last sermon, in robust health, on the 2d of April, 1854, on the Glories of Christ's Kingdom. Two days after this he made a short visit to Portland, and, as he was returning home, on the 8th, the boiler of the steamboat exploded, and he was killed instantly by a piece of iron striking his head. His wife and one of his children were present to witness the terrible catastrophe. His body was interred near the scene of his principal labours in Oregon. The Rev. Mr. Blain, on whom it devolved to occupy his pulpit first after his decease, delivered an appropriate Sermon from Titus ii, 12, 13.

Mr. Miller published, in 1839, an octavo volume, with the following title:—
"Biographical Sketches and Sermons of some of the First Ministers of the Associate Church in America: To which is prefixed a Historical Introduction containing an Account of the Rise and Progress of the Associate Reformed Church for the First Half Century of her existence in this country."

FROM THE REV. THOMAS HANNA, D. D.

WASHINGTON, PA., April 14, 1858.

Dear Sir: My acquaintance with the Rev. James P. Miller commenced in the fall of 1816, when he and I entered the Theological Seminary together under the charge of the Rev. John Anderson, D. D. From that time until about 1826, my opportunities for knowing him intimately were very favourable. His natural powers of mind were quite above mediocrity, and his attainments as a scholar were highly respectable—indeed, he seemed to have a natural taste for literary pursuits, and was admirably fitted, as well by his manners as his scholarship, for conducting a literary institution;—an employment to which he devoted himself with great success for several years previous to his licensure. His commanding personal appearance, his good temper, his readiness to communicate, all conspired to secure to him the respect and goodwill of his pupils.

Mr. Miller possessed fine social qualities, which, with his good taste and good sense, made him a very agreeable companion. He was a close observer of passing events, and he carefully treasured the results of his observation, to be appropriated as circumstances might afterwards require. He was a man of decidedly practical habits, and was never satisfied unless he was doing something that would tell benignly on the interests of his fellow-creatures. His friendships were sincere and ardent; and his incorruptible integrity secured to him the most unbounded confidence.

It was an evidence of his great benevolence as well as strength of character, that he should, at so advanced an age, have formed and carried into effect the purpose of migrating to a distant region in the character of a missionary. His sudden and sad removal from the world was indeed among the dark dispensations of Providence; but there is little doubt that his labours in that difficult field are destined to be gratefully remembered both on earth and in Heaven.

I am, Dear Sir,
Very respectfully yours,
THOMAS HANNA.

FROM THE REV. JOSEPH T. COOPER, D. D.

PHILADELPHIA, July 14, 1862.

Dear Sir: I cheerfully comply with your request for some of my recollections of the Rev. James P. Miller. Although his field of labour was remote from mine, and he was in the ministry many years before me, yet, as an Editor, I had much correspondence with him, and very frequently saw him in the Associate Synod, and for some days shared his hospitality.

As a Preacher, there was an earnestness and naturalness in his manner, that arrested the attention and kept alive the interest of the hearer. He had nothing of that sing-song tone, which, in former days particularly, was so common among the ministers of the Secession, and which so often acted as a lullaby upon the nerves of their hearers. It was not often my privilege to hear him, but I have sometimes heard him when I thought him impressively eloquent.

Occupying the post of an Editor, I had a favourable opportunity of becoming acquainted with Mr. Miller as a writer; and I can truly say that I always felt gratified on receiving a communication from him. His articles were characterized by great propriety and good sense. Instead of dealing in prolix introductions, he entered at once *in medias res*, and always showed that he clearly understood his subject. His manuscript was remarkably accurate, and, even when written in haste, scarcely needed any revision.

Mr. Miller was somewhat of an antiquarian, and took great pleasure in searching out the details of the history of the different branches of the Secession Church, both in this country and in Great Britain. His octavo volume, entitled "Biographical Sketches," &c., is a monument of his taste and labours in this direction. It was his purpose to bring down the history commenced in that volume to the present time; but this purpose was frustrated by his mission to Oregon. Previous to his departure, he placed in my hands the early Records of the Presbytery of Pennsylvania and of the Associate Synod, with an earnest request that I would prosecute the work which he had commenced. This I have been prevented from doing by the press of editorial and pastoral duties; but I earnestly hope that some one may yet be found who will undertake it.

Notwithstanding his deep interest in the past, he was intensely alive to all the movements of his own time. He was emphatically a Reformer. The cause of Temperance and Emancipation called forth his warmest sympathies, and received, through good report and through evil report, his effective co-operation. The use of tobacco, in all its forms, he reprobated as inconsistent not only with good manners but good morals; and it was his firm conviction that Christians, and especially Ministers of the Gospel, were bound to set their faces against it. Had I been disposed to take a smoke, I think I should have hardly ventured to do it in his presence.

Mr. Miller was a close and diligent student of the Bible in the original languages. He preferred to go to the fountain head to find out exactly the mind of the Spirit rather than trust to any translation. Both himself and some of his children were in the habit of using the Greek Testament in family worship. He bestowed much attention on the Prophetical Scriptures. He embraced, at least, in its outline, what has been called the Millenarian system of interpretation, believing that the Second Advent would be pre-millennial.

He was distinguished for his minute acquaintance with the forms and order of Ecclesiastical Courts. I have often heard him referred to by his brethren as being without a superior, or perhaps without an equal, in this respect, in the Secession Church.

Of Mr. Miller's social qualities it is not easy to speak in terms of exaggerated praise. He made every one in his company feel perfectly at ease, and there was a charm in his fine genial spirit that was quite irresistible. This, no doubt, had much to do with his great success as a Pastor, and the affectionate remembrance in which he is still held by those who once enjoyed the benefit of his ministry. His presence was highly prized and much sought for by the sick, not merely from the medical skill which he possessed, but from his cheerful and soothing manner in ministering to their spiritual wants.

He had a strong attachment to the principles of the Secession Church. In the latter part of his ministry, however, his attention seems to have been particularly directed to the divided state of the Church, and to the evils growing out of it, and he became earnestly desirous that different branches of the Presbyterian Church might be united in one Body. As might be expected, he appeared to some of his brethren, who viewed the subject from a different standpoint, to have declined in his love of the peculiar principles of the Secession Testimony. But to me it appeared not that he loved the principles of his

Church less than formerly, but that his love of all friends of the truth had grown much more fervent. His views of Prophecy contributed not a little to this state of feeling. He believed there were scenes of trial before the Church, and that God's people should be uniting their energies against a common foe.

I am, my dear Sir, yours fraternally,

JOSEPH T. COOPER.

FROM THE REV. S. F. MORROW.

ALBANY, July 8, 1862.

My dear Sir: My earliest recollections of the Rev. James P. Miller reach back to the time when I was probably not more than ten years old. He used then sometimes to be at my father's, and I distinctly remember the impression which his gigantic form and his capital jokes used to make upon me. A man with a larger frame than he had, I have rarely, if ever, met with. He could not have walked through Broadway, in New York, but that the eyes of many would have been turned upon him as a magnificent specimen at least of physical humanity. His weight was so immense that when, in the early part of his ministry, he used to perform journeys on horseback, he was accustomed to put in requisition two horses,—alternately leading one and riding the other. One of the stories which I heard him relate concerning himself, in my childhood, was, that, as he was riding on horseback, with a large blue cloak wrapped around him, a stranger who was coming toward him, and wishing to get off a good joke at his expense, made as if he would turn out, and said, as if discovering his mistake,—" Oh, I thought this was the stage coach." When I came to Albany, my relations with Mr. Miller became intimate, and our intercourse was frequent, until he left this part of the country for Oregon.

Mr. Miller had a countenance indicating strength of mind and of purpose; both of which qualities he undoubtedly possessed. His manners were urbane and gentlemanly, and revealed a heart of much kindliness and warmth. He was exceedingly hospitable, always giving his friends a cordial welcome, and always doing every thing in his power to render them happy. In his general intercourse with society he made himself popular by his intelligence, his good humour, his active habits, and his deep interest in whatever was going on around him. He had very decided political views, and he did not hesitate to express them, or to act upon them, whenever he thought occasion required. He was deeply interested in every thing pertaining to the History of the Church, especially of the Ecclesiastical Body with which he was immediately connected; and probably no person within the limits of his communion has done so much to rescue from oblivion the memories of our ministers who have passed away, as himself. He was a man of enlarged and liberal views in respect to whatever related to the general progress of human society. He was a well educated man, and I believe a good scholar; and he was a good Preacher withal; though the effect of his preaching was considerably diminished by a slightly hesitating manner. It was an evidence of his high tone of Christian public spirit that, at so advanced an age, he should have enlisted in an enterprise so arduous as that to which he may be said to have sacrificed his life.

Very cordially yours,

S. F. MORROW.

THOMAS BEVERIDGE HANNA.*
1848—1852.

THOMAS BEVERIDGE HANNA was born near Cadiz, O., on the 27th of March, 1823. His father, the Rev. Thomas Hanna, D.D., was, at that time, Pastor of the Associate Presbyterian Congregation in that place. His mother was Jemima Patterson, eldest daughter of Robert Patterson, of Mount Pleasant, O., afterwards of Wheeling, Va. He early discovered a fondness for books, and could not, on any light consideration, be persuaded to lose even a single day from his school. A considerable part of his English education, and the rudiments of Latin and Greek, he acquired under the tuition of several students of Theology, who afterwards became Ministers in the Associate Church. He commenced the Latin Grammar when he was nine years old, and, though he did not pursue his studies regularly from that time, he entered the Freshman Class in Franklin College, Ohio, in the autumn of 1840, at the age of twelve, and remained there, with little or no interruption, till August, 1844, when he was admitted to the degree of Bachelor of Arts. He graduated with the highest honours of his class, delivering the Valedictory Oration.

His mind seems to have received a decidedly serious direction from his earliest years, and it is probable that he scarcely remembered the time when he did not intend to be a Minister of the Gospel; but he did not make a profession of religion till the summer of 1844, when he became a member of the Church at Cadiz, then under his father's pastoral care.

In the autumn of 1844 he was admitted to the study of Theology by the Presbytery of Muskingum, and, immediately after, entered the Theological Seminary at Cannonsburg. Here he passed through the regular course, developing talents of a high order, prosecuting his studies with great diligence and thoroughness, and securing to himself the warm regard, not only of the Professors and his fellow students, but of many in the surrounding community. As there was but one session of the Seminary in the year, extending from the beginning of November to the close of March, he had the intervening seven months to himself. This time he divided between his theological studies, general reading, preparing Discourses for Presbytery, and teaching a few scholars in his father's neighbourhood.

In June, 1848, he was licensed to preach by the Presbytery of Muskingum. He commenced his public labours by fulfilling an appointment of Presbytery to supply vacant churches for three months within the Presbyteries of Muskingum and Chartiers; and on the 10th of September proceeded to Wisconsin, where he had had a field of labour assigned him by the Board of Home Missions. On his arrival there he found that his home was to be at Waterville, in Waukesha County. The people were generally poor, and the best accommodations he could obtain were barely comfortable. He took board at the village tavern, and, by the kindness of a young physician of the place, was allowed to use his office as a study.

In this field Mr. Hanna continued very laboriously occupied until May, 1849, when he visited Washington, then the residence of his father, and had the pleasure of spending a little time under the paternal roof. A meeting of the Synod took

* Memoir of his life, by Rev. T. H. Beveridge.

place at Allegheny about this time, at which a call was presented to him from Cambridge, O., and its connections, in the Presbytery of Muskingum, and another from the Associate Congregation of Clinton, Allegheny County, Pa., under the care of the Presbytery of Chartiers. The latter of these he accepted. He determined, however, in accordance with the advice of his Presbytery, as well as with his own inclination, before entering on his duties as Pastor, to labour a few months as a Missionary in the city of New York. He, accordingly, went thither in the month of June, and remained until the end of October, labouring, with great acceptance, in what is called the Mission Church. His condition here was rendered perilous, and his labours the more arduous, by the fact that the cholera was, at that time, prevailing, to a fearful extent, in the city.

About the first of November Mr. Hanna returned from New York, and commenced preaching at Clinton. After the usual trials, he was ordained, by the Presbytery of Chartiers, to the office of the Ministry, and installed Pastor of the Associate Congregation of Clinton, on the 13th of December, 1849. The Sermon on the occasion was preached by the Rev. Dr. McElwee, and the Charge to him as Pastor was delivered by his father.

Mr. Hanna now entered upon the duties of the pastoral office with great alacrity and earnestness, and with an evident purpose to make the salvation of his people his one all-absorbing object. The commencement of his labours seemed to give promise of a happy and effective ministry; but only two brief years had passed before his Master called him to give an account of his stewardship. On the 20th of January, 1852, he suffered a severe attack of bilious colic; but, as he had previously been subject to the same complaint, it excited no special alarm. The disease seemed to yield to some of the usual remedies, and, on Thursday, two days after the first attack, he supposed that he should be able to preach on the ensuing Sabbath. But, on Friday, his symptoms became more unfavourable, and his disease took the form of severe inflammation of the bowels. His family friends, being informed of his dangerous illness, hastened to his bedside, expecting to see him die; but, after their arrival, an apparently favourable change took place, which led his physicians as well as friends to indulge strong hopes of his recovery. These hopes, however, were but short-lived, as another change, of a different nature, very speedily followed. On Wednesday, the 4th of February, his most alarming symptoms re-appeared, and, in spite of all the appliances of medical skill, he sunk rapidly, and his death occurred about eight o'clock the next morning. The exercises of his mind were, to some extent, modified and rendered less satisfactory by the nature of his disease; but there was enough in his last hours to form a bright confirmation of the evidence that had been accumulating, in connection with his devoted life, that it was gain for him to die. The services at his Funeral, at which no less than fourteen of his ministerial brethren, of different denominations, were present, were conducted by the Rev. Dr. Anderson and the Rev. Nicholas Murray.

Shortly after Mr. Hanna's death, a Memoir of him, by the Rev. T. H. Beveridge, was published, in connection with fourteen of his Sermons.

FROM THE REV. S. F. MORROW.

ALBANY, July 3, 1862.

My dear Sir: I have very distinct and pleasant recollections of the Rev. Thomas B. Hanna, as I was associated with him as a student in my preparation for the ministry. My intercourse ceased with him after we left the Seminary, except that he paid me one short visit after my settlement in this city.

Mr. Hanna was of a tall and slender form, uncommonly youthful in his appearance, but with a fine, bright, benignant face, which predisposed everybody to like him. As you became acquainted with him, one of the first things that impressed you was his great modesty—you saw at once that he had formed no extravagant idea of his own abilities, and that he had no disposition to render himself unduly conspicuous. He had an uncommonly gentle and kindly spirit, never giving needless offence in his intercourse, and always ready to confer favours whenever he had an opportunity. He was marked for his ingenuousness and candour. Of any thing like unworthy management, or attempting to carry a point by indirect or unfair means, he was utterly incapable. No one could doubt that the object at which he was professedly aiming was the object which he really had in his eye; no one ever feared that he would circumvent or deceive him, even in the most unimportant concern or in the slightest degree. And he was as conscientious as he was ingenuous. He had but one rule by which to order his conduct, and that was the will of God, as indicated by his Word and Providence, and interpreted by an enlightened conscience. When he had once considerately answered to his own mind the question what the Lord would have him to do, his purpose was formed, and no earthly power was strong enough to move him from it. While his naturally amiable spirit made him condescending in all matters in which he did not feel that duty was positively involved, there was no sacrifice to which he would not submit rather than be false to his honest convictions. And to crown all, I must refer to his piety—it was not fitful, blazing to Heaven one day, and dying away into profound indifference the next; but it was consistent, intelligent, all-pervading—his faith was a living principle, that worked by love, and purified the heart, and overcame the world. It made him strong to perform the duties of life and strong to endure the trials of life; and its power was strikingly manifested when he was getting ready to put off his earthly house of this tabernacle.

Mr. Hanna's talents were remarkably well adapted to the pulpit. His sermons were rich in evangelical thought, expressed with great simplicity and clearness, and often with uncommon beauty. His manner was at once graceful, forcible and earnest; and you could not resist the impression that the preacher felt that he was dealing in eternal realities. His published sermons, though highly creditable to his taste, his culture and his piety, do not, after all, fully represent his power in the pulpit; for the latter part of his sermon, embracing his most earnest appeals to the hearts and consciences of his hearers, was usually left unwritten. Nothing, perhaps, in connection with his preaching, was more remarkable than the deep knowledge which it evinced of the workings of the human heart;—a knowledge which could never have been acquired but by a most diligent study of his own heart, in connection with the Word of God.

As a Pastor, he was eminently devoted to all the interests of his flock. He mingled with them with an affectionate freedom, that always secured to him a cordial welcome to their houses and their hearts. He was especially adapted to be a comforter in affliction—his sympathetic spirit quickly vibrated to every note of sorrow that fell upon his ear. He bestowed much care and attention on the young, conducting a Bible class on Sabbath morning for their benefit, and always keeping a watchful eye on the concerns of the Sabbath School. In short, he seemed ever intent on doing good among his people; and the deep grief which his early death called forth among them, showed how highly they appreciated his character and services.

I am yours truly, S. F. MORROW.

ALPHABETICAL INDEX.

NAMES OF THE SUBJECTS.

	PAGE		PAGE
Allison, Thomas	71	Hanna, Thomas Beveridge	132
Anderson, Abraham, D.D.	107	Henderson, Matthew	2
Anderson, John, D.D.	17		
Armstrong, Robert	68	Marshall, William	7
		Martin, James, D.D.	112
Banks, John, D.D.	52	Miller, James Patterson	126
Beveridge, Thomas	81		
Bruce, Robert, D.D.	90	Pringle, Francis	64
Carson, David	117	Ramsay, James, D.D.	77
Clarkson, James	15		
		Shaw, Joseph, LL.D.	85
Fulton, Andrew	56	Stark, Andrew, LL.D.	101
Gellatly, Alexander	1	Walker, John	95
Goodwillie, David, D.D.	40	Whyte, Archibald	47
		Whyte, James	121
Hamilton, Thomas	75		

NAMES OF THOSE WHO HAVE CONTRIBUTED ORIGINAL LETTERS.

	PAGE		PAGE
Baird, Robert, D.D.	110	Heron, Andrew, D.D.	57, 63
Beveridge, Thomas, D.D.	2, 17, 35, 61, 79, 95, 114	Mair, Hugh, D.D.	123
		Mathews, James M., D.D.	55, 76
Black, John, D.D.	91	McAllister, John, Esq.	13
Bower, Rev. Andrew	94	McClelland, Alexander, D.D.	23
Brownlee, Rev. John T.	74	McClure, Hon. William B.	68
Bullions, Alexander, D.D.	54, 92	McElwee, W. M., D.D.	108, 119
Bullions, Rev. David G.	83, 99, 106, 124	McIntyre, Hon. Archibald	89
Bullions, Peter, D.D.	46, 50, 87, 104	Miller, Rev. James P.	7, 73
Cooper, Joseph T., D.D.	129	Morrow, James, Esq.	60
Goodwillie, Thomas, D.D.	44, 47, 64	Morrow, Rev. S. F.	84, 116, 131, 133
Hanna, Thomas, D.D.	129		

NAMES INCIDENTALLY INTRODUCED EITHER IN THE TEXT OR THE NOTES.

	PAGE		PAGE
Banks, Joseph	53	Pringle, Francis, Jr.	66, 67
Barlass, William	38	Pringle, James	66, 70
Beveridge, Thomas Hanna,	34, 35	Pringle, Rev. William	43
Bullions, Alexander, D.D.	44	Ramsay, James Paxton	79
Clarkson, Thomas Beveridge	16	Smith, Thomas	52
Cree, John	32	Somerville, David	50
Henderson, Ebenezer	6	Walker, W. Houston	53
Kendall, John	127	Whyte, Archibald, Jr.	50

ASSOCIATE REFORMED.

PREFATORY NOTE.

Not a small portion of those to whom I am indebted for the material for this series of sketches, have passed away, and some of them have not only themselves become legitimate subjects for commemoration, but are actually among the worthies here commemorated. Of these I may mention particularly the Rev. Dr. McJimsey, whose early and warm approbation of the plan of my work helped to give me an impulse towards carrying it out, and whose intimate acquaintance with the Fathers of the Church, as well as his habit of accurate and impartial observation, has given great value to his communications. I am also under obligations to the Rev. Dr. Dales, of Philadelphia, and the Rev. Dr. Mathews, of New York, and to the Professors in the Allegheny Associate Reformed Theological Seminary, for much important information, besides the valuable letters which bear their names. And I cannot forbear here to repeat what I may have said elsewhere, that I owe much to the kindness of several distinguished ministers at the South, towards whom no adverse political relations can ever extinguish my gratitude. And, last of all, I beg to tender my warmest acknowledgments to the Rev. Dr. John Forsyth, whose identification with the Associate Reformed Body during nearly his whole life, and his perfect familiarity with the history of the denomination, together with the kindly interest he has taken in my enterprise, have rendered his services quite invaluable;

and his facile and graceful pen he has allowed me to put in requisition most freely, even beyond the limits of the denomination with which he has been more immediately connected. To all who have rendered me their assistance, in any way, I acknowledge myself a grateful debtor.

W. B. S.

HISTORICAL INTRODUCTION.*

The union of the Associate and the Reformed Presbyteries, constituting the Associate Reformed Church, may probably be traced, in some degree at least, to the War of the Revolution. The weakness of the congregations of the different sects of Scotch Presbyterians had, for some time, suggested the importance of consolidation for the sake of increased strength; and the Independence of the Colonies was thought by many to remove the previously existing causes of disunion. The question of a union came at length to be agitated with great earnestness, and several Conventions were held in reference to it; until, at length, in October, 1782, the Reformed Presbytery, the Associate Presbytery of New York, and a considerable part of the members of the Presbytery of Pennsylvania, met at Philadelphia, and formed themselves into a Synod, under the name of the Associate Reformed Synod of North America. The following articles constituted the basis of this union:—

1. That Jesus Christ died for the elect.
2. That there is an appropriation in the nature of faith.
3. That the Gospel is addressed indiscriminately to sinners of mankind.
4. That the righteousness of Christ is the alone condition of the Covenant of Grace.
5. That Civil Government originates with God the Creator, and not with Christ the Mediator.
6. That the administration of the kingdom of Providence is given into the hands of Jesus Christ the Mediator; and Magistracy, the ordinance appointed by the Moral Governor of the world, to be the prop of civil order among men, as well as other things, is rendered subservient, by the Mediator, to the welfare of his spiritual kingdom, the Church, and has the sanctified use of it and of every common benefit, through the grace of our Lord Jesus Christ.
7. That the law of nature and the moral law revealed in the Scriptures are substantially the same, although the latter expresses the will of God more evidently and clearly than the former; and, therefore, Magistrates, among Christians, ought to be regulated, by the general directory of the Word, as to the execution of their office.
8. That the qualifications of justice, veracity, etc., required in the law of nature for the being of a Magistrate, are also more explicitly revealed as necessary in the Holy Scriptures. But a religious test, any farther than an oath of fidelity, can never be essentially necessary for the being of a Magistrate, except where the people make it a condition of government.
9. That both parties, when united, shall adhere to the Westminster Confession of Faith, the Catechism, the Directory for Worship, and Propositions concerning Church Government.
10. That they shall claim the full exercise of Church Discipline, without dependence upon Foreign Judicatories.

* Sketch of the Assoc. Ref. Ch. by Dr. Forsyth.—Do. by Dr. Dales

The Body thus formed was composed of three Presbyteries, numbering fourteen ministers; though the number was immediately increased by the addition of the Presbytery of Londonderry, which remained in connection until 1802. One of the first Acts of the Synod, after its organization, was the adoption of a series of Articles, afterwards published under the name of the Constitution of the Associate Reformed Church; but these Articles were ultimately laid aside for a fuller exposition of the faith of the Church. The Synod, at its meeting at Green Castle, Pa., in May, 1799, issued its formal Standards, consisting of the Westminster Confession of Faith and the Catechism, with a revision of the Articles relating to the power of the Civil Magistrate. The Directory for Worship and the Propositions of Church Government remained unchanged; while the Rules of Discipline and Forms of Process were merely reduced to a regular system for the sake of more convenient application. The Book, as thus prepared, was published under the title,—"The Constitution and Standards of the Associate Reformed Church in North America."

For twenty years after the union, the Church greatly prospered, insomuch that the demand for labourers was greater than the Synod could possibly supply. While the Church was thus increasing its numbers and extending its boundaries, it was proposed that the Synod should be divided into subordinate Synods, and that delegates should be chosen, by each Presbytery, to attend an Annual Assembly, which should be called a General Synod. Accordingly, at the meeting in New York, in October, 1802, the Provincial Synods of New York, Pennsylvania, Scioto, and the Carolinas, were constituted; and in May, 1804, the first General Synod of the Associate Reformed Church met in Green Castle, Pa., in which there was a representation of the eight Presbyteries of which the Synod was composed,—namely, Washington, New York, Philadelphia, Big Spring, Kentucky, Monongahela, and First and Second Carolinas. This measure did not result favourably to the prosperity of the denomination. The Provincial Synods, on account of the wide extent of country covered by them, became irregular and delinquent in their meetings, and, after a few years, ceased to assemble altogether. There was an unfortunate centralizing of power, by means of which a spirit of jealousy was engendered in different portions of the Church, which brought in its train very serious evils. The Carolinas were, by their own request, constituted an independent Body, leaving the General Synod composed of only the Synods of Pennsylvania and New York. About the same time, the proposition for a union with the Reformed Dutch Church, having been the subject of protracted discussion, was laid aside. In 1821, at the meeting of Synod in Philadelphia, overtures were received from the General Assembly of the Presbyterian Church for a union of the two Bodies; and each Body appointed a committee to conduct the negotiation to its legitimate result. The joint Report of these committees recommended that "the different Presbyteries of the Associate Reformed

Church should either retain their separate organization or be amalgamated with those of the General Assembly, at their own choice;" that the Theological Seminary of the General Assembly and the Theological Seminary of the Associate Reformed Church should be consolidated; and that the Theological Library and funds belonging to the Associate Reformed Church, should be transferred to the Seminary at Princeton. This plan, having received the approval of the two Bodies, was sent down to the Associate Reformed Presbyteries for their action. At the next meeting of the General Synod, in 1822, it appeared that a large majority of the Presbyteries and congregations were decidedly opposed to the projected union. Notwithstanding this, however, the Synod resolved to proceed, and, after a debate of several days, the vote was taken, and there were six for union, five against it, and four silent. The vote was declared to be in favour of the union; the General Synod of the Associate Reformed Church was declared to be dissolved; its members were invited to seats in the General Assembly; and the Library of the Associate Reformed Theological Seminary was at once removed to the Theological Seminary at Princeton. This library was recovered, by a protracted law-suit, in 1838.

Thus terminated the General Synod, without, however, involving the extinction of the Church itself. The great mass of her ministry and membership remained true to her principles and interests, and set themselves at once to the work of endeavouring to heal her wounds and secure her perpetuity. The Western portions, comprising more especially the Presbyteries of Monongahela and Ohio, in the Synod of Scioto, had organized themselves, as early as 1820, as an independent Synod, under the name of the "Associate Reformed Synod of the West." In October, 1839, it was deemed advisable to form a new Synod, to be styled, "The Second Associate Reformed Synod of the West." In October, 1852, a third Synod was organized, called "The Associate Reformed Synod of Illinois." These several Synods were placed under the care of a General Synod, to be composed of delegates from the several Presbyteries; to have no appellate power, except in cases of doctrine; and to superintend the whole department of Missions. It was called "The General Synod of the Associate Reformed Church of the West;" and so rapid was its growth that, in 1855, when, by the union with the Synod of New York, it ceased to be known as the General Synod of the West, it included within its bounds three Synods and twenty-two Presbyteries. The Southern portion of the Church, composing the Synod of the Carolinas, was, after its withdrawal from the General Synod, in 1821, continued as an independent Body, under the name of "The Associate Reformed Synod of the South." This Synod has, within its bounds, eight Presbyteries and sixty-five ministers. About 1852 there commenced a correspondence between this Body and the General Assembly, with reference to a union; and the correspondence is still continued with the Southern portion of the

Presbyterian Church. The Synod of New York, having never withdrawn from the General Synod, and not assented to the Act of union with the General Assembly in 1822, occupied the ground, and claimed the rights, of the General Synod. Accordingly, its three Presbyteries,—New York, Washington and Saratoga, met as a Synod, at Newburgh, in September, 1822, and unanimously resolved to prosecute their appropriate work with undiminished vigour. Such was the increase of this Body that, in 1855, it numbered six Presbyteries, including fifty ministers. These several Synods,—the General Synod of the West, the Synod of the South, and the Synod of New York, though existing as three independent divisions. have adhered to the same standards and been united in a general co-operation. However, in May, 1855, a union was effected between the Synod of New York, and the General Synod of the West, in Pittsburg, Pa , under the title of "The General Synod of the Associate Reformed Church." This united Body entered upon its work both harmoniously and efficiently. At the time when the union with the Associate Church was consumated, in May, 1858, it contained 4 Synods, 28 Presbyteries, 253 Ministers of the Gospel, 367 Congregations, 31,284 Communicants, 8 Theological Seminaries, and 6 Foreign Missionaries. At the same time, there were, in this Body, the following periodical publications:—The Christian Instructor—a Monthly, published at Philadelphia; the United Presbyterian,—a Weekly newspaper, published at Pittsburg; and the United Presbyterian of the West.

As early as 1796 the Synod passed an Act in reference to a Synodical fund, one of whose objects was declared to be to "assist pious youth who, from poverty, cannot comfortably and successfully pursue their studies, and the establishment of a Professorship of Theology for the instruction of such as design the Holy Ministry." In 1800, in consequence of the increasing demand for ministers, it was resolved to take measures for the establishment of a Theological Seminary; and, in the mean time, in order to meet the then present exigency, efforts were to be made to obtain a supply of ministers from Scotland. For these purposes Dr. John M. Mason was sent as an agent to Great Britain in 1802; and he succeeded in obtaining funds to the amount of about six thousand dollars, the greater part of which was expended in the purchase of a library. He also brought with him five Scottish ministers, who came with a view to make this country the future theatre of their labours. At the first meeting of the General Synod, in May, 1804, Dr. Mason was chosen Professor of Theology, and it was agreed that the Seminary should be opened, in the city of New York, on the first Monday of November, 1805; and, accordingly, on that day, the institution commenced its course, under highly favourable auspices. In 1809, the Rev. James M. Mathews, one of the first class of students in the institution, was elected Assistant Professor of Biblical Literature and Church History—he held the office until 1818, and then resigned, with a view to becoming the Pastor of a Reformed

Dutch Church in New York. In 1821, Dr. Mason, having discharged the duties of his Professorship with distinguished ability for sixteen years, and finding himself broken down in consequence of his manifold and uninterrupted labours, was compelled to relinquish his place; and, at length, in May, 1821, the institution which had given to the Church no less than ninety-six ministers, was obliged, from various causes, to suspend its operations.

In 1825 the Synod of the West resolved to establish a Theological Seminary at Pittsburg, and the Rev. Joseph Kerr, D.D., was chosen its first Professor; but he had held the office only four years, when he was taken from it by death. In 1831,—the place having been somewhat informally supplied, during the two preceding years, by the Rev. Mungo Dick,—the Rev. John T. Pressly, D.D., of the Associate Reformed Synod of the South, was chosen to the office of Senior Professor. That office he has continued to hold till the present time, (1863,) his associates in charge of the institution being the Rev. A. D. Clarke, D.D., who was chosen to the Professorship of Biblical Literature and Criticism in 1847, and the Rev. D. R. Kerr, D.D., who was called to the chair of Ecclesiastical History and Church Government in 1851. Not less than three hundred young men have passed through their preparatory course for the ministry in this institution.

In 1829 the Synod of New York resolved to revive the Seminary that had been suspended in New York in 1821, and the Rev. Joseph McCarroll, D.D., of Newburgh, N. Y., was chosen the first Professor In 1839 a fine, commodious edifice was completed for the accommodation of the institution, and in 1852, the Rev. John Forsyth, D.D., was called to the Professorship of Biblical Criticism, Ecclesiastical History and Church Government.

In 1839 the Synod of the West resolved to form a second Synod of the West, and established a second Theological Seminary within its bounds. The Rev. Joseph Claybaugh, D.D, was chosen Professor of Theology, and the Rev. S. W. McCracken, Professor of Hebrew; and Oxford, O., was fixed upon as its location. Dr. Claybaugh died in September, 1855, and was succeeded by the Rev. Alexander Young. In 1858 the Seminary was removed from Oxford to Monmouth, Ill.

The Associate Reformed Synod of the South has a flourishing Theological Seminary at Due West, Abbeville District, S. C., which has furnished Pastors to a large number of churches within the bounds of the Synod, and has enjoyed the confidence of the Church at large. It has also under its care a highly respectable College, known as "Erskine College."

The Associate and Associate Reformed Bodies continued separate until 1858, when, with the exception of a few ministers and congregations of each side, they were united in one Body, under the name of the United Presbyterian Church of North America. This Body now (1863) consists of a General Assembly, 7 Synods, 44 Presbyteries, 462 Ministers, 671 Congregations, and 57,514 Communicants. It has 3 Theological Seminaries, and 6 Foreign Missionary Stations.

The Associate Reformed Church declared, in its standards, issued at Green Castle, in 1799, that it is "the will of God that the *Sacred Songs*, contained in the Book of Psalms, be sung in his worship, both public and private * * * * nor shall any composures merely human be sung in any of the Associate Reformed Churches." This law, though it has not always been rigidly adhered to, has never been repealed. The subject of *Communion* has, at different times, been under the consideration of the Church, and the action which has been taken in respect to it has varied with the diversity of circumstances. The General Synod, in 1811, passed a Resolution, recommending mutual forbearance, and evidently allowing some latitude on this subject; but this action, in connection with the remonstrances of Presbyteries against any thing like promiscuous communion, together with the publication of Dr. Mason's celebrated work on "Catholic Commmunion," combined with other circumstances to hasten the dissolution of the General Synod, and the resolving of the different Synods into separate and independent Bodies. In 1838 the Synod of New York, at its meeting at Salem, passed Resolutions, utterly disapproving the principle or practice of Open Communion, but still allowing, in extraordinary cases, occasional communion with themselves to members of other churches.

CHRONOLOGICAL INDEX.

[On the left hand of the page are the names of those who form the subjects of the work—the figures immediately preceding denote the period, as nearly as can be ascertained, when each began his ministry. On the right hand are the names of those who have rendered their testimony or their opinion in regard to the several characters.]

	SUBJECTS.	WRITERS.	PAGE.
1754.	James Proudfit	Robert Proudfit, D.D.	1
1761.	John Mason, D.D.	John B. Dales, D.D. Mrs. Joanna Bethune.	4
1761.	Robert Annan	John M. McJimsey, D.D. James M. Mathews, D.D.	11
1764.	Thomas Clark, M.D	John B. Dales, D.D. Thomas Beveridge, D.D	18
1774.	Alexander Dobbin	John M. McJimsey, D.D. James M. Mathews, D.D.	27
1784.	Matthew Henderson, Jr.	Rev. A. G. Wallace. Rev. H. Connelly	31
1789.	John Dunlap	J. D. Wells, D.D. John Gosman, D.D.	36
1790.	John Young	John C. Young, D.D. John M. McJimsey, D D	41
1792.	Andrew Oliver	Arthur Burtis, D.D. Hon. A. Oliver. Jacob Sutphin, Esq. James Thompson, Esq.	47
1793.	George Mairs	Peter Bullions, D.D. Rev. Peter Gordon.	52
1794.	John Riddell, D.D.	James Grier, D.D. Rev. H. Connelly	57
1794.	John Hemphill, D.D.	Rev. W. R. Hemphill David Macdill.	62
1794.	Alexander Proudfit, D.D.	John Gosman, D.D Ebenezer Halley, D.D	67
1794.	William McAuley	John Forsyth, D.D.	78
1794.	John M. McJimsey, D.D.	Robert Proudfit, D.D. Hon. William Kent John H. Morrison, D.D. Malcolm McLaren, D.D.	82
1796.	Alexander Porter	John T. Pressly, D.D.	93
1797.	James Gray, D.D	C. G. McLean, D.D. John M. Duncan, D.D.	94
1797.	John Steele	J. Claybaugh, D.D.	102
1802.	James Scrimgeour	John Forsyth, D.D. James M. Mathews, D.D.	105
1802.	Isaac Grier, D.D.	Rev. James Boyce. Rev. H. Connelly.	110
1802.	Robert Forrest	Robert Proudfit, D.D. John Forsyth, D.D.	114
1803.	Joseph Kerr, D.D	James Prestley, D.D. David Macdill, D.D Elisha P. Swift, D.D. Joseph Claybaugh, D.D.	117

SUBJECTS.	WRITERS.	PAGE.
1804. Mungo Dick	Rev. H. Connelly	126
1807. John Lind	J. M. Mathews, D.D. Joseph McCarroll, D.D. David Elliott, D.D John M. Krebs, D.D.	129
1809. George Stewart	J. M. Mathews, D.D.	135
1809. George Buchanan	Rev. John M. Galloway	138
1810. James Galloway	George Junkin, D.D. Jacob Van Vechten, D.D.	141
1811. John Mason Duncan, D.D.	Charles G. McLean, D.D. Jacob Van Vechten, D.D. William J. Sprole, D.D.	145
1820. James Lemonte Dinwiddie, D.D.	Joseph T. Smith, D.D.	154
1824. Joseph Claybaugh, D.D.	R. D. Harper, D.D.	156
1826. Richard Wynkoop	Hon. Daniel Weisel	158
1829. Joseph Reynolds Kerr	James Prestley, D.D Joseph Claybaugh, D.D.	161
1831. Moses Kerr	David R. Kerr, D.D. Rev. H. Connelly	166

JAMES PROUDFIT.*
1754—1802.

JAMES PROUDFIT was born near Perth, Scotland, in the year 1732. His parents were of respectable standing, and members of the Established Church of Scotland. They bestowed great care upon his religious education, and, as was common in Scotland at that time, taught him the Westminster Catechism with the Scripture proofs. Having evinced, from his childhood, a serious turn of mind and great fondness for study, as well as highly respectable talents, he was early destined to the Ministry of the Gospel, and, at a suitable age, was sent to the University for his education. Here he became acquainted with some members of the Secession; and, having become dissatisfied with the Established Church, especially from having witnessed the violent settlement of Ministers by patronage, contrary to the expressed wish of the people, he resolved to change his ecclesiastical connection, and, after mature deliberation, united with that branch of the Secession denominated Anti-Burghers. His parents earnestly protested against his taking this step, regarding it as fatal to his prospects of temporal preferment; yet, as he was conscious of being influenced by a strong sense of duty, he could not be persuaded to abandon his purpose, and, after completing his literary course, commenced the study of Theology under the direction of the Rev. Alexander Moncrieff,† Professor of Divinity in that denomination,—for whom, in token of his high regard, he afterwards named a son. Having completed the prescribed theological course, in 1753, he was licensed by the Presbytery of Perth and Dumferline to preach the Gospel. About this time frequent applications for ministerial aid were made to the Associate Synod in Scotland, by persons living in the British Colonies, who adhered to the principles of the Secession. The Rev. Alexander Gellatly and the Rev. Mr. Arnot had been sent out a few weeks before, in answer to their applications; the former for permanent settlement in this country, the latter to labour as a Missionary for a single year. Mr. Proudfit was deemed eminently qualified to occupy this then new field of labour; and, accordingly, in July, 1754, he was ordained to the ministry, with a destination for North America. The Ordination Sermon was preached by the Rev. George Brown, from Gal. i, 15, 16. The Presbytery then directed him to repair to the West of Scotland, and remain there until an opportunity should offer for sailing to North America.

A few days after this, Mr. Proudfit, in fulfilment of this appointment, embarked for America, and, after a favourable passage, reached Boston in the month of September; and, with as little delay as possible, proceeded to Pennsylvania, where he was to find his future field of labour. On reaching Philadelphia he met

---

* Christian Magazine, II.—Christian Instructor, New Series, V.—MS. from Rev. Dr. John Proudfit.
† ALEXANDER MONCRIEFF was born in 1695. As the eldest son, he inherited the estate of Culfargie, in the parish of Abernethy. He studied at St. Andrews, and then at Leyden under Mark and Wessel. He was ordained, and installed Minister of Abernethy, in 1720. He warmly sympathized with Ebenezer Erskine, joined in the protest against the censure inflicted on him, and was one of the first members of the Associate Presbytery. He died October 7, 1761, in the sixty-seventh year of his age and the forty-second of his ministry. He published An Inquiry into the Principle, Rule and End of Moral Actions; Christ's Call to the Rising Generation; Three Sermons; and two volumes of Miscellaneous Sermons.

the Rev. Mr. Arnot, who had completed his missionary tour, and was then returning to his charge in Scotland. Messrs. Gellatly and Proudfit were now the only ministers connected with the Associate Synod in these Colonies; and, after prosecuting their labours alone for about six years, they were at once gladdened and strengthened by the arrival of Dr. John Mason and the Rev. Robert Annan. Mr. Proudfit, after being occupied in itinerant service several years,—planting congregations and nurturing them, received a call from the Associate Church in Pequea, Pa., which he accepted, and thus, for the first time, became a stated Pastor. He lived in the immediate neighbourhood, and in most fraternal relations, with the Rev. Robert Smith, one of the most distinguished ministers of the Presbyterian Church of that day.

When the Associate Reformed Synod was constituted, about the year 1780, Mr. Proudfit cast in his lot with that Body. But, owing to a diversity of sentiment in relation to this movement among the people of his charge, and more especially owing to the desolating effects of the Revolutionary War, his congregation became greatly reduced in numbers, and he began to look out for a larger field of usefulness. Just at that juncture two calls were presented to him; one from a congregation in the interior of Pennsylvania; and another from Salem, in the State of New York. He accepted the latter call, and removed with his family to Salem in the autumn of 1783. There was not, at that time, a minister of his own denomination within a hundred and fifty miles, and scarcely a settled minister of any denomination North or West of Albany, in the State. His labours here were both multiplied and arduous. Though nominally Pastor of the Church at Salem, yet he preached occasionally at Cambridge, Hebron and Argyle, in Washington County, and in various places in the Counties of Saratoga and Montgomery; and he was spared to see what he found well-nigh a moral wilderness converted into a garden.

Mr. Proudfit having become quite advanced in life, and his health being seriously impaired, his congregation, in 1794, united in calling his son, the Rev. Alexander Proudfit, to become his colleague; and this union was, accordingly, happily consummated. He continued, however, notwithstanding his increasing infirmities, to share in the discharge of parochial duties until the year 1799, when he was visited with a paralytic shock, which terminated forever his public services in the sanctuary. From this time his powers of both body and mind rapidly decayed until the 22d of October, 1802, when he fell asleep, in the seventieth year of his age, and the fiftieth of his ministry. A Sermon was preached on the occasion of his death, by the Rev. Dr. Gray, of Hebron, from Psalm cxii, 6: "The righteous shall be in everlasting remembrance."

Of Mr. Proudfit's marriages there remains but a very defective record. When or to whom he was first married, I have sought in vain to ascertain—it is known, however, that by this marriage there were seven sons, one of whom was the Rev. Dr. Alexander Proudfit, three of whom entered the medical profession, two were merchants, and one a farmer. His second wife was a Miss Houston, who became the mother of one daughter, who still (1862) survives.

FROM THE REV. ROBERT PROUDFIT, D. D.
PROFESSOR IN UNION COLLEGE.

SCHENECTADY, June 4, 1855.

Dear Sir: The Rev. James Proudfit, concerning whom you inquire, was my father's brother, both having emigrated from Scotland to this country, a little after the middle of the last century. As, however, my uncle resided at Salem, N. Y., and my father in York County, Pa., my opportunities for seeing my uncle in early life were not very frequent, being limited to the occasional visits which he made to us, chiefly or entirely, when he attended the meetings of Synod at Philadelphia. Shortly after my graduation at Dickinson College, in 1798, I went to Salem, and took up my residence in his family, and pursued my theological studies chiefly under the direction of his son, the late Dr. Alexander Proudfit. I continued in his family nearly four years; and, though I had the opportunity of seeing much of him, he was, during much the greater part of the time, rendered quite helpless by paralysis. Though I had not the privilege of knowing him well in the days of his full activity and vigour, I had the best possible opportunity for witnessing the exercise of his passive graces; and I can truly say that in this respect he was "glorious" even "in ruin." After other subjects had well-nigh faded from his mind, the great truths of religion seemed to be as fresh and welcome to his thoughts as ever; and his command of Scripture, and his ability to refer to the place where any particular passage was to be found, were truly surprising. His religious experience was so deep, and his religious knowledge so thorough and minute, that when he had sunk back to the imbecility of childhood in relation to every other subject, he could still bear his part in religious conversation with the same apparent relish, and almost with the same degree of intelligence, as in his better days.

Mr. Proudfit was a tall man,—I think rather more than six feet high, and in the days of his health was well proportioned; though, when I knew most of him, he was somewhat emaciated by disease. Every thing about his appearance and manners betokened gravity. His countenance, though not marked by any thing like austerity, indicated an uncommonly thoughtful habit of mind. His movements were staid and deliberate, and his whole appearance, both in public and in private, eminently clerical. He was nevertheless of a kind and amiable temper, and was not destitute of humour, though it was rare that he thought proper to indulge it; and I might almost say, never, unless it were to administer a timely rebuke to impertinence. He was remarkable for having all his feelings and faculties under the most perfect control—I never heard of his being thrown off his guard by any sudden emergency, or of his being surprised even into an indiscretion.

If I were to describe his intellect in a single word, I should say it was eminently sound. He was not distinguished for imagination, nor, so far as I know, for a philosophical turn of mind; but he was remarkable for good judgment, excellent common sense, and enlightened, sober and practical views of whatever subject engaged his attention. He possessed also an extraordinary memory; having every part of the Bible at his command, beyond almost any other person whom I have ever known: insomuch that it used to be said that, if the Bible were actually to be lost out of the world, he could go very far toward replacing it. He was, in a very high degree, a practical man. The great object of his life evidently was to make the most of his faculties in doing good to his fellow-creatures, and promoting his Master's cause and honour.

His preaching was not what would commonly be called popular; but it was sensible, well considered and highly instructive. He preached from copious notes, which, I believe, were always written in short hand. He made much more use of the Scriptures in the way of proof and illustration than is common at this day, or, I believe I may add, than was common even in his own. He kept his hearers constantly impressed with the idea that he was delivering to them not only the mind, but to a great extent the very letter, of the Spirit. His voice, though sufficiently distinct, was rather feeble; his gestures were few and not particularly forcible; and his general manner by no means distinguished for extraordinary animation. But there was such evident sincerity pervading every thing that he said, and so much good sense, combined with rich evangelical instruction, that no one of a docile spirit could fail to be at once interested and edified by his ministrations. I ought to add that my impressions in regard to his preaching are derived more from the testimony of others than from my own observation. In my early life, when he used to visit my father, I remember hearing him preach in a barn in the neighbourhood in which we lived; but, after I came to live in his family, the only public service I ever heard him perform was at the Communion table, when his voice had become so feeble that it was not without great difficulty that he could be heard.

As a Pastor, he was a model of prudence, fidelity and affection. He estimated highly this kind of ministerial influence, and always aimed to make the most of it. His visits were, for the most part, strictly pastoral, and designed immediately to subserve the spiritual interests of his flock.

Though Mr. Proudfit was decided in his denominational preferences, he was a truly liberal minded man, and had a cordial welcome for all who seemed to him to bear the Saviour's image. As an illustration of this, I may mention that he cheerfully co-operated in the formation of the Northern Missionary Society, which was composed of Christians and Ministers of different denominations, and was its first President. Had he lived at the present day, when there is much more of commingling of the various Christian sects, I doubt not that both his principles and his spirit would have brought him still more largely and extensively in contact with other denominations.

In the Judicatories of the Church his modesty always diposed him to give place to others, and he was never a forward or noisy member of any Public Body. But he was always discreet and judicious, and accomplished more by wise counsels than most others did by long speeches. He was held in great respect not only by his own Body, but by Christians of all denominations, and by the community at large.

With great respect I am truly yours,
R. PROUDFIT.

JOHN MASON, D.D.
1761—1792.

FROM THE REV. JOHN B. DALES, D.D.

PHILADELPHIA, May 24, 1849.

Rev. and dear Sir: It gives me great pleasure to learn that among the honoured and useful ministers whom your work is designed to commemorate, is the venerable Dr. John Mason, (father of the late Dr. John M. Mason,) of New York. I have taken some pains to investigate his history, by a reference to Presbyterial and Synodical records, and have gathered also whatever traditionary information I could obtain, that seemed sufficiently authentic; and, though the materials, after all, are very scanty, I am inclined to think that I have succeeded in bringing together nearly all that now remains concerning this venerable man.

JOHN MASON was born near Mid-Calder, in the County of Linlithgow, Scotland, in the year 1734, being the eldest son of the family. His father was a farmer, and both his parents, who were eminently pious persons, died while he was quite young, but not till they had had time to impress him with the obligations of early piety.

His early training was under the influence of the Associate or Secession Church of Scotland, in its best days. On the 9th of April, 1746, this branch of the Church which, in thirteen years, had grown from a small Presbytery into a large and useful Synod, was unhappily divided, by what was termed the "Burgess oath,"* into the Burgher and Anti-Burgher parties, each claiming to be the true Associate Synod. With the latter of them Mr. Mason identified himself, and, after a thorough preparatory course, pursued his theological studies at Abernethy, with the Rev. Alexander Moncrieff, the first Professor of Divinity in the Anti-Burgher Synod. At the age of twenty he spoke the Latin language, in discoursing upon History, Philosophy and Theology, with as much ease as his mother tongue; and, at the age of twenty-four, was an assistant Professor in Logic and Moral Philosophy in the Theological Institution where he had himself studied. His piety also manifestly kept pace with his literary attainments; and, even at that early period of his life, he was remarkable for his spiritual fervour and devotion,—spending much of his time in his closet, and sanctifying all his studies and labours with the Word of God and with prayer.

At length the time arrived for his entrance on the work to which he had devoted himself. In the spring of 1761 the Synod, having received an earnest petition from a Congregation in New York, (long known as the "Cedar Street Church,") directed his Presbytery to ordain him to the office of the Holy Ministry. This was done; and he was immediately sent out, as one eminently fitted, by his intellectual and spiritual endowments, as well as by a warm attachment to the peculiarities of his Church, for that highly important and responsible place. He came in company with the Rev. Messrs. Robert Annan and John Smart†; and, arriving in June, was shortly afterwards installed in the pastoral charge of the people that had called him. His heart became deeply engaged in his work; and so much was he affected by the general destitution of the Gospel in its purity and power throughout the country, that the next spring he addressed several communications to the Synod in Scotland, soliciting, in the most earnest manner, for additional aid. Accordingly, the Synod designated a number to this field; only one of whom, however, Mr. William Marshall, a native of Abernethy, and at that time a student under Mr. Moncrieff, became an efficient labourer. By order of the Synod, he was licensed at an early day, and sent to this work; and, after

---

* This oath was the one administered to all town officers, and the clause which occasioned all the painful and disastrous results to the Secession Church, was as follows:—"Here I protest, before God and your lordships, that I profess and allow with my heart the true religion, presently professed within this realm, and authorized by the laws thereof; I shall abide thereat and defend the same till my life's end,—renouncing the Roman religion, called Papistry." The question was,—Can members of the Associate Synod profess, as the true religion, that which the State establishes in the Church from which the Secession was made? Burghers said Aye—Anti-Burghers said Nay.

† Mr. Smart, after remaining a few years in this country, returned to Scotland, where he spent the remainder of his life.

labouring for some time, was ordained to the pastoral charge of the Congregation of Deep Run and Neshaminy, Bucks county, Pa., August 30, 1765,—Mr. Mason preaching the Sermon from John iii, 10, and constituting the pastoral relation.

Shortly after this Mr. Mason became deeply interested in the relations between the Burghers and the Anti-Burghers in this Country; and, feeling that the matters which alienated brethren in Scotland ought not to separate them here, and that the hands of all would be strengthened by gathering these different Bodies together, he earnestly undertook to effect a union between them. The dispute which had long been carried on between the two Secession Synods at home, he characterized as "the dry, the fruitless, the disgracing and pernicious controversy about the Burgess Oath." He said,—" This controversy has done infinite injury to the cause of God in Scotland, and wherever it has shed its malignant influences. For my own part I cannot reflect upon it without shame and perplexity. Though we differ only about the meaning of some Burgess Oaths and Acts of Parliament. yet our mutual opposition has been as fierce as probably it would have been had we differed about the most important points of Christianity. The infatuation we have fallen into will amaze posterity." With this feeling he went forward, and though his course displeased the Synod in Scotland, and even caused his name to be erased from the roll, " as no longer entitled to a seat among them, until there should be an opportunity for bringing his case to a final trial," yet he saw much of his heart's desire and prayer granted,—the distinction between the Burghers and the Anti-Burghers, in this country, entirely broken down; and a consequent happy increase of vital godliness in the churches, and of saving knowledge among the destitute in various parts of the land.

Up to the month of May, 1776, there was but one Associate Presbytery in this country. This was the "Associate Presbytery of Pennsylvania, subordinate to the Associate Synod of Edinburgh," and there were thirteen ministers members of it. These were scattered over such a wide extent of country, and their meeting together was attended with so great expense of money and time, that they found it impossible to have that active co-operation which is necessary for most effectively advancing the cause of Christ. Mr. Mason, therefore, early favoured a division of the Presbytery, which, after some discussion, was effected with general unanimity. And though this division was blamed by the Synod in Scotland, inasmuch as it was made without consulting that Supreme Judicatory, yet, so far as this country was concerned, harmony and efficiency were happily promoted by it, and the good work was more energetically and successfully carried forward. The division of the Presbytery into two, and the facility which was thus afforded ministers of holding regular official intercourse, really promoted the unity and efficiency which Mr. Mason so ardently sought.

This movement, in behalf of what was supposed to be the best interests of the Scottish Churches in the Provinces, was early afterwards followed by another towards a union of an extensive and most important kind. Thus far the several Reformed Presbyteries,—the Associate which was organized in 1754, and the Reformed Presbyterian or Covenanter, in 1774, had been subordinate to Synods in Scotland. During the War of the Revolution, however, the communication with the mother country had been almost entirely interrupted, and the ministers in the several Presbyteries had been led to feel a painful necessity for Synods, and an ecclesiastical state of things adapted to their new condition in the land of their adoption. But they were weak in their separate and divided position. Mr.

Mason, therefore, readily listened to any proposition which had in view a union of brethren, of "like precious faith;" and after some years of prayerful conference and deliberation, he and his friends, the Rev. Robert Annan of Wallkill, N. Y., and the Rev. James Proudfit of New Perth, now Salem, N. Y., agreed to a basis which was accepted by the entire Reformed Presbytery, composed of the Rev. Messrs. Cuthbertson,* Dobbin and Lind. After further negotiations, these Presbyteries met with the Associate Presbytery of Pennsylvania, at Pequea, and on the 13th of June, 1782, agreed upon a general union. And that the very name of the United Body might be indicative of its origin, it was styled, "The Associate Reformed Church."

In all these movements Mr. Mason bore a leading part, drafting, as is believed, the leading articles of the basis of Union; and he was honoured with the office of Moderator, at the first meeting of the United Body in General Synod, October, 1783. Indeed, whatever tended to the unity of the visible Body of Christ was most congenial to his feelings. And, from the time that this union was consummated, he seemed to labour with even greater interest and success than ever. Nor was he without ample furniture for his work. He was a man of sound and vigorous mind, of extensive learning and fervent piety. As a Preacher, he was uncommonly judicious and instructive, and his ministrations were largely attended. As a Pastor, he was especially faithful and diligent. To great learning there were united in him meekness, prudence, diligence, knowledge of the world, and an affectionate superintendence of the interests, temporal and spiritual, of his flock. He so arranged his studies and other engagements in regard to time, that he had always some part of the afternoon to devote to visiting the families of his congregation. These visits were short, the conversation was serious, awakening, instructive and affectionate, and seldom did he leave a house without solemn prayer on behalf of its inmates. He did not consider any of his people's interests as beneath his notice, while his matured judgment and enlarged experience made him a wise counsellor and useful friend. On one occasion a lady, at whose house he called, in the spirit of a faithful Pastor, told him that she was sadly troubled by unworthy servants. "Ah, Madam," said he, "have you ever prayed to the Lord to provide worthy servants for you? Nothing which concerns our comfort is too minute for the care of our Heavenly Father."

* JOHN CUTHBERTSON was born in Scotland about the year 1720. He studied for the ministry probably under the Rev. John McMillan, the father and founder of the Reformed Presbytery of Scotland. He came to this country in 1752, and, for more than twenty years, was the only Reformed Presbyterian Minister in America. It is not quite certain whether he came hither on his own motion, prompted by his own missionary zeal, or by the formal appointment of the Reformed Presbytery. This Judicatory was constituted August 1, 1743, by two ministers, with their elders,—namely, Rev. Messrs. John McMillan and Thomas Nairn, and eight years afterwards (1752) the small Body was rent asunder by a dispute among its members regarding some doctrinal points. This was the very year of Mr. Cuthbertson's arrival in America; and the smallness of the Body, in its united state even, would have precluded the possibility of its lending him much aid in his mission. He seems to have established himself in Octorora, though, for twenty years, he had sole charge of the small Reformed Presbyterian Societies scattered over the Thirteen Colonies, and of course a very large portion of his time was spent in travelling. He entered cordially into the Union in 1782, and, until the close of his life, appears to have regularly attended the meetings of Synod. After the Union, his field of labour was restricted to his own immediate charge at Octorora, though he seems to have retained the habit, to some extent, of visiting many of the localities where Covenanters had settled. During the last visit of this sort that he made, some rumours got afloat prejudicial to his character for temperance, which were brought to the notice of Synod, by the Presbytery of New York. He had evidently acted indiscreetly, since his own Presbytery, after an investigation, administered a formal rebuke to him, and suspended him from the exercise of the ministry for four weeks. He died at Octorora, March 10, 1791.

On another occasion he met, in his pastoral charge, a difficulty which serious young persons often experience. A daughter of the excellent Mrs. Isabella Graham had wished to be connected with his church, but was afraid that her heart was not sufficiently engaged in the service of God. Her case was made known to him. With a peculiar kindness and solemnity of manner, he said,— "If the world, with all its wealth, pleasures and power were placed in one scale, and Christ alone in the other, which would your heart freely choose as its portion?" "Oh, Christ, Sir, Christ," said she. "Come then," said he, "and show this by professing Him before the world, trusting for the grace by which a weak faith may yet attain the full assurance." She came; and of her and her sisters their mother afterwards said,—"I have reason to think the Lord ratified their surrender of themselves to Him." Very similar was his faithful dealing with the late excellent Dr. Alexander Proudfit, in the character of a tender counsellor and friend. Just after graduating with much honour at Columbia College, New York, in 1792, and when somewhat excited with ambitious feelings and hopes, Mr. Proudfit called on Mr. Mason for advice in respect to his future course. In answer to an inquiry as to what profession he had chosen, Mr. Proudfit answered that he had not yet fully determined. Instantly, discerning the cause of his indecision, the venerable Pastor and friend replied,— "Alexander,—if you leave the service of Christ in the Ministry for the pursuit of worldly honours, He will raise up others to serve Him, but you may be lost." Immediately this "word in season" was blessed; and, from that short interview, the young student went forth to become a man whom many have risen up to call blessed.

As a public man, Mr. Mason was greatly respected and honoured, and exerted an extensive and benign influence. From 1779 to 1785 he was a faithful and useful Trustee of the College of New Jersey, and in 1786 received from that institution the honorary degree of Doctor of Divinity. In the time of his country's need he also showed himself his country's friend. Leaving the comforts of home, during the occupancy of New York by the British army, in the War of the Revolution, and placing his family at Pluckemin, N. J., he willingly encountered the dangers and hardships of the camp, that he might, as a Chaplain, counsel and encourage the American troops in their struggle for liberty and for right. Nor was he less zealous for what he deemed ecclesiastical rights,—for when an attempt was made some years before, to set up, on the model of the Established Church of England, an Archbishopric, he drew a strong pen in opposition to the measure, and perhaps had as much to do as any other person in defeating it.

In his own family Dr. Mason was eminently faithful and happy. Much of his time was spent in devotional exercises. His children were regularly instructed in the Scriptures, the Psalms versified, and the Assembly's Catechism with proofs; and often did his distinguished son, the late Dr. John M. Mason, ascribe his own ability, which every one knew to be most remarkable, to quote extended and appropriate passages of Scripture, to the early training which he received from his venerable father. In his intercourse with his ministerial brethren, however they might belong to a different denomination from himself, he exhibited the most kind and fraternal spirit, and studied in every way to promote their interests. When, for instance, the first movement was made, about the year 1770, for having English preaching in the Reformed Dutch Churches in New

York, under the ministry of the Rev. Dr. Laidlie, a great excitement prevailed. Some forty or fifty families were so disturbed by this innovation upon their long established order, that they determined at once to leave the denomination. Accordingly, they waited upon Dr. Mason, and informed him of their wish to attach themselves to his charge. His congregation was at that time comparatively feeble, and such an accession would have been of the utmost consequence to him. Without, however, hesitating a moment, he calmly told them that he thought them acting under the influence of improper feelings,—that they had better return to their church; and if, after six months or a year, they found error preached, or that their souls were suffering for spiritual things, and that God, and not merely their passions, pointed them to such a change as they now proposed, he would then consider the request to be taken under his pastoral care. The majority of them returned. Dr. Laidlie prospered in his ministry, and on Dr. Mason and his flock came the blessing of the Peace-maker. Indeed, his heart warmed with Christian love; and his counsels and energies were always ready for any work that promised good. This was so peculiar that, when he died, his venerable and attached friend, the Rev. Dr. Rodgers, of New York, said,—"I feel as if I had lost my right arm."

His labours were abundant,—often extending to distant places in his own and neighbouring States; and his ministerial services were attended with an unction which made them of a sweet savour to those who hungered and thirsted after righteousness. At length, however, the energies of nature gave way. After labouring nearly thirty years in his charge, his recollection suddenly failed him one day in the midst of his sermon, and he sat down in his pulpit, unable to proceed. Rising, in a few moments, he was enabled to say, in a peculiarly tender manner, that he considered this event as a call from his Heavenly Master to expect a speedy dismission from earth, and then solemnly admonished them to be prepared for the will of God. It was a touching scene. His people loved him as a father, and were dissolved in tears. He thence passed to his house, and was shortly attacked with his last illness. Patient and self-possessed, through the grace which he loved to magnify, the scene of his departure was joyful and triumphant. His views of Christ, in his grace and in his glory, were rich and refreshing, and next to these he loved to dwell upon the beauty and power of brotherly love in the Church of God. Calling his daughter to his side, he requested her to write a letter which should be directed to each member of the Synod. That letter was short, but how rich in the spirit of Him who said, "Love one another!" It was this:

"Dear Brethren:—Farewell; be perfect, be of good comfort, be of one mind, live in peace, and the God of love and peace shall be with you."

"Your dying brother,
"JOHN MASON."

At length, on the 19th of April, 1792, he died; and his death, like his life, was an honourable testimony to his Redeemer's power and grace.

Dr. Mason was twice happily married; and, by both marriages, became connected with respectable Dutch families in New York. His first wife was Catharine Van Wyck, who became the mother of nine children, of whom only three lived to maturity. The eldest of these (*Helen*) became the wife of Matthew Duncan, a merchant in Philadelphia, and the mother of John M. Duncan, D.D., for many years Pastor of the Associate Reformed Church in Baltimore. The second was the late *Dr. John M. Mason*, whose praise is in both hemispheres. The youngest (*Margaretta*) was married to the Hon. John Brown, one of the first Senators in Congress from Kentucky. Mrs. Mason died June 31, 1784. He was subsequently married to Sarah Van Alstine, who had no children, and survived him many years.

With much respect I am very truly yours,
JOHN B. DALES.

FROM MRS. JOANNA BETHUNE.

NEW YORK, June 26, 1849.

Reverend and dear Sir: In complying with your request for some account of my early friend and Pastor, Dr. Mason, I am forcibly reminded of God's word, Deuteronomy viii, 2: "And thou shalt remember all the way which the Lord thy God hath led thee these forty years in the wilderness, to humble thee and to prove thee, what was in thine heart, or whether thou wouldst keep his commandments or no."

My mother and family were introduced to the Rev. Dr. Mason, by the Rev. Mr. Ellis, of Paisley, in Scotland. He was the first to welcome us to a foreign land, and his kind attentions to the widow and the fatherless ceased only with his life. He was the first to persuade me publicly to acknowledge God as my Saviour and Redeemer. I was received into the communion of his church early in the year 1791. The next year I saw his remains consigned to the tomb, and ceased not to weep, and refused to be comforted, till his place was supplied by his distinguished son, the late Rev. Dr. John M. Mason.

Though more than half a century has elapsed since the death of the elder Dr. Mason, I have still a vivid recollection of his personal appearance and manner. He was of middle stature, not corpulent, had black hair, and a mild but penetrating black eye. He was distinguished for gentlemanly manners, staid deportment and decision of character. He was strict in his family discipline, uncommonly systematic in all his habits, and withal "given to hospitality." His sermons were thoroughly studied, his delivery was plain and energetic, and every thing, both in matter and manner, indicated a paramount regard to the glory of God and the salvation of souls. If an anecdote were admissible, the following might perhaps serve to illustrate his character more fully. A worthy Minister from Ireland, of somewhat eccentric habits and manner, travelled as a Missionary through the United States, and occasionally occupied Dr. Mason's pulpit. The good man was much annoyed at the fashionable style of the ladies' dress in those days, particularly their high head-dresses, and urged Dr. Mason to preach against them. "My dear Sir," replied the Doctor, "my business is more with the heart than the head. Looking to God to give effect to my preaching, I endeavour to convince my hearers that they are sinners, that they need a Saviour, and that they are bound to humble themselves before God, and give themselves wholly to his service. When this is effected, the head-dresses will come down of themselves."

I will only add the following brief notice of Dr. Mason's death, from a letter written by my beloved and venerated mother, Mrs. Isabella Graham, to a friend in Scotland:

"NEW YORK, April, 1792.—Sabbath noon.

"It is not my custom to take my pen on this day, even to write to a Christian friend, having occasion for my whole time with my family and with my God in secret; but I cannot go to dinner; I cannot eat; I cannot talk to my girls; my heart must bleed afresh upon the same altar where it has often been pierced. Oh, Madam, my dear Dr. Mason goes and leaves me here alone; in all probability, his course is nearly finished, and his crown awaits him. Five physicians now attend him closely. I have seen him often, and he says.—'All is well, and all *will be well*.' Of the physicians he said,—'Yes, yes, it is very well, they are useful men in God's hands. They may be useful in patching up this tabernacle a little. If it be raised to usefulness, I am content. If not to usefulness, I do not desire it. I feel no concern about the issue of this: the will of the Lord be done.'

"Sabbath Evening.—I have again seen my dear Pastor, and discern the clay dissolving fast. The words of dying saints are precious; and his are few. He thus accosted me:—'I am just awaiting the will of God; for the present, I seem a useless blank in his hand; I can say very little; be not too anxious for my life, but transfer your care to the Church; my life or death is but a trifle; if the Lord have any use for me, it is easy for Him to raise me up still; and if He do, it will be agreeable to observe his hand distinct from men; if He should not, you will all be cared for; leave all to Him and seek his glory.' He could say no more, nor will I to-night, but address myself to our Lord on his behalf, yours, my own and our dear concerns.

"April 23, Monday.—It is finished. My dear Minister's dying scene is over. On Thursday, the 19th of this month, a quarter before ten o'clock, A. M., the Lord received his spirit and laid his weary flesh to rest. He had a sore conflict with the king of terrors, who seemed allowed to revel through every part of his mortal frame. His legs were mortified to his knees. He had not been able to lie down for four weeks, and died in his chair. Like his Master, he groaned, but never complained. He had a draught of his Master's cup; but the bitter ingredient, *desertion*, made no part of it. I had the honour to close his eyes, and to shut those dear lips from whence so many precious truths have proceeded, and to mix with the ministering spirits who attended to hail the release. * * * This is a great work finished. Dr. Mason was a city set on a hill. He was with the army during all the War, after the evacuation of New York; had great influence over the soldiers; preached the Gospel of peace uniformly, but never meddled with politics, though he was fully capable. In every situation the Lord supported him in uniformity and consistency of character; and carried him through without a single spot or stain."

I have written under great infirmity, being now in my eightieth year; and I only regret that you have not found one more capable than myself of performing the service you have asked of me.

Wishing you success in all your labours of love,

I remain, Reverend Sir,

Yours, with Christian respect and regard,

JOANNA BETHUNE.

ROBERT ANNAN.*

1761—1819.

ROBERT ANNAN, a son of Robert Annan (his mother's maiden name was Landales) was born in the town of Cupar, Fife, Scotland, in the year 1742. Of his early history nothing definite can now be ascertained. After pursuing the usual course at the University of St. Andrews, he commenced the study of Theology under the venerable Alexander Moncrieff, one of the original Seceders. Among his fellow-students were Messrs. John Mason and James Proudfit, who afterwards became fellow-labourers with him in this country. He was licensed by the Associate Presbytery of Perth, when only about nineteen years old, and was, shortly after, appointed by the Synod to visit the American Colonies in the capacity of a Missionary. He was little inclined to accept the appointment, but it seems to have been scarcely at his option whether or not to do so, as the Synod, from their earnest desire to supply the waste places of the New World,

---

* Christian Instructor, 1845.—MS. from Samuel Annan, M.D.

had passed an Act, prohibiting the name of any probationer appointed to America from being proposed to any vacant congregation in Scotland.

Mr. Annan arrived in New York in the summer of 1761, and, after labouring as an itinerant about four years, was ordained and installed at Neelytown, N. Y., in 1765. Here he remained fourteen years, having charge at first of what are now the congregations of Hamptonburg, Little Britain, Graham's Church, and Bloomingburgh, though, ultimately, he confined himself to one of them.

When the War of the Revolution broke out, and through its whole progress, Mr. Annan showed himself a most earnest patriot, and not only in his private intercourse but in the pulpit vigorously defended the American cause. The following incident may serve as an illustration of his patriotic ardour:—In the fall of 1775 the people of Boston, being reduced to great straits in respect to provisions, sent over to the State of New York for aid; and, accordingly, a public meeting to respond to this application was held in the town of Hanover, (now Montgomery.) As no other person could be found who was able to speak to advantage in vindication of American rights, Mr. Annan, finally, though reluctantly, consented. The discussion, after a while, began to wax unduly warm, when, to prevent its becoming a bitter strife, Mr. Annan suddenly cried out,— "As many as are in favour of assisting the people of Boston and the cause of liberty, follow me." The effect was well-nigh electric—as he moved out of the house, nearly the whole assembly followed him.

Mr. Annan's fervid patriotism, and especially his denunciation of the British Government, during the period of the Revolution, made him a man of mark, and attracted the attention even of the Father of his country. On one occasion, while the army was in winter quarters, Washington, accompanied by Colonel Hamilton, the Marquis Lafayette and General Knox, paid him a visit. On their arrival, they found him engaged in teaching two of his sons the Greek Testament. They stayed a considerable time, Washington taking the lead in the conversation. Colonel Hamilton, after the other three had left the room, took up the Greek Testament and looked at it as if he were familiar with it. Mr. Annan supposed that he was the only one of the illustrious party that could translate a word of it.

Of the union by which the Associate Reformed Synod was constituted Mr. Annan was an earnest and efficient advocate. He was deeply impressed with the idea that the Providence of God had, by the Independency of the United States, so reduced the difference between the two parties that there was no sufficient reason why they should remain any longer asunder; and the final effecting of the Union, which was, in no small degree, through his instrumentality, was a consummation which he welcomed with devout joy. At a later period (in 1802) he expressed himself decidedly favourable to a Union between the Associate Reformed Synod and the General Assembly.

In 1788 Mr. Annan removed from Neelytown to Boston, having accepted a call from the congregation worshipping in Federal street. This was originally an Irish Presbyterian congregation, and was, for many years, under the pastoral care of the Rev. Mr. Morehead. Although the congregation was composed, originally, of very thorough Presbyterians, yet, in the course of years, as the emigration from Ireland and Scotland to Boston declined, it had so far yielded to the surrounding influences of Independency, that, when Mr. Annan took the pastoral charge, it was scarcely more than nominally Presbyterian. During his residence in Boston, which was for about three years, he had a high reputation as a Preacher, and was not altogether unknown as a man of scientific research. In the first volume of the Transactions of the American Academy of Science (Boston) there are several interesting papers written by him, one of which contains the earliest published accounts of the Mammoth remains discovered in Orange County.

In 1786 he received and accepted a call from the Old Scots Church, (Spruce Street,) Philadelphia. His relation to the Church in Boston had not been otherwise than pleasant; but as the Synod had made it imperative that he should "admit the Psalter used, and the mode of singing practised, in the Church of Scotland," and as he foresaw that this could not be done but at the expense of dividing the congregation, and as he had found it extremely difficult withal to maintain Presbyterian discipline in Boston, he thought it best, in view of all these circumstances, to avail himself of an opportunity to enter another field of ministerial labour.

Mr. Annan's removal to Philadelphia was little favourable to his personal comfort; as a portion of the Spruce Street Church, headed by the former Pastor, Mr. Marshall, had seceded in consequence of the union, and were, at this time, engaged in a legal prosecution for the recovery of the property; in which, however, they were unsuccessful. The contest between the parties was carried on in an earnest and even bitter spirit, and it is said to have operated, more than any other circumstance, to retard the growth of the Spruce Street Congregation.

Mr. Annan continued in this charge until 1801 or 1802, when he removed to Baltimore, to take the pastoral oversight of a congregation which had been then recently formed in that city. Here he remained until 1812, when he resigned his pastorship, and was shortly after succeeded by the Rev. John M. Duncan. He retired now to a place which he had purchased in York County, Pa.; but, though he never took another pastoral charge, he was usefully employed in supplying vacant churches in that region. He kept up his habits of study, and his powers of mind remained in full vigour, to the close of life. His death was occasioned by his being thrown with great violence from his carriage. He had preached on the previous Sabbath from Romans v, 2: "By whom also we have access by faith into this grace wherein we stand, and rejoice in hope of the glory of God." Not being able to finish the discussion, he had appointed the next Sabbath to complete it, and was on his way to the church when the fatal disaster occurred. He was taken up and carried home in a state of insensibility, and never rallied sufficiently to recognize any member of his family. He survived only two or three days, and died on the 5th of December, 1819. His remains were interred in the Octorora burying ground, now connected with the Associate Congregation.

The following is a list of Mr. Annan's publications:—An Overture illustrating and defending the doctrines of the Westminster Confession of Faith: prepared by appointment of the Associate Reformed Synod of North America, 1787. A Concise and Faithful Narrative of the various steps which led to the Unhappy Division among the members of the Associate Body in the United States, 1789. Animadversions on the Doctrine of Universal Salvation, 1790. The Connection between Civil Government and Religion, 1790. Mr. Annan had a long controversy with Dr. Rush, of Philadelphia, on the subject of Capital Punishment, in one of the newspapers of that city, in 1790.

Mr. Annan was married (it is believed in the year 1764) to Margaret, daughter of William Cochran, of Carrollsburg, York County, Pa. By this marriage there were two children, *Robert Landales* and *William*, both of whom became physicians—the former and the elder settled in Emmittsburg, Frederick County, Md., and died 1827; the latter settled in Philadelphia, and died in 1797. Their mother died on the 13th of October, 1793. The next year Mr. Annan was married to Elizabeth, daughter of Samuel and Elizabeth Hawthorne, who lived near the village of Strasburg, Lancaster County, Pa. She died in Lane County, Pa., on the 23d of July, 1813. The children of this marriage were six,—three sons and three daughters. *Samuel*, the second child, studied Medicine, partly in this country and partly in Edinburgh, and has been a medical practitioner successively in Emmittsburg, Baltimore, Lexington, Ky., and St. Louis, Mo. *John Ebenezer* and *William* were both graduated at Dickinson College in 1824; both entered the ministry of the Presbyterian Church; and the latter is now the Rev. Dr. Annan, of Pittsburg.

John Ebenezer Annan was born about the year 1803; and when he was in his ninth year removed with his father from Baltimore to his farm in Lancaster County, Pa. From early boyhood he was remarkable for his love of reading, though, up to his sixteenth year, he was principally occupied with the labours of the farm, enjoying no other advantages for education than are usually furnished by the common schools in the rural districts. Shortly after the death of his father, he entered the Classical School at Gettysburg, Pa., then under the care of the Rev. Dr. McConaughy, afterwards President of Washington College; and so rapid was his progress that, in about eighteen months, he was admitted to the Sophomore class in Dickinson College, then under the Presidency of Dr. Mason. In 1822 he became hopefully the subject of a revival of religion in College, and, some time after, made a public profession of his faith. He graduated in 1824 with the highest honours of his class. Notwithstanding he was now only in his twenty-first year, the uncommon vigour and maturity of his intellect, as well as his acknowledged rare acquirements, led the Trustees of Miami University, Oxford, O., to appoint him to the Professorship of Mathematics in that institution. Here he remained for several years, and, during this period, was vigorously engaged in the study of the higher branches of Mathematics, and wrote elaborate articles for several of the leading Scientific and Literary Reviews, including the "North American," and "Silliman's Journal of Science and the Arts." At this period also, he published Strictures upon Raymond's Political Economy, and Brown's Philosophy, which were written with great care and ability. But, as he was resolved to devote his life to the Ministry of the Gospel, he gave up his Professorship after a few years, and, having attended the Theological Seminary at Princeton during one session, was licensed on the 16th of May, 1829, by the Presbytery of Baltimore, to preach the Gospel. His first efforts in the pulpit were received with marked approbation. In July succeeding the period of his licensure, we find him on a missionary tour in Ohio, and labouring with great diligence and acceptance at Somerset, in Perry County, and throughout the surrounding country. He remained here until December, when he was ordained, by the Presbytery of Baltimore, as an Evangelist. Shortly after this he was invited to preach by the Presbyterian Congregation in Petersburg, Va., and, after supplying their pulpit a few Sabbaths, received a call to become their Pastor. He accepted the call, and was installed on the 10th of July following. He commenced his labours here under circumstances of great promise; but, in less than two months, was stricken down by the fever which is common in Southern latitudes, and especially dangerous to the unacclimated, and, after a very severe illness of a few days, closed his earthly career, on the 29th of August, 1830. He had gone to attend a Ministers' meeting at Lewisburgh, Greenbrier County, in the interior of the State, and it was there that the summons to depart met him. In his character were united a noble intellect, a warm and generous heart and a devoted Christian life, giving promise of the highest usefulness in the ministry.

FROM THE REV. JOHN McJIMSEY, D.D.

MONTGOMERY, ORANGE COUNTY, N. Y., July 12, 1848.

Rev. and dear Sir: In compliance with your request, I will now endeavour to give you a brief and faithful statement of my recollections and impressions in regard to the character and usefulness of the Rev. Robert Annan, one of the eminent fathers of our Associate Reformed Church. It was my privilege, early in life, to become personally acquainted with him, although it was a long period after his arrival in this country, probably thirty years,—the place of my birth and education being remote from the field of his ministry. He was, at the time I first saw him and heard him preach, at about, if not past, the meridian of life. He occupied the Moderator's chair when I was examined and licensed by the Presbytery, and addressed to me a solemn and affecting Charge on that occasion; and a letter of his, still in my possession, urging me to accept a call from Neelytown Congregation in Orange County, of which, in connection with Little Britain Congregation, he had himself been the Pastor, had no small influence in determining my choice; although I entertained a preference for Kentucky as the future field of my labours, which I had previously visited as a Missionary. As a Christian, he stood high with all who were acquainted with him; and the purity and integrity of his character as a Minister of Christ were never called in question; although, in particular instances, some might have thought that he scarcely paid sufficient deference to public opinion.

His ministry was highly acceptable, and there is reason to believe eminently useful, in the several congregations of which, for a longer or shorter period, he was Pastor. Although I took the pastoral charge of the Neelytown congregation long after the close of his ministry among them, I still found there abundant evidence of the happy effects of his labours. His memory, as an able, eloquent and faithful Minister, was still held, especially by aged and devout Christians, in the highest veneration.

As a Pastor, he was very instructive and very impressive. Erect and portly in his person, rising considerably above the common stature of men, with noble countenance and piercing eye, his whole appearance was commanding. He was not in the habit of fully writing out his sermons, and his speaking seemed extemporaneous; but he was always perfectly self-possessed, often rising to a high pitch of eloquence, his subject so animating and irradiating his countenance that one who was accustomed to hear him told me that it seemed to him that his face sometimes shone like the face of Moses when he came down from the Mount. The matter of his preaching was thoroughly evangelical, admirably uniting doctrinal instruction and practical Christian duty. He had a musical and well-regulated voice, and spoke with great ease and fluency; and though his gesture was not very abundant, it was natural and effective. While he delighted in preaching the evangelical doctrines, they were always so exhibited as to have a direct practical bearing. I heard him preach a sermon before the Synod from the text,—"Now the end of the commandment is charity out of a pure heart, and a good conscience, and of faith unfeigned";—the object of which was to illustrate the nature of evangelical obedience, which he said was emphatically charity; love to God and to our fellow-men; and he expressed his regret that the original word had not been translated *love*—*that* being its most proper and comprehensive sense: while the word charity, as now commonly used, is of a more vague and limited meaning. He mentioned to me, some time after, as a matter that deeply affected him, that one of his brethren came to him shortly after the delivery of his discourse, and inquired whether he had *him* particularly in his eye in some of his statements. This showed that his sermon had taken hold of at least one conscience.

It is admitted by all who knew Mr. Annan that he possessed uncommon ability and address in effecting reconciliation among brethren who were at variance, and in healing differences between ministers and their congregations. His speeches on such occasions were admirable, and breathed the most Christian and forgiving spirit. An instance of this kind occurred in the congregation of Salem, Washington County, during the ministry of Dr. Thomas Clark, he having been settled among them while Salem was yet a frontier settlement. Mr. Annan, after addressing the congregation on the subject of their difficulty in a tender and impressive manner, requested that all who wished the continuance of Dr. Clark's ministry among them would signify it by going out of the church at the East door, and those who felt differently to go out at the West door: the result was that the whole congregation, with the exception of one individual, went out at the East door, thus expressing, in the most public manner, their wish that their worthy minister should remain with them. Mr. Annan then, in no measured terms, administered a merited reproof to the individual who alone, and in the presence and against the express wish, of the whole congregation, could come out in this manner, against his Pastor, and a faithful Minister of Jesus Christ.

In the Judicatories of the Church Mr. Annan always took a prominent part, and exerted a powerful influence. He urged and defended his measures with great ability, and, as his natural temperament was warm and quick, he would sometimes, under a deep sense of the rectitude of his cause, be betrayed into expressions which could not be justified; but, as soon as he had taken time to reflect, he was always ready to acknowledge his error. With all his lofty bearing on some occasions, and severe as he was in his reproof of the conduct of wicked men, he cherished habitually a spirit of humility and meekness, and acknowledged to some of his Christian friends that the sallies of his temper gave him occasion for deep humiliation.

In his intercourse with his more intimate friends, his conversation sometimes betrayed a vein of pleasantry and wit, but in general it was marked by great dignity, and much of it was of a decidedly spiritual character. He seemed habitually to act under the influence of the Divine injunction,—"Let no corrupt communication proceed out of your mouth, but that which is good to the use of edifying, that it may minister grace unto the hearers." When dining one day with the late Dr. Mason, in company with several of the younger brethren in the ministry, the question was asked him, whether he had not been in the ministry half a century? He replied, "There about," and then said, with great gravity, "When I had been in the ministry forty years, that passage of Scripture came very forcibly to my mind, 'Forty years was I grieved with this generation.'" Dr. Mason, who was remarkable for repartee, immediately answered,—"I know not how that may be, but I believe that you have grieved some of this generation forty years."

With much regard,
I am sincerely yours,
JOHN McJIMSEY.

FROM THE REV. J. M. MATHEWS, D.D.

NEW YORK, August 6, 1861.

My dear Dr. Sprague: It costs me no self-denial to record my recollections of the Rev. Robert Annan,—for I remember nothing concerning him that will not well bear the light; and little effort,—for my impressions of him are so distinct that I can have no doubt of their correctness. My acquaintance with him began while I was a student in the Theological Seminary—he was one of the Superintendents of the Institution, and, on account of his age and standing, generally acted as their Chairman. Though I was a young man and he pretty far advanced, I became quite intimately acquainted with him at that early period, and our acquaintance ripened into a friendship which continued till he was called to his reward.

Mr. Annan had an uncommonly commanding personal appearance. He had a large, full, well-set frame, and was slightly inclined to corpulency. He had a bright, piercing eye, and his whole countenance was expressive of high intellectual powers and great strength of purpose. His manner was as commanding as his person; though there was nothing stern or forbidding in his demeanour, there was a dignity that always secured respect, even veneration. He had fine powers of conversation, and his presence was always recognized as a leading element of interest in any company. His mind was decidedly of a superior order, clear, logical, discriminating, comprehensive; and it had been subjected to the highest culture. His feelings were eminently kind and genial, and though I think he was naturally excitable, and was capable of saying severe things, and did sometimes say them under the pressure of exciting influences, he generally exhibited great self-control.

As a Theologian and a Minister of the Gospel, he held a very high rank, not only in his denomination, but in the Church at large. He had been all his life a diligent student, and, with such powers as he possessed, it was impossible but that he should have made immense acquisitions. He preached with great power, and scarcely any clergyman came to the city of New York who attracted larger congregations. The fact of his having been one of the original formers of the Associate Reformed Body from the Associate and the Reformed Presbyterian Church, had made him very extensively known, and contributed to greatly increase his influence; though, independently of this circumstance, his acknowledged high ability as a Preacher would have made him much sought after. His sermons were a model according to the old Scotch standard—they were full of Scripture truth, brought out with great clearness and force, and delivered with a simplicity and boldness and fervour that made them well-nigh irresistible. His voice was clear and strong, his intonations free and natural, and his action abundant and full of significance. I have heard sermons from him that would not have dishonoured Dr. Mason in the days of his greatest strength. I ought to add that he was capable of great tenderness as well as great boldness and force; and sometimes the exhortation with which he closed his discourse would be in the highest style of the pathetic.

As a Writer, Mr. Annan was probably distinguished above any other minister of his communion, during the period in which he lived, unless Dr. John M. Mason were an exception. He had great tact and ability in controversy, and I think also he was not wanting in polemical taste. He always met his antagonist with great fairness as well as force, and his friends generally had little doubt as to the issue of any contest in which he might engage.

I call to mind the interviews which I used to enjoy with him, with heartfelt pleasure. With a memory which retained almost every thing that had ever been lodged in it, with an exuberance of good-humour and kindly feeling, with a graceful facility of communication on every subject, and a most happy talent at adapting himself to every variety of character and condition, he seemed to me one of the finest specimens of intellectual and moral nobility which I had ever seen. He has impressed himself indelibly on the character of his denomination.

Very truly and affectionately,
J. M. MATHEWS

THOMAS CLARK, M. D.
1764—1793.

FROM THE REV. JOHN B. DALES, D.D.

PHILADELPHIA, June 24, 1849.

Reverend and Dear Sir: The position which the Rev. Dr. Clark long and usefully occupied in some of the most interesting portions of our country, I think, justly entitles his name to a place in your proposed work on the American Ministry. He was a faithful Minister of the Gospel, and a far-seeing and indefatigable labourer on behalf of the best interests of the community at large.

Of the particular time or place of his birth I have no certain information. That he was a native of Scotland, however, there can be no doubt; and that he early enjoyed the instructions and prayers of godly parents may be inferred from the fact that he always venerated the pious advantages of his youth, evinced a remarkable tenderness of conscience, and laboured in the ministry as if he had been thoroughly taught how to redeem the time by discovering and improving opportunities of doing good.

After a thorough course of study, he graduated at the University of Glasgow, and, during the War against the Pretender, in 1745 and 1746, did faithful service in the army.

According to a practice which was common with the young men preparing for the ministry a century since, Mr. Clark pursued a thorough course of Medical study also in the University, and took the degree of Doctor of Medicine. In this way he was often afterwards able to minister to the wants of the body, and thus more effectually reach the soul with his spiritual medicines. It was from this he obtained his usual epithet in this country,—"Dr. Clark."

The earliest public mention made of him is in connection with the first meeting of the Associate Burgher Synod at Stirling, Scotland, on the 16th of June, 1747. At this meeting Congregations and Societies in various parts of the country made application to the Synod for advice "in their present circumstances," and for a supply of preaching. In the unsettled state of things, and in the painful destitution of ministerial help, the Synod could give no immediate reply to these applications, but directed the Presbytery of Glasgow to take Thomas Clark and two other students of Theology, whom they also named, on trial for licensure. This the Presbytery did, and after pursuing his studies at Stirling, the next winter, under the Rev. Ebenezer Erskine, who was the first that had charge of the Burgher students, he was licensed in the following April, (1748,) to preach the Gospel.

At that time frequent and urgent petitions were sent from Ireland for ministerial aid. Three Congregations, Killency, Ballymoney and Ballybay adhered to the Burgher Synod, and were deeply anxious for supplies and for Pastors. On the 27th of the following June, therefore, Mr. Clark was appointed by the Presbytery to supply these vacancies, and immediately set out on his mission. His preaching was highly acceptable, and at a subsequent meeting of Synod in Stirling, a unanimous call was presented to him from this congregation, and also one from Clanannus and Scoon, near Perth, in Scotland. The former was accepted, and three members of the Presbytery of Glasgow having been appointed to fix the pastoral relation, he was ordained by them to the work of the Gospel Ministry, and installed over the Congregation of Ballybay, in the County of Monaghan, Ireland, on the 23d of July, 1751.

During the summer of 1751 he and two other ministers were formed into a Presbytery, styled the "Associate Presbytery of Down;" and now a wide field was opened before him. He loved it and his labours were abundant. But his very fitness for it soon threatened to be the occasion of his removal; for deeming him happily qualified for supplying the Institute, and having pressing callls from the Colonies of North America for ministerial help, the Synod appointed him, in 1754, to sail for Pennsylvania in the following August, and labour in the ministry there until the next April. To this he consented, for, having received a commission to "go into all the world and preach the Gospel to every creature," he held himself ready for any indication of the Divine will. Providence, however, interposed difficulties, and, by a new direction of Synod, he continued his labours at Ballybay. But while it was not yet the will of God that he should make known the riches of grace abroad, it *was* the Divine will that he should be a witness for his Master's cause at home. He lifted up his voice, with great earnestness, against what he considered defections from the purity of Christian doctrine and practice, and hereby brought upon himself a torrent of opposition. At length, as he refused to swear by kissing the book, which he believed was a Popish superstition, to which no Protestant could with propriety submit, and as he also would never consent to take the abjuration oath, in which the swearer bound himself to own the King as Head of the Church, and to help Bishops dethrone the King if ever he should become a Presbyterian; he was pursued by the hand of the civil law, and, as he was about to moderate a call in New-Bliss congregation, was arrested just as he closed his sermon. The people would have immediately rescued him, but he mildly bade them be calm and do no harm. All that night he was kept under guard in a tavern, and the next day was taken, amidst the tears of multitudes, along the road to Monaghan, and thrown into jail to await his trial. Thence he wrote letters of instruction and comfort to his people, and they came freely to him. Besides preaching to them while he was in prison, he baptized there thirteen of their children, and married one couple, who were afterwards under his pastoral care on the Catawba River in South Carolina. At length the day of trial came, but his commitment being found to have been erroneous, and his imprisonment false, he was immediately discharged; and, when he was urged to prosecute his persecutors, and had every assurance of a verdict in his favour, he gently lifted his eyes to Heaven with the exclamation,—' Vengeance is mine; I will repay, saith the Lord.' "

From that time, though often troubled, he was unfettered, and faithfully pursued his work. But his long imprisonment had served to wean him, in a great measure, from attachment to his country, which induced him to think of a field of labour in the wilds of America, where he could enjoy his religious sentiments free from the stringent arm of civil authority, which had been so powerfully thrown around him. In this feeling his people largely participated, and the Providence of God gradually made his duty clear to him. On the 18th of December, 1762, he was bereaved of his wife, who was an eminently godly woman, and not long afterwards two calls were addressed to him from America;—one from a small settlement in the Province of Rhode Island, and the other from a people near Albany, in New York. To these calls he felt disposed to listen, and the more so, as he observed a diminished attention in public worship among his people; a weariness among the youth in repeating the Scriptures and Catechism between sermons, as had been their custom under his ministry; a neglect of secret prayer by some in the intervals of public worship, and an engaging in unprofitable conversation by others; and " some," he said, " appeared in practice to adopt the Quaker's opinion, that very little or no salary should be paid to ministers, though it be God's express ordinance, saying 1 Cor. ix, 14,—'The Lord hath ordained that they which preach the Gospel should live by the Gospel.'" In view of these things, and particularly of the fact more painful to him than all others,—that " he had not heard of any person alarmed or edified by any of the public ordinances for a great while,"—he was led sorrowfully to suppose that his usefulness was at an end in that place, and to ask,—" What dost thou here, Elijah?" When, therefore, the above calls came, he concluded it was his duty to lay the matter before the Presbytery, and, on their acceding to his wish, and appointing him to supply in America for one year, he at once prepared to take his departure. On the last Sabbath of his ministry in Ballybay, he preached from 1 Cor. ii, 3,—" I was with you in weakness, in fear and in much trembling,"—a passage which " contains," said he, in a letter to them long afterwards, " the history of my sixteen years' sojourning with you."

Previous to this important step being taken, Dr. Clark opened a correspondence with the late Hon. Robert Harpur, of King's (now Columbia) College, in the city of New York, furnishing him with the names of one hundred families in the North of Ireland, that were desirous of migrating to America; and, on the 23d of November, 1763, Mr. Harpur obtained a warrant from the Government to survey a tract of forty thousand acres of land, North of the present towns of Kingsbury and Queensbury, Warren County, N. Y., for their location. Thus encouraged, Dr. Clark set sail from Newry, Ireland, on the 16th of May, 1764; but he was not alone—nearly three hundred of his people and their neighbours accompanied him. Not an untoward event occurred during the passage, and on the 28th of July they safely reached New York. Here the company divided, one portion proceeding South, and settling in the neighbourhoods of Long Cane and Cedar Spring, in North Carolina, and the other passing up the Hudson River to Stillwater, above Albany, N. Y., where they were to remain until the place of their permanent residence should be more definitely determined. To both of these companies Dr. Clark was drawn by the strongest ties of Christian sympathy and love, but his first choice was to labour with those that went North, and he was of the utmost service to them in various ways. A few of the families went on immediately to the tract in Warren County, for which Mr. Harpur had applied; but, after spending the next winter there, they were so disheartened by the dreary appearance of the country, as well as the deep snows and pinching cold, that, although Mr. Harpur obtained, on the 15th of May, 1765, a grant of four hundred acres for each family, they preferred abandoning all, if a more favourable location could be elsewhere secured, and returned to their friends at Stillwater. As the Pastor and friend of the Colony, Dr. Clark felt anxious for their best interests, and directed his attention especially to Washington County. In his exploration of that region, he visited what is now the town of Salem in the spring of 1765, and preached the first sermon ever heard there. It was in the house of Mr. James Turner,—the only house then erected on the plain where that beautiful village now stands; and the congregation was made up of a few individuals, who gathered in from the isolated dwellings in the surrounding region. To attend this service some females walked seven miles through the woods, having no other guide than marked trees.

At that time the entire township was providentially in a most favourable state for Dr. Clark's undertaking. On the 5th of January, 1763, Alexander Turner, James, his son, and twenty-two of their neighbours in Massachusetts, presented a petition to the Governor of the Province of New York for a patent, which was obtained on the 7th of August, 1764, conveying to them twenty-five thousand acres of land, which embraced the principal portion of the present town. Immediately afterwards, they conveyed twelve thousand acres of this tract to Oliver De Lancey and Peter Dubois, in the city of New York, and in the same year the patent was surveyed and divided into eighty-eight acre lots. All the parties then made divisions of their land by ballot,—De Lancey and Dubois drawing lots to the amount of twelve thousand acres; and all entered into mutual stipulations that three particular lots, situated near the centre of the town, which had been drawn by the "gentlemen," and three intervening ones, belonging to the "patentee," should be devoted to the support of a Minister and School-master. Just after these arrangements were completed Dr. Clark arrived, and, having examined the different tracts of land in that region, and ascertained the terms of their titles, he selected Salem as the most eligible spot for his Colony, and, in September, 1765, obtained from De Lancey and Dubois a grant of all the lands belonging to them in the township; they reserving a perpetual yearly rent of one shilling per acre when settled, and stipulating to pay the grantee a reasonable remuneration for procuring their speedy settlement. The way thus being prepared, the Colony removed from Stillwater, and every person who desired it received from Dr. Clark a farm, subject only to the annual rent just specified. Not long afterwards a church and school-house were erected on one of the church and school lots already described. This church was the first in the County, and, at that time, the only one in the State North of Albany. The name which the emigrants gave to the town was "New Perth," and the original tract was long known as "Turner's Patent."

In this place, which appeared so providentially prepared in the wilderness, the benevolent and devoted Pastor gathered his flock around him, and, corresponding with his friends in Scotland and Ireland, and even causing one of his people to revisit them, and lay before them the condition and prospects of this new home, he was instrumental in bringing out a number of emigrants during the following year. Nor was he unmindful of the spiritual interests of his people. With increasing diligence he gave himself to his ministerial work, and, mingling the religion of an intelligent and fruitful faith with all the affairs of the settlement, he was eminently useful, and, to this day, the savour of his name is precious throughout that region. His works do follow him, and many have risen to call him blessed.

As has been stated, Dr. Clark was a member of the Burgher Synod in Scotland, and was the first Burgher Minister who came to this country. None of his denomination were around him, and an isolated position was inconsistent alike with his feelings, his principles and his usefulness. Early in 1765, therefore, he applied to the Anti-Burgher Associate Presbytery of Pennsylvania,—the only Associate Presbytery in this country, for admission to its membership; and, after considerable delay, during which certain articles explanatory of the terms upon which he would join the Presbytery, and would be received by that Body, were drawn up and duly signed, he was admitted on the 2d of September, 1765, and thenceforward devoted himself with renewed zeal to his work. From the singular circumstance that the pastoral relation between him and the Church in Ballybay, Ireland, had never been formally dissolved by the Presbytery, that Church having risen up from Ballybay, and quietly settled down in Salem, there was never any formal organization of the Church, or installation of the Pastor, in this country; and in that situation he remained until his removal about fifteen years afterwards.

In May, 1776, the members of the Presbytery having increased to thirteen in number, and its bounds being now very extensive, it was agreed to form two Presbyteries,—the Presbytery of Pennsylvania and the Presbytery of New York. In the latter of these Dr. Clark was placed, with Rev. Messrs. John Mason, D.D., of New York city, and Robert Annan, of Wallkill, N. Y., and with them and men of kindred spirit in the cause of Christ, he laboured in making the Gospel known, and in prayerfully and anxiously seeking the unity and the prosperity of the Church. In this he was in his congenial element; and hence it was that, though his natural dislike for debate, and his multiplied labours throughout the missionary field as well as in the pastoral charge, prevented his attending the preliminary meetings of the Presbyteries, yet he was most cordially desirous of the union, which was effected between the Associate and the Reformed Presbyterian Churches, at Pequea, Pa., on the 13th of June, 1782; and by which the Associate Reformed Church was called into existence.

Thus he was at length permitted to see the church of his anxieties and prayers established, his people happily settled in their temporal concerns, and himself and them united in an ecclesiastical connection which he approved, and with brethren whom he loved, and in this situation he zealously watched for the good of the community. In various ways he planned and laboured for the public good, and a foundation was thus laid for a community which has been eminent to this day, for its intelligence, enterprize and high moral and religious character. Nor were his people ungrateful for his devotion to their interests—they loved him as the best of benefactors and friends, and their profiting under his ministry appears in their descendants to this day.

At length, however, the Head of the Church signified that he had work for him in another sphere. After several years, a few persons in his congregation conceived a prejudice against him, and, as he was at that time on a visit to the former members of his charge, who had settled in the South, and whom he found "fainting and scattered abroad, as sheep without a shepherd," he was overcome with their entreaties for the bread and water of life; and, concluding to demit his charge at Salem, he shortly after became the Pastor of the United Congregations of Cedar Spring and Long Cane, in South Carolina. Yet he never ceased to be deeply concerned for the people of Salem. He visited them several times and baptized some of their children. His last visit was in 1787, when he lectured in the church on the Thirteenth chapter of the Book of Judges, and, in a most affectionate and solemn manner, committed them all to the grace of God, until Pastor and people would meet in the Heavenly Sanctuary.

In his Southern field he gave himself to the most arduous labours. At first he preached in a rough log church, about two miles South of the present place of worship in that charge. Not long afterwards a commodious house was erected for him, and he was remarkably successful in gathering a congregation. In every place he had a message, and every incident and object furnished him with an occasion or a means of setting forth the Gospel. On one of his missionary excursions, he was overtaken, on a Saturday evening, at a tavern, in a place of great moral destitution, and not being willing to do the evil of travelling on the Sabbath, even that he might do the good of preaching, he was compelled to remain. In his closet he enquired what work the Lord would have him do in that place; and, without making himself known, waited until the Sabbath morning, when, finding there was no place of worship in the neighbourhood, and that multitudes of persons were to attend a horse-race near by, he mingled in the crowd, and at length raising himself in an elevated position, just before the race was to begin, called out, with a loud voice. " There is danger, my friends, there is danger here —let us ask God to take care of us and bless us ;" and immediately commenced a prayer, which produced a very general and powerful impression. This he followed with preaching, and that with such effect that the race was broken up, and the Gospel was effectually planted in that place.

In the discharge of his duty he was eminently faithful, and though his manner was oftentimes singular, it was generally most effective. One of his Irish members was in the habit of using minced oaths in her conversation. Having, at one time, a distressingly sore mouth, she asked him for a remedy. He gravely told her the disease probably came from the " faiths " and the " troths " and the " feign-a-bits " which she had brought over the sea, and that she could not expect to be better until she had sent them all back again.

He was remarkably attentive to the young. Catechizing was his delight, and even on a casual visit he would make some remark, or use some illustration, which would almost indelibly fix important principles in the tender mind. A venerable mother, recently deceased, in Newburgh, N. Y., could never divest herself of the impression made on her mind by his conversation, when, stopping at her father's one day for some refreshment, on one of his long missionary tours, he took her on his knee, (at that time about three or four years of age,) and in his broad dialect, and searching, but kind manner, said,—" My bonny gude girl, do you ever steal ony thing ?" " No, Sir," she lisped. " Never take a pin, or a wee bit o' riband or ony thing ?" " No, Sir." " Och, ye ha'e a bad heart, and must pray to God to tak it away for the love o' Christ, or the de'il will whop ye for ever." His letters to his different flocks were particularly instructive and impressive. He also wrote an able defence of the Scripture Psalms for the worship of God, and gave a solemn warning that a departure from what he regarded the Scripture plan would, in this, as well as in other things, be followed with the saddest results to the purity and the peace of the Church.

But the time of his departure came—it was sudden, but he was at his post. On the 25th of December, 1793, he had been sitting for some time in his study by himself, when a servant, on passing the door, heard a singular noise in the room, and, on entering, found him expiring. He was calmly sitting in his chair, apparently smitten with an apoplectic stroke. He died instantly. Before him was a letter, dated "Long Cane, South Carolina, March 15th, 1791," and addressed "to the members of his former charge at Ballybay, Ireland," as his "dearly beloved and longed for, whose great salvation from the power and practice of sin," says he, in the opening of the letter, " I have much longed for these forty years past. Some of you I still claim as my joy, even as my crown of joy." The last words were, "What I do thou knowest not now, but thou shalt know hereafter;" and the pen fell from his hand forever. He was buried amid universal regrets in the grave-yard of Cedar Spring. His resting place is near the church, and is enclosed by a brick wall and arch, while over the whole a sycamore and oak gently wave their sheltering boughs. His life was an eminently active and useful one; his death was peaceful; and there is no reason to doubt that " his rest is glorious."

I am, my dear Sir, truly yours,

JOHN B. DALES.

FROM THE REV. THOMAS BEVERIDGE, D.D.

XENIA, O., December 4, 1858.

Rev. and dear Sir: 1 have in my possession a very old and mutilated book of pamphlets, among which are two works published by Dr. Clark; and as one of them sheds some light upon his early history, it has occurred to me that some account of it might not be unacceptable to you.

The first (the title of which is lost) appears to be a republication of "The Last and Heavenly Speeches and Glorious Departure of John Viscount Kenmuir." There is a Preface to it, signed "Thomas Clark, Edinburgh, January 31st, 1749." The second is the one from which the statements in the "Church Memorial" were formed. The full title (and you will no doubt judge it sufficiently ample) is as follows:—" Some Letters from the Rev. Thomas Clark, Minister of the Gospel, to his Congregation at the New Meetinghouse in Ballybay, while Prisoner in Monaghan Jail, on account of his scruples of Conscience at some forms of expression in the Abjuration Oath, and the manner of Swearing by Kissing the Book. In regard it's judged that, as the Scotch and English Churches are, in many points, of very opposite principles, so it is inconsistent for any Presbyterian to be sworn by said oath, reduplicating in a clause of an Act therein mentioned to support the English Church principles, being formerly bound by his baptismal vows to support the principles of the Church of Scotland. Besides, it is certain that, as Kissing the Book is a superstitious form of swearing nowhere warranted in Scripture, lifting up the right hand being the form observed by God and his saints in swearing oaths, so all Christians are commanded to 'be followers of God as dear children,' i. e. in his imitable examples, Eph. vi, 1. 'And I have given you an example that ye do as I have done,' saith our Lord, John xiii, 15. Likewise a ministerial Warning and Charge to said Congregation against Sabbath-breaking, Profane-swearing, and other Vices too common in these times. 'Blessed are ye, when men shall revile you and persecute you, and shall say all manner of evil against you falsely for my sake * * * rejoice and be exceeding glad, for so persecuted they the prophets,' Matt. xi, 12. Dublin: Printed for Robert Johnston, Bookseller, 1754." On the back of

the title-page is the following: "N. B. Several of Mr. Clark's Elders, hearing of his arrestment, met him at a house on the road to jail, where they halted and agreed that the congregation should be warned to assemble, and observe the next day in Fasting and Prayer—wherefore he sent this first letter from jail to them the morning of said Fast day; and Mr. Thompson read it when public worship was over, having preached from Lam. ii, 19, "Arise, cry out in the night, &c." The congregation being very much moved, were mostly in tears that day. The "Preface to the reader" is as follows:—
'The Rev. Mr. Clark was educated in the principles of the Scotch Church from his infancy. He appeared in arms, a volunteer with the militia raised against the Pretender, Anno 1745 and 1746; having studied Divinity several years, was licensed by the Presbytery of Glasgow, 1748. Near two hundred families of Presbyterians in and about Ballybay did, about that time, leave their former teachers, because they could not find themselves edified by them, nor believe some things they taught; therefore applied to said Presbytery of Glasgow for supplies; who, considering their complaint and petitions, granted their request at last, and sent among others Mr. Clark to preach among them. Afterwards said families joined and sent commissioners to the Associate Synod in Scotland with a petition and call for said Mr. Clark being settled among them; whereupon the Synod laid aside another call that came before them for him, and appointed the Presbytery of Glasgow to ordain him at Ballybay, which, accordingly, they did, near the new meeting house, July 23d, 1751, in conformity to the rules of the Scotch Church in the like case. As the people had, for the above reasons, left their former teachers, so it is generally reckoned that spite and envy on that account moved them, particularly Mr. James Jackson of Ballybay and Mr. D. Hutchison of Monaghan, and their friends privately to be the instigators of procuring that warrant which was granted against him April 18th, 1753. Because they knew that Mr. Clark, as well as many other useful ministers, and very loyal subjects in Scotland, had, in conscience, scrupled at said oath, and kissing the Book, for the reasons foresaid; and so as the law is strong in that case, they no doubt hoped, by putting it in force, to ruin him; and so disappoint the people of his ministry, that they might be obliged to return with their stipends to their said former teachers, and be forced to take from them any sort of preaching they might be pleased to give them. Whereupon, one George Kerr, a hearer of said Mr. Jackson's, together with some others of his elders and hearers, did, on January 23d, 1754, at New Bliss, in the very time of public service, arrest Mr. Clark and carried him about fourteen miles to Monaghan Jail, escorted under a strong guard of horse and foot, raised by said Kerr for that purpose. He patiently remained prisoner in said jail until the 8th of April last, when the Right Hon. and Hon. the Lords Judges of Assize, finding the committal insufficient to detain him (Blessed be God) gave orders for his release. During his said imprisonment the following letters were sent by him to his congregation, and read publicly to them by Mr. John Thompson, probationer. Upon the people's frequent and earnest requests, Mr. Clark gave allowance to print these letters, with the Warning, which was only done in short-hand the week before his release, and extended since. He could not well refuse them to the people, seeing said letters and Warning are all the people have, instead of all those ministerial labours they had a prospect of, in case he had been at liberty of conscience which all others of his Majesty's subjects, under the name of Ministers in Ireland, yea, and the Popish priests also, enjoy, except himself only. There was again a new summons or writ issued against Mr. Clark, on or about the 24th of April last, notwithstanding what the judges had done, and is also presumed to be done chiefly at the instigation of the aforesaid New-light

teachers and their friends, in a private way, and what the end will be the Lord only knows."

After this Preface there follow four letters, dated January 24th, February 3d, March 16th and April 5th, 1754. The last is the Warning referred to in the Preface. The whole extends to fifty-two pages.

The only other publication of Dr. Clark, of which I have any knowledge, is a pamphlet entitled "Plain Reasons." It was in defence of the use of the Psalms in praise.

I will add a few anecdotes in respect to Dr. Clark, which used to be current, and which may possibly help to illustrate some of his characteristics.

On one occasion, when preaching, he took for his text Phil. iv, 13. He began by reading the first half of the verse,—"I can do all things;" and then abruptly added, "What's that you say, Paul, 'I can do all things'? I'll had ye a guinea o' that. But stop, let me see, 'I can do all things through Christ which strengtheneth me.'—Oh, yes, if that's all, I can do that, too, and I'll keep my guinea to mysel'." At another time, when preaching out of doors, having said something very pointed, he observed,—"How ye'll be all saying, 'That's very right, but it don't apply to me.' There's a man who thinks it don't suit him at all, but exactly suits that other," pointing to some individual in the Assembly; "that other man thinks it don't apply to him, but to another sitting behind him, and he thinks it don't suit him, but suits exactly that man sitting upon the fence," pointing to one in that position. On another occasion, when preaching with a brother behind him, who thought him rather tedious, and was about to give him a hint of this by pulling his coat-tail, he, very unexpectedly to the brother, remarked that, whenever Christ gave his servants any thing good to say, Satan was already behind them to pluck them by the coat-tail and get them to sit down. It is hardly necessary to add that the impatient brother did not think proper, in this way, to officiate for the Adversary. When travelling (I think in Vermont) he fell in company with a stranger with whom he rode a good part of the day. Coming at last to a place where their roads parted, they bade each other farewell, and rode each on his own way a short distance. The Doctor then halted and called to his fellow traveller to come back, saying that they had forgotten something. When met again at the forks of the road, the Doctor said to him,—" Sir, we have been travelling together some hours, enjoying each other's company, and may never meet again in this world. I think it would be well, before parting, to have a word of prayer." The stranger, though much surprised, made no objection. They dismounted, and, kneeling by the road side, the Doctor offered an appropriate and fervent prayer. He then proposed to the other that he should pray. The man declined this, and, being much importuned, at last acknowledged that he had never prayed in his life. The Doctor, however, would take no denial. He told him, if he had never prayed hitherto, it was high time to begin. The man, finding that there was no escape for him, at last kneeled down, and said,—"O Lord, thou knowest I can't pray at all." "That," said the Doctor, "is an excellent beginning—only persevere and you will do well." Many years afterwards, a minister, in his travels through Vermont, happened at a house where he lodged for the night, and finding himself in a praying family, made some inquiries, in reply to which the gentleman of the house related the above story as the history of his first attempt at prayer.

Dr. Clark, having set out with an Elder to fulfil an appointment, passed a night at a house some eight or ten miles from the place where he was to preach the next day. During the night their horses had wandered away, and in the morning the Elder insisted on setting out forthwith to hunt them. The Doctor, however, would not consent to his going till after worship, assuring him that nothing would be lost by prayer. The Elder, with great reluctance, yielded, and, much to his surprise, as soon as worship was ended, the horses were found coming up leisurely to the house. An old gentleman in Tennessee, who remembered having met Dr. Clark in one of the Carolinas, told me that, being at the time a small boy, the Doctor had taken him between his knees to talk to him. He said he had never forgotten the first question asked him:— "John, have the cats got any souls?" The above, I suppose, will suffice in the way of illustrative anecdotes.

I will only add that
I am sincerely yours,
T. BEVERIDGE.

ALEXANDER DOBBIN.
1774—1809.
FROM THE REV. JOHN McJIMSEY, D.D.

MONTGOMERY, N. Y., November 28, 1848.

Rev. and dear Sir: It gives me pleasure to comply with your request in furnishing you with some brief sketches of my excellent friend, long since departed, the Rev. Alexander Dobbin; and, in doing so, I shall avail myself of some notices of his life and character which I had occasion to prepare several years ago.

ALEXANDER DOBBIN was born in Londonderry, Ireland, February 4, (O. S.) 1742. Little is known of his parentage, or of his early religious education or exercises, excepting that his father was a sailor by profession, and probably a religious man; as it has been stated on good authority, that it was on account of the early piety of his son that he directed his studies with a view to the Ministry; and the purpose of the son to devote himself to this work was formed at the early age of seventeen. With this in view, he studied Latin and Greek in Londonderry, and then became a student in Glasgow, where he pursued his literary and theological course for seven years. On leaving College he was soon licensed to preach the Gospel, and was ordained by the Reformed Presbytery of Ireland, commonly known by the name of the Covenanters, on account of their attachment to the principles of the Covenanted Reformation in Scotland. He never had a pastoral charge in Ireland, and was ordained with the express design of leaving his native country, and preaching the Gospel in North America. From his early piety and the devotedness of his subsequent life to the interests of the Redeemer's Kingdom, there can be no doubt that he was influenced in the choice of the Gospel ministry, and of his ecclesiastical relations, by a deep sense of religious obligation. He was licensed, ordained, and married, and sailed for America,—all in the short period of six weeks. The Rev. Matthew Lind, a senior minister of the same denomination, accompanied him in his voyage, and they arrived in safety at New Castle in the year 1774. Both these excellent men were sent out by the Reformed Presbytery of Ireland to preach the Gospel in this country, in consequence of urgent solicitations for a supply of ministers, made by emigrants from Scotland and Ireland, who either had belonged to or preferred that denomination. These two ministers, soon after their arrival, with the Rev. John Cuthbertson, who had been sent to this country by the Reformed

Presbytery of Scotland as early as the year 1752, constituted themselves into a Presbytery, known as the Reformed Presbytery of North America.

Shortly after Mr. Dobbin's arrival in this country, he was settled as Pastor of a congregation at Rock Creek, near the spot where Gettysburg, Pa., now stands, although that town was not in existence until several years after his settlement in that vicinity. This was his home, and the centre of his labours, while he lived; though, for four years after his settlement at Rock Creek, he preached, the fourth part of the time, at or near Green Castle, Franklin County. In addition to his pastoral duties, which he discharged with most exemplary diligence and punctuality, he made several missionary tours, preaching the Gospel in more remote and destitute places.

Mr. Dobbin possessed an eminently catholic spirit,—an illustration of which we have in the early and prominent part which he took in the effort to heal one of the divisions of the Church; in other words, to effect a re-union between the Reformed Presbytery and the Associate Body in this country. The difference of views between these two Religious Bodies, previous to the Declaration of American Independence, related principally to the lawfulness of acknowledging the government of Great Britain, as it was constituted. This difference having been in a measure removed, in the providence of God, by the above important event, Mr. Dobbin was among the first and most efficient members of his Presbytery to countenance a union of the two denominations. As these two Ecclesiastical Bodies held substantially the same views in respect to doctrine, discipline and government, agreeably to the Westminster Confession of Faith, to which both professed their adherence and attachment, it appeared to judicious and unprejudiced men, in each of the separate Bodies, that there was no sufficient reason why they should remain distinct denominations. Both the Bodies now agreed in acknowledging the lawfulness of the civil authorities established in the United States by the Revolution, in the accomplishment of which the zealous and patriotic co-operation of the members of each of the denominations had been eminently instrumental. Mr. Dobbin, accordingly, as one of the ministers of the Reformed Presbytery, took an early and decided part in the deliberations and proceedings in relation to the proposed union. After the lapse of some years, during which several meetings of the two Bodies were held for conference and mutual explanations, the two Presbyteries of the Associate Body, (with the exception of two ministers who did not fall in with the measure,) and the Reformed Presbytery, were merged in one denomination, under the name of the Associate Reformed Synod.

Not far from the time when this union was consummated, there was an Associate Congregation at Marsh Creek, which had then recently become vacant, at the distance of a few miles from the place of Mr. Dobbin's settlement. This congregation presented a call to Mr. D., and obtained him for their Pastor for half of the time; and until the close of his ministry, he continued to preach alternately between that congregation and Rock Creek, now Gettysburg, where a new place of worship was erected for him some time previous to his death. Notwithstanding his new congregation had been formerly connected with the Associate branch of the Church,—a circumstance which might naturally enough have predisposed them to jealousy and dissatisfaction, especially as efforts were made by Ecclesiastical Bodies in fatherland to disparage the union and break it up,—yet such was the combination of gifts and graces in Mr. D.'s character, that the harmonious relations between him and his people are not known ever to have suffered the least interruption.

As an interesting and instructive Preacher, Mr. Dobbin was held in high estimation. His mode of preaching was, in some sense, extemporaneous. I do not mean by this that his sermons or lectures were not studied and well-digested; but they were not read, neither were they written out and committed to memory. His method was to make a brief analysis of his subject, and, after mature reflection, to trust to his feelings in the delivery for the appropriate language. The matter of his sermons was highly evangelical; and yet it was no further doctrinal than as it had an important bearing on Christian principles and a holy practice. His voice was strong and sonorous; his gesture striking and occasionally eccentric; and his manner, on the whole, highly acceptable. On Communion seasons he was especially appropriate and excellent.

As Mr. Dobbin had a large family to educate, and was unable, from his limited means, to send them abroad for this purpose, he was induced, chiefly by this consideration, to open a private classical boarding-school in his own house, and he continued it without interruption from 1788 to 1799. As there was no similar institution in the region, it soon came to be extensively known and patronized; and it proved in its results to be of incalculable benefit to many of the youth of that district, and through them to the next generation. He was much distinguished for his attainments in classical learning, particularly in the Latin, Greek and Hebrew languages. The late Dr. Gray, than whom it would be difficult to find a more competent judge, once said of him that, "at a meeting of their Presbytery, he gave a critical analysis of one of the Psalms, extempore, in which he displayed a profound acquaintance with the original language and with the rules of criticism." Many of his students have been distinguished in the different professions, and not less than twenty-five of them became Ministers of the Gospel. Previous to the period when the Theological Seminary in New York went into operation, under the instruction of the late Dr. Mason, Mr. Dobbin might be regarded as really the Theological Professor of his denomination; not indeed by the appointment of Synod, but by the voluntary selection of his students, and the implied approbation of the Ecclesiastical Body with which he was connected. His services in this department were of great value, and there are several clergymen still living, who can testify, from their own experience, to the ability and fidelity with which he discharged this important trust.

Mr. Dobbin was remarkably punctual in his attendance on meetings of Presbytery and Synod; and a full share of public duties, on these occasions, was always assigned to him. As a proof of the high estimation in which he was held by his denomination, he was chosen, at different times, Moderator of the Synod. This, however, was conferred upon him at the first meeting of the General Synod, held at Green Castle, in 1804; and, at the next meeting at Philadelphia, in 1805, he preached the Opening Sermon,—the last sermon, it is believed, that he ever preached in the presence of the Synod, though he attended several of its subsequent meetings.

In his private and social intercourse Mr. Dobbin was uncommonly agreeable. Being naturally of a cheerful and playful disposition, his company was always acceptable to the families in which he occasionally lodged. On one occasion, being asked by the lady of the house where he stopped, how many children he had, he pleasantly and respectfully replied,—" Madam, I have seven sons and every one of them has a sister." The answer at first excited astonishment at the size of his family, until he informed his hostess that, although he had seven sons, he had at that time only one daughter.

Mr. Dobbin was twice married. His first wife, whose maiden name was *Isabella Gamble*, he brought with him from Europe. From this union there were ten children,—seven sons and three daughters. One of the sons, *Daniel*, was a physician, and another, *James*, a lawyer. Mrs. Dobbin died on the 19th of August, 1800, in the forty-ninth year of her age. Mr. Dobbin was married, a second time, in 1801, to the widow of Daniel Agnew, of Adams County, Pa. Her maiden name was *Mary Irvin*. There were no children by this marriage. The second Mrs. Dobbin died August 21, 1824.

Mr. Dobbin continued his labours with great zeal, and no inconsiderable success, until October, 1808, when, on his way to church in Gettysburg, he ruptured a blood-vessel by coughing, and was unable to preach any more. His disease settled into consumption and terminated fatally June 1, 1809, when he was in the sixty-seventh year of his age. During the period of his decline, and in the near approach of death, he was full of peace and hope, and furnished a delightful proof of the all-sustaining power of the Gospel which he had preached. In his intercourse with his people he was very familiar, and did not scruple to play ball with them, and mingle with them in other amusements. He dressed in short pantaloons, with long stockings, and wore the wig. He had a large pointed nose, and a bright black eye. His speech was strongly marked by the foreign accent. With his great excellencies he combined striking eccentricities.

I am, dear Sir, with great respect, yours,
JOHN McJIMSEY.

FROM THE REV. JAMES M. MATHEWS, D.D.

NEW YORK. June 19, 1862.

My dear Dr. Sprague: The Rev. Alexander Dobbin, of whom you ask for my recollections, I did not know until he had considerably past his meridian; but, from the time that I was a student of Theology till his death, I had frequent and good opportunities of gathering material, from personal intercourse with him, for an intelligent estimate of his character.

Mr. Dobbin was rather small in stature, and was by no means imposing in his general appearance. His face, like his heart, was benignity itself,—his features were always lighted up with a most loving smile, and he could not open his lips but that you felt that you were in contact with a most loving spirit. Without the semblance of any thing that looked patronizing, he seemed to delight especially in acts of kindness towards his younger brethren in the ministry; never losing an opportunity to perform a kind act, or drop a cheering word, which would in any way minister to their comfort or advantage. I remember being once at a dinner party with him in Philadelphia; and, being seated next to him at the table, I took his tumbler to drink, supposing it were my own. Observing my mistake, he said to me, with great good-nature, in Scotch phrase,—what amounted to this,—" I am glad to share with you in any thing that will promote your enjoyment." He was very social and communicative, but always talked in a discreet and edifying manner. You could not converse with him, even casually, without being impressed with the idea that his soul was a fountain of pure sunbeams.

I think I never heard Mr. Dobbin preach, but he had a good reputation as a Preacher, being rather sound and instructive than brilliant or striking

Without any particular evidence in respect to his character as a Pastor, I venture to say, from what I knew both of his head and of his heart, that he was rarely excelled either in pastoral tenderness, diligence or fidelity. I often met him in Ecclesiastical Bodies, and was always impressed by the sound judgment and prudent forethought which he manifested on these occasions. Whenever he offered an opinion or a suggestion, he was always listened to by his brethren with deferential attention. Every where his simplicity, his integrity, his benevolence, his good sense, secured to him a large share of confidence and good-will, and an enduring memorial in the hearts of those with whom he associated.

Most affectionately,
J. M. MATHEWS.

MATTHEW HENDERSON, JR.
1784—1835.
FROM THE REV. A. G. WALLACE.

STEWARTSVILLE, PA., September 17, 1862.

My dear Sir: After having explored as diligently as I could the field of the Rev. Matthew Henderson's labours, (which is now my own field,) and gathered from some of the surviving members of his family whatever facts of interest they could furnish respecting him, I herewith send you the following sketch as the best result I have been able to reach.

MATTHEW HENDERSON the younger was born on Octorora Creek, Chester County, Pa., on the 10th of January, 1762; and, being the oldest child of the family, he received the name borne by his father and grandfather. He inherited from his father a large share of independence, combined with an amiable disposition and a high degree of reverence. He was carefully instructed in the knowledge of the Bible, and also of the devotional formularies of the Associate Reformed Church, but was not imbued with a sectarian spirit. His father was a liberal minded, self-sacrificing minister, who felt deeply the claims of the destitute, and therefore had a warm heart for all who earnestly laboured for their salvation. He infused the same spirit into his son; taught him to adhere firmly to his own convictions of truth, but to make the advancement of Christ's cause his primary object, and to love all who were fellow-labourers in his work.

A hundred years ago, educational facilities in this region were very limited; and hence Mr. Henderson's classical education was principally under his father. He began the study of Latin with a Mr. McGregor, a teacher of an English school, when he was about sixteen years of age. The Associate Presbytery, in order " to encourage pious and promising young men to pursue studies with a view to the Holy Ministry," appointed the Rev. John Smith " to instruct such as" might " offer themselves, in philosophy, as Divine Providence " might "lead the way." Mr. Smith being a fine scholar, and the ministerial neighbour and intimate friend of the elder Mr. Henderson, the young man was placed under his care. Of the time that he remained there, or of the progress that he made in his studies we have no account; but, as the father had a large family, and was frequently called to a distance to fulfil appointments, it is probable that the eldest son would be kept at home as much as possible. He never entered College. At the age of twenty he accompanied his father's family to the Valley of the Chartiers, and probably had charge of them during the journey. Among the earliest recollections of one of the younger brothers is the fact of his crossing the mountains, riding behind Matthew on a gray mare.

In those days the Pastor's house was sometimes, to the student of Theology, both Seminary and Home. Therefore, under his father's instructions, in the log cabin, in the scarcely disturbed wilderness, young Matthew Henderson had almost as good an opportunity of preparing for the ministry as if he had remained in the East. It is believed that he spent some time also under the care of the Rev. Mr. Smith, so that his theological course was probably more thorough than his classical. During this time the Associate and Reformed Churches were united; and, early in the summer of 1784, Mr. Henderson was licensed by the Second Associate Reformed Presbytery, which embraced the churches in Pennsylvania.

After licensure he returned to the West, and preached, by appointment, among the settlements in Westmoreland County, and part of what is now Allegheny. There Divine Providence appointed his future labours.

About seventeen miles above Pittsburg the Monongahela receivès a large tributary, called "The Youghiogheny," but locally known as "The Yough." The fine lands on these rivers attracted emigrants, who came by way of Cumberland. Those settlers who held, with characteristic tenacity, the faith of the Secession and Covenanting Churches, refused to form connections with other denominations, and, though their numbers were small, they formed Societies or Congregations of their own. One of these had their "Tent" mid-way between the rivers, about eight miles from their junction, and was known by the name given to the District, "*The Forks of Yough.*" It is now known as *Bethesda*. Across the Youghiogheny, about ten miles distant, another congregation had been formed, called *Brush Creek*, but now known as *Bethel*. In 1785 Mr. Henderson accepted a call from these congregations, and was ordained and installed in November of the same year. His field of labour was very extensive, the families who regarded him as their Pastor being scattered over a territory not less than forty or fifty miles long and twenty broad. Besides, he frequently preached in other settlements. As the population increased, other ministers came to the West, and his labours were proportionally reduced, but, for a few years, he and his father were the only ministers of the Associate Reformed Church, West of the Alleghenies.

In 1786 Mr. Henderson was united in marriage with Rebekah, the only daughter of Samuel Patterson, of Mountjoy, Lancaster County, Pa., and first cousin to Miss Patterson, who became the wife of Jerome Buonaparte. She was a lady of great personal attractions and uncommon loveliness of disposition. In her life she appears to have exemplified well what King Lemuel says concerning a virtuous woman. The heart of her husband trusted her, and many who visited in their house and enjoyed their generous hospitality, were loud in the praises of their happy family. Mrs. Henderson died in 1829,—the same year in which her husband retired from the pastorate.

About three years after his settlement, Mr. Henderson gave up the Brush Creek Congregation, and took in its place a small Society, a few miles below the present site of Brownsville. Unhappy divisions now arose. Men came in who were not satisfied with the Union, and the peace of many congregations was greatly disturbed. Mr. Henderson conducted himself with great mildness and prudence, and yet with equal firmness, and showed much ability in his discussions with those who condemned the position of the United Church. These dissensions so essentially weakened the congregations that it became necessary for him, in 1800, to resume the charge of the Brush Creek Congregation. In 1818 he was again released from it, and gave all his labours to the Forks of Yough until 1829, when he was permitted to give up the pastoral office altogether, on account of the infirmities of age. He, however, continued to preach, by appointment of Presbytery, some four years longer. About the close of 1833 his health became very feeble. In his memorandum book of sermons, opposite to the Sabbath, such notes as the following begin to appear, increasing in frequency with each successive month— "At home—cold and windy." "Heard Rev."—So and So—"Very unwell;" "In bed;" "Recovering;" "Sick;"—&c. His last sermon was preached on the third Sabbath of February, 1835, from I. Peter i, 18, 19. "Ye were not redeemed with corruptible things," &c. Three times afterwards he heard other ministers preach; and then the note, for several successive Sabbaths, evidently written each time with a most feeble hand, is, "At home, sick." The rest of the page is blank; his pen had made its last record. About two weeks before his death he took cold, under the influence of which he sank rapidly. His death-bed experience appears to have been what might have been expected from his life, hopeful and peaceful, without any remarkable demonstrations of triumph. On the afternoon of July 21, 1835, he sank to his rest, like the sun in a cloudless summer evening, without gorgeousness, but in softly blended tints, which fill our minds with glorious thoughts of Heaven.

Mr. Henderson had nine children, six sons and three daughters. One of his sons, *James P.*, received a liberal education, and is now an esteemed physician at Newville, near Mansfield, O. The other surviving members of the family remain in the vicinity of the old homestead, highly respected members of society and of the church.

Mr. Henderson was a person of commanding appearance. His voice was full and sonorous, and his delivery distinct and impressive, uniting calmness and deliberation with energy. He was not a profound scholar, but his general knowledge was quite extensive, and he had, in an unusual degree, the power of using it for the public good. He was somewhat acquainted with Medicine, and occasionally bled with the thumb lancet, and administered some of the more common and efficient medicines.

He possessed good executive ability, and managed his own affairs, and those entrusted to him, with prudence and skill. He was scrupulously faithful in fulfilling engagements. His name appears on the roll of members present at Presbytery almost as regularly as the date and place of meeting; and he was never absent without a satisfactory excuse. He often rode the Youghiogheny when the ice was running and the water was in the saddle skirts, rather than disappoint his congregation.* Sometimes, in mid-winter, he would come from the water with his feet wet, and ride to the church without stopping, and go through with two services in a house without fire,—a luxury not then introduced into

---

* In view of the times in which he lived, and the circumstances in which he was placed, it was fortunate for himself, as well as those to whom he ministered that, in the prime of life, Mr. H. was an accomplished horseman, and, when in the saddle, fully master of the situation.

meeting-houses. At an early period, he was appointed to visit some settlements in Kentucky. The greater part of his way was through a wilderness, held almost exclusively by the Indians. We now know little of the dangers and hardships of such a journey on horseback; but such considerations did not weigh much with the bold and hardy pioneers, like Mr. Henderson, and their appointments were almost sure to be fulfilled.*

In his domestic relations Mr. Henderson was exceedingly happy. His letters which remain are very brief, but they show his warm attachment to his family, and the deep interest he took in all that pertained to the prosperity of the Church and the welfare of the Country. He did not discard politics as unbecoming a Minister, and did not fear the desecration of the pulpit by the introduction of subjects of national interest. Some of his earliest impulses were received during the Revolution, and he often, in the pulpit, as in conversation, depicted the stirring scenes of that stormy period. Sensitive to every thing pertaining to the honour of the nation, he was a warm supporter of the Government in the War of 1812, and preached to the Volunteers on taking up their line of march for the defence of the country.

As a Preacher, Mr. Henderson, could not certainly be considered, in the higher sense of the word, eloquent. His sermons were unwritten. He made brief notes, but they were never before him. Even on special occasions, they were written only in outline; and hence nothing remains which could be published as a fair specimen of his discourses.† Possibly it might have been better for him to have written more; but the times in which he lived did not call for the graces of rhetoric and oratory so much as the simple and earnest exhibition of truth. His ministrations in the pulpit were instructive and edifying,—fitted to awaken the conscience and purify the heart.

---

* As Mr. H.'s visit, at this early period, to Kentucky was perhaps the most brilliant episode in his life, it may be proper perhaps to notice it a little more in detail.

Toward the close of the last century, the interior of Ohio was a savage wilderness, the white settlements being, for the most part, confined to the borders of the Ohio river, and a short distance up its tributaries. In 1794 General Wayne defeated the combined Indian tribes at Maumee Rapids; and in 1795 he concluded a treaty of peace with them at Greenville. In May, 1796, Congress passed a law authorizing Ebenezer Zane to open a road from Wheeling, in Western Virginia, to Limestone, now Maysville, Ky. In the following year, Mr. Zane, accompanied by his brother Jonathan Zane and his son-in-law, John McIntyre, both experienced woodsmen, proceeded to mark out the new road, which was afterwards cut out by the two latter. The cutting out, however, was a very hasty business, in which nothing more was attempted than to make the road passable for horsemen. This road was known as "Zane's Trace,"—about 230 miles in length, and was the one taken by Messrs. Henderson and Proudfit in their mission, in 1797, to Kentucky. What others accompanied them on this perilous expedition, going or returning, is not fully remembered; but Mr. H. had been heard to speak of a Captain Foreman as one of the party, who is believed to have been his only companion on the return. They experienced much hardship from the inclement season of the year, the fording of streams, in some instances swimming their horses through the swollen waters and floating ice, without opportunity of drying their boots and other clothing, and from the snow bending down the branches of the trees over their trail in the wilderness, and covering them sometimes several inches as they slept in their blankets at night. From his memorandum book it appears that Mr. H. preached at "Short Creek," on his way to Wheeling, September 15th and 16th, at "Sciota," or Chillicothe, on the fourth Sabbath of the same month, on his route to Kentucky, and again at "Sciota," on his return, on the fourth Sabbath of November. in the intermediate period having preached twenty-three times in Kentucky and the Southern part of Ohio, preaching twenty-seven times, in all, from the time of leaving home to his return, and baptizing twenty-nine children. His first discourse, after returning, was on the second Sabbath of December, and he must have been absent from home at least three months.

† In 1851 one of Mr. Henderson's sermons was published in the 2d vol. of the Pulpit of the Associate Reformed Presbyterian Church.

He excelled as a Pastor. He was eminently fitted for mingling with the people and moulding their character by his private influence. One, who had the opportunity of knowing him well, says,—" He was social and even gay. He was unusually beloved by the young. I distinctly remember that I never was happier than when I was in his company. He was clear in communicating instruction, tender to the sorrowful, attentive to the sick. While he was not censorious, he never even connived at what he believed wrong. He rebuked sin by gentle admonition or sad silence. He was no mischief-maker, tattling about the people, and insinuating evil of his brethren. He was prudent; and hence his influence was sought in removing jealousies and reconciling differences. He was not restless in his disposition—he mingled the conservative with the progressive, occupying the ground along the line which divides the two extremes in Church and State." None will venture to charge him with studying novelties, or attempting the introduction of new measures, yet he was deservedly ranked among the more liberal of his day. He adhered firmly to the old paths, but was among the earliest and warmest supporters of Bible Societies and other kindred Associations. He was a faithful Preacher—he did not wink at evils which he saw among the people; and he taught them to be faithful by exhibiting to them his own fidelity. But perhaps the greatest element of his power was his unquestioned piety. He made no parade of it; but it shone in all his actions, and was the spirit of his whole life. He lived in an atmosphere of love to God and man. He had a high relish for the ordinances of God's house. From the memorandum book, already referred to, it appears that, when not preaching himself, he embraced frequent opportunities of being present at the Communion in neighbouring congregations.

There were no remarkable fruits by which to measure Mr. Henderson's usefulness. There were no great revivals under his ministry. His influence, like his labours, was uniform and steady. His congregations grew in membership and in grace. Under his ministry, and that of his brethren in the General Assembly Presbyterian Church, the community in which he lived became, and continues, distinguished for its high moral character.

Assuring you of my interest in your great work, and my hope that you may be spared to complete it,

I remain your brother in Christ,
A. G. WALLACE.

FROM THE REV. H. CONNELLY.

NEWBURGH, June 19, 1862.

My dear Sir: When I was about seventeen or eighteen years of age, I began to attend on the ministry of the Rev. Matthew Henderson, and I sat under his preaching, either statedly or occasionally, during a period of five or six years. It was through his instrumentality that my mind first took a decidedly religious direction, and in due time he baptized me and admitted me to the communion of the Church. You will readily understand, therefore, why I cherish his memory with great affection, and why I am more than willing to do any thing in my power for the perpetuation of his name and influence.

Matthew Henderson was a large man, full six feet in height, of muscular frame and good proportions. His features were more than commonly large, but his countenance was expressive of ingenuousness and candour. His manners were far more cultivated than were those of the mass of clergymen, at that day, in the part of the country where he lived; indeed, I think he possessed great natural dignity, and it seemed never to cost him any effort to adapt himself most felicitously to any circumstances in which he was placed. His natural dispositions were kind and amiable, and his social powers of a high order, so that his presence was always welcome to any circle into which he might be thrown. He was, by no means, given to trifling in his conversation, and yet he was habitually cheerful, and was never offended by a witty saying or a good joke where there was nothing in the circumstances to render it unsuitable. He was exceedingly interesting in his own family. I used sometimes to visit at his house, and was struck with the fact that he was the revered centre of one of the most pleasant domestic circles that I had ever met with.

The great natural dignity, to which I have referred, gave a complexion to his professional as well as social character. In the pulpit he was the very personification of dignity. His air and manner, his mode of utterance as well as all that he said, had a sort of elevated character, well becoming the mission of an Ambassador of God. His preaching was chiefly in the way of exposition, and it was judicious, instructive and eminently successful in bringing out the mind of the Spirit. He moved about among his people in a manner that secured at once their respect, confidence and affection—it was difficult to say whether they admired, revered or loved him most. His presence in the Presbytery or Synod was always felt to be an element of strength and of safety. He adorned every relation that he sustained.

Very sincerely yours,
H. CONNELLY

JOHN DUNLAP.*
1789—1829.

JOHN DUNLAP, the eldest child of John and Margaret (Thompson) Dunlap, was born in Dolphinton, County of Lanark, Scotland, on the 15th of September, 1757. He was the eldest of five children. His parents were both members of the Church, though of different branches of it; his father belonging to that branch of the Secession called Burghers; his mother to the Church of Scotland. At the age of fourteen he was hopefully converted, and began almost immediately to have aspirations for the Gospel ministry; but there were, at that time, obstacles in his way that seemed insurmountable. His father, who was himself devoted to agricultural pursuits, was employed by a number of farmers, to go to America and purchase for them a tract of land, as a preparation for their migrating hither; he expecting to return to Scotland, and bring his family to this country, in company with those for whom he was to negotiate, the next year. Accordingly he crossed the ocean and landed in New York, in the year 1774, bringing his son John as the companion of his travels. On his arrival here he found the country in a state of deep political agitation, and he very soon entered warmly into the great controversy of the day, espousing earnestly the American cause. The next year (1775) he enlisted in the army as a volunteer, taking his son, then only fifteen years of age, along with him. They

---

* MS. Autobiog.—MS. from Rev. J. D. Wells.—Proceedings of the Fifteenth Anniv. of the Washington Co. Bib. Soc.

were at the siege and capture of St. John's, in connection with which they endured great hardships, encountered fearful perils and rendered important services. At the close of that campaign they went to Salem, Washington County, N. Y., and remained during the following winter. In the spring of 1776, notwithstanding the defeat of the American army before Quebec, and the death of General Montgomery, and the generally unpropitious state of affairs, such was the fervour of their patriotism that they again volunteered their services in the cause of freedom. It was only for a brief period, however, that the father was permitted to serve; for he was taken ill at Albany, of a disease known as the camp-distemper, and died in September, 1776, in the fifty-second year of his age. He carried his devotional habits with him into the army, observing regularly in his tent morning and evening worship, and cultivating Christian intercourse, as far as he could, with his fellow-soldiers. His wants, during his last illness, were kindly ministered to by some benevolent individuals in Albany, and he shared largely the consolations of Divine grace in the prospect of his departure, and in his passage through the dark valley. By his death the object for which he came to this country was entirely defeated.

The son was now left an orphan and comparative stranger in a strange land; and, at the close of the campaign, he retired from the army. He had never yet made a public profession of religion, though he had, for two or three years, as he believed, been living under its power; but, shortly after his father's death, he was examined and received to the communion of the Church under Dr. Thomas Clark, of Salem, who, ever afterwards, continued to treat him with a kindness scarcely less than parental. It was chiefly through Dr. Clark's influence that facilities were furnished him for obtaining an education preparatory to his entering the ministry.

From the time of his father's death until 1783 he was engaged chiefly in teaching an English school; and he had now begun to despair of ever attaining his long cherished object of entering the ministry, on account of his utter inability to meet the expenses of his education,—nearly the whole of the little property that he had received from Scotland having been lost in the depreciation of the Continental money. It was at this time that, through the conjoint influence of Dr. Clark, who had long been his steadfast friend, and Dr. John Mason, of New York, he was recommended to the favourable notice of Peter Wilson, LL.D., Principal of a very flourishing Academy in New Jersey. Dr. Wilson received him as a member not only of his school, but of his family; and there sprang up between the teacher and the pupil a degree of affectionate confidence that would not have dishonoured the relation between parent and child. Here Mr. Dunlap commenced the study of the Languages and Mathematics, and at the same time became an assistant in Dr. Wilson's school; performing his duties as a teacher during the day, and as a student during part of the night. He continued thus employed till he had finished both his classical and mathematical course, when an opportunity unexpectedly occurred, through the kindness of a benevolent individual in New York, for his prosecuting his theological studies under the direction of the elder Dr. Mason. Of this opportunity he most thankfully availed himself; and, after continuing his studies for two years, he was licensed to preach the Gospel, by the Associate Reformed Presbytery of New York, on the 13th of October, 1789.

After preaching for some time with much acceptance, as a candidate, he received a unanimous call from the Associate Reformed Congregation in Cambridge, Washington County, N. Y., which he accepted on the 13th of October, 1790,—one year, to a day, from the time of his licensure. The people composing this congregation were of different denominations,—many of them from the Ecclesiastical Body under the care of the General Assembly; and these latter, not being satisfied with the mode in which the government of the Church was there administered, very soon withdrew and formed a congregation by themselves; thereby considerably reducing the infant congregation of Mr. Dunlap. A congregation in Galway, hearing of the embarrassment to which he was subjected in connection with his charge, almost immediately made overtures to him to become their Pastor; but he declined the proposal, and actually remained with the congregation at Cambridge nearly twenty-six years.

Mr. Dunlap was one of the original Directors of the Northern Missionary Society, and its President in 1806. Having a comparatively small pastoral charge, he repeatedly undertook long and difficult journeys through the newly settled districts of the State, in behalf of this Society. By this means he acquired much familiarity with missionary life; and, accordingly, when the Young Men's Missionary Society of New York was formed, he was invited to enter into its service. With this in view, he resigned his pastoral charge in Cambridge, on the 3d of September, 1816. The field assigned him was chiefly the territory which now forms Oneida and Oswego Counties. Leaving his pleasant and commodious home in Cambridge, he removed first to Rome, and, after a few months, to Fairfield, N. Y. In the last mentioned place he preached about half the time,—his oldest son, then a student of Theology, reading a sermon and conducting the service during the other half. There was no church edifice or organization there, and their public service was held in the chapel of the Medical Academy. During the five years in which he was thus engaged in the work of Domestic Missions, he was instrumental in organizing eighteen churches, and fostering them in their infancy until several of them were able to support their own Pastors.

In 1822 Mr. Dunlap, finding his labours and exposure too severe for him, under the infirmities of advancing years, gave up his commission as a Missionary, and returned, with his family, to Cambridge. And now that he was again among the scenes of his earlier life, he resumed his active co-operation with the friends of the Bible cause in Washington County, and engaged in evangelical labours that were not interrupted until he was laid aside by disease. He was the first President of the Washington County Bible Society, from its organization in 1813 till 1816, when he left Cambridge; and his interest in this Society continued unabated till the close of his life. His chief employment, after his return to Cambridge in 1822, was supplying the vacant pulpits of the churches at Hebron, Arlington, Sandgate and Fort Ann, in each of which places his memory is still gratefully cherished.

He was laid aside from his public labours a little less than two years before his death; and, while suffering under a most painful malady, such was his love for the ministry, and such his desire to benefit his fellow-creatures to the last, that, until his strength was almost gone, he used to invite his neighbours, and especially the young people, to his house, that he might testify to the value of the Gospel, and instruct them in the things pertaining to the Kingdom.

The disease of which he died was cancer. In the fall of 1828 he submitted to a most painful surgical operation, which he endured with great fortitude. From that time until his death his sufferings were intense and almost uninterrupted, but his spirit was not only peaceful, but even triumphant. He died on the 7th of March, 1829, in the seventy-third year of his age, and the fortieth of his ministry. His Funeral Sermon was preached by the Rev. Dr. Alexander Proudfit, of Salem, who had been the companion of many of his early missionary labours, and was his faithful friend till the close of life.

His only publication was a Sermon entitled "The Power, Justice and Mercy of Jehovah, exercised upon his Enemies and his Friends"; delivered on board the Fleet at Whitehall, 1814. It passed to a second edition in 1823.

Mr. Dunlap was married, on the 11th of April, 1791, to Catharine, second daughter of Peter Curtenius, of the city of New York, the first Auditor or Comptroller of the State, after the adoption of the Constitution. They had six children, two sons and four daughters. His eldest son was educated for the ministry, but, after obtaining license to preach, was obliged to turn aside to agricultural pursuits, on account of the failure of his health. One of his grandsons, the Rev. J. D. Wells, D.D., is the highly respected Pastor of a Presbyterian Church in Williamsburgh, L. I.; and two of his grand-daughters have been married to Foreign Missionaries. Mrs. Dunlap died on the 24th of July, 1830, in the seventieth year of her age.

FROM THE REV. JOHN D. WELLS, D.D.

WILLIAMSBURGH, L. I., August 6, 1863.

My dear Sir: The Rev. John Dunlap, concerning whom you inquire, was my maternal grandfather. My recollections of him are those of a child from three to fourteen years of age. I remember him as a genial, kind-hearted old gentleman, a lover of children, a lover of good men, a friend of the poor, and a man ready for every good work.

He was fond of horticulture and agriculture, and planted trees, the shade and fruit of which he long enjoyed. He was so tender of robins and other birds that he would not have them destroyed, though we thought they had more than their share of the cherries. He loved books and had a good library. In the affairs of the nation he took the liveliest interest, having reached the country simultaneously with the sitting of our General Congress in Philadelphia, in 1774, and fought in several battles of the Revolutionary War, before he was seventeen years old. In the War of 1812 he served for a time as a Chaplain.

He was a liberal-minded and warm-hearted Christian and Christian Minister. Our family devotions were introduced by a short invocation. Then came the reading of Scripture, sometimes with exposition and exhortation. The Psalm or Hymn—for he loved the Hymnology of the Christian Church, and did not confine us to Rouse's version of the Psalms—was next; and the fervent prayer for ourselves and all men closed the service.

From the testimony of others I know that Mr. Dunlap was of a simple, confiding disposition, too honest and pure-minded to suspect others of any fraudulent intentions. For this reason he was imposed on in business transactions, and lost a portion of the property that came to him by marriage.

There was a Scotch bluntness and almost harshness of speech about him, by which, in his earlier years, he sometimes gave offence; but, in later life, his character mellowed into a pleasant and beautiful ripeness. Made perfect through suffering, he bore the image of Christ.

As a Preacher, he was plain, instructive, direct, evangelical and intensely earnest. Without a pleasant voice, he secured attention to the truths of the Gospel, by declaring them with sincerity, unction and great zeal.

It would be impossible to do justice to my grandfather's Christian or Ministerial character without making very prominent his great interest in the spread of the Gospel over the whole earth. A Domestic Missionary himself, and longing to see the land for which he had, at so early an age, put his life in peril, pervaded with the influence of truth, he watched, with ever increasing interest, the signs of the coming of Christ's Kingdom in Heathen lands. This was attributable in part—I would rather say chiefly—to his own sincere and earnest devotion to Christ, and partly also to his association with such large-hearted men as Dr. Alexander Bullions, Dr. Nathaniel S. Prime and Dr. Alexander Proudfit.

Such are some of my recollections and impressions concerning my venerable ancestor.

Very sincerely yours,
J. D. WELLS.

FROM THE REV. JOHN GOSMAN, D.D.

SAUGERTIES, November 13, 1863.

Rev. and dear Brother: You have asked me to communicate to you my impressions of the leading characteristics of the Rev. John Dunlap. My first acquaintance with him was in 1801. I had then commenced my theological studies under the direction of Dr. Alexander Proudfit, of the neighbouring town of Salem, and had frequent opportunities of seeing and conversing with Mr. Dunlap. The most prominent qualities by which he was distinguished as a Man and a Minister, were strongly indicated in his personal appearance. His countenance was expressive of great energy and strength of purpose; and while these traits were strikingly manifested throughout his whole ministry, they were specially demanded by the peculiar state of the churches in which he was called to labour.

There was in Mr. Dunlap a certain sternness of aspect, but it was only necessary to know him, to know that he was one of the most warm-hearted and genial of men. There was nothing morose nor sullen in his nature. He had a vigorous constitution, capable of great endurance. His voice was one of remarkable compass and strength. His gesture was free and appropriate, and helped to increase, in no small degree, the effect of his utterances. His aim evidently was to deliver the whole counsel of God. The trumpet in his hand never gave an uncertain sound. In the selection of his subjects he seemed most frequently to have in his eye the awakening of the careless and the unmasking of the hypocrite. When I listened to him I used often to be reminded of the voice of the stern Reformer in the wilderness,—" Repent, for the Kingdom of Heaven is at hand." But while his application of the truth to the sinner's conscience was most faithful and pungent, he was gentle to the mourners in Zion, and encouraged the Christian combatant to perseverance by holding up the promise of the sustaining sympathy of the Angel of the Covenant. In his intercourse with his brethren his great frankness and manifest sincerity inspired the utmost confidence, while his generous hospitality always secured to his guests a cordial welcome. In the Judicatories of the Church he was regarded as a wise counsellor, and an efficient co-operator in carrying into effect plans for the extension of the Redeemer's Kingdom. A careful student of his own heart, and a close observer of mankind and of the movements of Divine Providence, he was an expert casuist.

Cambridge was his first and principal charge. From his earliest ministry he was much interested in missionary efforts in the Home Department, always ready, in the destitution then prevalent in the Northern and Western parts of our State, to undertake toilsome journeys, thus laying the foundation of many churches which are now firmly established, and are active and liberal auxiliaries in spreading the Gospel at home and abroad. The labours and anxieties incident to the Pastorate, with the weight of years, led him to resign his charge. He had frequent invitations to visit vacant churches, and, in his own charge and in surrounding places, a migratory spirit prevailed which opened new and not unpromising fields of labour. Into these he entered not as a stranger, but as one who had already been to many, whom he found there, a spiritual father; and here no doubt he gathered gems which will forever adorn the Mediator's crown.

I have thus given you my recollections of one who was a friend of my youth, and whose memory I still gratefully cherish. I have no hesitation in assigning him a place with the "Elders who have obtained a good report through faith."

With sentiments of unfeigned regard I remain truly yours,
JOHN GOSMAN.

―――・・―――

JOHN YOUNG.

1790—1803.

FROM THE REV. JOHN C. YOUNG, D.D.

PRESIDENT OF CENTRE COLLEGE, DANVILLE, KY

DANVILLE, KY., May 9, 1856.

My dear Sir: It is a delicate service that you have assigned to me,—that of writing about my own beloved and venerated father. But my affectionate reverence for his memory, as well as my disposition to oblige you, will not allow me to decline your request. At the same time, I am bound to say that I was but a month old at the time of his death, so that I can say nothing in respect to his character except from the testimony of others.

JOHN YOUNG, born September 4, 1763, in York County, Pa., was the eldest son of William and Margaret (Schuyler) Young. His parents were both the younger children of families possessed of some wealth and rank in Scotland, and who had been, for generations back, distinguished for piety. After marriage they had migrated to Pennsylvania, where their means enabled them to live in comfort and independence. While both parents were distinguished for deep and fervent piety, the mother was remarkable for extraordinary intellectual endowments. Their eldest son had, from his birth, been prayerfully devoted to the service of God in the work of the Ministry. Both parents died, leaving six children, at the time when John was in his sixteenth year. The provision which had been made by will for the completion of his education, was defeated by the rapid depreciation of the Continental money, which had been received in payment at the sale of the estate. This misfortune compelled him, after closing his preparatory studies in Greek and Latin, under the Rev. W. Latta, to teach school for a time, and afterwards write in the Clerk's office at Annapolis, that he might obtain the means necessary for finishing his collegiate and theological course.

On graduating at Dickinson College, in 1788, he delivered the Valedictory

Oration, and immediately, in connection with some dozen others, commenced the study of Theology under Dr. Nisbet, the President of that Institution. He was licensed to preach April 26, 1790, by the Associate Reformed Presbytery of Pennsylvania. He was, from that period, engaged, by appointment of Presbytery or Synod, in supplying vacant congregations in the South and West, until the time of his settlement over the United Congregations of Timber Ridge and Providence, in Rockbridge County, Va., August 20, 1792. He continued in this charge until the year 1799, when he accepted a call from the United Congregations of Green Castle and West Conococheague. About the same time he received a call from Lexington, Ky., and another from the city of New York. The acceptance of the latter was strenuously urged upon him by Dr. John M. Mason, but he preferred a more retired field of labour. He continued to reside in Green Castle until his death, which took place in July, 1803. He died of bilious fever, induced by over-exertion in preaching thrice in the open air in a hot summer's day. He had, soon after his settlement in Virginia, married Mary Clarke, daughter of George Clarke, Esq., of Green Castle. He left two sons and two daughters. The oldest son, after graduating at Carlisle, at the age of seventeen, entered into mercantile pursuits, and died while still young. The daughters are still living,—one the widow of the Rev. John Lind, who succeeded my father in his last pastoral charge, the other the widow of J. P. Ramsey, a merchant of Philadelphia. My mother remained a widow till her death, a few years ago.

As a Preacher, I believe it was universally admitted that my father was more remarkable for strength and solidity than for elegance and ornament—though a strikingly fine personal appearance, a brilliant black eye that seemed to penetrate the soul of the hearer, a natural and somewhat impassioned delivery, with a pleasant voice, made his preaching as agreeable as it was instructive. He aimed to enlighten the understanding and awaken the conscience, and his preaching was greatly blessed. His sermons and lectures, even when not written, were prepared with great care; and more than one-half were written out, committed, and delivered from memory. While he was faithful and laborious in his pastoral duties, regularly visiting and catechising all the families of his various congregations, and while he devoted a considerable portion of time to discharging the duties of an Evangelist, by preaching in destitute churches, and building up new churches, he was so indefatigable in acquiring knowledge, and so thoroughly mastered all that he acquired, that his attainments, both as a scholar and a divine, were very superior in their extent as well as in their accuracy. His love of learning made study a pleasure to him, and few men have ever surpassed him in redeeming time to devote to literary and scientific pursuits.

In his general intercourse with society he so happily blended dignity with affability as to command universal respect and esteem; while, in the narrower circle of his private friends, his perpetual cheerfulness, affectionate disposition, playful wit and copious intellectual resources, made him an object of the most fond admiration and devoted attachment. There was in his character a singular union of the gentler with the sterner virtues. Uncompromising integrity, undaunted courage and inflexible principle, were found in him, in conjunction with a purity of sentiment, delicacy of taste and tenderness of feeling, that were almost feminine. To warm and generous affections he united a serenity of disposition, so unvarying that one who had lived for ten years in the closest daily and hourly intercourse with him, had never but once seen his temper in the slightest degree ruffled.

I have now given you the substance of what I know in respect to my father, and if it shall avail at all to your purpose, I shall be truly gratified.

Very truly your friend,
J. C. YOUNG.

FROM THE REV. JOHN McJIMSEY, D.D.

CRAWFORD TOWN, ORANGE COUNTY, N. Y., March 20, 1850.

Rev. and dear Sir: I am happy to learn that you propose to include in your intended work some account of the life and character of the Rev. John Young, whose ministry, in the all-wise but mysterious Providence of God, was brought to a close while he was yet in early life, nearly half a century ago. In accordance with your request, I take great pleasure in stating to you what I personally know in regard to him. Of his early life and history I have no knowledge, the place of our birth and residence being at some distance from each other. While a student at the Seminary of the Rev. Alexander Dobbin, I first saw Mr. Young, and heard him preach before Presbytery his first trial sermon, which was highly approved, and was considered as giving promise of future eminence. About the time I entered Dickinson College, or soon after, he, with seven other young men, finished their course of theological study, under the learned Dr. Nisbet.

As Mr. Young was soon after licensed and settled as the Pastor of Timber Ridge Congregation in Virginia, I had little opportunity of intercourse with him, or of hearing him preach, until the time of my own licensure. After that period, I met with him more frequently, and was always edified by his conversation, and pleased with his general bearing. Soon after my licensure I was appointed, by Synod, to visit Kentucky and preach for some months in places where my services might be desired, and where Mr. Young had previously been sent on a missionary tour; and, wherever I went, I found that both his preaching and his character were held in high estimation. On my return through Virginia, I called at his house, and was treated by him and his excellent lady in the kindest and most hospitable manner. I remained with him over the Sabbath,—it being a Sacramental occasion,—and heard him preach on the morning of that day. His text was Genesis, xlix, 26, in its connection; but chiefly the last clause of the verse—"They shall be on the head of Joseph, and on the crown of the head of him that was separate from his brethren." Christ, the Mediator, the subject of the prediction, and the great antitype, was the delightful theme of the sermon, and it was rich in evangelical truth, and delivered with great solemnity and pathos. I do not recollect that I ever heard him preach afterwards, although I saw him repeatedly at meetings of Synod.

As a Preacher, Mr. Young took a decidedly high rank. His enunciation was distinct and deliberate, but without hesitancy; his language clear and forcible, but not florid; the subject matter of his discourse doctrinal and instructive, but having a decidedly practical bearing. He had but little gesture, but that little was natural and appropriate. His whole manner was dignified, solemn and impressive. Like Cowper's favourite Preacher,—

"He was serious in a serious cause."

As an evidence of the deep interest which Mr. Young felt in the cause of Christ and his truth, I may here state an incident which occurred shortly before his decease, and when he viewed his death as very near at hand. As the General Synod was to hold its first meeting, after its organization at

New Castle, in May following, he left it as his solemn dying charge, to be given to his brethren, at the meeting of the Synod, that, as the cause and truth of Christ were committed to their care and keeping, they should be faithful to their trust, as they would have to give an account of their stewardship. This solemn charge of a dying brother was delivered from the pulpit, to the fathers and brethren in Synod assembled, by the late Dr. Mason, in the close of his Sermon, at the Opening of the Synod, in a very impressive manner. So solemn a charge, under the circumstances connected with it, came with an almost overpowering force.

Faithful and dignified as was Mr. Young in his character and deportment as a Minister of Christ, he possessed all those qualities as a Man, which were necessary to render him a most agreeable companion and valuable friend. With great decision he united great kindliness of spirit—he was meek, and modest and without pretension, while yet he was ready to every good work. His early death blasted many fond and cherished hopes.

With great respect and esteem,
Your friend and brother,
JOHN McJIMSEY.

As the Rev. Dr. JOHN C. YOUNG, the writer of the first of the preceding letters, has gone to his rest, and as he occupied a position of high influence in the Presbyterian Church, it is thought proper that some notice of him should appear in connection with the sketch of his father, notwithstanding his death occurred at too late a period to place him within the legitimate limit of this work.

JOHN CLARKE YOUNG, a son of the Rev. John Young, and Mary Clarke, his wife, was born in Greencastle, Pa., on the 12th of August, 1803. His father dying while *he* was an infant, he was brought up entirely under the direction of his mother, a wise and judicious woman, who was spared to see her only living son occupying a high position of honourable usefulness. Having gone through his course preparatory to entering College, under Mr. John Borland, an eminent teacher in the city of New York, he was for three years a member of Columbia College, but, at the end of that time, transferred his relation to Dickinson College, where he graduated in 1823, during the Presidency of Dr. John M. Mason. He had already united with the Church, and determined to prepare for the Ministry under Dr. Mason, having declined an offer to enter the profession of the Law, under the auspices of his maternal uncle, Matthew St. Clair Clarke, at that time an eminent practitioner and politician. He entered the Princeton Theological Seminary in 1824, and remained there two years; and then, in 1826, became a Tutor in the College of New Jersey, where he served till 1828. He was licensed to preach, in the spring of 1827, by the Presbytery of New York. After preaching in several Eastern cities, where he was strongly solicited to settle, he visited Lexington, Ky., and was elected and installed Pastor of the McChord Presbyterian Church in that city. In the fall of 1830 the Presidency of Centre College, at Danville, becoming vacant by the resignation of Dr. Blackburn, Mr. Young, though only entering his twenty-eighth year, was unanimously chosen his successor. For nearly twenty-seven years, and until his death, he occupied this honourable position with great credit to himself, and with the highest advantage to the institution.

In 1834 the Presbyterian Synod of Kentucky, at its meeting in Danville, passed some very decided Resolutions favourable to the gradual emancipation of the slaves. A very able Address, from the Committee, written by Mr. Young, was published, and widely circulated, and attracted great attention. He had subsequently an animated discussion with Messrs. Steele and Crothers, of Ohio, on Abolitionism, in which he drew a broad line between the Antislavery views of the Emancipationists of Kentucky and those of the Abolitionists. He continued until his death the advocate of gradual emancipation.

The Presbyterian Church in Danville having become vacant in 1834, he was invited by the congregation to supply their pulpit. He entered upon this duty, in connection with his duties to the College, as an experiment; and he continued its performance, with great acceptance and success, for twenty-three years—in the First church until 1852, and then in the Second church,—a branch of the same congregation, until 1857. The original congregation had grown under his ministry until the pastoral labour had become more than he was able, in consistency with his other duties, to perform.

In 1839 he was honoured with the degree of Doctor of Divinity from the College of New Jersey. In 1853 he was Moderator of the General Assembly of the Presbyterian Church.

Dr. Young's health was generally good up to the last two years of his life. During that period he was afflicted by a disease of the stomach, which finally terminated in a hemorrhage, causing his death on the 23d of June, 1857. He died, as he had lived, cheerfully and piously.

During his residence in Lexington he was married (November 3, 1829) to Frances A., the eldest daughter of Cabell Breckenridge, and grand-daughter, by her mother's side, of Dr. Samuel Stanhope Smith. By this marriage there were four daughters, three of whom are married to clergymen. Mrs. Young died in 1837; and in 1839 he was married, a second time, to Cornelia, daughter of the Hon. John J. Crittenden, by whom he had six children,—three sons and three daughters. His two eldest sons were graduated at Centre College—one of them is already (1863) in the ministry, and the other in a course of preparation for it.

Dr. Young published A Speech delivered before the Kentucky Colonization Society, 1831 or '32; An Address on Temperance, delivered at the Court House in Lexington, Ky., 1834; An Address to the Presbyterians of Kentucky, proposing a plan for the Instruction and Emancipation of their Slaves. By a Committee of the Synod of Kentucky; accompanied by an Appendix, entitled "The Doctrine of Immediate Emancipation Unsound, in reply to Brothers Steele and Crothers," which had at first been printed in the newspaper, 1835; The Duty of Masters: A Sermon preached in the Presbyterian Church at Danville, Ky., 1846; A Sermon on the Sinfulness, Folly and Danger of Delay, in a volume, edited by the Rev. Thomas P. Akers, 1851; An Address delivered at the Inauguration of the Professors of the Danville Theological Seminary, 1854. After his death, a Sermon on Prayer was published by the American Tract Society.

The following is an extract from a communication from the Rev. R. W Dickinson, D.D., dated Fordham, April 20, 1863.

"When Mr. John C. Young, on entering the Seminary at Princeton, took a room in the house in which I was boarding, I found myself prepossessed in his favour, no less by his personal appearance than from what I had previously heard of him. There was a quiet dignity in his person, an air of intelligent serious purpose in his countenance, blended with an expression of purity and benignity, that awakened an interest in him, and betokened more than ordinary promise: it was manifest, too, that he was scholarly and regular in all his habits, and withal consistently devout. Amiable, considerate, exemplary, he had few, if any, of the faults which, not unfrequently, may be detected in the character of students. He was seldom ruffled; never readily excited or depressed; equally removed from coarseness and levity; not unmindful of the feelings of others nor forgetful of his own dependence and responsibilities. Though highly valuing his time, he was not annoyed by interruptions, nor averse to inquiries, nor backward to aid others in study,—having equal facility in acquiring and communicating knowledge. Courteous to all whom he might meet, yet was he, in a sense, reserved; and it was only in the company of the few that he 'unbent'—having comprehended the significancy of Lawyer Pleydel's remark, 'that there are some people in the world who have too much malice or too little wit.'

"So far as I observed, Mr. Young was never troubled with doubts, which beset the minds of some of our number at the time,—doubts either in relation to his own interest in the Saviour, to the truth of Christianity, or even the truth of any articles of our faith. He never ventured beyond the limits of legitimate speculation, nor discussed a point for the sake of discussion. This was apparent in an Association composed of twelve members of the Seminary, (called the Round Table Club,) meeting once a month for the purpose of discussing various points. While some of us thought that we paid Truth but an easy homage if we contented ourselves with overlooking or underrating the weapons of her opponents, Young always opened or closed on the side of orthodoxy, and thought it better, if we must argue, to speak in the name of an opponent, not as if we held antagonistic opinions—so that, on one occasion, while I was contending that an ignorant ministry was more favourable to piety than a learned one, he virtually reproved me because I had spoken as if I really believed what I had said.

"His particular talent, however, seemed to be for the languages. He mastered the Hebrew with ease; read the classics with zest; appreciated their beauties; quoted with accuracy from both the Greek and Roman authors; drew from them and from Ancient History his happiest illustrations; and, having formed his taste on the best models, discriminated with precision and criticised with judgment. I do not think that he would have been regarded as either witty or ludicrous; though no one enjoyed the flashes of wit, or was quicker to perceive a vein of humour or to narrate an amusing incident, than he. While his sense of the ludicrous was never at fault, he had no sympathy with ridicule, much less with unnecessary or unjust severity. Thus, when, towards the close of a very serious meeting, in the 'Theological Chamber,' at which we were prayerfully considering the best means of promoting a Revival of Religion, a certain brother rose, and in a little, sharp, quick voice, said,— 'I think the best means would be for the brethren to pay their debts—I heard a storekeeper say that he could never become *pious* till some of the brethren paid him what they owed him'.—Young was painfully subjected to what good old Dr. Miller used to call the *contentio laterum*. On the other hand, when the late Dr. John M. Mason, the last time he ever moderated the Second Presbytery of New York, replied to a candidate for licensure who had modestly said (for the old gentleman's articulation was not then distinct) that he did not exactly understand the question,—'Can't help that, young man, can't help that—*can't give you understanding!*' Young had no sympathy with the suppressed laugh that pervaded the Body—he felt too much for the candidate.

"In short, it was Mr. Young's object, while he was at the Seminary, to fit himself for his work; to avoid every thing at variance with it, and to render all his studies subservient to the defence and illustration of revealed truth; and all this so diligently and quietly, without ado or ostentation, that it might have been difficult to say whether it was the result of grace or of early educational training; yet, though so studious and intellectual, he never lost sight of the importance of personal piety, nor neglected the cultivation of his spiritual nature.

"I heard him preach his first sermon in the old Cedar Street Church for the Rev. Dr. McElroy. It was characterized, as I presume all his subsequent discourses were, by just views and right sentiments, expressed in a clear, correct and rather ornate style; a steady advance of thought rather than by flights of eloquence or bursts of emotion; leading me to the conclusion that he would never fail to interest, to instruct, and to influence aright all whose privilege it might be to listen to his pulpit utterances or to cultivate his personal acquaintance.

"On leaving the Seminary I saw him but seldom, and then only for a short time, during his occasional visits to the North; yet I lost not my interest in him, nor was ever surprised to hear of his growing reputation and influence in the sphere in which he was so early placed after going to Kentucky, and for which he was eminently qualified by the whole course of his youthful studies."

R. W. D.

ANDREW OLIVER.
1792—1833.
FROM THE REV. ARTHUR BURTIS, D.D.

BUFFALO, October 8, 1864.

My dear Sir: I cheerfully comply with your request to send you some account, including my own recollections, of the life and character of the Rev Andrew Oliver.

ANDREW OLIVER was born in the parish of Abbotsrule, Roxburghshire, Scotland, on the 31st day of January, 1762. His father, George Oliver, of English descent, led the humble life of a shepherd. His mother, Helen Freeman, who was Mr. Oliver's second wife, was a woman of eminent piety. They had four children, of whom Andrew was the youngest. He attended for a season a classical school in the North of England, and it is said that he was engaged for a time in learning the printer's business. He seems to have been a child of God from his earliest years. He was so young when he became a subject of Divine grace that he could not remember the date of his conversion. At the age of fourteen he was received into the church. When about twenty-four years old, he married Elizabeth, daughter of Robert Ormiston, a substantial farmer of Eckford-East-Mains, Roxburghshire. Her mother's name was Mary Given. Shortly after his marriage in 1786, he came over to this country. After residing two years at Saco, Me., he removed to Londonderry, N. H., where he became acquainted with the Rev. William Morrison, by whose influence he was led to prepare for the Gospel ministry. He studied with Dr. Morrison and applied himself to his work with so much assiduity and devotion that he became almost blind. After his licensure by the Presbytery of Londonderry in 1792, he undertook a missionary tour on horseback to the State of New York, taking with him, on account of his blindness, a young man as a guide. Though labouring under this great disadvantage, his preaching was very acceptable and edifying. After his return in 1793, he was called to take charge of the Presbyterian Church in Pelham, Mass. During his ministry in this place, he enjoyed the society of the neighbouring ministers, and was an intimate friend of the Rev. Samuel Taggart of Colraine and Dr. Parsons of Amherst. Entering upon his work with large and liberal views of ministerial duty, and full of missionary zeal, he preached the Gospel in the region round about Pelham, and gratuitously supplied the pulpit of a neighbouring society at such times as would not interfere with his regular services at Pelham. He did not regard it as consistent with his notions of integrity and his pastoral relation to the church of Pelham to receive any compensation for these services. But the people whom he had served made him a present of about forty dollars. Instead, however, of accepting this gift, he divided it between the church of Pelham and the Society which had given it, and thereby both were offended,—the one because he did not keep the whole of the proffered gift, and the other because he shared it between the two Societies. To his honest and unselfish mind their displeasure at his conduct seemed quite unreasonable, and he was so troubled at this development of what appeared to him selfishness and injustice that he determined to resign his charge and seek a new field of labour. Leaving his family at Pelham, he set out in search of a new home, and extended his inquiries into the State of New York, where, several years before, he had laboured for a time as a Missionary. He spent several months in Springfield, Otsego County, N. Y. His services were so acceptable to the people of this place that they invited him to become their Pastor. He accepted the call, and, having made arrangements for his settlement, went back after his family. This consisted then of his wife and seven children, all of whom, except the oldest, were born at Pelham.

When Mr. Oliver came to Springfield in 1806, there was no Presbyterian house of worship. He preached in the Baptist Church on the hill at West Springfield, and also for a season half the time at Middlefield, in a barn. After about nine months, he purchased a small farm at East Springfield, and built a commodious house with money that was due to him from Pelham. His son William, then a boy fourteen years old, went after it on horseback, bringing the money home with him in his belt. Feeling the necessity of a house of worship, he urged the people to undertake the work of erecting one. When the frame was up, and the completion of the work was delayed, in order to arouse their zeal in the enterprise, he preached an earnest and stirring sermon on Haggai i, 4: "Is it time for you, O ye, to dwell in your ceiled houses, and this house lie waste," &c. He contributed of his own limited means to this undertaking, and encouraged the people until the work was finished. He laboured here with great faithfulness and success for several years, when an unhappy division arose, originated by persons who did not relish the Calvinistic doctrines of Mr. Oliver. They succeeded in driving away the venerable Pastor from the field, which he had cultivated with great faithfulness and with abundant tokens of Divine favour. On parting with them he preached an affectionate Farewell Sermon from II Cor. xiii, 11. "Finally, brethren, farewell; be perfect, be of good comfort, be of one mind, live in peace; and the God of love and peace shall be with you." The best of his flock, with an attachment and devotion to their afflicted Pastor rarely equalled, followed him, and afterwards united with the Associate Reformed Church which was organized under his auspices. On one occasion, after his removal from the Presbyterian Church, he so far controlled his feelings as to attend a Communion service on the Hill, in the church from which he had been ejected, and which had now called another minister. But he was passed by and not permitted to participate in the service. This treatment was a severe trial for his gentle forgiving spirit. His labors in connection with the Associate Reformed Church were richly blessed, and his associations with the ministers of that Body pleasant and peaceful. In the year before his death, during his illness, his pulpit was supplied for some time by the Rev. Malcolm N. McLaren, D.D. His congregation had erected a new house of worship at East Springfield, where their beloved Pastor continued to preach, until he was called to rest from his labours on the 24th of March, 1833.

To this event Mr. Oliver had long been looking forward with that sure and steadfast hope "which entereth into that within the vail." Living by faith and walking with God, he had been for years anticipating the time of his departure. In a letter to his son, Dr. Andrew F. Oliver, of Penn Yan, dated December 12, 1829, he thus alludes to the approaching end of his pilgrimage:—

"I am now in advanced life, and the increasing infirmities of old age notify me that my pilgrimage cannot be far from its close; and well will it be if I can say, with the great Apostle, when my journey is ended,—'I am now ready to be offered,

—I have fought a good fight, I have finished my course, I have kept the faith: henceforth there is laid up for me a crown of righteousness.' The great end of living should be to live well in order to die well, and those only die well who die in the Lord. The warfare is not yet ended, and the enemy appears very powerful at times, but the Captain under whom I serve, in whom I have long put my trust, I firmly believe, will finally gain for me the victory. And what an inconceivably glorious victory will it be when I shall stand on the verge of time, and through free grace be able to say, 'I have fought a good fight, I have finished my course.' If so, my passage through the Jordan of death will be far more glorious and happy than that of the ancient people of God through the river Jordan. It is true they had the ark of God, the symbol of the Divine presence; but I think I shall have the real presence of my great Immanuel, according to his own promise,—'I will never leave thee nor forsake thee, &c.'"

During Mr. Oliver's residence in Otsego County, he enjoyed the society and friendship of the Rev. Dr. William Neill, then of Albany, and the Rev. John Smith, of Cooperstown, Dr. James Carnahan, of Utica, Rev. Eli F. Cooley, of Cherry Valley, the Rev. Daniel Nash, of the Episcopal Church, and others, by each of whom he was highly esteemed. He was instrumental, with others, in forming the Otsego County Bible Society, which was organized March 7, 1813. The Rev. Daniel Nash, of Exeter, was the first President, and Mr. Oliver, the first Vice-President. In 1816 this Society appointed him, together with the Rev E. F. Cooley, of Cherry Valley, and James Fenimore Cooper, of Cooperstown delegates to co-operate with others in forming the American Bible Society.

The personal appearance of Mr. Oliver was dignified and commanding. He was tall and well-proportioned, with blue eyes and a full forehead, to which his habit of combing his hair back gave prominence. His countenance bespoke benignity and intelligence. He was plain and simple in his diet, and neat and becoming in his dress. His manners were gentle and conciliating; and his modesty and humility, his sincerity and guilelessness, apparent to all. His winning ways won the confidence of children, whom he often entertained with stories of the old country.

Deeply imbued with a missionary spirit, he made himself acquainted with the work and wants of the Church. It was his constant custom to ride over to Cherry Valley every Monday morning in his gig, and get from his daughter, Mrs. Morse, the New York Observer, Missionary Herald and other periodicals, which he read with avidity.

Though ardently attached to the doctrines of the Church of his fathers, Mr. Oliver had not a particle of bigotry. He loved all who loved the Saviour. He did not magnify indifferent points by making them vital articles of faith and terms of communion. During his ministry in the Presbyterian Church, he used Watts' Psalms and Hymns, though some of his people did not approve of the practice.

As a Preacher, he was simple, earnest and affectionate. It was no uncommon thing for him and for his hearers to be moved to tears. He rarely ever wrote out his sermons, but generally preached from very brief notes. His discourses were rather expository than topical; his arrangement quite methodical, yet natural, and his application pointed and practical. He was very fond of taking his texts from the "Songs of Solomon," and the "Revelations." His sermons, though marked more by simplicity, unction and earnestness, than by elegance or strength, made a deep impression on the minds and hearts of his hearers.

As a Pastor, he loved to visit the homes of his people. Few could minister so well as he the balm of consolation to the afflicted. His prayers were full, fervent and comprehensive, abounding in Scriptural language and breathing the spirit of adoption. But it was at Communion seasons that he was most effective, and came nearest to God and to the hearts of his people. He appeared then, as one of his people said of him, "as an angel of light." It was his custom to have a Fast on Thursday, the Preparatory Lecture on Friday, and also a service on Monday after the Communion. He always wore bands when he administered the Lord's Supper. He retained, for some time, the practice of the Scotch churches of giving tokens to the communicants, and he gave the token in such a manner as to impress the recipient with the great solemnity of the service, sometimes saying, as he gave it,—" When you receive this, may you also receive the grace of God in your heart." He administered also the sacrament of Baptism with great impressiveness, and pointed out to parents their covenant obligations with unusual clearness and earnestness.

Regretting that my time and opportunities have not permitted me to give you a more perfect sketch of one whose "memory is blessed" and worthy of all praise,

I am, Rev. and dear Sir,
Very truly yours,
ARTHUR BURTIS.

FROM THE HON. ANDREW OLIVER.

PENN YAN, N. Y., August 17, 1864.

My dear Sir: I remember very little of my grandfather, but that little is all beautiful. He appeared to me when a boy—and the memory is fresh to-day—as a true Christian Gentleman. He possessed great benignity of disposition. He was very kindly in his manners, venerable in appearance, and dignified in carriage. When he was excited in the pulpit, or out of it in family devotion and exhortation, which was in the old Scotch fashion, very common in those days, but very rare now, he expressed himself with a natural elegance and power truly eloquent. If all we leave after us really worth any thing is the memory of us, then certainly he left after him a precious and blessed legacy in one of the noblest and purest of memories,—one that is more true and worthy and really more deserving the monumental pile than that of the most successful gainer of earthly glory.

Very sincerely yours,
A. OLIVER.

FROM JACOB SUTPHIN, ESQ.

BROCKPORT, N. Y., August 11, 1864.

Dear Sir: My first recollections of Mr. Oliver began in 1806, when I was about five years old. I went with my mother to hear him preach in the old Yellow Meeting House. His text was: "Remember now thy Creator in the days of thy youth," &c. It was a sermon for children, and the first sermon I ever heard. Though my mother had not failed in teaching me the rudiments of Gospel truth, yet such was the power of the sermon that I resolved to be good, to make my salvation sure and to become a Minister. Soon after, he came to our house and left there a New England Primer; and we three, Joseph, Ellen and myself, began to commit the Catechism to memory. In the winter he came to catechise us as a family. I remember that he twice visited our school-house to catechise the neighbourhood, when he found it filled with parents and children, the parents standing in classes of about ten, and the children all seated in a row. He framed his questions so as to have the answer he wished, Yes or No. You perhaps may think that I have an uncommon memory; but it is not so. The reason is he made his mark on that generation. His manner was remarkably kind and gracious, and his heart full of love. This was the secret of his power. He was one of the "meek of the earth," as his after life clearly demonstrated. Under the greatest provocations he possessed his soul in patience.

His manner in the pulpit was calm, gentle, dignified and persuasive. His countenance always brightened when he found his hearers interested in his sermon, especially when he spoke to them of the love of Christ, a theme on which he always dwelt the longest. He was a profound student of the Prophecies. I retain more ideas concerning the "Man of Sin" from him than from all other preachers I have ever heard.

I remember that my mother would often say, as we were seated around the table after meeting,—"I wonder if there was any thing forgot or left out of the prayer this morning." He was pre-eminently a man of prayer; and though there might be a sameness in his prayers in the pulpit that was annoying to the worldly, they were full of unction to the godly.

His manner at Communion was truly impressive. He made the Sacramental services most solemn and affecting. I remember to have wondered why such men as old Deacon Sheldon and such women as old Mrs. Wilson should weep at "the gracious words which he spake;" but it is all plain to me now. He made more out of the Abrahamic Covenant than any man I have ever heard, and always availed himself of the ordinance of Baptism, to enforce the privileges, duties and blessings of that Covenant. He aimed at laying the foundation of a Gospel experience in a knowledge of what God has revealed.

I can only add that I am aware that this is a poor copy of the original. About the year 1820, soon after I united with his church, his deepest troubles began. In 1826 I left Springfield, and only visited the place twice after that during his life. When I heard of his death I could only exclaim,— "How are the mighty fallen and the weapons of war perished!"

I confess that to begin this was quite an irksome task, for it is a kind of work to which I am little accustomed; and I also confess that in the performance of it I have, as in the performance of many other duties, found much pleasure; for it has given me an unexpected opportunity of testifying to the worth and excellence of one of God's faithful servants.

Yours with much respect,
JACOB SUTPHIN.

FROM JAMES THOMPSON, Esq.

PENDLETON, N. Y., July 9, 1864.

Rev. and dear Sir: In answer to your request to give you my recollections of the Rev. Andrew Oliver, I would say that he was tall in stature and venerable in appearance. He seemed to be a man of feeble constitution. His manners were uniformly mild and agreeable. In conversation he was always interesting, yet grave and solemn. His style of preaching was much like that of the old Scotch divines, such as Boston and the Erskines. After taking his text, he would give a somewhat long introduction, then lay out the several heads, and, taking them up separately, would explain and enforce them with great clearness and ability, and lastly make the application. Though he never used written sermons, yet he was as systematic as any man I ever heard. In one branch of ministerial duty he excelled all I have ever known, and that is in the administration of the Lord's Supper. This ordinance was administered twice a year. He often had the assistance of the Rev. James Mairs of Galway on such occasions, and he made Communion seasons more solemn and interesting than any I ever witnessed before or since. He made it a point to visit all the families in the society twice every year. He would give notice from the pulpit that he would visit a certain section on a given week, and so would go through the congregation. Besides this, once every year he called the young people together at different times, in different parts of the town, for public catechising. In receiving members into the Church he was very close and careful in examining each candidate for admission.

   I am, Rev. and dear Sir,
     Your most obedient servant,
              JAMES THOMPSON.

GEORGE MAIRS.*
1793—1841.

GEORGE MAIRS was born at Drumbeg, Monaghan County, Ireland, in April, 1761, being the second son by his father's second marriage. Both his parents were devout and earnest Christians, and were especially careful in the religious training of their children. His father was a linen draper, and originally designed this son for the loom. One day, however, being somewhat vexed at his son's rather unpromising attempts to become initiated in the mysteries of this occupation, he rather abruptly told him to quit it, and never try his hand at it again. George, not feeling himself drawn very strongly toward the loom, was more than willing to yield to his father's prohibition; and he remained unsettled as to his future course until he had reached his sixteenth year, when his stepbrother proposed that he should enter upon the study of Latin, and, if he were thus disposed, should prepare for the ministry. His brother referred him for advice to an elder half-sister, who also had a son of about his age. On being consulted, she immediately fell in with the suggestion, and arranged that the two should pursue their studies under a private tutor in a room which she caused to be fitted up for the purpose in her own house. That young associate in study was William McAuley, afterwards a very useful Minister of the Associate Reformed Church, in Delaware County, N. Y.; and these two proved the nucleus of a school of a dozen boys, nearly all of whom became Ministers of the Gospel, and one of whom was the Rev. Joseph Kerr, D. D., who was, for a long time, one of the lights of the Associate Reformed Church in Pennsylvania.

From this preparatory school young Mairs went to the University of Glasgow. Here he applied himself to his studies with great diligence, and made very rapid progress, especially in the Latin language. Up to this time, though he had been designed for the Ministry, he had never been the subject of any permanent religious impressions; but, shortly after entering the University, he became deeply sensible of his guilt and ruin, and his mind was so powerfully wrought upon that his health failed, and he was obliged, for the time, to quit his studies and return home. But it was not long before the clouds which had gathered around him passed off, and the peace that passeth understanding gained possession of his soul. While he was upon his knees, earnestly supplicating God's gracious interposition in his behalf, he seemed to be suddenly lifted into a region of light and glory,

---

* Christian Instructor, vii.—MS. from his son, Rev. George Mairs.

and had the new song upon his lips, even the song of praise to a forgiving God. He immediately apprised his father of the happy change he had experienced, and received from him appropriate counsel and instruction. And now he was prepared to return to College, and to pursue his studies with a very different spirit from what he had ever done before. Having, in due time, honourably completed his college course, he placed himself, as a theological student, under the instruction of that great and good man, John Brown of Haddington. Here he remained, for some time, engaged almost exclusively in the study of the Bible; and, having completed the prescribed course, he was licensed to preach the Gospel by an Associate Presbytery in Ireland. After labouring as a probationer for eighteen months, he was ordained and installed in the pastoral charge of the Congregation of Cootehill, County of Cavan. Here he laboured with great acceptance, and not a few became the hopeful subjects of renewing grace through his instrumentality.

At that time frequent calls for help in spiritual things were heard from some of the new settlements on this side of the Atlantic. Mr. Mairs, partly from sympathy with those here who were destitute of religious privileges, and partly from his dislike of the interference of the magistrate in spiritual things, with which the Dissenting Churches in his own country had to contend, finally resolved on seeking a field of labour in this Western world. Accordingly, on the 2d of May, 1793, at a meeting of the Presbytery of Ballybay, he demitted his charge, and on the 12th of the same month, sailed for New York, where he arrived in August following, being accompanied by his brother, the Rev. James Mairs, who afterwards became Pastor of the Associate Reformed Church in Galway, N. Y. On the first Sabbath after their arrival, they preached for the Rev. John M. Mason, (the youthful successor of the Rev. Dr. John Mason, who had died the year before,) and, by his advice, set out the next day for New Perth, (now Salem,) Washington County, the residence of the Rev. James Proudfit. There they spent their second Sabbath; and the subject of this sketch, as he came from the pulpit, was not a little affected at finding numbers of persons gathering around him, and recognizing in him, with heartfelt joy, the minister they had heard in their native land. At the suggestion of Mr. Proudfit, he went, the next week, to a settlement at Galway, Saratoga County, and, finding there a people eager for the Word and Ordinances, he prepared the way for his brother to enter upon his long and useful ministry in that place. Returning to Salem, he thence proceeded to the present towns of Hebron and Argyle, where churches had been previously organized. Here his preaching met with such acceptance that, on the 27th of September, he was unanimously called to the united charge, and, on the 14th of November following, was installed as their Pastor, his brother preaching the Sermon from II Cor. iv, 5; and the Rev. James Proudfit delivering the Charges. Thus but a few weeks intervened between his leaving his people in Ireland and his being settled with good prospects of comfort and usefulness in America.

This charge he held for six years; during which time he laboured with great fidelity and success. By this time the congregations had so increased that each was able to support a Pastor, and each wished to remain under his pastoral care. Being warmly attached to both, he left the decision to the Presbytery; and, being directed to the Argyle portion, he was shortly afterwards installed over that flock. Here he held on the even tenor of his way, labouring noiselessly but faithfully and efficiently, through a long course of years.

As advancing age brought with it its infirmities, Mr. Mairs at length felt the need of having some one to share his labours, and, on the 3d of September, 1823 he was privileged to see his own son and namesake set apart as his colleague in the ministerial office,—this being the first collegiate charge in the history of the Associate Reformed Church. During the first five years after this connection was formed, he officiated only on Sabbath morning; and, after that, for five years more, he was accustomed to sit in the pulpit, and read the first Psalm that was sung, accompanying it with a lecture; but he did not attempt to preach. At length he became too weak to attempt any thing beyond the reading of the Psalm; though, as long as he was able to lift his trembling form into the pulpit, he was sure to be there. But he finally reached the weakness of a second childhood, and, for the last two or three years of his life, was incapable of any exertion, either bodily or mental; and yet, after his intellect had become a wreck, he would sometimes seem to catch a glimpse of the glory beyond the vail. On the 10th of October, 1841, the day on which the church to which he had ministered for almost half a century, were commemorating their Redeemer's death, he was seized with violent illness, and, after a brief period of extreme suffering, sunk calmly to his rest on the following day. His Funeral Sermon was preached by the Rev. Ebenezer Halley, of Salem, and was published.

Mr. Mairs was married, during his settlement in Ireland, to Sarah M'Fadden, an intelligent and godly woman, who became the mother of eleven children. She died on the 18th of February, 1818. He was united in marriage again, on the 14th of November, 1825, with Margaret, daughter of Thomas Whiteside, of Cambridge, N. Y., who, with one child, survived him. Two of his sons were graduated at Union College, and *George*, the elder, as has already been stated, became his father's colleague and successor.

Mr. Mairs had a brother, *James Mairs*, who was a pupil in Theology of John Brown of Haddington, came to this country about the year 1793, and shortly after became Pastor of the Associate Reformed Congregation of Galway, (now West Charlton.) He was a man of urbane and gentlemanly manners, was an acceptable preacher, and eminently devoted to his work; but, owing to some adverse circumstances, he resigned his pastoral charge about five years before his death, and then went to live with his children in the city of New York, where he died on the 18th of September, 1840.

FROM THE REV. PETER BULLIONS, D.D.

TROY, February 16, 1863.

My dear Sir: Of the Rev. George Mairs I can speak from a somewhat familiar acquaintance, commencing in the year 1818, and continuing till the close of his life. My appreciation of his character is such that it is a pleasure to me to do any thing to honour and perpetuate his memory.

Mr. Mairs was a man of low stature, of rather spare habit, with a round face, bright eye, and somewhat intellectual expression of countenance. His manners were free from all parade and affectation, and were characterized by great suavity, which was evidently the result of the workings of a most kind and genial spirit. His Christian character was marked by great purity, consistency and devotion; and to this no doubt was to be referred, in no small degree, the success that attended his labours as a Minister. He was most conscientious and diligent in the discharge of all his ministerial duties. His preparations for the pulpit were most mature and deliberate, and were the joint product of the intellect and of the heart; of careful study and earnest prayer. But while each sermon embodied a large amount of Scriptural thought, well digested and well arranged, and was therefore suited to the taste of the more reflecting and cultivated class of Christians, the style was so perspicuous and simple that the most illiterate never hesitated as to his meaning. Though his illustrations were chiefly drawn from Scripture, yet many of them were from the scenes of every day life; and were well fitted to secure the attention of his hearers. He was especially fond of lecturing on the Psalms; and every Sabbath morning through his whole ministry, unless there may have been some rare exceptions, he brought David to minister to the consolation and spiritual growth of his people.

Mr. Mairs had uncommon qualifications for the more private duties of the pastoral office. Possessing that simplicity of character that disarms suspicion, that wisdom that looks well to times and circumstances, that perseverance that never wavers or falters at the sight of obstacles, and that mild and gentle spirit that attracts and charms all who come within the range of its influence, to all which was superadded an earnest devotion to the cause and honour of his Master, it is not strange that it became a difficult matter to decide whether he accomplished more by his labours in the pulpit or out of it. He was particularly attentive to the children of his congregation, and could generally call each of them by name. He had catechetical exercises one half of the year for the benefit, not merely of the young, but of persons of all ages; and, during the other half, he was occupied in visiting from house to house. In making those visits he seemed like a father in the midst of his family, exerting himself to the utmost to promote the spiritual improvement of every member. He had a most happy talent at keeping his congregation in a state of peace; for though he dealt faithfully with wilful offenders, all that he did was so manifestly dictated by a spirit of love and good-will that it was not easy even for the offenders themselves to find fault. As might have been expected under such an influence, his congregation, though large and consisting of the usual variety of characters and tempers, was a model of harmony and peaceableness.

He had great influence in meetings of Synod, and his acknowledged good judgment, and firmness and integrity generally predisposed the Body in favour of any measure he might suggest. Whenever any subject of special importance presented itself, he was very likely to be placed at the head of the Committee to whom it was referred. All his influence was quiet and noiseless, but it was benign and often powerful.

In his more private and domestic relations he demeaned himself with great propriety, dignity and affection. His presence always diffused contentment and joy throughout his household. His friends confided in him without reserve, and he never deceived or disappointed them. The whole community in which he lived reverenced him, and when he died, it seemed as if there was mourning in every house.

With much respect and affection,
I am, Reverend and dear Sir, yours truly,
P. BULLIONS.

FROM THE REV. PETER GORDON.

SOUTH EASTON, N. Y., March 2, 1863.

My dear Sir : My acquaintance with the Rev. George Mairs began in 1828; and well do I remember how deeply I was impressed, on my first introduction to him, by his great simplicity of character, and that warmth and benignity of heart which glistened in his very eyes, and assured you at once of being in the presence of an Israelite indeed in whom there was no guile; and during the many years that followed, whether in private intercourse, or in our association as co-presbyters, he appeared uniformly the same as in this first interview. It was often my privilege to sit with him in his study, where he seemed most at home, and there enjoy those precious seasons of lively spiritual communion with him, which were always profitable, but only too brief. As I used occasionally to visit him, he would sometimes withdraw me from the company in the parlour, by whispering in my ear,—" Let us go to the study—we can enjoy ourselves better there;" and there, indeed, in the company of his old friends, as he used to call his favourite Ambrose, Owen, Flavel, and other authors, with a living friend also to commune with, he seemed in his native element. Stirring up the embers in his fire-place, if the weather was cold, and heaping on the wood,—pleasantly remarking at the same time that he knew how to build a fire,—he would sit and converse for hours so delightfully that I scarcely knew how to break away from him. He loved to dwell on the goodness of God towards himself all his life long, and the happiness he had enjoyed in his family, and among the people committed to his care; and, on one of these occasions, when I referred to the satisfaction which he must feel in having his son associated with him in the ministry, he replied with much feeling that he reckoned that among his greatest blessings, and then spoke of a sermon which he had heard him preach on the preceding Sabbath, from which he had derived great comfort.

My first appearance in public, after being licensed to preach the Gospel, was in his pulpit. I preached in the morning, which was all I had expected to do; but, in the intermission, he said,—" Now you must preach in the afternoon." This I declined on the ground that I was not prepared for another service, and was almost certain of a failure if I attempted it. He still insisted, remarking,—" There is no fear of you—only have faith; only have faith," he repeated—and preach I did; and never in my life have I felt more freedom and comfort in preaching than I did that afternoon. And often since, in hours of weakness and trembling, I have been comforted and strengthened by that simple expression of the good father, as if I heard his affectionate voice,—*only have faith.*

On returning home after the public services of the Sabbath, he would gather all his family, including domestics and visitors that might happen to be with him, and engage in prayer; and long shall I remember with what affectionate earnestness he commended all present to God, with fervent supplications that the word preached that day might be profitable, and that God would prosper his own cause in every part of the world. In these scenes of patriarchal simplicity and devout fervour, I have been sometimes reminded of Burns' inimitable " Cotter's Saturday Night." Such were the candour and honesty of that venerable man that the heart of his people trusted in him with the utmost confidence; and when any difficulty or doubt troubled them, they had recourse to him as children to a father.

I recollect asking him, when we were together in his study, and subsequently to my first settlement, how he had succeeded in building up and maintaining, almost without a rival establishment, so large and prosperous a congregation. He then went into a history of his labours from the very first,—stating that, when he came to Argyle, it was comparatively a wilderness; and as settlers came in, he sought them out, and made himself acquainted with their circumstances and wants, interesting himself in their temporal as well as spiritual welfare; and thus growing up with him, they naturally looked to him as their friend and counsellor, and they had never ceased to regard him with feelings of affection and confidence. He had much of that quiet good-humour which tends so powerfully to disarm opposition, and makes you pleased in spite of yourself. At a meeting of Presbytery, held in Dr. Proudfit's house,—an arrangement not uncommon in the winter season, I remember he arrived, in breathless haste, just as the Moderator had constituted the Court, and the Clerk was commencing to read the names of the members. He whispered to me at the door, with great glee,—" Just in the nick of time;" and, on being called to state his reason for absence from a former meeting, he said, with all gravity, and in a manner peculiarly his own, that he really did not remember *what* the reason was, but he was sure it must have been a *good* one.

As a Preacher, he was highly interesting and instructive; and his illustrations of Divine truth were frequently so apt and striking that they were little likely ever to be forgotten. It was, perhaps, in his prefaces, or "lecturing on the Psalms," that he was most distinguished; and this book of devotion furnished him an inexhaustible mine from which he dug the purest gold. He seemed himself conscious of his superiority here. "James," said he to his brother, on one occasion,—" James, you may beat me at preaching, but I can beat you on the Psalms."

I must not omit to say that he was peculiarly happy on Sacramental occasions. I have heard addresses from him at the table such as I have seldom listened to elsewhere. The last time I heard him in public was on such an occasion; and, though feeble in body, his whole soul seemed fired with Divine love, as if he had caught a glimpse of the glory hereafter to be revealed. His address was founded on the words of Ahasuerus to Esther,—" What wilt thou, Queen Esther, and what is thy request?" And then he proceeded, in a manner of which I can convey no adequate idea, to unfold the treasures of that Kingdom of Glory which God has prepared for them that love Him; saying, with great emphasis, that their happiness was not in receiving the *half*, but the *whole*, of the Kingdom.

But Mr. Mairs' sympathies were not all expended upon his own people or his own denomination. While heartily approving of his own order, he was kind and conciliatory towards those who differed from him in their views of Church polity. The eccentric Lorenzo Dow, who was, at one time, making a brief visit to Argyle, received tokens of Mr. Mairs' good-will, and was entertained at his house; and Dow expressed the highest admiration of his character. Eminently a man of peace, he not only enjoyed this precious blessing in his connection with his own people, throughout his entire ministry, but he was always on the alert to restore peace wherever it had been temporarily interrupted. He has been known to travel a considerable distance in old age, and in the depths of winter, to reconcile parties at variance; and these efforts rarely, if ever, failed of being successful.

I am very truly yours,
P. GORDON.

JOHN RIDDELL, D.D.
1794—1829.

FROM THE REV. JAMES GRIER, D.D.

NOBLESTOWN, PA., January 6, 1851.

Rev. and dear Sir; I have delayed a compliance with your request for some time, in consequence of finding more difficulty than I anticipated in collecting the materials requisite for such a document as you requested. I have endeavoured to explore the best sources of information concerning Dr. Riddell within my reach, and I think you may rely on the authenticity of every thing that I shall communicate. In the illustration of his character, as well as in the narrative of his life, I shall rely chiefly on those who were intimately acquainted with him ∙ as it is now twenty-one years since his death, and my own recollections of him are not sufficiently distinct or extensive to justify me in trusting exclusively to them as the basis of such an account as you desire.

JOHN RIDDELL was born in Monaghan County, Ireland; and if his age is correctly stated on his tomb-stone, he must have been born in the year 1758. He was the oldest of several children, all of whom received a good common school education. His parents, Hugh and Jane Riddell, were in easy worldly circumstances, and sustained a fair reputation for industry, morality and piety. They were regular members of a congregation then under the pastoral care of Mr. Rogers, a Seceder minister, to whose ability and faithfulness and other good qualities an aged sister-in-law of Dr. Riddell, now in this country, bears pleasing testimony. With such parents, and such a Pastor, it is not surprising that the subject of this notice should have been religiously educated. The aged lady already referred to has informed me that it was an early manifested and superior aptness to learn, which induced his parents to bestow upon him a liberal education. She states also that he never returned from College at the close of a session without a silver medal,—a testimony of his superior proficiency in college studies.

It is not certainly known, at least by any of his friends on this side of the Atlantic, in what year he commenced his collegiate course. His diploma, however, shows that he graduated at the University of Glasgow on the 10th of April, 1782. And it would seem, from a comparison of dates, that, almost, if not altogether, as soon as he had finished his collegiate course, he commenced, and prosecuted to a successful issue, the study of Theology. This he did under the supervision and instruction of the celebrated John Brown, of Haddington. He was licensed to preach on the 14th of June, 1788. On the 18th of November of the same year, he was installed Pastor of the congregation in Donaghloney, County Down. In this connection he remained till the spring of 1794, when he demitted his charge, and migrated to the United States. In August of the same year he was installed at Robinson Run, as Pastor of the United Congregations of Robinson Run and Union, in the vicinity of Pittsburg. As these congregations rapidly increased under his ministry, he was, in a few years, released from the charge of Union, and settled, agreeably to his own preference, and to the entire satisfaction of the people, for the whole of his time, at Robinson Run. The whole period of his ministry in this congregation was thirty-five years.

Dr. Riddell was a man of medium size; and though afflicted occasionally with sick headache, yet his constitution appears to have been sound and vigorous, and all his motions were light and quick. His visage was rather long and sharp; his eyes were dark and piercing; his lips thin and slightly compressed. Though not of a majestic corporeal appearance, yet there was something commanding in his countenance. It betokened independence of mind; it indicated decision and energy, and gave an expression of thoughtfulness. There was something in it, on account of which he would have been taken for a student, a man whose principal business is thinking—there was something in it, too, on account of which he would have been taken more readily than some others of the class for a clerical person.

He became naturalized not long after his arrival in the United States, and, from that time forward, he took a sober but steady interest in the welfare of his adopted country. His vote and his influence in other ways, so far as he thought proper to exert it, were in favour of the Federalist party, as it was called in those days. At some stage in the progress of the war of 1812, he preached a Sermon from the words,—"Oh, thou sword of the Lord, how long will it be ere thou be quiet? Put up thyself into thy scabbard, rest and be' still. How can it be quiet seeing the Lord hath given it a charge against Ashkelon, and against the sea-shore? There hath he appointed it." Jer. xlvii, 6, 7. This sermon was not preached on the Sabbath day, and, as it touched somewhat on politics, it was, as might have been expected, not universally acceptable.

Dr. Riddell was twice married,—once in Ireland and once in his adopted country. A Miss Margaret Arnold was the object of his first choice. She died about eleven years after his arrival in the United States. His second wife was a Mrs. Gabby, originally a Miss Mitchell, of Washington County, Pa. He reared a family of ten children, five by his first wife, and five by his second. His widow and most of his children are still living. One of his sons, *John*, graduated at Jefferson College, studied Law, and became somewhat eminent as a practitioner at the Bar,—first at Greensburgh, and then at Erie, Pa. His career of usefulness was cut short by a lingering illness, terminating in death. Another son, *George*, studied Medicine, and another still, *Joseph K.*, the youngest member of his family, studied Theology, but is not now in the exercise of the ministry.

Dr. Riddell was as quick as almost any other man in his discernment of what propriety required in any case, and he was prompt in obeying the dictates of a sound judgment, a generous disposition, a warm heart, a discriminating taste. He could accommodate himself to persons of all capacities, and, so far as it might be innocently done, to people of every character, taste and employment. He never forgot, however, the sacredness and lofty bearing of his calling; he never sacrificed, for the sake of making himself agreeable to any, the sobriety and gravity for which his religion and office called. He seemed to act on the principle that all with whom he had any intercourse must understand that he was an Ambassador of Christ as well as a man, an acquaintance, a scholar. Though disposed to maintain his social as well as civil rights, yet he was not supercilious, and he would have scorned meanness as well as injustice. He could utter a seasonable and delicate jest, and could appreciate genuine wit in others. As to manners, he had evidently read and studied a greater than Chesterfield, even Him who has said,—" Therefore all things, whatsoever ye would that men should do to you, do ye even so to them;" and who has taught his followers to be "pitiful" and "courteous;" to be "kind one to another, tender-hearted, forgiving one another."

His ministerial career extended through a period of forty-one years. It was characterized by diligence, faithfulness, zeal and courage. It was probably not long after his settlement at Donaghloney, that he went, at the request of an English gentleman, residing in that quarter, into the County of Mayo, in the Province of Connaught, to spend a few days there in preaching. This Province was almost exclusively Romanist, and it is easy to see the effect which his ministry would produce in such a community. When it was thought proper that he should return home, his English friend accompanied him a few miles, placed several guineas in his hand, and told him to make all the haste possible, as the

Romanists would doubtless pursue him. They did pursue him, and, at one time when his horse stumbled and partly fell, and of course lost some time in recovering his position and velocity, they were so near that some of the stones which they cast, fell within a short distance of him. However, he managed to keep in advance of them, and finally got clear of them altogether; but the race cost the life of his noble steed.

When Dr. Riddell came to the United States, he connected himself with that branch of the visible Kingdom of Christ, known then, as it still is, as the Associate Reformed Church. This Body had sprung into existence between the years 1780 and 1783, and was therefore in its infancy when he became a member of it. It passed through a period of great perplexity and trouble, betwixt the years 1811 and 1819; and Dr. Riddell took an active part in the management of its affairs, and did much to promote its enlargement and prosperity, as well as to preserve its distinctive character. He was amongst those who opposed, during the period referred to, some of the proceedings of the General Associate Reformed Synod, and who finally, in 1820, resolved to constitute themselves into an independent Synod, to be designated by the title of the "Associate Reformed Synod of the West." This was, in fact, the act of a subordinate Synod already in existence,—the Synod of Scioto, of which Dr. Riddell was a member. He was, from the first moment of his connection with the Body, zealously devoted to the constitution and standards of the Associate Reformed Church, with the final discussion and settlement of some parts of which, in the year 1799, he had something to do. He was an excellent member of Ecclesiastical Courts, having a peculiar talent for business, and being, at the same time, deeply interested in whatever seemed, in his view, to promise any advantage to the cause of truth and godliness.

He was a close student. Instead of retaining, as many have done, the peculiarities of pronunciation, style and method, which may have prevailed in his native country, at the time when he received his education, he conformed, in the literary qualities of his conversation and public exhibitions, to the country in which he lived, and he kept pace with the improvements of the age. His prevailing style of preaching is said to have been argumentative. He is admitted, by all who knew him, to have been an apt and acute disputant, a sound and judicious reasoner, and he was called, at least on one occesion, to try his powers in a public discussion of some points still in controversy betwixt Calvinists and Arminians. He was not, however, incapable of managing, to good effect, a pathetic subject; and though he never gained the reputation of being an orator, yet he could exercise considerable control over the feelings of an audience. His gesticulation was not always the most appropriate or graceful; yet his whole manner was indicative of earnestness, and he generally secured attention. I have often heard intelligent and pious men say,—"If you wish to have a difficult subject ably investigated and lucidly argued, employ Dr. Riddell." This shows in what his strength was supposed chiefly to lie.

He prepared for the pulpit with much care. Though the farm on which he lived, and which he owned, was large, consisting of about four hundred acres, yet he did not consume much of his own time in looking after it. He was mostly employed either in his study, or in the transaction of some business connected with his profession and office. He generally wrote his sermons, though he made no use of his manuscript or of notes in the pulpit. His memory, naturally good, was well trained, and he never appeared to have any difficulty in commanding the thoughts which he had previously committed to paper. He did not confine himself to any one manner of treating a text. His divisions were sometimes textual, but more frequently they were topical. It was an evidence of the high estimation in which his acquirements were held, that the Trustees of Washington College, Pa., conferred on him, several years before his death, the degree of Doctor of Divinity.

He was an excellent Pastor as well as an instructive Preacher. He was frequent in pastoral visitations and in catechetical instructions amongst his people. He was attentive to the sick, not only of his own congregation but of the community at large; and his conversation with the subjects of affliction of any kind was not only instructive but affectionate and impressive.

That he was not, and is not, more extensively known, in the Christian world, may be owing, in part at least, to the fact that none of the productions of his pen were ever published. It is thought that if he had lived a few years longer, he would have published a work on the subject of Religious Covenanting, as he has left behind him a large, though unfinished, manuscript on that subject. It has been examined by at least one competent judge, who has pronounced it to be worthy, so far as it goes, of its author.

Dr. Riddell had failed as little as almost any other man, when he was attacked by his last illness. The last public business to which he attended was the performance, a few miles from his own residence, of the marriage ceremony. He came home unwell, and became gradually worse, until the 4th of September, 1829, when he was released from his sufferings and taken to his eternal rest. He died of dysentery, in the seventy-second year of his age. He was confined thirty-one days, and at times suffered very much; but still he had, for the most part, the full use of his reason, in the exercise of which, and through the assistance of Divine grace, he "let patience have her perfect work," and waited in faith and hope the pleasure of his Master. Sensible of his own unworthiness, he relied upon the merits of Christ, and expired in the firm belief of the Gospel, and in the rich and sweet enjoyment of its consolations. His remains, on the day after his decease, were followed to the grave by a very great number of people, many of whom felt that they had sustained a loss which could not be easily made up, and amongst whom the general impression was that a star of no mean lustre had disappeared from the firmament of the moral and ecclesiastical world.

Yours with great respect,
JAMES GRIER.

FROM THE REV. H. CONNELLY.

NEWBURGH, June 26, 1862.

My dear Sir: My recollections of Dr. Riddell, though they date back to my early days, are still alike vivid and grateful. When I was at College I used sometimes to walk out to his church, a distance of six miles, to attend the Communion; and, on these occasions, I sometimes slept at his house. I had considerable acquaintance with him also, while I was a student of Theology, and had the opportunity of observing particularly his wisdom and energy, as they were displayed in the Presbytery. My personal knowledge of him ceased almost entirely when I was licensed to preach; but the impression he made upon me has thus far shown itself proof against the lapse of time.

Dr. Riddell's personal appearance was not imposing. He was rather beneath the common height, and within the common breadth; but his face, though rather inclined to be grave, was pleasant, and his eye penetrating. His manners were urbane and gentlemanly, and reflected what he undoubtedly possessed,—a spirit of great benevolence and candour. His mind was of a very superior order. He thought clearly, logically, profoundly; and he generally reached his conclusions by so luminous a path that it was not easy successfully to gainsay them. As a Preacher, he commanded great attention by his felicitous exhibition of Divine truth, and especially by his well-considered trains of argument. My impression is that he never carried a manuscript into the pulpit; but his thoughts were well-arranged in his mind, and he could expand them to any extent, and with great power. His mind, naturally fertile and inventive, had been subjected to very careful and thorough discipline; and it was difficult to place him in any circumstances, or present before him any subject, in respect to which he was not quite at home. I remember, on one occasion, witnessing the evidence of his high intellectual resources at a Communion season in his church. I had gone out with two or three of my friends, not only to be present at the Communion, but to attend the preparatory exercises on the preceding days. Dr. Riddell had made arrangements, as he supposed, to secure the presence and aid of one or two of his brethren, in the services of the occasion; but, by a misunderstanding, or from some other cause, no one came to his help. Thursday, Friday, Saturday came, and the exercises of each successive day devolved exclusively upon himself. The Sabbath came, and still he was without a helper. As the church to which he ministered was large, there was occasion to serve the table several times; and each time he introduced a fresh argument for the celebration of the ordinance. There was a richness, an appropriateness, an originality, a variety, in the addresses which he successively delivered, and which were evidently the unstudied effusions of his prolific mind, that marked him as an extraordinary man. I never knew of his proving inadequate to any emergency that he was called to meet.

I hardly need add, after the statements already made, that Dr. Riddell had great control in the ecclesiastical affairs of his denomination, and indeed exerted a powerful influence in society at large. He was a man of great shrewdness in worldly matters, and had unusual tact and skill in the management of property. He used sometimes to let some of his parishioners have the benefit of his sagacity in this line, and some even charged him with being more of a lawyer than was consistent with entire devotion to his professional duties. There was nothing, however, I believe, that interfered with his ministerial reputation or usefulness.

Fraternally yours,
H. CONNELLY.

JOHN HEMPHILL, D.D.
1794—1832.
FROM THE REV. W. R. HEMPHILL.
PRESIDENT OF ERSKINE COLLEGE, DUE WEST, S. C.

DUE WEST, S. C., December 8, 1850

Dear Sir: Your request for some account of my venerated father I will endeavour to comply with, though I confess to some embarrassment in doing it, growing out of my near relationship to the person of whom I am to write.

JOHN HEMPHILL was born in the County of Derry, Ireland, in the year 1761. His father, John Hemphill, visited this country in his youth, but, for some reason, returned to Ireland and remained there. Subsequently to his return, he was married, and became the father of two sons, both of whom migrated to this country. One of them settled in South Carolina, and the other enlisted in the American army during the struggle for Independence, and is supposed to have fallen in the battle of Brandywine. The mother of these sons having died, their father contracted a second marriage with Margaret, a daughter of William Ramsey. By this marriage he had four children, three sons and one daughter. The three sons (one of whom is the subject of this sketch) came to America, and all settled in Chester District, S. C. The daughter was married in Ireland, and remained, so far as is known, on her native soil.

The father of these children is represented as one of the strictest of the Covenanters;—so strict that he would break rather than bend from his perpendicular position. "He viewed the Crown of England" (writes a grandson) "as stained with the blood of our Reforming Fathers, and carried his testimony so far that he refused to pay the taxes imposed by the Government, and allowed his property to be taken and sold to pay his tax, rather than compound (as it was called.") Several letters addressed to his son John, prove him to have been a man of good sense and solid principles, and of strong parental affection. His son was a strict Covenanter before leaving Ireland, but, on reaching this country, was induced to connect himself with the Associate Reformed Synod, then recently formed. His father, in one of his letters to him, suggests a doubt in regard to the propriety of this step, but, after all, refers the ultimate decision to his own judgment and conscience.

Notwithstanding the excellent advantages for religious instruction which my father enjoyed under the parental roof, he determined, while he was yet at an early age, to leave his native country, and seek a home on this side the Atlantic. He landed at Philadelphia, shortly after the close of the American Revolution, destitute of funds, having but a single guinea to procure either the comforts or the necessaries of life. He was a tailor by trade; and, by untiring industry and rigid economy, he secured funds, and along with them friends, and eventually made his way to South Carolina, to the residence of his half-brother. Here he plied his needle, and likewise commenced his classical course, having obtained a common English education before he left Ireland. He began the study of Latin in Chester District; and an old drunkard, by the name of Warnock, taught him his first lessons; but his education, preparatory to entering College, was obtained chiefly under the direction of Dr. Alexander, of York District.

After finishing his preparatory course, he repaired to Dickinson College, Carlisle, then under the Presidency of the venerable Dr. Nisbet; but he seems to have been so far advanced in his studies that he was enabled to join the Senior class. His history at this period, and for some time afterwards, is contained in the following extract of a letter addressed to me by the Rev. Dr. McJimsey, of your State, who was my father's intimate associate in College:—

"My first personal acquaintance with your father took place at Dickinson College, Carlisle. We were in the same class and graduated in May, 1792; although he was several years older than myself. Of his classical attainments I possess no definite knowledge; as our studies in the class were of a philosophical character; and we were chiefly occupied in hearing and writing the Lectures delivered by the Professors. His general standing, as a scholar, I am sure, was respectable; while his attainments in scriptural and theological knowledge probably exceeded those of any other in the class; and it was one of the largest that had graduated.

"On leaving College, we spent some time together, in the study of Hebrew and Theology, under the instruction of the Rev. Alexander Dobbin, near Gettysburg, York County, now Adams. He pursued and completed his theological studies afterwards with the Rev. Matthew Lind, of Greencastle.

"We delivered our first trial discourses before the First Presbytery of Pennsylvania, at Big Spring, in August, 1793, and were licensed together in May, 1794,—the Rev. Robert Annan, Moderator, who gave us the Charge.

"As your father was to go on a mission to South Carolina, and myself to Kentucky, it was judged proper that our Ordination should take place in October following, at Greencastle. His, accordingly, did take place; but mine, at my own urgent request, was deferred. The members of Presbytery present on the occasion were the Rev. Messrs. Lind, Dobbin and Young. We then parted in cordial friendship, and, as our fields of labour in the Lord's vineyard were remote from each other, we had little opportunity afterwards for personal or ministerial intercourse. We had the pleasure of seeing each other occasionally at the meetings of Synod. The last letter I received from him affected me deeply, as he stated that he felt sensibly the infirmities of age, and that his memory had greatly failed him. Our mutual attachment was most cordial and lasting. I esteemed him as a faithful and excellent friend, —of unquestionable integrity and piety, of a clear understanding and sound judgment, zealous for the truth, and ready to defend it on all occasions,—of which he furnished a good specimen in his pamphlet on "The Duty and Occasions of Fasting."

After his Ordination at Greencastle he repaired to the South, and spent the winter and spring of 1794-95, preaching chiefly in vacant congregations, and returned to Greencastle in May, 1795.

In 1794 he was married to Jane, a daughter of the Rev. Matthew Lind, who had been his theological instructor. His family was left at Greencastle during his first visit to the South, but, in the fall of 1795, he removed to the South, taking with him his family, consisting of a wife and an infant daughter. The connection was a happy one to him, though not of very long continuance, as it was terminated by the death of his wife in 1809. Notwithstanding she is represented as having been a devoted Christian, yet, like some other good people, she seems to have been troubled on her death-bed with distressing doubts in respect to her spiritual state; but, before the final struggle took place, her doubts were all dissipated, and her soul was filled with the most ecstatic joy.

Being bereft of his partner and left with a large family, my father found it necessary ere long to seek another companion. Accordingly, in 1811, about two years after the death of his first wife, he was married to Mary, the widow of Dr. Andrew Hemphill, a physician of the same name, but not a relative. She was the daughter of Colonel Nixon, who fell in a skirmish with the Tories during the Revolutionary struggle. She still survives, but bears the marks of care and age. She proved an affectionate wife and a good stepmother.

My father was installed Pastor of Hopewell, Union and Ebenezer, in the year 1796. In this connection he remained until a short time before his death, when his charge was demitted to Presbytery. In his ministrations he was assiduous, faithful and energetic.

The following extract of a letter, from an excellent Ruling Elder, sets forth, in rather an unpolished but yet truthful manner, his character as a Christian Minister, and the estimation in which he was held by his brethren:

'Your father was not an orator; but all those who valued the matter were well pleased with his preaching. His practice was to explain a Psalm, or part of one, in the morning, in which he was practical and excellent. In the summer he frequently lectured in the forenoon and preached in the evening. He was considered a systematic and thorough Divine, and a great reasoner. No man was more punctual in family visitation and in catechising the children and others; in conversing and praying with and for them; and, as to attending meetings of Presbytery and Synod, there was no one who was more faithful, or whose opinions were more looked up to by his brethren. When he was providentially prevented from attending, they felt as if the Head was missing. In fact, he was an able and faithful Minister of the New Testament, always ready and willing to oppose innovations or errors, let them come from what quarter they might."

To this I may add that he was probably one of the best disciplinarians in the Synod; and his congregations, especially that of Hopewell, among whose members he resided, was perhaps under better regulations than almost any congregation in the State. Societies were formed in its different sections, and meetings were held in turn at the houses of the members on Sabbaths when there were no exercises at the church. The exercises of the Societies on these occasions consisted in reading the Scriptures and Sermons, in prayer and praise, and in catechetical instruction to both old and young, both the Shorter and Larger Catechisms being used. The Elders drilled the young people in the same Catechisms at church. In this way they became well acquainted with the doctrines of the Gospel, and they have generally proved to be substantial members, in whatever portion of the Church their lot has been cast. Many of them have removed to other States, and are now found, in considerable numbers, in the Associate Reformed Congregations of the West and North-west.

Though my father was, as his Elder has justly remarked, not reckoned an orator, yet he was not otherwise than an acceptable speaker. His attention was directed more to the matter than the manner. His power lay in argumentation, rather than in polished thoughts or pathetic appeals. He appears to have written out many of his sermons in the early part of his ministry; but in the latter part he satisfied himself with notes more or less copious. His sermons were more after the Boston and Erskine style than according to the fashion of the modern pulpit.

His constitution was firm and vigorous, and consequently he was enabled to endure much fatigue without exhaustion or injury. He frequently rode to one of his churches, (Union,) sixteen miles distant, on Sabbath morning, explained the Psalm and preached two sermons, and returned home the same evening.

He published nothing, so far as I know, except the Essay, above alluded to by Dr. McJimsey, on Religious Fasting, which, with an Appendix, consists of a hundred and sixty pages.

Being at Jefferson College at the time of his death, I am indebted to others for my knowledge of his closing scene. For several weeks previous to his demise, he was in a low and helpless condition; and, during this time, he was scarcely capable of holding any conversation. His mind, it seems, had lost its activity, and a sort of mental stupor had ensued. In consequence of this, his friends were denied the privilege of listening to his dying testimony in favour of the Gospel he had loved and preached, but the remembrance of his devoted Christian life remained to them, and in it they found the best of all evidence that he entered into rest. He died on the 30th of May, 1832, in the seventy-first year of his age.

By his first marriage my father had three sons and four daughters; and by his second, three sons and one daughter. Of the daughters but one (of the first wife) survives. Two of the sons have been removed by death. Three of them are graduates of Jefferson College. Hon. John Hemphill, Chief Justice of Texas, was, probably, the first graduate of that institution from South Carolina. James Hemphill, Esq., the eldest son by the second marriage, graduated at the same institution in 1833, and is now a practising attorney in his native district; and I was myself a member of the same class, and received my degree at the same time. From the same institution at which his sons were educated my father received the degree of Doctor of Divinity in 1828.

Hoping that the above sketch will answer your purpose, and wishing you entire success in your laudable attempt to preserve the memory of devoted ministers of the Gospel, who now rest from their labours,

I am, My dear Sir, yours in the bonds of Christian affection,

W. R. HEMPHILL.

FROM THE REV. DAVID MACDILL, D.D.

SPARTA, ILL., February 26, 1852.

Dear Sir: I cheerfully comply with the request contained in your letter which has just come to hand. I was born in Dr. Hemphill's Congregation; but before I had arrived at the age of eighteen, my father removed to the State of Ohio. Dr. H. was of about the ordinary stature,—rather slender,—what would generally be called a "handsome man." His countenance indicated cheerfulness, kindness, benevolence. In a controversial pamphlet having a bearing upon the union in which the Associate Reformed Church had its origin, I remember, he was designated, not with a sneer but in sincerity, "the amiable Mr. Hemphill." He was eminently a devout man. He frequently lodged at the house of my grandfather, who was a member of Session in a remote branch of his congregation. When a lad, like other grandchildren, I used to stay at my grandfather's; and having accidentally discovered the "solitary place," to which Dr. H. retired for secret prayer, I crept up so near that I could hear him, impelled by no higher motive than curiosity.

Having left the South at so early a period of life, my estimate of his mental character and ministerial qualifications is founded chiefly in the opinion of others, who were long and intimately acquainted with him, some of whom were his co-presbyters,—and from at least one production of his pen. In his more youthful days he was considered about on a par with the late Dr. Mason, of New York, as an expounder of Scripture, though he never possessed much of Dr. M.'s popular eloquence. Not having been launched into deep waters,—his situation not furnishing the same inducements to a very high order of mental effort, he could not be expected to keep pace with Dr. Mason. He seldom did an imprudent thing, and I am not aware that, under any combination of circumstances, he was ever induced to take a step, which impaired, in any degree, the confidence which his Christian friends reposed in him. Notwithstanding he was perhaps even strenuous in his religious views, and was a very staunch advocate of the peculiarities of the Associate Reformed Church, he still enjoyed, in a high degree, the esteem of good people of other Christian denominations around him. I have been credibly informed that young ministers of the General Assembly Presbyterian Church, and of the minor Presbyterian denominations, frequently sought his advice in matters of ecclesiastical polity and discipline.

I understand that you intend publishing a notice of Doctors Riddell and Kerr, of the Monongahela country. Compared with Dr. Kerr,—Dr. Hemphill's mind was more logical; he was a more close and profound thinker, but inferior as a pulpit orator. Had Dr. Kerr been settled in New York or Philadelphia in his youth, he would have ranked with the Masons, Romeyns, Milledolers, &c. Compared with Dr. Riddell, Dr. Hemphill's mind was less adapted to manage questions of subtle casuistry—his style was less polished and classical, though he was considered a more pro found scholar and theologian. In respect of popular talent, they were about on an equality.

In what follows you will of course make allowance for the partiality which a person always feels for the place of his nativity. I have had some acquaintance with all the Presbyterian denominations of the West, and in the middle Atlantic States, but if I am not mistaken, there was long a prevailing type of piety in Hopewell, (Dr Hemphill's congregation,) different from,—superior to what has come within my knowledge, any where else. Though every where there are congregations which contain a few, and sometimes more than a few, individuals, who are perhaps equally devoted. Near the beginning of the present century, ministers of another denomination, who had travelled extensively, were known to say that there was more serious practical piety there than in any congregation with which they were acquainted. Its members were numerous, and they were communing members—adherents were hardly known. But as they did not possess much wealth, and were generally a plain and unlettered people, they "dwelt alone and were not numbered among the nations." This tone of piety may be traced to two causes—First, the original founders of the church were generally from the North of Ireland, who had not only read their Bibles, but were intimately acquainted with the writings of Flavel, Owen, Boston, &c. Second, to the influence of Dr. Thomas Clark, who organized the congregation; of Rev. John Boyce,* a pious and pathetic preacher, who was its first Pastor; and, finally, to that of Dr. Hemphill. Old Hopewell has three daughters, in the West, who bear her name; one of which, previous to its division into three congregations, excelled the mother in wealth, numbers and Christian efficiency, though perhaps, from her dwelling places, there were, at no time, so many effectual fervent prayers sent up to the throne of grace.

Respectfully yours,
DAVID MACDILL.

ALEXANDER PROUDFIT, D.D.†
1794—1843.

ALEXANDER PROUDFIT was the fourth son of the Rev. James Proudfit, and was born at Pequea, Pa., in November, 1770. In his boyhood he was distinguished for vivacity, activity and resolution. In his thirteenth year he removed, with his father's family, to Salem, N. Y., and soon after began his preparation for College, under the instruction of Mr. Thomas Watson, a Scotchman, who had a high reputation as a classical teacher. Here he remained till the year 1785,—not far from two years,—when he was removed to an Academy at Hackensack, N. J., then under the care of that eminent scholar and teacher, Dr. Peter Wilson. His connection with this school continued till March, 1789, when he became a member of the Sophomore class in Columbia College, New York. Dr. Wilson, at the same time, became Professor of Languages in that institution;

---

* The father of JOHN BOYCE emigrated from Ireland about the time of the Revolutionary War, and settled in what was called the Long Lane Settlement in South Carolina. He graduated at Dickinson College in 1787; studied Divinity under the Rev. Matthew Lind, of Greencastle, Pa., and was the first Pastor of Hopewell congregation, Chester District, S. C. He died of consumption after a very brief ministry. He was highly esteemed both as a Man and a Minister.

† Memoir by Rev. Dr. Forsyth.—MS. from his son, Rev. Dr. John Proudfit.

and Mr. Proudfit continued to reside in his family, as he had done previous to his removal. There existed the most intimate relations between the venerable teacher and his pupil, until they were broken by death.

Mr. Proudfit was graduated in 1792, with the highest honours of his class. He had made a public profession of religion about the time that he entered College, with an intention of devoting himself to the ministry; but, soon after he graduated, his purpose in regard to a profession began to waver, and it was chiefly through the influence of his friend, the Rev. Dr. John Mason, that he was prevented from marking out for himself a different course of life. He soon entered on the study of Theology, under the direction of his father; and, after having remained at home one year, returned to New York, to avail himself of the Theological Lectures of the late Rev. Dr. John H. Livingston, then Professor of Divinity in the Reformed Dutch Church. He was licensed to preach on the 7th of October, 1794, at Galway, N. Y., by the Presbytery of Washington, of which his father was a member.

About three months after Mr. Proudfit's licensure he was called, by the congregation of Salem, to settle as colleague with his father. This call he accepted, and was ordained, and installed in that charge, on the 13th of May, 1795.

On the 2d of October, 1796, he was married to Susan, daughter of General John Williams, of Salem,—a lady of fine intellectual, moral and Christian qualities, who had received her education partly under that eminent female teacher, Mrs. Isabella Graham.

In the autumn of 1802, while Dr. John M. Mason was in Europe soliciting funds in aid of the Theological Seminary founded by the Associate Reformed Church, Mr. Proudfit, by appointment of Synod, supplied his pulpit about two months. During this time he laboured for the promotion of the spiritual interests of the congregation with as much zeal and diligence as if he had been their stated Pastor.

In 1812 he was honoured with the degree of Doctor of Divinity from both Middlebury and Williams Colleges.

In June, 1819, he was elected Associate Professor with Dr. Mason in the Theological Seminary of the Associate Reformed Church. He accepted the appointment; but, as the session commenced in November, he had little time to prepare for the arduous duties which he thereby assumed. His connection with the institution seems to have been a source of considerable disquietude to him, and it continued only during a single session.

In 1821 Dr. Proudfit experienced various severe trials, one of which was a greatly reduced state of health. In consequence of this he was obliged to abstain from preaching a considerable time, during which he was occupied chiefly in travelling in New England. After some months his health was so far restored that he was able to resume his accustomed labours.

The Theological Seminary in the Associate Reformed Church, after a suspension of its operations for seven years, was at length revived and established at Newburgh; and, during the summer of 1833, as well as at a later period, Dr. Proudfit was occupied, so far as his other engagements would permit, in endeavouring to further the interests of that institution. In 1835 the Synod appointed him Professor of Pastoral Theology; and, for a while, he entertained the idea that he might be able to spend so much time at Newburgh, during each session of the Seminary, as would suffice for the delivery of a brief course of

Theological Lectures; but, finding this to be impracticable, he resigned his office in 1837. He, however, still retained a deep interest in the institution, and often took part in the examination of its students.

Towards the close of the year 1833 he was earnestly requested, by the Young Men's Bible Society in the city of New York, to assist them in raising a considerable sum, for which they had become responsible, to aid the circulation of the Scriptures in foreign lands. He yielded to their request, and, at a most inclement season, undertook and performed this important service. The Society testified their grateful estimate of his labours in a series of Resolutions, the most honourable to his zeal and fidelity.

In 1835 Dr. Proudfit was chosen Secretary to the New York Colonization Society; and he immediately solicited and received a dismission from his pastoral charge with a view to accept the appointment. His congregation, in the acceptance of his resignation, manifested the highest appreciation of his services and the most affectionate respect for his character.

Having laboured in the cause of Colonization with most untiring zeal until 1841, Dr. Proudfit tendered the resignation of his office as Secretary of the Society; but, by the urgent request of the Executive Committee, was induced to retain the office till near the close of the next year.

In retiring from the service of the Colonization Society, it was by no means Dr. Proudfit's intention to withdraw altogether from the field of active Christian effort. He had still two objects which he was earnestly desirous of accomplishing —one was the bringing out of a new edition of his works, chiefly with a view to circulation in the destitute portions of our country; the other was the raising of an amount sufficient for the liquidation of the debt of the Theological Seminary at Newburgh. But these favourite objects it was not the design of Providence that he should live to accomplish. Shortly after he resigned his office, in the winter of 1842-43, he began to suffer from a serious affection of the eyes, which not only rendered him incapable of active labour, but confined him to his house, and almost entirely to his room. He, however, recovered from this affection, and, for a short time, both his health and spirits seemed to have regained their accustomed vigour. He had now taken up his residence with his son (Professor Proudfit,) at New Brunswick, N. J.; and he set out from home with a view to visit the Rev. Dr. Forsyth, of Newburgh, and assist him during a state of special religious interest in his congregation. He had reached New York, with the intention of going to Newburgh the next day; but when the next day came, he found himself so unwell that he judged it expedient to return to New Brunswick rather than proceed on his journey. He did accordingly return; and, on his arrival, immediately betook himself to his chamber, which he never left until he was carried from it a corpse. His disease proved to be a catarrhal fever, which, after a rapid course, terminated fatally, on the 17th of April, 1843. He was in full possession of his faculties to the last, and his sufferings and death were full of triumph.

Dr. Proudfit was the father of four children,—three sons and a daughter. His eldest son, *John*, was graduated at Union College in 1821; entered the ministry; was for several years Pastor of a Presbyterian Church in Newburyport, Mass.; and has since been a Professor, successively, in the New York University and Rutgers College. The second son, *James Owen*, was graduated at Union College in 1824, became a merchant in New York, and died at the house of his brother in New Brunswick, November 23, 1846, at the age of forty-one.

The following is a list of Dr. Proudfit's publications:—

The Gospel designed for all Nations: A Sermon preached before the Northern Missionary Society, at their Annual Meeting in Troy, and afterwards, by particular request, in Albany,	1798
An Act on the Kingly Authority of our Lord Jesus Christ, prepared by order of the Associate Reformed Synod,	1798
The Spiritual Steward: A Sermon preached in New York at the Opening of the Associate Reformed Synod,	1802
The One Thing Needful: In six Practical Discourses, designed for the Inhabitants of the Frontier Settlements,	1804
The Female Labourer in the Gospel, [This was re-published in Edinburgh.]	1805
The Barren Fig Tree cut down—also the Healing Balm administered to the Diseased Soul: Two Lectures. A New Year's Gift,	1806
The Ruin and Recovery of Man, in Sixteen Discourses: For Frontier Settlements,	1806
Our Danger and Duty: Two Sermons delivered on the Fast Day appointed by the Associate Reformed Presbytery of Washington, on account of the alarming aspect of affairs in our country,	1808
Ministerial Labour and Support: A Sermon preached at Middlebury at the Ordination of Henry Davis, D.D., and his Induction as President of the College,	1810
Life and Immortality brought to Light in the Gospel: The Substance of Two Discourses delivered in the North Dutch Church, Albany,	1815
Discourses on the Doctrines and Duties of Christianity,	1815
Tidings of Great Joy for all People: A Sermon preached before the Washington County Bible Society,	1816
The Extent of the Missionary Field a Call for the Increase of Missionary Labourers: A Sermon preached before the Middlebury College Society for Educating Indigent Youth for the Gospel Ministry,	1817
Personal Sobriety, Righteousness to Man, and Piety to God, our Duty, Glory and Interest: A Sermon preached in the South Dutch Church, Albany, before a Convention of Delegates from Moral Societies in the State of New York,	1820
Ministerial Duty and Encouragement: A Sermon preached in Cambridge, at the Ordination of Mr. Donald C. McLaren,	1820
Lectures on the Parables,	1820
The Duties of the Watchman upon Zion's Walls: A Sermon preached before the Associate Reformed Synod of New York, met at Galway: Also an Address delivered to the Students of Theology at the Seminary in the City of New York,	1822
An Address before the American Society for Meliorating the Condition of the Jews, in New York,	1825
An Address before the American Tract Society,	1825
An Address to the Coloured Emigrants embarking for Bassa Cove,	1836

In addition to the above he published the following Tracts, all of which have passed through more than one edition:—

A Word to Mothers on the Religious Instruction of their Children.
A Word to Children concerning their Everlasting Interests.
An Address to the Rising Generation.
An Address to the Inhabitants of the Frontier Settlements.
A Letter to a Member of my Church, on leaving my Pastoral care.
An Address to Mothers on the Importance of maintaining Family Religion when it is neglected by the Father.
A Short Method of occupying a Single Talent to the Best Advantage.

It is known that he projected Tracts on the following subjects, and that several, if not all, of them were actually published:—

On the Importance of Secret Prayer.
The Church in the House.
On the Importance of Attending Public Ordinances.
On the Advantages of Attending them.
An Address to Teachers of Common Schools.

In 1807 Dr. Proudfit edited a re-publication of A Scriptural View of the Constitution, Order, Discipline and Fellowship of the Gospel Church. By the Rev. Archibald Hall, of London; originally published 1769.

I saw Dr. Proudfit first, I think, in 1823, at West Springfield, where he spent a few hours with me, on his way to attend the meeting of the American Board of Foreign Missions at Boston. I was greatly struck by his staid and impressive manner, the kindliness of his spirit, and above all by the depth and fervour of his religious feelings. After I came to live in Albany, I became quite well acquainted with him, and often had the pleasure of seeing him at my house, and more than once of hearing him in my pulpit; and the more intimate my acquaintance with him became, the more were the impressions which I received concerning him, at our first interview, confirmed. His mind and his heart seemed always intensely set upon doing good. Sometimes when I saw him, the Colonization Society seemed uppermost in his thoughts, and then again the Bible Society; but whatever the particular object might be, he always addressed himself to it with the fervour and energy of a ruling passion. The force of his religious feelings sometimes led him to do things out of the common course; but if any had been disposed to criticise, his deep sincerity, which was manifest in every look and word, would have disarmed them. For instance, I remember, on one occasion, just as we were going to church, and the bell had nearly done tolling, he said to me and one or two other ministers who were staying with me,—" Brethren, let us not go to the house of God till we have had a word of prayer;" and instantly broke out in a fervent supplication for the Divine blessing on the services in which we were about to engage. When the American Board met in Albany, in 1829, the Annual Sermon was preached in the Second Presbyterian Church, by Dr. Archibald Alexander. Dr. Proudfit was in the pulpit, and the moment that Dr. Alexander sat down, *he* rose, and out of the fulness of his heart, spoke, for some eight or ten minutes, urging with great impressiveness and pathos some thought that had been suggested in the sermon. The same thing, done by another person, might have seemed strange; but, in his case, it was so evidently the simple workings of a spirit of fervent devotion to the cause, that it seemed natural and unexceptionable. I received marked kindness from him at different times, and I never think of him but with mingled gratitude and reverence.

FROM THE REV. JOHN GOSMAN, D.D.

GLASCO, June 26, 1855.

Rev. and dear Brother: I have too long delayed to comply with your request for my recollections of my excellent and honoured friend, the Rev. Dr. Alexander Proudfit. I was, for about three years, a resident in his family; accompanied him on many of his missionary excursions; had the opportunity of seeing him under a great variety of circumstances, and was in habits of familiar intercourse and correspondence with him during a considerable part of my life. It costs me little effort, therefore, to perform the service you have requested of me.

Dr. Proudfit was of medium height, slender in person, and when "the strong man bows himself," erect in attitude. His countenance bore unmistakable indications of reflective intelligence. Although he was, at no period of his life, in possession of very vigorous health, and any considerable exertion was sure to be followed by exhaustion, there was an elasticity which quickly restored the balance. He was an early riser—at early morn he was found in his study. He was a man of system; and his adherence to it contributed to his health, and prolonged his usefulness. He avoided that which has been injurious, and in many cases fatal, to persons of studious habits,—inattention to proper exercise. He was fond of nature—the fields and woods had attractions for him; and, by walking and riding, he sought a change, and returned to his studies with an increase of vigour. He had a love for retirement, and was a diligent student of the Word of God and his own heart, and a careful observer of the movements of Providence. He often quoted, and seemed to adopt as the motto of his life, the language of the ancient painter,—"*Nulla dies sine linea.*"

His manners were expressive of kind affections and cultivated tastes; they were formed on the Christian model, and presented a happy combination of "whatsoever things are true, whatsoever things are honest, whatsoever things are pure, whatsoever things are lovely, whatsoever things are of good report." The principles and spirit of the Gospel were so interwoven with his whole character, that he may be said to have been moulded by them, personally, relatively and socially. His manners reminded you of some of the fathers of the American Church—such as Rodgers, Livingston and Miller; between whom and himself there existed a warm regard and frequent intercourse. It was a style of manners that you felt had a sort of official appropriateness—it seemed adapted to the men and their position, and was in accordance with the views, habits and tastes of their contemporaries. The line of separation between the different ranks of society was, in that day, more distinctly marked than it is at present. This formality and precision affected only the exterior aspect, and were not incompatible with heartfelt courteousness. Their conversations were utterances of the heart. Dr. Proudfit's social affections were ardent and constant, and his animal spirits had that agreeable flow so happily described by his favourite Cowper—

> "A constant flow of love that knew no fall,
> Ne'er roughened by those cataracts and breaks
> Which humour interposed too often makes."

He was not the creature of impulse, nor chargeable in his attachments with fickleness or caprice. Generous in his confidence, distrust was painful to him; and although, from an extended intercourse with mankind, he had been exposed to the ordinary manifestations of human weakness and perverseness, yet they did not chill the genial current of his heart. He was an instructive companion; and, without any effort at display, could pour forth from his well furnished mind the treasures which he had accumulated by extensive reading, reflection and observation. He expressed his own opinions with frankness, but manifested a becoming deference to the opinions, and a delicate regard to the feelings, of those with whom he conversed. Familiar intercourse heightened the estimate of his gifts and graces. While grave, he was yet cheerful; and while he was distinguished for Christian sobriety in his deportment, he was still alive to the imaginative and witty. He was eminently "a lover of hospitality." His brethren of different denominations found in him a faithful friend and a judicious counsellor. The sympathies of the brotherhood were felt in all their sacredness, and the expression of kind affections was grateful to the guest, it seemed so manifestly a spontaneous effusion of the heart. All found in his dwelling the quiet enjoyment of a Christian home.

As a Preacher, Dr. Proudfit had a high place among the excellent Preachers of his day. His discourses combined the doctrinal and the practical in very happy proportions. He declared the whole counsel of God; there was no concealment or modification of the Gospel; and the attentive hearer could not but perceive that it was his earnest desire, in all his ministrations, "by manifestation of the truth, to approve himself to every man's conscience in the sight of God." His illustrations were clear and pertinent; he presented the truth with simplicity and force, and brought it home to the conscience in direct and pungent appeals. He was scrupulously careful to maintain the dignity of the pulpit. There was no ostentation or parade of learning in his discourses; and though they were elevated in their tone and spirit, they were so plain and simple that persons of humble capacities and little culture could easily understand them. He had great tenderness and earnestness of manner; and, though his voice was sufficiently loud and distinct to be easily heard through a large church, his mode of utterance was somewhat peculiar, and might have seemed at first scarcely natural, though I believe it was the legitimate result of his Scottish descent and his early education.

As a Theologian, he had no love of paradox, and never indulged the petty ambition of attracting attention by startling novelties. His mind was sound, clear and discriminating; and, while his views of the leading truths of the Gospel were well defined, and his adherence to them unshaken to the end of his earthly course, he loved the Saviour's image wherever he recognized it, and could enjoy fellowship with all who "love our Lord Jesus Christ in sincerity."

Dr. Proudfit was perhaps never more at home than in training young men for the ministry. He was eminently fitted for this by his high literary and theological attainments, and his earnest and active piety. While his superintendence was vigilant and kind, he endeavoured, both by his example and instructions, to place before them a high standard of spiritual attainment. He had an excellent literary taste, and had all the means of cultivating it that could be furnished by an extensive and well selected library. He was a thorough classical scholar—he discerned, as if by intuition, the beauties of the ancient Latin and Greek writers, and could quote, with readiness and appropriateness, whatever was necessary for illustration or embellishment. He was also familiarly acquainted with the Fathers of the Christian Church, and appreciated their distinctive merits; he read them with discrimination and independence, and, while he admired the good, and true, and beautiful, which he found in them, he never bowed implicitly to them or to any other human authority.

One of the most distinguishing features of his character was active benevolence and public spirit. He occupied a conspicuous position among those who may be considered as the pioneers in diffusing the Gospel in the destitute portions of the State of New York, and as having rendered important service towards its extension throughout the world. He brought to this great work all the ardour, activity, and persevering energy that belonged to him, both as a Man and as a Christian. He was accustomed amidst the labours incident to a large pastoral charge, to make missionary excursions into the destitute regions not only in the Western part of his own State, but in Vermont and Massachusetts also; and he not only preached frequently, but distributed tracts and standard theological works, which he carried with him for the purpose. In the prosecution of this benevolent work he performed long journeys, and submitted to great inconveniences, and even hardships, with a zeal which seemed to rise with the occasion, and which no difficulties could repress or exhaust. The interest which he subsequently took in establishing and sustaining the great National Benevolent Institutions of our country, such as the Bible, Tract, and Colonization Societies, will never be forgotten by his coadjutors, and its results can never be fully estimated on this side Heaven. And, in addition to these more general exhibitions of his benevolent spirit, I may mention that he assisted, by his contributions, many young men in the prosecution of their academic and collegiate course, some of whom have since been highly distinguished in the walks of literature, and others have occupied prominent stations of ministerial usefulness.

But that which constituted the crowning attraction of Dr. Proudfit's character, was his elevated spirituality. It was apparent to every one, who had an opportunity of observing his course, that he walked with God. In all his intercourse with his fellow men, whether with those who loved religion or those who neglected it, he always obeyed the command to let his light shine. He had an admirable tact in the introduction of serious remarks, and would often give a religious direction to ordinary conversation in so easy a manner that one would scarcely be sensible of the transition. He uniformly spoke of his own spiritual relations with the confidence of assured hope. Amidst the duties, temptations and vicissitudes of life, he endured as seeing "Him who is invisible," and, as the earthly tabernacle yielded to decay, he felt a joyful assurance that it would be exchanged for "a building of God, a house not made with hands, eternal in the heavens."

Very truly yours,
J. GOSMAN.

FROM THE REV. EBENEZER HALLEY, D.D.

ALBANY, February 15, 1858.

Dear Sir: In compliance with your request, I furnish you with a few reminiscences of the late Dr. A. Proudfit. I was indebted for my intimate acquaintance with him to the circumstance of being, at one time, Pastor of the same church in which he had so long and usefully laboured. From the period of my installation to his last illness, (embracing a space of nearly six years,) he annually made a visit to his beloved flock. Each of these extended to five or six weeks, and, as I was frequently, during this period, in his society, and accompanied him in many of his visits among his old parishioners, I am enabled to furnish some notices of his social and religious character. I shall confine myself almost entirely to what fell under my own observation.

No other attestation of his Christian excellence and the worth of his ministerial labours is needed, than the satisfaction which these annual visits gave to the people of his former charge. They were always fondly anticipated, and were enjoyed, through successive years, with unabated satisfaction. While the people joyfully welcomed back their venerable teacher, their faithful counsellor and friend, who had been ever prompt to allay dissension or relieve despondency, to impart instruction to the young and consolation to the aged, and who had visited them all in their dwellings in seasons of joy and bereavement, the visit was no less agreeable to himself. There he had spent the scenes of his youth. There he was installed over a people who had long enjoyed the pastoral labours of his venerable father. There, in his first and only charge, he had laboured for forty years, among an intelligent and excellent congregation, who had duly appreciated his sterling qualities and had greatly profited under his ministry. The annual trip therefore to Salem was always the subject of much previous converse and preparation. It was not only pleasant for Dr. Proudfit to exchange during the heat of summer the *"fumum strepitumque Romæ"* for the sweet repose and lovely scenery of his native vale, (and our country, amid its almost endless diversities of situation, has few more attractive sylvan retreats,) but it was still dearer to him as the spot where he could behold many fruits of his ministry, and enjoy those feelings which the heart retains the longest and cherishes the most tenderly.

During these visits, my pulpit, of course, was always open to him, and he was never reluctant to occupy it. Dr. Proudfit was entirely at home in vindicating the peculiar doctrines of the Bible, as the volumes which he has published abundantly testify,—but the discourses to which I listened were devoted not so much to the defence as the enforcement of Divine truth. He always secured the attention of his audience. Though he never aimed at any thing like startling antithesis or brilliant metaphor, designed to take the popular ear, and always delivered his sermons in a calm, dispassionate manner, often without gesticulation, and in a voice whose tones, though silvery, were in danger of becoming monotonous to a hearer, he was nevertheless a deeply impressive preacher. His conceptions were always clear and well defined. The arrangement of his subject was logical, and there was often a force and point in his expressions which not only arrested but riveted attention. His language, though always simple and chaste, was sometimes singularly beautiful. When we add to these a mind richly stored with Divine truth, from a devout study of the Scriptures and the most eminent Puritan writers, an impassioned zeal for the spiritual welfare of his fellow men, inducing an unction and fervour of manner rarely exceeded, it is not strange that he had a place among the most effective Preachers of his denomination.

At the close of every visit he was accustomed to take a solemn and affectionate farewell of the people from the pulpit. The scene was deeply affecting, nor did it lose its impressiveness by repetition, as each returning year diminished the probability of our seeing him again. I never witnessed a more thrilling scene in the house of God, nor listened to more solemn appeals, than on one of these occasions. Feeling that he must soon put off the earthly tabernacle, he reminded them of his long ministry among them, and of that solemn account which he and they must shortly render before the Judge of all; and then, summoning up all his energies, he, in a strain of deep pathos and fervour, addressed the several classes of his audience. The careless and impenitent were warned and reminded of their guilt in their habitual rejection of the Gospel; the young were affectionately counselled to remember their Creator; and the aged encouraged to steadfastness and zeal by the good hope in Christ Jesus. Some of the scenes of his past ministry, favoured, as it had been, with the signal testimonies of Divine grace were introduced, and notices of the eminently pious, who had gone to receive their reward during the period of his labours among them, were given with singular beauty and effect. He finally told them that this might be the last time they would ever listen to him; that their spiritual welfare, next to his own and that of his family, lay nearest to his heart; and that the next time they would hear his voice, might be at the judgment seat of God, where he must testify either for or against them. At the close of the address, when the solemn farewell was pronounced, the intensity of his feelings almost choked his utterance, and the emotions of the speaker were responded to by the tears and sobs of the crowded assembly.

In his intercourse with his people there was a happy union of dignity which commanded respect, and of kindliness which invited confidence. His manners were polished without being finical, and his general deportment partook more of the refinements of a city Pastor than of one reared amid the seclusion of a village. His eminence in the Church, and the deep interest he felt in the religious institutions of his country, had brought him into contact with the best society; and these advantages, united with a native delicacy of mind and feeling, rendered his manners singularly dignified, but never interfered with his cordial and confiding intercourse among his people. The village of Salem is small, and his hearers therefore chiefly came from the rural districts around it. Nothing afforded him greater pleasure than his pastoral visits among his people, all of whom were in circumstances of worldly comfort, and many of them thoroughly acquainted with the doctrines of the Gospel. One circumstance which often diminishes the interest of these visits is the want of sympathy between the people and the Pastor, owing, sometimes, to his deficiency of knowledge respecting their circumstances and habits. No such difficulty existed in his case. Not only had he been reared among his people, but, possessing the advantages of a quick eye and a tenacious memory, he rarely forgot a countenance; he could call each of his people, old and young, by name, and could readily call up the leading facts connected with the history of every family. No one could be more felicitous than Dr. Proudfit in taking advantage of these incidents, and engrafting upon them lessons of interesting religious instruction. Whatever the subject of conversation might be, it was almost certain to be used as the vehicle for communicating some practical hints. Among an agricultural population, the state of the seasons, as affecting the fruits of the earth, was naturally a frequent subject of conversation. How impressively, from the season of spring, did he inculcate upon parents the importance of instilling the truths of religion into the minds of their children, as the grand means of shielding them against the temptations of the world, and fitting them for spheres of usefulness in society and in the Church; and, as he saw them, in autumn, "bearing their sheaves," while he failed not to inculcate the duty of gratitude to God for the liberal distribution of his blessings, the important lessons which that season taught of the relations of this life to another, under the idea of sowing and reaping, were always enforced with great urgency and pathos.

There was one department in which Dr. Proudfit pre-eminently shone—I allude to his catechetical instruction of the young. He took a deep interest in this portion of his charge. He instituted various plans to elevate the standard of Christian education among them. And that Sabbath seldom, if ever, passed, on which their special instruction did not form a part of his ministrations from the pulpit. He was also wonderfully gifted in the ability to awaken the interest and fix the attention of children, by simplifying religious instruction to their easy comprehension. The doctrines of the Bible, and often the leading incidents in the Saviour's history, were the subjects on which he examined them. Particular passages in the life of Jesus were dwelt upon, difficulties were explained, allusions to oriental customs or natural productions clearly brought out and applied, interesting religious anecdotes narrated, and the service was closed in an affectionate address respecting the importance of their spiritual welfare. Many of his people attributed to these interviews their first enduring impressions of religion.

The habits of Dr. Proudfit were eminently devotional. He loved prayer, and lived in the habitual exercise of it—so much was this the case that when friends came to visit him, the circumstances must have been peculiar if the visit was not closed with a service of social prayer. This was sometimes repeated four or five times in an evening, so that his dwelling was indeed the House of God and the Gate of Heaven. The members of his Session have told me that when each of them, in rotation, have accompanied him in his pastoral visits, it was no unusual occurrence for him to order the wagon to be driven under the shade of a tree, by the road-side, where, sheltered from the rays of the sun, he would pour forth an affectionate prayer, embracing the interests of his family, his session and his flock, the welfare of his country and the diffusion of the Gospel over the world. For the last of these objects he always manifested the deepest interest. His name is honourably identified with the institution of Foreign Missions. He frequently preached on public occasions in their behalf, and continued a liberal supporter and a zealous advocate of them while he lived.

Dr. Proudfit was an ardent admirer of nature. This, which is usually felt only by the young and ardent, continued with him a passion to his old age, nor was he ever more elevated or gratified than when he had it in his power to communicate his emotions to others. A wild-flower by the way-side, a majestic tree standing alone in a field, a sunset, or the corn waving its graceful leaves, were objects from which he seemed to experience the highest delight. These pleasures were enhanced from the opportunities thus afforded him to expatiate on the indications of wisdom and benevolence which are seen in the works of the Almighty. One of his favourite studies eminently fitted him for this—it was the subject of adaptation. He had evidently read with great care such works as Derham's Physico-Theology, Rae on the Divine Wisdom, and Paley's Natural Theology. He would frequently, in his walks, pluck a flower, and point out the evidences of skill displayed in its general structure and separate arrangements, as a conclusive argument for a supreme cause.

Of the more active scenes of Dr. Proudfit's life, his valuable services to the Christian denomination with which he was connected, his prominent advocacy of most of the social and religious institutions of our country, the solicitude which he felt for the conversion of the Aborigines and the spiritual interests of the new settlers in our distant territories, his unwearied labours and successful agency in behalf of the Colonization Society,—of these and kindred spheres of usefulness I shall not speak, as I prefer to limit my notices to what fell under my own observation, or has been communicated to me by those under his pastoral charge.

Dr. Proudfit's life must have been a signally happy one. His wife was a lady of truly amiable and excellent character, who sympathized with him in all his schemes, and did much to lighten his labours. By the members of his family he was regarded with feelings of the deepest reverence and affection. The church over which he had so long presided looked up to him as their spiritual father, nor did his demission of his charge tend, in the least, to abate their affection. By the religious part of the community his services were deeply appreciated, as those of an eminent disciple of Christ, and even ungodly men were compelled to respect one whose life was so faithful a transcript of the truths which he preached.

As his life was thus happy, so his death took place under the most propitious circumstances. He endured his last illness under the roof of his son, in New Brunswick, where everything was done, that affection and medical skill could suggest, to alleviate his sufferings. He died in the hope full of immortality. His remains were brought to Salem for burial; and, on the day following, they were accompanied to the grave-yard by the largest number that had ever attended a Funeral in that village. The day was lovely, and the immense assemblage in the old burying-ground, on the East side of the village, presented a deeply imposing appearance. A hymn was sung before the last rites were performed, and the efficient choir of the Rev. Dr. Lambert, of the Presbyterian Church, led the devotions of the immense throng. The body was then consigned to the same grave where the ashes of his venerable father sleep, both to be partakers together of the same glorious resurrection.

On the following Sabbath, the Rev. Dr. Proudfit, of New Brunswick, preached, in the forenoon, an able and impressive sermon from I Cor. xv, 55, "O death, where is thy sting;" and the occasion was sought to be improved, in the afternoon, by him who has furnished this very imperfect tribute.

I am, Dear Sir,
Yours respectfully,
E. HALLEY

WILLIAM McAULEY.
1794—1851.
FROM THE REV. JOHN FORSYTH, D.D.

Rev. and Dear Friend: I send you with great pleasure my recollections of the Rev. and venerable WILLIAM McAULEY of Kortright, and I do this the more cheerfully, because I think that if his name did not appear on your roll of worthies of the Associate Reformed Church, the roll would be materially defective. You have often, I dare say, been reminded by your correspondents in all branches of the Church, of those well known lines of Gray, "Full many a flower is born to blush unseen," and have been surprised to find how many men of exalted talent, perhaps of genius, have lived and died in obscurity. You have had so many accounts of such persons, that you have possibly come to regard most of them as the exaggerations of friendship or affection. I confess that for myself I am inclined to believe that there is a good deal of truth in them—that a large number of those whose names would have been utterly forgotten but for the enduring monument which you have erected and on which they are inscribed, if their life "lines had fallen" in more favourable places, might have won for themselves lasting renown. Certainly that feeling is strong within me in regard to Mr. McAuley. Beyond the limits of the not very large Synod in whose communion he lived and died his name was unknown; so far as I know there is not a published page of which he was the author; in a word, his entire ministry in this country, stretching through more than half a century, was spent amid the sequestered hills of Delaware County, and yet, from what I know myself, but much more from what I have heard of him from his contemporaries, I am persuaded that if he had been called to labour in a different sphere, and in circumstances favourable to the full development of the man, he would have won for himself a distinguished reputation.

The Rev. WILLIAM McAULEY was born in the North of Ireland about the year 1765. At the usual age he repaired to the University of Glasgow, the institution in which most of the North Irish young men of that day, who intended to enter one of the learned professions, received their education. While a member of the University, Mr. McAuley gained very high distinction. He was regarded by his fellow students and the Professors as a youth of singular promise, and was the special favorite of Prof. Anderson, one of the most eminent scientific men of that time, and the founder of the Andersonian University of Glasgow. Having completed his academic course, he at once began the study of Theology under the well known and venerable John Brown, of Haddington, the Professor of Theology to the Associate Burgher Synod of Scotland, and was one of the last class of students taught by that great and good man.

Mr. McAuley was licensed by the Associate Presbytery of Armagh in 1789, and on this occasion a little scene occurred which showed the sort of stuff of which he was made. I had an account of it years ago, by a venerable parishioner of mine, himself a native of Ireland, and who happened to be present at the meeting and a witness of the affair. The Sermon and Lecture of the young candidate being under discussion, though better, I dare say, than many of the members of Presbytery could have preached, were most unmercifully criticised—according to the usage of Scottish and Irish judicatories of that day. Mr. McAuley endured the infliction as long as he could, but, at length, burning under a sense of the injustice done his productions, he arose, "bearded the lion in his den," demanded to be heard in reply, and then proceeded to give the astonished fathers and brethren a taste of the same sort of excoriation as that to which they had subjected him. The very sublimity of the impertinence, as it must have seemed to them, probably saved him from instant suspension. Certainly he must have been an uncommonly bold young man, who would venture, in that way, to face a Scottish or an Irish Presbytery in those times. In 1790 Mr. McAulay was ordained by the same Presbytery as Minister of the Associate Congregation of Tulliallan, and, during the four years of his residence in this charge, he performed his pastoral duties, in and out of the pulpit, with very great acceptance. He came to this country in the summer of 1794, was received by the Associate Reformed Presbytery of Washington, (in the Synod of New York,) on the 2d of September of that year, and on the 25th of June he was installed by the same Presbytery in the pastoral charge of the United Congregations of Kortright, Harpersfield and Stamford, in the County of Delaware, N. Y. The new field into which he entered was then one of the "new settlements," on the confines of the unbroken wilderness, if not actually in it, and must have presented the greatest possible contrast to that which he had left, amid the verdant and cultivated hills and valleys of Ireland. To reach Delaware County in that day, whether one started from Albany or Catskill, a long journey through the wilderness was necessary, and when one arrived there, he would find himself in just such a "lodge" as Cowper longed for, "a boundless contiguity of shade."

The history of Mr. McAuley's pastorate in Kortright, though it extended over more than half a century, is soon told. His parish originally embraced two or three townships, but the number of his parishioners was small, and most of them were so poor that it was absurd to think of their supporting a minister. Their Pastor, while watching over their spiritual concerns, was obliged to depend mainly upon his own exertions for the supply of his own temporal necessities. In process of time, Mr. McAuley's family grew to be a very large one; his salary hardly amounted to $300, and was irregularly paid; while preaching on the Lord's day, he was compelled to labour as hard as any of his hearers on every other day, and so he toiled, year after year, until he was past middle life, amid difficulties, privations, the pinchings of poverty, and the anxieties incident to a large family, such as few ministers or missionaries experience now-a-days. Ultimately his labours were confined to Kortright, which, while the mother of three or four respectable congregations itself, grew to be one of the largest and most substantial churches in all that region. In 1810 the Stamford branch of his original charge was set off as a distinct parish under the care of the Rev. Robert Forrest. His settlement in this place proved a great comfort and blessing to Mr. McAuley. No two men, in many respects, could differ more than these two Pastors, who, for nearly forty years lived and worked together within some six or seven miles of each other. They became the most endeared friends, and regularly twice a year they assisted each other at the dispensation of the Lord's Supper. There was no man whom Mr. McAuley loved more warmly than Mr. Forrest, and there was no man for whom Mr. Forrest had a profounder veneration as well as affection than Mr. McAuley. Mr. Forrest, carried with him to the then wilds of Delaware County, a fine library. He was a lover of books, and having the means to do so, he made constant and valuable additions to his collection. His settlement, therefore, in Stamford was a double boon to Mr. McAuley, for it gave him the companionship of a dear friend and fellow-presbyter, and also the access to books from which his remoteness from town and his poverty had shut him out for years. He had the happiness to see sundry colonies going forth from the mother church peacefully, and with their venerable Pastor's blessing, and to welcome, as his colleague and successor, my esteemed friend, the Rev. Clarke Irving, the present minister of Kortright. But so long as he himself was able to ascend the pulpit, and even when blindness and other infirmities of advanced age made it necessary for others to assist him into it, there was no one whom his people so loved to see there, or to whose voice they listened with greater delight. His death took place on the 24th of March, 1851.

About the year 1810 or '12, an earnest effort was made by the old Associate Reformed Church of Albany, (now the 3d Presbyterian,) to induce Mr. McAuley to become its Pastor. But, as the congregation was not a very strong one, and as his family had grown to be a large one, his friends thought that the risk involved in removal to a new sphere was too great for him in his circumstances to run, and the plan was consequently abandoned.

The first time that I ever saw him was in my childhood. There was a meeting of Synod at Newburgh, and Mr. McAuley was a guest of my father's. I have a dim remembrance of the sermon he preached on the Lord's day afternoon, though the fact might have faded from my memory if I had not so often heard the circumstances attending it repeated by my father and others who were present on the occasion. The leading men of the church had asked the Synod to arrange the services of the Lord's day, expecting, of course, that only the "big guns" would be employed,—to use a cant phrase—knowing as they did that the church would be crowded. The day came, and greatly to the mortification of the Elders and others, they learned that the person chosen for the service was the plain looking and rather humbly attired Mr. McAuley, of Kortright, who had not once opened his mouth in Synod, and from whom, judging by appearances, only a very ordinary sermon was to be expected. However the thing was done and could not be changed; they only hoped that there might be a thin audience, but in this too they were disappointed, for the church was as full as it could be. Mr. McAuley ascended the pulpit and began the service. The tone of his prayer surprised them a good deal, and they began to think, when it was ended, that they had possibly mistaken the man. He announced his text, I Peter i, 8. "Whom having not seen ye love," &c., and within five minutes he led the vast audience captive at his will. I have, as I said, a dim remembrance of that noble discourse, for I was only a child at the time, but I can never forget the profound stillness of the church, nor the delight with which I listened to his rich Irish voice. I need not mention that ever after, Mr. McAuley was a prime favourite in Newburgh, and that, on his occasional visits, necessity was laid upon him invariably to preach. As a member of Synod, the meetings of which he punctually attended until kept at home by the infirmities of age, he was one of the most modest and retiring of men. It was an exceedingly rare thing for him to take part in a discussion, although he was always in his place and a most attentive listener; but when he did speak, it was to give in a brief, clear and simple way, his judgment and the grounds on which it rested. But by the fireside of a friend, or in his own house, he was as genial and accessible as a child, and wherever he was a guest, the little ones were sure to find the way to his lap.

His head was one which would have filled a phrenologist with delight, and no one could look upon it without suspecting at least that it was the home of a superior intellect; and no one could look into his countenance without perceiving the traces of that love of humour for which his countrymen are generally noted. Indeed, I can well believe that in his earlier years, his native humour and wit often overflowed; but when I first knew him, he was past the meridian of life, and he had been called to drink deeply of the cup of sorrow, and consequently his humour came out in a quiet way. On one occasion when the Synod was to meet at Kortright, a large coach load of the brethren reached the parsonage about 8 P. M. We were of course warmly welcomed, but when some one was expressing his fears that there might not be beds enough for so large a company, Mr. McAuley with a humorous twinkle of his eye, replied that in any case we would not be so badly off as he was the first night he spent in Kortright, when, said he, "we had to sleep fourteen in a bed," *i. e.*, on the soft side of the floor. He was once called to marry the nephew of one of his neighbours, a worthy Covenanter of the old stamp, who was disposed to measure the value of religious services by their length. Mr. McAuley, as his habit was, made the marriage service quite short, and when, at the close, he pronounced the young couple husband and wife,—"Humph," said the uncle,—"they are nae mair married than they were before." Mr. McAuley overheard the remark, though it was not intended to reach his ear, but he did not notice it in any way. Some time afterward the uncle resolved to take to himself a wife, and as no minister of his own church could be got, he was forced, much against his will, to apply to Mr. McAuley, who cheerfully consented to "tie the knot" for him. When the evening for the marriage arrived and the parties had presented themselves, Mr. McAuley addressed the bridegroom (after a single word to the bride) in a discourse regarding his duties and responsibilities of such length that the poor man, fairly wearied out, was forced to take a seat, leaving the lady standing alone. Mr. M. thereupon closed the service, and, after the customary congratulations, he, with a significant smile, asked the worthy Covenanter,—" Do you think that *you* are married?"

But I must bring these reminiscences to a close. My letter is perhaps longer than it should be, and yet I feel that it will give your readers who never knew him, a very imperfect idea of the venerable man whom I have attempted to portray. That he was not an ordinary man all I think will admit, who consider the single fact that his " natural force " as a Preacher was considered as " unabated " by the grandchildren and the great-grandchildren of those who seventy years ago or more settled in a wilderness, which, through their instrumentality, has been made to blossom as the rose. You can easily understand how a man of the most brilliant natural genius, if compelled to toil in the fields during the entire week, and to elaborate his discourses while following the plough, and to do this for ten years, would come to feel a positive distaste for the pen. It seemed to have been so with Mr. McAuley. His fellow-presbyters who knew his powers often tried to get some product of his pen that might be preserved. With this view he was appointed by the Synod to prepare a Testimony on an important doctrinal point, about the year 1833; but the habits of a life-time were too strong, and the document was unwritten. So that only the memory of his sermons, his piety, his pastoral work, remains. *Stat nominis umbra.* And yet I am persuaded that, in the central portion of Delaware County, there are thousands, who, though they never saw him, yet from what their fathers have told them, will cherish with affectionate veneration the name, WILLIAM MCAULEY.

I am affectionately yours,
JOHN FORSYTH

JOHN M. McJIMSEY, D. D.
1794—1854.

JOHN M. MCJIMSEY, the eldest son of Robert and Mary (Harbison) McJimsey, was born near Carroll's Tract, York County, Pa., on the 18th of August, 1772. His parents were both of Scottish ancestry; though his father was born in the North of Ireland, and his mother in this country. His father was a farmer, and the family were in comfortable worldly circumstances. Both parents being devout Christians, he, with their other children, was carefully instructed in the principles of the Christian religion, and was required to recite the Westminster Shorter Catechism every Sabbath day. It was especially to the influence of a pious mother that he attributed those early religious impressions which ultimately gave the decisive complexion to his character.

When he was in his thirteenth year he was permitted, by his parents, at the urgent solicitation of some of their neighbours, to take charge of a small school. About six months afterwards he commenced his course of classical study under an Irishman, who taught a common English school in the vicinity; and, about a year after, he was placed under the tuition of the Rev. Alexander Dobbin, his Pastor, who had recently opened a private school in his own house, near Gettysburg, and who was regarded as a thorough classical scholar. Under his instruction he continued about two years, and then entered the Junior class in Dickinson College. A year previous to his entering College, however, he was employed as an assistant in Mr. Dobbin's school, at the same time pursuing his own studies, under Mr. D.'s instruction. He entered College in the autumn of 1790, in the eighteenth year of his age; and, after passing through the usual course of studies, graduated in May, 1792.

* MSS. from himself and his son, Rev. J. M. McJimsey.

Mr. McJimsey made a profession of religion at the age of about fifteen; and he seems to have had the Ministry in view at a still earlier period. Immediately after his graduation, he commenced the study of Theology under the direction of Mr. Dobbin, in connection with three of his classmates. After remaining here about a year and a half, he studied for six months under the Rev. John Smith,* of Octorora; and in May, 1794, was licensed to preach the Gospel, by the first Associate Reformed Presbytery of Pennsylvania, at the Hill-Meeting House, Marsh Creek, then York County.

After his licensure Mr. McJimsey was occupied more than a year under the direction of Presbytery, and, in accordance with his own desire, in preaching in different vacant churches within the limits of his denomination. By appointment, he went on a mission to Kentucky, then the only State organized in the South West, and spent the winter of 1795 in preaching in different destitute places in that State. After his return from Kentucky, during the summer of 1795, he visited, for the first time, the State of New York, preaching in several vacant congregations; but he declined the offer of a settlement, on the ground that it was his intention, at that time, to make Kentucky his future field of labour.

On his return from the North to the city of New York, about the beginning of September, 1795, he was attacked by the Yellow Fever, and brought to the borders of the grave, at the house of his friend, the Rev. Dr. John M. Mason; where he received every attention that the most generous sympathy could dictate. Having recovered from his illness, he took leave of his friends, among whom was Mrs. Isabella Graham, who kindly said to him, on parting,—"I wish you all prosperity, and affliction too, when necessary." About two months after his return to his father's,—on the 24th of December, 1795, he was ordained to the office of the Gospel Ministry, by the same Presbytery that had licensed him; the Sermon on the occasion being preached by his former Pastor and instructor, Mr. Dobbin. A call from a congregation in Kentucky had been previously put into his hands, and accepted by him; but as it was then too late in the season

---

* JOHN SMITH was born near Stirling, Scotland, about the year 1746. He was educated at the University of Glasgow, and studied for the ministry under Professor Moncrieff, of Alloa. In 1769 he was ordained by the Associate Presbytery of Stirling, with the special view of his going to America. He came to this country in 1770, and was soon afterwards settled in the pastoral charge of Octorora, Pa. He possessed fine pulpit talents, and his attainments as a scholar and theologian were more than respectable; and, for some years he had charge of the few candidates for the ministry then under the care of the Presbytery. He was a zealous friend of the union of the Associate and the Reformed Presbyteries, and took a prominent part in the conferences and discussions which preceded and led to it. He was chosen Moderator of the Associate Reformed Synod in 1788, and, during the first ten years of the existence of the Synod, was a member of nearly every important Committee. In 1787 he was appointed, in connection with Dr. John Mason and the Rev. Robert Annan, to prepare an Illustration and Defence of the Westminster Confession. The larger part of the work was done by Mr. Annan, but the Report of the Committee to Synod proves that both Mr. Smith and Dr. Mason performed some share of it. In 1793 Mr. Smith joined with another member in a sort of Protest against the action of Synod in refusing to recognize the binding obligation of the Solemn League and Covenant; but, as the Protest was withdrawn before the Synod adjourned, his difficulties were thought to have been removed. But, in 1794, he abruptly left the Presbytery of which he was a member, giving no reason for the step, and joined the Associate Presbytery. In announcing his purpose to his own congregation, he delivered a speech to them, which was considered so defamatory, that the Synod, in 1795, suspended him from the ministry. He remained in connection with the Associate Body for some years, but finally abandoned it, in consequence of some difficulties in which he was involved. He is believed to have spent his latter years in Western New York, and to have died about the year 1820.

to undertake so long a journey, his departure was necessarily delayed till the following spring.

Before the period of setting out for Kentucky arrived, the Presbytery to which he belonged, at the earnest request of the Presbytery of New York, reconsidered and revoked his appointment to Kentucky; and he was appointed to preach, a few Sabbaths, in the summer of 1796, to the then vacant congregation of Neelytown, in the township of Montgomery, Orange County, N. Y., where he had supplied for a short time the preceding summer. The result was that a unanimous call was soon made out for him by the congregation, which he accepted; and he was installed as the Pastor of the Neelytown Church, on the 22d of December, 1796, the Rev. Thomas Smith, Pastor of Little Britain Congregation, officiating on the occasion.

On the 12th of December, 1797, Mr. McJimsey was married to Ann, daughter of George and Mary (Bull) Wilkin, a member of the church of which he was Pastor. They had eight children,—five sons and three daughters. Two of the sons have been graduated at Union College, and are Ministers of the Gospel. Mrs. McJimsey was, for many years, bereft of her reason, but it was fully restored to her some time before her death. She died on the 12th of August, 1852, in the seventy-seventh year of her age.

When he became Pastor of the Neelytown Congregation, it was stipulated that he should preach a few Sabbaths in each year, in a neighbourhood about ten miles distant, where a few families resided, connected with the Neelytown Church, who had united in his call, and were pledged for a part of his salary. These people, in 1799, erected a place of worship, to which they gave the name of Graham's Church; and, after this, Mr. McJimsey preached, on alternate Sabbaths, there and at Neelytown; though he removed to a parsonage near Graham's Church, which had been bequeathed to the people by the individual for whom the church was named. The new church, however, was not fully organized until June, 1802.

Between these two churches he officiated as Pastor for about thirteen years from the time of his Installation at Neelytown; each Church gradually increasing in numbers during the whole period of his ministry. In 1809 he received a call from an Associate Reformed Congregation in Albany, which, by the advice of the Presbytery of New York, he accepted; and, on the 18th of October, his pastoral relation was dissolved. He removed immediately to Albany, and preached his first Sermon from Acts x, 29: "Therefore came I unto you without gainsaying, as soon as I was sent for; and ask, therefore, for what intent you have sent for me." His Installation, owing to some peculiar circumstances, did not take place till the 13th of July, 1810; when the Rev. Dr. J. M. Mason officiated, and preached a remarkably able and eloquent Sermon.

Mr. McJimsey exercised his ministry in Albany with a good degree of acceeptance and usefulness for more than three years; when, owing to some adverse circumstances, especially the inadequacy of his support, he applied to the Presbytery to release him from his pastoral charge. This request was granted on the 7th of October, 1813. As he was now not a little pressed in his pecuniary circumstances, and no opportunity for resettlement in the ministry presented, he resolved to open a private classical school in Albany. In this school, which was continued without interruption for about two years, he was eminently successful; and, during this period, he was occupied, a large part of the time, on the

Sabbath, in preaching to different congregations in the neighbourhood. He was finally induced to give up his school, chiefly by the consideration that an Academy was about to go into operation, and he was unwilling to hold an attitude that even seemed to be unfavourable to that important enterprise.

Shortly after he closed his school he received an invitation to become the Principal of the Dutchess County Academy, at Poughkeepsie; which he accepted. He, accordingly, removed to Poughkeepsie in November, 1815, where he remained in the successful discharge of his duties as Teacher for four years.

In 1819 he was invited to take charge of the Academy at Montgomery, and to supply, half of the time, the vacant Congregation of Graham's Church, in the vicinity of which he had had the pastoral charge, previous to his removal to Albany. As this furnished him an opportunity of resuming his labours as a Minister, he accepted the two-fold invitation; and, as the Church at Neelytown, which had formed the other part of his pastoral charge, was still vacant, he was soon employed to preach there every alternate Sabbath. He removed to Montgomery on the 1st of November, and immediately entered upon his varied and arduous duties. He found himself in the midst of a people still strongly attached to him, though they had become sadly reduced in numbers and strength during his absence. His labours among them, however, were now remarkably blessed, and a season of spiritual refreshing was enjoyed, in consequence of which each church received considerable additions.

After a few years Mr. McJimsey resigned the charge of the Academy at Montgomery, but his ministry was continued with both churches until the beginning of the year 1832, when his labours at Neelytown were brought to a close, in consequence of the congregation at Graham's Church making arrangements to secure his services during the whole time. As he was disposed to listen to their proposals, that congregation presented a request to the Presbytery that he might be installed over them; and, the request being complied with, he preached his Farewell Sermon to the Neelytown Congregation, on the 5th of February, 1832, and was shortly after regularly installed as Pastor of Graham's Church, the Rev. Dr. McCarroll,* of Newburgh, officiating on the occasion, by appointment of Presbytery.

---

*JOSEPH McCARROLL was born at Shippensburg, Pa., on the 9th of July, 1795. At an early age he united with the Associate Reformed Church of that place, of which his parents were members, and, as his mind was then turned towards the ministry of the Gospel, he began the usual course of study preparatory to entering College. He was thus engaged when the country was electrified by the tidings of the capture and burning of Washington by the British, and their threatened advance on Baltimore. The militia of that region marched in haste to the scene of conflict, and such was the patriotic ardour of the people of Shippensburg, that every man in the town, capable of bearing arms, hurried to the defense of Baltimore—among whom was Joseph McCarroll.

The regiment to which he belonged formed part of the reserves behind the entrenchments on the hills, about two miles from Baltimore, and hence did not go into action, though expecting to do so every moment. From this position Mr. McCarroll witnessed the bombardment of Fort McHenry, and the repulse of the British army and fleet—a spectacle which, in later years, he used to describe as one of the most imposing and magnificent he ever beheld.

Soon after his return home he entered Washington College, in Pennsylvania, and graduated in the class of 1815. For several years after leaving College, he was occupied as a Teacher in Bellefontaine, Greensburgh and Carlisle, and, in each of these places, won the warm regard of all with whom he was brought in contact. Meanwhile, he prosecuted the studies preparatory to the Ministry, in such intervals of time as he could snatch from the hours demanded by the school-room. But, though he had an iron constitution, he found the double work so hard and wearing that he was on the point of abandoning the Ministry, and perhaps might have done so, if he had not been encouraged to go forward by his friend, the Rev. John Lind, of Hagerstown, who used to call

Mr. McJimsey bore an active part in the reorganization of the Theological Seminary of the Associate Reformed Synod, in 1829. He acted as Secretary of its Board of Superintendents fourteen years successively, and drew up its Annual Reports to Synod respecting the state of the Seminary. As an agent in collecting funds for the institution, he visited a large number of churches, and obtained by subscription an aggregate of nearly seven thousand dollars.

He was honoured with the degree of Doctor of Divinity, from Rutgers College, in 1835.

Dr. McJimsey continued his pastoral connection with Graham's Church till the close of his life. His health was, so vigorous that he was able to discharge his ministerial duties till the Sabbath but one previous to his death ; and, on that day, he rode ten miles to fulfil an appointment. About the middle of August, 1854, he went to Newburgh to attend a meeting of his Presbytery, and, at the same time,.to visit his son and family, who were passing the summer there. While engaged in his official duties, he was violently attacked by the cholera morbus, which, in nine days, terminated his life. He died in the full possession of his faculties, and in the serene confidence of a better life, at the Powellton House, Newburgh, on the 26th of August, in the eighty-third year of his age ; and his Funeral Sermon was preached by the Rev. Dr. McCartee, of Newburgh.

Dr. McJimsey published Sermons under the following titles :—The Christian's Hope of Immortality ; Sin and Death, or Grace and Life ; The World no Equivalent for the Loss of the Soul ; The Christian's Privilege and Duty ; also a

him a "second Timothy." Accordingly, he entered the Theological Seminary of the Associate Reformed Church in New York, in the autumn of 1818. Before entering the Seminary he had mastered the Hebrew language, and had read the whole Hebrew Bible. Having completed the usual course of study, he was licensed by the Presbytery of Big Spring, on the 19th of June, 1821. For some months he supplied the Murray Street Church, New York, then vacant by the removal of Dr. Mason to Carlisle, with much acceptance. He was ordained by the Associate Reformed Presbytery of New York, and installed in the pastoral charge of the First Associate Reformed Church of Newburgh, on the 14th of March, 1823, where he continued his labours with great acceptance and success during the remainder of his life. In the autumn of 1829 he was elected Professor of Theology in the Theological Seminary of the Associate Reformed Synod of New York, which had been revived a short time before and removed to Newburgh. This office he continued to hold till his decease, which occurred on the 29th of March, 1864.

The following is a list of Dr. McCarroll's publications :—A Sermon preached at Salem, N. Y., before the Domestic Missionary Society of the Associate Reformed Synod of New York, 1826. Answer to a Discourse preached by Dr. William E. Channing at the Dedication of the Second Congregational Unitarian Church, New York, 1827. Address on the Sabbath, 1827. Speech before the General Assembly of the Presbyterian Church of 1831, in support of a Claim of the Associate Reformed Synod of New York, to the Property transferred to the General Assembly by the General Synod of the Associate Reformed Church in 1822, 1831. The Way of Salvation : A Discourse delivered at Newburgh, 1834. Ministerial Responsibility : a Sermon preached in the Associate Reformed Church, Philadelphia, 1834. Review of the Opinions of Dr. N. W. Taylor, 1834. Review of Stuart on Romans, 1835. The Atonement : A Sermon on John i, 29, 1837. A Sermon preached at the Funeral of Mr. D. N. Carithers, 1838. An Address to the Students in the Theological Seminary, Newburgh, 1839. Bible Temperance, in Three Discourses, 1841. The Seraphim : An Address to the Students of the Theological Seminary, 1847. Fishers of Men : An Address to the Students of the Theological Seminary, 1848. The Book : An Address before the Students of the Theological Seminary, Newburgh, 1849. The Christian's Hope : A Sermon on I Peter i, 3-5, 1850. An Essay on Capital Punishment, 1852. A God-sent Ministry the World's Great Need : An Address to the Students of the Theological Seminary, 1852. An Essay on The Geology of the Bible, 1856. The Cherubim : A Sermon on Genesis iii, 24.

Dr. McCarroll, though a quiet and undemonstrative man, possessed high intellectual ability and rare goodness. He won not only the respect but the warm affection of his Students. In the pulpit his manner was usually unimpassioned, but his utterances were so weighty as to command the fixed attention especially of the more intellectual portion of his audience. He was decidedly a man of mark, not only in his denomination but in the Church at large.

Sermon occasioned by the Death of his Wife. He edited the American edition of Dr. Lawson's Lectures on Ruth.

I first knew Dr. McJimsey about the year 1830, when, happening to pass a a Sabbath in Albany, he preached half a day in my pulpit. I had barely heard of him before, and knew nothing of his character as a Preacher. His text was "Those that be planted in the house of the Lord shall flourish in the Courts of our God." The Sermon was equally rich in evangelical thought, and simple and beautiful in construction; and I could not but marvel that the man who was capable of writing it, and delivering it with such graceful simplicity, should not be occupying one of the higher places of Zion. In private, I found him then and ever after, one of the loveliest of men,—warm-hearted, ingenuous and confiding. I had often occasion to put his kindness in requisition, and the first intimation of my wishes always brought from him a prompt and favourable response. I never had an interview with him, or received a letter from him, that did not deepen my impression of his great moral worth.

FROM REV. ROBERT PROUDFIT, D.D.

SCHENECTADY, June 5, 1855.

Dear Sir: There may be others whose relations with Dr. McJimsey were more intimate than mine, yet there are probably few whose recollections of him reach back to so early a period. I saw him first at my father's, in York County, Pa., when I was quite in my boyhood. I became further acquainted with him the next year, when I was a pupil at the Rev. Mr. Dobbin's school, he being, at that time, a licensed Preacher. After I had graduated I came to reside permanently in the State of New York; and then I found him settled as Pastor of Graham's Church, in Montgomery County, where he spent the greater portion of his ministerial life. Though we were never thrown into the same immediate neighbourhood, I often met him in Synod and at other times, and was always on terms of familiar and fraternal intercourse with him as long as he lived.

Dr. McJimsey could hardly fail to impress you favourably, the moment you set eyes upon him. He was of about the medium height, rather inclined to be slender, of an expression of countenance at once intelligent and benignant, and almost always, in social intercourse, taking on a bright and winning smile. He was easy and light in his movements, social in his disposition, and ready, fluent and agreeable in conversation. He impressed you at once as a man without guile: and you could not, by any effort, work yourself into the least apprehension that he would ever, in any way, prove unkind or unfaithful to you. While he was a good talker, and was always ready to bear his part in any conversation that might come up, and always spoke intelligently and to the point, there was nothing that seemed monopolizing in his manner,—least of all was he disposed to make himself the hero of his own story.

Dr. McJimsey's mind was uncommonly symmetrical. His perceptions were quick and clear, his judgment sober, and his taste formed after the best models. He was not an impassioned Preacher, nor yet was he a frigid and lifeless one; but there was a simple, dignified sort of earnestness that could hardly fail to secure the attention of any audience. And then there was a rich vein of evangelical sentiment running through his discourses, accompanied not unfrequently with striking and ingenious illustrations, which gave him favour with intelligent as well as devout hearers. He was a vigorous Preacher, even in his old age; and a sermon which he preached after the death of his wife, and not long before his own death, and which has been published, is distinguished not more for its pathos and elevation of sentiment, than for its chaste and faultless style.

Dr. McJimsey was always much at home in Public Bodies, and was always an active and useful member. While his judgment was regarded with high respect, he had great facility at communicating his thoughts, especially with his pen; and whenever there was any Report to be prepared, the committing of it to him was always considered as a pledge that it would be done in the most felicitous manner. He was perfectly familiar with all the forms of ecclesiastical business, and would detect almost instinctively the least departure from rule, while yet he was, by no means, a stickler for indifferent usages. He possessed, in the best sense of the word, a *catholic* spirit; one evidence of which was that other denominations honoured him as truly as his own.

His Christian character was a lovely compound of the various Christian graces, especially of the more quiet and retiring ones. He was the subject of a protracted and most severe domestic affliction, of which it was natural that he should not be much disposed to speak. Once, however, when I was riding with him, he introduced the subject, and, while he evinced the deepest, tenderest sensibility, he showed also the most unqualified and cheerful submission to the Divine will. His course through the world was comparatively a noiseless one, but it was marked by great consistency, purity and Christian elevation. Respectfully and truly yours,

ROBERT PROUDFIT.

FROM THE HON. WILLIAM KENT.

NEW YORK, December 16, 1854.

My dear Doctor: I have left unanswered too long your letter respecting the late Dr. McJimsey. I have endeavoured to recall something which might be of use to you in your proposed biography; but really I can find little to say beyond my expression of deep respect for this excellent and venerable man.

I was very young when I entered his school. It was established, I think, in 1814, when I was only eleven years of age, and I remained under his care, according to my recollection, about two years. He removed from Albany, I think, immediately after the commencement of the Academy to which I was transferred; and, during the residue of his life, I saw him only once or twice, when he casually visited New York.

I remember him with great affection and respect. He was not, I imagine, a deep scholar, and the education we received in his school did not approach the English standard, nor that of our classical schools in America of the present time. But he was a patient, intelligent and judicious teacher. The little Latin, and much less Greek, which I retain, I owe principally to his tuition; and more than this, he taught his scholars how to study, and formed in them habits of self-relying investigation. This, you will doubtless agree with me in thinking, is the most important gift of education.

Of his moral qualities,—of the purity and excellence of his life, no praise can be too high. I did not know till long after our personal intercourse had ceased, how much sorrow and misfortune this mild, amiable and pleasing man had borne with uncomplaining fortitude and undisturbed equanimity. To his sweetness of temper, his patience with the waywardness and wantonness of youth, his firm and just government of his school, and to the deep and unobtrusive piety of his daily life,—to all this I bear heartfelt testimony.

I was fond of him while I was his pupil, and years and reflection added gratitude to my attachment.

This brief and simple expression of feeling is all I can give in answer to your request

Believe me, with great respect, your most obedient servant,

WILLIAM KENT.

FROM THE REV JOHN H. MORRISON, D.D.,
MISSIONARY TO INDIA.

NEW YORK, August 4, 1863.

My dear Brother: My recollections of the Rev. Dr. McJimsey are of a very general character, and are confined chiefly to the years of my boyhood. I remember his once showing me his Record of Baptisms, and pointing to my name on the list. This, if I recollect right, was on one of only two or three visits which I paid him after my attention had been turned towards the Ministry of the Gospel. It seemed to afford him the utmost joy to see any one of his baptized children devoting himself to the service of Christ—indeed I never knew any minister of whom it could be more appropriately said that he seemed to have no greater joy than to see his children walking in the truth. He was anxious to have me go out as a Missionary from the Presbytery of which he was a member, but was met by difficulties which he was unable to overcome.

The three features of his character that have impressed themselves most vividly on my memory are his wonderful cheerfulness, his uniform kindness and courtesy, and his perfect dignity. I never saw in him the semblance of any thing to indicate the least tendency to gloom or depression. The heavy afflictions with which he was visited, during the whole period of my recollection of him, would have crushed many to the dust, and disabled them for a course of active usefulness; but I never saw him, even under his severest trials, when so much as the semblance of a cloud seemed to be resting upon him. He was evidently sustained by an indwelling, invisible power, that kept his heart in constant contact with the things that are not seen and are eternal. He seemed a noble illustration of God's faithfulness to his promise that his grace shall be sufficient for every time of need. But, though always cheerful, I doubt whether any one ever saw in him the slightest approach to levity or trifling. His heart overflowed with kindness. None were so young and none so old, none so rich and none so poor, none so virtuous and none so debased, but that he was on the alert to do them good whenever it was in his power. He was especially kind in his treatment of children. I never felt afraid to approach him, nor was I ever made to feel that he was so great, or so far above me, that I might not go and talk with him with perfect freedom. With all his kindliness and familiarity, however, he was uniformly dignified. His words, his manner, every thing pertaining to his deportment, evinced a calm and thoughtful habit of mind, and was fitted to awaken respect and veneration. He was a fine model of a Christian Gentleman. His self-respect never degenerated into arrogance, nor his courtesy into obsequiousness or flattery. In the pulpit and out of the pulpit, his demonstrations were all worthy of an Ambassador of God.

Believe me, very truly,
Your brother in the Lord,
J. H. MORRISON.

FROM THE REV. MALCOLM N. McLAREN, D.D.

NEWBURGH, October 24, 1856.

My dear Sir: It gives me pleasure to comply with your request for a sketch of my impressions of the late Dr. McJimsey. I wish I could do more justice to the subject,—which I certainly should do, could I transfer to this sheet the image of that excellent man as it exists in my own mind.

Although I had not perhaps so close an intimacy with him as some others of his clerical brethren who were nearer his age, yet I knew him well. Our fields of labour were adjacent. I was his successor in one of the Societies in which he had long and faithfully laboured. We often met on social and religious occasions. He was a not unfrequent visitor at my house, and I was quite as often at his. Even though my opportunity for knowing him had been much less favourable, I could scarcely have failed of a correct perception of his character,—so free was he from any thing like disguise, and so much and truly did the man himself appear in his every day and every where deportment. This remark is not designed to convey the idea that he was unguarded and imprudent in action or in speech, garrulously throwing out expressions of thoughts and feelings as they arose in his mind, or flitted in lights and shadows over it—he was conscientiously careful what thoughts and feelings he harboured, and no less so what words he uttered. Reserved where reserve was proper,—in regard to all that others had a right to know, he was unveiled and open. His good sound sense and self respect preserved him from the weakness of affectation; his ingenuous nature shrunk from the least approach to dissimulation. Partly from principle and partly from the impulse of his nature,—either alone was sufficient to produce the effect—he carried in his very appearance the features of his real character.

His manners were plain and simple, and at the same time dignified, and perhaps I might add, courtly. He was every inch a gentleman. I will not say he belonged to the old or the modern school, although he united the precision and dignity of the former with the easy and graceful urbanity of the latter. He belonged rather to that higher school, where true politeness is taught, not with reference to movement and attitude, but by implanting the spirit of Christian courtesy in the heart. The courteous bearing which always marked his conduct was not the result of studied attention to conventional rules—it was the effect of his instinctive perception of the proprieties of life; of his correct impulsive appreciation of what becomes the Man, the Christian and the Christian Minister; and of that true kindness of spirit which prompts its possessor every where, and under all circumstances, without ostentation or without effort, to promote the comfort of others. His politeness, like his breathing, was not the effect of design, of plan, of effort,—it was natural, spontaneous, unavoidable, a necessary function, an attribute of the man.

He was a man of remarkable equanimity. Whatever may have been his natural temperament, grace had schooled and subdued it into great evenness and self-command. If he did not often rise into great elevation of spirits, he seldom sunk into great depression. If what the old Scotch folks call *pouther* had a place in his bosom,—and he was not wholly destitute of that commodity,—he was generally careful to keep it stowed away in its proper magazine, where the attrition of a careless foot, or the advent of a floating spark, might not produce ignition. Though, during a large portion of his life, he was sorely tried by severe affliction of members of his family, yet such was his ordinary composure and calmness of spirit that those not acquainted with his history might be daily conversant with him without suspecting that he was enduring heavy trouble. Never, excepting in the closest intimacy of most confiding friendship, did he give any verbal intimation, and seldom did his countenance indicate, that he was daily drinking the cup of affliction. This did not arise from any lack of tenderness—few men possessed quicker or finer sensibilities. Neither did it arise from pride, affecting a stoical apathy, or a philosophical superiority to the sorrows of life. Such pride had no place in his heart. Nor was it any want of conjugal or fatherly regard. In these and in all the relations of life, he was considerate, attentive, gentle, affectionate. It was the piety of a sanctified soul shining out in his life. It was the meekness of a subdued spirit acquiescing in the will of his Lord and Master. It was the power of faith rejoicing in the wisdom and goodness of a Covenant God, and giving a practical utterance to the sentiment of Job,—"Shall we receive good at the hand of the Lord, and shall we not receive evil?"

Dr. McJimsey was a godly man. Probably it would not be transcending the bounds of truth to say he was eminently so. No one who knew him could entertain a doubt of his piety. It proved itself, not by ostentatious exhibitions, but by the general tenor of his life. It was not confined to times and places. At all times, and wherever he went, it went with him, as the radiations of light move with the moving of a lamp that burneth. If it was not always equally full and clear, it was always unequivocal. It was removed as far as possible from that which is spasmodic and fitful. Staidness was an attribute of his piety, as well as of himself. It was not a monthly—blooming and fading with the changes of the moon; nor was it an annual, which, however beautifully adorned with foliage under the summer sun, withers into barrenness at the approach of the wintry blast. It was an evergreen, retaining its beauty and manifesting increasing attractiveness amidst the storms and snows of winter. Although like every thing connected with our poor humanity, it sometimes varied in its appearance, it always exhibited a good degree of the freshness of "the tree planted by the rivers of water, that bringeth forth his fruit in his season." And although, like the tall mountain pine, it sometimes bent before the force of the storm, yet, in all its swaying to and fro, it always pointed and reached towards Heaven. I have seen him in various circumstances, and sometimes amidst exciting elements, and himself excited, though not often; but I never saw him when he appeared to be unmindful of what became him as a Man, and an Ambassador of our Lord Jesus Christ.

As a man of talents and substantial mental furniture, Dr. McJimsey occupied a highly respectable standing. He possessed a sound mind, well cultivated and well stored. Not at all deficient in general intelligence, he was particularly well informed in whatever pertained to his own profession. He was familiar with the Sacred Scriptures, and made much use of them in his pulpit exercises. His understanding was clear and discriminating. If his imagination was not quick and lively, it was always chaste. His position among educated men, and his general influence in society, are not to be attributed so much to any one prominent talent as to the general harmony of his intellectual powers. He had that happy combination of mental and moral properties which qualifies less for occasional dazzling exhibition than for steady and permanent usefulness. Good sound judgment had more to do in making up the aggregate of his usefulness than originality of thought or elegance of expression. If his mind did not move as fast as the minds of some others, it moved as sure. If it did not come as quickly to its conclusions, it usually came to them quite as correctly. What was lacking in celerity was compensated in strength. No one who knew him would ascribe to him the mental qualities that glitter; but he had, in more than usual degree, those which are practical and useful. He seldom let fly those scintillations which, however brilliant at the moment, so often prove, when subsequently examined, to be nothing but cinders. But whether in the coolness of reflective conversation or in the animation of heated debate, his mind always gave out the ring of the true metal.

Whether he should be pronounced eloquent or not, would depend, of course, on the taste of the hearer. If eloquence consists in fluent thoughts, glibness of utterance, theatric attitudes and violent gesture, or in sentiments adorned with florid imagery, and very prettily and gracefully delivered, Dr. McJimsey was at a respectable remove from eloquent. But if it consists in appropriate and connected thought, clearly conceived, and clearly, forcibly and feelingly expressed, then he was eloquent beyond the majority of his compeers.

If he was not what is commonly termed a *great* Preacher, he was what is far better, a *good* one. He showed both his wisdom and his piety in the selection of subjects for his pulpit discussions, or rather in confining himself to those which the adorable Master has Himself assigned. Familiar as he was with the truths of the Bible, he had no need, and, loving those truths as he did, he had no desire, to occupy the sacred hours of the Sabbath and the Sanctuary in the discussion of political, scientific or literary matters. He never introduced secular subjects into the pulpit. The Bible furnished him with texts not only, but with subjects, and suggested the mode, or at least the spirit, in which they should be handled. The themes which engaged his most frequent attention, and on which he most delighted to linger, were those which cluster around the Cross. He was not ashamed of the Gospel of Christ, nor of any of its doctrines, however unpopular, or however contrary to the pride and wisdom of the world. He gloried in them, and made them the glory of his discourses and of his life. He was thoroughly of the old Scotch School in his Theology, a Calvinist of the Calvinists, as Paul was a Hebrew of the Hebrews,—pure and full-blooded. By the unyielding tenacity with which he clung to what he believed to be the truth, and the tolerance and kindness with which he treated those who differed with him, he showed that the spirit of truth was enshrined in his heart.

In the pulpit, offering the prayers of the people to God, or delivering the message of God to the people, he was always serious and affectionate. It is rarer praise, and no less deserved, to say he was always serious and affectionate *out* of the pulpit. Even his cheerfulness had an air of seriousness about it, which savoured strongly of the fragrance of the closet, and his seriousness was characterized with a cheerful elevation of spirit, which betrayed the sacred source whence it was derived. Seen any where, he would be recognized as a Minister of Christ. None who attended his ministry, or heard him but occasionally, could fail of receiving the impression that the principle that governed him was love to God and to the souls of his fellow-men. Those who heard him oftenest, and knew him best, carried this impression deepest in their hearts.

Whether we contemplate our departed friend as to his natural endowments, his educational acquirements, his general intelligence, his habits of thought, his elucidations of Divine truth and his faithful application of it to his hearers, and the happy illustration of the power of grace which he gave in his life; he appears to have been admirably fitted for the work in which he was so long and so faithfully engaged.

Wishing you success in the enterprise to which this is a trifling contribution, and the blessing of our Lord and Saviour upon all your labours,

I am, dear Sir, very sincerely yours,

MALCOLM N. McLAREN.

ALEXANDER PORTER.
1796—1836.
FROM THE REV. JOHN T. PRESSLY, D.D

ALLEGHENY, February 13, 1863.

Rev. and dear Brother: In conformity with your request, I furnish the following brief sketch of the life of my old friend and Pastor, the Rev. Alexander Porter.

ALEXANDER PORTER was born in South Carolina in the year 1770. After receiving the rudiments of a classical education in his native State, he took his collegiate course in Dickinson College, Carlisle, during the Presidency of Dr. Nesbit. There being, at that time, no Theological Seminary under the care of the Associate Reformed Church, he pursued the study of Divinity under the direction of the Rev. John Jamison, of Indiana County, Pa., and was licensed to preach the Gospel in the year 1796. In the following year he was ordained to the office of the Holy Ministry, and was installed Pastor of the United Congregations of Cedar Spring and Long Cane, in Abbeville District, S. C. In a few years after Mr. Porter entered upon his pastoral labours, the congregations under his care increased to such an extent that one of them was sufficiently large to occupy the whole of his time. Accordingly, the pastoral care of the Congregation of Long Cane was relinquished, and his undivided attention was devoted to Cedar Spring. Here he laboured with much acceptance, and with a good degree of success, until the year 1814, when he removed to the State of Ohio; and, in the year following, was installed Pastor of the Congregation of Hopewell, in Preble County. Here he continued to labour assiduously and successfully, in a large congregation, till the year 1833; when, in consequence of declining health, he relinquished his pastoral charge. After this, he preached occasionally, as the state of his health would permit, for somewhat more than a year; and finally closed his active and useful life on the 29th of March, 1836, in the confident expectation of a glorious immortality.

Mr. Porter was an interesting and acceptable Preacher. His tall and erect form, his solemn and dignified appearance, his placid countenance and penetrating eye, his clear and melodious voice, and his simple and persuasive manner, all combined to inspire the hearer with awe. He excelled particularly in a plain, simple exhibition of God's Word, possessing the happy faculty of unfolding the truths of the Gospel in a manner intelligible to the common people, while it was never otherwise than acceptable to the cultivated mind. Easy and familiar in his manners, he was an agreeable companion; social in his disposition, he was always welcome to the domestic circle; and both the young and the aged eagerly sought his society. While he filled the pulpit with dignity, his deportment in his intercourse with society was such as became a good Minister of Jesus Christ. As a necessary result, his influence, both with the people and with his brethren in the ministry, was very great, and there are probably few men who have been instrumental in introducing into the Church of Christ, a greater number of persons who have adorned their Christian profession by a consistent deportment.

Mr. Porter was an active and useful member of the Board of Trustees of Miami University from 1819 till his death.

Mr. Porter's only publication of which I have any knowledge was a pamphlet of considerable size on the Arminian controversy, in reply to one from a Mr. Glenn, a Methodist Preacher. Indeed, during the active period of his life, the facilities for printing in South Carolina were so limited that few comparatively of the ministry published any thing.

Mr. Porter was married, in 1796, to Mary, daughter of John and Nancy Cochran, who resided in Abbeville District, S. C., within the limits of his pastoral charge. They had nine children,—four sons and five daughters, six of whom survived their father. His second son, *Alexander*, is a respectable Physician and a Ruling Elder in the Church, and resides in Fairhaven, Preble County, O. His third son, *James C.*, is a worthy minister in the United Presbyterian Church, residing in Little Rock, Ill. In consequence of declining health, he has recently demitted his pastoral charge.

Such, Dear Sir, is a very meagre sketch of the history, and a very imperfect delineation of the character, of a singularly excellent man, whom I knew well, under whose ministry I had my early training, and whom I succeeded in the pastoral care of the Congregation of Cedar Spring, of which I had the oversight for the first fifteen years of my ministerial life. I have stated nothing which any one who knew him would consider extravagant. Though he was not a man to excite the wonder of the world, he was a good scholar, an agreeable speaker, and profoundly acquainted with the Holy Scriptures. With serious persons, whether in humble life or in cultivated society, he was a favourite Preacher. And it is a fact worthy of notice that there are now persons who were trained under his ministry in Cedar Spring, or their off-spring, who are members of our Church in Georgia, Alabama, Tennessee, Mississippi, Illinois, Indiana and Ohio, and, to a remarkable extent, they exemplify the life and power of religion.

But you will see that I possess little skill in drawing a character, while I have a good model before me. If these few hints can be of any service to you, they are at your disposal.

Wishing you great success in your labours, I am, with great regard, your friend and brother,

JOHN T. PRESSLY.

JAMES GRAY, D.D.

1797—1824.

FROM THE REV. C. G. McLEAN, D.D.

FORT PLAIN, N. Y., December 20, 1848.

My dear Sir: I am happy to comply with your request, in sending you such notices of the life of my beloved and venerated relative as are within my reach.

JAMES GRAY was born December 25, 1770, in Corvoam, County of Monaghan, Ireland. He was descended of families of great respectability and substantial wealth. His father was the late Capt. John Gray, of the above mentioned place, and commanded a company of the celebrated Irish volunteers under Lord Charlemont. His mother's maiden name was Niblock. He was himself the first born of the family, which consisted of four sons and three daughters.

From childhood he was devoted to study, and had no taste for any other employment. His father was disposed to fall in with his predilections thus early manifested, and gave him every opportunity for the culture of his mind that his ambition coveted. He was himself a person not only of great compass and soundness of mind and decision of character, but of genuine and earnest piety; and it was his highest ambition, in respect to his son, that he should be an able and faithful Minister of the New Testament. He lived to witness the accomplishment of this pious desire.

After going through the elementary branches of his education, he entered the College of Glasgow, in 1790; and, having distinguished himself in the several classes he attended, he graduated in April, 1793. His diploma bears the signatures of fourteen Professors.

His theological studies were prosecuted principally under the direction of one of the Fathers of the Secession in Ireland, the late Rev. John Rogers, of Ballybay. He was licensed by the Presbytery of Monaghan. After preaching some time to vacant churches of the denomination of Burghers, with great acceptance, he took his letter of dismission and recommendation from the Presbytery of Armagh, of which, in the mean time, he had become a member, (May 10, 1797,) with a view of finding a home on these Western shores. Having, in the course of this year, married the widow of John McLean, M.D., he, with his wife and her two children, shortly after, embarked from Newry, and, in the month of June, landed in New York. In the succeeding autumn he was settled in West Hebron, Washington County, N. Y., in connection with the Associate Reformed Presbytery of Washington. There he remained, in a retired and even obscure field of labour, until the fall of 1803, when, having received a unanimous call from the Church in Spruce Street, Philadelphia, in connection with the Associate Reformed Synod, he accepted the call and removed to that city.

In 1805 he received the honorary degree of Doctor of Divinity from the University of Pennsylvania.

Next to Dr. Mason, he had probably the most important agency in establishing the Theological Seminary of the Associate Reformed Church in the city of New York. That institution he always regarded with the deepest interest, and in various ways lent it his cordial and efficient support. Knowing, as he did, the value of the highest intellectual qualifications for the ministry, it was a favourite object with him to increase the facilities of theological education as far as possible.

In 1808 he took an active part in the formation and management of the Philadelphia Bible Society, (the oldest institution of the kind in the country,) and, after the first year, was, for a long time, its Corresponding Secretary.

About this time he, in connection with Dr. S. B. Wylie, opened a Classical and Scientific Academy, which was well sustained for several years. At length, however, Dr. Gray came to feel that his labours in the Academy interfered too much with his appropriate duties as a Minister; and, as he had accomplished the principal object for which he had embarked in the enterprise, he and his associate, by mutual consent, dissolved the connection. Shortly after this he demitted his pastoral charge of the Spruce Street Church and removed to the city of Baltimore.

Having long contemplated publishing his views on certain points in Theology, he determined not to enter again into the pastoral relation. But, to support himself and his family, he opened a select school in Baltimore, which was very prosperous during the whole time that he presided over it. Here he composed and published his "Mediatorial Reign of the Son of God." He began, also, his Theological Review; but, as this was not sufficiently patronized, and as he had no funds to throw away, it was not continued beyond the first year—four numbers only were issued.

In the spring of 1823 he, with his family, came to reside with me at Gettysburg, Pa., where he continued till his death, which occurred September 20, 1824, in the fifty-fourth year of his age.

Dr. Gray's published works are a Sermon entitled Present Duty; A Dissertation on the Priesthoods of Melchisedec, Aaron and the Lord Jesus Christ; The Fiend of the Reformation Detected; Concio ad Clerum; The Mediatorial Reign; and the Theological Review. Had his life been spared, he had intended publishing another work or two, provided sufficient encouragement had been given to justify it.

His habits as a student were in some respects remarkable. His devotion to his studies was so intense as not to be disturbed by any thing about him. He was as collected amid confusion and uproar as when he was sitting alone in his study. When he was not reading or writing, he would often be walking, running or leaping, and still prosecuting his studies in connection with this bodily exercise. When on horseback, which was his favourite mode of travelling, his friends had little difficulty in determining whether or not he was engaged in deep thought by the gait of his horse: if it was slow, it was an indication that he was relaxing his faculties,—if rapid, it indicated, with equal certainty, that his mind was occupied in profound contemplation. So perfectly were his faculties under his control that he could stop at any point in his course, attend to what turned up at the moment, and then resume, as if his thoughts had suffered no diversion. These characteristics he retained even to the last. Few men kept up the whole circle of thought, traversed by the three professions, more completely than he did. With Hebrew, Greek and Latin he was perfectly familiar. Whatever was best worth knowing in Sacred or Profane History he had at hand. With the natural and abstract sciences he was so familiar that he was able to converse and even to debate to advantage with their respective Professors. His personal appearance was striking. In height he was about five feet, eight inches; muscular; without any tendency to corpulency; every limb fully developed, and all the joints well knit together, and every thing about his frame indicating great activity, strength and power of endurance. His complexion was fair, inclining to the florid; his lips thin and compressed; his nose aquiline; his eyes blue, and his forehead fully developed in the perceptive and intellectual regions. His temperament was sanguine, his friendships ardent and enduring, his antipathies few and short lived. He rarely lost a friend in the most exciting and protracted debates, and as rarely made an enemy. Moral truth, particularly as it lies in the inspired page, was the great central attraction of his soul. For that he lived and laboured and prayed. He held it with the utmost tenacity, and brought all the energies of his mind and heart to its vindication.

In all the relations of life, as Husband, Father, Pastor, Citizen, he was faithful, amiable and conciliatory. The rich respected and the poor loved him. The intelligent found an instructive companion in him, and the ignorant, one whom they might ever approach without fear. And though he had never any children of his own, he found in his step-son and daughter two whom he could not have loved more fervently, if they had been his own; and they merely knew that he was not their father according to the flesh—in every other respect they felt that they were not fatherless. His memory they cherish in their love, gratitude and veneration, in the fond hope of ere long meeting him in glory.

Your very sincere friend,
C. G. McLEAN.

FROM THE REV. JOHN M. DUNCAN, D.D.

BALTIMORE, October 28, 1848.

Dear Sir: Your letter of the 10th instant requests me to furnish you with my "recollections" of the late Dr. Gray. The appeal has worked up sensibilities which, originating with my early years, when Divine Providence ordained his right to a moral parentage over my undisciplined mind, and remaining through the toils and struggles of my maturer life, I would most sacredly cherish, *now* that his Master has called him home. I knew him well, loved him dearly, and confided in him without reserve. But I wield not the pen that is adequate to do him justice. You say well, when you speak of him as "one of the *greater*," I would say one of the *greatest* "lights of the American pulpit." The late Dr. Mason was in my house, when the news of his loved companion's decease reached our city, and, on being told of it, bowing his head, the big tears rolling down his cheeks, he observed,—"the greatest man I ever knew." Leaving me the next day, feeble and tottering as he was, he bade me farewell, saying, not only in words, but with his own expressive countenance,—the finest I ever beheld,—"I shall soon be with Dr. Gray."

His Creator had richly endowed him. His mind was of the first order, and his heart of equal claims,—both nicely balanced, and properly adjusted in his high character. The delicacies and refinements of intellectual intercourse he knew well how to appreciate,—rendering due respect to age, willing that equals should rise to any eminence to which talent or providential circumstances apparently called them; kind and condescending to the young, whom he was ever ready to encourage and assist; "compassionate to the ignorant and them that are out of the way;" never indulging the habit of speaking evil of others, yet making others see and feel that he had a high and keen sense of honour. One circumstance in connection with the first class of these, and which you may take as a guaranty for all the rest, I heard him relate, when advance in life allowed me the intimacy which the remark implies. When the venerable Dr. Reid, for whom he entertained the most unqualified respect, appeared upon the College Green, the students always took off their hats, to which this beloved Professor uniformly responded by the corresponding token. This, the youthful Gray determined he would not do; assigning to me, as his reason, that he exceedingly disliked to give the feeble old man so much trouble. Many would not so accurately discriminate between a fashionable custom and so happy and appropriate a moral reason for omitting it.

On second thought, it seems to me that I may as well inform you of another circumstance, illustrative of his regard for the young. It occurred to myself, during a period of toil and sorrow that I am destined never to forget, and through whose results I am still passing on to the judgment-seat, full of hope, and without any personal regrets. In the midst of my painful investigations, I said to him,—"Doctor, I am somewhat offended with you." "And what about, pray, Sir?" he replied. "Why you know I am walking through troubles, through which you have given me much reason to believe you have yourself passed in your early years. I come to you with my problems and seeking relief. Instead of sympathetically relieving me, you put me under a course of catechism, until you find out how far I have gone, and then you leave me." He answered to the following effect,—"I know it; I have done so on purpose, and have treated my son in the same way. You have your own work to do,—your own place to fill. We are in an unkind and misjudging world. After a while, when circumstances may require you to tell your own thoughts, that world will be mean enough to say you got your ideas from me; and I am determined, so far as my conduct can do it, to deprive that world of the power of saying so with truth. Go on, and God bless you." I answered,—"Oh, if that is your reason, I forgive you." In the midst of my struggles, or rather when others discovered what I was about, he died. Have I not good cause to remember him, after having been brought so close in contact with a mind so superior, and that was honourable enough to entertain such prospective views? He always treated the young student with kindness, desirous that his honours might be high and well-deserved. I heard him ask, in one of his speeches before the Synod, when the Act to establish a Theological Seminary was under discussion, and when it was by some urged that thereby the older ministry would be thrown into the shade,—"What father ever regretted that his son should be a wiser and better man than himself?"

The education of his early years must have been thorough; his college life must have been a laborious one. In other words, the foundations must have been laid deep and broad; for the intellectual superstructure he so assiduously reared in after life was mighty. He was a ripe scholar, a profound metaphysician, an original, accurate and incessant thinker. His reading was extensive; his researches were various; his views ofttimes startling; his communications prompt, never betraying any deficiency by stereotype thoughts or phrases, but always fresh and vigorous. No one, it seems to me, who can estimate mind, particularly when it is in full action, whether corresponding with him in general sentiment or not, would hesitate to accord all this to Dr Gray, and more. Let his works speak for themselves.

I have often endeavoured to form for myself a full idea of this noble man, and have as often retreated into his own description of one whom, in his "Fiend of the Reformation Detected," he styles "the INVESTIGATOR." "The ADVOCATE of truth," which is another character most inimitably portrayed in that book, he certainly was; but then he grew into the INVESTIGATOR. He never could have drawn these so entirely to the life had he not learned the exercises of their various intellectual powers from experience. Nor do I wonder that Dr. Mason expressed the opinion of him that I have already referred to, and that, in relation to his annual visit to Philadelphia, during the winter recess of the Seminary, he should assign one of his reasons to be that he might have a chat with Dr. Gray.

Dr. Gray belonged to the Calvinistic school, and has pronounced the highest eulogy upon the spirit of that sect. He says: "The peculiar attribute which has distinguished the Calvinistic sect in all nations, and in all ages, is a firm and stubborn faith. I use these epithets in their fullest and most favourable sense. A Calvinist will believe God's Word, but he will believe nothing else, in matters of religion." Yet high as this estimate is, he did not consider that any right existed in that sect, nor does he suppose that it had ever been legitimately assumed, to cripple his powers of thought or to control his conscience; but adds,—"Talk to him (a Calvinist) of the decisions of ten thousand councils, he cares nothing about them, and indeed rarely gives himself trouble to know any thing about them." Again, he says, "All the world should know that we are not disposed to surrender to any authority the liberty with which 'Christ has made us free;' the liberty of submitting our consciences to no authority but his own, and of knowing no law of duty but his law, which is the perfect law of liberty. Those who know this conscientious liberty, should be open and candid, but at the same time modest in asserting it." He freely availed himself of this liberty, as his writings abundantly show. How far this INVESTIGATOR might have used this liberty, had it pleased God to have spared him to this day, when the *mass* of mankind may be seen marshalled in polemic strife, and the question of right in every form is convulsing both Church and State, it is not for me to say.

There is a mental faculty which is rare, and which he possessed in an eminent degree—it is that which enabled Solomon to acquire his peculiar fame, even among inspired writers, and which has afforded so rich a repast to the Church in the book of Proverbs. Here Dr. Gray stands almost unrivalled. His knowledge of human nature was profound, and his observation on society and social manners was keen and accurate. Here he had often a tangled skein to unravel, but he unravelled it. This power, so peculiar and yet so valuable, gave him great advantages in enabling him to illustrate to the common sense of men general principles on which he ever reasoned, and great confidence in the prospective views he took. It fully explains a remark I once heard him make, which might seem to many quite enigmatical. He had taken a long journey on horseback, having been sent to preach to a vacant congregation. The Presbytery to which he belonged was small, and long rides were frequently assigned to the several members. He was complaining of his fatigue and dissipation of thought, occasioned by the rough and protracted exercise. A young clergyman or student, knowing that he never wrote his sermons, asked him how he could preach under such circumstances. He replied, "I make every man I meet study my sermon for me." Thus he was always *observing* ; reading society instead of books, studying man instead of the volumes he had left behind.

As a Preacher, he was a lecturer or expositor, rather than a sermonizer. We have his views on the comparative merits of these modes of pulpit exhibition, detailed in the conclusion of his " Mediatorial Reign." See page 431, 432.

" Preparation for the weekly exposition of Scripture compels a minister to be a diligent student. It keeps him habitually engaged over the whole field of literature, languages, criticism, history, chronology, laws, antiquities, every thing. A good expositor of Scripture must become a learned divine, according to the measure of his faculties. Who enjoys the benefit? Himself first, and next the Church. Young preachers are apt to shrink back from the difficulties which attend a commentator. It would be nothing to diminish their fears by cherishing false hopes. The difficulties lie in the nature of things; and he who tries the work may expect to meet them. The only true encouragement is this :—That if the labour be difficult, the pay is glorious. The clear and assured view of evangelical truth, which the practice of Scriptural exposition produces ; the intellectual and spiritual riches which is the result ; the promptitude and facility with which Divine subjects will, by and by, be grasped, discussed and handled,—these are a few, and only a few of the precious rewards which God bestows on all the diligent students of his own Word. The minister who has conquered the difficulties of a commentator; I mean he, who can, with reasonable industry, expound a chapter, or half a chapter of the Bible, on the Sabbath, has, in reality, conquered all the most formidable difficulties of his office. Sermons cost such a man almost nothing. Saturday is divested of all its terrors. He never trembles about a few leaves of manuscript. He can check for thousands, and is not afraid of failing for small change. If his heart be only right with God, he can hardly ever be unprepared for preaching the Gospel. Thus, before he has reached the meridian of life, he finds himself a man, and carries his sermons in his heart, not in his pocket."

He was not what, in familiar phrase, is called a *popular* Preacher The mass could not find in him that which they commonly call eloquence; which they professedly seek after; ofttimes do not attain; and do not know it when they hear it. There was a want of *Demosthenic* action,—of those dulcet and thundering tones which exert a sort of *mesmeric* influence, convert some deformity into a beauty, and end in a "bodily service," leaving the soul under the dominion of animal passion. He understood all this, and well describes it when he says,—" The age in which we live, too, is fastidious in its taste. It exacts—it can hardly tell what it exacts; novelty, figure, pathos, rhetoric. We refuse to put up with sound good sense; the man who rests the weight of his discourse upon the importance of the truth which he utters, will be suspected of some defect in genius or erudition. Never was an age less concerned about what is spoken; but we insist it shall be spoken well. We demand, in composition, the pomp of Johnson, the magnificence of Burke, or the pathos of Curran; and in utterance, we demand the attitudes, tones and thunders of the stage." Notwithstanding this public and injurious mistake, there was about him an eloquence of sentiment, often clothed in appropriate and most sublime language, which held his audience in rapt attention. I remember, when the Associate Reformed Church was terribly agitated on the subject of Catholic Communion, he was a delegate to the General Synod; though he was prevented by scholastic engagements from attending constantly on their deliberations. On one of the afternoons, while this discussion was in progress, a pause had occurred, and, at the moment, Dr. Gray came in suddenly and rapidly. He inquired what was the subject before Synod; and, on being informed it was Catholic Communion, he began. Before he finished I saw candles brought in, but without particularly noticing the circumstance, until I heard him observe,—" I beg pardon of the Synod for detaining them so long; but I really had not time to make a shorter speech,—my school demands so much of my attention." I was surprized at the apology, thinking it entirely uncalled for; as he could not, I thought, have occupied more than half an hour. On referring to my watch, I found he had been speaking an hour and a half. One of the most eloquent sermons I ever heard from him was delivered under similar pressure.

During that speech he observed that "communion could be held no further in any religious service, than that service went; and that, therefore, no Christian brother, in enjoying fellowship in the ordinance of the Supper with the brethren of another denomination, did thereby sanction the errors of that denomination;" and then he rose in his majesty of thought to represent the wilting character of sectarian disputations, and said,—" Why, Moderator, there are the Fishers, and the Erskines, and such like men—give them some great scriptural doctrine to handle, and they speak, they write like angels—give them some Secession peculiarity,—the burgess oath, or a like sectarian trifle, and they speak, they write like children."

It was his lot to be the object of ill-natured remarks,—who is not? He might have readily replied to these, and in a manner that no critic of this order of slanderers could have forgotten. No man possessed keener wit, power of quicker retort, or could have employed more scorching satire. But his Christian feelings held him in check. He generally observed,—" Let such things alone, they'll die of themselves." A man of such various gifts and noble feelings must have been a most interesting companion—and such he was, whenever circumstances called him out or sufficiently interested him. Particularly was this the case when he met an INVESTIGATOR like himself, or, to use his own language, " when he met an artist, who had laboured at the same trade and given it up fairly; they go in (to his workshop) and laugh at their folly; and wonder how like to wisdom folly can look, and how very much the follies of different men may resemble each other." I have heard ardent wishes expressed, and often felt them myself, to be present at such interviews. But he writes,—"They would not let a young artist in, lest he should fall in love with one of their machines, (systems laid aside as useless,) and either steal it, or go home and make something like it."

A young clergyman whom he greatly loved, and whose feelings he would have deeply grieved to wound, once undertook to reprove him for sleeping while he was preaching. "It was a poor compliment to me, Doctor, and might lower me in the estimation of my people." I was curious to know what excuse he would make for the apparent impropriety, or how he would blunt the edge of the remark, well understanding that there may be great difficulty in such an exalted man listening to an inferior mind, and that, not uncommonly, Preachers are most restless hearers. "Tut, man," he replied, "I never slept under a blockhead in my life; when I was a young man, I remember two Professors in College, on whose lectures I was obliged to attend. One of them possessed the highest order of intellect, and his exhibitions were of the most finished description. I uniformly fell asleep during his interesting exercises. I was sorry for it, but could not help it. The other was an ordinary man; and his lectures were dull and insipid. Under him I never could sleep, though I had tried it." Any man might feel himself gratified to hear from such lips that his preaching could so far interest such a mind as so to affect the physical action of the brain by which it worked. Perhaps a great deal of this was honest compliment—his character would guarantee that; but Dr. Gray was a man of great bodily activity,—ever elastic and in motion,—rarely still, except when at his desk and laboriously engaged in composition; and even there he would frequently and suddenly start up, and take a run or two around the premises as far as they would afford him room. Under some powerful and rapid impulses, he would frequently act so during his meals—his active, bounding mind could hardly brook restraint, but he would thus unexpectedly start off, impelled by some thought, suggested by a book he might be reading or by some of his own musings. His strong mind had its own peculiarities, and these might often amuse those who were but slightly acquainted with him.

On one occasion, when ecclesiastical business had called him to a sister city, he was returning during the evening to his lodgings. But not having fixed his landmarks with sufficient distinctness in his mind, or being in one of those absent moods, which he says are not uncommon with INVESTIGATORS, he mistook the door, and went into the next house; nor did he discover his mistake until he found himself in the parlour, and in the midst of a party of gentlemen and ladies. It was no difficulty to him to make the best of such an unlooked-for circumstance, but immediately apologized, and so handsomely that he was invited to spend the evening. He accepted the invitation, quickly made himself at home, and soon became "the life of the company."

But I detain you too long in reading my hastily written sketches. If, however, they can afford you any aid in delineating a character which richly deserves to stand out in bold relief before the American public, they are entirely at your service. If not, throw them among your papers. In some future year they may afford you no unpleasing remembrance of one, who, though not personally acquainted, was willing to respond to your call, and afford such aid as he could in your contemplated work. Or, perchance, they may meet the eye of some candid young student, who will be pleased to discover that, in a preceding age, and before his own important advent, such a man had lived in our country. "In the morning sow thy seed, and in the evening withhold not thy hand; for thou knowest not whether shall prosper either this or that, or whether both shall be alike good." I thank God that

I ever knew Dr. Gray, and that I can never fall so low in my own estimation as to forget him.

I am, My dear Sir, faithfully yours,
J. M. DUNCAN.

JOHN STEELE.
1797—1837.
FROM THE REV. J. CLAYBAUGH, D.D.

OXFORD, September 26, 1850.

Rev. and dear Sir: In complying with your request for some notice of the life and character of the late Rev. John Steele, of the Associate Reformed Church, I shall venture to avail myself of a brief biographical sketch of him, from the pen of Dr. Bishop, late President of Miami University, and for many years a Co-presbyter with Mr. Steele, in Kentucky. The sketch is as follows:

"William Steele and his wife were originally from Ireland. He was one of the first explorers of Kentucky, and had some very narrow escapes from the Indians. He, on one occasion, went, by himself, in a canoe, from the place where Maysville now stands to Pittsburg. He finally settled with his family, at a very early period, on the Hinkston Fork of the Licking River, near Millersburg, Bourbon County, where he and his wife lived till they were gathered to their fathers in a good and honourable old age.

"Their son, JOHN STEELE, was born in York County, Pa., December 17, 1772. He received his grammar-school education in Kentucky, and his college course at Dickinson, under Dr. Nisbet, where he graduated in 1792. He studied Divinity under the Rev. John Young, of Greencastle, Pa., and was licensed by the First Associate Reformed Presbytery of Pennsylvania, May 25, 1797, and ordained by the same Presbytery, in August, 1799.

"He returned, very soon after his Ordination, to Kentucky, and devoted himself exclusively to the discharge of his ministerial duties. During the first years of his ministry, he had the pastoral charge of four congregations, in four different counties. By the arrival of additional ministerial help, he was, in 1808, relieved from two of these congregations; but the two that he continued to serve were thirty miles apart. The state of society in Kentucky, during the whole of his residence there, was very unfavourable to the spread of the Gospel; and there were, besides, some local difficulties of considerable magnitude, which were peculiar to the Associate Reformed Church. In 1817 he removed to Xenia, Greene County, O., where he remained till October, 1836. Here, also, he had the charge of two congregations—one in Xenia, and the other in Springfield, Clark County, eighteen miles distant.

"Mr. Steele was one of the first, if not the very first, of the sons of Kentucky, who devoted themselves to the work of the ministry. He was, in early life, and during his prime, a close student. He had an active and independent mind; was an excellent member of Church Courts; had peculiar qualifications as Recording Clerk; never grudged any ministerial service which he could perform in any of his own congregations, or in any vacancy, and hence he was, in some seasons of the year, in the earlier part of his life, fully one half of his time on horseback. He continued a faithful and labourious Pastor and Preacher, till the infirmities of age admonished him to retire. He had just moved to Oxford, and had made some arrangements for the accommodation of his family, with a particular view to the education of his two youngest sons, when, without a groan or a struggle, he was called home to his Father's house, on the morning of the 11th of January, 1837, in the sixty-fifth year of his age, and thirty-eighth of his ministry."

The above, I consider, a very faithful sketch. My acquaintance with Mr. Steele began in 1822, when he was appointed to superintend my theological studies, our Seminary in New York having been suspended. For two years I was familiar with him as my Theological Instructor, and was afterwards a member of the same Presbytery with him till his death. He had, in early life, enjoyed educational opportunities about as good as the country afforded, which he had diligently improved; so that he occupied a very respectable position in the ranks of an educated ministry. He had, while a student at Dickinson, taken full short-hand notes of all Dr. Nisbet's lectures on Intellectual and Moral Philosophy, Divinity, &c., of which he had several volumes (in short hand) carefully bound and preserved as an invaluable treasure. For the memory of Dr. Nisbet (by the way) he cherished a profound respect. Indeed, he was almost the only man from whose opinions, in some point or other, I never heard him venture to express his dissent.

Mr. Steele had also, through Dr. Mason, early in the century, procured from Europe a number of valuable theological works, not procurable at that time in this country; and his library was among the very best ministers' libraries in the West, and with it he had made himself very familiar. He was an able, clear-headed Theologian, well-read in Church History, and versed in Ecclesiastical affairs. Great reliance was placed on his judgment in matters of discipline and Church-order. He served long, with ability, as Clerk both of his Presbytery and of Synod.

His mind was logical, somewhat scholastic. He was a close reasoner, careful in laying down his principles, and boldly and rigidly pursuing them to their legitimate results; giving no range to imagination nor dealing at all in analogies, but pushing straight forward and marking very distinctly every step to his conclusion. He admitted less of what may be called the logic of the heart, than some men who were his inferiors in intellect, and by no means superior in moral and Christian worth. Hence he perhaps failed in modifying his principles in their application to circumstances, and was less popular as a Preacher than a man of his powers should have been, and had less visible success. By this, I would, by no means, intimate that he was not a successful minister—on the contrary, he has left his mark on an extensive and growing portion of the Church. The slow growth and subsequent decline of the churches which he served in Kentucky was owing to peculiar causes; and then these churches are, in a manner, reproduced in several large and flourishing congregations, which have sprung from them in Ohio and Indiana; and though the churches he last served did not become large during his connection with them, they yet were in a thriving state, and have since become among the largest and most influential in any Presbyterian connection in the West. The fruit of his labour has been gathered since he left the field and is still being gathered. He may be reckoned among those who sow while others reap. Certainly he laboured and others entered into his labours.

Mr. Steele was characterized by quick penetration, decision, energy, firm adherence to principle and fearlessness in doing what he thought was right, and in maintaining what he believed to be God's truth. Yet he was a lover of peace, fond of making peace, and was very tender of both the feelings and reputation of others. He was a prudent man, and remarkably sparing both in praise and in censure. His stern integrity and independence, combined with modest self-respect, forbade him to be obsequious; yet he was companionable, and was likewise familiar and free in his intercourse with his neighbours and fellow-citizens, as well as with his parishioners, ready to converse on all subjects—for he was a man of general information, and took a deep interest in public affairs. With some sternness of countenance and manner, he was yet a man of great tenderness and of fine sensibilities, and was kind, obliging and generous; and truly hospitable, but without ostentation. The naturally rugged features of his character were much softened by age; and I think I have never known such a delightful mellowing of the mind and heart as was exemplified during the latter years of his life.

In the pulpit Mr. Steele was very doctrinal and argumentative, yet animated and earnest. In later years he became more practical. In pathos he seldom indulged, and generally, when betrayed into it, his utterance was choked. His voice was strong and masculine, and his enunciation distinct and clear, but rather nasal. He was a methodical preacher,—his heads and inferences being distinctly stated, but he was not tied to any particular method, though he generally followed what is called the *scholastic* division. What his practice in early life was I am not able to state; but in later years his only written preparation was in brief short-hand notes. He never read his sermons,—a practice indeed which has never been introduced in the pulpits of the Associate Reformed Churches West, and which the worthy subject of this notice decidedly condemned. He never played the orator, nor was he often called eloquent, yet his discourses occasionally, especially at Communion seasons, would compare well with those of the most distinguished Preachers of the day, in vindicating the Glory of the Cross, and bringing to view the Wonders of Redeeming Love.

I would suppose that Mr. Steele was about five feet eight inches high. His head was large and thickly set with coarse black hair, which became silvered as he became old; his beard was heavy and black; forehead low but rather broad and well marked with the lines of thought; his eyes small, black and piercing; features marked, but regular; look, collected and resolved. He was remarkably *light-built;* well made for activity and strength. In youth he was slender and neat; when I became acquainted with him, he had become somewhat fleshy, though not corpulent, and was very plain; rather careless, yet genteel, in his person and manners. He was a most estimable man of God. His death was sudden, but not unanticipated. He had come to feel that his work was done, and was quietly awaiting the call of his Master to enter his eternal rest.

Shortly after he entered the ministry, Mr. Steele was united in marriage to Jane, daughter of Walter Cunningham, of Staunton, Va., who was an officer in the army of the Revolution. In this marriage he was most happy, having obtained, as the companion of his life, a lady distinguished for intelligence, energy of character and devoted piety, who yet survives. They had eight children,—four sons and as many daughters. Of the sons one is a physician; two are ministers in the United Presbyterian Church; one, a youth of great promise, died while a student of Theology, and the only surviving daughter is the wife of the Rev. Robert Brice, of Chester, S. C.*

Yours very truly,
J. CLAYBAUGH.

JAMES SCRIMGEOUR.†
1802—1826.

JAMES SCRIMGEOUR was born in the year 1757, in the neighbourhood of Edinburgh, Scotland. His mother, who was a member of the Secession Church, is represented as having been a lady of remarkable intelligence and piety. After the usual preparation for College, he entered the University of Edinburgh in 1772, where he became distinguished for his classical attainments. The University, at that time, had Dr. Robertson at its head, and most of the Professors were among the greatest lights in literature and science of their day.

In 1777 Mr. Scrimgeour commenced the study of Theology at the Hall of the Associate Church, then under the direction of the celebrated John Brown, of Haddington, who is said to have formed a high idea of Mr. S.' talents and qualifications for the work to which he was devoted. Under the instructions of this admirable Teacher and model, he prosecuted his theological course; and, having performed his several parts of trial to unusual acceptance, was licensed by the Associate Presbytery of Edinburgh, in April, 1782.

For two years after his licensure he preached in different parts of Scotland, and was among the most popular young men of his denomination. In Aberdeen, particularly, multitudes thronged to hear him, and his preaching left an impression of deep solemnity. Early in 1784 he was ordained as Minister of the Associate Congregation of North Berwick, a sea-port on the coast of East Lothian,—the Sermon on the occasion being preached by his venerable instructor in Theology. Here he laboured with much fidelity and considerable success for several years. In some of the neighbouring towns, particularly Dunbar and Haddington, he officiated occasionally at the administration of the Lord's Supper, and his labours on those occasions were highly appreciated.

In 1794 Mr. Scrimgeour was visited with a severe trial, by means of which his mental and physical constitution became so much affected that he felt obliged to resign his pastoral charge and retire from the active duties of the ministry. After his health was somewhat recruited, fearing to return immediately to the sedentary habit of a student, he resolved, to the deep regret of his people and of his brethren of the Presbytery, not to resume his charge in North Berwick. By the advice of his intimate friend, the late Rev. Dr. James Hall, then Minister of Rose street Congregation, but afterwards of Broughton Place, Edinburgh, he undertook the superintendence of a Theological bookstore in that city. This was his occupation for several years; but he still preached occasionally in the city and the neighbourhood, and always with much acceptance.

In 1802 the Rev. Dr. John M. Mason visited Great Britain, partly with a view to induce ministers in Scotland to migrate to this country. Several ulti-

* This paragraph has been added in 1863.
† Christian Instructor, 1847.

mately agreed to his proposal, and among them was Mr. Scrimgeour. He sailed in company with the Doctor and other brethren, and reached New York in October, 1802. Soon after his arrival on our shores, he was installed Minister of the Scottish Church, Newburgh, where he remained until 1812, when he received and accepted a call to the adjacent Congregation of Little Britain. Here he remained till the growing infirmities of age compelled him to resign his charge. This he did a few months before his decease, which took place in the winter of 1825.

During his incumbency at Newburgh Mr. Scrimgeour entered into the marriage relation with Miss Boyd, the eldest daughter of Robert Boyd, Esq., a lady eminently qualified for the place to which she was thus introduced. She died about three years after their marriage, leaving an only son.

Mr. Scrimgeour's only publication, so far as is known, is a Sermon entitled "Christ Forsaken on the Cross," published in the Associate Reformed Pulpit, 1817.

FROM THE REV. JOHN FORSYTH, D.D.

COLLEGE OF NEW JERSEY, PRINCETON, May 10, 1852.

Rev. and dear Sir: You desired me, when we last met, to send you my recollections of the Rev. James Scrimgeour. As he died while I was a mere youth, the reminiscences, which I cheerfully transmit to you, cannot, of course, be expected to include many incidents illustrative of his character in the public or private relations of life, of which I was myself personally cognizant. I have, indeed, heard a good deal respecting him from those who knew him long and well. I have a perfectly distinct recollection of his personal appearance, his manner in the pulpit and his usual style of sermonizing. His image is before my mind quite vividly, and if I could only describe on paper the features which are so distinctly drawn on the tablet of boyhood's memory, though I might still fail in making a very readable epistle, I am sure you would get at least a tolerably correct idea of the venerable man whom you have chosen as—so to speak—one of the representatives of the Associate Reformed Church.

Let me, at the outset, say, in order to guard against possible misapprehension, that, while Mr. Scrimgeour had some peculiarities which I may presently mention, he was not by any means "*a character*,"— to use a common and convenient term. He was very far from being one of those *oddities* of whom even children will retain a lively remembrance, when men of less salient traits will be quite forgotten by them. Scotland has produced her share of this class of persons, and the churches of Scottish origin in this country have received from the mother land not a few ministers noted for their eccentricities. But Mr. Scrimgeour was not one of them. He was fond of retirement, the largest portion of his time being spent in his study, and this disposition, probably a natural one, was much strengthened by the trials to which he was subjected. Some circumstances connected with the death of his father, which took place not long after his entrance into the ministry, made so deep an impression upon his mind that, for a time, he was quite overwhelmed by the shock. Though he ultimately so far recovered from the effects of this heavy stroke as to be able to resume the work of a Pastor, his mind seems never to have regained completely its original tone. Besides this early affliction, he lost his wife—a woman every way qualified to make his home happy—within two or three years after his marriage. Yet he did not, like the misanthrope, shun society, nor was he accustomed, when in company, to indulge in those indelicate revelations of his griefs which are sometimes heard. No one, however, could look upon his grave countenance without at least suspecting that he was a man who had been called to drink largely of the waters of Marah.

During the period of my personal knowledge of him, he was minister of a retired country congregation, and had few opportunities of mingling in general society. But he was often in Newburgh, and I may almost say, as often in my father's house. I cannot give you any thing like a detailed account of his social characteristics—all that I remember is, that he was ready enough to chat with his friends; that, like many of the good old Scottish ministers, he had a vein of quiet humour, which now and then "cropped out," and of course no one relished better than himself the exhibition of the same quality by others in reasonable measure.

It was, however, mainly as a Minister of the Gospel that I remember him. Shall I say that, though comparatively little known, he was really one of the greatest Preachers of his day? Perhaps if I did, I should only be repeating what a great many reminiscents have already said to you, but I shall say no such thing, and shall leave you to form your own judgment respecting the preaching abilities of my venerable friend. Formed in the school of John Brown, of Haddington, all who knew him would admit that he was an excellent specimen of its peculiar style of Preachers. His sermons, several of which I possess, were evidently written with care, and yet, if you should eliminate from them all their Scriptural quotations, you would find the remainder like the worthy Professor Brown's Body of Divinity, under a like process, to consist of nothing but a skeleton. I have no doubt that many of our young preachers, fresh from the Seminary, would turn up their noses at the sight of these sermons, under the impression that it is the easiest thing in the world, with the help of a Concordance, to get them up; but if they once made the experiment, they would find that, unless they were very familiar with the Bible, they could much sooner elaborate a discourse from their own brain than fill up the Scripture complement of one of Mr. Scrimgeour's skeletons. Judging from the sermons that have come into my hands, as well as from my own recollections, I should say that Mr. S. never attempted metaphysical discussion nor deep argumentation, though he was probably not unequal to the task of dealing with the class of topics that require to be thus handled. He was trained in a school remarkable for its high estimate of the simple word of God, and, with the old-fashioned sort of Christians to whom he preached, no argument was half so convincing and edifying as a "thus saith the Lord."

Those who knew him in the earlier years of his ministry have told me that he was then one of the most popular Preachers in the denomination to which he belonged,—the Burgher Seceders; and, from what I know of the taste of Scottish Christians, as well as from my own recollection of his manner in the pulpit, I can easily credit the statement, and various reasons might be assigned, if it were worth while to dwell upon the point, why his ministrations were not so generally acceptable in this country as in his native land. Not to mention others, his strong Scottish accent, if not positively distasteful, would not be particularly pleasing to most Americans; while the seclusion in which he lived prevented him from taking part in those philanthropic and religious schemes which serve as mental stimulants to those engaged in them, and, at the same time, help to give variety to the exercises of the pulpit. His own people, however, were strongly attached to him, and, in other congregations, containing a large Scottish element, as in that of his old friend Dr. Mason, of New York, in Newburgh, and elsewhere, his appearance in the pulpit always gave pleasure to his audience. When he visited these places, he very well knew that he would be required to preach, and he always went from home with an ample equipment,—that is, with from fifty to a hundred sermons in his portmanteau. On one occasion an excellent lady of my acquaintance travelled some fifteen miles to hear Dr. J. M. Mason, who was expected to preach in one of the Associate Reformed Congregations, back from Newburgh.

When she reached the church, to her great disappointment, she saw Mr. Scrimgeour ascend the pulpit. Her first impulse was to quit the place and return home, but the "sober second thought" of the Christian kept her in her seat. You may well suppose that she was not in the most favourable mood for appreciating the preacher, (whom she had often heard,) yet she afterwards declared that she went away quite captivated with the sermon, and fully persuaded that even Dr. Mason himself (whom she also knew) could not have better recompensed her for her long journey.

Boy as I was, I would have gone any day a good long distance to hear Mr. Scrimgeour, nor would any thing have kept me from the church in which he was to preach but absolute inability to get to it. His majestic figure, the solemn yet kindly expression of his venerable countenance, kept my eye riveted upon him, while his deep-toned voice, his strong Scottish accent, and the fine old semi-chant or "intoning" with which his sentences were uttered, filled my ear like the richest music. But it was not his manner alone that fixed my attention. To this day I retain a lively remembrance of several sermons preached by him in the old Scots Church of Newburgh, especially of one from Psalm xxiv, 7-10. In answer to the enquiry of the text,—"Who is this King of Glory?" he collected all the choicest types and similes of the Scriptures that set forth the manifold relations and grace of our Redeemer, arranged them in admirable order, quoting in full the passages in which they occur. You may imagine that there must have been something above the common run of sermons in this one, which could thus arrest the attention and fix itself in the memory of a boy. Often have I heard the older members of the congregation speak of this discourse, as one of rare richness. I may here mention that Mr. Scrimgeour studied brevity in all his pulpit exercises, and I have no doubt that many of his hearers were half amused and half vexed at the frequency with which his watch was pulled from his fob, and at the complaint, which always accompanied the act, of the extreme scarcity of time.

While Mr. Scrimgeour retained a good deal of the old Scottish feeling about the proprieties of clerical costume, he seems to have fallen, during his latter days, somewhat into the free and easy style which obtains in some parts of our land. I once heard him, on a fearfully hot day, in his shirt-sleeves, an uncanonical sort of semi-surplice, in which he not unfrequently appeared in his own pulpit during the summer heats. It was at Newburgh, at the opening of the Associate Reformed Synod of New York. During the sermon, Mr. S. came near fainting; the service was suddenly suspended, and, for a few moments, considerable alarm was felt. After a little, one of the Reverend fathers present proposed to relieve him of the service, but Mr. S., feeling himself by this time sufficiently recovered to continue his work, declined the offer, rose in the pulpit and resumed his discourse at the very sentence where he had broken off. Occasionally, in his own pulpit, little episodes would occur savouring largely of the ludicrous. He once observed one of his hearers in a profound slumber, when he stopped in his sermon and asked a parishioner sitting near to wake him up. The nudge, however, was so gentle as to make no impression on his somnolent neighbour. The good Pastor, perceiving how the case stood, exclaimed, with the greatest gravity and the broadest Scotch, " *Shak* him, Dawvid.—Shak him."

Like many of his countrymen, Mr. Scrimgeour was an inordinate consumer of snuff. Even while preaching, he would make large and frequent drafts upon his "mull." I remember to have gone with a young companion into the pulpit of the Church at Newburgh after a sermon by Mr. S., when we found on the carpet so much of this nasal stimulant that each of us collected a decent handful. You might suppose that this practice would produce some injurious effect upon his voice; but such was not the case—the current of sound was too deep and strong to permit the snuff, largely as it was thrown in, to settle in the channel and harden into shallows; no, it was borne along upon the surface of the mighty stream.

Let me only add that Mr. Scrimgeour was an out-and-out Presbyterian, noted for his punctuality in attending Church Judicatories, and for his promptitude in performing all assigned duties. My knowledge of him in this respect is, of course, wholly derived from the accounts of others; but all unite in testifying that he was a most conscientious attendant at meetings of Presbytery and Synod, and, though not given to speech-making, took an active share in the business of the Court. One of my old fellow-presbyters told me that Mr. S. once gave him quite a fright. He was giving in to the Presbytery his trials for licensure, and had just read his Latin Dissertation, when Mr. Scrimgeour arose and asked, "Moderator, shall we impugn it?" and then went on to say, in explanation of the formidable term, that, in former days, members of Presbytery were called upon to make their objections to the essay in Latin, to all of which the candidate was obliged to make, in the same language, an extempore reply. Mr. S. himself could have gone through the process with great ease; but the other members, either out of kindness to their young brother, who had expected no such ordeal, or perhaps suspecting that they would themselves be found rather rusty in their Latin, concluded to dispense with the impugnation. But I must close these reminiscences lest I make myself tedious; and I do so with the assurance that I remain

Very affectionately yours,
JOHN FORSYTH.

FROM THE REV. JAMES M. MATHEWS, D.D.

NEW YORK, January 26, 1861.

My dear Dr. Sprague: When I was licensed to preach, in New York, in 1807, the Rev. James Scrimgeour was one of the leading members of the Presbytery; and the acquaintance which I commenced with him then was always kept up as long as he lived. He was full six feet high; had a decidedly Scotch face, though not otherwise strongly marked; stooped slightly as he walked; and was rather staid and deliberate in his movements. His mind was distinguished rather for a symmetrical combination of all the faculties, in a good measure of strength and activity, than for the extraordinary development of any one of them. And his preaching was what you would expect from such an intellectual constitution, taken in connection with a Scotch education of the strictest order. He divided, and sub-divided, almost without a limit; but all that he said was luminous and sensible, and not a small part of it in the very words which the Holy Ghost teacheth. His system of doctrine was the sternest type of Calvinism; and I doubt whether he ever preached a sermon by which this would not be revealed. He had but little gesture, and that little, as I remember, was not particularly impressive. His utterance was very distinct and deliberate, and yet was characterized by a good degree of earnestness. He was not much given to speaking in Public Bodies, though, when he did speak, it was always with good judgment and good spirit, and he was listened to with attention and respect.

For nothing was Mr. Scrimgeour more remarkable than his unfailing good will and kindness. An instance of this now occurs to me, with which I happened to be associated, which was of a somewhat ludicrous character, and might have been very serious in its consequences. I was going with him from Newburgh to visit the church at a place called Shawangunk; and we were both riding on horseback. As we approached a school-house, the little children formed themselves into a line by the side of the street, to pay their respects, the boys by a bow, the girls by a courtesy, to the venerable man, as he passed. The old gentleman's horse, not being used to such an array of civility, suddenly shied off, and with so much rapidity as to leave the rider almost literally licking the dust; and the first thing he said, before I had time to overtake and bring back his horse, was—"My gude children, you see that your gude manners had well-nigh cost me my life." The spirit of good-will towards his fellow creatures always came out, wherever there was an opportunity to manifest it.

Very truly and affectionately,
J. M. MATHEWS.

ISAAC GRIER, D.D.
1802—1843.
FROM THE REV. JAMES BOYCE.

FAIRFIELD DISTRICT, S. C., February 12, 1851

My dear Sir: I cheerfully comply with your request for some brief notices of the life and character of the late Rev. Dr. Isaac Grier. I was born within the limits of his pastoral charge, and received my early training under his ministry. It was my privilege to be frequently in his company, both before and since I reached mature years,—in his own house, in social parties, by the bedside of the sick, in ecclesiastical meetings, and on journeys of several hundred miles; so that my opportunities for knowing him were, by no means, inconsiderable. I shall, in accordance with what I understand to be your wish, attempt not an elaborate and critical analysis of his character, but only some brief and simple memoirs.

ISAAC GRIER was descended of a worthy parentage. His father, Robert Grier, was a native of Pennsylvania, and a member of the Reformed Presbyterian Church. In 1775 he removed to North Carolina, and in the same year married Margaret Livingston, an emigrant from Ireland. Immediately afterwards he repaired to Georgia, and settled in Greene County, where his son, the subject of this notice, was born in the eventful year 1776, being the first Presbyterian Minister born in that State. On the head stone placed over the grave of Margaret Grier, who lies in the burying ground of Sardis, Mecklenburg County, N. C., are inscribed these words—"The mother of the First Presbyterian Minister born in Georgia." The interior of Georgia was, at that time, regarded as frontier country, and was, therefore, much exposed to Indian depredations; and, consequently, to escape those dangerous hostilities, Mr. Grier, with his family, retreated to Cabarras County, N. C., where his son Isaac was baptized by the Rev. Mr. Martin, an itinerating Minister of the Reformed Presbyterian Church. As soon as the hostilities on the frontier had ceased or abated, he returned to his former residence in Georgia. The youthful training of the son is presumed to have been of the strictest and most orthodox character, for his parents and preceptor were decidedly of the old school type. His academical education, preparatory to entering College, was conducted partly by Dr. Moses Waddell, who taught with some celebrity many years in the South, but chiefly by the Rev. Messrs. Cunningham and Cummins, of Georgia, Ministers of the General Assembly Presbyterian Church.

Having completed his preparatory studies, he repaired to Dickinson College, Pa., where he graduated in 1800, under the Presidency of Dr. Nisbet. He studied Theology under the direction of the Rev. Alexander Porter, of the Associate Reformed Synod of the South, Pastor of Cedar Spring and Long Cane Congregations in Abbeville District, S. C., and was licensed at Long Cane, by an Associate Reformed Presbytery, September 2, 1802. After itinerating among vacant congregations for two years, he was called to take the pastoral care of the Congregations of Sardis, Providence and Waxhaw, in North Carolina, and was ordained to the Gospel Ministry at the first mentioned place, some time in the year 1804. He continued Pastor of these three Congregations until 1808, when he resigned the Congregation of Waxhaw, in consequence of its inconvenient distance from the other two churches, and united the Congregation of Steele Creek, which had been demitted by the Rev. William Blackstock,* to those of Sardis and Providence. In 1815 he resigned the Providence Congregation, but retained his charge at Sardis and Steele Creek until 1842, when the infirmities of age rendered it necessary for him to resign his entire charge. From that time his health gradually declined till the 2d of September, 1843, when he was removed by death, after having laboured in the ministry about forty years.

In 1837 he received the degree of Doctor of Divinity from Jefferson College, Cannonsburg, Pa.

In person Dr. Grier was of about the ordinary stature. He was broad and well-built, possessing an erect and manly form, and well fitted for hardships and fatigue, being neither afflicted with leanness nor burdened with corpulency. Though he passed several ordeals of the severest sickness, and of medicines which took an unfortunate and well-nigh ruinous turn upon him, yet he wore, even to old age, the unwrinkled face and ruddy countenance of youth.

Dr. Grier was a man of more than ordinary firmness; but whether he was so constitutionally or from education and habit I could scarcely venture an opinion. When his mind was once made up, whether in relation to truth or duty, it was with difficulty that it could be changed. What he believed to be right and true he adhered to with the utmost tenacity, even though it may have subjected him, in some quarters, to the charge of bigotry.

Punctuality was another of his prominent characteristics. It was a standing rule with him to fulfil all his appointments, whether they related to secular or ministerial engagements; so that if ever absent from an Ecclesiastical Judicatory of which he was a member, or from a Congregation where it was announced that he would preach, he generally had the credit of being detained by circumstances beyond his control.

The labours of Dr. Grier were signally blessed in one department where all ministers are not successful. While he had the pleasure of witnessing very considerable numbers making a profession of their faith under his ministry from

---

* WILLIAM BLACKSTOCK was born, educated and licensed to preach in Ireland. He migrated to this country about 1794. The Presbytery of the Carolinas report—that William Blackstock, a probationer from the Presbytery of Down, in Ireland, had been received by that Body, and was ordained on the 8th of June, 1794, over the United Congregations of Steele Creek, Ebenezer and Neeley Creek, S. C. Here he continued till the year 1804, when he resigned his charge and became a stated supply to the Churches of New Perth, New Sterling and Rocky Spring. He seems to have remained here till 1811, when he was settled at the Waxhaws, N. C. He subsequently accepted a call from Tirzah, S. C., and died in 1830 or '31. He had a highly respectable standing in the ministry.

year to year, yet, peradventure, in the whole course of his ministerial life, there was nothing more gratifying to him than the spectacle of so many young men among his parishioners turning their attention to a course of education preparatory to the Ministry, and, in due time, being actually introduced into it, and afterwards raised to stations of usefulness and respectability, and some of them to eminence, in the Church. Nearly two-thirds of the Presbytery to which he belonged consisted of ministers who had been born and reared within the limits of his ministerial charge.

Probably no minister in the denomination with which he was connected took more pains than he in the religious instruction of the coloured people. In addition to the catechetical exercises which were conducted at the church, during the intermission of public service, in the Summer, for their special benefit, he was accustomed, for a number of years, after preaching two discourses to his congregation, to deliver a third to the blacks, assembled at a given place, near his own house, some five miles distant from the church.

His pulpit performances were simple, perspicuous and instructive, and generally of a medium length. He was scarcely ever tedious in his public ministrations. He was fond of reading and conversation, and was never more pleased than when engaged with his favourite authors or conversing with his friends. Few divines were more conversant with History or better informed in Theology. Possessing excellent conversational powers, he was supplied with an almost inexhaustible fund of amusing and instructive anecdotes, and possessed the ability of rendering himself agreeable and interesting to his companions and fellow-travellers in journeys of weeks and months, as I am able myself to testify.

In 1806 he was married to Isabella Harris, daughter of a Ruling Elder in his charge,—a lady distinguished for her fine intellectual and moral qualities, and for a most exemplary Christian character. She died in 1842, about a year previous to the death of her husband. They had three children, one of whom, the Rev. Robert C. Grier, is a minister of the Associate Reformed Church, and a Professor in Erskine College.

Yours with Christian regard,
JAMES BOYCE.

FROM THE REV. H. CONNELLY.

NEWBURGH, July 2, 1862.

My dear Sir : After my graduation at College, I was, for two years, the Teacher of an Academy in Lancaster District, S. C.; and then and there it was that I had the pleasure of an acquaintance with the late Rev. Dr. Grier, who was so well known and so highly esteemed, especially throughout the Southern churches. Though he lived near the borders of North Carolina, some thirty miles distant from the place of my sojourn, I used to meet him at Presbytery, and occasionally at other times, and once I remember that he took me home with him after a Presbyterial meeting, and treated me with great hospitality and kindness. For one year I was a theological student, under the care of the Presbytery to which he belonged, and this brought me into nearer relations with him, and secured to me, on one occasion at least, the benefit of his criticisms upon a sermon which I was required to deliver as a theological exercise.

Dr. Grier was of about the ordinary height, rather inclined to be stout, with a round full face, a benignant light eye, a mild, pleasant expression of countenance, and a general healthful appearance. He had a well balanced and well cultivated mind, and was more distinguished for the reflective and practical than the imaginative. He had an uncommonly gentle and kindly spirit, and was always on the alert to do good and communicate happiness whenever it was in his power. His manners were not formed after any standard of artificial refinement, but were the simple acting out of strong benevolent feelings, under the combined influence of good sense and good taste. From the first hour you came in contact with him, you could not help being impressed with the sincerity, kindliness and dignity of his character; and the more you knew of him, the more of admiration and veneration would these qualities elicit.

Dr. Grier's preaching was sober and instructive, not brilliant or startling. It was very much of an expository character, and never failed to throw much light upon the portion of Scripture which he had under consideration. His voice was distinct and pleasant, but not of remarkable compass. In Public Bodies he always seemed at home, observed carefully all that was passing, and mingled freely and advantageously in any important discussions that might come up. Much deference was paid to him by his brethren, all regarding him as a clear-headed, right-minded, thoroughly practical man. I never had much opportunity of knowing what he was as a Pastor; but, from my knowledge of his general character, I am quite sure I should hazard nothing in saying that he adorned the pastoral relation with the most graceful kindness and the most unremitted devotion.

There was no feature in the character of Dr. Grier that I think of with more interest than his marked kindness to the slaves. He was a man of considerable property, and, in common with almost every body around him, was the owner of a number of negroes. But if all masters were like him, the system of Slavery would be shorn of its most offensive features. He seemed to me to exercise towards them an almost parental kindness. At morning and evening family worship, they came together as regularly as any other members of his household. He did not, as is common, employ a white overseer, but appointed the most intelligent of their own number to take a general direction of affairs, and this one reported to *him*, and received suggestions and instructions from him, as often as there was occasion. I believe he was the first in that region to change the order of things in regard to the accommodation of the negroes in public worship. Formerly their inferiority in the house of God had been virtually recognized by their occupying seats in the remote part of the house; but Dr. Grier introduced the practice of dividing the day between the blacks and whites, giving the afternoon to the former; and then, instead of occupying seats in the rear where they were nearly hidden by a high intervening partition, they were allowed to come forward and occupy the front seats, while the white people, if they chose to be present, took the less favoured position. I remember being there, on one occasion, at a Communion, in a forest, at which he presided, and at the last table there appeared an imposing array of blacks, to whom he administered the ordinance with the utmost tenderness and appropriateness. He seemed always to seek to promote the benefit of the coloured race, as if that had been his peculiar mission.

Very respectfully yours,
H. CONNELLY.

ROBERT FORREST.*

1802—1846.

ROBERT FORREST was born at Dunbar, Scotland, about the year 1768. He was brought up under the ministry of the Rev. John Henderson, of the Burgher Secession Church, the author of a work entitled "The Legal Temper displayed in its Nature and Tendency." Of this excellent Pastor he retained, even to his old age, an affectionate remembrance, often referring in terms of the greatest respect to his piety and learning. At what precise time he first felt the power of Divine grace upon his heart, or consecrated himself to the ministry of reconciliation, I have not been able to ascertain. After attending, during the usual period, the Grammar School of Dunbar, he became a member of the University of Edinburgh about the year 1787.

Having completed the usual classical and scientific course at the University, Mr. Forrest commenced the study of Theology, under the late Dr. George Lawson, of Selkirk, at that time Professor of Divinity in connection with the Associate (Burgher) Synod, and the successor in that office of the eminent John Brown, of Haddington. Dr. Lawson was a man of profound and varied erudition, mighty in the Scriptures, of deep and earnest piety, and of singular simplicity of character and manners,—"an Israelite indeed, in whom there was no guile." By all his students he was not only respected as a theologian but loved as a father. Mr. Forrest, to his latest day, was accustomed to express his deep sense of the value of his instructions, and, indeed, he could hardly mention his name without giving some token of the veneration he felt for his memory. Among his fellow students at the Hall were Dr. Henry Belfrage, of Selkirk, author of "Sacramental Addresses" and other popular and practical works, and Dr. Andrew Marshall, the Father, as he has been called, of the "Voluntary Controversy."

In 1796 Mr. Forrest was ordained and installed in the pastoral charge of the Associate Congregation of Saltcoate, a small town in the West of Scotland, on the coast of Ayrshire. Here he remained in the diligent discharge of his ministerial duties until the visit of Dr. John M. Mason to Great Britain to obtain funds for the Theological Seminary, and a competent number of evangelical ministers to meet the pressing demand made upon the Associate Reformed Church for the supply of ordinances. As all the documents connected with this important mission have been published, it is not necessary, in this connection, to enter into any details of its history. It is sufficient to say that Mr. Forrest was one of the first to listen to the cry for help from the American Church. This offer was gratefully accepted, and, on the 1st of September, 1802, he sailed from Greenock, in company with the Rev. Dr. Mason, Dr. James Laurie, Messrs. James Scrimgeour, Alexander Calderhead, Robert Easton and Robert H. Bishop. They had a prosperous voyage and reached New York in time to attend the meeting of the Synod, which commenced its sessions in that city on the 21st of October, 1802; and, having presented their letters of dismission and other credentials, were at once received into Christian and ministerial communion.

* MS. from Dr. Forsyth.

During the first year after his arrival in this country Mr. Forrest visited various destitute portions of the Church, and, it is believed, spent some months in Lower Canada. On the 26th of April, 1804, he was installed Pastor of the Pearl Street Congregation, in the city of New York. He remained in this charge until the 14th of June, 1808, when, at his own request, the connection was dissolved. After labouring, for some time, as an itinerant, in Central and Western New York and in Upper Canada, he was admitted to the pastoral charge of the Congregation of Stamford, Delaware County, on the 15th of January, 1810. Here he remained, performing with great diligence and faithfulness the duties of the ministerial office, until the growing infirmities of age induced him in 1843 to ask for a dissolution of his pastoral relation. During the following year he resided in the city of New York, but, finding the climate injurious to his own health, and also to that of his wife, he returned once more to the scene of his labours amid the pleasant hills of Delaware. But his race was well-nigh run. For half a century he had been permitted to preach the glad tidings of Redemption, and on the spot where he had so long testified the Gospel of the grace of God he was at last gathered to his fathers. Though his health was feeble during the last two years of his life, he was able occasionally to appear in the pulpit, and, with the utmost readiness, lent his aid to his brethren, of whatever name, when his strength allowed him to do so. In the autumn of 1845 he was seized with an illness which confined him to his chamber from that time up to the day of his death. He bore his protracted and often very severe sufferings with exemplary patience, and died on the 17th of March, 1846, in the seventy-eighth year of his age and the fiftieth of his ministry.

He bequeathed his large and valuable library to the Theological Seminary, formerly at New York, now at Newburgh.

The following is a list of Mr. Forrest's publications:

Conversion of an Aged Sinner: A Narrative Tract, - - - - 1807
Great Encouragement to Perseverance in Missionary Labours: A Sermon delivered before the Northern Missionary Society at their Annual Meeting in Lansingburgh, - - - - - - - - 1815
A Testimony on the Doctrines of Original Sin and of Atonement, prepared by order of the Associate Reformed Synod, - - - 1831
He was also a liberal contributor to the Christian Magazine, - - 1832–42

FROM THE REV. ROBERT PROUDFIT, D.D.

UNION COLLEGE, April 2, 1850.

Rev. and dear Sir: I became acquainted with the Rev. Robert Forrest in the winter of 1802–03,—shortly after his arrival in this country. We were afterwards co-presbyters for about thirty-six years, and of course I had the opportunity of frequent intercourse with him. My earliest impressions concerning him, which were never afterwards essentially changed, were that the characteristics of the true Gentleman and of the Christian Minister were as happily blended in him as in any one with whom I was acquainted. His talents were rather solid than brilliant. He did not exhibit much original thought; but, having time and opportunity for much reading, and having both a sound judgment and a retentive memory, he possessed very extensive information, particularly upon theological subjects. His preaching was calculated to enlighten the understanding, rather than to affect deeply the emotional nature; and hence he seemed better fitted to edify saints than to extend the visible Church. His piety was deep and uniform, but altogether unobtrusive; and his aversion to the extravagance sometimes accompanying revivals led him perhaps too far in the opposite direction; but never to underrate the genuine appearances of vital religion. While firmly attached to the Church with which he was connected, he was liberal in his views of other denominations, whom he considered as holding the fundamental truths of religion; but I think he sometimes imagined errors in doctrine when there was nothing more than verbal inaccuracy, or indistinct statement.

The most strict and unyielding integrity was a striking feature in his character. He was utterly incapable of any thing approaching dissimulation, meanness or unworthy artifice. Possessing considerable property, he was generous in bestowing gifts upon those who were in need; and, while indulgent himself to those who owed him support, he strenuously inculcated the liberal maintenance of Gospel Ordinances as a Christian duty. He was exemplarily punctual in attending Ecclesiastical Courts, and, indeed, in all his engagements. In his deliberations and decisions he was strictly conscientious; but, often, from a momentary impulse, proposed measures which appeared to others unwise, and which he himself, upon a little reflection, would readily abandon. In our long and frequent intercourse in Presbytery and in Synod, he and I often differed in judgment upon measures under consideration, but I do not believe that either of us was ever the subject of an unkind feeling on that account.
Yours truly,
R. PROUDFIT.

FROM THE REV. JOHN FORSYTH, D.D.

THEOLOGICAL SEMINARY, NEWBURGH, April 10, 1856.

Rev. and Dear Sir: In complying with your request to send you my recollections of Mr. Forrest, I feel that I am only obeying the Divine precept,— "Thine own friend, and thy father's friend, forget not." He was both. For many years, my father's house was his home, on the occasion of his annual visits to Newburgh, as one of the Superintendents of the Seminary; and in his own modest parsonage on the banks of the Delaware, and amid the green hills of Delaware County, I spent some of the happiest days of my life when a student. I can never forget the pleasant fellowship with him at my father's fireside and his own, or the various talk in which he delighted, about books and passing events, and the men whom he had known in his native land, or those with whom he had become acquainted during his residence of forty years or more in America. His image is as distinctly before my mind's eye, his very attitude, as he used to sit with his snuff-box in his hand, or with the snuff between his fingers, or in the act of carrying it, as he did with exquisite grace, to his nose,—as distinctly as if I were looking upon his portrait.

Yet I find it, by no means, an easy task to transfer this image to paper, inasmuch as it had few salient points. Mr. Forrest had no eccentricities, unless, indeed, you reckon as such his intense dislike of long speeches and sermons,—very good ones, of course, excepted,—a feeling which sometimes became objective—to use a Germanism—in the form of a vigorous yawn, which was neither agreeable to the Preacher nor stimulating to his eloquence. Once, and only once, I remember to have endured the infliction. It was during my first year in the Seminary, on the occasion of my class preaching before the Superintendents. I had the misfortune to be the last preacher of the evening. A moment's thought might have convinced me that the emphatic evidence of weariness that greeted and horrified me, was not occasioned by my sermon; for I had not spoken three minutes, and I was, besides, rather a pet of my good old friend: but I can never forget the electric-like shock which that yawn produced. But let me pass to more serious matters.

Mr. Forrest afforded a striking illustration of the extent to which a mind, naturally of no great power or compass, can be invigorated and enriched by persistent industry in scholarly culture. He had not a spark of that quality, so often noticed in pen-portraits, so rarely met with in real life,—originality. He had no tendency to speculation, and no special aptness for elaborate reasoning. He could not be called an independent thinker, yet he was, by no means, a slavish imitator of the models which he most admired. The principles of faith and polity in which he had been trained, by his venerated theological instructor, Dr. Lawson, of Selkirk, he adhered to through life with undeviating consistency. It were an injustice to his memory to say that he took them upon trust. He stood where he did, immovably firm, because deeply convinced that he was standing on the rock of truth; but the weapons by which he defended his position were derived from armories constructed and replenished by the heads and hands of others. He took care to surround himself with the best books in the various branches of Theology and Literature, and he made their contents his own by hard and constant study. Even in his old age he kept up his habits of reading and of careful writing, and during the thirty-five years of his residence in Stamford, he always carried home with him from the city of New York—which he was accustomed to visit semi-annually—a goodly supply of the best productions of the British and American press. In his large library there was hardly a volume with whose contents he was not acquainted. The consequence was that his mental vigour, like his Christian graces, was renewed, day by day, even when the outward man was perceptibly decaying. And his friends in Newburgh were wont to say, from year to year,—"That last sermon is the best he ever preached here." Indeed, the last half dozen which I had the privilege to hear were truly noble discourses.

In personal appearance Mr. Forrest was a man of presence. A stranger meeting him anywhere, in the street or the drawing room, would, at the first glance, conclude that he must be a Minister, and a Minister, too, worthy of all respect.

Leading, as he did, the retired life of a student and rural Pastor, Mr. Forrest necessarily lacked that knowledge of men which can be got only by close and constant contact with men:—

Fluctibus in mediis, et tempestatibus urbis.

He thus became occasionally the victim, as I may say, of prejudices against individuals, which would, now and then, vent themselves in a hasty word. But if the very persons whose opinions or public conduct he perhaps was sharply condemning, had, the next moment, knocked at his door, it would have been instantly seen how evanescent were all his personal dislikes, and that on his heart the law of kindness was deeply engraved.

Believe me to remain very truly yours,

JOHN FORSYTH.

JOSEPH KERR, D.D.
1803—1829.
FROM THE REV. JAMES PRESTLEY, D.D.

PITTSBURG, March 3, 1862.

Dear Sir: I have been requested to send you a memorial of the Rev. Joseph Kerr, D. D., formerly Pastor of the First Associate Reformed Congregation in this city, of which I at present have the charge, and first Professor of Theology in the Theological Seminary of the Associate Reformed Presbyterian Church in the West. It is compiled in part from my own recollections, as I was under his pastoral care all the time he had charge of this congregation; in part from information derived from the surviving members of his family; in part from those who studied Theology in his classes; but principally from obituary notices of him published shortly after his decease. His memory is cherished still in th: hearts of all who knew him, and is like precious ointment poured forth, to this day, in the denomination of Christians with which he was connected. I am altogether of opinion that his life is well deserving of a more public and general remembrance, and I am glad that you propose to give his name a place among those of the many eminent divines whose names you are embalming in the "Annals of the American Pulpit."

JOSEPH KERR, son of the Rev. Joseph and Elizabeth (Reynolds) Kerr, was born in County Derry, near the border of County Tyrone, Ireland, in the year 1778. His father was an eminent Minister of the Gospel, connected with the Burgher division of the Associate Synod in Ireland, and greatly esteemed in his day for his great abilities in the pulpit. Of the instructions and example of this eminently pious father his son was deprived, while yet a child. He was accustomed to retire for meditation and study to a secluded walk in his garden. To this place he had gone early in the morning of the day on which he died, and, on being sought for at the breakfast hour, was found lying in the walk, dead. Mrs. Kerr was left with a family of small children, over which she watched with great tenderness and care. Being possessed of some means, she was able to afford to the subject of this memoir facilities for acquiring an education. Having passed through a suitable preparatory course, he entered the University of Glasgow, Scotland, about the year 1794. From this Institution he graduated when he was about twenty years of age.

From early childhood he was the subject of religious impressions, and was esteemed by all who knew him as a pious and promising youth. He made a public profession of religion early in life. In what particular year cannot now be ascertained; but, as is supposed, when he was about sixteen years of age, when he left home to enter the University of Glasgow. On his return,—after graduating, he was taken under the care of the Associate (Burgher) Presbytery of Derry, as a student of Theology, and prosecuted his studies for a time under the Rev. Dr. Rogers, of Ballybay, County Monaghan, Professor of Theology for the Associate (Burgher) Synod in Ireland.

He came to the United States in the year 1801, and put himself under the care of the First Associate Reformed Presbytery of Pennsylvania, as a student of Theology. In the year 1802 he was, at his request, and before he had delivered all the trials which had been assigned him by that Presbytery, dismissed to the Second Associate Reformed Presbytery of Pennsylvania. He was received by that Presbytery at its meeting in Robinson's Run Church, in April, 1803; the same meeting at which its name was changed to "The Presbytery of Monongahela," in accordance with an order of the General Synod. At this meeting, on the 27th day of April, 1803, Mr. Kerr was licensed to preach the Gospel. His licensure may be regarded as an epoch in the history of the Associate Reformed Church in the West. It seems to have inspired the fathers of the Presbytery with new life and hope. They were few in number and widely separated. At this time Western Pennsylvania was comparatively a wilderness, congregations were small and scattered widely apart, and settled Pastors were very few. Mr. Kerr laboured among these dispersed vacancies, extending from the ridges of the Alleghenies on the East, far into Ohio on the West, and from the Northern Lakes below Mason's and Dixon's line on the South, with unheard-of popularity. Wherever he went he was admired and beloved. Calls for his labours were sent into Presbytery from a great number of neighbourhoods, and from several places that had not been previously recognized by Presbytery as any part of their charge. Indeed, his name rendered savoury that section of the Church to which he belonged. He laid, during his missionary labours in the extended bounds of the Presbytery, the foundation not only of the congregations where he first settled, but of many others which not only still exist, but continue to flourish, and some of which have been subdivided into two or more large and flourishing congregations.

After riding thus as a Missionary, for a year, Mr. Kerr was regularly invested with the sacred office. He was ordained by the Presbytery of Monongahela, at a meeting held at Short Creek, Va., on the 25th day of April, 1804. He continued to supply the vacancies in the bounds of the Presbytery some months longer; and, having declined several calls which, in a pecuniary view, were far more inviting, he, at length, from a prospect of usefulness rather than gain, accepted a call from the United Congregations of Mifflin and St. Clair, in the vicinity of Pittsburg; and, on the 17th of October, 1804, at the house of Nathaniel Plummer, was installed Pastor of these congregations.

In a few years each of these congregations declared itself able to support its own Pastor, and desired to obtain his undivided labours. The matter was postponed, from time to time, until, in the year 1817, Mr. Kerr, considering his health inadequate to the labours required by two Congregations as large as these had become, demitted the charge of Mifflin Congregation, and the whole of his labours were given to the Congregation of St. Clair. Here he still continued to enjoy the smiles of his Divine Master, and laboured for several years with great success.

In the mean time, an organization, with good prospects, had been effected by order of Presbytery in the city of Pittsburg, which, under the pastoral charge of the Rev. Joseph McElroy,—now Dr. McElroy, of the Presbyterian Church, Fourteenth street, New York city, had grown to be a large and influential congregation. On the removal of Mr. McElroy to New York the attention of this congregation was directed to Mr. Kerr, and, notwithstanding the affection known to exist between him and the people of his charge, a call was made out for him and presented through the Presbytery. Pittsburg was, at that time, considered one of the centres of influence in the Associate Reformed Church; the position was a desirable one, and the pecuniary support large for that day. It may have been thought by some that these considerations would have weight with Mr. Kerr, but they did not. On the presentation of the call, he stated that he entertained a high regard for the people of the Congregation of Pittsburg, and most heartily desired their prosperity; yet, inasmuch as he had always been of the opinion that a minister, who was comfortably settled in a congregation, with a mutual good understanding existing between him and his people, ought not, excepting under very imperious circumstances indeed, to think of removal, he could not separate himself from his congregation without doing violence to his feelings and to all his principles—he, therefore, begged leave respectfully to decline the call from Pittsburg.

In the year 1825 the Associate Reformed Synod of the West resolved to establish a Theological Seminary, and elected Mr. Kerr their Professor of Theology. As Pittsburg was generally esteemed the most suitable locality for the Seminary, and as the Synod could not support the Professor, unless he had also a pastoral charge, the Congregation in Pittsburg, after taking the advice of some of the members of the Presbytery, renewed their call to Mr. Kerr to become their Pastor. When the matter came before the Presbytery, that Court, by its own act, transferred him from his then present charge to the charge of the Congregation in Pittsburg. In this decision of the Presbytery he acquiesced, and, having also accepted the Professorship, commenced his preparations for an immediate removal to Pittsburg, and was installed as Pastor in his new charge in October, 1825. Previously to his removal to Pittsburg, that congregation, through frequent disappointments and discouragements, was considerably weakened. His settlement among them had an electrical effect in quickening them to new life and vigour. From a desponding, disintegrated handful they, in a very short time, became one of the largest and most respectable congregations in the city. Thus, wherever this good man was called to labour, it pleased the Head of the Church to bless his labours and to make manifest the savour of his knowledge by him.

Shortly after entering on the duties of his Professorship of Theology in Pittsburg, he received the honorary degree of Doctor of Divinity from the Western University of Pennsylvania.

My personal recollections of Dr. Kerr, though I was but a lad when he died, are very distinct. His personal appearance was very imposing and attractive. He would have been marked any where, not because of obtrusion, for he was singularly modest, but from his general appearance. He was tall, straight, symmetrical, with good features and well-formed head. His air was almost military. In him dignity was blended with great amiability. His countenance beamed with benevolence, and his eye, especially when he spoke, was remarkably expressive of deep interest in what he was saying. In society he was very complaisant, and in cases of affliction very sympathetic. With his fine powers and liberal culture, he could condescend, without any effort, to the humblest person or smallest child.

As a Preacher of the Gospel he excelled. His appearance in the pulpit was always attractive. He was clothed there with the dignity of his office, and, sometimes, when greatly moved, rose to grandeur. His voice was sonorous, never offensively loud, and could be distinctly heard through every part of the largest church edifice. It could melt into the lowest tones of sorrow, and rise in trumpet tones to the highest pitch. I was not so capable at the time, being but a youth, of judging correctly of the matter of his discourses; but I recollect that I was always interested. I never felt lassitude while he was preaching. Young as I was, I could understand him, and could carry home to the evening examination a good deal of what he said. This was not strange—the whole congregation appeared to hang upon his lips. He was, as the result, unusually successful in edifying his people, and in adding to the Church. One contemporary with him, writing of him, says,—" As a Pulpit Orator, he soon excited attention, and in his new field of labour he was unusually successful; and he filled the Professor's chair with great acceptance. * * * But let there be no misapprehension. Dr. Kerr was not a *showy* preacher, on whom a crowd would gaze in stupid wonder and then go away sure of nothing but that they had heard a great sermon, if they only knew what it was about; but like Aaron he could 'speak well,' which John Quincy Adams says is the perfection of eloquence. Every speaker has some peculiarities of manner. When Dr. Kerr hesitated for a word to express his idea, he paused, cast his eye downward, and in a moment the word, the very right word, came."

Dr. Kerr was eminently a pious man. He was decided in his views and consistent in his practice. Of an ardent temperament and of a very susceptible nature, yet such was his habitual self-control that I have never heard any one say that he had spoken in anger or unadvisedly with his lips, on any occasion, no matter what the provocation. He was withal a very benevolent man and much "given to hospitality." It was no uncommon thing for him, when living on a farm, to assist a young minister just starting out on his first tour to preach the Gospel, to a horse or equipments. He not unfrequently gave away the last dollar in the house. When elected to the Professorship of Theology, which he held for only four years, he, for the first two years, gave his salary, two hundred dollars, all that the Synod could afford to pay him, to commence a fund to assist young men in needy circumstances in prosecuting their theological course, and, during the last two years, he gave a hundred and fifty dollars each year toward the same object, besides large contributions toward procuring a necessary library for the Theological Seminary.

In his intercourse with the people of his charge he was remarkably prudent—his counsels were eminently judicious and his influence was very great. His memory is still fondly cherished among those of his congregations who survive, and they speak of him as a model to be imitated. As a Father, the lives and deaths of his children attest his fidelity. In Church Courts he did not often speak, but when he did, it was with power. He had great strength in debate, but appeared to be unconscious of it. He was incapable of any thing like indirection. Mr. McFarland, of Chillicothe, O., a man of considerable power in debate, who had sometimes encountered him in the Synod, once said,—" I like Mr. Kerr for an opponent, *for you can see all of him.*" As a Man, in all the relations of life, there was no one more kind, more universally cheerful, or more instructive. He was a good man, and his " memory is blessed."

One of his contemporaries, in an obituary notice, says,—" As this sketch may be handed down to a future age, it may not be amiss to state some of those personal and moral qualities that rendered him so universally admired and beloved. His personal appearance was highly respectable and pleasing. He was tall of stature, straight and portly. He possessed a large share of social cheerfulness, and was, at the same time, very sympathetic and tender with the suffering. His ideas were lucid, and he communicated them with the greatest facility. He was always pleasant and ready in speech, but in public speaking his fluency acquired an ardour which fascinated his audience. He had a well-balanced and capacious mind. His pulpit exercises were most remarkable for embodying a large amount of the richest evangelical matter. In the exercise of prayer he excelled. In his ministerial calling he was diligent in business; fervent in spirit; serving the Lord."

One of his students of Theology, writing to me recently, says of him:

" His best and noblest appearance was in the pulpit. Goodness, true greatness, and eminent godliness characterized him at all times and in all places, but especially in the sacred desk. He looked and spoke like a messenger fresh from the Divine Throne, whose soul overflowed with love to God and man. His lectures and sermons were lucid and forcible expositions of the Word of the Lord. The language was so plain, and the matter so important and attractive, that the ordinary hearer was edified and delighted, and the most cultivated and fastidious listener not displeased. A seeming unconcern in regard to the rules of oratory marked his delivery. At times his beseeching utterances were solemn and persuasive; at other times his burning words were awful and soul-harrowing. He kept his subject always between himself and his auditors; so that they saw and analyzed *it* rather than *him* The application of his discourses was searching and impressive. In this he excelled. He came near, in God's name, to every hearer, young and old, saint and sinner; and to each he addressed a suitable word in season. The application was always the warmer and better half of the discourse. I loved, admired and revered him: and so did all his students without exception."

As a Professor in the Theological Seminary, Dr. Kerr was very successful, and gave universal satisfaction. In his intercourse with the students he was courteous and dignified. He was a mild critic, considerate of the feelings of the student, and yet faithful. He was careful not to wound while he corrected. He was an excellent instructor, clear, sufficiently concise, and had a happy faculty of bringing to view all that was legitimately connected with the subject in hand. He had great discernment of character, and could not be easily deceived as to the capacities, diligence or attainments of his students. He, by his urbanity, kindness and faithfulness, rendered himself very dear to them all; and this is perhaps one of the best testimonials of his real worth as a Professor.

In the year 1806 Mr. Kerr returned, for a short time, to Ireland, where he was united in marriage, on the 6th day of April of that year, to Miss Agnes Reynolds, who still lives, at the advanced age of eighty years. He had, by this marriage, eleven children,—five sons and six daughters, all of whom survived him and lived to adult years. Three sons became Ministers of the Gospel, only one of whom survives,—*Rev. David R. Kerr, D.D.*, Professor of Ecclesiastical History and Church Government in the Theological Seminary of the United Presbyterian Church, Allegheny City, Pa.; and editor of "The United Presbyterian," a weekly religious newspaper in the interest of the same denomination. Four of the daughters married clergymen. Only four children,—one son and three daughters, now survive.

Dr. Kerr's last illness was short and very severe; but death did not find him unprepared. He could say,—"For me to live is Christ, and to die is gain." He was taken ill on the evening of Thursday, the 12th day of November, 1829; and died on the evening of the following Sabbath. His disease was bilious colic. During the night of Thursday he suffered excruciating pain. The best medical skill the city could afford, was exerted in his behalf, but without avail. He sustained his affliction—and the pains were sometimes extreme—with astonishing composure and resignation. His countenance was lighted up during the whole period of his sufferings, as if he continually realized the hand of God in them, and rejoiced to suffer at the hand of Him with whom he expected, in a short time, to reign. He appeared to be entirely free from any anxious concern about the world. When he saw his family and friends weeping around him, he comforted them and admonished them not to grieve for him. He assured them that, though his conflict was sharp, it would not be long; that he was not unsustained; that if God had any thing more for him to do in this world, He would raise him up; and, if not, he was satisfied. He continued to suffer, thus sustained by the grace of God, until the evening of the Sabbath. A short time before his departure, he

summoned all his strength, and spoke for some time, with great feeling, on the heinousness of his sins, and on the greatness, grace and preciousness of his Saviour; of the goodness and forbearance of God to him through life, and of his personal unworthiness. A few minutes before he died, he was asked by his brother if he had any fears in view of the near approach of death. He replied,—
"No, no, I am a great, *great sinner*, but I have a great, *great*, GREAT Saviour." Having said this, and asking to lean more entirely upon a friend,—one of the Elders of his church, who was partially supporting him in that posture, (for he sat in a chair, not being able to recline on his bed,) without a struggle, he fell asleep in the bosom of that great Saviour whom he so ardently loved, and so diligently and faithfully served. "Thus died," says one of his brethren, "an amiable Man, a pious Christian, a talented Professor, and an able Minister of the New Testament." "Blessed are the dead that die in the Lord:—yea, saith the spirit, that they may rest from their labours, and their works do follow them."

Affectionately yours,
JAMES PRESTLEY.

FROM THE REV. DAVID MACDILL, D.D.

SPARTA, Ill., April 8, 1852.

Dear Sir: My acquaintance with the Rev. Joseph Kerr, D.D., commenced about the year 1818, and continued till his death. He was a good Preacher of the Gospel. Few indeed understood the plan of salvation better. He had what old Mr. Baxter called a "rousing voice." His talents, though not what would be called brilliant, were eminently solid and useful. He was, in the best sense, an eloquent man, and yet the graces of oratory he seemed neither to study nor regard. His prevailing moral qualities were candour, gentleness, kindness, goodness. I can hardly think that any person could have heard him speak without being convinced that he was listening to a sincere man. These qualities gave him great influence among the people. It was commonly said that, when a difficulty arose in any of their congregations, which required the services of a peace-maker, the Presbytery to which he belonged would appoint him to go and attend to the call. While Pastor of a country congregation, before his removal to Pittsburg, I have heard that when he saw any respectable looking man travelling the road which passed near his house, he would frequently enter into conversation with him; and if he found him, in some degree, a man of a kindred spirit, would invite him in and lodge him courteously.

Every public speaker has perhaps some gestures which may be called mechanical, but which are often very expressive. The late Dr. Mason, of New York, when he was labouring to bring forth some vast idea in all its power and grandeur, had a peculiar manner of rubbing his fore-finger on his forehead; and when, from some momentary confusion, he could not at once get hold of the idea, or the word, which he wanted, he would bring his hand briskly before his eyes, as if he were brushing away some insect which obscured his vision. When Mr. Kerr was in search of a word, he cast a broad earnest look downwards, as if he were looking for something at his feet. It was never long before the word was found; and when found, it was exactly the right one. The congregation of which he had the charge in Pittsburg flourished under his ministry. In the Theological Seminary, in which he was sole Professor, his labours were highly acceptable both to the students and to the Synod.

Respectfully,
DAVID MACDILL.

FROM THE REV. ELISHA P. SWIFT, D.D.

ALLEGHENY CITY, PA., January 17, 1862.

Dear Sir: To recall the fading reminiscences of those departed servants of the Lord, whom we once knew and esteemed, is not an unpleasant office; and I, therefore, cheerfully comply with your request to state what may occur to my thoughts in reference to the late Rev. Dr. Joseph Kerr. In view of the fact that it is now thirty-two years since his decease, and that my acquaintance with him was neither of long continuance nor very intimate, you will expect nothing more from me than a brief statement of my own impressions of his character.

I distinctly remember him as a man of about the medium height, erect in stature, slender in person, with a countenance at once thoughtful, benignant, intellectual and suggestive of his sacred office. In his general appearance and manner there was much to indicate a studious habit, blended with great modesty and self-distrust, and a most gentle and kindly spirit. He did not strike me as a man of very original powers, or varied learning, or commanding eloquence; but rather as one who, with a vigorous, well-balanced and well-furnished mind and pleasing address, was qualified to be a judicious, instructive and interesting Preacher of the Gospel, and a successful former of the theological principles and mental habits of the rising ministry. When the Associate Reformed Synod of the West determined to found a Theological Seminary within their own bounds, all eyes seem to have been directed to Mr. Kerr, as the person who should be chosen first Professor in the infant institution; and he was accordingly elected to that office with great unanimity. It was deemed expedient that the Seminary should be opened in the city of Pittsburg; and the First Associate Reformed Church in the city being then vacant, and wishing to avail themselves of the pastoral labours of the Professor elect, made out a unanimous call to him to take charge of that large and flourishing congregation.

A very flattering testimony to the personal worth and ministerial qualifications of Mr. Kerr, in the estimation of this congregation and that of St. Clair, five miles from the city, of which he was then Pastor, grew out of this occurrence. This latter church made the most earnest and persevering opposition to his translation to the Pittsburg charge, while the former were equally intent on the prosecution of their call. The reluctance of the St. Clair congregation to give him up became so strong as to threaten the very existence of the church; but matters finally settled down in the event of his removal to the Pittsburg charge. In this relation he was held in the same high estimation among his people as had existed before; and the congregation grew under his ministry until the close of his life. He, at the same time, took the entire charge of the education of such students of Theology as the Synod was able to collect. In this new and responsible office, his thoroughly evangelical views, his excellent judgment, and exemplary and even parental bearing, united with good theological attainments, rendered him at once highly acceptable and useful. He enjoyed the affectionate respect and confidence of his pupils; and the infant Seminary flourished under his care.

But neither the congregation nor the Seminary were permitted long to enjoy his useful labours. After a few years he passed away, having served his generation faithfully and acceptably, and leaving a name which continues fragrant to this day.

Yours very truly,
E. P. SWIFT

FROM THE REV. JOSEPH CLAYBAUGH, D.D.

OXFORD, O., June 26, 1850

Dear Sir: My recollections of Dr. Kerr date as far back as 1812. He was then comparatively young in the ministry, but in high repute as a superior Preacher and an agreeable, gentlemanly man. In the summer of that year he was to assist our minister, the Rev. Matthew Henderson, in the dispensation of the Supper, at Brush Creek; and when it was given out that Mr. Kerr was to take part in the service, expectation ran high, and it seemed as if the whole surrounding country turned out. So much was said that, though I was only a lad of nine years of age, I had a great anxiety to see and hear him. His health was delicate at the time, and he did not preach till Saturday. I recollect well his appearance then,—a tall, pale-faced man, with large features and open countenance; thoughtful, yet full of kindness and good-nature; and though evidently sickly, yet very erect in person. In his latter years he appeared to me broader and stouter than he did at that time. Of his sermons on the occasion I only remember that they were much admired. Of his familiar and pleasant manners I have a more vivid impression. I happened to be standing in the path which led from the place where he hitched his horse to the meeting-house, or rather "the tent"; and, as he passed along, he noticed me, and, asking me my name, laid his hand on my head, and, giving it a gentle rub, bade me be a good boy, and added, " You may be a Preacher some day." A year or two after this, my father moved to Ohio, and I neither saw or heard of him again till I met with him in Synod, in the spring of 1825, when he was chosen Professor of Divinity. But I had often heard his name mentioned in connection with current events in the Church, as one of the leading ministers. In the troubles that occurred about the time that the Synod of the West withdrew from the General Synod, he was looked up to by the people with great confidence, as a man of unusual stability, and yet of a mild and pacific temper.

His post as Professor of Divinity he filled with great ability, commanding the respect and love of the students and the unbounded confidence of the Church. At his suggestion, the fund for aiding young men in prosecuting their theological studies was founded, and to this fund he generally, from year to year, contributed a considerable portion of his salary as Professor. Some of the most useful men in the Church took their theological course under him.

In Synod he was seldom on the floor, and showed no ambition to have the pre-eminence; yet he manifestly watched the course of proceedings with great interest. His speeches were short and directly to the point; and when he differed with any of his brethren, it was with a modest reluctance and a manly good-nature that disarmed opposition. On these occasions he showed himself familiar with the institutions and historical incidents, as well as the doctrinal proof-texts, of the Bible; thereby evincing that, however well acquainted he was with systems and standard authors, he was more than all a Bible student. In measures he was prudent and cautious, yet investigated with candour, honesty and openness to conviction. This was especially noticeable in his course on the Slavery question, which was warmly discussed in the Synod of 1829,— only a few weeks before his lamented death.

The only time I heard him preach, after I came to mature years, was at this meeting of Synod, at which he gave the Opening Sermon. It was characterized by clearness, strength and method. His manner was manly and earnest, but not impassioned; his voice full, commanding and agreeable; his utterance deliberate, yet unhesitating and impressive. He would have been marked in any place as a Preacher of a high order.

Yours very truly,
JOSEPH CLAYBAUGH.

MUNGO DICK.*
1804—1839.

MUNGO DICK, a son of Mungo and Matilda Dick, was born in Fifeshire, Scotland, in the year 1792. His father was a farmer, and the son is believed to have spent his early years on his father's farm. He, however, discovered a decidedly intellectual turn, and, in due time, having passed through the preparatory course, he became a student at the University of Edinburgh. Here he took high rank as a scholar, as was indicated by the fact that he took every honour of his class save one. After prosecuting his theological course, he was licensed to preach by the Associate Burgher Presbytery of Perth.

In the summer of 1804 he migrated to this country. On the 19th of September of that year he joined the Associate Reformed Presbytery of New York, at a meeting held in Graham's Church, Orange County. In November following he went to labour within the bounds of the Monongahela Presbytery, in the Synod of Scioto; and, at a meeting of that Presbytery, on the 10th of April, 1805, he was received under its care as a probationer, on certificate from the Presbytery of New York. Shortly after this the Presbytery assigned to him his trials for Ordination; and, having performed the several exercises with acceptance, he was ordained to the work of the ministry on the 10th of April, 1806,—the Sermon on the occasion being preached by the Rev. David Proudfit,† from Gal. iv, 4, 5. This meeting of Presbytery was held in St. Clair Church, Allegheny County, Pa. On the first day of the meeting a call was presented to him from the Congregation of Butler and of Deer Creek, and one from Sewickly and Mount Pleasant; both of which were held for consideration. At a meeting of Presbytery, on the 26th of August following, a call was presented to him from Mercer, Neshannock and Sandy Creek, and this also was held for consideration. At this meeting the Congregation of Denniston's town requested that they might be united in a pastoral charge with the Congregations of Sewickly and Mount Pleasant; and, the Presbytery having signified their consent to the proposed measure, the union was consummated at the next meeting. The call from this united charge was then accepted by Mr. Dick, and the other two calls declined. At a meeting of the Presbytery held at the house of John Milligan, in the Sewickly Congregation, April 1, 1807, he was installed Pastor, the Sermon on the occasion being preached by the Rev. Matthew Henderson, and the Charges delivered by the Rev. David Proudfit.

---

* MS. from his son, Rev. J. M. Dick.

† DAVID PROUDFIT was a native of York County, Pa., where his parents, Andrew and Sarah (Wallace) Proudfit, who were natives of Scotland, settled on their removal to this country. He was licensed to preach the Gospel by the Associate Reformed Presbytery of Monongahela in the year 1796. After being employed for about two years in missionary labours in Kentucky and Ohio, he was settled in the pastoral charge of Laurel Hill, Fayette County, Pa. Here he continued to labour with much acceptance as a Preacher, and especially as a Pastor, for twenty-six years, when he removed to Muskingum County, O., and took charge of the Congregation of Crooked Creek. Here also he laboured with much success, enjoying the affection and confidence of a large congregation, during the remainder of his life. He died on the 11th of June, 18:0, in the fifty-ninth year of his age. In June, 1798, he was married to Sarah, daughter of William Patterson, by whom he had nine children,—six sons and three daughters. Four of the sons became Ruling Elders in the Church, and one a Deacon. Mr. Proudfit was tall in stature and of a dignified and commanding personal appearance. He was a plain, affectionate, earnest Preacher, and was especially felicitous in his treatment of the conscience-burdened and distressed.

At a meeting of the Presbytery, on the 11th of September, 1816, the Mount Pleasant Congregation requested that one half of Mr. Dick's time should be devoted to them; and their request was granted; and about the same time he demitted the Dennistou's town branch of his charge. At a meeting in Harmony, on the 10th of September, 1823, he was, at his own request, released from his charge of the Mount Pleasant Congregation. At the St. Clair Church, on the 8th of September, 1824, a petition for half of his time was presented from Turtle Creek and Brush Creek;—one-quarter of this to be given to the former, and three-quarters to the latter. Shortly after this, he received a call for half his time at Brush Creek; which was accepted. During his ministry there Brush Creek changed its name to that of Bethel. At a meeting of Presbytery, on the 14th of April, 1835, he requested to be released from this part of his charge, on account of increasing bodily infirmity.

On the 1st of December, 1829, he was appointed to superintend the studies of the students of Theology during the following winter. In 1830 he was appointed, by a unanimous vote of the Synod, Professor (*pro tem*) in the Theological Seminary; but, as his failing health would not permit him to go to Allegheny City, where the Seminary had been located, the students repaired to his residence that they might avail themselves of his instruction. The next year, however, he was relieved from this duty by the regular appointment of a Professor. From this time his health declined more rapidly, and, at a meeting of the Presbytery, on the 27th of April, 1836, he asked to be released from the only remaining part of his charge, (Sewickly,) and the request was granted. He, however, continued to preach occasionally to this congregation until near the time of his death. He lived to see his successor ordained and installed, but he survived that occasion only two days. He finished his course on the 2d of May, 1839, in the sixty-seventh year of his age,

Mr. Dick was married, in or about the year 1815, to Elizabeth, daughter of Jeremiah Murray, of Murraysville, Pa. They had eight children,—two sons, *John N.* and *Jeremiah M.*, who entered the ministry in the Associate Reformed Church, and one daughter who is married to the Rev. James Grier, a minister of the same church. Mrs. Dick still (1862) survives.

FROM THE REV. H. CONNELLY.

NEWBURGH, June 24, 1862.

My dear Sir: I spent several of my early years in the congregation of which Matthew Henderson was Pastor, and, as he occasionally exchanged pulpits with Mungo Dick, I had the opportunity of hearing him, though I was too young to form an intelligent estimate of his character as a Preacher. I remember, however, the deep interest with which I used to listen to him even then, and the impression that seemed generally to prevail throughout the region,—that he was one of the ablest Preachers of his day. I used to hear of him frequently while I was in College, though I am not sure that I saw him during that time; but, after I became a student of Theology at the Pittsburg Seminary, I was accustomed to meet him at Presbytery, where he was sure to exhibit some of his most striking characteristics. After my licensure I became quite well acquainted with him. On one occasion I went to hear him preach, and when, on entering the church, he discovered me in the audience, he approached me and said, with a sort of authoritative though not unkindly air,—"Connelly, you must preach." "I cannot preach, Sir," said I; "I came to hear you." "You must preach, Sir," said he, and, taking me by the hand, led me into the pulpit. I did preach; and his remarks upon my youthful performance were alike creditable to his taste, his fidelity and his generous consideration.

Mr. Dick was of about the middle stature and of a well proportioned form. He had a bright black eye, high forehead, full cheek and an expression of great intelligence and earnestness. Altogether, his personal appearance was decidedly imposing and attractive. The movements of his body were not rapid, but strong and steady, indicating stability of character and purpose. In conversation he was free and affable, and expressed himself with great facility and propriety. Though I should not say that he was generally of a jocose habit, there was evidently a rich vein of fun in his nature, which would occasionally reveal itself in something that left it at nobody's option whether or not to keep sober. There was a Mr. M——, a native of Ireland, settled near the Allegheny River, who was rather remarkable for pathos in his public services, and was especially felicitous in the administration of the Communion. Father Dick and he, though in pleasant fraternal relations, did not think alike on all subjects, and especially on politics. On one occasion they met at the house of a mutual friend, and slept in the same room, and, if I mistake not, in the same bed. Mr. Dick awoke first in the morning, dressed himself and left the room, his brother M—— being still fast asleep. Discovering in the yard a flock of geese, he caught one of them, and opening the window of the room in which he had slept, (it being on the lower floor,) threw in the goose as a companion for his friend, closed the window again and passed away. It was understood to be intended as an illustration of the old sage maxim,—

"Birds of a feather
Flock together."

Mr. Dick was a man of great strength and comprehensiveness of mind, and capable of taking profound views of any subject that engaged his attention. He was never superficial in any thing, never satisfied till he had fathomed the depths of his subject, so far as it came within the range of his faculties. If he had any considerable degree of imagination, it must have been kept in abeyance to his reasoning faculty, as I do not remember ever to have witnessed any marked exhibitions of it. He was a man of liberal and varied acquirements, and though he made no ostentatious display of his learning, it was impossible to associate with him without discovering it.

As a Preacher, Mr. Dick commanded great respect from all classes. His voice was loud and sonorous, and he was so intensely Scotch in his accent that it had almost the effect of a monotony. His manner was very earnest, and his countenance singularly solemn, and he impressed you irresistibly with the conviction that every word that he uttered came from his inmost soul. His sermons were rich in evangelical truth, comprehensive, logical, and fully exhaustive of the subject discoursed upon. No intelligent hearer was likely ever to grow weary under his ministrations.

In a Deliberative Assembly or Church Judicature he was never forward or unduly officious, but was always attentive and watchful, and ready to exert a decisive influence wherever it was needed. He was a man of goodness, wisdom and power.

Very sincerely your friend and servant,

H. CONNELLY.

JOHN LIND.*
1807—1824.

JOHN LIND, the son of the Rev. Matthew Lind and Jennett Fulton, was born in Franklin County, Pa., March 14, 1784.

The father, *Rev. Matthew Lind*, was born in the County of Antrim, in Ireland, in 1732. He completed his education at Glasgow, and was settled as a Minister near Colerain, in the County of Londonderry, about the year 1760. His wife was the first cousin of Robert Fulton, of steamboat memory. He came to this country in the year 1774, and soon after his arrival accepted a call from a Congregation in Dauphin County, Pa. In 1783 he was released from his charge, and accepted a call from the United Congregations of Greencastle, Chambersburg, West Conococheague and Great Cove. Here he continued in the faithful discharge of the duties of his office, until about three years previous to his decease, when, in consequence of bodily infirmity, heightened by the effect of a fall from a horse, he resigned his pastoral charge. He died greatly lamented on the 21st of April, 1800.

There was a remarkable event in the history of Mr. Lind, previous to his leaving Ireland, which some have supposed had some influence in leading to his emigration. A rumour got abroad that he had officiated in a clandestine marriage of a young gentleman of high birth and expectations to a farmer's daughter. Mr. Lind denied unequivocally the alleged fact; but the circumstances were such that even his denial did not, by any means, allay suspicions. So strong was the feeling on the subject that the case was eventually brought to the notice of the Presbytery in Scotland, to which he was attached, and a committee was sent to investigate the rumours against him. By this time, two men were found to come forward and state that they had seen Mr. Lind celebrate the marriage, and they named the place at which it was done. Mr. Lind persevered in his denial, and also succeeded in adducing testimony respecting his movements on the evening when the marriage was said to have taken place, which availed so far that the committee could not venture to condemn him. But, though he was thus ecclesiastically acquitted, public opinion was still strongly against him; and he felt deeply the embarrassment of his condition. It is more than probable that, when there was an application sent to Ireland from this country for a number of ministers, this was one of the circumstances that disposed Mr. Lind to be one of the number. Many years after he had left Ireland, and subsequently, it is believed, to his death, an aged and eminently pious man, who had long been under Mr. Lind's pastoral charge, was one evening sent for, in great haste, to visit a neighbour, like himself an old man, but notoriously wicked, who was supposed to be lying at the point of death. He hastened to the house, and, as he entered the chamber where the dying man was, he begun to address him with reference to his condition and prospects. His remarks seemed to be entirely unheeded, and the aged sinner requested that he might be alone, for a few moments, with his neighbour. The room being cleared, he proceeded to say,—" I am dying, but I cannot die without making to you a statement that will sur-

---
* Obituary by Rev. James Buchanan.—MS. from his son, Mr. R. S. Lind.

prise you. You have often no doubt remarked the very striking resemblance between myself and the Rev. Matthew Lind. You remember also the report that he had married (naming the parties), and how earnestly and perseveringly he denied the charge. Mr. Lind was innocent—I am the person who committed the offence—for a bribe, and under the strongest obligations of secrecy, I personated Mr. Lind. I dared not reveal the truth until now. I leave it with you to use after my death; for you will use it wisely." His astonished auditor left him, but did not himself make the matter public till some time after. This statement is made on the authority of the Rev. Dr. Stanley, a highly respectable clergyman who resided in the immediate neighbourhood of the place where the circumstance occurred.

In March, 1796, John Lind, being twelve years of age, was sent to a Grammar School at Gettysburg, Pa., under the care of the Rev. Alexander Dobbin, where he remained a year. In 1797 he attended the school of a Mr. Borland, of Green Castle; and in 1798 and 1799 he was again at the school of Mr. Dobbin. In the autumn of 1800 he entered the Junior class of Dickinson College, of which Dr. Nisbet was then President, and graduated with the highest honours of his class in 1802. Being in delicate health when he left College, he travelled to the South, and spent some time, pursuing his theological studies under the direction of his brother-in-law, the Rev. Dr. Hemphill, and returned in the autumn of 1803. In 1804 he was under the care of the Big Spring Presbytery, and pursued his studies, partly under the Rev. Alexander Dobbin and partly under the Rev. John Young. He became a student in Dr. Mason's Seminary at its opening in 1805, being admitted at an advanced stage in the course, on account of his previous studies. His connection with the Seminary continued until May, 1807, when he received the regular certificate from the Superintendents that he was qualified to be taken on trial for license to preach the Gospel; and he was licensed, by the Presbytery of Big Spring, on the 4th of August following. His public labours being, from the beginning, very acceptable, he soon received a call from the United Congregations of Hagerstown, Green Castle, West Conococheague and Great Cove, which had become vacant by the death of the Rev. John Young, who was the successor of Mr. Lind's father in that pastoral charge. Mr. Lind, having accepted the call, was ordained, and installed as Pastor of those congregations, on the 4th of October, 1808. Here he exercised his ministry for a number of years with great fidelity and acceptance. But the labours incident to so extended a charge being found to overtask his constitution, and the Congregations of Hagerstown and Green Castle believing that it would tend to promote their growth and spiritual edification to have a greater portion of his ministerial labours secured to them,—they made application to the Presbytery to have the connection which existed between the Pastor and those parts of his charge known by the names of West Conococheague and the Great Cove dissolved; and to have the whole of his services appointed to themselves. In June, 1817, the Presbytery complied with this request, thus reducing the field of his labour from four congregations to two. Here he continued labouring with increasing success till the close of life.

The circumstances of Mr. Lind's death were deeply affecting. He had preached on Saturday, September 5th, in reference to the Communion which was to take place the next day; but, before leaving the pulpit, he was seized with a violent chill. During the night and the next morning he was severely ill, but when he heard that the people had assembled at the church in large numbers, he made an effort to meet them, though he was obliged to omit the Sermon, and attempt nothing more than the Communion service. This he performed with great interest and solemnity; though, instead of the usual address at the close, he simply quoted a passage of Scripture, and pronounced the Benediction. He was immediately taken home in a carriage, and was not free from suffering afterwards till death came to his release. He manifested perfect submission to the Divine will, though, for the last four days, he was deprived of the power of utterance. He died at Hagerstown, on the 20th of September, 1824, after an illness of about two weeks, in the forty-first year of his age. His Funeral Sermon at Hagerstown was preached by the Rev. Joseph McCarroll; and another Funeral Sermon was preached at Green Castle by the Rev. James Buchanan.

Mr. Lind was married May 22, 1807, to Ann Washington Smith, of the city of New York. She died at Green Castle, Pa., February 19, 1819, leaving five children, one of whom (*John Y.*) was graduated at Jefferson College in 1837, and subsequently at the Jefferson Medical School at Philadelphia, but migrated to California in 1849, where he has since occupied important stations in civil life. Mr. Lind was again married, May 7, 1822, at Green Castle, then his residence, to Margaretta St. Clair C. Young, daughter of the Rev. John Young, for many years Pastor of the Associate Reformed Congregation of that place. By this marriage he had two children.

Mr. Lind is not known to have published any thing except a Sermon preached before the Bible Society in Franklin County, Pa.

As an evidence of the high estimation in which he was held by his brethren, it may be mentioned that he was one of the Superintendents of the Theological Seminary of his denomination for a number of years. He was also one of the Commissioners, appointed by the General Synod, with Dr. Mason and the Rev Ebenezer Dickey, and some respectable Elders, to visit the Synod of Scioto, and especially the Presbytery of Kentucky, to take cognizance of the state of the churches under the care of the Synod, and particularly to settle some matters of difference between two of its prominent members.

FROM THE REV. J. M. MATHEWS, D.D.

NEW YORK, May 21, 1852.

My dear Sir: The Rev. John Lind and myself were classmates. We were the only students belonging to the first class in the Theological Seminary which Dr. Mason opened in this city in 1805, under the care of the Associate Reformed Church. We were intimately acquainted with each other; and the intimacy was kept up till the time of his death.

Mr. Lind had not only great purity of mind but an affectionate, kind spirit, that was seen in every word and deed. His very countenance secured your confidence at once; and such was the uniformity and consistency of his whole character that you would never find reason for changing your first favourable opinion of the man. Every faculty of his soul was embodied in the Ministry of the Gospel, and no sacrifice of comfort, health, or even of life, was deemed too great, if it promised usefulness to the welfare of his fellow men. His mind, like his heart, was distinguished for its perfect transparency. He made every thing plain which he touched, and to every class of hearers his preaching was of course edifying and profitable. He was a growing man in the ministry as long as he lived, for he was always a close student and a diligent observer of men.

Mr. Lind's mind was one of great delicacy, and he evinced it particularly in his considerate regard to the feelings of others, never giving offence where it could be avoided in consistency with a regard to his duty. I should have supposed that he had naturally perfect sweetness of temper; but he once told a friend of mine that what seemed natural in his case was the result of the most rigid self-discipline; that when he was a little boy, he became so much incensed, on one occasion, with one of his playmates, that, for several hours, he was deadly sick; that, during that time, he was deeply sensible of the sin and folly of his thus giving loose to his temper, and he resolved that, by the grace of God, he would subdue it; and that, by the grace of God, he had been enabled to keep his resolution.

Mr. Lind's truly liberal spirit made him always ready not only to extend his intercourse beyond his own denomination, but to co-operate freely with Christians and Ministers of other communions for advancing the common Christianity. He had an eye that was quick to discern the Saviour's image; and wherever he discovered that, neither his heart nor his head recognized any obstacle to Christian fellowship.

I have heard, on good authority, one or two anecdotes in respect to his childhood and youth, that were at least an index to his future character. An old man, by the name of A——n, was cursing a piece of wood; and Mr. Lind, then a small boy, who was unused to hearing such language, looked up very earnestly in the face of the profane man, and burst into an immoderate fit of laughter. Mr. A. asked him what he was laughing at. "Why," said the boy, "at your being so foolish in getting angry and saying bad things to a piece of wood that don't know any thing, and don't care for you." The individual reproved afterwards said that the remark, taken in connection with the manner, from that little boy, was the severest reproof he ever received.

His Teacher, Mr. James Borland, whose school at Green Castle he entered in 1797, writes thus concerning him:—" John Lind, both boy and man, was certainly one of the most amiable characters I ever knew. He appeared to love every body and every thing but sin. He would step aside to avoid treading on an insect. An anecdote which was current in the neighbourhood about him will serve as an illustration. He was, one day, when a boy, hoeing corn, and a snake made its appearance. Feeling the impulse of the enmity existing between the seed of the woman and the seed of the serpent, he struck it with his hoe and killed it; but afterwards, reflecting on what he had done, he fell sick."

No man was less ambitious than Mr. Lind to sit in high places, or to have the public eye specially turned upon him. He had overtures made to him with reference to several important posts of usefulness in the Church, but he refused to listen to them, preferring a more retired field of labour. His commanding desire evidently was to do all that he could, and in the most quiet way that he could, to benefit his fellow men and build up and extend the cause of his Master.

In the inscrutable providence of God, he was removed from the Church below, at a period of life when he seemed more than ever qualified for useful service; but he still lives in the memory of his people. I am told that many accessions made to the church since his death can be traced to his faithful labours, while he was yet among them.

Very truly yours,

J. M. MATHEWS.

FROM THE REV. JOSEPH McCARROLL, D.D.

NEWBURGH, December 20, 1849.

Rev. and dear Sir: I knew the Rev. John Lind well, and held him in such high regard that it gives me pleasure to testify in any way my respect for his memory. He ended his ministry and his days on earth in the midst of a people many of whom were seals of his ministry, and all of whom he had, by the Divine blessing upon his labours, been instrumental of gathering around him. It was my lot, in the providence of God, to preach his Funeral Sermon, at the first opening of the church at Hagerstown after his death, and also to baptize his youngest child; and many a moistened eye that day bore witness to the deep and strong attachment which had subsisted, for many years, between this devoted servant of Christ and the people to whom he had ministered. His last ministerial act was the dispensing of the Lord's Supper a short time before his death. He died at his post, and with his armour on; for the disease which carried him off was even then preying upon his vitals. It might truly be said of him, as of the proto-martyr Stephen, that "devout men carried him to his burial, and made great lamentation over him."

Mr. Lind held a standing among the first ministers of his age for talents, attainments and a natural and graceful eloquence. But it was in his moral and religious character that his distinction more especially consisted. All who knew him loved and revered him. I think I may safely say that I have never known a more amiable person, or one who furnished a more attractive example of the beauty of holiness. He was in the habit of assisting the Rev. James Walker, of Shippensburg, at his Communion service; and I well remember that, whenever it was known that Mr. Lind was to preach, the church was crowded with deeply interested and attentive hearers.

The following incident illustrative of his successful fidelity as a Pastor, occurred at Hagerstown:—A Physician, of high standing in that place, but of infidel opinions, had sustained the loss of several daughters by death. The last of his family, on her death-bed, earnestly desired the conversation and prayers of Mr. Lind; but her father was utterly opposed to it and forbade his coming to the house. The afflicted young woman, however, under deep solicitude about her eternal interests, sent for Mr. Lind during her father's absence. While the servant of God was engaged in prayer, her father returned; and, overhearing the affectionate and solemn intercessions presented at the throne of grace for his dying child, was completely melted and subdued; became deeply concerned for his own salvation, and, in due time, gave evidence of a radical change of character, and connected himself with the church under Mr. Lind's pastoral care; and, as a testimony of attachment and gratitude to the instrument of his salvation, he took the whole charge of the maintenance and education of Mr. Lind's youngest son, who is now a respectable physician.

As an evidence of the estimation in which he was held by his brethren in the ministry, and of that modesty which graced his many other excellencies of character, it may be stated that when Dr. Mason became unable to attend to the duties of Professor in the Theological Seminary, it was proposed to appoint Mr. Lind to the place; but he utterly declined being considered a candidate, on the ground that, in his own opinion, he did not possess the requisite qualifications.

Cut down in the vigour of his years, he has left a character for prudence, for intelligence, for amiability of temper, for suavity of manners, for high moral excellence and for genuine godliness, which attracted many hearts to him, while he lived, and has verified, in his case, the Divine declaration,— "The memory of the just is blessed."

Very respectfully yours in the Lord,
JOSEPH McCARROLL.

FROM THE REV. DAVID ELLIOTT, D.D.

ALLEGHENY CITY, February 27, 1852.

My dear Sir: My only regret, in attempting to comply with your request, is that I am not able to do it to better purpose. Although it is true that the excellent man concerning whom you inquire and myself were on terms of the most affectionate intercourse, yet, as we lived at some distance from each other and belonged to different Ecclesiastical connections, that intercourse was only occasional. I can state, in general, that all my impressions of his character were of the most favourable kind. He was extremely amiable, affectionate and cautious in his intercourse with others. He evinced a tender regard for their feelings, and seemed scrupulously to avoid any expression or act which would give them pain. He was a plain, sensible, affectionate and evangelical Preacher, much loved and respected, not only by the people of his own charge and denomination, but by those of other congregations and other denominations also. He was catholic in his feelings, and never indulged in bitter expressions against those who differed from him in their ecclesiastical or religious views. Indeed, his views of doctrine and order were so entirely in harmony with those held by our own Body, that he had made up his mind to connect himself with us, which (as I now recollect) he intended to do at the next meeting of the Carlisle Presbytery, and doubtless would have done, had not death prevented. He assisted at the formation of the first Bible Society which was organized in Franklin County, Pa. In answer to a call, written by myself, and inserted in the Franklin Repository, a meeting was held in Chambersburg; Mr. Lind and others attended, and a County Bible Society was formed—he was elected one of the Managers, and preached the Sermon before the Board at their first meeting after their organization. He was punctual in his attendance at the meetings of the Board, and entered heartily into every measure fitted to insure the success of the enterprise. I allude to this circumstance chiefly as illustrative of that catholic, earnest, devoted spirit, which pervaded his whole ministry, and which, if he had been longer spared, would have been a pledge of prolonged and still greater usefulness. He was a man of whom all who knew him cherish a grateful remembrance.

Very truly yours,
D. ELLIOTT.

FROM THE REV. JOHN M. KREBS, D.D.

NEW YORK, October 25, 1860.

My dear Sir: I have mentioned to you, elsewhere, that my birth and baptism were in the German Reformed Church; but, while I was yet quite young, my father's family frequently attended the ministry of Mr. Lind, and finally we became connected with the Presbyterian—at that time the Associate Reformed—Church in my native town.

Thus he became the Pastor of my boyhood; and when I was about eighteen years old I was by him admitted to the Lord's table; and I was with him when he died. It was by him also that I was instructed in the rudiments of Latin, before entering upon the regular course of the Academy and the College. He was a good classical scholar; and I was indebted to his personal care for an earlier insight into the structure of the language than I could have gained in the mere routine of the school.

The Church of Hagerstown was gathered by Mr. Lind. His first settlement was in the Associate Reformed Church at Green Castle, in Pennsylvania. A few Presbyterian families were settled in and about Hagerstown, and, at their invitation, he would visit them, and preach in the German Reformed

Church on the afternoon of every other Sabbath, riding nine miles for that purpose, after preaching in his own church. He usually spent Monday in visiting the families who attended his ministry; and, among them, as everywhere else, he was a welcome guest.

These labours resulted in organizing a congregation, and in the erection of a very neat, substantial and commodious church edifice, which, during his ministry, was always well filled. He served the two congregations, at first giving us one Sabbath in three, and afterwards, as the congregation prospered, two in three, still keeping up his regular pastoral visits, and at length removing his residence to Hagerstown. When, in 1822, a considerable portion of the Associate Reformed Church united with the Presbyterian General Assembly, Mr. Lind preferred to remain in his original connection; and out of the same regard to him which, from the first, determined the congregation that way, it also continued in it until his death, when, under the pastoral care of his nephew, the late Rev. Matthew Lind Fullerton,* it united with the Presbyterian Church.

Mr. Lind was tall in person, neat in dress, and quietly dignified in manner. His countenance was inclined to paleness, as I recall it, but not unhealthful. His aspect was sweetly grave, serene and cheerful. I would describe it as the repose and peace, the love and sympathy, of a truly devout and holy man. No man could have been more beloved than he by young and old. His manner was very winning and attractive. The children gathered to him, for he was gentle, condescending and affable, and we all trusted him who so constantly and kindly entered into all our feelings and interested himself in our welfare. It used to be said to him jocosely, by a brother clergyman and fellow-townsman of Mr. Lind, and a relative by marriage,—" Woe unto you, John Lind, for all men speak well of you." His house, in which I spent many a pleasant hour, was the seat of a genial and refined hospitality. His conversation was instructive and not without a certain quiet humour. His manner in the pulpit was calm, yet solemn and tender; his sermons thoroughly studied and scriptural; and his hearers listened, attentive, edified and impressed with a thorough conviction of his sincerity and the truth of his message. I cannot recall a man to whom so justly and thoroughly applies Goldsmith's description of " The Village Preacher."

Truly yours,
JOHN M. KREBS.

GEORGE STEWART.*

1809—1818.

GEORGE STEWART, a son of Hugh and Margaret Stewart, was born at Green Castle, Pa., in the year 1782. His father was a farmer in moderate circumstances, and able but partially to meet the expenses of his education. The early years of the son were spent upon a farm; and, even after he commenced his studies, he was able to devote only so much time to his books as he could com-

---

* MATTHEW LIND FULLERTON was a native of Green Castle, Pa.; was graduated at Union College in 1820; received his Theological education at the Princeton Seminary; was settled Pastor of the United Congregations of Green Castle and Hagerstown in 1825; and died in 1833. He was a highly acceptable Preacher, and was regarded as a young man of much promise.

*MSS. from his daughter, Mrs. Turner, and Mr. A. Dimmick.

mand in the intervals of labour. As the result of much careful painstaking, he was at length fitted to enter College, and became a member of Dickinson College, Carlisle. At this institution he maintained a highly respectable rank, and was graduated with honour in 1805. In November of that year he became a member of the first class that entered the Associate Reformed Theological Seminary in New York, under the care of Dr. John M. Mason. Here he took the regular four years' course, and was licensed to preach, by the Associate Reformed Presbytery of New York, in June, 1809. In April, 1810, he was settled as Pastor of the Associate Reformed Church in Bloomingburgh, Sullivan County, N. Y.

Mr. Stewart continued in this relation till the close of his life. He was the first Pastor ever settled over that congregation, though they had erected a church edifice some twelve or fifteen years before; and it required what Mr. Stewart actually possessed,—a large amount of wisdom and energy, to give character and stability to the infant congregation. Besides labouring with great diligence at home, in his preparations for the pulpit and in his private pastoral duties, his services were frequently called for in other congregations, and, when it was possible, were always freely rendered. He was also, for several years, the principal teacher of an Academy in Bloomingburgh—an institute which was in such repute as to draw students from some distinguished families in the city of New York. And, in addition to all his other labours, he had the general superintendence of a small farm, and the oversight of the building of a large house. There is no doubt that his unceasing and diversified engagements tasked his faculties beyond their power of endurance; and thus probably originated the disease (consumption) which terminated his life. Owing to his declining health, he was taken off from his labours for a year or more previous to his death; but, during his whole decline, he was an example of tranquil and trusting submission to the Divine will. He died among the only people to whom he had ever sustained the pastoral relation, on the 20th of September, 1818, in the thirty-seventh year of his age.

Mr. Stewart's congregation flourished greatly under his ministry, and he enjoyed, in a high degree, their confidence and affection. While he was valiant for what he believed to be important truth, he was disposed, on some points, to go farther in the way of conciliation or accommodation than suited some of his brethren. For instance, in the last year of his ministry, he introduced the use of the Dutch Church Psalmody; and though a few of his people regarded it as an unwarrantable innovation, to the majority it was not otherwise than acceptable.

Mr. Stewart was married, in 1815, to Ann P., daughter of Colonel John Carr, of Hagerstown, Md. He left one daughter, about two years old at the time of his death, who is now (1863) the wife of a Mr. Turner in Maryland. Mrs. Stewart, who was a lady of uncommon excellence, died at the house of her brother-in-law, Alexander Mitchell, near Hagerstown, Md., on the 29th of March, 1827.

FROM THE REV. J. M. MATHEWS, D.D.

NEW YORK, April 6, 1863.

My dear Friend: You ask me to tell you what I remember concerning the Rev. George Stewart. My acquaintance with him began in 1805, when, having just graduated at Dickinson College, he came to New York to study Theology in Dr. Mason's Seminary, of which I was myself at that time a member. I was very soon attracted to him by his fine intellectual and moral qualities, and thus commenced an acquaintance which ripened into an endearing and enduring friendship. As he chose his field of labour in this part of the country, and remained here till the close of his life, we often met, both in public and in private, and I can truly say that the more I knew of him, the more he became an object of my respect and even admiration.

Mr. Stewart was a man of medium stature, of a well proportioned frame, of a bright, penetrating eye, and of a countenance grave and intellectual rather than highly animated. His movements were deliberate and dignified, and indicated a calm and thoughtful habit of mind. His manners were courteous and gentlemanly, and would leave you with the impression that he had not been unaccustomed to intelligent and refined society. He possessed a very kindly and generous spirit, and was not otherwise than social and cheerful in ordinary intercourse, though he rarely indulged in any thing like sport or merriment. He conversed with ease and fluency, and always to edification; and you would see at once that he spoke out of a richly furnished and well cultivated mind. His mind was not brilliant or highly imaginative, but it was solid, reflective, discriminating; he would hold a subject to his thoughts in patient investigation to excellent purpose; and he very rarely failed of reaching the right conclusion. He was distinguished for his earnest and successful devotion to study while he was in the Seminary; and I believe it is safe to say that no one of his fellow-students exceeded him in the extent and thoroughness of his acquisitions. He was essentially a studious thinking man; and I believe he never relaxed in his habits of study till the close of his life. He was especially distinguished for a deep and all pervading piety. He lived habitually as seeing Him who is invisible. He cultivated intimate communion with God and a deep sense of his dependence upon Him, and reverently, gratefully, submissively, acknowledged his hand in every stage of his experience.

Mr. Stewart had deservedly an excellent reputation as a Preacher. Others might carry the multitude with them much more than he; but few would be more acceptable to the most thoughtful and intelligent class of hearers. His discourses were of a deeply evangelical tone, were thoroughly logical in their construction, simple and chaste in style, and every way fitted to render intelligible and impressive to the mind of the Spirit. They were carefully composed and written, but were delivered without the manuscript. His voice was clear and agreeable, but without any remarkable compass. He could extemporize readily, though on these occasions his utterance was always very deliberate, as if the thoughts he uttered were the result of his meditations while he was speaking. As a Pastor, he probably had few superiors. The best interests of his people were always near his heart, and there was no labour or self-denial to which he was not ready to submit for the promotion of them. His death was justly regarded as the extinction of one of the lights of his denomination.

Your affectionate friend and brother,
J. M. MATHEWS.

GEORGE BUCHANAN.*

1809—1855.

GEORGE BUCHANAN was the youngest child of John and Jane Buchanan, who were originally Covenanters, but fell in with the union in which originated the Associate Reformed Church. At the time of his birth they resided in the "Barrens of York." They were both distinguished for their piety and died at a good old age. The exact date of the birth of the son cannot now be ascertained, though it appears, from the Baptismal Record, that he was baptized on the 3d of April, 1783. His religious education was what might have been expected from the earnest and devoted piety of his parents. He commenced his academical studies at Gettysburg, under the instruction of the Rev. Alexander Dobbin, and in due time entered Dickinson College, where he was graduated in the fall of 1805. He made a public profession of religion, at the Big Spring Church, about the close of his college life. Shortly after his graduation he entered the Theological Seminary of the Associate Reformed Church in the city of New York, then under the care of Dr. Mason, and was a member of the first class organized in that institution. Having completed the prescribed course of study, he was licensed by the Presbytery of Philadelphia, at a meeting held in Washington City, in December, 1809.

Agreeably to the injunction of the General Synod, his Presbytery appointed him to supply, four months from the 1st of August, within the bounds of the Presbytery of Monongahela. But he did not re-cross the Mountains till he was sent as a delegate to the General Synod which met in Philadelphia in May, 1812, —the Monongahela Presbytery having detained him after his appointment had expired; for doing which they were formally censured by the Synod, on the complaint of the Presbytery of Philadelphia. In the fall of 1810 he preached in the old Court House in Pittsburg, and laboured in the vacancies of the Monongahela Presbytery till April, 1811. At a meeting of that Presbytery, held in Mercer County, Pa., in the barn of Peter Mitchel, when Mr. James Galloway was ordained, three calls were presented to Mr. Buchanan. He accepted the one from the United Congregations of Steubenville, Yellow Creek and Hermon's Creek. The line between the States of Pennsylvania and Virginia, and the Counties of Washington and Brook, passed through the church edifice of the last named congregation.

His Ordination and Installation took place at Steubenville, O., on the 4th of June following. Thus commenced a pastoral relation which, in regard to the Steubenville Congregation, remained unbroken for upwards of forty-four years; and was then dissolved by death. As an illustration of some of the hardships incident to his ministry, he is said to have often ridden in the depths of winter from Steubenville to Hermon's Creek, (seven miles,) and preached to his congregation without feeling the influence of fire; and sometimes to have spent a tedious hour on the bosom of the Ohio River, while the boatmen battled their way across through the drifting ice, in what would now be called a crazy craft.

During a portion of his life Mr. Buchanan added, with good success, the labours of a Teacher to those of a Pastor. Among his pupils who became eminent were

* MSS. from Rev. Dr. George Junkin and Rev. John M. Galloway.

the Rev. John Newton, D.D., the Missionary, and the Hon. E. M. Stanton, now (1863) Secretary of War.

Mr. Buchanan's health was gradually declining during the whole of the last summer of his life; but he continued his ministerial labours until the second Sabbath before his death. On the last Sabbath that he spent on earth, though he was able, during the day, to walk about in his room, he intimated to his wife that he should not live through the following night. In the course of the afternoon a change took place so decidedly unfavourable that it was thought that the dying moment had come; but he quickly revived, and was spared a few hours longer to render a yet more distinct and triumphant testimony to the value of the Gospel in life's darkest hour. A short time before his departure he gave utterance to these words:—"When this struggle is over I shall be freed from contending with a sinful world; from resisting temptations and fighting with spiritual wickedness in high places. I shall be done with warning sinners, and if they will not heed my admonitions but cast them from them, they must bear the consequences. And now, what wait I for? I know that I shall receive the crown of righteousness which God will give to him who is faithful to the end, and shall be received to that city which is in Heaven, whose builder and maker is God." This was nearly his last deliverance. He passed gently and triumphantly away on Sabbath evening, October 14, 1855; and on the Tuesday following, his Funeral was very numerously attended, and an Address delivered on the occasion by the Rev. C. C. Beatty, D.D.

On the 28th of April, 1812, Mr. Buchanan was united in marriage with Mary, third daughter of Joseph and Eleanor (Cochrane) Junkin, then of Mercer County, Pa. They had seven children,—four sons and three daughters. Two of the sons,—namely, *John Junkin* and *Joseph*, entered the ministry of the Associate Reformed Church. Of the remaining two sons one studied Medicine and the other Law. Mrs. Buchanan died at the house of one of her daughters in Keokuk, Iowa, on the 4th of August, 1861.

JOHN JUNKIN BUCHANAN, was born in Steubenville, O., January 24, 1817; was graduated at Franklin College, New Athens, O., in 1838; studied Theology in the Associate Reformed Seminary, Allegheny City, and was licensed to preach, by the Presbytery of Steubenville, in 1841. The next year he accepted a call from the United Congregations of Racoon and Hanover, Beaver County, Pa., and was ordained by the Presbytery of Monongahela. He was married May 5, 1842, to Jane, daughter of Philip Mowry, of Allegheny City. Having laboured in his first charge about two years he accepted a call from the Congregation in Mifflin, Allegheny County. After a few years he was obliged, from failing health, to give up this charge also, and from this time he confined himself to preaching in vacant congregations, at the same time performing some literary labour. In June, 1852, he was obliged to desist altogether from the exercise of the ministry. He died of consumption, in Allegheny City, on the 27th of July, 1853, in the thirty-first year of his age, leaving a widow and four children. He was a good scholar, a well read theologian, and a plain, earnest and instructive preacher.

FROM THE REV. JOHN M. GALLOWAY.

CLEARFIELD, PA., February 18, 1863.

Dear Sir: I had some knowledge of the Rev. George Buchanan for many years before I knew him intimately; but my relations with him became more close in the year 1836; and for the last seventeen years of his life, perhaps I was as familiar with his views and feelings as any other person. We were co-presbyters; and, residing most of that time but a few miles from each other, and the remaining portion in the same place, we had the most intimate ministerial and social intercourse, and usually accompanied each other on our journeys to the meetings of Presbytery and Synod.

It was Mr. Buchanan's intention that we should be associated in the administration of the Lord's Supper on the day which proved to be his last on earth. On that day, whilst serving the last table, I was requested by Mr. M. O. Junkin, a brother-in-law and a member of his Session, to bring the services to a close as soon as convenient, as we were wanted at Mr. Buchanan's. Thus we were summoned from the solemnity of the Communion table to the solemnity of the Pastor's death-bed.

In person, Mr. Buchanan was rather above the medium size, not fleshy but of a good muscular development, with black eyes and hair, and altogether a well-formed and fine looking man. In the later years of his life he grew spare, and lost that appearance of vigour which he had possessed at an earlier period. His countenance was habitually sedate and expressive of sincerity and earnestness. His manners were easy and natural, but rather grave than elegant. He possessed a sound judgment, and reached his conclusions with deliberation, but when once they were formed, he adhered to them with great tenacity. He rarely erred in his opinions of men or things. He managed his own affairs and those of his congregation with remarkable discretion, and was a judicious counsellor to such as sought his advice. His imagination was not strikingly vivid or poetic.

His discourses were expository and didactic, with few illustrations from any other source than the Bible. The love of God in giving his Son, and the love of Christ in giving Himself, to die for sinners, he dwelt upon with great interest and tenderness. His habit was not to use texts in the way of accommodation, but to present what he believed to be the mind of the Spirit, and then deduce and enforce such practical lessons as were legitimate to the doctrines taught. Few would complain that this part of his discourse was not sufficiently practical; but a certain Mr. M., who occasionally attended on his ministrations, did once find fault. "Mr. Buchanan," said he, "I like your sermons very well, but they would be better if they were a little more pointed." "I do not know how I can make them more pointed," replied Mr. B., "unless I say plainly, Mr. M., if you do not cease getting drunk, you will certainly go to perdition." The poor man had fallen into a habit for which this was an appropriate rebuke.

He was an attentive and kind Pastor, ready to hear of the temporal as well as the spiritual wants of his people. He took a special interest in the young, and they, in turn, were most warmly attached to him. In addition to his regular pastoral visits, he made frequent calls, and was accustomed to visit, on Monday, those of his people whom he had missed from the sanctuary on the preceding day. He was especially kind and attentive to the widows under his pastoral care, of whom there were a goodly number; and in cases where he judged there was a lack of pecuniary means, he would quietly hand a receipt for pew-rent,—an act never revealed except by the recipient.

His salary, always small, was so wisely used by himself and his excellent wife, that, though his house was noted for its hospitality, there was no lack of family comforts apparent; and the remark was often made that a special blessing rested on his basket and his store. In some two or three instances he received, as tokens of regard, handsome legacies from persons who were not of his kindred or congregation.

As a Presbyter, Mr. Buchanan was not given to much talking; but when he did speak, he was listened to with deference, and his opinions, which were always conservative, had great weight with most of his brethren. He was perfectly open in all that he said and did, and had no patience with any thing like concealment or trickery in the carrying of any measure.

He received, *ex animo*, the Westminster Confession of Faith, as adopted by his Church, and viewed all additions to it as unwise and retrogressive; and hence he was unwilling to form a union with sister churches on the basis of any considerable additions to that document.

I will only add that his friendship was ardent and abiding, and not to be overthrown by the unfavourable surmises or opinions of others. He who once enjoyed it, might reckon upon its continuance ever after, unless he proved himself unworthy. He was, in the best sense, a firm friend and a true man.

Yours with much regard,
J. M. GALLOWAY.

JAMES GALLOWAY.
1810—1818.
FROM THE REV. GEORGE JUNKIN, D.D.
PRESIDENT OF WASHINGTON COLLEGE, LEXINGTON, VA.

WASHINGTON COLLEGE, September 18, 1850.

My dear Sir: If the following brief notices of my lamented friend Galloway are in accordance with the design of your work, they are quite at your service. His was not what may be called an eventful life; and yet there was that in his character which was a source of no inconsiderable attraction while he lived, and in the record of which, though dead, he yet speaketh.

JAMES GALLOWAY was born in Bedford or Westmoreland County, Pa., on the 4th of August, 1786. His father, John Galloway, lived in Bedford, and removed to Westmoreland, but whether before or after the birth of this son, I do not know. He was graduated at Jefferson College in 1805, and soon after commenced the study of Law. The gentleman with whom he entered died, when his course of life took the happy turn which threw him into the higher pursuit of the sacred office. Immediately he conferred not with flesh and blood, but offered himself to the Associate Reformed Presbytery of Monongahela. In 1806 he entered the Theological Seminary of that Church in New York, then under the sole care of the Rev. John M. Mason, D.D., where he prosecuted his studies until 1810. On the 28th of June, he was licensed by said Presbytery,— Matthew Henderson, Moderator. On the 17th of December of the same year, a call was made out for him from Mercer, Mahoning and Shenango Churches, and he was ordained, in the following spring, over these united congregations where he continued to minister, with great acceptance, till within a few months of his decease. He was released, at his own request, from his pastoral charge, in April, and died on the 21st of May, 1818, in the thirty-second year of his age.

Mr. Galloway was married, in the spring of 1812, to Miss Agnes Junkin, a daughter of Joseph and Eleanor (Cochran) Junkin, of Mercer County, Pa. Her father, in command of a company of militia, was wounded at the battle of Brandywine, in 1777. Mr. and Mrs. Galloway had three sons. The eldest, *John Mason*, has long been a useful and efficient minister of the Gospel; first in the Associate Reformed Church, and now in the Presbyterian Church. Mrs. Galloway was subsequently married to Hugh Bingham, of Mercer, and died in September, 1858.

Mr. Galloway was of middle stature; of full face; florid complexion, hazel eyes, bright and sparkling with good-humour; broad and high forehead, light brown hair, inclined to curl; and under lip somewhat curled downward. His general manner was frank and manly; his bosom was open to friendship for all disposed to meet him as a friend; and he was familiar and easy of access. In company he was lively and sportive, and made all around him easy at once. None could live near him without being sociable.

As to his intellectual character, his mind was clear and discriminating, though not remarkable for the power of logical arrangement. His preaching was doctrinal and argumentative, and whilst the hearer felt that the conclusions at which he arrived were undoubtedly true, yet sometimes the steps by which he led you to them were indistinctly marked. In the application of his doctrines to practical use he was generally very happy. His elocution was clear and distinct; although, from an original and probably organic defect of the ear, the finer properties of an eloquent delivery were beyond his reach.

Mr. Galloway was incapable of distinguishing musical sounds, and of course unable to sing or enjoy the beauties of music. This gave a stiffness to his modulations of voice, and prevented much of that effect from his delivery, which the excellence of his matter and the gracefulness and energy of his action were calculated to produce. Whilst he was often animated and warm, he was defective in mellow pathos. This was the only element wanting to constitute him an eloquent Preacher.

His theological system was that of the Westminster Confession, and he held to the liberal views of Dr. Mason whom he greatly admired and fondly loved. His faith discovered itself in the spotless purity of his life, the general buoyancy and brightness of his moral feelings, the open, unsuspecting confidence of his social affections, securing to him the good-will and friendship of all around him.

Mr. Galloway's piety was unassuming, calm, deep and humble. He rarely rose to great ecstasies or sunk into great depths. The spirit of his piety will be shown best, perhaps, by some brief extracts from a few of his last letters to me.

He was a Commissioner from his Presbytery to the General Synod at Philadelphia, in May, 1817. In June following I travelled with him, on horseback, from that place to New York, and thence to Newburgh, where we parted for the last time. The Rev. A. D. Campbell (now of Allegheny) here fell in with him, according to arrangement, and accompanied him home by the Northern lakes, health being then the object of his pursuit.

In a letter from him, dated at Mercer, October 1, 1817, he writes thus:—

"As to flesh and strength, I am much as when you saw me last, though my cough is at present much worse. My complaint regularly has its changes; I will be better for two or three weeks, and I then become worse. The weather, for two weeks past, has been cloudy and rainy. I have felt rather worse than usual. I am now convinced that my disorder is a confirmed consumption; that it has pleased the Head of the Church to say to me that He has no more use for me in the Vineyard. I have revolved this dispensation of Providence with prayer, and am convinced that it remains for me, by a patient and cheerful submission to his will, to glorify that Redeemer whom, with much weakness, I have preached unto others. Oh that God would so strengthen,—would so afford his comfortable presence, that I may not be permitted to bring a disgrace upon that cause which it is the wish of my heart to honour. I feel now a comfortable assurance in the Redeemer, and trust that He will never leave nor forsake me.

"My friend, I would be glad to see you and converse a while; but that pleasure I never expect to enjoy in this world. If we are both fitted to enjoy each others' society forever in those mansions prepared by the Redeemer, it will be of little loss to us,—the short separation in this world. I would like to have some person to converse with me on the subject of death. But my friends all act as if any such conversation would injure me by depressing my spirits. But I can assure you they are mistaken. I oftener view my approaching dissolution with pleasure than with dread. The Lord will do all things well for those that love Him. The ties which bind me to the world have been weakened in the death of my little Joseph. He died about three weeks before I came home, of a dropsy in the head. I trust I have been enabled to say, in this dispensation, with the servant of God of old,—'The Lord giveth, and the Lord taketh away; blessed be the name of the Lord.' Yet the conflict of natural feeling is often severe."

Under date of November 24, 1817, he writes thus:—

"Dear Brother: I have received two letters from you since I have written. I have read your first letter and have meditated upon it. It was a subject that I had often deeply, and as a dying man, considered. My dear friend, Death I consider as at no great distance. I have endeavoured to realize him in his last attack, and were it not for the hopes which the Gospel affords, his approaches would be terrible indeed. Who can dwell with everlasting burnings? Who could enter with fortitude into that unknown world? But how abundant the consolations of the Gospel! How cheering the promises! How precious the Saviour! Yea, how precious that Saviour to me after examination of myself by that Word of God, which is truth. I trust that I can say, without deceiving myself, that I know in whom I have believed, and that He is able to keep that which I have committed to Him. Such, my friend, is my habitual confidence—then for me to die will be gain. But think not that I have nothing to disturb my repose. Alas! how little love for a Redeemer who has performed so much for me! How cold generally my affections! How little of that sensible communion with God do I enjoy! I expect yet to meet with temptations. I expect that yet the adversary may be permitted to disturb my repose. And were it not that my Redeemer is pledged as my second, dreadful indeed would be my defeat. But I *know* that his word is pledged that I shall obtain the victory. Upon that word, and upon that word alone do I rely, while I feel that I am nothing and know that He is all-powerful. And I hope that I shall not only obtain the victory finally, but that in death I shall be able to glorify God in showing forth to others the efficacy of those truths upon myself, which I have so often preached to them. My friend, pray for me that I may be enabled thus to glorify God."

He then gives his reasons for tendering his resignation, urges me to think of succeeding him, tells of his removing for the winter to his father's, about twelve miles distant, and expresses a purpose, should he acquire strength, of removing to Carolina in the spring. The letter closes thus:—

"I rejoice with you on the return of the Doctor (Mason). I would be glad to see him once more. Give my love to him ; and it is a love which must remain as long as my heart continues to throb. Our friends here are all well. And now, my friend, remember the importance of that work unto which you are called, and that to whom much is given of them shall much be required. Our time here is short and uncertain. Oh! may we then, when we meet, if we are never permitted to meet in this world, be prepared to take our seats on the right hand of Jesus in glory.
'Your brother in Christ,
"JAMES GALLOWAY."

On the 18th of March, 1818, Mr. Galloway again changed his abode from his father's to his father's-in-law, and the next day he writes me thus:—

"Dear Brother: I rode up to town yesterday without stopping to rest, which was an exertion much greater than I expected I was able for. I had the happiness of meeting with your letter. But before I make any observations on your letter, I will give you some account of myself. The complaint has been making regular advances since I wrote to you. I find myself weaker every week or two. I am very much troubled with shortness of breath. I have been troubled for a few days past with a diarrhœa, which accompanies the last stage of this disorder. My spiritual concerns are much as they were when I wrote last. I feel generally a calm peace of mind, relying not on myself, (alas, I find my heart filled with corruptions,) but his blood is sufficient to cleanse from all sins. Oh! my dear friend, to have our hope sure in Christ is what we ought all to seek. It is this alone which can afford true peace and joy in the hour of death."

The remaining part of this letter regards the question of his friend's settlement, where he presses the claims of his charge, showing the deep anxiety of his heart for the dear flock to which, for seven years, he had ministered. The penmanship of this letter betrays the palsy of death near at hand, and the next still more so.

"MERCER, April 25, 1818.

"Dear Brother: With a trembling hand I take my pen to address you, a hand that speaks loudly that our correspondence is near at an end. My weakness has increased very much in the last two weeks. But God is very gracious to me. As to pain, I scarcely feel it. But the more you and I live up to this principle,—'It is the will of our Heavenly Father—let it be done,'—the more spiritual comfort and joy will we experience under all our trials, and find our labour in the Lord to be sweet indeed. I am persuaded that for me to die would be gain. But the Lord's time is best, and oh! that the little time I have to be on his footstool I may spend more to the glory of the blessed Redeemer, who has done so much for me, that, even in death, I may be able to show forth the honour of his name. Pray for me that I may not lose the consolations of the Holy Spirit. Though we are separated at a great distance from each other, we have the consolation that we can pour out our supplications before the same throne of grace. I do not think that I always feel the same warmth of sunshine. I often feel languid in the service of my dear Master,—a law in my members warring against the law of my mind. Satan often takes advantage, and though he sometimes disturbs my peace, blessed be God, he has never been able to shake my trust on the Rock of Ages."

These extracts will enable you and your readers to judge of his spirit and faith. Twenty-six days after he wrote this last extract, he breathed his spirit into the hands of God,—Brother A. D. Campbell sustaining the clay tabernacle, whilst its occupant passed away into a more tender embrace.

The Lord direct your pen till his own time shall come for calling you up to join the society of our departed brother.

Your brother in Christ,
GEORGE JUNKIN.

FROM THE REV. JACOB VAN VECHTEN, D.D.

ALBANY, February 16, 1863.

My dear Sir: I fear that my recollections of the Rev. James Galloway are not sufficiently extended to be of much service to you, but such as they are I am quite willing to communicate them. They are confined almost entirely to a single year which I spent with him in the Theological Seminary in New York,—it being the last year of his course and the first of mine.

I remember Mr. Galloway as a man not above the ordinary stature, with a rather square face, large eye, and kindly expression of countenance. His mind was not brilliant, but exceedingly well balanced, a sound judgment being perhaps the predominating faculty. His moral qualities were in full harmony with his intellectual; and among the most prominent of them were sterling integrity, prudence and kindliness. His opinions were deliberately and carefully formed, and were held with a proportional tenacity, though not with that dogged obstinacy which ignores argument and is incapable of conviction. He was eminently discreet in all his intercourse, never impulsive, never betrayed into a wrong course by any sudden change of circumstances. His earnest desire always to do right kept his moral vision so clear that he was in little danger of ever being misled. His heart was evidently in the great work to which he had devoted himself; and though I had no opportunity of witnessing his subsequent course, I am quite sure that it was that of an earnest and highly useful minister. I cannot say that he was distinguished particularly in respect to any one faculty; but he possessed them all in such respectable measure, and such symmetrical combination, and all were so manifestly moved by a conscientious regard to the Divine authority and in humble dependence on the Divine teaching and guidance, that I cannot doubt that, in a quiet and unostentatious way, he accomplished far more for the Church than many a man of higher pretension and more glittering and attractive qualities.

Very truly your friend and brother,
JACOB VAN VECHTEN.

JOHN MASON DUNCAN, D.D.*
1811—1851.

JOHN MASON DUNCAN, a son of Matthew and Helen (Mason) Duncan, was born in Philadelphia, in July, 1790. His parents were every way respectable, and were especially distinguished for great moral worth. Of his paternal grandmother, Mrs. Margaret Duncan, the following well authenticated fact is stated: On the passage of the family from Ireland to this country,—the provisions of the ship being exhausted,—the grave question arose how they were to get along, and their deliberations resulted in the appalling conclusion that they would determine by lot who should be sacrificed to keep the rest alive. Mrs. Duncan was one of the persons upon whom the lot fell. She then made a solemn vow that if God would spare her life by bringing the ship to land, she would, by his help, erect a church in commemoration of this supplicated deliverance. That very day the Capes of the Delaware were discovered, and the crew and passengers were all saved. She fulfilled her vow in building the church, and it now stands on Thirteenth Street, between Market and Filbert, in Philadelphia. The subject of this notice was, by the maternal line, the grandson of the Rev. Dr. John Mason, and the nephew of the late Rev. Dr. John M. Mason, both of the city of New York.

He received his classical and scientific education altogether in Philadelphia, and graduated at the University of Pennsylvania in the year 1805. At a very early period he became intimate with the Rev. Dr. Gray, who then lived in Philadelphia; and, after the death of his father, which occurred in the same year that he was graduated, he went to live in Dr. Gray's family. In 1807 he became a member of the Theological Seminary of the Associate Reformed Church, in the city of New York, of which his uncle, Dr. Mason, was the principal Professor; and he boarded in his uncle's family during the period of his connection

* MSS. from his family and Rev. Drs. Knox and C. G. McLean.

with it. He was licensed to preach by the Associate Reformed Presbytery of Philadelphia in 1811, having completed the constitutional course of four years in the Seminary. His first efforts in the pulpit betokened a brilliant career. He preached to great acceptance in several places, and received a call from Gettysburg, Pa., which he declined. In August, 1812, he was ordained and installed Pastor of the Associate Reformed Church of Aisquith Street, Baltimore. Such was his popularity that it soon became necessary to erect a larger edifice for the accommodation of those who wished to attend upon his ministry; and, accordingly, a new and spacious building was erected in what is now the centre of the city, in which he continued to officiate as long as he lived.

It the autumn of 1815 he was married to Eliza, daughter of the Hon. John McKim, Jr., of Baltimore. They had eight children, one of whom, *John McKim*, became a Congregational, and ultimately a Presbyterian, clergyman, and settled in Elkton, Md., but is now (1863) deceased. Mrs. Duncan died on the 19th of August, 1855, in the fifty-eighth year of her age.

When the Union took place between the General Assembly of the Presbyterian Church and several Presbyteries of the Associate Reformed General Synod, in 1822, the Associate Reformed Presbytery of Philadelphia, taking the name of the Second Presbytery of Philadelphia, was allowed to continue its old organization until it should deem it expedient to dissolve; and whenever that time should come, it was authorized to give certificates of dismission to its members, that they might join whatever Presbyteries belonging to the Assembly they might prefer. At length it was unanimously voted to dissolve, and certificates were accordingly made out; and, among others, one for Mr. Duncan to join the Presbytery of Baltimore. But before he had an opportunity to present his certificate to the Presbytery, he had published a Sermon entitled "A Plea for Ministerial Liberty," delivered before the Directors of the Theological Seminary at Princeton, in which he put forth certain views that were considered as not exactly in harmony with the principles and spirit of Presbyterianism. Accordingly, when the Presbytery met and his certificate was presented, they refused, by a unanimous vote, to receive him. The matter came before the Synod of Philadelphia, at its meeting in Baltimore in 1825, and, though a committee, appointed to look into the case, reported, after a conference with Mr. Duncan, favourably to his being received by the Presbytery of Baltimore, yet the Report was not adopted. Mr. Duncan then avowed himself no longer responsible to any of the Courts of the Assembly, while, at the same time, he declared himself always ready to meet any overture for reconciliation and restoration to the Presbyterian Church, that would consist with an adherence to his honest convictions. The Synod then declared the pastoral relation between him and his church dissolved, annexing the church to the Presbytery of Baltimore. But the majority of his congregation remained with him, and shared his fortunes to the last. A Commissioner, having been appointed by the Presbytery to declare the congregation vacant, he went to the church, though, such was the state of the congregation that he did not even enter the pulpit, or attempt to discharge the duty to which he had been designated. A small minority seceded from the church, and afterwards instituted a suit for the recovery of the church edifice, in which, however, they were unsuccessful. The majority employed the late William Wirt for their defence, and his effort on the occasion is said to have been one of the most splendid in his whole professional career.

The degree of Doctor of Divinity was conferred upon Mr. Duncan, in 1843, by Columbia College.

Dr. Duncan could not be said to enjoy vigorous health for many years previous to his death; and yet he was enabled, without much difficulty, to go through the ordinary routine of pastoral duty. About 1826 or 1827 he went to Europe, chiefly for the benefit of his health, and returned, considerably invigorated, and highly gratified, by his tour. In March, 1849, he went to New York to attend the Funeral of his cousin, the Rev. Ebenezer Mason; and, as he was on his way to the house of Dr. Erskine Mason, after his arrival in the city, he was struck with paralysis in the carriage. The attack did not seem at first very severe; but it ultimately proved fatal. He lingered along, sometimes apparently a little better, but gradually sinking in strength. His mind was less affected than his speech and locomotion. The last official act which he performed was to baptize his grandchild, and the last words which he uttered were " The Lord is my portion." He died on the 30th of April, 1851, in the sixty-second year of his age and the thirty-ninth of his ministry. An Address was delivered at his Funeral, by the Rev. John Chambers, of Philadelphia.

Dr. Duncan's publications are A Plea for Ministerial Liberty; A Sermon delivered before the Directors of the Theological Seminary at Princeton, 1824; A Reply to Dr. Miller's Letter to a Gentleman in Baltimore in reference to the case of the Rev. Mr. Duncan, 12 mo., 1826; An Essay on the Origin, Character and Tendency of Creeds and Confessions of Faith, as Instruments of Ecclesiastical Power, 12 mo., 1834; Lectures on the General Principles of Moral Government, as they are exhibited in the first three chapters of Genesis, 1832, (Two Editions); The Eunuch's Confession, or Scriptural Views of the Sonship of Jesus Christ; A Sermon delivered on Fast Day.

FROM THE REV. CHARLES G. McLEAN, D.D.,

FORT PLAIN, N. Y., February 13, 1852.

My dear Friend: My opportunities for knowing Dr. Duncan have probably been equal to those of any other living man. We came together in the fall of 1803; and, from that time, until his decease, our intercourse was frequent, endeared and confidential. We went to the same church and were admitted to membership by the same Pastor,—my father, the late Dr. Gray; we were educated at the same College, though in different classes; we were fellow-students in the same Theological Seminary, were licensed and ordained by the same Presbytery; ate at the same table and slept in the same bed. If I do not therefore meet your wishes, I certainly cannot plead ignorance; and I am affectionately alive to the place he is to occupy on that scroll which you are soon to unroll to the gaze of the world.

Dr. Duncan, from the very commencement of his ministry, commanded great attention by his efforts in the pulpit. He was eminently an attractive Preacher, and certainly ranked among the finest pulpit orators of his day, in this country. And there were many tokens of the Divine blessing attending his labours. Not that there was any thing like a revival, in the technical sense of the word, but there were continuous accessions to the church; and very few of those who became members returned to the world. Scores and hundreds of members left the church and city to reside in other places and unite with other churches; but their pews and seats at the Lord's table were soon filled again. No minister in the city had among his hearers, on the Sabbath, a larger number of distinguished strangers than he; and they generally went away expressing the highest satisfaction. His peculiar mode of preaching gave him uncommon command of Scripture truth, fact and example. He adopted the Scottish practice of continuous exposition or analysis;—that is, he began a Book and went regularly through it, making this exposition the exercise for Sabbath morning, and if he felt that his subject was not exhausted in the morning, he either resumed it in the evening or on the next Sabbath morning. Following this course, he expounded nearly the whole New Testament once, and some portions of it two or three times. Various parts of the Old Testament also he treated in the same manner. He always consulted the original Scriptures, with the best helps he could obtain from his own or other libraries. He studied the Bible for himself; and no man was ever farther than he from becoming the victim of mere technicalities or the idolater of other men's opinions. In the progress of his inquiries he undoubtedly reached some conclusions that were somewhat in conflict with the accredited orthodoxy. As to the correctness or incorrectness of his peculiar opinions I have nothing at present to say. He has spread them before the world, through the press, with all that ingenuousness which formed a prominent a trait of his character; and however differently they may be viewed by different persons, no one who knew him will doubt that he was thoroughly convinced of their truth.

From a boy, his inclination and taste prompted him to become, if possible, a finished orator. This was evidently his leading characteristic; and, apart from this, I cannot say that there was any thing remarkable in his intellectual developments, either in College or in the Theological Seminary. Whatever he said, he wished to be *well said*. As his mind ultimately developed itself, his prominent characteristic, I think, was ingenuity; sometimes running, as was thought, into needless refinement and subtlety, and bringing out the complaint of obscurity from those who were not familiar with his mode of expression and illustration. Next to this was imagination, which frequently originated new forms of thought, clothed in rich and beautiful drapery, by means of which the graver part of his hearers were delighted, and the more susceptible well nigh entranced. Added to all this was a heart glowing with warm affections, and deeply impressed with the importance of the truths which he was delivering. He was uncommonly attentive to the spiritual interests of his flock. He managed the concerns of his church very prudently and successfully, but chiefly in a private manner.

Owing to imperfect health, occasioned by a torpid state of the liver, Dr. Duncan not unfrequently appeared gloomy and dispirited; and this gave to strangers the impression that he was unsocial and austere. Those who knew him well, however, could easily draw him out from under the cloud into some sunny spot, where he would be as joyous as a lark. He never entered into the athletic exercises of other youths, at School, College, or Seminary; but he was fond of walking, and riding on horseback. Though his appearance out of the pulpit, owing to the circumstance to which I have adverted, was not always in his favour, yet *in* the pulpit he may be said to have been not less a splendid looking man than he was a finished orator. His posture was erect and commanding; his eye was peculiarly expressive and brilliant; his hair dark, glossy and disposed to curl; his articulation perfectly accurate and distinct; his intonations full and varied, according to emotions, and his gestures perfectly appropriate and graceful. When his mind became highly excited, his voice would sometimes break; but the general effect was rather increased than diminished by it. He was nowhere else so entirely in his element as in the pulpit and at the communion table.

Such are my views of Dr. Duncan's character, as gathered from an acquaintance that has reached through much the greater part of my life.

Very truly yours,
CHARLES G. McLEAN.

FROM THE REV. JACOB VAN VECHTEN, D.D.

ALBANY, February 14, 1863.

My dear Sir: You ask me for my recollections of Dr. Duncan. They go back to the beginning of the year 1810, when I became a student in Dr. Mason's Seminary, and found him there two classes in advance of me. My attention was first specially drawn to him by his remarkable gift in prayer, as exhibited at a weekly prayer-meeting held by the students of the institution. I very soon made his acquaintance, and was intimate with him till the close of his theological course. And though our fields of labour were remote from each other, I knew him quite well as long as he lived, and the better probably from the fact that my marriage brought me into affinity with him.

Dr. Duncan was rather tall; had a long face and nose; a dark eye, expressive of uncommon strength, and features which would instantly take on the prevailing hue of his thoughts or feelings. I have rarely seen a face which was so true a mirror to the soul, or that co-operated so effectually with the life, both in public and private, as his. His manners were well formed and gentlemanly, and showed that he had been familiar with the best society. In his ordinary intercourse he was somewhat reserved, and sometimes even distant; but to his intimate friends he unbosomed himself with the utmost freedom, and was a very model of a genial and confiding spirit. His powers of conversation, when brought into exercise under favourable circumstances, were very remarkable; and yet he would sometimes sit an hour in a company and scarcely open his lips. Perhaps it is only fair to admit that the strong views which he took of certain subjects made him, in some cases, less tolerant than could have been desired towards those who differed from him, but he was essentially a man of ardent affections, and this gave an intensity to his utterances on any subject that strongly interested him.

As a Preacher, Dr. Duncan had very great and deserved popularity. His preaching was nearly all of it extemporaneous; and it was well that it should be so, as he could extemporize far better than he could write. When he took the pen, there was apt to be a want of simplicity in his productions; and sometimes there would be a splendid haze over his sentences that you would have to penetrate before you could get at his true meaning; but when he spoke without writing, his thoughts were presented with great clearness and force, and sometimes with remarkable beauty. His manner in the pulpit was singularly attractive. He had a voice of uncommon power, and yet of equal melody; and it partook of the same character with his face—it was so flexible as to express every variety of emotion with the greatest ease. He spoke with remarkable fluency, never hesitating for a word; and rarely, if ever, failing to get the word best suited to his purpose. His gestures were rather abundant, but they were perfectly simple, and graceful, and full of meaning. Indeed, I think he might be called, as truly as almost any man I have known, a natural orator.

Dr. Duncan was, by no means, remarkable for a comprehensive knowledge of the world. He scorned every thing like management, and whatever he did was done in perfect simplicity, though not always in careful or successful adjustment to the object he had in view. Without any definite knowledge on the subject, I might almost venture to affirm that he never had much to do with any of the public affairs of the Church; and perhaps it would be safe to presume that there was that in his constitution which went far towards accounting for the painful embarrassment to which he was subjected in his ecclesiastical relations.

With every consideration of respect and esteem,
Your brother,
J. VAN VECHTEN.

FROM THE REV. WILLIAM J. SPROLE, D.D.

NEWBURGH, September 12, 1864.

Reverend and dear Sir: In compliance with your request, I herewith send you a brief statement of my personal recollections of the late Rev. Dr. J. M. Duncan, whose memory I have ever cherished as that of one of my best earthly friends.

After he had become Pastor of the church in Baltimore with which my parents were connected, I saw him for the first time in the country house of one of the congregation, where I had been sent some days previous, for the benefit of my health. At that time I was a very young child,—not more, if I recollect aright, than five years of age; and well do I remember the impression made on that occasion by the kindness and gentleness of his manner, as well as the readiness with which he helped me in my childish pastimes. This was during the earlier years of his ministry, and at a time when he was regarded by the people of my native city as one of its most eloquent and popular preachers. A new and spacious church had been built for him, which was thronged every Sabbath day with an interesting and interested audience; and, although too young to be taken to it, I remember to have heard not only my parents, but many others who were frequent guests in my father's house, speak about him very often, pronouncing him one of the greatest preachers they had ever heard. In those days, at least in the church in connection with which I was raised, part, and no trifling one either, of the Christian education of the children consisted in teaching the lambs of the flock to respect and love the under shepherd. His was, to them, always an honoured presence, and they were consequently prepared to esteem and appreciate the slightest expression of kindness as something to be treasured in memory, and talked about with pride. Such being the case, it was natural that the attention paid me on the occasion to which I have referred, should make a deep impression on my young heart, and inspire me with a love that succeeding years, and more intimate relations, only served to strengthen.

I have heard many speak of him, after I entered the ministry, as taciturn, and at times cold, if not repulsive, in his intercourse with others. That he was ever cautious in his utterance, never frivolous and always dignified, whether mingling with bosom friends, or comparative strangers, is true; but his was a warm heart, and few men could have been more genial, courteous and entertaining when the occasion called for it. His treatment of me, when a child, was a fair type of his whole manner during the years I was subsequently permitted to pass with him as my Pastor and Teacher; and the opinion I ever entertained of his frankness, gentleness and kindness, in the social intercourse of life, is, I am satisfied, cherished by all who had like opportunities of knowing him.

Not long after the incident I have mentioned, I was taken to hear him preach on the Sabbath; and, long before I was prepared to understand or appreciate his sermons, his manner and voice in the pulpit would keep my attention fixed during the whole service, and incline me to revere the man I already loved. From him I derived my first serious impressions, and under his luminous expositions of the Divine Word, I was persuaded, I trust, to give my young heart to God. Joining his church brought me into intimate relations with him, and when I had resolved to devote myself to the ministry, he became, during the first two years of my preparation, my teacher. At the fireside and in his study, I had the amplest opportunity of becoming well acquainted with his character, and, during the whole time the connection lasted, I received the treatment of a son, the anxious care and faithful instruction required by a pupil. In all that time I never recollect to have heard from his lips what might be termed a trifling remark. His constant effort seemed to be, and doubtless was, to set before me an example worthy of imitation, and to improve my preparation for the great and responsible work to which I had devoted myself. He was a constant thinker, made the Bible not only his text-book but his most favourite companion, and from it, as his loved and chosen treasury, he took delight in deriving themes that filled up his moments of leisure, as well as the time spent in the toil of preparation for the pulpit.

He often remarked to me that he made his sermons while rambling over the hills—he was a great walker—by pondering the truths which he had gathered in the quiet of the closet; and he would say, with emphasis and earnestness,—"The Bible, the Bible, William, must make up the largest half of your library!" In the early years of his ministry it was his habit to write and memorize his Sermons; but for some time before he received me as a student he had discontinued it, contenting himself with gathering facts and thoughts, and trusting to the impulse of the moment for language. His memory was both tenacious and accurate, and such was his mastery of his mother tongue that I never knew him, in his most elaborate and longest discourses, to hesitate for a moment. His sermons were mostly expository, and seldom hortatory. He delighted in setting forth the great truths of the Gospel, relying upon their exhibition, as he understood them, to make their own impression on the hearts and consciences of his hearers. He never repeated, had no pet figures, dealt but little in the flowers of rhetoric, and made up his discourses of matter which compelled his auditors to think, and not seldom to feel. The inattentive hearer might as well have stayed at home: those who came to be instructed seldom retired without the distinct consciousness of having been fed. The result was that he had a decidedly intellectual congregation. Some of the first minds of the city were incorporated in it, and even the occasional hearers from other churches, who were drawn to his by the power of his eloquence,—though many of them differed from him on points of polity and doctrine—were ever ready to speak of him as a Preacher of unusual ability. It was no uncommon thing, on Sabbath evenings especially, to find his church—at that time the most commodious in the city—crowded to excess, not with the floating mass who are ever eager to run after novelty, but with men of age and culture, many of whom filled learned professions, and strangers of note, whom business or pleasure had drawn to the city,—and this continued for years.

His appearance in the pulpit was imposing, his manner commanding—in short, there was, if I may be allowed the expression, an air of majesty about it that forcibly reminded many of his uncle, the Rev. Dr. John M. Mason, in his palmiest days.

On one occasion, riding in a rail-car from Baltimore to Washington—I sat near two gentlemen, one of whom was giving the other an account of a clergyman, whom a friend had taken him to hear the previous evening. As the speaker was talking with earnestness, I had no difficulty in learning that my old instructor was the subject of his remarks. After a somewhat extended account of the discourse, he closed by remarking to his companion,—"So he is in the pulpit what Daniel Webster is in the Senate." I refer to this incident as illustrating the impression he was calculated to make on minds prepared by culture and observation to appreciate his sermons. The speaker evidently belonged to that class. The only criticism I ever heard unfriendly to his style and manner of treating subjects in the pulpit, related to an excess of verbiage and prolixity in argument. The first may have arisen from his mode of preparation and his wealth of language, the second, from the tax he laid upon the attention of the hearer. As already intimated, to be benefitted by his sermons you were compelled to think with him.

There was one feature in his character worthy of all praise, and entitling it to the close imitation of his brethren, and that was the great tenderness he ever manifested in speaking of those who differed with him. The spirit of fault-finding could never be detected, nor the slightest indication of jealousy, nor was he ever known to betray the least suspicion of unworthy motives. On one occasion, when there was much to try his temper, and fill him with honest indignation—he had been most unjustly and wickedly charged with denying the Lord who bought him—to the friend who recited the story of another unkindness, he simply remarked,—"Ministers are but men." If, in speaking of others, he found but little to commend, he never condemned; and wherever occasion required him to refer to their public acts, in which he was personally interested, he was a beautiful illustration of that charity which "suffereth long and is kind."

It was a sore trial to him when he felt constrained to dissolve his ecclesiastical relation with brethren with whom he had often taken sweet counsel; and though denounced by some, both in public and in private, as a heretic, he bore it with a meekness of spirit which never allowed him to retaliate or enter upon a defence of his reputation. Neither from the pulpit, nor in his most unrestrained intercourse with his most intimate friends, was he known to call in question the honesty, sincerity, or general excellence of those who had both written and spoken against him. He believed that his views were biblical, and in strict accordance with the teachings of the Spirit, and that if right, the Master would care both for them and him—consequently it seemed to be amongst the least of his anxieties what others said of him, and the treatment his books received at their hands. And it was doubtless owing, in a great measure, to this beautiful trait in his character that many who considered his published writings as containing sentiments at variance with the truth, were constrained to regard him as a God-fearing, pious man, though, as they supposed, strangely misled in his mode of explaining some of the essential doctrines of the Gospel.

He was a man of much prayer, and I have been told by those who were qualified to make the comparison, that, in the performance of this service in the pulpit, the social circle, in the home of sorrow and at the bed of death, he very much resembled his distinguished uncle Mason—him I never heard, and it is equally true I never listened to one who equalled Duncan in addressing the throne of grace, for the pathos, copiousness, variety and appropriateness of his utterance. There was a winning method about it I am unable to describe, which left the impression on Christian hearts that he talked with God as if standing in the audience chamber of his almighty but nearest and best friend. Long continued intimacy with Him who seeth and heareth in secret, showed itself when leading the devotions of the people in public; and not a few who came with prejudice to hear him preach, found themselves disarmed during the preliminary service, and were constrained to receive with affection what they anticipated hearing with dislike.

Of all the men I ever knew, he entertained the strongest abhorrence of the least departure from the truth. The recital of a story, intended to harm no one, but not in strict accordance with facts, was distasteful to him; the quotation of a text, not in the exact words of the Bible, gave him pain, while the semblance of a falsehood was enough to excite his disgust. Scandal was a thing in which he never indulged, and if others attempted it in his hearing, they seldom escaped without the application of that "excellent oil" which leaves the head unbroken. The tale bearer who intruded on his presence was not likely to seek a second interview. There was something in his look and manner, when subjected to such an infliction, that administered wholesome chastisement without the utterance of a word, and which made the story-teller feel, before his recital was ended, that he had mistaken the place where his news was in demand.

Living much at home, seldom going abroad, and devoting his whole time and energies to the care of his flock, he was probably less known to the Church at large, by personal intercourse, than any Preacher of his day, of equal ability. Hence many were disposed to regard him as unsocial, if not morose,—inclined to be morbid, unduly selfish, and entertaining but little concern for intercourse with his brethren. Finding enough to occupy his whole time in the duties of his large congregation, and living not only in the affections of his people, but for them, he had but little leisure to roam abroad, and for a number of years previous to his death, less inclination to do so. His peculiar position in the Ministry may have had something to do with it. Being in a great measure isolated from his brethren, having no ecclesiastical connection with any denomination of Christians, he naturally confined himself to intercourse with those who waited on his ministry and by whom he was best appreciated. But no one ever formed his acquaintance or shared his hospitality, without carrying away the impression that he was a frank, generous, companionable, high-toned Christian Gentleman.

Though a man of considerable attainment in general literature, and an accurate scholar, so far as his scholarship extended, he never made a parade of learning in his public discourses, nor could any one in private life have known the extent of his acquirements, had not some subject been introduced which compelled him to take advantage of those stores of knowledge, which he had commenced to acquire under the tuition of his illustrious uncle. And what was true of his learning might be said of the mother wit with which the Creator had endowed him—had he been disposed to indulge in it, few could have excelled him in repartee, or in uttering words which provoke to laughter and are said to sting. This keen weapon, which has so often inflicted wounds past healing, was, in his case, under beautiful control. The blade was ever wreathed in flowers.

There were times, though of rare occurrence, in which he indulged in harmless pleasantry, and with a witty utterance could so completely foil an antagonist that what might otherwise have proved a source of pain, became the occasion for merriment. I can recall no better illustration of this than what occurred during an interview at which I was present. I had accompanied him, in the city of W—— to make a call of friendship on an old acquaintance whom he had not seen before for many years. We found the Rev. Dr. —— who was a staunch Old School Scotch Presbyterian, in his office, and after some little time had been spent in the interchange of mutual enquiries about times and friends that had passed away, and after the recall of some of the reminiscences of their early acquaintance, the old gentleman, who was the senior of Duncan by a score of years, referred to a Book on the principles of the Divine Government, as contained in the first three chapters of Genesis, and which Duncan had recently published. I thought this allusion most unfortunate, since there were many things in the book which did not meet with the endorsement of the Old School men, and was perfectly aware that the old gentleman maintained sentiments in decided opposition to those which Dr. D. had put forth. As our visit was prompted by friendship, without anticipating any thing like controversy while it lasted, I feared that our interview might terminate unpleasantly. For some little time I listened with uneasiness to what was said, lest some disparaging remark concerning the book might fall from the Doctor. He was what we term an outspoken man, and though a good one, there was very little of the *suaviter in modo* about his manner of expressing himself concerning a thing which was distasteful to him. Duncan allowed every thing advanced by the Doctor to pass unchallenged, and, when the time he had set apart for the interview had elapsed, with a sweet smile which ever played upon his countenance when talking with a friend, rising from his chair, remarked,—" Well, Doctor, we have had enough of Genesis,—now for the Exodus." The pleasant laugh in which we all shared, restored the Doctor to the same genial mood in which he received us, and we parted in the best of humour.

The last time I saw him was some five years before his death, when he made me a visit during my pastorate at the seat of Government. Time had dealt kindly with his face and person. He looked, I thought, as young and healthful as he appeared when I left his study for the Seminary at Princeton, and which was some fifteen years before. In his silken locks I could not detect a thread of grey—his eye was as bright, his carriage as erect, his step as firm, and his voice as sweet as when I parted with him for the "School of the Prophets." During that period he had seen much affliction, but no trace of it could I detect in his personal appearance; and after a few days of most delightful intercourse, we parted again to meet no more in this world. He was then fast ripening for his rest, and now realizes the blessedness of that communion of saints which is never jarred nor broken by the imperfections of the flesh.

Very truly yours,
W. J. SPROLE.

JAMES LEMONTE DINWIDDIE, D.D.

1820—1849.

FROM THE REV. JOSEPH T. SMITH, D.D.

BALTIMORE, January 10, 1851.

Rev. and dear Sir: It is with great pleasure that I attempt, in compliance with your request, to furnish you with some notices of the life and character of the late Rev. Dr. J. L. Dinwiddie. My earlier studies were pursued under his direction. I have had a knowledge of his history, and frequent personal interviews with him, up to the period of his death. I have also conferred freely with his daughter, Mrs. Smith, of this city, on some points in respect to which I was in doubt, so that I believe the entire accuracy of every thing which I shall communicate may be relied on.

JAMES LEMONTE DINWIDDIE, a son of William and Anna (Lemonte) Dinwiddie, was born in Adams County, Pa., February 23, 1798. His parents were both devout members of the Associate Reformed Church. He was early the subject of religious impressions; but, beyond this general fact, I have no information concerning the incipient stages of his Christian experience. He entered Jefferson College in 1813, and remained there till the next year, when his relation was transferred to Washington College, where he graduated in 1816, under the Presidency of the Rev. Dr. Brown. In 1817 he entered the Theological Seminary at New York, where he continued for two years; and then, in consequence of Dr. Mason's being partially disabled by bodily infirmity for the discharge of his duties, he completed his theological course under the Rev. Dr. Kerr, of Allegheny County, Pa. He was licensed to preach by the Associate Reformed Presbytery of Monongahela, at its sessions in Mifflin township, Allegheny County, Pa., in May, 1820.

Being very popular as a Preacher, from his first appearance in the pulpit, calls were addressed to him from several vacant congregations; but that which he accepted was from Mercer, the County seat of the County of Mercer, Pa. Here he was ordained and installed on the 22d of November, 1820; and here he laboured with much acceptance for about fourteen years. In May, 1834, he demitted his charge, much against the will of his congregation, and removed to Philadelphia, and took charge of a congregation in connection with the Presbyterian Church—it was the Sixth Presbyterian Church of Philadelphia, now under the pastoral care of the Rev. Dr. Janeway.

After continuing in this connection about seven years, he returned to his mother Church, and was again received as a member of the Presbytery of Monongahela, on the 26th of July, 1841. Shortly after this he received a call from the Second Associate Reformed Church of Pittsburg, Pa.; and, having accepted it, was regularly installed as Pastor of that Church, on the 27th of September, 1842. On the 13th of September, 1843, he was elected to the Professorship of Biblical Literature and Sacred Criticism in the Theological Seminary of the Associate Reformed Church at Allegheny. This appointment he accepted, and, that he might give his whole time to the duties of his Professorship, he demitted his pastoral charge in April, 1844.

He was honoured with the degree of Doctor of Divinity, from Jefferson College, in 1844.

Dr. Dinwiddie entered upon the discharge of his duties in the Seminary with great zeal, devoted himself assiduously to his work, gave promise of eminence in his department. He suffered from frequent attacks of headache, and, by his intense application to study, it is supposed that he brought on a paralysis of the brain, in February, 1846, which unfitted him for his duties in the Seminary and for preaching. In January, 1849, he had another attack which terminated his life in a few hours.

The last two years of his life were spent in this city, with his daughter, Mrs. Smith. His wife was Rachel Cochran, of Allegheny County, who became the mother of three children and died six years after her marriage.

I will venture to subjoin a few hints towards a general estimate of Dr. Dinwiddie's character.

He was a finished Gentleman. There was a charm in his address which attracted all who approached him. Indeed, he was indebted for no small part of his influence over a large class to the polish of his manners.

He was an accurate Scholar. He was familiar, beyond most, with our sterling old English literature. He was quite thoroughly versed in the classics. The impulse his mind had received from Dr. Mason was never lost. He was through life a diligent student. And his labours in the Seminary justified the high estimate his brethren had placed on his attainments. He was an enthusiast in the science of Geology, and had amassed a large stock of materials for a work which he proposed and had commenced on that subject. This, to the great regret of his friends, he destroyed, when he found himself incapacitated for its completion.

He was eminently a Biblical student. His exigetical lectures, delivered in the Seminary, the notes of which are still preserved, were truly admirable. His sermons, beyond those of most preachers, were enriched with copious quotations of Scripture words, and illustrations drawn from Scripture subjects.

As a Preacher, his gracefulness of manner and propriety of address would perhaps first arrest the attention of a stranger. Indeed, with some the force of his ministrations was impaired from this cause; as it left the impression of something like coldness or mannerism. As a Pastor he was greatly beloved;—a welcome visitor at the fireside, the kindest of friends in affliction, and a minister of mercy at the death-bed. In the domestic circle he was a model of tenderness, dignity and fidelity.

If the above should prove, in any degree, what you desire, I shall rejoice at it; for I do not think so good a man should be left to perish without a memorial.

Yours very truly,
JOSEPH T. SMITH.

JOSEPH CLAYBAUGH, D.D.*

1824—1855.

JOSEPH CLAYBAUGH,, a son of William and Barbara (Keifer) Claybaugh, was born in Frederick County, Md., July 1, 1803. His mother was an eminently godly woman, but his father did not make a profession of religion until late in life, though he finally became an Elder in the Associate Reformed Church. While he was yet a child, his father removed with his family to the State of Ohio. Joseph's health having been impaired by scrofula, the disease that finally terminated his life, he was placed, at an early age, at the Chillicothe Academy, then under the care of the Rev. John McFarland. Having completed the usual course of study in that school, he was entered as a student at Jefferson College, where he maintained a high standing and graduated in the year 1822. Almost immediately after leaving College, he was taken under the care of the First Associate Reformed Presbytery of Ohio, as a student of Divinity. The Synod of Sciota having then recently withdrawn from the General Synod, and resolved itself into an independent Synod, under the name of the Synod of the West, the few students she had under her care pursued their studies privately under the direction of some of her members. The Rev. John Steele, then Pastor of the Church at Xenia, was appointed by the Presbytery to superintend the studies of Mr. Claybaugh. In 1824 he was licensed as a probationer for the Holy Ministry; and the next year received and accepted a call from the Congregation at Chillicothe, which had been vacant since the removal of Mr. McFarland, at the time of the separation of the Synod of Sciota from the General Synod. In May, 1825, he was ordained, and installed Pastor of that congregation. At the same time, or shortly after, he took charge of the Chillicothe Academy.

For a year or two Mr. Claybaugh discharged his duties, in connection with both the Church and the Academy, with a good degree of ease and comfort. But

---

*Christian Institute, 1855.—MS. from his son, Rev. W. M. Claybaugh.

his health became so seriously impaired as to render all active engagements a burden. So feeble was he that he would often leave his bed to go and preach, and, as soon as the service was over, would return, and throw himself upon it again. By the advice of his physician, he made a journey to the East to try the effect of sea-bathing, but returned without having received much benefit. His congregation were warmly attached to him, but, from causes over which he had no control, their numbers were not greatly increased under his ministry.

In the year 1839 Mr. Claybaugh was called to take charge of the Theological Seminary, then recently organized in Oxford, O., and about the same time the degree of Doctor of Divinity was conferred upon him by the Board of Trustees of Miami University. The congregation which he had served, in so much bodily feebleness, and yet with so much fidelity, were reluctant to part with him, but they yielded from a regard to the more general interests of the Church. With his labours as Professor he associated the pastoral charge of the Congregation at Oxford; and continued in both relations till the close of life, discharging the duties belonging to each with most exemplary fidelity and to great acceptance.

He died at Oxford on the 9th of September, 1855, after having held the Professorship sixteen years, and, with the exception of a single session, performed the duties during the whole time, without assistance. His last words were, "I see the King in his Glory." His Funeral Sermon was preached by the Rev. William Davidson, of Hamilton, O.

Dr. Claybaugh published, a short time before his death, a small work entitled "The Christian Profession," which has been received with much favour.

Dr. Claybaugh was married on the 25th of October, 1825, to Margaret Cunan, daughter of David and Ellen (Johnson) Bonner, of Greenfield, O. They had eleven children, five of whom, with their mother, still (1863) survive. Of the two sons who survive, one (*William M.*) is a clergyman, settled in Hartford, Conn.; the other (*Joseph*) is a lawyer, in Frankfort, Ind.

FROM THE REV. R. D. HARPER, D.D.

XENIA, O., May 1, 1863.

Dear Sir: In compliance with your request, I herewith transmit to you my personal recollections and impressions of the late Joseph Claybaugh, D.D.

My acquaintance with this excellent man commenced in the year 1845. He was, at that time, residing in Oxford, Ohio, having charge of a congregation, and being Professor of Theology in the Seminary of the Associate Reformed Church. My first favourable impressions of his character were confirmed by an intimate acquaintance which continued until his decease. He was a man of vigorous and cultivated mind. He was an original thinker; a superior scholar; an accomplished Professor; an eloquent Preacher; a Christian Gentleman, and a man of high toned and exemplary piety. He loved the Church, and had enlarged charity for all the followers of our common Saviour. Those who knew him best loved him most. His memory is redolent of good. Long will he be cherished in pleasing remembrance by those who shared his friendship and received his instructions. Few men have lived to better purpose. He acted well his part in all the relations of life. He rests from his labours, and his works do follow him.

With great respect yours sincerely,

R. D. HARPER.

RICHARD WYNKOOP.*

1826—1842.

RICHARD WYNKOOP was born in the city of New York, on the 16th of December, 1798. His parents were Peter and Margaret (Quackenbos) Wynkoop, and his paternal grandfather was Judge Derrick Wynkoop, of Ulster County, N. Y. His studies preparatory to entering College were prosecuted at the Grammar School of Joseph Nelson, then a well known teacher in the city. Integrity and a high sense of honour were among the marked characteristics of his early years. He took much delight in active exercise, and the manly sports to which he then addicted himself contributed much to the vigour of his constitution in after life. He entered Columbia College in 1815, and graduated in 1819; on which occasion he delivered a somewhat satirical Address on the "$Κυνοκεφαλοι$ of Herodotus, and the probability of their being the ancestors of our common dandies." He entered upon the study of Theology in the autumn succeeding his graduation, at the Seminary of the Reformed Dutch Church in New Brunswick. He had naturally a strong predilection, amounting well-nigh to a passion, for debate; and his mind was so much occupied in forming lines of attack and defence, and adjusting arguments on various theological questions, that he was, to some extent, delinquent upon the regular course of study; and this brought him temporarily into relations with some members of the Faculty of the Institution which were not altogether agreeable. He was dismissed from the Seminary, at his own request, in September, 1833, and then went to New York and prosecuted his theological studies, for two or three years, with great diligence, under the direction of one of the clergymen of the city. Meanwhile he had placed himself under the care of the Second Presbytery of New York, and was licensed to preach by that Presbytery, on the 5th of April, 1826.

In October following he was appointed, by the Directors of the Missionary Society of the Reformed Dutch Church, to labour, as a missionary in the church at Cato, N. Y. After labouring in this field for three months, he was reappointed, in March, 1828, for a like term; but, preaching on his way, by invitation, to the Presbyterian Church at Yorktown, Westchester County, N. Y., that church immediately tendered him a call, which he accepted, furnishing, at the same time, a substitute for the missionary station at Cato.

Here he remained till February, 1834, when he received a call from the Presbyterian Church in Hagerstown, Md., to become their Pastor. This call he, on the whole, thought it his duty to accept, though it is said that he subsequently doubted the propriety of the decision. The Presbytery of Bedford dissolved his pastoral relation, dismissed him, and recommended him to the Presbytery of Carlisle, in April following.

He was installed Pastor of the church in Hagerstown, on the 25th of June, 1834. After he had been in charge of this church for some time, several of its members became the subjects of discipline. An appeal to Presbytery having been made, the decision of the Session was reversed, and the suspended members declared in regular standing. The Pastor and Elders, believing that this step

---

* MSS. from his son, Richard Wynkoop, Esq., and Hon. D. Weisel.

of the Presbytery was a sacrifice of principle to the love of peace, applied for dismissal from the General Assembly connection. The Presbytery were willing to dismiss the Pastor, but not the congregation—whereupon, after a statement of the case by the Pastor, the Associate Reformed Presbytery of New York, on the 6th of March. 1830, re-admitted the congregation, (for they had formerly belonged to that Body,) and added Mr. Wynkoop's name to their roll. The church-members who had been the subjects of discipline, with others who had been dissatisfied, commenced a suit in Chancery, in September, 1838, for the possession of the church property. Mr. Wynkoop prepared a very full and elaborate answer, which was filed in June, 1839. He obtained permission from the Chancellor to conduct the defence, in behalf of the other defendants as well as for himself. He prepared himself for the trial, but the cause never came on.

In 1838 he favoured a union of the Associate Reformed and the Associate and Reformed Bodies. He was a vigorous opposer of all secret societies. In October, 1839, he preached a sermon on the subject, which drew forth some very severe strictures in a newspaper; and this, with some other circumstances, led him to preach another sermon, in July, 1840, of a yet more decisive and searching character, from Isaiah xxix, 15—" Wo unto them that seek deep to hide their counsel from the Lord, and their works are in the dark; and they say, Who seeth us, and who knoweth us?"

Mr. Wynkoop's last sermon was preached from Malachi iv, 1—" For behold the day cometh," &c. The day and the church being chilly, he contracted a cold, with fever, which became highly congestive, and in the brief space of four days terminated his life. Though perfectly prostrated by disease, his mind remained as clear and vigorous as ever; and, being fully aware of his approaching dissolution, he conversed with his family and friends with great solemnity and tenderness, and with his wonted composure. He died on the 5th of April, 1842. His Funeral Sermon was preached by the Rev. Jonathan Dickinson, then of Williamsport, Md., who had been his early and constant friend, from the words,—" I have fought a good fight, I have finished my course, I have kept the faith," &c.

On the 10th of August, 1825, he was married to Catharine, daughter of the Hon. James Schureman, of New Brunswick, N. J., and sister of the Rev. Dr. John Schureman, Professor in the Theological Seminary of the Reformed Dutch Church. She was a lady of vigorous intellect and earnest piety. They had six children,—two sons and four daughters. One of them, who bears his father's name, was graduated at Rutgers College in 1849, and is now (1863) a lawyer in the city of New York. Mrs. Wynkoop died among her friends in New Jersey, on the 18th of May, 1847.

FROM THE HON. DANIEL WEISEL.

HAGERSTOWN, Md., July 7, 1849.

Dear Sir: My opportunities for knowing the Rev. Richard Wynkoop were such as you would expect from my sitting under his ministry, and being intimately associated with him in various ways, during a period of several years. The impressions which I then gained in respect to his character are still fresh, and I cheerfully, in compliance with your request, communicate them to you.

Mr. Wynkoop was a man of stern principle, and an ardent and devoted champion of what he believed to be the truth. Truth was the object and aim of all his investigations, and to his researches he brought a mind quick, penetrating, strong and logical. He would seize upon the points of inquiry with the rapidity of lightning, and trace them through mazes of difficulty with the ease and quickness of intuition. Rarely is a mind ever so well fitted or so well equipped for theological discussion as was his. Ever on the alert to detect error, he was sure to expose it on every proper occasion, often using the weapons of sarcasm and ridicule, which he wielded with great skill, and sometimes with prodigious effect. Probably he carried this to an extreme; and the free use of these weapons in his encounters with his brethren, either at the fireside or in the Councils of the Church, no doubt excited against him much of prejudice and unkind feeling.

He studied the Scriptures carefully in the original languages, and thus became, to a great extent, his own commentator. His general reading was limited, but he was well versed in all the branches of theological learning, and was familiar with the best writers in each department. In the distinctive belief of the Presbyterian Church, no one that I have met with could more clearly, ably and satisfactorily expound its mooted points. He possessed the reasoning faculty in uncommon power. His sermons were among the finest specimens of logic; and this character was awarded to them by many gentlemen of the Bar and other professions, who were attracted by his remarkable powers, and whose praise any one might value. There was no variety in the method of his sermons—in respect to their frame-work they were all alike. On any one occasion, the services, throughout, all pertained to the subject of his discourse, and derived their complexion from it. The psalms, prayers, &c., bore upon the truth to be discussed. The chapter read was invariably that from which the text was taken. The text was read twice; and the exordium of the sermon was a running commentary on the preceding context. This was often the most interesting and instructive portion of his discourse; and the text, by the time he reached it, seemed as clear as if it had actually been the subject of a formal discussion—all that followed was amplitude and illustration. He then proceeded to divide the text into its appropriate heads, observing, in the order of these, that connection which would exhibit the proper dependence of one upon the other. The filling up consisted of proofs from reason, analogy and Scripture; and the conclusion was a brief application of the truths presented. His preaching was a preaching upon texts, not upon subjects. His object was to communicate instruction, and in this he never failed. The most difficult passages opened before the rays of his penetrating intellect, and no one who listened attentively left his pew without a substantial addition to his stock of religious knowledge. He never *accommodated* his texts, as it is termed. He was not in the habit of writing out or committing his discourses. But he *thought* them out, and that fully and effectually. His arrangement, proofs, &c., were committed, in neat and precise form, to a slip of paper, which always lay before him; and within the limits of this analysis he strictly confined himself. His manner was plain, simple, but dignified. He never affected style or oratory in the pulpit. In proportion as he had reflected on his subject, and according to the degree of interest it had excited in his own mind, were the impressiveness and power of his delivery. His whole manner and appearance in the pulpit indicated his own sense of the solemnity of the errand on which he stood there, and awakened corresponding emotions in those whom he addressed. No one could fail to infer from his prayers the distinctive character of his faith; many of them were beautiful epitomes of Theology within the range of the subject before him.

In physical structure he was muscular and athletic, formed for labour and endurance; and the movements of his body, like the operations of his mind, were quick and agile. But strong and powerful as his frame was, it soon gave way before the fearful malady that consigned him to the grave.

Of the difficulties in the church, which resulted in its separation from the General Assembly, and with which Mr. Wynkoop had much to do, I do not wish here to express any opinion further than to say that I have the fullest confidence that he acted from honest, conscientious conviction. That his peculiar constitution may have sometimes led him into mistakes on this and other occasions, I am far from denying; but of the purity of his motives and the general integrity of his character, his whole life is the voucher.

Your friend and servant,
D. WEISEL.

JOSEPH REYNOLDS KERR.
1829—1843.
FROM THE REV. JAMES PRESTLEY, D.D.

PITTSBURG, PA., March 7, 1862.

Dear Sir: The account which I am about to give you of the Rev. Joseph Reynolds Kerr is compiled from the recollections of those contemporary with him; from obituary notices of him at the time of his decease; but, chiefly from my own recollections. As I enjoyed the advantages of his ministry and pastoral care for years, and at a time of life when I was better able to form a correct opinion than I was when I sat under the ministry of his father, I think I have a proper appreciation of the Man and the Minister. To me his labours, in the pulpit and out of it, were invaluable; and I manifested my appreciation of them in the strictest attendance, day by day, on his ministrations in the pulpit, and in seeking his counsel on all proper occasions. There were other very able Ministers of the New Testament, and very dear friends too, on whose ministry it would have been a profit and a pleasure to attend; but these were years of my life, in which, I think, I was never absent from my accustomed seat, and heard no other than my beloved Pastor, unless some one ministered in his stead. Having him, I had all I desired, and was content. It affords me a melancholy pleasure to contribute these lines, at this late day, to his memory, and to assist in rescuing his name from earthly oblivion, by placing it among the other worthy names that grace the pages of your "Annals." I feel assured that his name is in the "Book of Life," and, therefore, feel no apprehension of its being forgotten among those in Heaven, who walk with Christ in white, because they are worthy; and of whom, individually, he says, "I will confess his name before my Father and before his angels."

JOSEPH REYNOLDS KERR was a son of the Rev. Dr. Joseph and Agnes Kerr, and was born in St. Clair township, Allegheny County, Pa., on the 18th of January, 1807. His father was, in his day, one of the most influential ministers of the Associate Reformed Presbyterian Church, and contributed largely to the building up of the cause of Christ in a wide region of comparatively new country, from fifty to seventy-five miles in different directions from his place of residence. Joseph was early dedicated to God, and devoted to his service in the Gospel of his Son, by these pious parents, who coveted no higher honours for their sons than that they might serve the Lord in the ministry of reconciliation.

He was the oldest of five brothers, three of whom became Ministers of the Gospel in the Associate Reformed Presbyterian Church. One, with his father, was taken to his reward before him; the others still survive.

He received his classical education at the Western University of Pennsylvania. He attended that Institution in the days of its highest literary character; when five of the most eminent and learned men in the city of Pittsburg composed its Faculty; when its curriculum was as extensive, and the grade of the scholarship of its students stood as high, as in any Institution in the Western country. He was an indefatigable student during the whole period of his college course; and, in acknowledgment of his superior talents, his great industry in the pursuit of knowledge, and his literary attainments, he was awarded the highest honours of his class, at the time of his graduation, in July, 1826.

About one year after leaving the University, he was, on his application, taken under the care of the Presbytery of Monongahela as a student of Theology; and was directed by the Presbytery to prosecute his studies under the direction of his father, at that time Professor of Theology in the Seminary founded by the Synod a short time before. He entered the Seminary in the fall of 1827. Here the same unwearied diligence, and the same superiority in the acquisition of knowledge and in mental cultivation, characterized him as in the University. Such was the success with which he prosecuted his studies that, at the end of two sessions in the Seminary, the Presbytery deemed him worthy to be taken on trial for license. He delivered the usual pieces of trial to the entire satisfaction of the Presbytery, and was accordingly licensed to preach the Gospel, as a Probationer for the Holy Ministry, on the 2d day of September, 1829.

In less than two and a half months after his licensure, and while absent on his first preaching tour, his father was removed by death. Returning home immediately on hearing the sad tidings, he was not only called on to minister consolation to his bereaved mother and brothers and sisters, but to feed his father's disconsolate flock. They thought the mantle of his deceased father had fallen on him, and transferred to him almost immediately the affection and esteem which they had for his father. They immediately petitioned the Presbytery for his labours as a stated supply, and not long after they directed a unanimous call to him to become their Pastor and take the care of their souls. After mature deliberation he acceded to their request; and, after having delivered the usual pieces of trial for Ordination, to the entire satisfaction of the Presbytery, he was ordained to the office of the Holy Ministry, and installed Pastor of the congregation, on the 29th day of July, 1830. Thus called by Providence to fill the pulpit of such a man as his father, he succeeded, from the very first, in giving entire satisfaction to his people, and soon became one of the most, if he was not altogether the most, popular of the preachers in the city; but it was at the expense of such exhausting toil as contributed slowly but surely to undermine a constitution at best but delicate. From being a student of Divinity, and without any experience, he entered at once on the pastoral oversight of a large congregation, and all the duties connected with the office of the Christian Ministry. In his preparation for the pulpit he was a close, unwearying student. He was ambitious of excellence in whatever he attempted, connected with his office, and became a workman that needed not to be ashamed.

As a Preacher of the Gospel, Mr. Kerr was very like, and very unlike his father. In some respects not equal, and in others superior to him. There was in both the same commanding and yet attractive bearing in the pulpit; the same richness of voice, somewhat softened in the son; the same intellectuality; the same richness of evangelical matter; and the same fluency. Neither was ever at a loss for something worthy to be said, pertinent to the subject in hand, or for suitable language in which to express it. The father had the more directness and force,—he had better health and more physical energy,—the son the more feeling and polish. The father drew but seldom on the imagination, and seldom dealt in long sustained descriptions; the great characteristic of the mind of the son was ideality; and he excelled, and frequently indulged, in long and well sustained descriptions and flights of the imagination. His discourses abounded in figures, comparisons and illustrations; and all this without extravagance, for while his imagination was brilliant it was chaste. Every thing was in place, perfectly natural and in good taste. He was remarkable for the clearness with which he presented and illustrated a difficult subject; for the interest with which he could invest, and the sentiments he could extract from, one that appeared to be barren; and for his happy combination of language, look and gesture, in the pulpit. He blended, with great skill, in his sermons, doctrine and duty, principle and practice, that he might through the understanding reach the heart. He sometimes used the terrors of the law to warn the sinner, to scourge the presumptuous, and startle the unwary; but he principally delighted to preach the Gospel; and he excelled in presenting it in its unrivalled attractions. Jesus Christ, and Him crucified, in all the bearings of that great subject, was his darling and continual theme. If the Crucifixion of the Saviour was the theme of his discourse, he would not unfrequently transfix his audience, and bring them into such sympathy with himself and the sufferer that their very hearts were broken; or if the Ascension and Glorification of the Saviour was the theme, he would bear them on high in the train of their ascending Lord, until, enraptured, they were drawn, as it were out of the body, and stood amid, and in sympathy with, the assembled multitude that beheld Him enthroned and crowned; and hailed Him, "Lord of all." His physical powers were not equal to such heavy drafts without manifest suffering; and the pallor of his countenance, his streaming eyes, and quivering, tottering frame made new drafts on the sympathy of his audience, and brought them into that close union with him that enabled him to move them as he himself was moved. In him this was not art—it was natural; and all the more irresistible, because it was, evidently, natural. Thus, at once instructive, convincing, persuasive and eloquent, and, with all these qualities, richly evangelical, his preaching possessed a charm for all ranks and classes of society. Many owe to him their first convictions of sin, and their clearest conceptions of the way of salvation; and their hearts have burned, day after day, with those emotions which his eloquent presentations of Divine truth were the means of exciting within them.

In his pastoral intercourse he was affectionate and considerate. There was no reserve between him and his people. Wherever he entered he was received with unfeigned pleasure, and admitted to all their councils and their hearts. He could sympathize with every class of his flock in their afflictions. In the sick chamber and at the bed of death he was peculiarly happy. He could come near to the person he addressed, gently and without effort remove all unbecoming reserve, and present the instructions, advice and comfort the case demanded. He handled the wounds of the spirit with a skilful, faithful and tender hand. He could probe, and deeply, where it was necessary; but he always had at hand the balm of consolation to be poured into the wound; the great object being to heal thoroughly, not slightly, the wounds of his people. He recognized the fact that he had the care of souls, and he made it his study to care for them.

In the social circle Mr. Kerr was uniformly kind and courteous. His tact in delicate conjunctures, his prudence, his unruffled equanimity, his, in many respects, even childlike simplicity of manners, his playful yet instructive conversation, all combined to impart an attraction to his society that drew toward him all hearts, wherever he went, and made his own house the abode of peace and happiness. As a consequence, he had no enemies. All persons appeared to entertain for him the kindest sentiments.

Great as were his mental riches,—the result of natural gifts cultivated by hard study and diligent reading; great as were his social qualities; they did not and they could not distinguish him as did his humble and uniform piety. In all his troubles—and they were not few, for death had early taken away from him his father, and continued his ravages in his father's family, and had entered, once and again, his own family circle and left him childless; yet, amid all, his trust was in the Rock of Ages. He was a man of prayer, and, from a child, devout. Nothing, even in childhood, was permitted to hinder his private devotions, and the same carefulness characterized him through life. "He was a good man, full of the Holy Ghost, and of faith;" and, by his instrumentality, "much people was added unto the Lord," as all who knew him can testify.

In personal appearance, he was tall,—about six feet high,—and slender, with good features, forehead broader than high, and a dark grey eye, that was soft when at rest, but could sparkle and blaze under excitement. His mental endowments were superior. He possessed a clear, active, comprehensive intellect; a very tenacious memory; correct taste, and great powers of application. His thought flowed copiously, and whether in the pulpit or elsewhere, in literary or theological discussion, he was a sound reasoner and good debater. He was well furnished, mentally and by education, to be a pleasing, edifying, and therefore popular, Preacher of the Gospel. To this his attention had been directed from early life, and this was the great object kept in view in all his preparatory course. He cheerfully, nay thankfully, devoted all his powers to the service of his Divine Master, to the illustration of his truth, and the commendation of the Saviour to his perishing fellow men; and the Lord blessed him in his work of faith and labour of love.

In the year 1835, on the 24th day of August, he was united in marriage to Miss Harriet Snowden, daughter of Hon. John M. Snowden, an old and respectable citizen of Pittsburg. By this marriage there were three children,—two daughters and one son. The daughters died in infancy and before their father; the son, born after his father's decease, and bearing his father's name, *Joseph R. Kerr*, still lives with his widowed mother, and is prosecuting, as a student of the second year,—in the Seminary where his father studied, and of which his grandfather was the first Professor,—his theological course, with a view to entering the Christian Ministry. It is the earnest prayer of all his friends that the mantle of his father and grandfather may fall on him. Should he live to enter the ministry, he will be the fourth minister in regular succession in the Kerr family,— and all bearing the name of Joseph,—his father, grandfather, and great-grandfather, having been ministers of the Gospel, and all eminent.

Mr. Kerr's publications are an Address before the Alumni Association of the Western University of Pennsylvania, on "The Responsibility of Literary Men," published by the Association, 1836; and a Sermon on "Duelling," published by his congregation, 1838.

About this time he received the literary degree of Master of Arts from the Western University.

Mr. Kerr preached his last sermon in March, 1843; and from that time his strength rapidly failed. He wasted away without suffering, while his mind retained all its usual vigour and serenity. His transition from life to death was attended with few variations; one day or week being almost precisely like another. During all his last illness, his piety appeared very eminent. His hopes were unclouded. He was not troubled with doubts or fears. His trust, firmly based upon the Rock of Ages, was quiet and tranquil; but, like still waters, clear and profound. Toward the last he appeared to be anxious to be gone. "Having a desire to depart and to be with Christ, which is far better." Not only was he thus resigned himself, but, by his well-timed exhortations, he armed his relatives with Christian fortitude against the loss they were about to suffer; while his uniform cheerfulness banished melancholy from his chamber, and imparted strength and comfort to the numerous friends who came to condole with him. The peace of God appeared to reign in his soul, and, when his hour came, without a struggle he passed through death to life. He died on the 14th of June, 1843, in the thirty-seventh year of his age and fifteenth of his ministry. "He lived," says one who knew him well, and was no flatterer, "as a Minister of the Gospel and an humble and experienced Christian ought to live; and his death was like his life. The last enemy found him with his loins girded and his lights burning. His death was, therefore, the triumphant consummation of his life. He died to live for evermore." "Mark the perfect man, and behold the upright; for the end of that man is peace." Very truly yours,

JAMES PRESTLEY

FROM THE REV. JOSEPH CLAYBAUGH, D.D.

OXFORD, O., June 26, 1850.

My dear Sir: I became acquainted with Joseph Reynolds Kerr at the house of his father, Dr. Joseph Kerr, in the summer of 1828. He was then a student of Divinity, very young, but evidently of a precocious and aspiring mind. He was tall; of a delicate, elastic frame; light and graceful in his movements; with a well-defined face; a dark, rolling, speaking eye; an air of more than common thoughtfulness; and a deep, mellow, musical voice. It was evident that he was no ordinary youth; and, as in conversation he gave evidence of a sanctified and devoted spirit, entertaining high views of the work of the Ministry, and setting before himself a high standard, he left upon my mind the impression that he was destined to become no ordinary Preacher. Though he was licensed before he had reached the age of twenty-one, his first efforts in the pulpit fully met the high expectations of his friends. Though subsequently called to be his father's successor in a large and important congregation in Pittsburg, he immediately acquired, and retained during life, not only in Pittsburg but throughout the Church, a popularity not surpassed by that of any other man. Being near the Theological Seminary, his ministrations were much attended by the students, and he was evidently the popular model. The students unavoidably carried away with them the impress of their favourite Preacher.

I had the pleasure of hearing him repeatedly; and with the method and clearness of his father he united a softer, more musical and more flexible voice, was more rapid and impassioned in his utterance, and I should say was, on the whole, a more thrilling and captivating Preacher. His eloquence was generally of the soft and winning type, though it was sometimes scorching and terrible. He was a man of amiable, generous temper; but I should suppose he had more fire in his constitution than his father. Had he lived, and mingled, as doubtless he would have been called to do, in the great religious movements of the day, I have no doubt that he would have taken his place among our most influential clergymen, as well as the most distinguished of our pulpit orators. I am, with kind regard,

Yours very truly,
JOSEPH CLAYBAUGH.

MOSES KERR.
1831—1840.
FROM DAVID R. KERR, D.D.,
PROFESSOR IN THE THEOLOGICAL SEMINARY, ALLEGHENY.

PITTSBURG, July 26, 1862.

My dear Sir: Agreeably to your request, I now undertake the somewhat delicate task of furnishing you with a brief narrative of the life, and my general impressions of the character, of my lamented brother, the Rev. Moses Kerr. While I will endeavour to be faithful to his memory, I trust I shall not allow any statements I may make to be unduly coloured by fraternal partiality.

MOSES KERR, the third son of the Rev. Joseph Kerr, D.D., was born in St. Clair, Pa., on the 30th of June, 1811. Naturally of a serious and thoughtful cast of mind, and manifesting in very early life decided piety, his education was directed, from the first, with a view to qualifying him for the sacred ministry. He was the first of the family to enter upon a classical course. But, in a short time, signs of failing health led to a suspension of his studies and thoughts of some other calling less trying to a feeble constitution. He was induced to devote himself, for a time, to preparation for mercantile life. For this he had no taste, and it soon proved as unfavourable to his health as his application to study had previously done. He then engaged in ordinary farm work, and in this he appeared to grow strong; and, feeling now that he had the prospect of comfortable health, he again turned his attention to the profession on which he had first set his heart. He now entered the Western University of Pennsylvania, in which he prosecuted his studies without interruption until he was honourably graduated in 1828. In the fall of the same year he began the study of Theology in the Seminary then under the care of his father. He had completed one session, and entered upon a second, when his father died. He finished his theological course under the instruction of the Rev. Mungo Dick, a learned and excellent Minister, who consented to take charge of the students of the Synod of the West until a Professor to succeed Dr. Kerr could be formally chosen. Here he had not only the regular instructions of Mr. Dick, delivered to his class, but the advantage of living in his family and enjoying familiar intercourse with him, from which he was often heard to say that he derived very important advantage.

He was licensed to preach as a probationer for the holy ministry by the Presbytery of Monongahela, on the 28th of April, 1831. The same year the First Congregation of Allegheny was organized, and he was chosen its first Pastor. He accepted this call on the 24th of April, 1832, and, from this date, preached to this congregation, until the fall of the same year, a short time before the meeting of Presbytery, at which it was expected he would be ordained and installed. But when the Presbytery met, he returned the call, on account of a hemorrhage of the lungs, which made it necessary for him to refrain from public speaking,—he knew not how long. The Presbytery released him from his acceptance of the call to that particular congregation, but proceeded with his Ordination to the office of the ministry. This was on the 9th of October, 1832.

In his short term of service in Allegheny he was quite successful. And, while his health continued, he was very happy in his work there. His brother Joseph was Pastor of the mother church in Pittsburg, from which Allegheny city is separated by the river from which it takes its name. The two brothers still lived together in the parental home, were warmly attached to each other, and were mutual counsellors and aids in their respective fields of labour. The termination of these happy relations was a great affliction to both brothers. Upon Moses it fell almost as heavily as the failure of his health.

For a time he was much dejected. Friends did what they could to encourage him, and, after some time, led him to hope that, with a little rest, and by the application of proper remedies, the disease with which he was threatened could be overcome. It was recommended to him to take a sea voyage, and, accordingly, shortly after his Ordination, he sailed for Europe. After an absence of about seven months, most of which were spent in the salubrious air of Ireland, he returned with every appearance of restored and established health. After his return, he resumed preaching, but was unwilling to accept a pastoral charge until his strength should be in some manner tested. After more than a year's trial of preaching to vacant congregations, he concluded to accept a call that had been tendered him by the large and influential congregation of Robinson's Run, in the vicinity of Pittsburg, that had been rendered vacant by the death of Dr. John Riddell. He accepted this call September 2, 1834, and was installed as its Pastor on the first Thursday of the following month. But he had served this congregation but a little more than six months, when he was again attacked with hemorrhage of the lungs, in consequence of which, on the 15th of April, 1835, he demitted his pastoral charge.

Again he was cast down as much in spirit as in body, though it was not the loss of health, so much as of ability to exercise his ministry, that made him despondent. This he was now called to endure for a longer time, and in greater discouragement, than before. Yet he did not give himself up to indolence. During this period he performed some very important service. He discharged for a time the duties of Professor of Languages in the Western University of Pennsylvania; afterwards of Biblical Literature and Criticism, in the Theological Seminary, Allegheny. But his taste and talents were for the pulpit. To this he returned. He appears to have become satisfied that a complete restoration of his health was no longer to be expected; and he seems now to have resumed the full exercise of his ministry, resolved to give it all that remained of his health and life,—to die as a good soldier of the cross with the harness on. At this time he accepted a call from the Third Church, Pittsburg. This was on the

18th of October, 1837. With that congregation he closed his life, having served it, under much bodily infirmity, but with great acceptance and success, for more than three years. He died on the 26th of January, 1840, in the twenty-ninth year of his age and the tenth of his ministry.

Moses Kerr was a man of fine personal appearance, and of noble and generous qualities. While not indifferent to the good opinion of others, he would never depart a hair's breadth for it from what he believed to be true and right. His independence in this respect sometimes made him trouble in circumstances through which men of more supple character would have passed without annoyance. He knew no fear but of God. And yet he was not austere. He was grave and dignified in his manners, but bland and courteous. Presumption and arrogance sometimes felt a rebuke in his presence, as did all unmanly or unworthy conduct. But sincere and honest worth always met with the kindest greeting. The humblest and the weakest could approach him with confidence, and invariably found him ready to listen, sympathize, counsel and aid. For the relief of the suffering poor he would part with his last farthing.

His intellectual character partook of like manly qualities. His bodily infirmity, and the frequent interruptions of study and active service consequent upon it, did not allow him to display fully, perhaps, at any time, the power which he really possessed. His mind, too, was very gradual in its development. From the beginning of his public career he had a respectable standing; but, before the close of his life, short as it was, he had a strength, compass and vigour of mind, which they who knew him only at the outset of his ministerial life would have scarcely deemed possible. He was a student from the love of study; and a careful reader of the best writings not only in Theology, but in literature generally. With a becoming appreciation of the demands of his profession, he aimed to store his mind, not only with the matter of text-books in Theology and the works of past ages, but the fresh discussions of living divines; and, at the same time, keep up with the general advance of literature and science in the world. The result was that his mind became thoroughly furnished and highly cultivated. As a Preacher he had capabilities, which, with ordinary health and an ordinary length of life, must have rendered him eminent in his profession. He began preaching when quite young,—not yet twenty years of age; and his early performances, with other marks of youthfulness, were perhaps unduly florid. But, as his mind matured, and his knowledge enlarged, and the responsibilities of his profession became more sensibly felt, he settled down into a style of preaching in which the instructive, the argumentative, the descriptive and exhortatory, were very happily blended. In sermonizing, he made it his first object to ascertain precisely what the text was intended to teach; he then sought the order of discussion best adapted to declare, establish and apply that truth, in the precise form and phase in which it was revealed in the particular passage under consideration. To this he scrupulously confined himself, and made his preparation with all the care which circumstances permitted. The result was that his sermons were usually marked by precision, unity, clearness and conclusiveness of discussion and closeness of application. His whole manner in the pulpit was expressive of solemnity and earnestness. His voice was strong but soft, very flexible and capable of almost every variety of intonation. When he explained, it was with calmness and clearness of utterance as of thought. When he argued, it was with all the strength and emphasis of his voice as of his mind. When he described, it was with the living colours of a master of the art. When he came to the application of his discourse, his voice would soften down into tones of inexpressible sweetness and power. It was here that he generally became most impassioned. Some of his appeals to perishing sinners, I well remember, were characterized by a solemnity and tenderness, a pathos and power, which I never heard surpassed. His preaching was not uniformly of this order. He depended much on careful preparation; and the state of his health often imposed restraint upon both his preparation and delivery. At times he would speak under a constant fear of an over-exercise of his lungs. But when in his best health, and sometimes when not, but when carried away with his subject, he would rise to a display of pulpit power of a very high order.

Such are my recollections of this departed brother, and I may add that the most discriminating of the few yet surviving of his ministerial acquaintances, received and still retain substantially the same impressions of his character as a Man, and as a Preacher, as these which I have now recorded.

I am yours very truly,
DAVID R. KERR.

FROM THE REV. H. CONNELLY.

NEWBURGH, June 20, 1862.

My dear Sir: I had seen Moses Kerr as far back as 1822, or '23, while I was a member of College, but I cannot say that I was acquainted with him till we became fellow-students in the Theological Seminary. There, during two sessions,—that is, from 1827 to 1829, I was in the habit of frequent intercourse with him; and though, after we left the Seminary, our intercourse was comparatively rare, yet I met him occasionally till near the close of life. In stature I think he must have been fully six feet. His frame was rather large and muscular, though he had, by no means, an exuberance of flesh. His countenance was expressive of gravity and sound judgment rather than of any startling or brilliant mental qualities; and herein I think the countenance was a true index to the character. He could, however, sometimes be a little impulsive, and in one instance I remember this occurred in a case that occasioned us some amusement. He had written a sermon for an exercise on a text that had previously been assigned to him, which, for some reason, he did not particularly fancy; and he had to deliver it, standing in a very narrow place, usually occupied by the chief singer. It so happened that both his father, who was Professor, and his fellow-students, criticised his sermon with more than ordinary freedom. Being rather annoyed by the criticisms, he replied that he did not see how any body could write a good sermon from such a text as that, or deliver a sermon well in such a place as that. His mind, though not rapid in its operations, possessed, I think, more than ordinary strength; and it had been trained by a course of vigorous application. He was decided in his opinions, and resolute in his purposes; and never relinquished an object to which his attention was once directed, but for what he deemed the most satisfactory reasons. I do not think that he was remarkably free in his ordinary intercourse with society, and yet his friends always found him sociable, and I believe sufficiently confiding. As a Preacher, he aimed rather to enlighten men's minds, and reach their consciences and hearts, than to make a powerful impression that should immediately pass away. His manner in the pulpit was simple and natural, attended with but little gesture, though not wanting in animation. His voice was uncommonly clear, and sufficiently loud to fill a large church without effort. His preaching was, I think, very acceptable and well fitted to be useful. His general character inspired respect and confidence.

Very truly yours,
H. CONNELLY.

ALPHABETICAL INDEX.

NAMES OF THE SUBJECTS.

	PAGE.		PAGE.
Annan, Robert	11	Kerr, Moses	166
Buchanan, George	138	Lind, John	129
Clark, Thomas, M.D.	18	Mairs, George	52
Claybaugh, Joseph, D.D	156	Mason, John, D.D	4
		McAuley, William	78
Dick, Mungo	126	McJimsey, John M., D.D	82
Dinwiddie, James Lemonte, D.D	154		
Dobbin, Alexander	27	Oliver, Andrew	47
Duncan, John Mason, D.D	145		
Dunlap, John	36	Porter, Alexander	93
		Proudfit, Alexander, D.D	67
Forrest, Robert	114	Proudfit, James	1
Galloway, James	141	Riddell, John, D.D	57
Gray, James, D.D	94		
Grier, Isaac, D.D	110	Scrimgeour, James	105
		Steele, John	102
Hemphill, John, D.D	62	Stewart, George	135
Henderson, Matthew, Jr	31		
		Wynkoop, Richard	158
Kerr, Joseph, D.D	117		
Kerr, Joseph Reynolds	161	Young, John	41

NAMES OF THOSE WHO HAVE CONTRIBUTED ORIGINAL LETTERS.

	PAGE.		PAGE.
Bethune, Mrs. Joanna	10	Harper, R. D., D.D	156
Beveridge, Thomas, D.D	24	Hemphill, Rev. W. R	62
Boyce, Rev. James	110		
Bullions, Peter, D.D	54	Junkin, George, D.D	141
Burtis, Arthur, D.D	47		
		Kent, William, LL.D	83
Claybaugh, Joseph, D.D	102, 125, 165	Kerr, David R., D.D	166
Connelly, Rev. Henry,	35, 61, 112, 126, 169	Krebs, John M., D.D	134
		Macdill, David, D.D	66, 123
Dales, John B., D.D	4, 18	Mathews, James M.., D.D	17, 30, 100
Duncan, John M., D.D	97		131, 135
		McCarroll, Joseph, D.D	133
Elliott, David, D.D	184	McJimsey, John M., D.D	15, 27, 43
		McLaren, Malcolm N., D.D	89
Forsyth, John, D.D	78, 106, 116	McLean, C. G., D.D	94, 147
		Morrison, John H., D.D	89
Galloway, Rev. John M	138		
Gordon, Rev. Peter	55	Oliver, Andrew, Esq	50
Gosman, John, D.D	40, 72		
Grier, James, D.D	57	Pressly, John T., D.D	93
		Prestley, James, D.D	117, 101
Halley, Ebenezer, D.D	74	Proudfit, Robert, D.D	87, 115

ALPHABETICAL INDEX.

	PAGE.		PAGE.
Smith, Joseph T., D.D.	154	Van Vechten, Jacob, D.D.	144, 149
Sprole, William J., D.D.	150		
Sutphin, Jacob, Esq.	50	Wallace, Rev. A G.	81
Swift, Elisha P., D.D.	124	Weisel, Hon. David	159
		Wells, J. D., D.D	39
Thompson, James, Esq.	51		
		Young, John C., D.D.	41

NAMES INCIDENTALLY INTRODUCED IN THE TEXT OR THE NOTES.

	PAGE.		PAGE.
Annan, John Ebenezer	14, 15	Mairs, James	54
Blackstock, William	111	McCarroll, Joseph, D.D	85, 86
Boyce, John	67	Moncrieff, Alexander	1
Buchanan, John Jenkin	139	Proudfit, David	126
Cuthbertson, John	7	Smith, John	83
Fullerton, Matthew Lind	135	Young, John Clarke, D.D.	44, 45, 46
Lind, Matthew	129, 130		

REFORMED PRESBYTERIAN.

PREFATORY NOTE.

In commemorating the prominent ministers of the Reformed Presbyterian Church, I deem it a special favour that I have been able to secure, in respect to each of them, the original testimony of some living person or persons, every way competent to judge of the character. Two venerable men, the Rev. Drs. McMaster and Wylie, are here as both writers and subjects; and Dr. Black, who is also here commemorated, has paid his tribute to the memory of a brother of another communion. The Rev. Samuel Wylie and the Rev. Gavin McMillan, of the West, have both placed me under great obligations by their very satisfactory compliance with my numerous requests —the latter especially by the frequent exertions he has made in my behalf, in a state of health which might have fully excused him from attempting any thing. From the Rev. Dr. E. D. MacMaster, who, though connected with another denomination, had his birth and education in this, and is familiar with the details of its history,—I I have received essential aid at various points. The Rev. Dr. McLeod, of New York, whose stores of minute and valuable information in respect to his Church seem wellnigh inexhaustible, has never grown weary—at least has given me no evidence of it—of answering my inquiries. The Rev. Dr. T. W. J. Wylie and the Rev. S. O. Wylie, of Philadelphia, the Rev. Dr. Sproull, of Allegheny, the Rev. David Scott, of Rochester, and the Rev. Dr. Forsyth whose services I have so often had occasion to acknowledge, have all lent their cheerful and effective aid to the promotion of my enterprise. Notwithstanding the original Body is now divided into two Bodies, I beg here to tender my acknowledgments to the members of both indiscriminately for the valuable service they have respectively rendered me. W. B. S.

ALBANY, 15th December, 1863.

HISTORICAL INTRODUCTION.*

The "Revolution Settlement," by which, in 1688–'89, the Presbyterian Church was again recognized as the Established Church of Scotland, was so unsatisfactory to some of those who had just come out of the fires of persecution that they declined to accede to it. Being without a ministry, their organization, as a distinct branch of the Church, was, for several years, necessarily imperfect. In 1706 they were joined by the Rev. John McMillan, and in 1740 by the Rev. Thomas Nairn, by whom the first Presbytery, known as *the Reformed Presbytery*, was formed, on the 1st of August, 1743.

The first minister sent to America by the Reformed Presbytery of Scotland was the Rev. John Cuthbertson, who arrived in this country in 1752. For more than twenty years he laboured alone among the widely scattered Societies of Reformed Presbyterians; but in 1774 he was joined by the Rev. Messrs. Mathew Lind and Alexander Dobbin, and thus the way was opened for the constitution, in the same year, of a Reformed Presbytery in America.

In the War that gave us our Independence the Reformed Presbytery felt a deep interest and took an active part; being, both in principle and in feeling, decided opponents of the British Government. Our own form of Government, which was the grand result of the Revolutionary conflict, met their hearty approval.

As the Reformed Presbytery was merged in the Associate Reformed Synod in 1782, the few and widely scattered Societies of Reformed Presbyterians who declined to enter into the union, by which this new Body was formed, were left without any regular Gospel ministrations. Thus they continued till 1789, when the Rev. James Reid* was sent to

---

* MS. from Rev. Dr. Forsyth.—Reformation Principles.—Ref. Pres. Ch. by Dr. McLeod, in Rapp's Hist. Denom.

† JAMES REID was born in the Parish of Shotts, August 12, 1750. He was licensed to preach at Foulyet, in the Parish of Bothwell, April 27, 1780, being then in his thirtieth year, and was appointed to preach his first sermon at Edinburgh, on the 7th of May following. After preaching in different places for about three years, he received a call from the Reformed Presbyterian Church in the Counties of Wigtown and Kirkcudbright; and was ordained at Lead Mines, in the Parish of Monigaff, on the 10th of July, 1783. He was married on the 26th of December, 1786, to Helen, daughter of James Bland, of Calside, Parish of Anwoth. When the mission to America was proposed to him, though the acceptance of it involved many personal sacrifices, he could not doubt that it was his duty to accept it. He left Scotland for America in August, 1789, and reached Scotland, on his return, in July, 1790. He resumed his labours with his accustomed diligence,

them as a missionary from the Reformed Presbytery of Scotland; though, after a few months, during which he peformed much acceptable service, he returned to his native land. In 1791 the Rev. Mr. McGarragh was ordained by the Reformed Presbytery of Ireland for the Church in America, and the same year he landed in South Carolina. He was followed by the Rev. Mr. King in 1792, and by the Rev. James McKinney in 1793. These gentlemen, as a Committee of the Reformed Presbytery of Scotland, were empowered to manage judicially the concerns of the church in America; which they continued to do until the constitution of "The Reformed Presbytery of the United States of North America," in the city of Philadelphia, in the spring of 1798. But as the territory covered by the Presbytery was very wide, the members were subdivided into three standing committees, each of them being invested, to a certain extent, with Presbyterial powers.

Soon after the organization of the Presbytery, Messrs. Wiley, Black, McLeod and Donnelly were licensed to preach the Gospel, and they became very efficient missionaries in different parts of the United States. On the 24th of May, 1809, all the ministers of the Reformed Presbyterian Church in America being convened at Philadelphia, with Ruling Elders from the respective Sessions, they agreed to constitute themselves into a Synod. Whereupon, the Rev. William Gibson, the senior member, did, as Moderator, constitute the Synod under the name,—"The Synod of the Reformed Presbyterian Church in America." All the Acts of the Reformed Presbytery were ratified and adopted; and the three Committees were erected into Presbyteries under the inspection of Synod, and to be known as the Northern, Middle and Southern Presbyteries. In 1823 the Constitution of the Supreme Judicatory was re-modelled by an Act which ordained that a General Synod of the Reformed Presbyterian Church, to meet biennially, be formed by delegations from the several Presbyteries. At this time there were 24 Ministers, 2 Licentiates, and about 40 Congregations, connected with the Body. The Doctrines, Discipline and Modes of Worship of the Reformed Presbyterian Church are, in the main, identical with those of the Associate and Associate Reformed Bodies.

though, after a few years, his field was somewhat reduced by a separate congregation being formed within its limits. About the year 1825, in consequence of a decision of the Reformed Presbyterian Church, which Mr. Reid regarded as involving a departure from its former Testimonies, he judged it his duty to withdraw, and actually did withdraw, from the communion of the Synod, and maintained his separate standing, in connection with a few others, till his death. In the spring of 1828 he removed from Newton Stewart, which had been the place of his residence, to Glasgow, where he afterwards lived with his daughter, Mrs. Stuart. He continued, for some time, to preach once on the Sabbath to such as adhered to his views of the Testimony of the Church; but even this came soon to over-task his strength. He died, at length, of a sudden and severe illness, on the 4th of November, 1837, in the eighty-seventh year of his age. He was distinguished for great gravity, kindliness of manner, and regularity in all his movements. He published The Lives of the Westminster Divines, in two volumes; and a Sermon on the Divinity of Jesus Christ.

to be the Reformed Presbyterian Church, the Supreme Judicatory being known in the one case, as the General Synod of the Reformed Presbyterian Church; in the other, as the Synod of the Reformed Presbyterian Church. The division still exists, though a few years ago, an effort for re-union was attempted, but without success.

Within the General Synod of the Reformed Presbyterian Church are 61 ministers; 1 Theological Seminary, at Philadelphia; a Board of Domestic Missions, a Board of Foreign Missions, and a Board of Education. Within the Synod of the Reformed Presbyterian Church are 70 ministers; 1 Theological Seminary at Allegheny, Pa.; a Board of Domestic Missions, and a Board of Foreign Missions.

In the arrangement of the subjects of this volume, I have found it most convenient to reckon them all as Reformed Presbyterians, placing them in chronological order, without recognizing the different classes into which they are divided. It may be proper, however, to state, here, the respective positions which they have severally held. Of those who had passed away before the division took place are James McKinney, Campbell Madden, and John Reily. Of the members of the General Synod of the Reformed Presbyterian Church are Thomas Donnelly, Alexander McLeod, Samuel J. Wylie, Gilbert McMaster, John Kell, and John Black. Of the members of the Synod of the Reformed Presbyterian Church are William Gibson, James R. Willson, Robert Wallace, John Cannon, Robert Gibson, James Blackwood, Moses Roney, Hugh Walkinshaw, and John McKinley.

CHRONOLOGICAL INDEX.

[On the left hand of the page are the names of those who form the subjects of the work—the figures immediately preceding denote the period, as nearly as can be ascertained, when each began his ministry. On the right hand are the names of those who have rendered their testimony or their opinion in regard to the several characters.]

	SUBJECTS.	WRITERS.	PAGE.
1798.	James McKinney	Gilbert McMaster, D.D. / Samuel B. Wylie, D.D.	1
1797.	William Gibson	Rev. William Sloane	6
1799.	Alexander McLeod, D.D.	Gilbert McMaster, D.D. / Samuel B. Wylie, D.D. / John Black, D.D. / Samuel Miller, D.D.	9
1799.	Thomas Donnelly	Rev. Gavin McMillan	25
1799.	John Black, D.D.	John N. McLeod, D.D.	28
1799.	Samuel Brown Wylie, D.D.	Samuel B. How, D.D. / Hon. William B. Reed / John Forsyth, D.D.	34
1807.	James Renwick Willson, D.D.	James M. Willson, D.D. / John Forsyth, D.D.	39
1807.	Gilbert McMaster, D.D.	Erasmus D. MacMaster, D.D. / T. W. J. Wylie, D.D. / William James, D.D. / James C. Moffat, D.D.	46
1809.	John Reily	Rev. Samuel Wylie	60
1809.	John Kell	Rev. Gavin McMillan / Rev. Samuel Wylie	62
1814.	Robert Wallace	Thomas Sproull, D.D.	66
1815.	John Cannon	Thomas Sproull, D.D.	68
1818.	Robert Gibson	Rev. David Scott / Thomas Houston, D.D.	71
1820.	Campbell Madden	Hugh McMillan, D.D.	75
1824.	James Blackwood	Thomas Sproull, D.D.	77
1829.	Moses Roney	Rev. Samuel O. Wylie	79
1832.	Hugh Walkinshaw	Thomas Sproull, D.D. / Rev. R. Hutcheson	83
1835.	John McKinley	Hon. James Pollock, LL.D. / T. W. J. Wylie, D.D.	87

JAMES McKINNEY.*
1793—1804.

JAMES McKINNEY, a son of Robert and Elizabeth (McIntyre) McKinney, was born in Cookstown, County of Tyrone, Ireland, in the year 1759. After pursuing his preparatory studies in Ireland, he entered Glasgow College, where he took a regular course, and remained there several years after, engaged in the study both of Theology and of Medicine. In due time he was licensed to preach in the Reformed Presbyterian Church in his native country, and was ordained, and constituted Pastor of a Congregation at Kirkhills, in the County of Antrim. Shortly after his settlement—about the year 1781—he was married to Mary, daughter of John and Jenny (Trowbridge) Mitchell, of the County of Derry, a lady of fine talents and accomplishments, and of excellent character.

In 1793 he migrated to the United States, leaving his family in Ireland until he should obtain a settlement here and be ready to receive them. The first four years after his arrival he spent in the capacity of a Missionary, travelling from New York to Carolina, and preaching wherever an opportunity presented. Mrs. McKinney, with her five children, arrived in 1797, and the year immediately succeeding they spent in Philadelphia, and Mr. McKinney had, at one time, expected to remain there; but, being obliged to leave temporarily on account of the Yellow Fever, he concluded to come North, and, shortly after, became the Pastor of a Reformed Presbyterian Church in Galway and Duanesburgh, N. Y., which had been gathered by himself. Here he remained until May, 1804, when he accepted a call from a church of the same denomination in Chester County, S. C. He was installed, in due time, as Pastor of that Church, though his ministry there was of very brief continuance. He died, after an illness of a day or two, on the 10th of September, 1804.

Mr. McKinney had not removed his family to Carolina previous to his death, so that their only residence has been in the State of New York. He had eight children in all, three sons and five daughters. Mrs. McKinney died on the 30th of April, 1847.

Shortly after his arrival in this country, Mr. McKinney published a long and very elaborate Sermon, entitled "Rights of God," which passed to a second edition in 1833.

FROM THE REV. GILBERT McMASTERS, D.D.

OXFORD, O., December 6, 1848.

Rev. and dear Sir: If the statements which I am now about to record, concerning a man whose name ought not to be forgotten, can, in any degree, promote the enlightened, liberal, and, permit me to add, pious, aim of your proposed work, I shall feel happy in having had it in my power to comply with your request. I am so imperfectly acquainted with the facts necessary to form a narrative of his life, that I must ask you to seek them from some other source; and will only attempt to give you an idea of some of his leading characteristics.

As a friend of liberty, civil and religious, Mr. McKinney saw and felt, with disapprobation, the oppression of his native land; and, in reference to the

* Communications from his family.

claims of the Prelacy, and the Erastian invasion of Zion's rights by the British Crown, in usurping a Headship over the Church, he, as an ardent advocate of her spiritual independence of all secular power, could not be an indifferent or a silent spectator. In virtue of that assumed Headship, the Throne held the power of establishing, tolerating, oppressing, or persecuting religion, according as a temporizing policy might dictate. Mr. McKinney and his brethren, fearlessly and without compromise, asserted the exclusive Headship of Christ over his own House. He was known, too, to have sympathized with the United States in the contest for their Independence; and, in common with the friends of rational freedom every where, he looked with favour on the early movements of the French in 1789. Under these circumstances, as a lover of liberty, a man of education, commanding talents, large public spirit, impressive and persuasive eloquence, great fearlessness and incorruptible integrity, he was, to the powers that then ruled his country, an object of jealousy. It is true he committed no treasonable act; and while he abhorred the measures that goaded so many of the best men of the country,—men not inferior in love of country to the purest patriots of any land,—to unite in order to break the British yoke, yet he did not identify himself with the Society of United Irishmen. His views were more extensive than theirs, and his principles of higher bearing. But orderly as his views and principles were, they still furnished a pretext for a prosecution, which might, as in the case of some of his brethren, have consigned him to the prison house for years, or even to the grave. From the arrest of the minions of oppression he narrowly escaped.

On his arrival in the United States, he was cordially received, not only by the ministers and people of his own denomination, but by the friends of liberty and oppressed humanity generally. For the employment of his talents and energies our country furnished a wide and appropriate field; and it was impossible that, with such a spirit as he possessed, he should stand by with folded hands. Inquisitive, adventurous, active and zealous in the exercise of his ministry, he repeatedly (not by railroads and steamers, as now) made laborious and dangerous journeys from the place of his residence in the State of New York, to the Canadian borders on the North, and to the Carolinas on the then nearly extreme South of the Union.

Of the character of Mr. McKinney, as a Preacher, and of the power of his eloquence, the very large assemblies that every where attended on his ministry, and the uniform testimony of well informed and serious men, of various denominations, leave no room for doubt. Thus, of those who had attended on his ministry, you would hear one declare,—"His sermons were a continued stream of thought;"—another,—"I never can esteem any Preacher as I did Mr. McKinney;" and yet another,—a man of mind, and a scholar, and well qualified to judge in such matters, affirmed to me,—"For grandeur of thought and depth of feeling, such displays of eloquence I never expect again to hear on earth."

In his discourses, it is understood that, while he dwelt with emphasis, and to a great extent, on the claims of the Divine law on man, and on the righteousness and grace of the Redeemer, as meeting those claims, together with their bearing on the social interests of man, he was peculiar in the range of his views of the administrations of Divine Providence; and, in the light of revealed truth, of the relation of those dispensations both to the character and plans of God and to the concerns of the inner man. By tried and experienced Christians his ministry was highly appreciated. These considerations induce me to suspect the correctness of the suggestion of some, that there was less spirituality in his ministrations than in those of some other distinguished men. Is there not some reason to apprehend the existence of mistake on this subject? Which are the more spiritual administrations,—those which are confined to a few, say important, points of the Gospel scheme, giving prominence to the several articles of this little circle, and the agency of the Spirit of God by them, in the production of their appropriate effects; or those in which are brought to view the entire system of salvation, in the fulness of its parts; its origin, its arrangements, its harmony and results, as these are revealed in the oracles of God? In both classes, the Redeemer, the Spirit, and the means of grace, are brought into view; but in the one partially—some portions of the Redeemer's character remain unseen; a part only of the means and instrumentalities by which the Spirit goes forth and acts appear; and of course his developments are imperfect. In the other, the Mediatorial character of Jesus shines in full-orbed splendour; the Law, the Gospel, the Ordinances, the Providences, the revealed character of God, and the agencies He appoints, and over which the Holy Ghost presides, and by which He puts forth his energies, producing his blessed effects on the whole man, are brought to light. Which of these forms of administration is the more spiritual, it seems to me is not difficult to perceive.

His moral courage and constitutional intrepidity have often been noticed. A gentleman who had been intimate with him once remarked to me,—"He is like Leviathan, made without fear." Whilst strong in his passions, as in his mental powers, he was practically the friend of order. This was especially manifest in judicial proceedings. If, at any time, advised of a trespass on decorum, by the Presiding Officer, though a junior brother, his reply would be,—"You are right; I am a friend of good order, and bow to your authority." With strangers he was distant; and hence was sometimes thought to be proud and stern. Such, however, he really was not.

He lived in revolutionary times. Of the tyrannical establishments of Europe his judgment disapproved, and with them his heart was dissatisfied. Revolutions in States he considered as God's decreed means of removing the rubbish of the falling or fallen fabric, in order to the rearing of a better edifice. With him the desire of revolution was not the effect of a restless spirit, or the mere love of change. In the preface to a publication of his, at the close of the last century, where are impressed some of the strong characteristics of his powerful mind, he remarks,—"Were it not for the persuasion I entertain that Christianity will purify and support the rights of man, fond as I am of liberty, I do not believe I would give a shilling to bring about a revolution in any nation upon earth." The robbers of the earth he abhorred, and the shabby train of infidel reformers he loathed.

One feature of his ministerial character may perhaps be inferred from the plan of a work which he proposed to publish, the introductory portion of which only he lived to complete. The proposal was a discussion of the Rights of God, the Rights of Christ as Mediator, the Rights of the Church, and the Rights of Humanity in general. Taking the part published as a specimen of the whole, the reader will regret the failure of the purpose. The work would have been worthy of the man;—not only sound in matter, but deep in thought and impressive in style. For two sentiments of an incidental character, and not necessarily belonging to his subject, party zeal assailed him at the time of the publication of the part referred to, with what would now be considered undue acrimony. In vindicating the ways of God, he adverts to the mysterious arrangement that permitted the existence of evil in the dominions of the Creator; and, alluding to the sufferings of more sensitive existences, after various deeply interesting observations, he remarks,—"Nay, though we are far enough from adopting the doctrine of transmigration in its full extent, yet, as we have no reason to believe the annihilation of any creature that has once existed, it is not unreasonable to suppose that many of these animals, after having regularly passed through the lower orders of existence, shall pass to Heaven in the bodies of the saints, and shine in the brightest orbs of intellectual bliss without end." It is offered only as an incidental conjecture, and, however it may be regarded as fanciful, it seems not to be, as some were disposed to represent it, a fatal heresy. Others had offered it without blame. Professor Brown, of Haddington, a sound and very sober divine, in his system of Divinity, (p. 111,) presents the same idea. And again, Mr. McKinney, illustrating the evidence of the Divine goodness, as seen in the felicities of the empire of God, adds,—" Perhaps, on the great map of being, the region of misery will scarcely form a perceptible point, when compared with those on which an unfading spring of everlasting glory shall pour forth its balmy sweets with unbounded profusion."—p. 28. Such conjectures, whether well or ill founded, in a Presbyterian Calvinist of the oldest school, indicate any thing rather than a cold and an unfeeling heart.

In the place of his residence, nearly sixty years since, the help needed in the labours of the field could not always, even for wages, be obtained. In such cases Mr. McKinney did not withhold his own hand. In his forest clearing, amidst the half burnt logs, in company with his hired man, he might be seen putting forth the strength of his muscular frame at the heaviest end of the log. But near by were the implements of the scholar and the man of reflection,—the paper, the ink-stand and the pen. His table was the stump of the tree that had lately been felled by the axe in his manly hand; and, while his man, amid their common toils, was taking breath, McKinney was at his unpolished stand making a record of his thoughts,—those deep meditations on the Rights of God and Christ, of the Church and of Humanity in general, on the mysteries of the Divine plans, providence and grace, that he might "justify the ways of God to men." Thus, in the charcoaled field, and with his bodily frame blackened with its dust, the soul of this great man was roaming abroad among the works of the Divinity,—his thoughts winging their way to Heaven,—the whole man in communion with God.

James McKinney lived in troublous times, underwent great labours, suffered great ills, was exposed to many temptations, and strange would it be, indeed, had he been exempted from all the frailties of our frail humanity. For this he put in no claims himself. He knew the infirmities of his nature; for, strong as this great man was, he had his infirmities. In the confidential hours of unreserved friendship, he would confess them. Thus he has said,—" Tenfold the amount of grace that would be adequate to make a Christian of another man, constituted as men generally are, would be requisite to sanctify me."

Before concluding, I may be permitted to make an extract from a respectable Foreign Journal,—a Journal of his native land, in which a sketch of his character is found. It is as follows:—

"The character of James McKinney never was exceeded in the boldness of its outline and in the distinctness and prominency of its features. His eloquence was in perfect character. His heart, possessed with the love of the truth as it is in Jesus, was ever set upon its recommendation and enforcement; and it was when descanting upon the grand Gospel theme of a crucified Saviour or asserting the Church's rights; or when, with well sustained pathos, he mourned the wrongs of Zion, that his mind assumed a gigantic attitude, and put forth its wonderful energies. His diction was clear, copious, strong, and full of pertinent and often brilliant figures. He has frequently, in his public discourses, caught a flame from the working of his judgment, imagination and feelings; and then his conceptions, conveyed in simple, energetic language, or in bright imagery, and in bold and apt allusions, produced an astonishing effect. In America, whose republican institutions he had long loved, the land of enterprise and freedom, was the field which just suited the genius of McKinney; there his powers had full scope for development and exercise," &c. "An eminent Trans-Atlantic divine (American) has been heard to say that he had met with many considerable, and some great, men, but not one equal to James McKinney."

His own brethren who knew him well, say;—

"He possessed an intrepidity of character that could not be seduced by friendship or overawed by opposition. An extensive acquaintance with men and with books furnished his mind with various and useful knowledge; and his inventive powers never left him at a loss for arguments to defend the system to which he was piously attached. The sublimity of his conceptions, the accuracy of his judgment, the fervour of his devotion, and the vehemency of his eloquence, qualified him to rouse into the most active exertions for the good of Zion those lonely societies" of his Church, which he visited and addressed.*

After making all due abatement from these representations for the partiality of friendship, enough will remain in them to prove the subject of these notices no ordinary man. But these testimonies stand not alone—the universal voice of intelligent and good men in his native land, and in our own country, of every denomination, who had access to his ministry, with one consent, sustained them as correct. In the exercise of a living faith he rode out the storms of time, and amidst the pains of dissolution, with the place of final rest in view, his last words were,—" Now is the time to have the anchor cast within the vail."

I never heard him preach but three times, and I was then scarcely old enough to form an intelligent estimate of his merits in the pulpit. And in one instance only had I the privilege of social intercourse with him. That interview was to me very pleasant, giving no indication, on his part, of the stern and distant manner that was sometimes attributed to him. His communications were such as became the Scholar and the Christian Gentleman of experience, to make to a youth engaged in his course of study. His remarks I still remember. But little, at that day, did either of us suppose that I should be his immediate successor in his then pastoral charge. It is proper to add that the testimony of that people, as to the talents and character of their late Pastor, was in accordance with that of the public; and I think I may say with confidence that those friends who knew him best esteemed him most.

With affectionate respect,
I am very truly yours,
GILBERT McMASTER.

FROM THE REV. SAMUEL B. WYLIE, D.D.

BELLEVUE, (near Philadelphia,) January 11, 1849.

Rev. and dear Sir: I most cordially comply with your request for my reminiscences of the Rev. James McKinney; and you will see from the estimate that I form of his character that I think him well worthy of a place in your forthcoming work.

I knew him in Ireland, the country of his birth. He was a most ardent Patriot and Republican, having no sympathy with British domination and Irish vassalage. He thought correctly as an enlightened patriot, and spoke undauntedly as he thought. He became, of course, obnoxious to the tools of Government, and left his native land for a country whose liberty he appreciated and dearly loved. Some years after his arrival here, I had the honour of being associated with him in a mission to the South and West, to organize congregations and abolish slaveholding among any of our members who practised it. In these duties we succeeded so far as to have no slaveholder a member of our communion. I had, therefore, a pretty fair opportunity of knowing Mr. McKinney. He was my friend, my brother and my companion on a journey of more than five thousand miles.

Mr. McKinney possessed a strong and vigorous mind, and I should say that his talents were of the highest order. He was naturally eloquent, but his

---

* Brief Historical View, pp. 114, 115.

eloquence was independent of technical rules or artificial erudition. It was the spontaneous flow of a cultivated intellect. It proceeded from a full knowledge of his subject, and an ardent desire to produce a beneficial effect on his hearers. His Sermon on the "Rights of God" gives a good specimen of his powers. His bearing was manly, his language bold and nervous,—its effect powerful and often electric. His doctrinal discussions were lucid, and his arguments weighty and convincing. In private discussion, however, if the first thunderbolt did not completely discomfit his antagonist, he might be vanquished by a greatly inferior opponent, who had prepared himself on the minutiæ of the subject, to which Mr. McKinney had not seen cause to attend. I witnessed this myself in several instances. He had seized the grand cardinal points; but it required time and deliberation to attend to and digest all minor ramifications.

As a Pulpit Orator he may be said to have been in a high degree peculiar. His eloquence was his own. He had few competitors, and perhaps still fewer superiors. He was constitutionally a man of strong passions, and these were developed (though this is to be taken not *in malam partem*) in his public character.

I have written this letter amidst the infirmities of age, having now reached my seventy-sixth year; but it has nevertheless given me pleasure to bear my testimony to the ability and worth of an ancient and honoured friend.

Believe me, My dear Sir,
Yours in our common Master,
S. B. WYLIE.

WILLIAM GIBSON.*
1797—1838.

WILLIAM GIBSON, a son of Robert and Susanna (McWhirr) Gibson, was born near Knockbracken, County of Down, Ireland, in 1753. His parents were members of the Presbyterian Church in connection with the Synod of Ulster. He, however, on arriving at early manhood, connected himself with the Reformed Presbyterian Church, the views of that Body appearing to him, in some respects, more scriptural than those of the denomination in which he had been trained. His early education was in Ireland, but he completed his classical course at Glasgow College. He was licensed to preach by the Reformed Presbytery of Ireland in 1781, and soon after was constituted Pastor of the United Congregations of Kellswater and Kallybacky. These congregations increased much under his ministry.

He bore a solemn and earnest testimony against what he believed to be the corruptions of the various churches in upholding the Government of the British Empire; and, more than that, he is said to have encouraged the private associations of United Irishmen, which aimed at nothing less than the independence of Ireland. In the failure of the plan, he arrayed against himself the prejudices and the power of the Government, and if he had not fled from the country, it is supposed that his life would have been sacrificed. He came to the United States, landing at Philadelphia, in 1797, in company with two Reformed Presbyterian

---

*Presbyterian Almanac, 1862.—MS. from Rev. W. Sloane.

students of Theology, who had been educated in Glasgow College. There had already been formed, by the Rev. James McKinney, Societies of Reformed Presbyterians, both in Philadelphia and New York; and these Mr. Gibson organized into congregations by ordaining Ruling Elders. Until this time, all ecclesiastical business of the Reformed Presbyterian Church had been transacted by a Committee, subject to a British Judicatory. Mr. Gibson and Mr. McKinney, with Ruling Elders, constituted the Reformed Presbytery in North America, in Philadelphia, in the spring of 1778. Mr. Gibson preached frequently in the vacancies at Philadelphia, New York, Coldenham, and also in Vermont, and his labours were generally acceptable, and were accompanied with manifest tokens of the Divine blessing.

In Ryegate, Vt., a Society of Reformed Presbyterians had been in existence several years. A few families of Covenanters had settled there shortly after the Revolution, and their numbers had so far increased that they were at length organized into a congregation. Mr. Gibson accepted a call from them, and was installed as their Pastor in 1799, between two and three years after his arrival in America. The congregation grew and prospered under his ministry, while other congregations which were vacant, and some of them quite distant, had the benefit of his occasional labours. When the Synod was constituted in Philadelphia, in May 1809, eleven years after the constitution of the Presbytery, Mr. Gibson. as the senior Minister, was called to preside.

Mr. Gibson remained at Ryegate till 1817, when he accepted a call from the Congregation of Cannonsburg, Pa. This was quite an extensive field, embracing several places of preaching, and some of them quite distant from each other. Here he remained in active service nearly thirteen years, until the infirmities of age disqualified him for the occupancy of so wide a field. His pastoral relation to this congregation was therefore now dissolved; whereupon he returned to the East, and, for more than two years, preached as a stated supply to a Congregation in Patterson, N. J.

From the meeting of the Subordinate Synod in May, 1834, until about a year before the death of his son, the late Rev. Robert Gibson, he spent nearly his whole time in Philadelphia. After the son became disabled for labour, by the disease which finally terminated his life, the father, for more than a year, supplied his pulpit, usually preaching twice every Sabbath. In the spring of 1838 he administered the Lord's Supper in the same congregation, being then in his eighty-fifth year. From that time his health rapidly declined, though he still continued to preach on the Sabbath till about midsummer, when his infirmities became so great that he could no longer venture into the pulpit. He was, however, habitually sustained during the whole period of his decline, and spent much of his time in private devotional exercises. The sessions of the General Synod were held in New York while he was upon his death-bed; and, on two different occasions, a delegation from the Synod waited upon him to tender to him the assurance of the sympathy and prayers of his brethren. He met their kind salutations with the warmest gratitude, expressing, at the same time, his deep interest in the prosperity of the Church, and especially of their own denomination. He died in New York, in great peace, on the 15th of October, 1838, in the eighty-sixth year of his age. Soon after his settlement in Ballymore, Mr. Gibson was married to Rebecca Mitchell, of Derry County, Ireland, by whom he had nine children,— five sons and four daughters. Mrs. Gibson died in Philadelphia in 1835.

During his residence in Vermont Mr. Gibson published a Discourse of which the following is the title: "The substance of a Sermon preached at Barnet, designed to expose some Dangerous Errors contained in a Sermon lately preached and published in this neighbourhood. When the enemy shall come in like a flood," &c. He subsequently published another pamphlet, in the form of a Dialogue, on the same subject.

FROM THE REV. WILLIAM SLOANE.

WARRISTON, ILL., October 22, 1863.

Reverend Sir: The Rev. William Gibson, whose leading characteristics you ask me to describe to you, was ordained over a congregation in the County of Antrim, Ireland, the same year in which I was born; and my father was among those who subscribed his call. After I entered the ministry I preached nine years to what had once been a part of his congregation. The first time I saw him in this country was at a meeting of Presbytery in New York, in the year 1827, when age had rendered his appearance venerable. When I was in Philadelphia, in 1835, I saw an old gentleman very much bowed with age, walking in the street, and the thought instantly occurred to me,—"There go the remains of a great Man." I met the same man, shortly after, at the house of a common friend, and found it was Mr. Gibson.

He was a tall, good looking man, and I distinctly remember, when I was not more than ten years old, hearing a gentleman, (not of our persuasion,) after listening to one of his sermons, speak to my father of the fine appearance his minister made in the pulpit. His mind was of the solid rather than the brilliant cast, and he liked arguments better than metaphors. He was reputed a good scholar and a well-read theologian; and in general conversation he evinced a good degree of intelligence. He was naturally benevolent in his disposition—his hand opened readily as well in dispensing charities to the needy as in extending a generous hospitality to both friends and strangers. He was warm and steady in his friendships, and void of every thing like dissimulation. He seems to have been of a sanguine temperament; and it was his inculcating and defending Republican principles, with so much vigour and earnestness, that finally led him to quit his native country, and seek a home on this side the ocean.

I remember two or three anecdotes concerning him, which, perhaps, may give you some idea of his peculiar turn of mind. In the early part of his ministry he had been preaching against Popery—a Romanist who had heard him manifested his violent dislike to his discourse, by going to his lodging on Monday morning, before he was yet up, and challenging him to a boxing match. When Mr. Gibson was informed of the challenge, he came out of his chamber with a Bible in his hand, and said to the man,—" That is my sword, and I will never fight with any other weapon;" whereupon the man's wrath cooled down, he listened to what Mr. Gibson had to say to him, and finally became a Covenanter. While he lived in Ireland, he had, at one time, a very severe attack of the jaundice; and a woman, who lived in the neighbourhood, gravely proposed to cure him by a charm. He replied, "I am ill of the jaundice, very ill; but not so ill that I will go to the devil for a cure." Having differed with one of his hearers in Vermont, and parted with him in a state of considerable excitement, as he saw the sun near setting, he said to his wife,—" I must go and be reconciled to Mr. W." He did go, and the reconciliation was effected. The first time he preached in Vermont was in 1799, in warm political times, and the majority of his congregation were Federalists. Being a cordial hater of the British Government, he pleaded the cause of Democracy with so much fervour that the people said he was no minister, but an emissary of France.

I think you may rely upon the above statements as correct, as they contain nothing but what I either knew personally or received upon unquestionable authority. I am, Rev. Sir, with much respect, yours,

WILLIAM SLOANE.

ALEXANDER McLEOD, D.D.*
1799—1833.

ALEXANDER MCLEOD was born at Ardcrisinish, in the Isle of Mull, Scotland, June 12, 1774. His father was the Rev. Niel McLeod, who was connected with the Established Church of Scotland, and was Minister of the United Parishes of Kilfinichen and Kilvichewen. His mother was Margaret McLean, daughter of the Rev. Archibald McLean, who was the immediate predecessor of his son-in-law, Mr. McLeod, in the same charge. Both his parents were eminent for talents and piety. The great Dr. Johnson, in his tour through the Western Islands, was a visitor at his father's house, and, in referring to the circumstance, Johnson says,—" We were entertained by Mr. McLean," (by mistake he used the name of the lady for that of her husband,) "a minister that lives upon the coast, whose elegance of conversation and strength of judgment would make him conspicuous in places of greater celebrity."

At the age of five years, Alexander McLeod lost his father; but, even at that early period, his mind seems to have been alive to religious impressions; for when the tidings of his father's death were announced to the family, the child was upon his knees in prayer. From that time for several years the general conduct of his education devolved upon his mother, than whom perhaps no mother could have contributed more effectually to the development and right direction of his faculties. His mother, however, employed a tutor in the house, who immediately superintended his studies; and his uncommon quickness of apprehension and facility at acquiring knowledge, were indicated by the fact that he had mastered his Latin Grammar before he had completed his sixth year. He subsequently attended the parish school of Bracadale, in the Island of Skye, for three or four years, and availed himself also of the advantages furnished by other schools, with reference to particular branches, which were understood to be taught in them with unusual efficiency. He lost his mother at the age of about fifteen, when he was absent from home at school. So deeply was he affected by the tidings of her death, that, for a time, there were serious apprehensions that it would be the occasion of depriving him of his reason. As he was consecrated to the ministry in the intention of his parents, he seems, before he was six years old, to have formed a distinct purpose of carrying out their intention; and of that purpose he never lost sight, amidst all the subsequent vicissitudes which he experienced. He was always remarkable for an intrepid and adventurous spirit, and was not unfrequently confined by injuries which he received in consequence of too freely indulging it.

* MS. from his son, Rev. Dr. J. N. McLeod.

Having reached his eighteenth year, and enjoyed the advantages of an excellent education, it became necessary that he should engage in some occupation that might yield him a support; and, after having two or three places offered him, neither of which possessed many attractions, and one of them, involving some connection with the slave trade, being repulsive to all his feelings, he resolved to migrate to the United States. Accordingly, in the year 1792, he crossed the ocean, and landed in the city of New York. Shortly after his arrival he ascended the Hudson, and, in the autumn of that year, was employed as a Teacher of the Greek Language at Schenectady. He entered Union College in 1796, immediately after it was established, and was a member of its second graduating class. Here he maintained a high reputation as a student, and enjoyed a close intimacy with several men who were afterwards among the leading spirits of the day in the different professions.

It would appear, from a Diary that he kept, during his residence at Schenectady, that his mind was at this period deeply interested and exercised in spiritual things. The probability is that he had made a public profession of religion in his native country, though of this there seems to be no certain evidence. It is, however, matter of record that within nine months after his landing in the United States, and when he was in his nineteenth year, he became a communicant in the Reformed Presbyterian Church. The immediate occasion of this was a sermon which he heard at Princetown, in the neighbourhood of Schenectady, from the Rev. James McKinney, who had emigrated from Ireland to this country with a view to diffuse the principles of the "Covenanted Reformation." That denomination was then in the feebleness of its infancy; and it was certainly a striking evidence of young McLeod's great integrity and conscientiousness that he should have connected himself with a Body which was then only beginning to be recognized among the denominations of the country, when, by joining a different communion, he might have avoided many inconveniences, and commanded at once a much more extensive, and what would generally be considered more promising, field of ministerial labour.

He was licensed to preach at Coldenham, near Newburgh, by the Reformed Presbytery, the first organized in this country,—in June, 1799; and, as he graduated only the year before, he could not have had an opportunity for very extensive or mature preparation for the ministry. Dr. Wylie of Philadelphia and Dr. Black of Pittsburg received license at the same time; and an affectionate intimacy between him and them was kept up to the close of his life.

He was ordained in the year 1800; and shortly after received a call from the Congregation of Coldenham, Orange County, to become their Pastor. Among the persons who signed it were several who held property in slaves; and so strong was his repugnance, even at that early period, to slavery, that he found in the fact referred to a sufficient motive for rejecting the call. He, however, on being assured that the evil would be immediately redressed, consented to take charge of the congregation; and as this brought the subject regularly before the Presbytery, the result of their deliberations upon it was an enactment that no slave-holder should be retained in their communion. This regulation has always continued down to the present day. About a year after, he preached and published a Sermon entitled,—" Negro Slavery Unjustifiable;" in which he expressed his views on the subject with great clearness, and defended them with great power. This Discourse has passed through several editions, both in this country and in Great Britain. At a later period in life, he carried out the principles which it maintains in the efficient support which he rendered to the American Colonization Society.

He remained at Coldenham but a short time; for, in 1801, he became the Pastor of the Reformed Presbyterian Church in Chambers Street, New York. The church was in its infancy, and he was its first Pastor; but, under his able and earnest ministry, it increased rapidly both in numbers and in influence. He himself, also, soon came to be known for his remarkable powers, and took his place in a constellation of the most gifted minds which perhaps the city of New York could ever boast.

In 1809 he was honoured with the degree of Doctor of Divinity from Middlebury College.

It was not strange that Dr. McLeod's brilliant career should have rendered other denominations than his own desirous of securing his permanent services. Accordingly, in 1812, he received a call from the Reformed Dutch Church in Garden Street, of which the Rev. Dr. Mathews afterwards became Pastor; but he felt himself constrained to decline it. Shortly after this, the First Presbyterian Church, having become vacant by the removal of the Rev. Dr. Miller to Princeton, as Professor in the Theological Seminary, it was unanimously resolved, at a joint meeting of the Session and Board of Trustees, to nominate Dr. McLeod as his successor; but this procedure was arrested by an intimation from the Doctor that he could not be induced to leave his people or change his ecclesiastical relations. About the same time also he received an invitation from the Trustees of Princeton College to the Professorship of Mathematics, in connection with the office of Vice President. But this also he declined, still remaining steadfast to the determination to live and die among the people of his charge. Subsequently to this, however, he did lend an ear to a project started by the late Vice President Tompkins for the establishment of a University on Staten Island, and, had the plan taken effect, he was to have been the first President of the Institution; but the purpose was ultimately abandoned.

Dr. McLeod's health had, for several years, suffered from his excessive labours; but, in the year 1824, he had a violent inflammation of the lungs, which continued for some months, and in which it was supposed originated a disease of the heart, which finally had a fatal termination. In the hope that a voyage across the ocean, and a visit to his native land, might do something to recover his energies, he embarked at New York in February, 1830, and reached Liverpool, after a remarkably quick passage, early in the month of March. He spent the spring and summer chiefly in Scotland and Ireland, and was every where met with the greatest cordiality, and was cheered by seeing the faces of some of his near relatives and the companions of his youth, from whom he had been separated nearly forty years. Wherever he went, he awakened a deep interest by his commanding powers, by his strong religious sensibility, and especially by his earnest efforts to unite Christians, holding substantially a common faith, in a closer fellowship. He returned home in the autumn of 1830, with his health so much improved as to encourage the hope that his life might be continued for many years. It, however, soon became evident that the improvement was more in appearance than in reality; but he resumed his labours with considerable zeal, and when his friends urged him to desist, he would reply,—"I wish to die with the harness on." In the beginning of the year 1833 the congregation, which he had served with great fidelity for more than thirty years, called his own son, the Rev. (now Dr.) J. N. McLeod, to be his associate in the ministry; and, upon the consummation of this relation, in which one of the strongest desires of his heart was fulfilled, he withdrew almost entirely from all public labours. Within three months after this event he preached his last sermon, on the text,—"To die is gain." He addressed his people in public but once after this, and that in serving a table on a Communion occasion, within about two months of his death. The subject of his remarks was the "Tree of life;" and, while his audience were listening to him with most earnest and solemn attention, he abruptly concluded with this declaration,— "But I feel that my labours in the sanctuary below are about to close. I shall soon go away to eat of the fruit of the 'tree of life,' which is in the midst of the paradise above."

From this period he undertook no public service, but spent his time in retirement, occupied chiefly in those devout exercises which so well become the spirit that is about to mingle in the scenes beyond the vail. From the nature of his disease he anticipated a sudden departure. In conversing on the subject with his son, he remarked,—" You need not be surprised, at any time when you leave me, to find me gone when you return." But he added, with most serene composure, " Be not unduly moved; by the grace of our God, I am ready for the change. They speak of the grave as the gate of death, but I call it the gate of life; and I know that when the earthly house of this tabernacle is dissolved, I have a building of God, a house not made with hands, eternal in the Heavens."

The death scene of Dr. McLeod was tenderly and sublimely interesting. On Sabbath morning, while his son was preparing for the pulpit, a request came from the father, then on his way through the dark valley, that the family should be collected, and once more approach unitedly the throne of grace. The son led in the exercise; the twenty-third Psalm was sung, and the dying husband and father joined in it with an audible voice. When the prayer was ended, he turned himself in the bed, fixed his eyes on each individual in the room, and then, lifting up his hands, pronounced distinctly the apostolical benediction. The family having retired, he said to his wife beside him,—" It is the Sabbath, and I am at peace." In less than two hours from that time the earthly tabernacle had fallen. While his son was in the pulpit, conducting the devotions of the sanctuary, the service was interrupted by the mournful announcement that the Father and Pastor was gone. The voice of weeping soon filled the house, and the people were dismissed to their homes. He died on the 17th of February, 1833, in the fifty-eighth year of his age and the thirty-fourth of his ministry.

Dr. McLeod was the efficient patron, if not the originator, of various Charitable Associations. Upon no one perhaps did he look with deeper interest than the American Colonization Society; and some have claimed that the first conception of that enterprise belonged to him. He had a primary agency in the establishment of the New York Society for the Instruction of the Deaf and Dumb; and the American Society for Meliorating the Condition of the Jews also received no small share of his attention and regard. He appeared on various public occasions, as the advocate of the interests not only of piety but of humanity; and he was ready to co-operate with men of every name in doing good, on the broad basis of general philanthropy.

The following is a list of Dr. McLeod's publications:—

Negro Slavery Unjustifiable: A Discourse, - - - - - 1802
Messiah Governor of the Nations of the Earth: A Discourse, - 1803
The Ecclesiastical Catechism, - - - - - - - 1806
The Constitution, Character and Duties of the Gospel Ministry: A Sermon at the Ordination of the Rev. Gilbert McMaster, in the First Presbyterian Church, Duanesburgh, - - - - - 1808
Lectures upon the Principal Prophecies of the Revelation, - - 1814
A Scriptural View of the Character, Causes and Ends of the Present War, - - - - - - - - - - 1815
The Life and Power of True Godliness: A Series of Discourses, - 1816
Address to the Synod of the Reformed Presbyterian Church in America, on their submitting to their consideration the Plan of Corresponding with the General Assembly, - - - - - - 1827

 He also wrote the Historical part of the Testimony of the Reformed Presbyterian Church, the Book of Discipline, Form of Covenant, and other public documents; Six Essays on the Atonement; besides contributing largely to the Christian's Magazine, Evangelical Guardian, Evangelical Witness, American Christian Expositor, and other periodicals.

 Dr. McLeod was married, on the 16th of September, 1805, to Maria Anne, daughter of John and Anne (Stavely) Agnew, of the city of New York. Mrs. McLeod died on the 16th of April, 1841, in the fifty-second year of her age. They had eleven children, only four of whom—three sons and a daughter—survived their parents. The eldest, the *Rev. John Neil McLeod, D.D.*, is Pastor of the First Reformed Presbyterian Church in New York, and also Professor of Doctrinal and Practical Theology in the Seminary of the Reformed Presbyterian Church. *William Norman* graduated at the University of Pennsylvania in 1834, studied Law in New York, and went to Michigan, where he entered into political life. He was successively a member of the House of Representatives and of the Senate, Assistant Geologist to the State, Geologist-in-chief to the Hudson Bay Company, in which service he was engaged for three years, and ultimately, having returned to Michigan, United States Attorney for the Northern District of that State. While holding this office, he died of a decline, at Mackinaw, December 29, 1853, in the thirty-ninth year of his age. The third son, *Cornelius Donald*, entered the University of the city of New York, but did not stay to graduate, first studied Law and afterwards took orders in the Episcopal Church, and is now (1863) Professor of English Literature in St. Mary's College, Cincinnati. The daughter, *Margaret Ann*, is married to the Rev. J. R. Johnstone, a Presbyterian clergyman now residing in Philadelphia.

FROM THE REV. GILBERT McMASTER D.D.

OXFORD, O., December 7, 1848.

 Rev. and dear Sir: An intimate and confidential intercourse with Dr. McLeod for more than a quarter of a century furnished me with opportunities of knowing him well. To do justice, however, to the character of a distinguished man, he must be seen and described in the several relations he sustained, in the actions arising out of those relations, the principles and conditions of those actions, their mutual bearing on one another and on the whole tenor of his life. To give such a delineation of character is the province of Biography; but, in the present case, it would be too serious and extended a task for me to attempt. Not having either time to review the records of an extensive correspondence, or space to contain their contents, all that can be given in this letter is a reference to some general points of character, a few extracts illustrative of them, and from recollections and connections that cannot yet be fully developed.

In general it may be stated—and this was acknowledged by all who had any considerable acquaintance with him—that he was a man of very powerful mind; well informed in the various departments of literature and science, of liberal sentiments, comprehensive views and great activity. Though peculiarly ardent in his constitutional temperament, he was at the same time remarkable for his self-command. The superiority of his intellectual powers and his kindness of heart, uniting with a sense of duty, saved him from being betrayed, under provocation, either into passion or utterance of unguarded language. Of either of these the manifestations were rare, and then in a very measured degree. To his credit it ought to be recorded that his great mental powers and acquisitions were put in requisition to subserve the interests of true religion and the principles of moral order among men. As a consecrated offering they were laid on the altar of the Church.

The eighteenth century, in the latter part of which Dr. McLeod entered upon the field of public action, did not, in our country, furnish Theological Schools, for preparing candidates for the Christian Ministry. To direct his course of study, the student, at the recommendation of Presbytery, usually selected the best qualified Pastor to whom he had access. After having finished his collegiate curriculum, young McLeod enjoyed the advantage of the guiding care of an able and eloquent man,—the Rev. James McKinney. The "*Institutio Theologiæ Elencticæ*," of Turretin, was his theological text-book; and an extensive and well selected library furnished him with material for illustration of the subjects of his inquiry. He was a very laborious student. The structure of the minds of the Preceptor and the Scholar were, in many respects, alike. The strong and comprehensive grasp of Mr. McKinney's mind, the grandeur of his conceptions, his enthusiastic love of liberty and admiration of the great principles of the Presbyterian Reformation, with his full assurance of their final triumph in the settlement of the moral order of our world, in both Church and State, exhibited in his masculine and impressive eloquence, were well adapted to the rousing into action of the yet latent, though by no means inferior, powers of his youthful pupil.

Dr. McLeod's mind was peculiarly fitted for the investigations of Mental Science, and in those inquiries he had special delight. Of the writings of the Scottish school of Metaphysics he was master; but of the distinguished Doctors of that school he was no servile follower. With Reid, in his views of the Will, he of course differed. Of the gorgeous style of Stewart and Brown he disapproved, as being ill adapted to the precision of metaphysical thought. Of Campbell's Philosophy of Rhetoric he thought much better. Of the Senior Edwards, of our own country, both as a divine and a mental philosopher, he was a great admirer; though, as I have reason to know, by his criticism in manuscript on some of the speculations of that distinguished man, his admiration was not indiscriminate. Dr. McLeod, then a young man, and very young in the ministry, is the "ingenious and learned friend" to whom the venerable author of the Retrospect of the Eighteenth Century refers, vol. II. p. 453, and whose notes are found pp. 253–256. The first of these notes respects the misapprehension of supposing President Edwards to be the first *Calvinist*, who fully and thoroughly avowed the doctrine of moral necessity. Edwards was eminent in vindicating this doctrine, but was by no means its discoverer—it had been fully asserted long before his day.

With the younger Edwards, while President of Union College, Dr. McLeod had a personal and intimate acquaintance. The Scotch metaphysicians, especially Dr. Reid, on the subject of Moral Agency, Dr. Edwards did not greatly esteem. In a conversation with him, adverting to the "Dissertation on Liberty and Necessity," Mr. McLeod ventured to ask Dr. Edwards if, on an important point, he did not differ with his father. The Doctor inquired,— "On what point?" Mr. McLeod having specified it, the reply was,—" Yes; but though my Essay has been twenty years before the public, you are the first person I have heard notice the difference." The part of the Essay in which Dr. Edwards dissents from his father's views, is the eighth chapter, on the relation of the Divine agency to the existence of moral evil.

I have adverted to these facts as indicating the character of the associates and mental employments of Dr. McLeod when he had just entered on the ministry. The acute and playful note in the "Retrospect," on the speculations of materialists, as well as that which refers to the relation of motive to volition, intimates to us, that at that early day of his public life, his acquaintance with subjects of deep philosophical and theological inquiry.

Into the various departments of liberal research his studies were perseveringly carried. His study of History was not to ascertain a mere detail of facts. His inquiries were directed to the philosophy of that study. He sought the principle that connected the facts, and that influenced the recorded events of time; that he might trace their connection with the page of Prophecy, the policy of States, and their bearing on the moral and social interests of man, and especially on those of the Church of God. How well he succeeded in this course of inquiry may, in some measure, be ascertained from his expositions of Prophecy, his Discourses on the War of 1812 with Great Britain, and by those displays of judicial talent witnessed by his friends and others in the Courts of the Church and other places. As an instance of this, I might refer to a delicate, difficult and important case of discipline, some forty years since, in one of our Presbyteries, in the investigation and disposal of which he was called to take an active part. Among others who attended as spectators was a distinguished Judge; who, afterwards, in a private party, having occasion to refer to the process, turned to the Doctor and remarked,—" I knew that you were a *divine*, but I did not before know that you were a *lawyer*." At a later date,—the day after he had exhibited great mental power in a legal case, though not in the forum, he was met by the late Chancellor Kent, who, in his own familiar and peculiar manner, addressed the Doctor, saying,— "Why Judge P—— tells me you are an able lawyer." "And why not, Mr. Chancellor?" was the reply. "Really," added his Honor, "Judge P—— says you conducted and argued that cause with great ability." If an acquaintance with the great constitutional principles of moral and social order that lie at the foundation of the State, and that ought to regulate the policy of nations, constitutes such a character, then indeed Dr. McLeod was a lawyer and a statesman too.

It was his decided opinion that a Minister of the Gospel, to be fully qualified for his work, should have the attainments of a jurist and a statesman. That the State is a moral person, the moral creature of God, and a subject of his moral government, and that Christian "ministers have the right of discussing from the pulpit those political questions which affect Christian morals," is his recorded and published avowal. But to exercise the right, the minister of religion who undertakes it must have the requisite qualifications. As an apology for ignorance and rudeness in the ministry, he always heard with great impatience a reference to the Apostles as illiterate and unpolished men. Such, he said, they were not. He held them to be no strangers to the literature of their country, and to belong to a respectable rank in society. He ear nestly maintained that every clergyman should not only be a good and learned man, but a gentleman also. Of such a character he was himself a fine example.

He was well versed in Physical Science also; and on it he set a high value. As I was once speaking to him of *Physiology* and *Metaphysics*, as two interesting and noble subjects of study, he said,—" Yes, they show man's relation to Heaven and earth; for in his constitution Heaven and earth unite." His opinion was that no man could be a sound and thorough physiologist, who was not a sound and well instructed mental philosopher. To a defective acquaintance with mental science he ascribed the tendency of so many of the Medical Faculty to a low materialism.

In his habits Dr. McLeod was remarkably retiring; in mixed companies comparatively silent; at all times peculiarly reserved and delicate in speaking of himself or his actions. When, however, he deemed it proper to enter into private discussion, he never indulged in prolonged altercation. The first principles of a subject would be educed or referred to, and if the opposing party had sense to see their application, the controversy was ended; if not, the argument would not be pursued. In the discussion of subjects, he was somewhat impatient of entering into very minute details. The principle he would distinctly state; and in such a manner as to carry to the man of mind the evidence of its truth; but if, in the perception of his position, there happened to be great dullness, he would seldom repeat what he had said or attempt to make it plainer. In such cases, it seemed to be his purpose, by leaving the individual to himself, to induce him to exercise his own mind. Thus I recollect that, more than thirty-six years ago, when a candidate for the ministry, in a private conversation, expressed some difficulty in reference to the doctrine of the Ruling Elder, as generally held in the Presbyterian Church, the Doctor, in his usual manner, stated the principle, and briefly, though distinctly, referred to the proof; but to a continued detail of little objections made no reply. Upon the retiring of the individual, I asked the Doctor why it was that if, in these matters, one requested of him a hundred dollars, he would readily give them, but if he asked a cent, it would not be granted. His reply was,—" He may either make the cent himself or do without it."

To modest weakness Dr. McLeod was peculiarly indulgent; but to the obtrusiveness of shallow pretensions, or the impertinence of knavery, when they came before him, he would sometimes administer an exemplary castigation; never, however, in a manner unbecoming the high bearing of a Christian Gentleman. Of this an example may be given. On a journey in the neighbourhood of one of our chief watering places, we were obliged, early in the afternoon, in consequence of a thunder storm, to seek a shelter, and to take lodging for the night, at a boarding house and half tavern, kept by a man who had once been a Preacher, and, if I mistake not, still held a license to preach. Of this landlord Dr. McLeod had no previous knowledge, but the impression made on his mind by our host was far from favourable. The company present, however, was respectable; and, in the course of the evening, the conversation turned on the relations and policy of England and the United States, and the principles and results of the then late War, (that of 1812,) still fresh in the public mind. The conversation approximated towards an argumentative discussion, to which occasion was given by the sentiments of an aged and venerable gentleman from New England, expressed in favour of the cause of the United States. In support of the views of this truly respectable person, Dr. McLeod had taken a part in the conversation; and while he was stating some facts bearing on the subject, our preacher landlord, in a tone and manner not the most courteous, interposed, saying,—" I do not know that your statement is correct." The Doctor, turning upon him his penetrating eye, replied, in his own emphatic manner,—" Who doubts your ignorance, Sir? What right have you to interrupt this conversation?" The rebuke was felt, and seemed to be regretted by none but its subject. At my private suggestion to the landlord, who had requested me to perform that service, Dr. McLeod was called upon to conduct the social devotions of the evening. Solicitude for the health of his family, disappointment in not receiving letters from home, and the previous animated conversation on the moral and social interests of the country, prepared the way for a prayer such as is seldom heard. In the combination of devotional sentiment, comprehensive views of the Kingdom of Christ, embracing the concerns of the Divine glory and the happiness of man, and a strong expression of faith in the promises of God in reference to those subjects, I have never heard its equal. The impression on all present was deep and solemn. Our venerable New England friend appeared delighted; drew up his chair close to that of the Doctor, and entered into an interesting conversation on the prospective bearing of American institutions, policy and character, and on the political and moral condition of the other nations of the world.

Dr. McLeod was a *Caledonian* by birth, and he loved his native land. He was likewise, on principle, and in heart, an American Republican. An enthusiastic admirer of the Government of the United States, he always heard the suggestion of its weakness with impatience, and used to say with emphasis that it is the strongest Government on earth, inasmuch as it is sustained by the people. And while he saw and lamented the ignorance, the weakness and the vices which were abroad in the land, he had strong confidence in the existing intelligence and moral power of the community, under the benign providence of the Prince of the kings of the earth, as adequate to the saving of the country.

In the spirit of these sentiments, while the port of New York was blockaded by a British fleet, he composed, preached and published his Discourses on the War of 1812; in which was found, perhaps, the ablest defence of that measure which had been given to the public. He vindicated the Government of the United States, on the principles of our Independence, by the law of nations, and above all, by that of the Bible. It is due to the memory of Dr. McLeod, as a Minister of Christ, to state that it was not in the spirit of a mere political partisan that he put forth his gigantic powers in defence of the American cause. Irrespective of all mere party considerations, he saw in the matter of contest great principles of political and national right, and he believed that with those principles were connected the interests of the Kingdom of Christ. In that conflict between the United States and the most powerful nation on the globe, he recognized a carrying out of a portion of the old Presbyterian principle of the Reformation; and to aid in its maintenance and progress he was willing to lend the labours of his head, his heart and his hands, together with the influence of his name. What his views were in writing and publishing his Discourses may be seen from the following extract of a letter addressed to myself a short time before they were published : "My object is to spread the knowledge of Reformation principles in matters civil and religious. The good of my country is the next object to the good of Zion." And in another letter, on the issuing of the second edition of the Discourses, he remarks,—" You will not be so much disappointed about it as many others. It was intended as a display of Reformation principles; and I dare say you will think it the best I ever made. The War is but the carriage and the equipage in which the Old Covenanter travels among the cities of the land. I venture to reveal to you the secret which could not be long concealed from your own sagacity."

A partial alienation of some of his friends was, for a time, one of the results of these Discourses. This caused some of our common friends of other denominations to regret their publication, because of the impairing of his influence among them in what they deemed matters of greater importance. On once asking him if he was apprized of the extent to which his War Sermons had alienated some of his friends and produced regret in others, his reply was,— "Yes, 1 know it, but when they need me they will come back." It is, however, but justice to state that among those who thought differently from him on the causes of the War, were still found a full proportion of his most attached friends.

But it was as a Theologian and an Ecclesiastical man that Dr. McLeod was especially distinguished. As a Divine and a Preacher, he may be judged by his published works,—his Expositions and Sermons. In the pulpit he was eminently powerful—lucid in his explanations ; logical, candid, animated and vigorous in his arguments ; and in the practical application of his doctrinal discussions, distinct, brief and generally vehement. "God," I have heard him say, "has given me sensibilities ; and when the occasion calls for their expression, the attempt to suppress them is to do violence to my nature." After his powerful and impressive discussions, I have seen the respectable Preacher, a stranger to him, who was to follow him in the same place and before the same audience, not a little embarrassed and agitated, and reluctant to proceed to the fulfilment of his appointment. Yet, while others were delighted and edified, this strong man was often evidently dissatisfied with his own performances. He rarely spoke of them farther than, in confidential conversation, to express the opinion that his talent for the edification of the Church lay rather in the use of his pen than in preaching. For a precise expression of his thoughts with his pen he was very remarkable. His manuscripts he had rarely occasion to correct for the press. He studied while others slept, and while many talked he thought. Often have I heard him express, in other terms, the substance of the declaration made in a letter of November 21st, 1820, in which he says,—"The Sabbath is my only day of recreation and enjoyment; or rather the pulpit itself is the principal place of my rest on earth. If I did not love it, I would be most miserable." He loved the employment of the pulpit, because he loved Christ, the Gospel of Christ, and the souls of men: yet he was dissatisfied with his own services there, because of their defects; defects which his audience neither saw nor felt.

Profound in his theological knowledge, he was decidedly opposed to all novelties in religion, and to all curious speculations in the things of God. His impression was that, since the middle of the seventeenth century, the science of Theology had been on the decline. He was averse to the introduction of new and ill-defined terms in religious discussion, holding that the authorized standards of the Church contained her only legitimate vocabulary. The old doctrines of the Reformation, in their deep principles, but in new combinations, illustrations and practical application, as exhibited by him, often surprised, while they edified, the hearer. He was indeed an eloquent preacher. With simple elegance, in vigorous, precise and appropriate language, of which he had a remarkable command, he habitually expressed himself in the pulpit. On the various subjects of mental and theological inquiry, he had settled in his mind and always had at command a few first principles, guided by which, in new discussions, he often gave exhibitions that, to minds otherwise constituted than his own, appeared as intuition. The power of discrimination he possessed in an unusual degree; and he was much inclined to connect in discussion the principles of mental science with experimental religion. It was at his suggestion that the Theological Professor in the School of his Church was instructed to deliver to "the class of students in Pulpit Eloquence a course of Lectures on Metaphysics, including the science of the Human Mind and Christian Experience." And in his own ministry some of his most instructive discussions evinced how much he was at home on those subjects; not in idle or amusing theories, nor in dry speculations, but in the unfoldings of the living soul under the influence of a true and living religion.

In labours he was abundant. Few constitutions could have borne up under them. Three discourses every Sabbath, an evening lecture every week, and a catechetical exercise of the youth of his church on another evening, together with stated pastoral visits to the families and fellowship prayer meetings of his congregation, until a late period of his life, formed the usual routine of his services. He was still a diligent student and a close observer of events. He slept but little and rose early. Naturally of a fine constitution, he was nevertheless subject to attacks of indisposition; but he rarely complained, judging the idea of a sickly minister to be injurious to his official reputation and influence. The fruits of his labours were found in the intelligence, piety and orderly deportment of the people of his charge. His church, though not at that time among the most numerous and wealthy, was peculiarly well ordered and ecclesiastically strong. Upon others their example was salutary. The character then impressed upon that church, through the Agnews, the Giffords, the Nelsons, the Clarkes, and their associates,—names of rare excellence of a past generation, is still found in the congregation now under the pastoral care of his worthy son and successor, the Rev. John N. McLeod, D.D.

As an Ecclesiastical man he was not less distinguished than as a Theologian. His views of the Church, as an organized Body, were enlarged and comprehensive. And when, in his public ministrations, he expatiated on the glories of the Redeemer, his Mediatorial fulness, the extent of his dominion, the riches and power of his grace, and on the origin, constitution, relations, claims, influence and destiny of Zion, he was commandingly grand. Of the universal extension over the world of the religion of the Bible, and the visible, organical union of the whole Church, his confidence was unwavering; and in order to do this, he believed in the perfect adaptation of the principles and forms of moral order, as revealed in Scripture, to the intellectual, moral and social constitution of man,—God being the author of both. And that He with whom is the residue of the Spirit, will, in due season, redeem his pledged promise, and that Zion shall then be *one* united, peaceful and blessed habitation, he did not doubt. In the mean time, while he disapproved of a thoughtless amalgamation of discordant materials in the Church of God as unprofitable, he was an advocate of a generous intercourse among all whom he considered as holding to the Head, Christ, without compromise of recognized principle.

The estimation in which he was held beyond the boundaries of his own department of the Church, may be inferred from the repeated calls made upon him by both the Presbyterian and Dutch Churches; and by the offers made him of distinguished places in their literary institutions. An acceptance of any of these offers would have greatly improved his financial circumstances; and his respectful refusal of them at least proved that, with him, neither avarice nor ambition was a governing motive.

Notwithstanding Dr. McLeod, in his writings and in his public ministry, was accustomed to deal only with principles and characters, without descending to offensive personalities, he was himself frequently the object of personal and violent attack. In writing to me in reference to one of these assaults that had been made upon him, he says,—" I fear not enemies—I fear not even Satan himself—but I fear the destitution of that greatness of soul, which alone can build the walls of Jerusalem in troublesome times." Of character he had a high estimate, and of ministerial character he was peculiarly tender. Of those who acted towards him an unworthy part, he seldom spoke, and never in the language of vulgar abuse. As a proof of his lofty bearing in this respect, I may mention that he once stated to me that, though he had been sixty times attacked, in his public character, through the medium of the press, yet he had never replied or taken any public notice of the attack in a single instance. When, however, character was assailed, he deemed it right that it should be vindicated; but its vindication, he thought, belonged to the friends of the injured rather than to himself; as a man is not likely, in his own case, to be the most impartial judge.

In his devotional feelings and spiritual exercises there was a peculiar intensity. The constitutional decision of his character was carried into its religious actings. Of himself, as a *sinner*, he evidently thought and felt with deepest humility—of himself as a *saved* sinner he never appeared to doubt. The provisions of Redemption by the Lord Jesus he well understood; the gracious overtures of the Gospel assured him of his right and his obligation to go to the Saviour; and under the influence of the Spirit of God he went to him in faith, and knew what he was doing. He was a stranger to that indecision of mind, that languor of action, that leaves the deed in a state of uncertainty whether it be performed or not.

Dr. McLeod sensibly felt the ills of life, but he evinced under them the most meek and quiet spirit. As an illustration of this, I may be allowed to give the following extracts from a letter dated December 9, 1815, shortly after being bereaved of two amiable and beloved children by scarlet fever:—

"Your favour reached me at a time in which private grief overcame the force of public interests. On Tuesday morning, my fine daughter breathed her last. She now lies beside her younger sister, where not the fever nor the storm shall disturb them. Blow upon blow falls upon my offending head and my deceitful heart. You know how long I have desired a release from this body of death and world of trials; but my God—for yet I shall call Him mine—refuses my wishes and my prayers, and beats me on the sorest part, by slaying my beloved babes, one by one, before my eyes. I have seen in the tortures of my infants the hatred of the Divinity against sin; and my works and my prayers, my knowledge and my experience, start up before my alarmed conscience, as a thing in which I cannot hope. Decked in their impurity and imperfection, it is I who have sinned more than these afflicted children who are torn from my bleeding heart; and both the experience and the labour of my life are a burden instead of a pillar on which my soul can rest. Oh, my brother, how inestimable is that word of truth upon which the faith of God's elect may and doth rest! To that word I refer my all. It is my only comfort, and, resting upon the offer of the gift of God, I say,—'Though He slay me, as He did my children, I will trust in Him.' Excuse these effusions of a wounded spirit. You know the feelings of a father."

Such was the Rev. Dr. Alexander McLeod. Yet he was but a man—great and good indeed, but still a man. The sun has his spots, and my illustrious friend had his imperfections. They were, however, only such as are incident to our diseased nature in its present state;—the occasional manifestation of the remains, in the saint, of "the old man,"—"the body of sin and death," where the graces and virtues that constitute the Christian character were greatly predominant and confessed of all.

To the pages of his biography it belongs to tell of his fine constitutional proportions, of his manly gait, his commanding voice, and persuasive tones; to tell that when he wrote or spoke, it told; that, when he acted, a great man was there; and that his moral worth was in full accordance with his mental power. To them too pertains the record of his connection with the benevolent institutions of his time; of his relations to many of the great men in Church and State of the last generation; and to note his place in that constellation, whose benign and splendid light, in a by-gone age, was so profusely shed on the Churches of New York, and throughout the land. And when the distinguished names of Rodgers, Livingston, Mason, Romeyn, Linn,

Milledoler, Abeel, and others, are mentioned, and the register of his connection with them and of their high and mutual regard for each other shall be fully made out, the reputation of Alexander McLeod, as an able minister of the New Testament, will suffer no eclipse.

I am, with affectionate respect,
Truly yours.
GILBERT McMASTER.

FROM THE REV. SAMUEL B. WYLIE, D.D.

BELLEVUE, NEAR PHILADELPHIA, December 28, 1848.

My dear Sir: My acquaintance with the Rev. Dr. McLeod, concerning whom you ask for my reminiscences, commenced in 1798, and continued without interruption until the close of his earthly labours. I had formed a very favourable opinion of him from the representations of the late Dr. J. B. Smith, President of Union College, where young McLeod had graduated shortly before. To this was added the testimony of the Rev. James McKinney, who, for a short time, had been his Theological Preceptor, after he had finished his collegiate curriculum. I longed for a personal interview with one, of whose character I had been led to form so high an estimate. This desire was gratified, in the city of New York, in 1798; and then all my anticipations in respect to him were more than realized. I found a countenance beaming with no ordinary degree of intelligence; a heart fraught with true Celtic nobility; and manners at once courteous and entirely unaffected. As I take for granted that you do not expect from me any thing like a narrative of his life, I will proceed at once to give you my recollections of what he was in some of his various relations.

As a Pulpit Orator, Dr. McLeod's character is not, in my opinion, of easy delineation. He was an original. He imitated nobody. He had no model. He uttered the effusions of an elevated intellect and a sanctified heart, in all the simplicity that nature dictated. His talents were of the first order. His mental energy never flagged, even under the influence of great bodily debility. In his exhibitions in the pulpit he was not exclusively exegetical, didactic, hortatory, terrific, persuasive, but all these characters were so appropriately blended as to meet the respective conditions of the auditory. It was not the melody of his voice, nor the flow of his sentences, that fascinated the hearer; but there was an unction diffused from his discourse which was generally felt by the whole audience. His vigorous and masculine mind seized on the cardinal points of his subject; and he enforced them with an eloquence so fervid and vehement that few could withstand it. It often descended, like the mountain torrent, sweeping all before it; sometimes regardless of laws, and wrapt up in the excellence of its own originality. On doctrinal and didactic subjects, his arguments were strictly logical, and always cogent. While his mind was acutely metaphysical, it was never trammelled by what may be called the *ultraism* of that science. His was not the metaphysics of the Scholastic Doctors of the Dark Ages, or of the Aristotelian School; not the jargon of unintelligibility, but clear, conclusive, irresistible deductions. During almost the whole period of his ministry in New York, he delivered, on Sabbath evening, discourses in which he discussed some of the most important topics of Didactic Theology. These subjects he treated with so much acumen and strength of argument that large and respectable audiences, including not only many members of other congregations, but also ministers, licentiates, and students of theology, were in steady attendance.

Dr. McLeod loved to preach Jesus Christ and Him crucified. Often has he said to me, in private conversation,—" How I do like to preach the Gospel." He seemed, when in the pulpit, in his favourite element. For myself, I can truly say that there was, in his pulpit services, a degree of evangelical power and attraction, which, so far as my observation goes, has been rarely surpassed.

In his application of doctrinal discussions, the truths presented were closely pressed home upon the conscience. Here he was searching, pungent, affectionate and hortatory. While there was consolation administered to the penitent, the sinner, pricked to the heart, was forbidden to despond, and affectionately pointed to the Balm in Gilead and the Physician there.

In Ecclesiastical Judicatories he was always cautious, judicious and unassuming. He expressed his views of important subjects with firmness, dignity, and withal with that modesty which is characteristic of superior minds. Though he could climb to the mast-head, and command a wide view of any subject, he never arrogated to himself any superiority. His arguments of course were always listened to with attention and respect.

In the social circle he was a universal favourite. His manner, though dignified, was not distant. He was ever courteous, kind and respectful to all. His conversation was always instructive and pleasing; and, although he could not be said to be *full of anecdotes*, yet, on suitable occasions, no one could introduce an anecdote more appropriately than he, or relate it in a manner more gratifying to the company.

Dr. McLeod was among the more eminent writers which this country has produced. His published works are an enduring monument of his talents, learning and piety. His Sermon on Slavery, his Ecclesiastical Catechism, his War Sermons, his Treatise on the Revelation, his True Godliness, &c., all bear the marks of a master mind, acting under the influence of a heart warmed with the love of God.

One or two anecdotes concerning Dr. McLeod occur to me, with which I will close my communication.

Some considerable time before his decease, he was seized by a violent disease, and was given up to death by his relatives and friends. I was written to, in the most pressing manner, by several persons, to come on, if I would see him again among the living. I started on Saturday, at a moment's warning, but, from the state of the roads and stages, did not reach Dr. McLeod's house till Sabbath afternoon. On his first recognition of me, as he lay on his bed, apparently in a dying state, he immediately sat up and exclaimed,—"My dear Billy,"—a familiar name by which we were in the habit of addressing each other,—and from that time he began perceptibly to recover. Some believed that the old associations connected with "Billy" had formed the crisis of the complaint, or that it led to its taking a new turn.

In his admission of members to Church Communion he was particularly tender and judicious. On one occasion a certain woman appeared before the Session, and, on examination, was found so very defective in knowledge that the Elders were hesitating about admitting her; though all believed her to be truly pious. The Doctor, having heard them all state their opinions, observed,—"This woman appears to me like a sieve that can retain nothing, but yet may be purified by the water that passes through it."

With much respect, I am, dear Sir,
Yours in the bonds of our common Lord,
S. B. WYLIE.

FROM THE REV. JOHN BLACK, D.D.

PITTSBURG, December 4, 1848.

Reverend and dear Sir: Understanding that you are engaged in preparing for the press a work to consist of memoirs of distinguished American clergymen, and believing that a few reminiscences of my dear friend, the late Dr. Alexander McLeod, would not be unacceptable to you, I send you the following:

My acquaintance with the Doctor commenced in 1798, when we were both on trials for licensure. This acquaintance soon ripened into friendship, which continued in unabated and increased vigour till the day of his death. He was a friend to whom you might entrust your whole heart. He was an Israelite indeed, in whom there was no guile. As you left him, you found him, the same steady, unwavering friend. Dr. Wylie, of Philadelphia, Dr. McLeod and myself were licensed together. An unbroken and indissoluble friendship subsisted among the three. Cæsar, Pompey and Crassus formed no such triumvirate as ours, for friendship, good feeling and real enjoyment. Our meetings were a jubilee.

Dr. McLeod was a scholar,—a truly scientific man. He was well acquainted with the Philosophy of the Human Mind. That he was a divine of the first order his writings bear abundant testimony. His works praise him in the gates. He was thoroughly imbued with the spirit of the Reformers. He had deeply digested the system of Theology, as he found it in the Bible, and heartily espoused it. His Lectures on the Revelation, and his Sermons on True Godliness, exhibit a master mind in the exposition of Scripture, and a Christian at home in the life and practice of a true believer. His triumphant vindication of the Universal Government of the Lord Jesus Christ, in his "Messiah, the Prince of the Kings of the Earth," evinces the deep concern which possessed his soul for the honour of his exalted Redeemer. Nor was he unmindful of the rights of man. In his politics he was an unwavering Republican; besides, he was a Christian man, and therefore felt an interest in the concerns of humanity. In his "Negro Slavery Unjustifiable," he maintains, with great ability, the position that Negro Slavery is alike at war with every principle of humanity and with the revealed will of God.

In Church Courts Dr. McLeod was pre-eminent. His chief excellence here consisted in a deep and quick perception of the point and bearing of an argument. In this respect his mind acted as if by intuition. He saw, at a glance, the strength or weakness of a position, and no sophistry could elude the ordeal of his keen perception. The fallacy, however specious, his sound penetration instantly detected.

He was a punctual and most profitable correspondent. His letters were always most welcome to his friends. The spirit of Christian charity, liberality and evangelical piety, breathed in all, even his most familiar communications.

As a Preacher, I can honestly say I never heard a man who could enchain my attention like him. His was no studied eloquence, but it was the eloquence of a great mind and a great heart, acting in all the simplicity of nature. It never could have been the product of art. He addressed every power of the soul, going down into the very depths of the heart, but it was always through the medium of the understanding and the judgment. Some speakers we admire while we are listening to them, but we bring nothing away with us. Not so in respect to Dr. McLeod. You could carry his sermons home with you and digest his arguments at your leisure. Take him all in all, we seldom meet his like. He is gone, but his memory is embalmed in the hearts of his brethren, who are soon to follow him.

With kind regards and best wishes for the success of your undertaking, I am, Dear Sir, Yours respectfully,

JOHN BLACK

FROM THE REV. SAMUEL MILLER, D.D.

THEOLOGICAL SEMINARY, PRINCETON, January 30, 1849.

Rev. and dear Sir: In thinking of the appropriate subjects of the large work on Clerical Biography in which you have for some time been engaged, I of course expected you to include a notice of the life and character of the late Alexander McLeod, D.D., of the city of New York. Few names among the departed have a higher claim to a place in your list, than the name of that distinguished divine. When, therefore, I was requested, as one who had enjoyed the privilege of an early acquaintance and friendship with him, to make my humble contribution towards embalming his memory, I felt as if an honour had been conferred upon me, which I could not too promptly or cordially acknowledge.

You will no doubt be furnished from another source with all the desirable historical notices concerning his nativity, his education, and the leading events of his literary and ecclesiastical life. On these, therefore, I shall not dwell; but shall content myself with merely stating my general impressions and estimate of his character, as a Man and as a Minister of the Gospel.

My acquaintance with Dr. McLeod commenced in the year 1801, soon after he had accepted a pastoral charge in the Reformed Presbyterian Church in the city of New York, where I then resided. I had never before heard of him; but my first interview with him gave him a place in my mind seldom assigned to one so youthful. His countenance beaming at once with intelligence and benevolence, his attractive manners and his conversation, though marked with a modesty becoming his age, yet abounding in evidence of intellectual vigour and unusual literary culture, mature theological knowledge and decided piety, made an impression on me which I shall never forget. This impression was confirmed and deepened by all my subsequent intercourse with him.

At the period of which I speak, there was a Clerical Association in the city of New York, which was in the habit of meeting on Monday morning of each week. This Association comprehended most of the ministers of the different Presbyterian denominations in the city. The exercises consisted of prayer, conversation, both general and prescribed, and reading compositions on important subjects. In this delightful Association I was so happy as to enjoy, for ten or twelve years, the privilege of meeting with Dr. McLeod weekly, and seeing him in company and conversation with the Pastors venerable for their age and standing, in that day; and I must say that the longer I continued to make one of the attendants on those interviews, the higher became my estimate of his various accomplishments as a Scholar, a Christian, and a Divine.

Dr. McLeod had a remarkably clear, logical and comprehensive mind. As a Preacher, he greatly excelled. For, although he seldom wrote his sermons, and never read them in public, yet they were uncommonly rich and instructive, and at the same time animated, solemn, and touching, in their appeals to the conscience and the heart. As a Writer, his printed works are no less honourable to his memory. His Lectures on the Prophecies, his Sermons on the War of 1812, and his Discourses on the Life and Power of true Godliness, to say nothing of other publications of real value, though of minor size, all evince the richly furnished Theologian, the sound Divine, and the experimental Christian, as well as the polished and able Writer. So great indeed was his popularity in the city of New York, far beyond the bounds of his own ecclesiastical denomination, that several of the most wealthy and respectable churches in the city, in succession, invited him to take the pastoral office over them. His attachment, however, to that branch of the Presbyterian Body in which he began his ministerial career, was so strong that he never could be persuaded to leave her communion.

After I left New York, on my removal to Princeton, in the year 1813, I rarely visited the city, and almost always in the most transient manner, so that, after that year, I seldom saw Dr. McLeod. I had only two or three short interviews with him at different and distant intervals. In a few years his health became impaired, and not long after so fatally undermined, that he exchanged his ministry on earth for the higher enjoyments and rewards of the sanctuary above. In the retrospect of my life, I often call to mind the image of this beloved and cherished friend, and dwell upon his memory as that of a great and good man, from my intercourse with whom I am conscious of having derived solid advantage as well as much pleasure. But I, too, must soon "put off this tabernacle," and then I trust we shall be re-united in a better world, and be permitted to study and to enjoy together, to all eternity, the wonders and the glories of that redeeming love, which I have so often heard him exhibit with feeling and with power while he was with us.

That you and I, my dear Sir, may be more and more prepared for that blessedness, is the unfeigned prayer of your friend and brother in Christ,

SAMUEL MILLER.

THOMAS DONNELLY.*
1799—1847.

THOMAS DONNELLY was born in the County of Donegal, Ireland, in January, 1772. He evinced an early love of study and a strong desire to obtain a liberal education. Accordingly, having gone through the preparatory studies, he was entered, in due time, as a member of Glasgow College. How long he remained in connection with that institution is not known; but he left it before he had completed his regular course, and, in 1791, migrated to South Carolina. He soon found his way to the North, and was, for some time, a student at Dickinson College, Carlisle, though, as his name does not appear on the Catalogue, it is presumed that he did not graduate. On leaving the College, he returned to the South, and commenced the study of Theology under the direction of the Rev. William King,† of South Carolina, who was one of a Committee of the Reformed Presbytery of Scotland, judicially authorized to manage the concerns of the Reformed Presbyterian Church in America. The members of this Committee having, in 1797, constituted themselves into a Presbytery, under the title of the "Reformed Presbytery of the United States of America," Mr. Donnelly, in connection with Messrs. Black, Wiley and McLeod, was licensed by that Body, at Coldenham, N. Y., in June, 1799.

On the 3d of March, 1801, he was ordained and installed Pastor of the Congregation about Rocky Creek, Chester District, S. C., or "such part of that people as he should be able to superintend." Here he laboured with great diligence, often visiting remote congregations, not only in Carolina but in Georgia. About the year 1813 the congregation of which he was Pastor was divided, and the Rev. John Reily was placed over a portion of it, the part which remained to Mr. Donnelly being known as the "Brick Church." Here he continued to labour for several years; but, after a while, in consequence of some difficulty, another division took place, which left Mr. D. with a still smaller charge, though they

---

* MS. from Mr. Thomas Smith, of Bloomington, Ind.
† The Rev. WILLIAM KING came to this country from Ireland in the year 1792, arriving first in South Carolina. He then came to the North, and spent some time in Pennsylvania and New York, after which he returned to South Carolina, and became Pastor of a Church in Chester District. He was invited to a Conference, at Alexandria, with the Northern Ministers, Messrs McKinney and Gibson, but died before the time of meeting. His death took place on the 24th of August, 1798, at the age of about fifty.

were scattered over a wide extent of territory, and the due care of them furnished him ample employment. The strong dissatisfaction which these people felt with the institution of Slavery led many of them to migrate in large numbers to the Northwestern States; but, as the infirmities of age were now upon him, he thought it not best to remove to a new country, and, therefore, he continued his labours among the few that remained, until he was too feeble to perform any further service.

Mr. Donnelly continued to preach until about one year previous to his death. His last sermon was preached on the first Sabbath in November, 1846, and his last public act was to baptize his grandson, whose death a little preceded his own. On the 1st of January, 1847, he was attacked with paralysis, affecting deeply his mental as well as his bodily powers, from which he only partially recovered. He was able, however, after some little time, to walk about, but he scarcely recognized his old friends, and could speak only in a whisper. In the autumn following he was prostrated by a bilious affection, which, after a few weeks, terminated fatally on the 27th of November, 1847.

On the 6th of March, 1801, Mr. Donnelly was married to Agnes Smith, a member of the church to which he ministered, and a lady of great moral and Christian worth. They had five children, four of whom survived him. Mrs. Donnelly, who was greatly distinguished for her spirituality and active Christian life, died on the 4th of April, 1848.

FROM THE REV. GAVIN McMILLAN.

MORNING SUN, PREBLE COUNTY, O., June 26, 1862.

Rev. and dear Sir: Your request for my recollections of the Rev. Thomas Donnelly has, I confess, somewhat embarrassed me; for though he was the beloved Pastor of my youth, and I have many reasons for being more than willing to pay a tribute to his memory, yet, as I am now seventy-six years of age, and as it is nearly half a century since I last saw him, I have little confidence of being able to do justice to his character. I will, however, do the best I can in presenting you with a portraiture of him, and I am the more willing to attempt it, as I could hardly direct you to any one, at this late day, whose opportunities for knowing him were better than my own

My first acquaintance with Mr. Donnelly was when I became a pupil in his school in my father's neighbourhood, in Chester District, S. C. I entered his school at an early age; and as he was my first teacher, (my parents excepted,) so he was also among the last. Under his tuition I studied the elementary branches, such as reading, spelling, etc., and recited to him the Larger Catechism. The Bible was not then excluded from the school, on the ground of its being a sectarian book, nor was the school trammelled with Trustees or Directors, which, however, are, no doubt, often very requisite. The afternoon of every alternate Saturday was spent in reciting Catechisms and portions of Scripture, which had been previously committed to memory. He was a rigid disciplinarian of the Old School, recognizing the rod as a Divine ordinance, and never substituting for it modern inventions. He was a man of great inflexibility of purpose. About Christmas there were several well grown young men in attendance at the school, who had become acquainted with the Popish practice, too prevalent among the Scotch Irish, of barring out the master,—as the phrase was,—to make him treat the scholars. They barred him out, and called upon him to treat; but he peremptorily refused.

They even tied him, and carried him down to the creek to duck him; but all their efforts were unavailing—he would not yield a particle.

Though he was firm in his opinions, he could not be called either a bigot or an extremist. He was generally of a cheerful and social turn, and at weddings, and on other festive occasions, his presence was always peculiarly welcome. In advanced life, through the influence of disease and troubles of various kinds, he became somewhat reserved and distant in his intercourse, and perhaps somewhat less genial in his spirit.

Mr. Donnelly was a man of medium size, of rapid movements and of unassuming manners. He had great generosity and nobleness of heart, and as there were but few benevolent institutions at that day in the part of the country in which he lived, he found full scope for the exercise of his individual beneficence. He was a decided and earnest Anti-slavery man, but by no means an ultra Abolitionist.

When the Reformed Presbytery met at the house of Mr. John Kell, father of the late Rev. John Kell, Rocky Creek, Chester District, Mr. Donnelly, being then a student of Theology, under the care of the Rev. William King, acted as Clerk of the meeting. One of the deliverances of this Presbytery, on the subject of Slavery, in connection with a publication on the causes for Fasting, is as follows:—

"That abominable species of murder, even enslaving thousands of fellow-creatures for life, and their posterity without end, and degrading them below the brutes, is now reduced to a system, and seems, by a long prescription, to outbrave a remedy. There is, for the present, power on the side of the oppressors; but no power on the side of the oppressed. What humane mind but will mingle his tears with those of his fellow mortals, when he sees them shut out from every source of rational happiness, banished far from their native home, torn from their dear relations, and wallowing in the most abominable uncleanness, while every means of meliorating their condition is artfully kept from their view, by their insolent and murderous masters. Oh, America, what hast thou to account for both to God and man on the head of Slavery alone!! Alas!!! When shall God arise for the cries of the oppressed?"

To these strong, bold sentiments, Mr. Donnelly gave an unhesitating and cordial assent.

Mr. Donnelly had the reputation of being a correct logician and a good Oriental scholar; but he was undoubtedly most at home in the science of Theology. His knowledge of the Scriptures was exceedingly minute and exact. And he could tell the story of the Cross to as good purpose as any other man;—if not in the most finished and polished style, yet in a manner to make the attractions of the Cross most powerfully felt by all classes. You could not but feel that every word he uttered came fresh from his heart; and this it was especially that constituted the power of his manner. He wrote nothing but brief notes, and from these he spoke with great facility and effect. Dr. Black, of Pittsburg, used to say that all he wanted to ensure a good sermon was one of Donnelly's skeletons; and it is said that, in hearing him preach, he would sometimes take notes of his discourse, and avail himself of them, to some extent, in his preparations for the next Sabbath. At times he had a good deal of the Scotch or Scotch-Irish tone, or the Covenanter and Seceder sing-song; but there was nothing, after all, that seemed like affectation. He was never verbose or tautological; never gave sound for sense, or attempted to be any body else than himself. He was not always equally interesting, and sometimes was perhaps a little tedious. It was thought by many that, if he failed at any point, it was in the want of sufficiently close and pungent application. When he commenced preaching as a licentiate, he was greatly lacking in confidence. The first or second discourse which he ever delivered was in the Red Tent, on the Stony Ridge, below Carlisle, on the way to Harrisburg, Pa. I have been informed that he kept his eye constantly upon his little Bible, scarcely looking his audience in the face at all. An old lady who heard him that day, on being asked, after the sermon, what she thought of Mr. Donnelly, replied,—"He did pretty weel; but he read ower muckle." He got the better of this extreme diffidence afterwards, and greatly improved every way in his pulpit exhibitions.

Mr. Donnelly was, in other respects, a good Minister of Jesus Christ. He was particularly attentive to the interests of his flock, visiting from house to house, and thus making himself acquainted with their spiritual condition, and adapting his instructions and counsels to their various circumstances. In the Session of the Church, (of which my father was a member,) he was most considerate, and never disposed to lord it over his brethren. He was an excellent Presbyter, was familiar with the details of ecclesiastical business, and was once, if not more than once, Moderator of the Synod. He was undoubtedly to be regarded as one of the lights of his denomination.

Your brother in Christ,
G. McMILLAN

JOHN BLACK, D.D.
1799—1849.
FROM THE REV. JOHN N. McLEOD, D.D.

NEW YORK, August 20, 1861.

My dear Sir: I cheerfully comply with your request for some account of the life and character of my venerable friend, the Rev. Dr. Black. My relations with him were such that I am at no loss for material from which to form the desired sketch.

JOHN BLACK, a son of John and Margaret (McKibbin) Black, was born in the North of Ireland, County of Antrim, October 2, 1768, and he made his home there until after he arrived at manhood. The son of respectable parents, he received from them the rudiments of an excellent education, which he completed at Glasgow College, in Scotland. Having graduated at that seat of learning, he returned to his own country, but it was only to leave it for the home of his adoption. In the year 1797 he embarked for America, an exile for liberty. I have known many individuals, in almost every condition in life, from the simple farmer or artisan to the eminent physician, the eloquent lawyer, and the dignified minister of religion, who had more or less concern in the Irish Insurrection of 1797–98; and I have never known a mean man among them all. Coming to the United States, instinct with the love of liberty, and ardently admiring our republican institutions, they formed a fine and highly useful element in our growing population, and contributed their part to the formation of our national character. Of these was Dr. Black, who was all his life an intelligent republican, and at home in every thing that related to the science of government, the rights of man, and the constitution and laws of his country. It has often been said of him, by good judges, that, had he been of the legal profession, he would have made an acute Lawyer, a discriminating Judge, or a profound and influential Statesman. As it was, he enjoyed the society of some of the ablest jurists and civilians of his own and other States, and upon subjects of practical morality, such as Slavery, Punishment, Citizenship, War, Privateering and Lotteries, his pen was often and effectively employed in the periodicals of the day. Having come to the United States in the fall of 1797, he was employed for some time as a teacher of the Classics in the neighbourhood of Philadelphia, and latterly in connection with the University there. Having been licensed to preach the Gospel by the Presbytery of the Reformed Presbyterian Church, in 1799, he immediately devoted himself to this work, soon passed to the Western country, and settled in Pittsburg, then a village of a few scattering houses. On the same day, and from the same authority, the late Rev. Drs. Alexander McLeod and Samuel B. Wylie received their license as preachers, and the three constituted a triumvirate of honourable and honoured Ministers of Christ, whose personal friendship continued while life lasted, and whose eminent abilities and usefulness secured to them a large measure of the public confidence. Dr. Black remained for forty-eight years, and until he closed his life, on the 25th of October, 1849, in the same pastoral charge in Pittsburg. He was identified with almost all the literary and benevolent institutions of that city and vicinity, having assisted in laying their foundations; and he deserves to be recognized by posterity as one of the early moral pioneers of that important section of our country.

Dr. Black was rather below the middle stature; but his intellectual head, his penetrating and lively eye, his rapid and even restless movement, and, withal, the decision that showed itself in all his conduct, marked him out at once as a superior man, who had a purpose, who could carry it out with fearless energy, and who was formed to exercise great influence over others. He was an eminently social man. No one could be more serious than he when seriousness was required, and yet he was courteous, and even witty and playful, when time and place allowed the indulgence of these qualities. All kinds of persons sought and enjoyed his companionship, and his place in the various institutions with which he was connected was always the working department.

Considered in his public and social relations, Dr. Black may be truly said to have been all his life a teacher of others. Beginning with the primary school, he marched upwards to the Tutorship, Professorate, and Presidency of the College. Classes of Theological students of his own and other denominations waited upon his instructions, gratuitously tendered, and when themes of peculiar difficulty were to be handled, he was the man to whom his brethren in the ministry would apply among the first to state and elucidate them before the public assembly. Well-read in physical science, in medicine, and in general literature, and a proficient in the Hebrew tongue, he was also thoroughly versed in the Greek and Latin languages. With the latter he was specially familiar. He spoke it well, and could, with ease and elegance, transfer the English into it, and *vice versa*. I have known him prepare, at a sitting, a form of diploma for a College, and at another a preface for a book in that language. The Latin introduction to Rabbi Leeser's issue of the Hebrew Bible, last printed, Philadelphia edition, is from his pen. In his teachings Dr. Black showed great power of analysis. He aimed at making his pupils understand fundamentals, and, accurate himself in every thing, he sought to give a taste for accuracy to others. It is rare that a philosophical acquaintance with the genius of the language taught, and a minute knowledge of its grammatical mechanism, are found together in the same man, as was the case with Dr. Black. He never heard a grammatical blunder committed that he did not, if possible, correct; and his dear friends, Drs. Wylie and McLeod, were accustomed familiarly to call him "*grapho*," the

Greek word from which grammar is derived, as expressive of his attainments in this kind of knowledge. Dr. Black, too, took delight in communicating knowledge to others. I have known him spend an hour in teaching the letters or the stops to a little child in the house of a friend where he was as a visitor; and again and again sitting up all night to elucidate an abstruse subject in Theology to an enquiring Divinity student. No wonder that his pupils loved him, and that there are so many, East and West, who cherish his memory with profound affection.

Dr. Black held the Chair of Latin and Greek in the Western University at Pittsburg, from its establishment until his resignation, on making a visit to Europe in 1832; and, on the death of his early friend, the Rev. Dr. Bruce, he was chosen to succeed him as President of Duquesne College, Pittsburg: of this, he accepted, only to graduate the then existing Senior Class, and then retired altogether from the field.

As a Controvertist, with both tongue and pen, Dr. Black was for years distinguished. He attacked the errors and vices of the day with entire fearlessness, and was never at a loss for weapons of offensive or defensive warfare. Few men wished to encounter him a second time in argument, and he had great tact in discovering the character of his opponent and his audience. It is narrated of him that he thus disposed of a noisy, obtrusive individual, who called himself a —— Preacher. They were travelling together in a steamboat on the Ohio River. The Preacher had gathered a crowd around him, and had confounded one or two plain men who had attempted some reply to his declamation. He proposed to prove his doctrine from Scripture, quoted large portions of it, and, in closing, challenged all present to reply if they could, to his arguments. At this moment Dr. Black, who had been looking on from the edge of the crowd, stepped forward and said that he had a word to say. He then, with great gravity, began and repeated nearly the whole of the first chapter of I. Chronicles, composed almost entirely of hard names. The wonder of the people was excited; and, as the Doctor ceased abruptly, his opponent asked, with excitement,—" What has all this to do with the subject?" " N·thing at all," said the Doctor, " but you quoted Scripture, and so have I, and mine is just as much to the purpose as yours." The ridicule told effectively, the company dispersed with a shout of laughter, and the Doctor, who judged that this was the only proper mode of disposing of the matter, retired to his state-room.

On the floor of a Church Judicatory few men were superior to Dr. Black. He had studied minutely the principles and usages of Presbyterial regimen. He understood the order of judicial proceeding. His recollections of precedents was remarkably accurate, and therefore cases of discipline were disentangled from their difficulties, and reduced to their equitable principles, with great facility, by his judicious remarks and management. He demanded punctiliously the observance of the due order, and viewed the proper forms of judicial proceeding as the safeguards of personal, conscientious liberty. When the judicatory of which he was a member would become confused and at a stand, as such Bodies often do, he was the man who could show them the way of consistent evasion. "The Directory for Worship," in the Reformed Presbyterian Church, is from the pen of Dr. Black, and he served for many years as the Stated Clerk of her Supreme Judicatory.

But the exercise of the Christian Ministry was Dr. Black's chosen employment. This engaged all his versatile talents, and to this all his other engagements were subordinated. When he took charge of some dozen families of Reformed Presbyterians in Pittsburg and its vicinity, they composed the only congregation of that Christian denomination, West of the Allegheny Mountains. He lived to see three Presbyteries of that Church in what had been his personal field of missionary labour. Over this field he often rode thousands of miles each year. He every where preached the Word, and was universally acceptable to the people, who gathered, in large numbers, to hear him.

Dr. Black's preaching talents were of a high order. He was a distinct, plain, fluent speaker, always interesting and often eloquent and powerful. Full of knowledge of his subject, argumentative, learned, original, self-possessed, he was equally at home whether discussing a doctrine, urging a duty, solving cases of conscience, or elucidating the experiences and dispensing the consolations of the Christian life. Having a lively imagination, he dealt largely in allegory, and would sometimes enrapture his audience with his descriptions of Scripture scenery, and figurative exhibitions of the evils or graces of their own hearts. As he advanced in life, his spirituality and directness increased, and aged Christians were specially delighted with his ministrations. One of his most marked characteristics as a Preacher was his extreme readiness. It was commonly said by his brethren that Dr. Black never refused an invitation to preach, and this was almost literally true. By day or by night, in the house or by the way, to a handful or a crowd, and often in circumstances that would have deterred most men from a public appearance, he was ready to stand forth and proclaim the Gospel of his Saviour. Often has he released from a trying service a younger brother, who had not had time to make his needful preparation, and when others failed in discharging their public appointments, he was ready to become their substitute. At a certain time he was engaged to preach in the country, at a distance from his own house. He had selected from a number of scraps of paper, one on which was the subject that he designed to speak upon. Having set out on horseback with a brother, the time was engrossed in conversation, until they came within sight of the place, where the people were already assembling. On looking for his Bible and memorandum, it was found that both were forgotten, and the subject had slipped from his memory. "What shall I do?" said the Doctor to his brother, with some emotion,— "I have forgotten not only my sermon, but even my text." "It is likely there will be a Bible there," said the brother laconically,—"there are texts enough in it, and I expect you will be able to find one, and a sermon too." And so it was. He preached with great freedom upon a different subject from the one intended, as was afterwards ascertained. After sermon, an intelligent female came to him with joy, told him she had been greatly troubled on the very subject of which he had been treating, and thanked God for sending him there to quiet her disturbed heart. On another occasion, when, on a visit to Belfast, in Ireland, in 1832, being in the house of the late Rev. John Alexander, D.D., of the Reformed Presbyterian Church there, he was informed by his host that he had an appointment to preach and baptize at a short distance from town, and was asked to accompany him. Other ministers were present, and, as they came within sight of the place of meeting, Dr. Alexander inquires,— "Who is to preach?" "Yourself," says Dr. Black. "No," replies Dr. Alexander, "the people must hear the stranger." Though at first displeased at being so much taken by surprise, Dr. Black yielded to the importunity of his friends, who knew their man, and, although not expecting to preach, he discoursed most ingeniously and satisfactorily, for nearly an hour, on the subject of Infant Baptism, until all were delighted or surprised. But I will give one other example. Dr. Black had been appointed by his church to represent them in the Union Convention of Reformed Churches. Its annual meetings were opened by a Sermon appointed the previous year. At one of these meetings the person appointed did not appear. The hour had arrived, and a large congregation, including many ministers of the Gospel, were present, but no Preacher presented himself. Dr. Black was appealed to and urged to preach. He said,—" No, I am at home,—some of the strangers must do it ;" and thus he declined. He, however, added, as the person who applied to him was passing away, " If no one else can be found to do it, you may come back to me." All excused themselves—it did come back to the Doctor. With great solemnity he took the pulpit, and preached a most admirable sermon, and what was especially striking to all, was its remarkable appropriateness to the time, place and circumstances; and the whole produced a great impression.

Dr. Black was, indeed, a man for all occasions. And this characteristic and uncommon readiness was the result, not of recklessness nor love of ostentation, nor reliance on good memory,—for he never wrote out or memorized his discourses,—but it came from his possessing very many of the higher order of mental and gracious qualifications. He was ready, because he had a full mental storehouse,—the power of abstraction, the gift of language, a great command of the resources of his own mind, and, above all, a strong, humble and unwavering dependence on the help of God's Holy Spirit. He preached because he loved the work, and had found, by repeated trial, that he had from God the ready power to perform it. And, yet, Dr. Black *prepared* to preach. He was always preparing. His studies were never finished, and, to the close of his life, he was a laborious student. His views of the Christian ministry were too high to admit of the attempt to serve God with what had cost him nothing. He selected his subject, elaborated it in his mind, used all available helps, wrote upon paper an extended skeleton, and so went to the desk to speak on God's behalf to sinners. He preached for nearly fifty years, and then died with the harness on.

Dr. Black's life was too active, and too much engrossed with multifarious cares, to effect much as an author. And yet few men are more frequently called to print their spoken discourses. He wrote largely for the newspapers and periodicals of the day, and he left behind him, as more permanent monuments of his industry and learning, an extended Discourse on " Church Fellowship ;" " The Bible Against Slavery ;" " Two Discourses on the Baptist Controversy ;" and one on " The Duration of the Mediatorial Kingdom." This last is a remarkable production. It was preached at the request of several ministers of various denominations in Pittsburg and the vicinity, and, although written when the author was entering his eightieth year, shows all the freshness and activity of earlier days. " Is Dr. Black wearing out ?" a mutual friend inquired of Dr. Gilbert McMaster, his old associate. " Dr. Black will never *wear out*," replied Dr. McMaster; " when the time comes, he will *go out*." And so it proved. The lamp of life was suddenly blown out by the storm of disease, sent immediately from God. It was not left to wear down and expire, after long flickering in its socket. And Dr. McMaster has gone out too. But stars set to rise again— they do not perish.

Dr. Black was married to Elizabeth Watson, daughter of Andrew and Margaret (Thomson) Watson, of Pittsburg. They had ten children, eight of whom survived both parents. Three of the sons became Clergymen, and one a Lawyer, and one a Physician. *John* died on the 15th of August, 1828, in the twenty-third year of his age, soon after becoming a licentiate of the Reformed Presbyterian Church. *Andrew Watson* was graduated at the Western University (Pittsburg) in 1826; was licensed to preach, by the Reformed Presbytery of Pittsburg, in the winter of 1828; and, after travelling extensively in the West and South, was Ordained, and installed Pastor of the Congregations of Shenango and Neshannock, Pa., on the 18th of January, 1832. He was married on the 1st of January, 1835, to Margaret, youngest daughter of John Roseburgh, of Pittsburg. In 1839 he accepted a call to the then newly organized Reformed Presbyterian Church in Allegheny City, Pa. While Pastor of this church, he received the appointment of Chaplain, or Moral Instructor, in the Penitentiary of the Western District of Pennsylvania, and for several years discharged its duties with success. In 1852 he was honoured with the degree of Doctor of Divinity from Rutgers College. In 1855 he resigned his charge in Allegheny, and accepted, for a year, the agency of the American Bible Society, for several of the Northern Counties of Pennsylvania and Ohio; and, in the mean time, received invitations to settle in Chicago and several other places, all of which he declined. At a meeting of the General Synod of the Reformed Presbyterian Church, held in Cedarville, O., in June, 1857, he received the appointment of delegate to the sister churches of Britain and Ireland, and also of the representative of the Church to which he belonged, to the Conference of Evangelical Christians meeting in Berlin, Prussia. These appointments he fulfilled with great fidelity and acceptance. At the meeting of the General Synod of the Reformed Presbyterian Church, held in Eden, Ill., in June, 1858, he was appointed Professor of Exegetical, Historical and Evangelistic Theology in the Theological Seminary under their care. He was preparing for the duties thus devolved upon him by a unanimous act of the highest judicatory of his Church, when he was called to his reward. He died on the 10th of September, 1858, just entering his fifty-first year. He was an able, learned and judicious man, and an earnest, eloquent and popular preacher.

Samuel Wylie was graduated at the Western University in 1835, became eminent in the profession of Law, was a Judge, and Governor of Nebraska Territory. He was also a Colonel of Volunteers in the Mexican War. When the Southern Rebellion broke out he accepted the command of a Regiment of Volunteers from his native city, and proceeded at once to the field. He was killed by a rifle ball, when gallantly leading his regiment in a charge against the enemy, before Richmond, on the 27th of June, 1862, in the forty-sixth year of his age. He was highly gifted, learned, eloquent, courageous, and intensely patriotic.

Robert John, the fifth son, was graduated at the Western University in 1840 or 1841; studied Theology partly under the direction of his father, and partly in the Seminary of the Reformed Presbyterian Church, under the direction of the Rev. Dr. S. B. Wylie. He was licensed, by the Reformed Presbytery of Pittsburg, in October, 1843, and, having preached with acceptance in various parts of the Church until January, 1847, he received a call, at that time, to become the Pastor of the Third Reformed Presbyterian Church in Philadelphia. Having accepted this call, he was ordained and installed on the 22d of April following.

In August, 1853, he was united in marriage with Susan Julia Maria, daughter of the late Dr. S. B. Wylie, and they became the parents of three children. Mr. Black continued to labour with great diligence and fidelity till he was disabled by the malady which terminated in his death. He died on the 10th of October, 1860, in the forty-fifth year of his age, and the fourteenth of his ministry. He was an able, eloquent and highly popular Preacher, and his early demise was deeply lamented. One of Dr. Black's daughters is married to a clergyman, the Rev. Samuel Wylie, of Eden, Ill.

Very respectfully yours,
J. N. McLEOD.

SAMUEL BROWN WYLIE, D.D.*
1799—1852.

SAMUEL BROWN WYLIE, a son of Adam and Margaret Wylie, was born in Moylarg, near Ballymena, County of Antrim, Ireland, May 21, 1773. His father was a farmer in easy circumstances, and both his parents were exemplary members of the Reformed Presbyterian Church. His religious education was very carefully attended to in the family, and the influence of an elder sister had much to do in moulding his Christian character and determining his choice of the ministry for a profession. After having gone through the requisite course of preparation,—during which time he was himself engaged as a teacher,—he entered Glasgow College, where he distinguished himself much as a scholar, and graduated as Master of Arts in April, 1797. After his graduation he engaged in teaching a school in Ballymena, and continued thus employed until he was compelled to fly from his native land in consequence of his connection with the efforts made in favour of Irish independence.

Mr. Wylie landed at Newcastle, Del., on the 18th of October, 1797, after a passage of twenty days. Notwithstanding the Yellow Fever was then prevailing in Philadelphia, he, with one of his fellow-emigrants, after a few days, started for the city on foot, and arrived there on the 31st. Within about six weeks, through the kindness of a venerable man of the Society of Friends, he was engaged in teaching a school in Cheltenham, about ten miles North of the city. Here he remained until the fall of 1798, when he was appointed a Tutor in the University of Pennsylvania. He afterwards established a private academy, which he taught with great success for many years. In 1828 he became Professor of the Latin and Greek Languages in the University of Pennsylvania, and held the place until 1845, when he ceased from its active duties, and became Professor *emeritus*. On the organization of the Theological Seminary of the Reformed Presbyterian Church, in 1808, he was appointed a Professor in that institution, and held the office until his resignation of it in 1851. He was engaged as a teacher, with only some slight interruptions, during a period of upwards of sixty years.

He studied Theology, after he came to this country, under the care of the Reformed Presbytery, and was licensed to preach, by that Body, at Coldenham,

---

* MS. from his son, Rev. Dr. Wylie, of Philadelphia.—Dr. McLeod's Fun. Disc.

Orange County, N. Y., on the 24th of June, 1799. He preached some time in Walkill, N. Y., and assisted Mr. McKinney at a communion in Galway, and, in the winter of 1799–1800 returned to Philadelphia, where he preached for a while to a small congregation of the Reformed Presbyterian Church, which had been organized in 1798. He was ordained at Ryegate, Vt., on the 25th of June, 1800, and immediately after made an extensive tour to the West and South. He was sent on this mission, in company with the Rev. James McKinney, to carry into effect the decision of the highest judicatory of the Reformed Presbyterian Church, prohibiting any of its members from holding slaves. In 1802 he was sent as a delegate from the Reformed Presbyterian Church in the United States to the sister Churches in Scotland and Ireland; and he visited those countries again in 1845. His first and only pastoral charge was in Philadelphia, to which he was called in 1802, and which he retained till the close of his life. He was, however, partially relieved from his labours in 1843, by having his son, the Rev. Theodore W. J. Wylie, associated with him as a colleague.

He was chosen a member of the American Philosophical Society in 1806. The degree of Doctor of Divinity was conferred upon him, by Dickinson College, in 1816. He was chosen Professor of Languages in that College, but declined the appointment.

In 1847, the fiftieth anniversary of his arrival in this country, his many friends, in his congregation and out of it, held a public meeting in the church, and presented him, in token of their affectionate respect and veneration, with a service of plate and a purse of five hundred dollars in gold.

Dr. Wylie continued to preach with unabated mental power, and with his usual earnestness of manner, until within four months of his death. In the immediate prospect of his departure he exhibited the utmost composure of spirit, the deepest humility, and the most joyful and triumphant confidence in his Redeemer. He died, from general debility and suffusion of the heart, on the 13th of October, 1852, in the eightieth year of his age. He was buried in Woodland Cemetery, his Funeral being attended by crowds of mourning friends from all ranks and professions. A Discourse, commemorative of his life and character, was delivered shortly after, by the Rev. John N. McLeod, D.D., of New York, and another by the Rev. Gilbert McMaster, D.D., which were published.

Dr. Wylie's publications are two Sermons, 1804; a Greek Grammar, 1838; and a Memoir of the late Rev. Alexander McLeod, D.D., 1855.

He was married on the 5th of April, 1802, to Margaret, eldest daughter of Andrew Watson, of Pittsburg, Pa. They had seven children, four of whom, with their mother, still (1863) survive—two daughters, one of whom became the wife of the Rev. J. N. McLeod, D.D., of New York, and the other of the Rev. Robert J. Black, of Philadelphia, (now deceased); and two sons, both Ministers in the Reformed Presbyterian Church, the elder,—*Theophilus A. Wylie*, being also a Professor in the University of Indiana, and the younger, *Theodore W. J. Wylie*, who has succeeded his father in his pastoral charge, being also his successor as Professor in the Theological Seminary of the Reformed Presbyterian Church.

FROM THE REV. SAMUEL B. HOW, D.D.

NEW BRUNSWICK, N. J., March 25, 1857.

Rev. and dear Sir: Agreeably to the promise I made you, I now furnish you with some of my recollections of the Rev. Samuel B. Wylie, D.D., whom

I knew well, especially during the time that he was associated with Mr. James G. Thompson, as a Teacher in the Grammar School of the University of Pennsylvania. Both of these gentlemen were highly accomplished classical scholars, and most thorough and accurate teachers. The school flourished greatly under them, and consisted of more than one hundred scholars, all studying in one of the very spacious rooms of the old University building. The discipline and mode of teaching adopted by both these eminent instructors were the same.

As a Teacher, Dr. Wylie insisted upon the greatest possible thoroughness, and was never satisfied until every difficulty in the lesson had been mastered, and the most minute details had been intelligently and accurately grasped. His mode of teaching brought into exercise not merely or chiefly the memory, but the faculties of reflection, combination and association—indeed, each student, as the mysteries of the Latin and Greek were gradually unfolded to him, was, at the same time, undergoing a process of thorough mental discipline. I have often thought that a recitation to Dr. Wylie, especially in Greek, was, merely in relation to the power of reflection, as severe and improving a mental process as the solution of a long and difficult problem in Mathematics.

Dr. Wylie was a strict, and even severe, disciplinarian in the government of his school, and often, as well as Horace's teacher, Orbilius, deserved the epithet of "*plagosus*." No interference of parents with the management of the school was permitted. But he was considerate and discriminating in his discipline, and often kind and generous. The studious and well-behaved had nothing to fear. In his strictest discipline it was manifest that he was influenced by a conscientious regard to duty, and a sincere desire to effect the reformation and promote the welfare of those whom he punished. I consider him as having been a fine model of a Teacher. Thoroughly qualified for teaching the Latin and Greek languages, holding the profession of a Teacher in high esteem and thoroughly devoted to it, relying for success on the fearless and conscientious discharge of duty, he was highly esteemed while living, and is held in grateful remembrance by his surviving scholars.

I had the opportunity of hearing Dr. Wylie preach but a few times. Once was when he lectured, or gave a continuous comment, on the First Chapter of the Epistle to the Hebrews. His thoughts were clear and vigorous, his criticisms able, and his expositions thorough. I remember to have been taken somewhat by surprise at his proving, by learned grammatical criticism, that $O\ \Theta\varepsilon o\varsigma$, in the eighth verse, is in the vocative, and not in the nominative, case. He concluded his criticism by saying,—"These remarks are for those present who understand the learned languages." He was undoubtedly an able Preacher as well as an able Teacher.

With high regard and esteem, yours truly,
SAMUEL B. HOW.

FROM THE HON. WILLIAM B. REED.

PHILADELPHIA, September 8, 1859.

My dear Sir: I have not been unmindful of your request as to Dr. Wylie, but have been trying to gather materials out of which to frame an answer. I am under the impression that, in directing your inquiry to me, you have confounded me with my brother Henry, who was a fellow Professor with the Doctor in the University of Pennsylvania, and who knew him well and loved him much. I had very little acquaintance with the old gentleman and never was his pupil, and could give you very little but what lawyers call "general character," which was that of a single-minded, devout clergyman, and of an accomplished scholar. He was a man of large fortune, or would have been so but for his profuse generosity to all around him,—family, parishioners and friends; and some rather grotesque traditions exist of his credulity on the side of generosity and charity. More than this I cannot say.

On Dr. Wylie's death in 1852, my brother Henry wrote a sort of Obituary Review for a Church newspaper with which he was connected. I will transcribe two or three paragraphs from that article, which may give you an idea of some of the more prominent features of his character :—

"Dr. Wylie was a life-long student—even when between seventy and eighty years of age, his active mind was opening for itself new spheres of study. His acquirements as a linguist were very extensive—besides the Greek and Latin and Hebrew, to the teaching of which so many years of his life were devoted, some of the Oriental languages were known to him. Of several languages he had a mastery, and is said to have understood, in all, no less than fourteen.

"It is interesting to know that all this profound scholarship and earnestness of ministerial labour were joined with unfailing Christian cheerfulness and a freshness of character that was most attractive. The paragraph in Mr. McLeod's Sermon, which describes Dr. Wylie in his home, may be quoted as a very pleasing picture of a clergyman's domestic life:

"'In domestic life he was simple in his habits, cheerful in his intercourse with all, strict in carrying out his family regimen, careful in the instruction of his household, faithful to warn and rebuke, prompt and punctual to an extraordinary degree, and yet attracting all by his honest and exhaustless affection, which he poured forth as from a horn of plenty. His heart was always young. A household, almost prostrated by their bereavement, show how they loved him. We never knew a man more attached to his own home than he was; and where he was, there his family desired and loved to be also. His house was the abode of friendship, and its hospitalities were dispensed without stint and without murmur. For his charities he was proverbial, and if they were not always discriminating, they were as cordial as they were ample. Caring nothing for money except as a means of usefulness, a very considerable portion of his income, which was sometimes large, was all his life expended in works of beneficence to others. Even ingratitude, from which he did not always escape, could not divert from its course the stream of his bounty.'

"We have rarely met with any thing more beautiful—so full is it of an old man's wisdom and a child's innocence—than the expression of the feeling with which this good Christian, bringing together in his thoughts a retrospect of near eighty years, and a close prospect of his last hours, contemplated life and death. To Mr. McLeod's qestion,—'What are the exercises of your mind now, and in immediate view of death?'—he answered,—'I cannot say that I am anxious to die, as I have heard some Christians say they were,—for life is still pleasant to me. I feel no serious decay of my mental powers; I am not oppressed with poverty; I find nothing in the conduct of my family to make me think they wish me away; my congregation is peaceful and prosperous; and I have better hopes of the Church than I had. I do not feel like a burden as yet. I am, therefore, willing to live. But, on the other hand,' he continued, 'I am nearly fourscore; I feel of course that my earthly pilgrimage is near its end; I can do little more for God, and I know that to depart and be with Christ is far better than to continue here. I am perfectly willing to die. I leave the whole matter in the hands of my Redeemer. My faith, I think, is taking the form of entire submission to the will of God. I rest with perfect confidence in Jesus Christ.'"

In the hope that these extracts may avail to the object contemplated by your request,

I am, my dear Sir, very sincerely yours,
WILLIAM B. REED.

FROM THE REV. JOHN FORSYTH, D.D.

NEWBURGH, November 6, 1859.

Rev. and dear Friend: I send you my recollections of the late Dr. Samuel B. Wylie, such as they are, with a great deal of pleasure.

I became acquainted with him while I was serving as a licentiate; and, though he belonged to a different branch of the Church, he kindly assisted at my Ordination as a Pastor of a Church in Philadelphia. I was an inexperienced youth, and almost from the moment of my introduction to him, the venerable man treated me with paternal kindness. His library was placed at my command, and, having no domestic hearth of my own, I had at all times freest access to his. A native of Ireland, he had all the best traits of his countrymen,—a genial temper, an open hand, and a heart full of the milk of human kindness. But he had other qualities, for which Irishmen are not specially noted, and among them I should name an indomitable patience, a persistent energy, which no difficulties could affright or exhaust.

One of his older parishioners told me that when Dr. Wylie was called to Philadelphia, his congregation was the merest handful,—indeed, so small that, (as Dr. W. himself told me,) on the first Sabbath after his Ordination, the members of it met for sermon in the bed-room of one of them who happened to be sick. Even then they were not in the least crowded. He was, of course, obliged to depend upon his own efforts for support, and he, accordingly, opened a school. But he was a stranger in Philadelphia; he knew nobody except a few poor Covenanters; and when the session of his Academy began, not a solitary scholar darkened its door; he had no one to teach but himself. However, he stayed in the room from 9 A.M. till 3 P.M, then "closed his school," and went home. This he did with punctual regularity, day after day, for a week or more, until a gentleman, living in the vicinity, struck by the oddity of the affair, or curious to learn something about a teacher who seemed so laboriously engaged in doing nothing, called upon him. He was so well pleased that he sent him, the next day, a pupil, who speedily brought more, until Dr. Wylie's school became one of the largest, the most renowned, and the most successful in the city. Such it continued to be until its Principal was transferred to the chair of Ancient Languages in the University of Pennsylvania. He had filled this office for many years when I became acquainted with him. The Latin and Greek authors, read by his classes in College, must have been familiar to him as household words; but he made it a rule, as he himself told me, never to meet a class without a previous and careful reading of the lesson of the day.

During a long life he was a most laborious student. He was a thoroughly old fashioned Presbyterian in his notions about a learned ministry. He collected a noble library containing several thousand volumes, and particularly rich in theology, classic literature, and science. There were few books in it of which he could not give you a good account. If he were at leisure, and you were disposed to draw him out in regard to a book, he would have charmed you with his curious and exact information, respecting the subject or the author, yet unmixed with the slightest spice of pedantry, but seasoned with occasional sallies of Irish humour.

Though unable to devote much time to pastoral labour, he gathered a large congregation; but he continued his academic labours, which, indeed were a sort of second nature to him, even after his people had become numerous enough to have afforded him an ample maintenance. Occupied as he was during the day in his school, and subsequently in College, he could not have done what he deemed justice to his pulpit duties, if he had not resorted to a somewhat singular expedient. He went to bed immediately after tea, slept soundly until twelve o'clock, then rose and studied for three or four hours. He escaped the invasion of visitors, to whom—such was his kindness—he could not have denied himself had he been awake, and he thus found time to enrich that treasury of knowledge out of which he brought things new and old, from Sabbath to Sabbath, to delight and edify his hearers.

For many years Dr. Wylie held the office of Professor of Theology to the Reformed Presbyterian Synod, and frequently had a dozen or more theological students under his care. I have reason to believe that those trained by him for the ministry will compare, both as Theologians and as Preachers, with the alumni of any other Seminary in our land. You will be ready to say, What an iron constitution he must have had to enable him to discharge such multifarious duties, for so long a period, and to discharge them all so well. He was a person of large frame, well-built, and stately,—a man of presence, who could scarcely fail to arrest the eye of a stranger, in the street or elsewhere. At threescore and ten, he was as erect in his bearing as a soldier, and having all the marks of robust health, so that he looked much more like a hearty old country gentleman whose days were spent *sub Jove*, than a hard working student. In a word, even unto old age he was a noble illustration of the oft-quoted words, *sana mens in corpore sano*.

Dr. Wylie was not an eloquent Preacher in the sense in which that phrase is commonly understood. His voice, though strong, was wanting in flexibility, and his manner was perhaps somewhat modified by the necessity he was under of preaching extempore. But no one could listen to him without feeling that he was in the presence of a man of massive sense, thoroughly versed in Scripture, and master of the topic under discussion. From the few opportunities which I had of hearing him, I should judge that his sermons, in the main, were better adapted to instruct, console, edify the believer, than to arouse the careless; though the latter class was by no means overlooked. They had the rich unction of the Gospel, so that they could be relished by the humblest as well as the most cultivated Christian; but they were argumentative and expository rather than hortatory or sentimental. He won, and kept until his dying day, the devoted and reverential love of his congregation, which, under his able ministrations, became very numerous. A better instructed congregation, or one more fruitful in all good works, it would be difficult to find in Philadelphia or elsewhere.

I remain very truly yours,
JOHN FORSYTH.

JAMES RENWICK WILLSON, D.D.*
1807—1853.

JAMES RENWICK WILLSON was born, April 9, 1780, in "the Forks of Yough," the neck of land between the Monongahela and Youghiogheny Rivers, about fourteen miles from Pittsburg, Pa. His paternal great-grandfather had emigrated from the County of Down, Ireland, in 1721, and settled near Back Creek, Dauphin County, Pa.; but the family subsequently removed to "the Forks," where they still resided at the birth of the subject of this notice. His father, Zaccheus Willson, was a Ruling Elder in the Reformed Presbyterian Church. His mother, whose maiden name was Mary McConnell, was also of Irish extraction. Both his parents were distinguished for earnest piety, for great vigour of mind, and, considering their limited opportunities, for a large measure of general intelligence.

His father was a farmer; and he himself pursued the same occupation until he had reached his twenty-first year. But, from his early youth, he evinced a decided intellectual taste, and was never satisfied unless he was adding something to his store of knowledge. His mind also early took a religious direction, as was evinced by the fact that at the age of fourteen he officiated in the family devo-

*MS. from his son, Rev. Dr. S. M. Willson.

tions, in the absence of his father, and a year later made a public profession of religion. He originally joined the Associate Reformed Church; but, when he was in his eighteenth year, he transferred his membership to the Reformed Presbyterian Church, in connection with which he continued ever afterwards. He received his education at Cannonsburg, Pa., and the early part of it was chiefly under the Rev. Dr. McMillan. The institution of which he became a member was, at that time, only an Academy; but, after a year or two, it was incorporated as Jefferson College; and, having passed through the regular collegiate course, he was graduated in 1805. He was a most vigorous student, rarely allowing himself much more than four hours for sleep, and graduated with the highest honours of his class. During the last year of his collegiate course, he was employed as a Tutor in the institution. Shortly after he left College he went to New York, where, for some time, he prosecuted the study of Theology under the direction of the Rev. Alexander McLeod. In 1807 he was licensed to preach by the Middle Committee of the Reformed Presbytery.* From 1809 to 1815 he was the Principal of an Academy at Bedford, Pa., and, during his residence here, he made the first analysis of Bedford Springs, the result of which was published. In 1815 he removed to Philadelphia, where he was engaged in teaching a Select School for about two years. During this period he often occupied the pulpits of several of his brethren, and, for a long time, preached regularly on Sabbath afternoon at what was called "the Neck," where he found a very interesting field of labour.

In September, 1817, he was installed Pastor of the Coldenham and Newburgh Congregation, in the State of New York. In 1824 a distinct Congregation was formed at Newburgh, and he remained in charge of the Coldenham Congregation until 1830, when he removed to Albany, and took charge of a very small church in that city. He, however, returned to Coldenham in 1833, and resumed his pastoral charge there. He was engaged, more or less, during the greater part of his ministry, in giving instruction to theological students; and, in 1838, was appointed, by the Synod, Professor in the Eastern Theological Seminary. In 1840 the Eastern and Western Seminaries were united and fixed at Allegheny, near Pittsburg; in consequence of which he resigned his pastoral charge at Coldenham, and removed his family to Allegheny. In 1845 the Seminary was removed to Cincinnati; and, in 1849, into the interior of the State, he moving along with it.

He continued his labours as Professor till about a year and a half previous to his death. His constitution was uncommonly vigorous, and his health almost uninterrupted until 1847, when he experienced a partial stroke of the sun, from the effect of which he never fully recovered. The winters of 1851–52 and 1852–53 he spent with his son in Philadelphia. The last public service which he performed was "serving a table" at the Communion in the Reformed Presbyterian Church in Philadelphia, on the 18th of March, 1853. He spent the summer of 1852 and also of 1853 with his friend, Mr. John Beatrice, at Coldenham, eleven miles west of Newburgh; and here he closed his earthly career. The immedi-

---

* The Reformed Presbytery, which had been constituted in 1798, had, in 1803, become too widely extended to allow its members to attend meetings with sufficient frequency; in consequence of which they formed three Committees,—Northern, Middle and Southern, which met twice a year or oftener, and attended to the ordinary routine of business, reporting to Presbytery at its annual meetings. The Middle Committee was located in the State of Pennsylvania.

diate cause of his death was a fall, which fractured the neck of his thigh-bone. His system did not react, and, after a gradual decline of six weeks, he sunk calmly to his rest, on the 29th of September. 1853.

He was honoured with the degree of Doctor of Divinity (from what College I have not been able to learn) in or about the year 1828.

The following is a list of Dr. Willson's publications:—

Historical Sketch of Opinions on the Atonement, interspersed with Biographical Notices of the Leading Doctors, and Outlines of the Lectures of the Church from the Incarnation to the Present time. With translations from Francis Turretin on the Atonement, - - - 1817
The Subjection of Kings and Nations to Messiah: A Sermon preached in the Reformed Presbyterian Church, New York, - - - - 1819
Civil Government: A Sermon preached at Newburgh, - - - 1821
Dr. Watts an Anti-Trinitarian, demonstrated in a Review of Dr. Miller's Letter to the Editor of the Unitarian Miscellany, - - - - 1821
Honour to whom Honour is Due: A Funeral Eulogium delivered at Goshen, at the Interment of the Bones of those who fell at the Battle of Minisink, - - - - - - - - - 1822
Anniversary Address delivered before the Newburgh Lyceum, - - 1823
A Sermon on the Book of Life of the Lamb; preached in New York, 1824
The Glory and Security of the Church of God: A Sermon preached in New York, - - - - - - - - - 1824
Dissertation on the Musquito, read before the Newburgh Lyceum, - 1824
Political Danger: A Sermon preached on a Fast day observed by several Churches in Newburgh, - - - - - - - - 1825
The American Jubilee: A Discourse delivered at Walden, N. Y., on the Fourth of July, - - - - - - - - - 1825
Alphabetical Writing and Printing: An Anniversary Address before the Walden Library Association, - - - - - - - 1826
The Sabbath: A Discourse on the Duty of Civil Government in relation to the Sanctification of the Lord's Day, preached in Coldenham, - 1829
The Bow: A Sermon preached in Newburgh, - - - - 1831
Prince Messiah's Claims to Dominion over all Governments, and the Disregard of his authority by the United States in the Federal Constitution: A Sermon preached at Albany, - - - - - 1832
Tokens of the Divine Displeasure in the late Conflagration in New York, and other Judgments: A Sermon preached at Newburgh, - - 1835
An Address before the Newburgh Library Association on its First Anniversary, - - - - - - - - - 1836
The Written Law, - - - - - - - - - 1840

He was also the editor of The Evangelical Witness, a Monthly, from 1822 to 1826; of the Christian Statesman, a Weekly Journal, 1827–28; and of the Albany Quarterly from 1831 to 1833. In connection with the last mentioned he published a History of the Church of Scotland, of three hundred octavo pages.

In 1807 he was married to Jane, daughter of John Roberts, a merchant of Cannonsburg, originally from Ireland, but immediately from Pendleton County, Va. They had nine children,—three sons and six daughters. The eldest son died in 1838—the two that survive are ministers, and one of them,—*James M.*,

D.D., is Professor in the Theological Seminary of the Reformed Presbyterian Church, at Allegheny. The three surviving daughters are married to Reformed Presbyterian Ministers. Mrs. Willson died in March, 1839.

I was quite well acquainted with Dr. Willson during the two or three years that he lived in Albany, and had much pleasant intercourse with him. I was always greatly impressed with the vigour of his intellect, the extent and variety of his knowledge, and I may add with his genial and kindly spirit. I do not remember to have ever heard him utter an expression that savoured of undue harshness concerning any body. But it was currently said that in the pulpit he seemed to breath another atmosphere; and sometimes his eloquence there combined both the majesty and the fury of the tempest. I remember his preaching here on one public occasion—I think it was before the Albany County Bible Society—when his denunciations against certain forms of evil were perfectly terrific. Hence those who saw him only in the pulpit, while they could not but admire and reverence him as a power, were not likely to give him credit for those finer and gentler qualities which he really possessed. I recollect his showing me, on one occasion, letters from some prominent clergymen in Scotland, which evinced a very high estimate of his talents and acquirements.

FROM THE REV. JAMES M. WILLSON, D.D.

PHILADELPHIA, February 15, 1865.

Rev. and dear Sir: Your request for my recollections and impressions of my ever venerated father I will comply with in the best way I can, though I am quite sensible of the delicacy of the task it has imposed upon me.

His appearance indicated no common man. His frame, large and massive, but not corpulent; his stature considerably above the ordinary standard; his elevated and expanded forehead; his dark, piercing eye; his thin, firm, compressed lips; his grave and thoughtful visage; his vigorous and elastic step; all gave evidence of extraordinary physical and mental energy. In his youth he delighted and excelled in the athletic sports so common in the then frontier portions of the country, and, by these, in connection with the toils of the farm, his naturally strong constitution was admirably developed, rendering him, in after life, until enfeebled by advancing years, almost a stranger to fatigue. Though he did not commence his literary course until he had attained his majority, yet, when he had once begun, he studied with untiring diligence, and soon passed all his competitors. His studies took a wide range —his learning became in a few years varied and extensive. He acquired some knowledge of from twelve to fifteen languages, ancient and modern—most of these he could read with ease and pleasure—of some of them he was a master. He conversed in French and German. History ho had read largely. He was quite familiar with the modern sciences. In Belles Lettres he was a finished scholar. In early life he studied Medicine more or less for several years. But Theology was his principal study. He resorted constantly to the original fountains of Divine truth, and to the weighty tomes of the Reformation. He began the day, for many years, with the Hebrew Bible, and closed it with the Greek Testament, studying each critically.

His habits were social, and he was never happier than when bringing forth his stores of knowledge for the benefit of those with whom he conversed. In his frequent travels he never hesitated to accost strangers, either to give or to obtain information. He cared little for etiquette; and, though free from any thing like rudeness or coarseness of manner, he was not what would be styled a polished gentleman. His original rusticity never fully wore off. He associated much with distinguished men, and abounded in anecdotes illustrative of their character and times; and he could relate them well.

His imagination was peculiarly powerful and excitable. He *saw* every thing. He dealt with no abstractions—all was, to him, concrete, living reality. Hence some of his peculiarities. The invisible world of the good and the bad had to him not only a real but a present existence. In this I have often been struck with the resemblance between him and Luther.

Intellectual activity was one of his most remarkable traits. He was always busy, but never seemed wearied with mental effort. I never saw him listless—whatever he did, he did with his might; and, partly from the force of his imagination, which invested every thing with its own radiance, and partly from his habit of referring every thing to God's providential agency, nothing seemed trifling to him.

He had great discernment of character, and yet he was unsuspicious. Indeed, a certain childlike simplicity was one of his striking characteristics. He was no financier—the accumulation of property he never thought of.

Of his moral character I should say that the most marked trait was unwavering fidelity and integrity. He knew nothing of a calculating expediency. Duty, right, faithfulness—these were his mottoes. He was incapable of artifice or intrigue. He was vehement in his denunciations of sin, and never hesitated to trespass upon what might be regarded as the sphere of politicians, when the occasion demanded stern rebuke. His passions were originally strong, partaking of his constitutional energy and ardour. At times he was impatient, nor could he ever bear with equanimity opposition to what he deemed important truth.

He had every physical attribute of the Orator,—great bodily vigour, a powerful and sonorous voice, a flashing eye, an elastic frame. These, with his wide range of information, enabling him to gather from every quarter arguments and illustrations, his vivid fancy, his ready command of the best language, his highly cultivated reasoning powers and absorbing earnestness, rendered him a commanding and attractive public speaker. He was equally at home in the pulpit and on the platform, and never declined a call either to the one or the other, when he *could* respond to it. He always spoke extemporaneously. His notes, which he never used in speaking, did not occupy more perhaps, than a hand-breadth of paper. But he meditated closely, and was never at a loss.

He was eminently a man of prayer, and not unfrequently spent hours together in devotional exercises. He was accustomed to carry all matters, even the least, to the throne of grace. This gave to his prayers, both in public and in the family, somewhat a peculiar character.

He was a very ready writer, and wrote legibly but not beautifully. Except in respect to his journal, which he attended to daily, he had no fixed hours for composition. Indeed, times and seasons had little influence upon him as a student.

Though he had no disrelish for social pleasantry, he was not, either by nature or habit, a wit. His mind, from the time I became capable of observing, was almost constantly occupied on themes which he deemed of momentous import. I may add that he was an ardent friend of the Bible Society, and took an active part in the cause of Temperance, and in opposition to Slavery, preaching and writing abundantly on all these subjects. His death was singularly serene and happy.

With best wishes, I am, Rev. and Dear Sir,
Yours truly,
JAMES M. WILLSON.

FROM THE REV. JOHN FORSYTH, D.D.

NEWBURGH, November 16, 1858.

Rev. and Dear Friend: I send you, with much pleasure, my recollections, such as they are, of the late Dr. James Renwick Willson—at the same time you will allow me to express the hope that you have secured the aid of some one who was brought into closer contact with him than I ever was, and therefore better qualified than myself to portray his character.

When Dr. Willson first came to Newburgh, I was too young to be cognizant of his arrival and settlement as a Pastor. My father, though not one of his parishioners, often went to hear him of a Sabbath evening, and regarded him as a valued friend. My earliest recollection of him is on this wise. For some reason I had been allowed to sit up with my mother, one Sabbath evening, much beyond my bed-time, while my father was away hearing Dr. Willson. On his return home he gave what must have been a glowing account of the sermon—for he was an excellent *raconteur* of such matters—and I well remember with what childish wonder, not unmingled with terror, I listened to the startling intelligence that "a city, New Jerusalem, was coming down out of Heaven," and asked what in that case was to become of Newburgh. The words first quoted, I dare say had formed the theme of the Doctor's discourse. Dr. Willson was then Pastor of the Reformed Presbyterian Congregations of Coldenham and Newburgh—the latter consisting of a mere handful of people, though it rapidly increased under his able ministrations. I cannot recall the time when I first heard him; but, though too young properly to appreciate his preaching, I distinctly remember how eager I was to accompany my parents whenever they attended his church. There was nothing in the forms of the service to attract me, there was no well-trained choir, nor organ "breathing its distant thunder notes or swelling into a diapason full." Our Reformed Presbyterian brethren, as you know, abjure such aids to devotion, as savouring of will worship. The Preacher was the great attraction, and you will agree with me that his eloquence must have been of no mean kind, when it could thus draw a mere child, as well as the crowds of men and women who thronged his church.

When I was old enough to appreciate him, Dr. Willson was in the full maturity of his powers, physical and mental—a man of imposing presence, with a bodily frame capable of enduring almost any amount of work or of study, and in neither respect was he sparing of himself. He had attracted attention in Philadelphia before he came to Newburgh, and Dr. Ely, who was then on terms of intimacy with him, in a review of one of his publications, (Willson on Atonement,) described him as a "man of genius, whose fancy sometimes runs away with his judgment—a man of fervour, faults, and powerful intellect." The whole passage sounds like an outburst of admiring friendship, but those who knew Dr. Willson will recognize the truthfulness of the description of the man; and you will thus see that he had some of the most essential elements of the Orator. It has been my good fortune to hear Melville, of Camberwell; Neale, of Liverpool; James, of Birmingham; Candlish and Guthrie, of Edinburgh; Monod and Coquerel, of Paris; and I can honestly say that, in the power to arrest and fix the attention of an audience, the ablest of these distinguished men were scarcely superior to Dr. Willson. The first time I heard Adolphe Monod, his style of speaking reminded me of my old Newburgh friend. Both were eminently natural in manner. In the exordium and the expository parts of his discourse Dr. Willson was quite colloquial, though never vulgar in his tone,—a tone which he maintained until he reached some elevating sentiment. Then he began gradually to rise on the wings of a fine imagination, like a bird, so perfectly conscious of its mastery over its pinions as to seem unconscious of the least effort in using them. There were no violent transitions, nor sudden outbursts of passion, no extravagant emphasis, nor over-strained declamation. You rose with the Preacher as high as he chose to go, and were then brought down to the ordinary conversational plane of the discourse. Soon again, and almost before you were aware of it, you found yourself borne away on a second and somewhat higher flight. And so it went on, the levels, if I may be allowed the word, becoming shorter, and the flights higher, as you advanced, until the sermon ended in a prolonged and grand, but never grandiloquent, climax. Such, in the main, was Dr. Willson's style of speaking, even in his ordinary services; but it was on the evening of a Sacramental Sabbath, or when discussing "the signs of the times," or the predicted glories in the future of the Church of God, or the Millennial reign of Messiah the Prince, that the qualities of the Preacher were best brought out, both in the matter and manner of his discourse; and then he exemplified the kind of eloquence described by Cicero—" *Quod non solum delectet sed etiam sine satietate delectet.*" You were sorry when he said *Amen*.

The reputation and the influence of Dr. Willson as a public man were necessarily limited by reason of the smallness of the denomination to which he belonged, and its distinctive views in regard to ministerial and Christian communion. Within the County of Orange, however, he was widely known in all branches of the Church; and on those public occasions when a special Sermon or Oration was expected, Dr. Willson was generally the man to whom the community looked to perform the service.

Let me add that in private life he was no less attractive than in the pulpit. His conversational powers were of an unusually high order. He had a pretty large acquaintance with public men. He had travelled extensively in our own country and the British Provinces, and no object of interest, physical, agricultural, educational or religious, escaped his notice. He examined them not only with the curiosity common to travellers, but with the eye of a man of science. He was a zealous student of Natural History and Chemistry; and his reading had taken a wide and various range. The bent of his own mind and his habits as a Covenanter had made him specially observant of the "sings of the times" in the old world and the new, in politics, literature and social movements. A tenacious memory gave him perfect command of the materials of instruction or entertainment gathered from so many fields. Then, too, he was of a very companionable temper, dignified in bearing but never starched, his talk plentifully seasoned with wit, humour, anecdote, so that his hosts or his guests would often find their converse kept up with such interest that midnight had come and gone ere they were aware, and they were ready to say of him what Dr. Ely said to him—" Thou man of genius."

Although precluded by the rules of his Church, and his own views of order, from communion with other denominations, Dr. Willson was not wanting in catholic sympathies. He loved good men of every name, and was warmly loved by not a few in return. In all that related to the cause of our common Presbyterianism, and the welfare of the Church Catholic, he ever felt a lively concern. For the "Cloud of Scotland's Witnesses," especially those who lived and died in "persecuting times," he had an almost unbounded veneration. Few things would sooner rouse his indignation than a sneer at their principles, or a slur upon their memory. He was familiar with the minutest details of their history, and I have no doubt that he had imbibed, in some measure, their heroic faith and courage. Whatever faults he may have had, cowardice, certainly, was not one of them. In avowing what he deemed truth, and in denouncing what he deemed sin, no one could be bolder—he neither feared the face of man nor ever stopped to count consequences.

His views of the relations between Christianity and Civil Government, and of the duty of nations to own Christ as King, naturally led him to comment on civil constitutions and the conduct of public men, so that many would have charged him with bringing politics into the pulpit. Those who heard him only on such occasions might have gone away with the notion that his preaching was too polemical and political to be edifying. If so, I am sure they would have done Dr. Willson injustice. The staple of his preaching, as I have reason to believe, was the simple Gospel, and though his fine fancy might sometimes carry him into the region of speculation, when treating matters pertaining to "the Church of the future," yet his sermons were, in general, and in a high degree, scriptural in structure as well as sentiment.

His published discourses, if collected, would make a handsome volume. Most, if not all, of them were written out for the press, after their delivery in the pulpit. None of them, however, would give the mere reader a proper conception of his abilities as a Preacher. Though he wrote a great deal on various subjects, scientific and theological, the style of his sermons is somewhat stiff and dry, as if the author was not much accustomed to handling the pen,—a fact all the more remarkable, considering his copious command and felicitous use of language on the platform and in the pulpit. I will only add that the savour of his ministry still survives in this region, and his memory is cherished by many who "for a season rejoiced in his light," though they were never under his pastoral care.

Believe me, very affectionately yours,
JOHN FORSYTH.

GILBERT McMASTER, D.D.*
1807—1854.

GILBERT McMASTER, a son of James and Mary (Crawford) McMaster, was born in the Parish of Saintfield, a few miles from Belfast, Ireland, on the 13th of February, 1778. His ancestors, who held a respectable standing in both civil and religious life, and who were distinguished for their uncompromising adherence to the system of doctrine, worship and Church polity, of the period of the Westminster Assembly, and for their hatred of all political usurpation and oppression, removed from Scotland to Ireland about forty years before his birth. His father was a man of intelligent and earnest piety, and of singular and even scrupulous probity of character. His mother was very respectably connected, was a person of superior intellect and great force of character, of fine womanly virtues and graces and of an exemplary religious life.

The subject of this sketch enjoyed the advantages of a most faithful Christian education; and the appropriate fruits of this culture began, in due season, to appear. From an early age he was the subject of serious thoughts and impressions which never left him. These, with the advance of years and the development of his natural faculties, became gradually more clear, constant, habitual and controlling; issuing in a settled religious character of great exemplariness, and, about the eighteenth year of his age, in a public profession of religion;—a profession sustained with much uniformity and consistency by the whole tenor of his subsequent life.

* MS. from his son, Rev. Dr. E. D. Macmaster.

In the year 1791 his father came, with his family, to the United States, and, after a short sojourn near Wilmington, Del., settled as a farmer in Franklin County, Pa. Here Gilbert prosecuted a liberal course of study—which indeed had been commenced at an earlier period—at the Franklin Academy, then under the Rectorship of the late James Ross, LL.D., a distinguished teacher of the Latin and Greek classics, and author of the Grammars which bear his name. Here he remained about two years; then spent a year and a half as a tutor in Shippensburg; and then (in 1801) entered Jefferson College. There he continued about two years and a half, an earnest and successful student, nearly completing the usual curriculum of studies. Some temporary pecuniary embarrassment, to which he was subjected, induced him to leave the College for a time; and, for reasons not now known, he did not return. By both Mr. Watson and Dr. Dunlap, who successively presided over the College during his connection with it, he was treated with marked kindness, of which he ever afterwards cherished a grateful remembrance. The latter gentleman sought, by the offer of a Tutorship, to engage him in the service of the College, with a view to a permanent connection with the Faculty; but he preferred other prospects.

On leaving College Mr. McMaster entered upon a course of medical studies, which being completed, he was regularly admitted to the profession in 1805, and settled himself as a Physician in the borough of Mercer, Pa. Here he was successfully engaged in medical practice for about two years and a half.

The thoughts and wishes of Mr. McMaster had been early directed towards the Gospel Ministry. But, from the very high estimate which he had formed of the sacredness of the office and the qualifications necessary to it, in connection with his own self-distrust, he shrank from the idea of assuming its responsibilities, and therefore entered the medical profession. The duty of devoting himself to the ministry had been, through a course of years, often and earnestly urged upon him by his clerical and other friends, and the subject had deeply exercised his own mind. At length, in September, 1807, the late Dr. Alexander McLeod, of New York, and Dr. Samuel B. Wylie, of Philadelphia, sought an interview with him at Pittsburg, and informed him that the Presbytery of which they were leading members, had, at an informal conference, resolved to exercise their Presbyterial authority, and require him to yield his scruples and prepare to enter the ministry. In this decision he recognized the voice of Providence; and, as his studies had always had a special direction to the various branches of theological learning, after passing the customary parts of trial, he was, in October, 1807, licensed to preach the Gospel. Having declined some other calls, he was ordained to the work of the ministry in the Reformed Presbyterian Church, and settled as Pastor of the Congregation in Duanesburgh, N. Y., on the 8th of August, 1808.

From his settlement at Duanesburgh he continued to minister to that church for a period of nearly thirty-two years; holding a distinguished position in his own community and in the friendly and respectful regards of other denominations, building up a large and flourishing congregation, and exerting a benign and powerful influence over the region. In 1828 he was honoured with the degree of Doctor of Divinity from Union College. In 1840 he accepted a call from the church in Princeton, Ind., and removed to that place, leaving his former charge, for what appeared to him sufficient reasons, amidst the universal and strongly expressed regrets, not only of his own congregation, and others of the same ecclesiastical connection with himself, but of the whole community, of all denominations and classes. At Princeton he continued usefully and pleasantly employed in his pastoral work for six years. In no period had he more evident tokens of the blessing of God than he enjoyed during the whole time of his residence there, in numerous accessions to the full communion of the church, in the edification of a more than usually religious people, in the establishment of kindly relations among the different churches of the place, and the extending of a strong moral and religious influence over the whole region far beyond the immediate sphere of his personal labours. An enfeebled state of health compelled him, in 1846, to withdraw from the quiet scene of these pleasant and fruitful labours, and to demit the pastoral charge of a warmly attached, grateful and affectionate people. From the time of his leaving Princeton, he resided, until his decease, with his son, the Rev. Dr. Erasmus D. MacMaster, first at Oxford, Ohio, and afterwards in the city of New Albany, Ind. He died, after a painful illness of nine days, on the 17th of March, 1854, closing a consistent Christian life with Christian dignity and composure.

In June, 1863, Dr. McMaster was married at Cannonsburg, Pa., to Jane, daughter of Benjamin Brown, belonging to a family of high respectability. With this lady, who entered with the deepest interest into all his views, and was every way suited to the place she occupied, he lived most happily till the end of his days. He had eight children,—four sons and four daughters. Two of his sons* are distinguished ministers in the Presbyterian Church. One is a farmer, and one an editor.

Mrs. McMaster died, greatly lamented, at the residence of her son, the Rev. Algernon Sydney MacMaster, D.D., in Poland, Ohio, March 15, 1860. Of his daughters, the eldest died in infancy; the other three in mature age, after adorning their Christian profession by a most exemplary Christian life.

The following is a list of Dr. McMaster's publications:—
The Duty of Nations: A Sermon on a Day of Public Thanksgiving, -
The Embassy of Reconciliation, with its Occasion and Ministry: A Sermon delivered at the Ordination of the Rev. James Milligan† in the Church of Coldenham, N. Y., - - - - - - 1812

---

* One of them, the Rev. ERASMUS D. MACMASTER, D.D., has died since this sketch was written. He was born in Mercer, Pa., in February, 1806; was graduated at Union College, Schenectady, in 1827; studied Theology under the direction of his father; was licensed to preach in the Reformed Presbyterian Church in 1829, and was ordained to the full work of the ministry in the Presbyterian Church in February, 1831, when he became Pastor of the Ballston (N. Y.) Presbyterian Church. Here he continued, an eminently faithful and acceptable Minister, until 1838, when the great interest which he felt in the cause of Western Education, led him to resign his charge and accept the Presidency of the College at Hanover, Ind. This office he held until 1845, when, in consequence of some unexpected embarrassments in connection with the College, he resigned his place and accepted the Presidency of Miami University, Oxford, O. After more than four years of intense and complicated labour in this institution, he reluctantly accepted a call to the Professorship of Systematic Theology in the Seminary at New Albany, Ind. After a few years this Seminary, owing to various unpropitious circumstances, ceased to exist, and in place of it came two others,—one at Danville, Ky., and one at Chicago, Ill. To the Professorship of Theology in this latter institution he was appointed by the General Assembly of 1866. He was inaugurated in September of that year, and entered upon his labours with great zeal and fidelity, and with every prospect of the best success; but before the close of the year his earthly course was finished. He died in perfect peace, after a brief illness, on the 11th of December. He possessed a massive intellect,—clear, acute, powerful; an unwavering fidelity to his own convictions of right; a kindly and benevolent spirit, and an earnest and devoted piety. In any community in which his lot might have been cast he would have been a man of mark.

† JAMES MILLIGAN, a son of John and Margaret Milligan, was born in Dalmellington, Ayrshire, Scotland, August 7, 1785. His early tendencies were decidedly religious

An Essay in Defence of Some Fundamental Doctrines of Christianity, (an octavo volume,) - - - - - - - - 1815
The Shorter Catechism Analyzed, with Proofs from Scripture, (three editions,) - - - - - - - - - - 1815
An Apology for the Book of Psalms: in Five Letters, addressed to the Friends of Union in the Church of God, (a duodecimo volume, four editions), - - - - - - - - - - 1818
Ministerial Work and Sufficiency: A Sermon preached at the Ordination of the Rev. John McMaster, in the Reformed Presbyterian Church, Schenectady, - - - - - - - - - 1832
The Moral Character of Civil Government: Considered with reference to the Political Institutions of the United States; in Four Letters, - 1832
A Brief Inquiry into the Civil Relations of Reformed Presbyterians, according to their Judicative Acts: Addressed to those of that Communion, - - - - - - - - - - 1833
Speech in Illustration of a Report on the Doctrine of Civil Government: in the General Synod of the Reformed Presbyterian Church in the city of Pittsburg, - - - - - - - - - 1835
The Obligations of the American Scholar to his Country and the World: An Address delivered at Hanover College, - - - - 1841
Thoughts on the Union of the Church, - - - - - 1846
Speech in Defence of the Westminster Confession of Faith against the Charge of Erastianism: in the General Synod of the Reformed Presbyterian Church in Pittsburg, - - - - - - 1847

and, at the age of fourteen, he was a communicant in the Established Church. At sixteen he migrated to America, on account of being dissatisfied with the Government of his native country. He made his way to Westmoreland County, Pa., where he had a half-brother settled, and he became a partner with him in a mercantile establishment. Though he had belonged to the National Church in Scotland, he then was led now, as the result of diligent inquiry, to cast in his lot with the Covenanters; and, by the advice of Dr. Black, and some others in whom he was disposed to confide, he determined to abandon his secular employment, and, if possible, obtain a liberal education. He, accordingly, entered Jefferson College; but his funds were very quickly exhausted, in consequence of which he went to Greensburg, and opened a school there, which he taught with good success for eighteen months. He then resumed his place in College, joining the same class he had left, and graduating in 1809 with the first honour. On leaving College he went to Philadelphia, and placed himself, as a theological student, under the care of the Rev. Dr. Samuel B. Wylie, and, at the same time, was a Teacher of Languages in the University of Pennsylvania. He was licensed to preach by the Northern Presbytery in 1811, and was ordained Pastor of Coldenham Congregation, Orange County, N. Y., by the same Presbytery, in 1812. During his residence here he performed much missionary labour in the State of New York, and organized many congregations which have since become large and influential. In 1818 he resigned his charge, and was installed Pastor of the Scotch Covenanter Congregation in Ryegate, Vt. Here he continued labouring with great diligence, and encountering many hardships, for nearly a quarter of a century. During this period he laboured throughout the whole region, and made many tours into Canada to visit poor Covenanters scattered through the Provinces. He was intensely Anti-slavery in his views, and was always ready to show his faith by his works. He was translated from Ryegate to New Alexandria, Pa., in 1839; thence to Eden, Ill., in 1848; and, in 1855, he demitted his pastoral charge, and, from that time till the close of life, resided with his sons in Pennsylvania and Michigan. He died at the house of his son, in Southfield, near Detroit, Mich., on the 2d of January, 1862, aged about 77. In 1820 he was married to Mary, daughter of Robert Trumbull, a soldier of the Revolution. They had six children,—five sons and one daughter. Three of the sons are in the ministry of the Reformed Presbyterian Church, and the daughter was married to a minister of the same communion. He was honoured with the degree of Doctor of Divinity; but when or by what College I am unable to ascertain. He published a Defence of Infant Baptism, in a volume of three hundred pages; A Narrative of the Secession Controversy in Vermont; and a Sermon on Grace and Free Agency, and another on the Prospects of a True Christian in a Sinful World. He was a man of decided ability, intense industry and extensive usefulness.

The Great Subject of the Christian Ministry: A Discourse at the Opening of the General Synod of the Reformed Presbyterian Church in the city of Philadelphia, - - - - - - - - 1852
The Upright Man in Life and at Death: A Discourse delivered on the Occasion of the Decease of the Rev Samuel Brown Wylie, D.D., 1852

In addition to the above, he published various ecclesiastical papers, articles in several periodicals, &c.

I quote from the tractate on Civil Government the author's statement of the fundamental principles of his theory, which may serve both to indicate his habit of thought, and to exhibit his views on a subject which he held to be one of great moment,—the application of Christianity to the constitution and administration of political society. It is as follows:—

"POSITION I.—Civil Government is the ordinance of God, as the Creator and Governor of the world, for good to man, founded in the law of our social nature, the principles of which law are the standard of its actual constitution and administration.

"POSITION II.—Political and Ecclesiastical society are essentially different from each other, in their nature, government, and immediate ends.

"POSITION III.—It is not the mere fact of the existence of a political power, but the possession by it of those attributes which fit it to answer the ends of its institution, that makes it the moral ordinance of God.

"POSITION IV.—Mere defects in high and ultimate moral attainments, if fundamental attributes be in conformity with, and in nothing contrary to, moral principle, will not render illegitimate a constitution of government.

"POSITION V.—Every nation in its civil character, to which the Revelation of the Son of God as Immanuel, is made, and which, according to that revelation, is summoned to submit to Him, is bound to confess his name, not merely in words, but substantially, really, and practically, as Lord of all.

"POSITION VI.—In perfect accordance with the last position, it is held that until a nation make it so by its own deed, the recognition of no principle peculiar to the system of grace can be considered as necessary to the validity of its actual constitution as a moral ordinance of God."

Each of these positions is illustrated in a clear and concise discussion. This is followed by like discussions under the three subsequent heads:—" The Moral Estimate of the Political Institutions of the United States"; "Character of the Federal Government"; "Objections Considered";—the object of the whole being the vindication of the political institutions of the country from the charge of irreligion and immorality.

I had some personal acquaintance with Dr. McMaster during the latter years of his life, which has left upon my mind a deep impression of his superior worth and ability. The qualities which seemed to me most patent in his character were his great modesty and utter absence of all pretension; his thoughtful and benevolent spirit, disposing him to all kind offices; his intellectual vigour and comprehensiveness, and large and varied resources; and a perfect simplicity of thought and feeling and manner, that gave complexion to all his external demonstrations. I never heard him preach but once—his discourse then, as I remember it, was of a highly evangelical type, was constructed with logical accuracy and full of weighty, consecutive thought, and was delivered with characteristic simplicity, showing that the dependence for its effect was upon the matter rather than the manner. He impressed me altogether as a man of mark, and fully justified to my mind the high estimate of his character which I had formed from living in the same region with him, and from the testimony of those with whom he had been in intimate relations for many years.

FROM THE REV. ERASMUS D. McMASTER, D.D.

NEW ALBANY, December 31, 1855.

Reverend and dear Doctor: While I am duly sensible of the delicacy of the task which your request has imposed upon me, I am prompted to comply with it, as well by a feeling of filial reverence and affection as by an unwillingness to decline what you so kindly desire. I confess I do this the more willingly, as there are some things touching my father's relation to the Reformed Presbyterian Church which require to be specially noticed in order to a correct appreciation of his character.

The whole ecclesiastical position, standing, and, I may say, character, of Dr. McMaster arose out of, and were determined by, the idea that the Church of God is one in all times, a spiritual Body having perpetual succession, a moral person possessing personal identity; and hence that, whatever attainments may have been made in the public profession of the Christian doctrine, order and worship, and whatever obligations may have been in this behalf assumed by the Church, or by any branch of the church, in any preceding times, it is incumbent upon the Church, or such branch of the Church, in succeeding times, to recognize, to bring down, and, along with later attainments, in a progressive course of moral and religious reformation, to transmit to the generation following, and through it to the ages to come; and that it is only thus that the Church can properly realize her own high character as "the pillar and ground of the truth." To understand, therefore, the views under which he acted in his connection with the Reformed Presbyterian Church, it is necessary briefly to refer to the historical relations of this Ecclesiastical Body.

The Reformed Presbyterians in America, though fifty years ago few in numbers, and widely scattered through the country, having only a few organized congregations, and some smaller societies not yet organized, Dr. McMaster held to be the legitimate descendants and proper representatives of that minority in Scotland, who, adhering to the principles of the Presbyterian Reformation in that country prior to 1649, dissented from the Revolution settlement of William III. on account of its Erastian assumption of dominion over and in the Church; and of those earlier witnesses for the truth, under the two preceding reigns of Charles II. and James II. who, openly and boldly denouncing the usurpation by those tyrants of supremacy in all ecclesiastical cases, spurning all "tolerations" and "indulgences" proceeding from this usurpation, and at last because of their subversion of the Constitution of the State as well as of the Church, and their oppression and persecution of the true religion, disowning, as on the same grounds did the whole nation a few years later, their civil authority, were hunted through the land and given as sheep to the slaughter. "It was felt," says Dr. McMaster, speaking of the Church in America before the Revolution in 1776, "by the consistent friends of the Reformation, that the waters of the Atlantic had neither sanctified the Erastianism of the British Establishment, nor as to themselves absolved them from the authority of Messiah's claims. To the principles of civil and religious liberty, of the Church's spiritual independence of all secular power, and to that vital truth, of such extended practical bearing, the alone universal Headship of the Christ of God, their adherence, as at other historical periods of deep interest, was unshrinking."

The American Revolution, which dissolved the political connection of this country with Great Britain, and which the Reformed Presbyterians had hailed with joy, and, according to their numbers and means, efficiently promoted, forever separated the United States from all subjection to an Erastian and immoral Crown. But, before that auspicious event, the different parties into which the Presbyterians of the Old World had been unhappily divided had established themselves in the New. To some extent, different historical relations and traditions, different habits of thinking and feeling on religious and ecclesiastical matters, different usages, and perhaps mutual misapprehensions, had grown up; which, though all parties would have held them to be insufficient to justify the making of divisions in the household of faith, yet stood in the way of a reunion after these divisions had taken place. The principles which underlay, were embraced in, and gave character to, the Presbyterian Reformation, Dr. M. thought were best represented by the Old Dissenters from the Revolution Church of Scotland, known, from their adherence to the Solemn League and Covenant, as "the strict Covenanters." The circumstances of the several Presbyterian Bodies in this country, since the era of the American Revolution, are indeed widely different from those of their predecessors in a former age and in another hemisphere. This fact Dr. M. clearly apprehended, and has every where in his writings strongly represented. But the great principles of the Presbyterian Reformation, divested of all which is local, temporary and incidental, he held to be general in their import, and of universal application in every age and in every nation. To the course of the Covenanted Reformation his family were, from education and principle, attached. The Christian heroism of the Scottish martyrs had enkindled, at an early age, in his young mind, a burning love of religious and civil liberty. In his early manhood he addressed himself to the study of the history of the Reformation in the land of his fathers, and of the principal controversial writings of the times. "The system of Reformed Presbyterianism," says Dr. M., "appeared to me to occupy more decidedly than did any other the ground of the martyrs. By it the Bible system of doctrine, order, discipline and worship seemed to be more consistently held. Especially the great principle of the Headship of Christ over the Church, and over all things for the Church's sake, appeared to me to be more consistently exhibited in it than elsewhere. The clear, full and explicit acknowledgment of this great principle seemed to me to comprehend at once a proper recognition of the rights of God, and security for the rights of man; and to furnish a ground of assurance of the ultimate union of the divided Church upon a proper basis; and of the well-being both of the Church and of States. Such was the light in which Reformed Presbyterianism presented itself to me, and, without much of consultation with flesh and blood, I embraced it."

Dr. McMaster regarded the Presbyterian Reformation of the seventeenth century in Scotland as an inchoate movement arrested almost at its beginning; whose particular *measures*, some of which he thought marked by grave errors and mistakes, belonged exclusively to that Church and Nation and to those times. But in respect to the essential *principles* of that movement and the prevalent *spirit* by which it was pervaded, he was more than willing to be regarded as a follower of the Scottish Covenanters even of "the stricter sort."

I have thought it right that Dr. McMaster's own views of his ecclesiastical position and relations should be truly and fairly given. Of these views I am the reporter, not the critic. But I may be permitted to say that, whatever in either hemisphere there may have been of error and mistake in its management, the time draws on when "the good old cause" of the Scottish Covenanters will lift up its head in the Church and among the Nations.

The ordinary course of Dr. McMaster's pastoral ministration was in conformity with the customary order of many of the Scottish Presbyterian Churches. Usually the Sabbath morning service was an exposition of some Book of Scripture in course, with doctrinal and practical observations, accompanied by the ordinary devotional exercises. The subject of the afternoon's discourse was either some branch of the morning's exposition, selected for fuller development, elucidation and application; some head of Christian doctrine, or some theme suggested by the various circumstances and occasions of his congregation or of the times. These services of the Sabbath he supplemented, during the week, by regular pastoral visitation and by biblical and catechetical instruction of the young at stated times. His usual written preparation for the pulpit consisted only of short notes, filling from two to four pages of a small duodecimo volume, and briefly marking the heads of his discussion, and the more important particulars, with references to apposite Scriptures for illustration, confirmation and enforcement. His subject, thus briefly noted, he carefully thought out in its matter, relying on the occasion of the delivery for the language.

As a Preacher, he was distinguished for the clearness of his method, the fulness of his Scriptural expositions, the solidity and abundance of his matter, and the appropriateness, tenderness, and richness of his application of Christian doctrine to the diversified exigencies of the Christian life. While his presence was commanding, his manner dignified, his voice full and good, his language always correct and appropriate, and his delivery often impressive, yet he judged the enticing words of an over-wrought and excessively ornate rhetoric to be out of place in discussing the momentous themes of the pulpit, and he sought not the lighter graces of a fascinating oratory. To the serious-minded, the earnest, the inquiring, seeking to profit by the Divine Word, and to the old saint far advanced in his pilgrimage to the city of God, though often found in different ecclesiastical connections, his ministrations, especially during the last twelve or fifteen years of his ministry, were peculiarly acceptable, and to many such, in various parts of the Church, there is reason to believe that they were the means of great blessing.

In the business of the Ecclesiastical Judicatories and the general affairs of the Church, though very retiring in his disposition, he always bore a principal part. The General Synod, as well as some of the Subordinate Judicatories, expressed in strong terms their high estimate of his character, their affectionate and reverential respect for his person, and their sense of the loss they sustained in his death.

He was throughout life and habitually a man of reading and of thought. His information was various and extensive. A general scholar of good attainments in the different departments of learning, he possessed a special and intimate knowledge of Theology, the Constitution, Polity, and History of the Church, and of Ethical and Politico-ethical Philosophy. All who knew him acknowledged his worth as a gentleman and a scholar.

His character, habits, and manners were in many respects more those of an Irish or Scottish gentleman than of a Cis-Atlantic. But, brought to this country while he was yet a child and growing up under its formative influences, while he retained an affectionate regard for the land of his nativity and for that of his forefathers, in all his controlling predilections he was intensely American. The principles of the old British Whigs were part of his ancestral inheritance; and from his youth he was an ardent admirer of the political institutions of the United States, of which his tractate on that subject is a defence against the charge of irreligion and immorality; and in the political affairs of the country he always took an intelligent and lively interest.

That Dr. McMaster was capable, in a wider sphere of action and under external circumstances more propitious, of achieving as a public man more than he actually accomplished, those who knew him well, believe. The extent and the measure, however, of the influence exerted by an unobtrusive and retiring man of thought, who has not occupied the most conspicuous position in public affairs, by means of his private and quiet intercourse with other men, cannot be known with precision. The springs of the mountain fastnesses feed the rivers and the sea.

Leaving to yourself and your other correspondents the general estimate of his character, I may be permitted to say that Dr. M. was, in all his intercourse with his fellow-men, true, just, honourable and magnanimous. In social life he was conversable, genial and very attractive. In his special friendships he was most constant, faithful and generous. In his family, while his word was law, towards the wife of his bosom, a woman in whom the heart of her husband did safely trust, he cherished a most tender and affectionate respect, and to his children he was a revered and loving father. If he had faults, as all men have faults, I had no eye to see them when he was living, and I have no heart to remember them now that they are buried in his grave.

I may say, in concluding these reminiscences, that Dr. McMaster, having in early youth, and probably in yet earlier childhood, committed himself to God as his Covenant God in Christ, was practically religious throughout life, feeding in himself and others the springs of that life which is hid with Christ in God. His piety was eminently manly, as well as Christian. During the last few years of his pilgrimage, those who were near him could not fail to observe a marked and delightful maturing in him of the graces of the Christian character. The last two or three years, the Scriptures were more than ever his daily study. The few weeks immediately preceding his last illness, he addressed himself anew to a careful study of the Prophecies of Isaiah, in which he expressed the deepest interest. The animating visions in the sixtieth, sixty-first, and sixty-second chapters of that Prophet, of the glory of the Church in the accession of the Gentiles; the great office of Christ in her redemption; and the satisfying joy of Zion in her union with Jehovah, were the last passages of the Scriptures which he read in the morning worship of the family, only a few days before his departure to enter into the joy of his Lord. His prayers in the family worship, the last few months, and especially the last few weeks, for himself and his family, for the Church and the world, were very comprehensive, fervent, solemn and impressive. His death was every way worthy of his life. Calm, self-possessed, confiding, he went home to the house of his God on high. We had the fullest confidence, when we saw him passing in dignified tranquillity through the dark valley, that it was to enter the gates of immortal life.

With great respect and esteem,
Yours most truly,
E. D. MacMASTER.

FROM THE REV. T. W. J. WYLIE, D.D.

PHILADELPHIA, November 5, 1861.

Rev. and dear Sir: The affectionate regard with which I cherish the memory of the late Rev. Dr. Gilbert McMaster overcomes the feeling that I am quite incompetent to do justice to his character, and leads me to submit the following reminiscences to your disposal. I am not without the hope that even this imperfect delineation may excite greater admiration of the power and excellence of the Spirit's sanctifying grace, and lead some one to imitate the virtues of a person so pure and noble as he was.

Dr. McMaster was a frequent and always welcome visitor at my father's house, from the days of my childhood, and I had the happiness, when a boy, of making a short visit to his own retired country home. As he was so prominent a Minister of the Reformed Presbyterian Church, and so intimate a friend of my father, it was natural that my attention should be closely directed to him. The impression was early made upon my mind, which time and reflection have only deepened, that he was "one of Nature's noblemen," "a holy man of God."

At the period of my earliest recollection of him, Dr. McMaster was a person of portly and commanding aspect. Though corpulent, there was nothing languid in his appearance; but the sprightliness of his manner and the firmness of his step indicated that the mental was not subservient to the physical organization, but held it in complete control. He was remarkably prompt in all he undertook. His commanding appearance was sustained by a dignity of manner which never yielded to querulousness, while the nobleness of a warm and generous mind rendered him exceedingly agreeable in social intercourse with all who enjoyed his friendship. He took great pleasure in the society of men of learning, with whom his own well cultivated mind prepared him to converse with ease and propriety. There was sometimes a reserve, and occasionally an abruptness, in his manner, among those with whom he was not very intimate; but this, I doubt not, arose from the effort to overcome his native modesty, while the unobtrusiveness of his own character caused him to view forwardness with displeasure, and repel it with severity. He was very affable with those whom he esteemed and loved, but his sound and honest heart rendered him averse to affect for any an interest which he did not feel. There was a delicacy in his kindness which required the quietude of the family circle for its exercise and evidence. On two occasions, Dr. McMaster was, for a considerable time, in our house. Both these were seasons of affliction, arising, in the one case, from a severe accident my father had met with, and which disabled him for some time from preaching, and in the other from my father's death. In both instances, Dr. McMaster manifested a warm, deep, soothing sympathy, which we can never forget. There was a simplicity and unaffectedness in his kindness, which rendered it most acceptable. He was warmly attached to my father, and, when he called to see him during his last illness, he suddenly went out of the room, and, without returning, shortly after left the house. On following him, I found him quite overcome, and he told me that he felt unable to utter any parting words, as he had the impression that he would never meet my father again on earth,—an expectation which proved sadly correct.

As a Preacher, Dr. McMaster was thoroughly evangelical in doctrine and affluent in ideas, but his style was somewhat involved, and his utterance, though impressive, was not animated. His composition was ponderous. Like a heavily loaded carriage, he moved slowly and carefully. He required the close attention of his hearers, but he richly rewarded it. He was averse to display, especially in the solemnities of the pulpit, and was reluctant to submit himself to the public gaze. "I am no *talker*," was his reply, when urged to speak on some public occasion.

As an Author, Dr. McMaster did much to benefit the Christian community which his writings reached. Several of his Sermons and Addresses were printed by request, and display the characteristics of a well-stored and discriminating mind. His Analysis of the Shorter Catechism of the Westminster Divines has passed through several editions, and, notwithstanding a number of publications, of the same kind, have since been issued, it still retains its value. A Controversial work occasioned by the peculiar views of Elias Smith, issued early in his ministerial career, presents a discussion of some of the most important doctrines in Theology. His "Apology for the Book of Psalms" is undoubtedly the most valuable of his works. It is designed to show the suitableness of this portion of Sacred Scripture for the use of the people of God in singing his praise, in every age, and in every land; but it is free from the spirit which pervades many publications with this avowed object. While Dr. McMaster was strongly attached to the principles and usages of the Reformed Presbyterian Church, of which he was a prominent Minister, he properly appreciated and applied that article in her terms of Communion, which requires "a recognition of all as brethren in every land, who hold a Scriptural testimony in behalf of the attainments and cause of the Reformation, against all that is contrary to sound doctrine and the power of godliness." The generous instincts of an enlightened and elevated development of Divine grace led him to love the brotherhood of saints, and to seek, on a broad and solid basis, the union in one organization of all evangelical churches. Some of the ripest and most valuable productions of his pen have reference to this subject.

During the discussions which distracted the Reformed Presbyterian Church, in regard to the moral character of the United States Government, he issued several valuable Essays in which this subject is treated with the acumen of a Lawyer, the profound thoughtfulness of a Statesman, and the conscientious, reverential spirit of the Christian. He did much to bring the Reformed Presbyterian Church to the position she now occupies on this subject, asserting the duty of the Civil Commonwealth to conform its constitution and the administration of its laws to the Scriptural standard, and recognizing in the political system of this land such elements as authorize obedient subjects of the Mediatorial Crown to participate in their obligations and advantages.

Dr. McMaster excelled as a letter-writer. His correspondence was very extensive, and embraced many persons of eminence in the religious and political world, both in this country and Europe. His views of current events, as presented in this way, are exceedingly interesting, and a collection of his letters, I am sure, would form a very valuable publication.

Dr. McMaster's last days were spent in delightful serenity in the house of his accomplished son, the Rev. E. D. MacMaster, brightened by the companionship of the wife of his youth, one of the kindest and purest of Christian women, and sustained by the respectful love of his sons, and the soothing attentions of his two amiable daughters. The habitual modesty and reserve of his character continued unaltered to the last, but his long, self sacrificing, useful and holy life was his best testimony for God.

With great respect truly yours,
T. W. J. WYLIE.

FROM THE REV. WILLIAM JAMES, D.D.

ALBANY, June 28, 1854.

My dear Sir: In the winter of 1831 I attended an Installation at Schenectady, in which all the services, including the Sermon and two Charges, were performed by Dr. McMaster, then in the fifty-fourth year of his age. As his residence, from the commencement of his ministry in 1808, had been within twenty miles of my native city, from my boyhood I had often heard of him as the Corypheus of his own small denomination, and at the same time as being not less remarkable for his general character, than for the zeal with which he maintained the peculiarities of the Covenanters. This was my first sight of the man, and the only occasion on which I ever saw him in the pulpit. My knowledge of him indeed was never intimate, being derived from casual and not very frequent interviews. But his qualities were of a cast which it required no nice analysis to discover, nor a special intimacy to appreciate.

In person he was large, well formed, and of a full habit, with an open countenance and ruddy, the effect of which was heightened by contrast with the whiteness of his hair, a full head of which he retained to the last. He had large eyes, of a dark, hazel colour, with a grayish tinge; and a bass-toned voice, which added sensibly to the weight of whatever fell from his lips. The impression made by the nobleness of his person and countenance was increased by a natural urbanity, which (though any thing but a modish man) appeared even in the general neatness of his dress, and equally in the style of his social intercourse. Underneath the antique sentiments in which he had been educated, and the professional tendency of his mind to subjects of grave import, there was a large vein of masculine sense, and of sympathy with the common ideas of mankind, which made him quite at home in general society; and indeed there was about him such an air of secular respectability, that a person, not knowing him to be a clergyman, might easily suppose he was some eminent civilian.

Next to these more obvious traits of manner and appearance, the orderly method and discipline of his mind, as apparent in his conversation, could not fail to attract the notice of a stranger. He soon discovers that he is talking with a person of scholarly aptitudes and liberal acquirements; with one who is critical in his use of language, ever ready for a discussion, and particularly versed in the conduct of one. All things considered, person and voice, as well as style and matter, he concludes very certainly that this portly and high-minded gentleman, buried all his life in an out-of-the-way country parish, is very far from the position which nature designed for him. The remark probably was common among his acquaintances that he was a man far more in himself than he had opportunity to show in action. Accomplished in all that pertained to the literature of the Bible, and an adept in Ecclesiastical History, his conversation frequently discovered that civil studies also, and particularly those of Law and Politics, were not alien to him. It was probably his interest in physical inquiries which led him to adopt the Medical as his first profession. But our esteem of the man did not arise so much from his actual attainments as from the native character of his mind, which, though not distinguished by the remarkable development of any particular power, was admirable for two things;—for its general strength, and for its happy combination of the speculative with the practical, the latter decidedly predominating. Thoroughly ratiocinative, yet not particularly analytical, while it spared no pains to reach general principles, it wasted none in pursuing refinements. If he wanted originality or brilliancy of conception, he possessed the more important power of clearly comprehending the whole of a subject, and of seeing the relation of all its parts to each other. In reading any of his pieces, you may not be delighted by novelty, but you are always satisfied both with the clearness and the fullness of the general representation. In addition to this, a good classic taste gave a form to his sentiments, which made his conversation as graceful as it was edifying. If he had any natural humour, the disposition to indulge it was generally repressed. Though of a buoyant, cheerful temperament, and very communicative, he was not at all given to anecdote, nor to talk about small things. He was always upon subjects which invited discussion, and which reflected the truth-loving earnestness of his nature. A predominant logical tendency, always doing service to some elevated practical end, is the best idea which can be given of his intellectual character.

But if, as a man of ideas, he won the respect of his acquaintances, that sentiment was greatly heightened by his natural virtues, which were as strongly distinguished, and seemingly as finely balanced, as the powers of his mind. That he was a man of striking virtues was obvious enough, but the crown of these was their symmetry. There was in him especially a remarkable combination of self-reliance with deference to the wisdom of others, of firmness with moderation, of warm and generous instincts with the power of regulating their action. But the word which best expresses what was most noticeable, not in his character alone, but in his very physiognomy, is magnanimity. You could not believe that a man of such a countenance could be capable of any kind of meanness; and this was the report which he obtained universally. It was the common remark of those who were frequently associated with him in engagements of a public nature, that, however trying the occasion, he was never known to falter between principle and expediency, and yet that he was always among the first consulted in any emergency which peculiarly required the exercise of wisdom. The same superiority to selfishness and sophistry is seen in his controversial writings, in reading which one is at a loss whether most to admire the firmness with which he maintains his own convictions, or the fairness with which he treats those of his opponents. He was singularly free from those vices, both of mind and character, which one rather expects to find in the representatives of peculiar or unappreciated opinions. It seems almost a solecism—but it is true—that while he was a most loyal servant of one of the smallest religious bodies in Christendom, the unity of the Church seemed about as dear to him as its purity. Witness the following extract from one of his charges to a Pastor, which recalls the spirit of much of his conversation: "For the factions and schisms which deform, weaken and perplex the Church of God, you and I, my brother, are not responsible. They exist independently of us, and most of them had their origin before we were born. But for their evils we shall be held accountable, should we employ our influence, whatever that may be, to perpetuate them. Our actings should be directed to the healing of the wounds of the daughter of Zion," &c. The explanation of the solecism is, that whilst Dr. M.'s convictions made him zealous for the principles of his own Church, he was by nature a man of the most capacious sympathies. His persistent maintenance of tenets, so little appreciated, only proved that truth was more to him than all temporalities, and that he served his Master for no earthly reward. For one, I should have honoured him less, considering the catholic tendencies of his nature, had he been less decided in his attachment to the principles of his own Church. It is not exactness of opinion on the one hand, nor liberality of feeling on the other, but the union of the two, which constitutes Christian magnanimity; and it was this, in a rare degree, which distinguished our venerated friend, and which, in connection with his mental endowments, gave him the large place which he held in the estimation of the religious public.

I have not known many clergymen who were so well fitted, both by mental and moral constitution, for exercising a commanding influence in religious society as Dr. McMaster. And I have always regretted that one whom nature seemed to have designed for a leader of men, should have had to pass his life in comparative obscurity. The reason, however, of this comparative seclusion will be obvious enough, if we consider the peculiarity of his ecclesiastical position. Sympathizing profoundly with the ideas and principles of the Scottish Reformation of the Seventeenth Century, believing in the Sovereignty of the Messiah for the Church's sake over States, as such, as over all other things, he believed also in the corresponding duty of States to acknowledge this Sovereignty in their political constitutions and administrations, and that public covenanting is an ordinance of God to be observed on proper occasions both by Churches and Nations. It was indeed one labour of his life to divest his own Church of a certain exotic character which belonged to it from its historical connection with Scotland, and to bring it, unembarrassed by any thing of a foreign nature, to the maintenance of its own standards in their application to the actual circumstances of our own time and country. But the principles embodied in the Transactions of the Scottish Reformation on the National Covenant of 1580–81, and in the Solemn League and Covenant of 1643–48, divested of all which is merely local, temporary and incidental in their application, he believed to be of universal obligation and of momentous importance; and therefore, although, as already intimated, no one could have a more delicate sense of the relations which ought to exist among Christian brethren, or feel more keenly the evil of multiplied divisions, or pray more earnestly for the period when all shall be one, yet, with a view to the revival, in a more auspicious age, of these great " Reformation Principles," he chose to dwell within that enclosure of the great Presbyterian fold, which, with the smallest prospect, perhaps, of any immediate enlargement, was most redolent of the spirit of the Past, and most pregnant, as he doubtless thought, with the destinies of the Future. Though not expecting the extensive prevalence of these principles in his own day, yet believing their general prevalence to be the indispensable condition both of the security and well-being of States in reference to their appropriate ends, and of the reunion of the broken and divided Church, as well as of her proper efficiency in her great mission to the world, while fully acknowledging the fidelity of other and larger churches to other parts of the doctrine of Christ, and rejoicing in their prosperity and usefulness, yet, for the sake of maintaining the above principles, so generally neglected, if not impugned, he chose to abide with that section of the Church universal, which was alone distinguished by their formal and explicit maintenance. In the hope that in a future and better age these principles should obtain a general acceptance, and that over the whole field of God's husbandry their fruit should shake like Lebanon, our venerated friend lived and died — not having received the promises, but having seen them afar off, he was persuaded of them, and embraced them, and confessed that he was a stranger and pilgrim on the earth.

Yours very truly,
WILLIAM JAMES.

FROM THE REV. JAMES C. MOFFAT, D.D.,
Professor in the Theological Seminary at Princeton.

Princeton, April 29, 1868.

Rev. and dear Sir: My acquaintance with the Rev. Dr. Gilbert McMaster pertains to only the latter part of his life. For a few years—between 1845 and 1849—we both resided in the town of Oxford, Ohio. His son, the Rev. Dr. E. D. MacMaster, was then President of Miami University, where I was a Professor. During that time I saw him often and familiarly. The recollection of his venerable appearance is peculiarly agreeable to me.

In person Dr. McMaster was portly of stature, rather above the medium, and of gait, even in old age, firm and erect. The prevailing expression of his countenance was solemn and tender, which, in social intercourse, frequently relaxed into kindly playfulness.

The feature of his character first to arrest my special notice, was that whereby, although then quite advanced in years, he entered into cordial sympathy with the tastes and enterprises of young men. The world of toiling minds, from which his own efforts were gradually being withdrawn, had not ceased to be the object, not merely of a lingering interest, but of a warm and genial affection.

Neither had he outgrown a love of nature, nor of things beautiful therein. And they always seemed to have a message from God for him. A garden, in those days, one of my favourite recreations, was occasionally the scene of our interviews, where the conversation, by his guidance, would ascend, through the most natural transitions, from fruit, and trees and lawn, to the blessedness of the spiritual life, and of that land of promise, in which even our vile bodies shall be changed into the likeness of Christ's glorious body. Several delightful summer evenings are thus in my mind associated with him. His soundness of mental and bodily health maintained, even unto old age, the best feelings of young and hearty manhood. And in full accordance with this feature was the considerate tenderness which he always evinced for the feeble and suffering. I should be ready to believe that he might be stern in discipline, inflexible in defending the truth and repelling error, but the severer manifestations of his character fell not under my observation.

He also kept up acquaintance with the progress of literature and science, and the general intelligence of the time. I never knew a man more free from unreasonable prejudice, or more willing to consider the claims of the new, while intelligently maintaining the respect presumptively due to the old. He undoubtedly had, as all men have, more or less, his bias, which, in some directions, usurped the place of judgment; but the character of his mind was eminently open and liberal.

A favourite field of discussion with him was that department of Philosophy, which underlies Systematic Theology. Here his conversation was most instructive and entertaining, and when circumstances favoured, was sometimes considerably prolonged. In one instance which fell within my knowledge, where he met with a congenial spirit in that respect, an amicable discussion was carried on by two or three hours at a time, from day to day, for several weeks, with Socratic good-humour and urbanity on both sides, and on his, throughout, with a view to spiritual edification.

His style in conversation was remarkably copious and complete in structure. Had it been printed from his lips there would have been little to alter in the proofs. And yet there was not the slightest appearance of effort at precision. Its entire fitness to the man was one of its beautiful properties.

Although not largely endowed with the gift of humour, his enjoyment of it in others was quick and hearty, and added much to the light and kindliness of his manner.

I never heard him preach but once, and that effort, in those advanced years, could be no fair specimen of his pulpit abilities. He appeared in the black silk gown and bands, after the Scotch fashion; and delivered his sermon entirely without notes, in a full deliberate flow of language of impressive solemnity. His voice was still unbroken, rich, deep and harmonious. I should think that, in earlier years, it might have been one of great power. He always dressed well and his deportment and manner were at once dignified and cordial.

Upon the whole, the impression which remains to me of the Rev. Dr. Gilbert McMaster is that of a venerable and warm-hearted Christian gentleman of the old style.

With sentiments of the highest esteem,
Yours truly,
JAMES C. MOFFAT.

JOHN REILY.
1809—1820.
FROM THE REV. SAMUEL WYLIE.

EDEN, ILL., April 21, 1863.

My dear Sir: My grateful remembrances of the Rev. John Reily, of whom you ask me to give you some account, predispose me to comply with your request; and yet I fear that my information concerning him is hardly sufficient to avail to

JOHN REILY.

your purpose. I believe, however, I can state the leading facts of his life, and can at least give you my impressions of his character.

JOHN REILY was a native of Ireland, and was born about the year 1770. He came to this country when he was about seventeen years old, in company with the Rev. Messrs. John Black and Samuel B. Wylie; and after his arrival prosecuted his studies for a considerable time with a view to becoming a Teacher. In due time he entered on this vocation, and continued thus engaged in Philadelphia and its vicinity for several years. He also became an Elder, in the Reformed Presbyterian Church in Philadelphia under the care of Dr. Wylie, in which capacity he was eminently useful. At length he resolved to devote himself to the Ministry of the Gospel, and, having studied Theology, for some time, under the direction of Dr. Wylie, he was licensed to preach by the Special Presbytery, at Philadelphia, on the 24th of May, 1809. On the 15th of August, 1812, at Pittsburg, the Presbytery were required to take him on trial with a view to Ordination; and, when ordained, to send him as a Missionary to the States of South Carolina, Kentucky and Ohio; and on the 5th of May, 1814, at Philadelphia, the Presbytery reported that they had ordained Mr. Reily, and sent him on a mission as directed. His Ordination took place some time in the year 1813.

Though he was ordained and sent forth as a Missionary, he had not been long in South Carolina before he was installed as Pastor of the United Congregations of Beaver Dams, in Chester District, and Wateree in Fairfield District, where he laboured with great acceptance and success till the close of his life. He also organized a Congregation at Turkey Creek, in York District, and preached for some time in Winnsborough, Fairfield District, and Columbia, Richland District. He died, of Bilious Fever, greatly lamented, in August, 1820. The maiden name of his wife was Jane Weir—she was extremely delicate in her physical organization, but she survived him for some time; and such was the strength of her affection for him that she could never be induced to leave the neighbourhood where he died, on the ground that she wished her remains and those of her husband might rest side by side. They had no children.

My acquaintance with Mr. Reily commenced while I was yet in my *teens* and a student in the University of Pennsylvania, and he the teacher of a school in Frankfort, a few miles North of Philadelphia. As the Communion season was approaching in Dr. Wylie's Church, he took me aside, and, with the earnestness of a loving parent, urged upon my consideration the great importance of religion, showing that, while the heart believes unto righteousness, the tongue makes confession to salvation, and proving the necessity of putting on the livery of Christ, and openly avowing myself a Soldier of the Cross. I followed his counsel, and my name was accordingly entered on the list of members of the First Reformed Presbyterian Church in Philadelphia, in the year 1810. For the wise and judicious counsel he gave me I have reason to bless his memory and to thank God to this day.

In the spring of 1818 I visited the Carolinas, and preached in several congregations, spending most of my time in Mr. Reily's family, and often accompanying him on his parochial visits; and I also travelled with him from Carolina to Pittsburg, Pa., to attend a meeting of Synod. This gave me an opportunity of becoming more intimately acquainted with his character and habits as a Minister of the Gospel.

Mr. Reily was distinguished for gentleness and kindness, and this was manifest in his manner of speaking; while yet the tones of his voice were strong, bold and commanding. He shunned not to declare the whole counsel of God, testifying against all immorality in both Church and State, and denouncing with special severity the practice of holding and buying and selling human beings as chattels. Whilst his whole course manifested a childlike simplicity and godly sincerity, his singleness of purpose and undaunted intrepidity in maintaining and defending his own views commanded the respect even of those who differed from him, especially in respect to God's law and human rights.

He was a close observer of human character, and his doctrine was brought home and powerfully applied to the hearts and consciences of his hearers. Many felt that, under his ministrations, the Gospel came to them not in word only but in power, and in the Holy Ghost and in much assurance.

Mr. Reily's name is savoury and his memory dear to many old disciples, who in youth sat under his ministry. Members and descendants of members of his congregation are scattered through the different congregations of the Western and Ohio Presbyteries, and the prefix name *Reily* is found in many a household. His attention to the young, the lambs of Christ's fold, was unceasing and most vigilant. His character as a citizen and friend was so exemplary, and his character as a man of God so strongly marked, that his name is well worthy of an enduring memorial.

In person he was of the middle size, and his manner, both in and out of the pulpit, was agreeable. He was particular in his attentions to strangers, and, by his bland and genial spirit towards them, was quite sure to gain their good-will. He was a good Hebrew scholar, and had, in general, a well-cultivated mind, and exerted a decided influence in his denomination.

I remain, Dear Sir, with sentiments of regard, yours truly,

SAMUEL WYLIE.

JOHN KELL.*

1809—1842.

JOHN KELL, a son of John and Jane (Morton) Kell, was born at Rocky Creek, in Chester District, S. C., in the year 1772. Among his recollections of his very early childhood was the fact that his mother hid himself and his little brother in the bushes, at night, from an apprehension that their house was in danger of being burnt by the British or Tories. His father was a farmer, and this son worked with him upon his farm until he had reached the age of seventeen or eighteen, when the partial loss of his health disqualified him for the business of husbandry, and led him to form the purpose of acquiring a liberal education. He prosecuted his course preparatory to College under an accomplished teacher from Ireland, by the name of John Orr; but, as there were no Colleges in that part of the country at that early day, he crossed the ocean and pursued his studies at Glasgow College, Scotland. Having completed his

* Obituary notice in the Missionary Advocate, V.—MSS. from Mrs. Kell and Rev. G. McMillan.

course there, he engaged in the study of Divinity under the direction of the Rev. Dr. McMillan, of Stirling, Professor of Theology in the Reformed Presbyterian Church. He returned to South Carolina in the fall of 1808, and in June of the next year was licensed to preach in the Reformed Presbyterian Church, by what was then known as the Middle Presbytery.

From this time till his Ordination he was employed in travelling through the Western States and Territories, visiting the small settlements of Reformed Presbyterians, as well as solitary families scattered about the country, and preaching wherever he could find those who were disposed to attend on his ministrations.

On the 10th of November, 1811, Mr. Kell was married to Jane, daughter of Joseph and Mary (Crawford) Hartin. They had emigrated from the County of Antrim, Ireland, to South Carolina, in 1790, but, in 1807, they removed to Preble County, O., from their preference for living in a free State.

Mr. Kell was ordained to the work of the ministry, in South Carolina, by the Rev. John Black and the Rev. Thomas Donnelly, a little before the close of the year 1811. His Ordination was with special reference to his becoming a Missionary in the Western States and Territories, though he was allowed to select his own place of ultimate settlement. He was first settled (though not installed) in Beech Woods, Butler County, O., but afterwards removed to Princeton, Gibson County, Ind., where he took charge of a small congregation. Here he had his home during the residue of his life, though he still performed a great amount of missionary labour in Illinois, Kentucky and Tennessee. In 1837, he was, at his own request, released by Presbytery from his pastoral charge. His life was one of most untiring activity, and, under his faithful ministry, many a spot in the wilderness was seen to bud and blossom as the rose. His health was generally good, and he experienced little interruption of his labours until he was attacked by the malady that carried him to his grave. His last sermon was preached just four weeks previous to his death, at a place called Whitehall, as he was returning from a meeting of his Presbytery at Bloomington. He died at his own house in Princeton, of an affection of the heart, on the 6th of November, 1842, being perfectly conscious to the last, and committing his soul, with humble confidence, into his Redeemer's hands. His Funeral Sermon was preached by the Rev. Dr. Gilbert McMaster.

Mr. Kell left a widow who still (1862) survives; but he had no children.

FROM THE REV. GAVIN McMILLAN.

MORNING SUN, O., June 26, 1863

My dear Sir: My recollections and impressions in respect to the Rev. John Kell are such that it is only a pleasure to me to record them. I will state what I remember concerning him in the order in which it occurs to me.

In person he was above the common size, and somewhat athletic. When he was quite a young man, he and one of his young friends, by the name of William Hughes, agreed to try their strength in wrestling on the sandy beach of Rocky Creek. Hughes held him down in the sand in spite of his utmost exertions; and the bodily system of Kell was, as he believed, seriously injured in consequence of the struggle. This circumstance, I have understood, was chiefly instrumental in bringing him to serious reflection, which resulted in his entering into a solemn covenant with God, and ultimately in his forming a purpose to devote himself to the ministry.

Mr. Kell, being cordially attached to Reformation principles, was zealous and laborious in his efforts to promote them; nor could he be tempted by any consideration to give up the Banner of the Covenant. Still he was constitutionally and habitually generous and liberal. His manners were courteous and pleasant; and these, with his well cultivated mind and kindly disposition, rendered him, as Dr. Bishop once said, "a noble companion." Having once espoused a cause which he considered just and laudable, his zeal in the promotion of it was not easily quenched. Witness his efforts in the cause of Temperance, and Missions, and Colonization, and Emancipation, and Prayer Meetings, and Music in the Church. When asked what tunes he would have sung, he said humourously,—"Any thing, from 'Old Coleshill' to 'Fire in the Mountains, Boys.'" He had, however, no relish for human composure nor instrumental music in the worship of God.

He delighted greatly in the communion of saints. A sacred unction accompanied his devotional exercises, which always rendered them savoury. He was greatly given to ejaculatory prayer, insomuch that he would sometimes be engaged in it even in company. When I first noticed this in Mr. Kell, I confess it impressed me unfavourably—it seemed to me to savour more of ostentatious sanctimony than of genuine devotion. But I had occasion very soon to change my opinion; and I became satisfied that what I witnessed was the irrepressible fervour of an eminently devout spirit. He used to say that, after becoming familiar with a person's devotional exercises, he thought he could decide with tolerable certainty whether or not he was a true saint. Some thought that he was at times a little visionary; and others complained of what they regarded his excessive liberality towards other denominations; but, however this may have been, there can be no doubt that his standard of religious character was much above that of ordinary Christians. I heard him preach an excellent sermon to my congregation from I. Peter ii, 11, in which he opened up a good deal of the mystery of sanctification. He seemed to delight in selecting those texts which had special reference to the operations of the Holy Spirit and to communion with God. He was at once a doctrinal, experimental and practical Preacher. He could not, perhaps, in the common acceptation of the word, be called *eloquent* in the pulpit; but there was such a hallowed unction pervading all his utterances that his preaching could hardly fail to make an impression. In controversy he was exceedingly patient and persevering; but his reasonings were sometimes less lucid than could be desired.

With all his deep religious feeling and devout fervour, he was far from being a gloomy Christian—on the contrary, he had a keen relish for social enjoyment, and would sometimes laugh heartily. He used sometimes to say with the poet,—

> Religion never was designed
> To make our pleasures less."

Mr. Kell was remarkable for his sympathy for the African race. He viewed the Colonization Society with great favour, regarding Liberia as the best home for the coloured man. He encouraged this unfortunate people, so far as he could, to migrate thither, that they might enjoy all the rights and privileges of freemen, and withal might prove a blessing to their father-land. He considered it a matter of great moment that some of their number should be educated, that they might be the instructors of others of their race, both at home and abroad. He evinced great public spirit in connection with different objects of Christian charity, and was always ready to spend and be spent in behalf of any cause with which he believed that the glory of his Master or the best interests of his fellow men were connected.

Very truly yours,
GAVIN McMILLAN

FROM THE REV. SAMUEL WYLIE.

EDEN, RANDOLPH COUNTY, ILL., March 30, 1863.

Reverend and dear Sir: I cheerfully comply with your request for my recollections and impressions of the Rev. John Kell, who, besides being an early acquaintance, was, for many years, my fellow-labourer and co-presbyter. I knew him first in Ireland. Though a native of South Carolina, he, for a time, pursued his literary course in Scotland, and, after that, spent some time in Ireland, when I, as a pupil, read Latin and Greek to him at the house of the Rev. William Stavely.

After returning to America and receiving Ordination, he travelled extensively through the West and the South. In 1818 I was myself ordained as a Missionary and sent to Illinois. From that time till his death, he and I were together as co-presbyters in the Reformed Presbyterian Church.

When I first visited the West as a Missionary, I found Mr. Kell settled in a congregation in Princeton, Ind. The bounds of the Western Presbytery included a large extent of territory in the West, then but sparsely settled. Families and individuals, in connection with the Reformed Presbyterian Church, were scattered through the new States and Territories, and Mr. Kell, as a dauntless pioneer, plunged into the depths of the wilderness, visiting lonely societies and solitary families, and bearing to the wretched and destitute the offers of a free salvation. Naturally of a frank and sociable turn, he soon became a favourite wherever he was in the habit of calling. On leaving the humble but friendly cabin, the urgent inquiry would be made,—" When will you come back to us?" And to that was very sure to be added,—" Do come soon."

He was particularly attached to children, and, as a natural consequence, he drew them very near to him; and they would press around him with eager and loving looks, and drink in his heavenly teachings. In his pulpit exhibitions there was perspicuity of style, orderly and natural arrangement, Scripture truth unalloyed by human wisdom, direct and forcible arguments, and, to crown all, a deep and all-pervading piety. It was impossible to be familiar with him without perceiving that he lived habitually under a deep impression of his responsibility as a Minister of Christ, and that his highest ambition was to save the souls committed to his care. He was obedient to the Apostles' direction,—" Preach the Word; be instant in season and out of season." Wherever he lodged, his conversation was like a sermon by the fireside or in the social circle. At the same time, there was nothing about him that savoured of gloom or moroseness. He could, on proper occasions, be playful and facetious, and had at his command a large store of anecdotes and entertaining reminiscences, particularly of his early journeyings in the West.

In the latter, as in the earlier, part of his ministry, Mr. Kell was engaged much in missionary labour. He spent several months here and hereabouts. At this period of his life, it was remarked that the Bible was his constant companion. All other books, I might almost say, were discarded, and the Book of books was almost always in his hand, and its precious contents formed his heart's richest treasures. His whole Christian character, as was indicated by this fact, became more mature, earnest, elevated, and it was manifest to all that he was waiting in faith and hope till his change should come.

I will only add that, in his early travels in the South and West, Mrs. Kell, deeply imbued with a missionary spirit, often accompanied him, braving all the difficulties of new settlements and a pioneer's life.

I am yours truly,
SAMUEL WYLIE.

ROBERT WALLACE.*
1814—1849.

ROBERT WALLACE was born in the parish of Loughgilly, County of Armagh, Ireland, in December, 1772. His parents were intelligent and exemplary members of the Antiburgher Secession Church. He, in common with the other children of the family, was carefully instructed in the great truths of religion, as well as in the distinctive principles of the Church in which he was baptized. At the age of nineteen Robert, the third son of his parents, made a public profession of his faith, and devoted himself to the service of Jesus Christ in his Church. Shortly after this his attention was directed to the question whether it was lawful to receive the *Regium Donum*, or *King's Bounty*;—a question which, at that time, was agitated extensively and with no small degree of interest. In endeavouring to attain to the truth concerning it, he was led to a careful examination of the whole doctrine of Civil Government, searching diligently the Scriptures, and reading the best authors on that subject within his reach. He became convinced, as the result of his inquiries, that he could not conscientiously subscribe to the doctrine of passive obedience, and non-resistance for conscience sake, to the Government of Great Britain, and he therefore soon left the Body in which he had been baptized and nurtured, and joined the Reformed Presbyterian Church.

Having now reached the age of about twenty-four years, he was united in marriage with Margaret, second daughter of James King, one of the most respectable and wealthy men in his neighbourhood; and about this time he resolved to become a Minister of the Gospel. Though he foresaw that he should have to encounter many difficulties in his preparation for the sacred office, he addressed himself to the work with great zeal, and, after a while, entered the University of Glasgow, from which he graduated in the year 1810. In the spring of the next year he crossed the ocean with his family, consisting of a wife and four children, with a view to find a permanent home in this country. Having, for some time, pursued his theological studies under the direction of the Rev. Dr. Wylie, of Philadelphia, he was licensed to preach the Gospel in May, 1814, and in the autumn of the same year received a call from two Societies, one on the waters of Licking, and the other near Chillicothe, O. Having accepted the call, he was ordained in the vicinity of Pittsburg; and shortly after removed West, and was installed Pastor of the Churches to which he had been called.

He continued in this relation till 1820, when he resigned the Licking part of his charge. As the congregation with which he was now connected was small, and required but a part of his time, he employed himself extensively in missionary labour, and was instrumental of organizing Societies in the vicinity of Walnut Creek, Brush Creek, Jonathan's Creek, Tomica and Salt Creek—indeed his field was the great and growing West. In this work he suffered great toils and privations. The country was but sparsely settled; the roads were often well nigh impassable; the bridges over rivers and creeks were few; and every thing seemed adverse to the comfort of the traveller. There were but few Covenanters, and

---

* MS. from his son, Mr. David Wallace.—Reformed Presbyterian, 1849.

they were widely scattered; and though they were anxious to have the Gospel preached to them, they seem not to have practically received the doctrine that they who preach the Gospel must live by the Gospel. Still he endured hardness as a good soldier of Jesus Christ. He laboured earnestly and patiently, amidst the most adverse circumstances, for the conversion of sinners and the edification and enlargement of the Church, looking for his reward in a better country, even an heavenly.

And his labours were not in vain—he was uncommonly successful in winning souls to Christ. He sought out individuals and families in different parts of the country far distant from each other, who were favourably inclined towards the truth, and by his affable and friendly manner and the seriousness and spirituality of his conversation, he won their confidence, taught them the way of God more perfectly, and was instrumental of bringing them into the Church. These individuals and families he organized into Societies, and some of them, under his fostering care, grew into flourishing congregations. One of these is the Congregation of Salt Creek. Here there were only two families belonging to the Reformed Presbyterian Church, when he first visited the place; but, as the result of his diligent and faithful labours, their number increased until they formed three distinct Societies. In 1822 these Societies united in giving him a unanimous call to become their Pastor. This call he accepted, and, having demitted the charge of the Utica Congregation, was shortly after regularly introduced to this new field of labour.

Although his travelling was, from this time, much less extensive than it had been, yet he still continued to occasionally visit and minister to the several congregations which he had been instrumental of planting, and which still regarded him as their spiritual father. Thus, though naturally of a feeble constitution, he performed, for many years, the double duty of a Stated Pastor and a Missionary. The care of several churches was upon him. His own congregation continued to increase in numbers until it became one of the largest in the denomination. He laboured, and others entered into his labours. With some interruption on account of ill health and his growing infirmities, he continued to discharge pastoral duties until a few months before his death, when he fell from his horse as he was going to preach on Sabbath morning, and experienced so severe a shock that he was never able to preach again. He declined gradually until the 19th of July, 1849, when he passed gently to his final rest, in the seventy-seventh year of his age. During his last days and weeks his confidence in the promises of God never faltered, and he had the most cheering foretastes of the glory that was soon to be revealed to him. His neighbours and the members of his congregation generally abounded in their manifestations of good-will and affection towards him, both while he was living and after he was dead.

He had a family of six children,—three sons and three daughters,—all of them now (1864) living. The oldest and youngest of his sons, and one grandson, are ministers of the Reformed Presbyterian Church.

FROM THE REV. THOMAS SPROULL, D.D.

ALLEGHENY, November 25, 1864

Rev. and dear Sir: My acquaintance with the Rev. Robert Wallace began when I was a student of Theology, perhaps in 1830. His oldest son, John Wallace, and myself, were classmates in the Western University, graduated at the same time, and studied Theology together. The Rev. Robert Wallace, although he lived more than a hundred and fifty miles from Pittsburg, and travelled on horseback, rarely failed to be at the meetings of the Presbytery, which were usually held in that place. From 1833 to the time of his death, he and I were co-presbyters, meeting frequently in the Courts of the Church and also on other occasions.

The traits of Mr. Wallace's character that always seemed to me more prominent than any others were kindness and cheerfulness. He was a true philanthrophist, wishing well to every body, and, so far as he had opportunity, carrying out his wishes in deeds. He was a favourite with all the families among whom he was accustomed temporarily to sojourn. He had a pleasant word for every body, and an almost exhaustless store of amusing and instructive anecdotes, which he would tell in a way peculiarly his own. I well remember, however, that he was always careful neither to wound feelings, to injure reputation, or give any countenance to a censurable or sinful frivolity.

An incident, that he was fond of relating, will exemplify the above statement concerning him. Once travelling in a neighbourhood where he was a stranger, he stopped at a house to inquire for the family which he was seeking. An old man, with long white hair, neatly combed back, in clean dress, gave him the desired information. He seemed so patriarchal that Mr. Wallace turned away, admiring him, and pronouncing him, in his view, the prettiest old man he had ever seen. On arriving at the house whither he was going, which was but a short distance off, in conversation with his host, he referred to the old man he had met, and added some expression of admiration. "That man," replied his host, "is one of the most profane men I ever knew." Mr. Wallace, on his return the next day, passed by the same house, and saw the same old man in the same place. And he would finish the story by saying,—"I thought he was the ugliest old man I ever saw."

Yours truly,
THOMAS SPROULL.

JOHN CANNON.*
1815—1836.

JOHN CANNON was born in Dungiven, County of Derry, Ireland, on the 19th of November, 1784. His parents were both communicants in the Presbyterian Church. In 1788 the whole family migrated to this country, and settled in Westmoreland County, Pa. Owing to their dissatisfaction with the use of Watts' Psalms in the Presbyterian Church, they joined the Associate Reformed Church, under the pastoral care of the Rev. Mr. Jameison. John, who was their youngest child, evinced an early fondness for books, and a more than ordinary facility at acquiring knowledge. After studying, for a considerable time, under private teachers, he entered Jefferson College, where he took the regular course and graduated in September, 1810. In the autumn of 1811 he commenced the study of Theology, under the Rev. Samuel B. Wylie, Professor of Theology in the Reformed Presbyterian Church. He was licensed to preach the Gospel by the Philadelphia Presbytery on the 23d of May, 1815. In due time, he received and accepted a call from the Congregation of Greensburg and vicinity, and, on the

* Reformed Presbyterian, 1837.

16th of September, 1816, was ordained to the work of the Ministry, and set apart as the Minister of the said Congregation.

At a meeting of the Synod in 1821, he was appointed to visit the Church in South Carolina to aid in settling certain difficulties that existed in that quarter. In the course of five weeks, he and his fellow Commissioner had succeeded in settling the existing disputes, and rectifying the disorders complained of; had ordained Messrs. Campbell Madden and Hugh McMillan, administered the Lord's Supper, and organized the Southern Presbytery.

Within about six years from the time of his settlement, his charge was divided into two distinct congregations. Over one of these he remained as Pastor, labouring with all fidelity, and zeal, and self-denial, till the close of life.

For several years before his death, he suffered not a little from an affection of the liver; and his disease was aggravated by the fatigue and exposure incident to his professional duties. Still nothing could induce him to desist from preaching, so long as he could command strength enough to go through the service. To a member of his Presbytery who had written to him, advising that he should suspend his labours till his health should be restored, he replied, in a letter dated February 12, 1835, as follows: "God has again restored me to a comfortable measure of health, except that I have at present contracted a cold. My health was not injured by my attempts to preach. Friends have said that I exposed myself too much in preaching. But, dear brother, I am persuaded I have been too remiss in ministerial duty, and I think that my affliction has been more for this than any other cause."

On the last Sabbath of August, 1835, he dispensed the Sacrament of the Lord's Supper; but his health was now much reduced; and this proved to be the last public service that he ever performed. From this time he became greatly debilitated, and his disease took on the form of dropsy. Medical skill now proved unavailing; but, knowing in whom he had believed, he was not afraid to die. He lingered till the 2d of February, 1836, and then peacefully took his departure.

It was a mark of the high estimation in which he was held by his brethren that, at the memorable Synod of 1833, he was chosen Moderator.

Shortly after his settlement in Greensburg, he was married to Martha, eldest daughter of Robert Brown, a member of his Session. They became the parents of eight children, all of whom, with their mother, survived him.

FROM THE REV. THOMAS SPROULL, D.D.

ALLEGHENY, Pa., November 6, 1863.

Rev. and dear Sir: Your request that I should furnish you with some of my recollections of the late Rev. John Cannon for your forthcoming volume of "Annals of the American Pulpit," devolves upon me a service which it is only a gratification to me to perform. Some of my most cherished reminiscences are those which have respect to my intercourse with this esteemed minister of Christ. His was the first preaching of which I have any distinct recollection. In 1816 he became the Pastor of the congregation of which my parents were members. I knew him well from that time till his death; and our acquaintance ripened into a friendship intimate and endearing.

Mr. Cannon I regarded as a model Man, Christian and Minister. Kindness, candour and firmness were prominent traits in his character. The needy ever found in him a friend. He was "given to hospitality." Such was the estimation in which he was held that his death spread a gloom over the entire neighbourhood. To many it was the loss of a benefactor; to all that of a kind friend. He was as far as possible from attempting to secure favour by flattery—no man was more faithful than he to his honest convictions of duty. The wrong-doer rarely escaped a rebuke for an evil deed done in his presence. Of this I have heard many instances; two of which, as they happened to come under my observation, it may not be out of place to describe.

In 1833 he and I travelled by stage to Philadelphia. Descending into the valley of the Juniata, we received a passenger, a young man of no promising appearance. He took his position in the middle seat, Mr. Cannon and myself occupying the one in the rear and two other gentlemen the one in front. When the driver stopped to water the horses, our new passenger hailed some one on the porch with the inquiry, "Have you any thing to drink?" No reply being made, he put the same inquiry again with greater emphasis. Thus receiving no attention, he exclaimed, in an angry tone, "Why the devil don't you answer me?" Mr. Cannon, immediately repeating the words,—"Why the devil," asked him if he travelled in the name of the devil. He replied, with an impudent look, "Yes." Mr. Cannon then said to him,—"You had better, my friend, take care what kind of words you utter, as there are persons behind who will take account of them." He answered, (the profane expletive I will not record,) "Then you'll have a pretty busy time of it between this and Philadelphia." The coach moved on, and nothing more was said. During the day, however, the same person managed to get into a conversation with Mr. Cannon and seemed quite pleased with his new acquaintance.

The other incident took place on the evening of the same day, and in connection with the same person. Just as it was beginning to get dark, and when within twelve miles of Harrisburg, the coach stopped, and a female passenger was admitted, whose whole appearance indicated that she was a grossly depraved character. Almost immediately there was apparent a mutual attraction between her and the passenger referred to, and there were very significant indications that they did not intend to remain strangers to each other. They being observed by Mr. Cannon, he turned to her and asked if she had no male friend to see that she received no improper treatment among strangers. She replied, in a whispering tone,—"No, Sir." Mr. Cannon then told her that she need be under no apprehension of insult while she was in the coach, for there were gentlemen there who would be sure to protect her. This unexpected announcement took both aback, and they drew up within as narrow limits as possible, at the opposite ends of the seat.

The personal appearance of Mr. Cannon was very pleasing. He was of about the middle height, with dark eyes, hair and complexion. His forehead was high and somewhat bald; but, by a skillful arrangement of his hair, his baldness was tastefully covered so as to give to his countenance quite a youthful appearance. He was scrupulously neat in all his habits.

I will only add that Mr. Cannon's ministry, which continued about twenty years, was eminently successful.

I remain yours in the Gospel,
THOMAS SPROULL.

ROBERT GIBSON.*
1818—1837.

ROBERT GIBSON, a son of the Rev. William Gibson, was born at Ballymena, Ireland, on the 1st of October, 1793. In 1797 his parents, on account of dissatisfaction with the British Government, migrated to the United States, landing at Philadelphia. His father, soon after his arrival in the country, became the Pastor of the Reformed Presbyterian Congregation at Ryegate, Vt. At an early age, he commenced the study of the Languages under his father's instruction, and very soon proved himself an excellent scholar. Having gone as far in his classical course as was deemed necessary, he went to Philadelphia to prosecute his theological studies, in the Reformed Presbyterian Theological Seminary, under the care of the late Rev. Dr. Samuel B. Wylie. He was licensed to preach in 1818, it is believed by the Middle Presbytery of Philadelphia, and his first efforts in the pulpit awakened much more than ordinary attention. On the 6th of September, 1819, he was ordained and installed as Pastor of the Beaver Dam Congregation, by the Pittsburg Presbytery. Here he laboured with great acceptance and success for twelve years. In 1831 he accepted a call from the Second Reformed Presbyterian Church in the city of New York, and was installed as its first Pastor in May of that year. In this new and extensive field he found much to encourage and quicken him. In labours he was abundant,—preaching three times every Sabbath, besides delivering a weekly evening lecture, attending prayer-meetings, and being most faithful in the duty of family visitation and catechizing. The effect of his diligence and fidelity in his work was that his congregation grew in numbers and in graces, and the tie that bound him to them gradually acquired great tenderness and strength.

In the controversy which issued in the disruption of the Church in 1833 he bore a prominent part. He published three pamphlets vindicating the course of the Synod, and showing that he considered the question at issue as having a vital bearing on the best interests of the Church.

During his ministry in Pennsylvania he had been subjected to great exposure in the discharge of his duties, by means of which he had contracted an incipient disease of the lungs. It was confidently hoped that the climate of New York would serve to counteract these tendencies; but the result proved otherwise. In 1836 the symptoms of decline appeared in an unmistakable form. He visited Vermont, in the hope that, by spending a little time among his father's parishioners and the scenes of his own early life, he might recruit his waning vigour; but his labours in the pulpit were so often put in requisition that, when he returned to New York, his health had in no degree improved. In the spring of 1837 he made a visit to his native land, where the Reformed Presbyterians gave him a cordial welcome, and he, in turn, impressed them most favourably in respect to both his talents and virtues. As his health, however, was not benefitted by his sojourn in Ireland, he made but a short visit there, and returned in the autumn of 1837.

It was apparent, when he came back to his people, that the days of his usefulness, and even of his life, were well-nigh numbered. He conducted once the

* Presb. Alm., 1862.—MS. from Rev. S. O. Wylie.

morning service, and, on the 12th of November, took part in the administration of the Lord's Supper. This was the last public service he ever performed; and it was an occasion of most tender interest to his congregation. From this time he continued gradually to decline until the 22d of December, when he closed his earthly career. He left a widow and four children.

Mr. Gibson's only publications were the three controversial pamphlets already alluded to. He, however, was, for some time, joint editor with the Rev. Mr. Irving, of the Associate Church, of a weekly paper in New York, afterwards edited by the Rev. Dr. Brownlee, entitled the "American Protestant Vindicator."

Mr. Gibson was married in 1817 to Mary Ann Harvey, of Philadelphia, by whom he had five children,—four sons and one daughter. She died in 1824. He was subsequently (it is believed in 1827) married to Mary Ann Lindsay, of Philadelphia, by whom he had one child,—a son. She survived her husband some two or three years.

FROM THE REV. DAVID SCOTT.

ROCHESTER, December 4, 1863.

Rev. and dear Sir: I became acquainted with the late Rev. Robert Gibson, on going to the city of New York, in the summer of 1829. A short time before that, he had come from the Western part of Pennsylvania, where he had been settled as the Pastor of a congregation. From this period till the close of his life, we were often brought together through our ecclesiastical relations. During the greater part of this time we were co-presbyters, and frequently associated in the business of the Church.

Mr. Gibson was rather above the medium height, of dark complexion, of an open, manly, agreeable countenance. His appearance, especially in the pulpit, was prepossessing. He had many of the elements of a popular and successful speaker; and not only among the people of his own charge, but wherever he ministered, his preaching was highly acceptable. He had a good voice, with a clear and distinct utterance, and a manner of address well adapted to attract the attention of the masses of the people. He was distinguished more for quickness and acuteness than depth of thought; and this characteristic sometimes betrayed him into hasty conclusions, which, however they might be accepted at the time, would not always stand the test of deliberate reflection. To this feature of his intellectual character may possibly be attributed the fact that, while he was very generally acceptable as a Preacher, and influential as a member of Presbytery and other Church Courts, there were not wanting those whose estimate of him did not come up to the popular standard. Indeed, I have seldom known one, of his acknowledged intellectual endowments, in respect to whom there has existed so great a difference of opinion; though, with much the larger class, not only within but outside of his own ecclesiastical connection, he took a high rank as a Preacher. The popular elements, embracing a large vein of irony, which were embodied in his mode of thinking, his manner of address, and forms of expression, were all in sympathy with the public mind.

Mr. Gibson took a decided and prominent part in the controversy respecting Civil Relations, which terminated in the disruption of the Reformed Presbyterian Church, in the United States, in the year 1833. In the earlier stage of the controversy, and before it reached its culminating point, his influence seemed to be thrown on the side of those who wished to change the position of the Church in regard to her relation to the State; subsequently, however, he took a different view of the case, and acted with great decision on the other side. It was characteristic of the man, when the path of duty seemed plain to him, to pursue it earnestly. Indeed his ardent temperament made this a necessity. His course in reference to this matter alienated from him some who had been his devoted friends; but no considerations of friendship or interest could prevail against the honest convictions of his own judgment.

I am, Dear Sir, yours in the Lord,
DAVID SCOTT.

FROM THE REV. THOMAS HOUSTON, D.D.

BELFAST, IRELAND, November, 1864

My dear Sir: The Rev. Robert Gibson, late of New York, was my correspondent several years before he visited this country. We were led into the first interchange of sentiment from the internal troubles that disturbed the peace of the Reformed Presbyterian Church in the United States, and that resulted in the division of the Body in 1833. About the same time there arose a controversy in the Covenanting Synod of this country, chiefly in relation to the extent of the Power of the Christian Civil Magistrate in matters of Religion, and some other kindred subjects. As Mr. Gibson took a warm interest in the matters in debate, and in the manner in which the discussion was conducted, and as I was called to occupy a somewhat prominent position in the controversy, from being the Editor, at the time, of the *Covenanter*, the periodical in which some articles appeared that were called in question by brethren who afterwards separated from the Church—this led to frequent and free correspondence between us.

This intercourse was the more cordial as it was begun without any previous acquaintance, from mutual esteem and from our entertaining the same views in relation to great principles that were involved in the discussions that were carried on in the Church on both sides of the Atlantic. It may be mentioned that Mr. Gibson's sentiments were in harmony with the Westminster Confession and Catechism, according to the strictest interpretation, and were those held by our Presbyterian forefathers of the Second Reformation, by those who weathered the Prelatic persecutions, and who, as the intrepid advocates of Civil and Religious Liberty, dissented from the corrupt Erastian establishment of the Revolution, both in its civil and ecclesiastical departments.

In Mr. Gibson's letters I chiefly admired his cool, comprehensive judgment, his sterling honesty and integrity, and his candour. He always showed singular acuteness in grasping the proper limits of a subject, in perceiving the strong points of an argument, and in detecting sophisms, or inconclusive points in reasoning. He had a generous, confiding nature, and a genial disposition. I admired much his nobility of mind—he ever avoided personalities in controversy, and could appreciate what was excellent and praiseworthy in an opponent, and he did not fail to give expression to his esteem on fitting occasions. However one might differ from him in sentiment, he made no personal enemies among his opponents. The letters that I received from him contained so much valuable information, conveyed in so easy and natural a style; so closely stated and so ably vindicated important principles, and were withal so brotherly and loving, that I felt, at the time of our correspondence, and since, that I had no brother with whom I was privileged to enjoy a more interesting and profitable intercourse.

In the early summer of 1837 Mr. Gibson came to this country, in very impaired health. He was labouring under bronchitis, and his bodily system had become much exhausted, through continued ministerial work, before he left America. He was considerably recruited by the voyage; but it was evident to me and other friends in this country that he had not strength to engage in preaching and other public duties of the ministry. Our esteemed brother, however, led in part by the consciousness of restored strength, and more by the earnest desire to glorify the Master whom he loved, undertook, soon after his arrival among us, too frequent engagements to preach; and though he was often warned of the peril of such a course by the great prostration of strength occasioned by these labours, and the restless nights that followed, he persevered in preaching nearly every Sabbath during his sojourn in this country.

His public discourses were much liked, and were, I trust, blessed to not a few who heard them. It was sufficiently evident that—so far as the manner of delivery was concerned—he was unable to preach as in his days of unimpaired strength and vigour. But on all occasions he displayed an extensive acquaintance with the great truths of the evangelical system, and an intense concern for his Master's glory and for the salvation of souls. His manner was solemn and impressive—he always seemed to realize his nearness to eternity, his Redeemer's presence and his final account. Those who heard him could not fail to feel that they were listening to one who possessed abilities of a high order as an Expounder of the Word and a Preacher of the glorious Gospel;—who, knowing the terrors and love of God, persuaded men.

On one occasion, while at this place, and preaching to my congregation, he appeared to rise above his bodily weakness, and gave a remarkable display of his eminent power as a Preacher. It was on the Monday after our Communion. It was in the middle of summer; and, from the length of the services, and the heat in the house—owing to the large congregation that was present— Mr. Gibson appeared much exhausted. In the opening of the services on Monday he explained or lectured on a part of the sixty-eighth Psalm,—chiefly from the twenty-second to the thirty-first verse. For graphic power of description, exalted views of the Covenant of Redemption, of the Mediator and his work, the Government of Providence, the privileges of God's people, the doom of their enemies, and a testimony in relation to national sins and judgments, it was altogether a singular display of massive and compact thought—of holiness in preaching the truth; of eloquence of the most effective kind. The congregation, that had before sympathized with him in his weakness, listened to this discourse with wonder and delight. It was spoken of by many with admiration long after he left us, and salutary impressions were made by it on the minds of not a few who were present. There were other occasions on which Mr. Gibson, while he remained in this country, took part with brethren in the vicinity in sanctuary services, and his discourses were spoken of as displaying abilities of a high order, and as having been productive of valuable practical effects.

In his private intercourse with brethren in the ministry and their families, and with others throughout the Church, Mr. Gibson was highly esteemed and greatly loved. He was always frank, confiding and genial. His conversation was lively and deeply interesting. From the stores of a well cultivated mind, and from extensive information acquired by reading and close observation of men and public measures, he could enter fully into discourse on a great variety of subjects. His sentiments were always expressed with clearness and candour, and his reasoning and conclusions discovered high intellectual power and moral earnestness, such as to command respect, and to produce in many instances strong conviction.

There was an attractive influence in Mr. Gibson's whole manner of intercourse, in the families where he rested for a time, during his stay in this country. He was so firm in his attachment to principle, and yet so candid and charitable in judging of others; he was at the same time so confiding and loving and so grateful for kind attentions, that all who were familiar with him felt towards him as a brother or a most endeared friend. Not a few of our most pious people considered it a privilege to sympathize with him in weakness and toil, and by acts of kindness to do all that was in their power to alleviate his sufferings and promote his comfort. When he parted from us, he was followed by the affectionate regrets and earnest prayers of many who regarded him as a tried and honoured servant of Christ, who had been called to suffer for his sake, and whose life and strength had been spent in labours for advancing his glory.

While here, Mr. Gibson was able to be present at one of our Synodical meetings, and to take part in the proceedings. The Address which he delivered on the occasion was singularly judicious and affectionate, and fitted to have the best effect in advancing the truth and promoting harmony among brethren, at a time when the peace of the Church was endangered by controversy. On all sides his presence among us was regarded as beneficial, as his farewell taken of the Synod was solemn and affecting. I can never forget the last interview which I and a few other attached friends had with this beloved brother, and our parting from him on the deck of the vessel that conveyed him from our shores towards the land where were his family and flock. While we sorrowed at the thought that we should see his face on earth no more, and that in all likelihood his days were nearly numbered, he appeared, as before, calm, resigned, loving and joyful. He was called to the rest of the faithful servants of Christ, in about a fortnight after he had returned to his family and an attached congregation.

Very truly yours,
THOMAS HOUSTON.

CAMPBELL MADDEN.
1820—1828.
FROM THE REV. HUGH McMILLAN, D.D.

XENIA, O., July 1, 1850.

Dear Sir: I will do the best I can to comply with your request for some account of the Rev. Campbell Madden, though I regret to say that my knowledge of the history especially of his early life is only of the most general character. I would gladly refer you to some one more competent to the service than myself; but I do not know of any such person. In my general estimate of his character I shall be in little danger of mistake; for though I cannot say that my acquaintance with him was very intimate, yet I often met him in Church Courts, and, as our congregations joined upon each other, we were frequently together in preaching, assisting each other especially on Sacramental occasions. I had thus an opportunity of seeing him under different circumstances and influences, which enabled me to form a definite idea of his leading characteristics.

CAMPBELL MADDEN was a native of Ireland, where he received both his literary and theological education, and in due time was licensed to preach the Gospel in the Reformed Presbyterian Church. In 1820 he migrated to America, and took up his residence in South Carolina, and connected himself with the Reformed Presbyterian Church in that State. He soon received a call from a congregation in Chester District, S. C., which he accepted, and was ordained, and installed Pastor of that congregation, in 1822. Here he remained till the close of his life. He brought with him to this country a fine physical constitution, which gave promise of a long course of active usefulness. But he was not aware of the danger of living in a Southern climate, and therefore neglected the necessary precautions. He was attacked first with fever and ague, and, after that, suffered from great weakness of the breast and repeated hemorrhages. He was obliged at length to desist altogether from the labours of the pulpit, and, soon after this, it became apparent both to himself and his friends that he had not much longer to live. But there was nothing in the future to disturb or alarm him. His death, which took place in the year 1828, was singularly peaceful and triumphant. He died greatly lamented by all who knew him, and especially by those who had enjoyed the benefit of his ministrations.

Soon after he came to this country he was married to a Miss Cothcart, of Winnsborough, Fairfield District, S. C., who survived him, and, I believe, still lives. They had three children, a son and two daughters.

Mr. Madden's labours, as a Minister of the Gospel, were highly acceptable and useful. He possessed a mind of very considerable discrimination and force, and could present a difficult subject with such simplicity and clearness that persons of the humblest intellect could hardly fail to be instructed. His voice was rather feeble, but his articulation was perfectly distinct, so that he could be heard in any ordinary place of worship without effort. His exposition of Scripture was remarkably clear and satisfactory; his division of his subject natural; and his treatment of it logical and exhaustive. The general style of his preaching was argumentative and didactic; and yet he was very felicitous in his illustrations, and was sometimes quite descriptive and imaginative. Though he dwelt much on the peculiar doctrines of the Gospel, he never failed to exhibit them in their practical bearings, and to show their connection with the various duties of the Christian life. He was especially happy in detecting the first inroads of error; in guarding the avenues of the mind against its reception; in distinguishing between true and false religious experience; and his ministry, on the whole, was eminently fitted to promote the edification and purity of the Church.

Mr. Madden had, with great sincerity and heartiness, adopted this country as his own. Educated, as he had been, under a Monarchy, and by no means insensible of the blessings connected with it, he yet greatly preferred our Republican institutions. He was not indeed insensible to the evils connected with our form of government, and sometimes spoke of them, both in public and in private, yet he always spoke cautiously, and would sometimes, in the same connection, say, with characteristic modesty, that it did not become a stranger to speak too freely of that of which he had at best but an imperfect knowledge. I may add here that modesty was one of his most striking characteristics, and that it gave complexion to his whole character, and diffused a charm over all his intercourse.

Before leaving Ireland Mr. Madden received the elements of a Medical education. After he came to this country, and even after his settlement as a Pastor, he still gave a portion of his time to the study of the healing art. He spent one winter at Lexington, Ky., in attendance on the Medical Lectures, where he was highly esteemed by all who knew him, and especially by the Medical Faculty. He often expressed the opinion that the advantages of the medical profession in this country were fully equal to those enjoyed on the other side of the water. Though not giving himself formally to the practice of medicine, he did not fail to turn his medical knowledge to good account in the community in which he lived, and he had the reputation, even among medical men, of being a skilful Physician.

Regretting that I am not able to do better justice to a man so justly entitled to grateful commmemoration, I remain, with great respect,
Yours in the Gospel,
H. McMILLAN.

JAMES BLACKWOOD.*
1824—1851.

JAMES BLACKWOOD, the third son of Thomas and Jane Blackwood, was born in the County of Tyrone, Ireland, a little before the close of the last century. His excellent parents early devoted him to the Ministry of the Gospel, and, with a view to this, gave him the requisite advantages for a thorough education. In 1811 he entered Glasgow College, where he remained three years. in 1818 and 1819 he prosecuted his studies still farther, including especially the Hebrew language, at the College of Belfast; and, having completed his theological course, he was licensed by the Southern Presbytery of the Reformed Presbyterian Church, in Ireland, to preach the Gospel.

In the year 1824, some time after having received licensure, he, in company with two of his brothers and two of his sisters, migrated to the United States. His brothers having settled in Belmont County, O., within the bounds of the Reformed Presbytery of Pittsburg, he placed himself under the care of that Presbytery, and, on the 8th of May, 1826, was ordained by it to the work of the ministry. The same year he received a call from the Congregation of Brush Creek, Adams County, O., which he accepted, and the next year he was installed its Pastor. Here his labours were received with great favour, and a very cordial attachment grew up between him and his people; but, from the unsuitableness of the locality to his constitution, his health soon became impaired; and this, with some other circumstances, led him, in April, 1829, to seek and obtain a dissolution of his pastoral relation. In August, 1833, he was married to Jemima, daughter of John and Isabella Calderwood. He remained unsettled for nearly five years, during which time he was actively employed in visiting and administering ordinances to vacant congregations in Western Pennsylvania and Ohio. In May, 1834, he took charge of the United Congregation of Little Beaver, Austintown, Camp-Run, Slippery Rock, West Greenville, &c. In this extensive field, the extremities of which were forty miles apart, he laboured, with great diligence and success, till 1838, when the Little Beaver, Greenville, and Austintown branches were separated from the rest, and organized as a distinct congregation. In 1850 the congregation was farther reduced by the separation of the Springfield and Sandy Lake branches. In the portion of the original congregation that now remained he continued to labour till within two months of his death.

Mr. Blackwood's health had been perceptibly declining for a year previous to his decease, though his naturally cheerful and hopeful temperament disposed him to make as little of his unfavourable symptoms as he could. In the winter immediately preceding his death, he was, for several weeks, unable to preach, on account of debility; but he subsequently rallied, so that his friends had strong hopes of his

* Ref. Presb., 1851.

recovery. During the meeting of Synod, in the following summer, though taking the deepest interest in the proceedings, he spoke much less than usual, thereby indicating, what was otherwise manifest, a very decided abatement of his physical vigour. Shortly after his return from Synod, it became evident that his disease was taking on the form of dropsy. He soon became unable to walk, and, for several weeks before his decease, was almost entirely helpless. His sufferings were at times very severe, but he endured them with unqualified resignation. He died in the utmost composure on the 8th of October, 1851, leaving behind him a widow and six children.

FROM THE REV. THOMAS SPROULL, D.D.

ALLEGHENY, PA., December 8, 1863.

Reverend and dear Sir: In complying with your request for some personal recollections of the late Rev. James Blackwood, I find the material so abundant that I really feel embarrassed in making a selection. With Mr. Blackwood I became acquainted first in 1829, while I was a student of Theology. He was a member of the Pittsburg Presbytery, under the direction of which I prosecuted my studies. At my Ordination I became his co-presbyter, and enjoyed his friendship and his confidence till his death.

By those who did not know Mr. Blackwood intimately his character was not readily understood. With strangers he was somewhat formal and distant. He had a remarkable faculty of judging men at first sight. If his impressions of them were favourable, he would be very likely to seek an intimacy—if not, he would treat them with polite kindness. This was not mere caprice. His keen observation would detect something that a less scrutinizing eye would fail to notice. And with him the turning point of a man's character was his manhood, his truthfulness and his piety. If he found a person right in these respects, mere adventitious circumstances were overlooked, and the individual was received to his friendship.

He was of an ardent temperament,—strong in his attachments, and not less strong in his antipathies. If, in a moment of excitement, he should wound a friend by a keen remark,—and few could handle the weapon of sarcasm better than he,—as soon as the excitement subsided, he would make it manifest that he deeply felt the wound which he had himself inflicted, and would seek the earliest opportunity to remove the unpleasant feeling which he had unwittingly occasioned. This, within the circle of his intimate friends, was no difficult matter; for none but honourable men were admitted into it.

The personal appearance of Mr. Blackwood was dignified; and to a stranger it might possibly give the impression of something like superciliousness. But such an impression would do him great injustice. Few men whom I have known, occupying so high a position, and accustomed, as he had been, in the course of his education, to the most cultivated society, were more accessible to those who were in the humbler walks of life. This was especially manifest in his pastorate. The elderly men were addressed by him as *uncles*, and the elderly women as *aunties;* and it was a common saying, by his acquaintance, that Mr. Blackwood abounded in uncles and aunts. This was no mere movement of policy to secure influence. It was just the dictate of his warm and loving heart.

He was a man of exceedingly pure sensibility. This might be called his weak point. The knowledge of suffering never failed to draw forth his sympathies in a practical form. Yielding for the moment to feeling, without taking counsel of judgment, he could be easily imposed on. The same characteristic rendered him, at times, less useful in comforting the afflicted than otherwise he would have been. He could weep with those that weep, and rejoice with them that rejoice, as few other men could. But often, in the house of mourning, his utterance would be impeded by the welling up of sympathy from the fountain of his great heart. And, at times, in preaching, when the grand theme of Christ and Him crucified filled his soul, he would be forced to stop from the gush of feeling, that silence and tears, not words, can express.

Punctuality was a marked trait in Mr. Blackwood. I was a member of the same Presbytery with him for eighteen years, and I recollect only one meeting from which he was absent. I heard him say, not long before his death, that he had rarely been absent from any of the sessions of Synod at roll-call, and never absent from any of its meetings. In the Courts of the Church he was an active and useful, but not a noisy, member. He had the happy faculty of condensing his thoughts within narrow limits, and presenting the result of his reflections with great clearness. He loved the peace of Zion. The Pittsburg Presbytery, after the division of 1833, was composed of but five members. These Mr. Blackburn, in after days, often called "the old team," with reference to their harmony in judgment and action. Of these but two now survive.

In stature Mr. Blackwood was perhaps a little less than six feet. His form was quite erect, and his bearing soldierly. His hair was red, and his complexion exceedingly fair. He had clear blue eyes, overshadowed by heavy brows, and a highly intellectual forehead.

The social qualities of Mr. Blackwood were of the first order. His disposition was lively. Few men could contribute more to while away in pleasantry an hour of relaxation. But he could also entertain and profit in those seasons of religious intercourse when heart talks with heart. Though far enough from ostentation in religion, he would tell to the ear and to the experience of the confiding friend what God had done for his soul.

With kind regards your brother in the Gospel,
THOMAS SPROULL.

MOSES RONEY.*
1829—1854.

MOSES RONEY was born in Washington County, Pa., on the 20th of September, 1804. His parents were members of the Reformed Presbyterian Church, and were careful to train him up in the nurture and admonition of the Lord. In his fourteenth year he entered the Grammar School connected with Jefferson College, and in due time became a member of the College, where he graduated with the highest honours of his class in 1823. After his graduation he spent some time in teaching, in Baltimore, and then prosecuted the study of Theology under the direction of the Rev. Dr. Willson, at that time one of the most distinguished ministers of the Reformed Presbyterian Church. He was licensed to preach on the 8th of June, 1829, and at once took rank among the most popular preachers of his denomination.

After preaching in different places a few months, he was called to the pastoral charge of the Church in Newburgh, N. Y., and was ordained and installed there on the 8th of June, 1830.

* Ref. Presb., 1854.

In 1832 Mr. Roney was married to Elizabeth F., daughter of James Beattie, a Ruling Elder of the Coldenham Congregation.

Shortly after Mr. Roney's settlement, the great controversy took place in the Reformed Presbyterian Church, concerning the relations of the Church to the constituted authorities of the United States. Regarding the proposed changes with decided disapprobation, as an essential infringement upon the vital principles of the Church, he took strong ground in favour of adherence to the ancient landmarks. Though he was but a young man, he was among those who were most prominently identified with this controversy.

In 1836 he was unanimously chosen, by the Synod, to be the editor of a contemplated Monthly Magazine. The first number of this periodical,—"The Reformed Presbyterian,"—was issued in March following. He conducted this work with much ability, with the exception of a single year when he was at the South, until he had reached about the middle of the eighteenth volume, when this and all his other labours were terminated by death.

In the spring of 1843 Mr. Roney had a severe attack of inflammation of the lungs, which prepared the way for a hemorrhage in January of the next year. Though he partially recovered from these attacks, it was apparent to his friends that he was already the subject of an incipient pulmonary affection. In 1848 his health had become so much impaired that he felt constrained to resign his pastoral charge; though he did it with great reluctance and much to the regret of his people. In the autumn of 1847 and of 1848, he went South to avail himself of a milder climate during the winter; but, though this retarded the progress of the malady, it did nothing towards its removal. In 1849 he removed to Allegheny, Pa., having accepted an invitation from the Pittsburg Presbytery to take charge of their literary institution. Here he continued, labouring often beyond his strength, till the time of his departure had nearly come. The following letter addressed to his intimate friend, Mr. Andrew Bowden, of New York, and believed to be one of the last, if not the very last, that he ever wrote, will give some idea of the state of his mind in the prospect of the final change:—

PITTSBURG, June 20, 1854.

Very dear and highly esteemed friend: I have for months longed to communicate with you, but have been unable. In the expectation of friends, and in my own opinion, I was near the end of my earthly journey. It has pleased my Heavenly Father to give me a little respite, and I have been for a few days tolerably comfortable. I have no expectation that it will be of long continuance, but still it gives occasion for thankfulness to God, and is a ground of satisfaction. On two occasions I was really brought low; but though the Lord chastened me sorely, He did not give me over to death. My prayer is that, while I live, I may call on Him who is my only support and my only portion. I trust that, by his grace, "for me to live is Christ, and to die is gain." Oh that I may find the presence of the Good Shepherd when I come to enter the dark valley. My only trust is in the righteousness of Christ. My dependence is on the aid of the Holy Spirit. Oh, my friend, pray for me and that I may die in a triumphant faith. Mrs. R. is much fatigued from want of rest. &c. Still she and the children are mercifully kept in health. Give my warmest love, and what may perhaps be my last farewell, to Mrs. B. and all the family. My kind remembrance to all inquiring friends.

With love and esteem, I remain
Affectionately and truly yours,
M. RONEY.

From this time he gradually declined till the 3d of July following, when his earthly career closed in perfect peace.

Mr. Roney was the father of eight children, five of whom, with their mother survived him.

FROM THE REV. SAMUEL O. WYLIE.

PHILADELPHIA, November 3, 1863.

Reverend and dear Sir: It gives me pleasure to furnish you, for your forthcoming volume of the "Annals of the American Pulpit," some recollections of the late Rev. Moses Roney. My acquaintance with him extended through a period of fourteen years, beginning in 1842, at his own house in Newburgh. I had known him by reputation for years before; but this was the time and this the place of our first meeting. Subsequently he was often in my house, and I often in his; and our correspondence by letter was constant up to the time of his death. I can truly say that I had no more esteemed and valued friend.

The personal presence of Mr. Roney was more than ordinarily commanding. He was about six feet in height and large in proportion. His form was erect and remarkably well developed. His complexion was dark, eyes full and jet black, forehead high, face broad, and the whole expression highly intellectual and full of benignity and kindly feeling. His gait was advised and deliberate —he never seemed to be in a hurry. He had fine gentlemanly manners, and in every position was completely at his ease. He was extremely affable, inviting confidence and freedom from all whom he met. I have often been struck, in walking with him through the streets of Newburgh, to notice with what a large number of persons he seemed to be acquainted. He was singularly free from every thing like respect of persons. He had a salutation for every one; and it was offered as cordially to the man in tattered garments, covered with the dust and sweat of toil, as to the man of opulence and refinement. This polite deference which he showed to others did much to secure for him universal esteem and good will. As an evidence of the respect entertained for him, I may mention that, when he was on the eve of leaving Newburgh for Allegheny City, several persons, outside his congregation altogether, attended the sale of his furniture, and purchased small articles to be kept purely as mementos. His social qualities were admirable. His house was always open to his friends, and his numerous visitors always felt assured that he was glad to see them. He was gifted with rare powers of conversation, having, in this respect, few equals and scarcely a superior.

Mr. Roney gave early indications of an uncommonly vigorous mind. When a student in Jefferson College, his proficiency merited and received the commendation of his teachers, and his example was recommended by them to the imitation of others. It is known that his very rapid progress arrested the attention of the President of the College, the Rev. Dr. Brown, who spoke of him as a youth of remarkable promise. His mind was distinguished for strength and keenness, rather than originality. He possessed a large fund of general knowledge. He was remarkably well read, and was accurately posted as to current events, both at home and abroad. He was ready in debate, and could detect and expose a sophism with most damaging effect to an opponent. In the pulpit he appeared to excellent advantage. His manner was graceful; his gesture appropriate; his voice sonorous, well-tuned and of large compass; his eye brilliant, and his countenance at times wonderfully expressive He possessed, in a high degree, the elements of the Pulpit Orator, and, prior to the failure of his health, almost every sermon was marked by occasional bursts of impassioned and thrilling eloquence. It was a fault, perhaps, that occasionally, in his moments of fervid utterance, his voice seemed to be upon a strain. He belonged to the class of extemporaneous preachers. He seldom, and, in the later period of his ministry, perhaps never, wrote out a discourse. He did not even use notes in the pulpit. His sermons were commonly logical in arrangement, always instructive and thoroughly evangelical. The Royalty of Messiah was a favourite theme with him, and he insisted much on his claims as "Prince of the kings of the earth," and the duty of nations to acknowledge and submit to Him, and receive the law of God from his hand. He was a true patriot,—loved his country ardently, but was not blind to its faults. The omission to incorporate into the Constitution of the United States a formal recognition of the being of God, of the supremacy of his Law, and the dominion of Christ, he deemed highly criminal; and, not unfrequently, in his public discourses, he inveighed against the compromises of the Constitution in the interests of Slavery. I have heard him say that the fearful guilt of Slavery would be washed out by the best blood of the American people.

As a Pastor, Mr. Roney was greatly beloved. He was unwearied in his efforts to do good to his people, and to promote their temporal as well as spiritual welfare. Having considerable knowledge of Medicine, his advice was often sought and cheerfully given, though it was a point with him never to stand in the way of the Physician, but rather to encourage application to him. His executive abilities were superior, and he was frequently consulted on points of business. Cautious and sagacious, he was an eminently wise counsellor. His faculty for business was happily illustrated in the Councils of the Church. There was no better Presbyter. His knowledge of ecclesiastical law and forms of procedure was accurate and extensive. On these points he was looked up to as an authority. In Church Courts he occupied the floor less frequently than many others; but he was gifted with the faculty of knowing at what time to speak so as to make his influence tell to the best advantage. He seldom failed to carry his point. Before entering the ministry, and after the demission of his pastoral charge in consequence of shattered health, he was engaged in teaching. I have been told by those who had the best opportunities for judging, that his competency as a Teacher was unsurpassed. The Rev. Dr. Sproull, of Allegheny City, one of the Trustees of Westminster College, an institution of which Mr. Roney had the charge, assured me that he never knew an instance in which a Teacher commanded, to an equal extent, the reverence and affection of his pupils.

Mr. Roney was a lively and growing Christian. His piety was earnest but not obtrusive. Every thing like ostentation in religion was disgusting to him. With intimate friends he conversed freely in regard to personal religion, and in his private correspondence often referred to it. In prayer he breathed a filial spirit, and was happy in adapting himself to particular cases and circumstances. His patience under affliction was extraordinary. In this regard he had, as much as any one I ever knew, the mind of Christ. During the later years of his life he was greatly afflicted with difficulty of respiration, often gasping for breath; but ask him how he was, and he was always "very comfortable," or "very well for me." No one, I believe, ever heard a murmuring or complaining word escape from his lips. As his disease advanced, the difficulty of breathing was aggravated to such a degree that it was found necessary to keep him from sleeping more than a few minutes at a time, lest suffocation should be induced. He was compelled to sit most of the time in his chair. In this posture he was when death came to his relief, and found him rapt in vision as was Stephen, whose dying words he made his own.—"Lord Jesus, receive my spirit!"

Truly yours,
SAMUEL O. WYLIE.

HUGH WALKINSHAW.*
1832—1843.

Hugh Walkinshaw was born in the County of Antrim, Ireland, on the 15th of June, 1803. His parents were, at that time, members of the Presbyterian Church; and they seem to have designed him, from his early childhood, for the Ministry of the Gospel. In about his eighth year he commenced the study of Latin, which, with other kindred studies, he prosecuted, as he had opportunity, as long as he remained in Ireland. In 1819 his father, with his whole family, migrated to the United States, and settled in Belmont County, O. Some time after this he entered Franklin College, where he took the regular course, and graduated in the spring of 1827, being the second graduate of that institution. The next winter he commenced the study of Theology in Pittsburg, under the direction of Dr. Black; but, in the spring following, went to Philadelphia, where he completed his theological course under Dr. Wylie. In the summer of 1832 he was licensed to preach by the Philadelphia Presbytery. In 1834 he came within the bounds of the Pittsburg Presbytery, where he supplied vacancies, with much acceptance, till the following spring, when he received a call from the United Congregations of Brookland, North Washington, Union, Pine Creek, &c., and was ordained, and installed their Pastor, on the 15th of April, 1835. In 1841 his pastoral charge had so much increased as to render it desirable that it should be divided—the division, accordingly, took place, and he chose the part comprising Brookland and North Washington. Here he continued, a most laborious and faithful Pastor, till the close of his life.

About a year previous to his death, he was confined, for several weeks, by a fracture of one of his limbs. The effect of the bodily inactivity consequent upon this was the development of an organic disease of the liver. A dropsical affection, first in the extremities, and then in the body, ensued, which carried him gradually down to his grave. During the whole of his illness his spirit seemed in beautiful harmony with the Divine will, and he was evidently waiting in faith and hope and patience till his change should come. He died on the 19th of April, 1843, in the fortieth year of his age.

Shortly after his settlement in the Ministry, he was married to Lydia Jane, daughter of Robert Sproull, a member of his congregation. They became the parents of three children,—a son and two daughters.

FROM THE REV. THOMAS SPROULL, D.D

Allegheny, December 25, 1863.

My dear Sir: My acquaintance with the Rev. Hugh Walkinshaw was so intimate that I have no fear of making any erroneous estimate of his character, while yet my relationship to him by his marriage with my sister was so near that it may possibly seem to some a matter of questionable delicacy that I should undertake any account of him for the purpose for which you have requested it. I shall not, however, suffer any scruples of this kind to prevail against your request, but will with pleasure communicate to you my impressions of my lamented brother-in-law, availing myself, to

* Ref. Presb., 1843.

some extent, of something that I wrote concerning him when my recollections of him were more fresh than at present.

Mr. Walkinshaw possessed many desirable natural endowments. He had not only a sound judgment and retentive memory, but a clear discernment also. And his mind was well cultivated. His learning was more solid than showy; rather enriching with its real worth than dazzling with its superficial splendour. But all his acquirements he made subservient to the great work of glorifying God in the salvation of men. With this view, he was a diligent student of the Scriptures in their originals; and the importance of this he endeavoured to impress on the minds of others. The Hebrew Bible was among the first books which he put into the hands of young men who sought to avail themselves of his instruction.

Mr. Walkinshaw was highly favoured also in respect to his moral constitution. Between fickleness and obstinacy he kept the proper medium,—neither the subject of changeful caprice, nor the slave of perverse determination. But he was as true to his own convictions as the needle to the pole—the path of duty once ascertained, nothing remained for him but calmly and diligently to pursue it, no matter what measure of opposition might be arrayed against him. Naturally fond of society, his manner and spirit and whole character rendered him at once an agreeable and profitable companion. He possessed also a high sense of honour—his noble spirit could never stoop to a mean action. And his heart warmed with genuine benevolence towards his fellow-men—his hand opened instinctively to aid the children of want, and he was always on the alert to avail himself of opportunities for doing good.

He was strongly attached to the distinctive principles of his own Church. With these he made himself thoroughly acquainted before he embraced them; and they were always prominent in his pulpit exhibitions. Every thing that seemed to him like a removal of the old landmarks he watched with a jealous eye. To any connection of the Church with voluntary associations for promoting morality he was opposed, believing that their tendency was to lessen her power, and that they would ultimately fail of accomplishing their proposed end. On his death-bed he said,—"I am sensible that my ministry has been very imperfect, but I can truly say that I am now thankful that I have never been a member of any of those voluntary associations." Not that he had any sympathy with those who made this a pretext for leaving the Church—on the contrary, he viewed their conduct with strong disapprobation—both his conversation and his prayers evidenced the strongest desire that the integrity of the Church might be preserved.

He was a diligent and faithful Pastor. Naturally active and enterprising, he was placed in circumstances favourable to the development and exercise of these qualities. At his Ordination he was placed over a congregation of more than two hundred members, and scattered over an area of many miles in circumference. To discharge pastoral duty to such a flock was no easy task, and yet no murmur of dissatisfaction from his people was ever heard. So tenderly were they all attached to him that, when the congregation was divided, both parts strongly urged their claims to him as their Pastor. Nor did he find it easy to submit to a separation from any part of a flock which he so tenderly loved.

He was an instructive, earnest, deeply evangelical Preacher. His discourses were neither fitted nor designed to captivate the multitude, but to impress Divine truth, in all its purity and power, upon the heart and conscience. And many who heard the Word from his lips will no doubt be at once witnesses to his fidelity and gems in his crown. Though he was not inclined to be communicative in respect to his own religious experience, those who were on terms of confidential intimacy with him, knew that he lived in near and constant communion with God, and there is no doubt that this was one of the leading elements of his power in the pulpit. Among his last discourses was one from John xvii, 24: "Father, I will that they also whom thou hast given me be with me where I am, that they may behold the glory which thou hast given me." This discourse, which was delivered under great bodily infirmity, and heard by many under the impression that it would be his last, produced a powerful effect. It was worthy to be his last testimony in honour of the cause which was dearer to him than life.

Mr. Walkinshaw, as he was deeply interested in all that involved or pertained to the welfare of his own Church, was prompt and regular in his attendance upon her Judicatories, whenever his health would permit; and his influence on these occasions we always felt to be in the right direction. His brethren were attracted by the kindliness of his spirit, while they confided in his wisdom and sound judgment.

Yours in the Gospel,
THOMAS SPROULL.

FROM THE REV. R. HUTCHESON.

Grove Hill, Iowa, March 4, 1864.

My dear Sir: I very gladly comply with your request that I should send you some personal recollections of the Rev. H. Walkinshaw, a Minister of the Reformed Presbyterian Church. My personal acquaintance with him commenced about the time of his call to the congregation of which he took charge, and continued till his decease. For nearly four years I was a student, reciting to him almost daily, in the Languages and Theology; and, during most of that time, I resided with him as a member of his household. His father was a Ruling Elder, and one of those faithful men who seldom or never give to the world so much as an hour that belongs to the service of religion. He owned a mill, and whether it was family-worship, prayer-meeting, sessional or congregational assembly, or week-day preaching, the mill was always certain to be shut down. Whatever was the occasion, he and his family were there, and there in time.

As to Mr. Walkinshaw's personal appearance, he was of about the middle height, of a slender figure, spare face, and youthful visage. In dress and general aspect he was remarkably genteel. His countenance, when at rest, wore a slight cast of melancholy, but, on meeting an acquaintance, this readily gave way to a smile of easy cheerfulness. The air of sadness to which I refer was probably occasioned by a disease on the liver which terminated his life.

His manners were free from all stiffness and formality, and were evidently an expression of the sincerity and honesty of his heart. He hated every thing that savoured of pretence; cheerful and free in conversation, he was the same at home as abroad. In discussion he could maintain his own views firmly without being dictatorial. He wasted no time in company which was required for his studies. The only thing in connection with his manners that I ever heard subjected to criticism, was his reserve on the days that he devoted to his preparation for the pulpit. In public he was never at a loss—while he appeared to feel the weight of his responsibility, he seemed always fully master of the subject in hand. His visage wore a very pleasant aspect in the pulpit,—solemn in prayer, bright and earnest in preaching.

His habits were all ministerial. He engaged in no speculations or employments aside from his appropriate work. If he laboured an hour or two in his garden, it was to invigorate body and mind for higher service. In training a few students, he did not consider himself as stepping out of his direct course any more than in examining, licensing and ordaining them. Even in our literary preparation he required us to study *theologically*. During our study of the Greek language, we read the New Testament largely and closely, with an exercise occasionally in the Septuagint. Simultaneously with the Greek we commenced the Hebrew Grammar,—not exactly as a study,—a kind of semi-recreation in the place of light reading—it wasted no time. While others were debating, in public speeches and periodical essays, the propriety of Christian classics, he was quietly inaugurating the system, as far as the range of his influence extended. He expected his students to read Hebrew fluently before entering the Theological Seminary; and an acquaintance with the original Scriptures he preferred to a College Diploma, where both could not be obtained. One of his students, the Rev. R. J. Dodds, is a Missionary in Latakieh, a town at the foot of Mount Lebanon, and is considered one of the best Arabic scholars now in Syria.

His preaching was always interesting—he entered into his subject with earnestness, and studied diligently to know for himself what was the mind of the Spirit on each particular theme. In lecturing on portions of Scripture, he studied critically the originals, but made no parade of learning—he would neither startle us with new translations, nor alarm us with errors in the old. He endeavoured to give doctrine and practice their due proportion, and spoke fully and boldly of the evils of the time, and of the place where he preached. His discourses were rather intellectual than emotional, and his arguments addressed to the judgment rather than to the feelings. The distinctive principles of our Church received their due share of his attention—he was a *Covenanter*, and could give a clear exposition of his principles,—their nature, their foundation, their practical bearing, their importance, without giving unnecessary offence to persons of other communions. The standards of the Church were no impediment to him in preaching—he never had occasion to run against them—he was attached to all the attainments of Scotland's Second Reformation. He was nothing intimidated by the hue and cry of " politics in the pulpit," but exhibited the Divine law in all its bearings, whether it touched the politics of the nation or the conscience of the individual.

When his congregation became so large as to render a division necessary, each branch wished to engage him for their Pastor, all regarding him with strong affection. In the Courts of the Lord's House he was highly respected. The great weight which he possessed there was not the result of profound intellect, splendid eloquence, or any one, two or more accomplishments—it arose from an orderly balance of all the powers, intellectual, moral and spiritual. He spoke little of himself, either in public or private. I do not remember ever to have heard him drop a word about his own Christian experience, previous to his last illness. His spirituality was not of the same type with that of McCheyne or Harlan Page; but every one acquainted with him felt that there was a good man there. Once, when he had received an appointment to preach in a certain locality, a lady of his acquaintance charged the people to be kind to him, urging, as a reason, that, if there was a good man living, he was one. How much I have seen men labour to make the same impression; and how often I have seen them fail. His last remark, when I visited him on his death-bed, threw much light upon the inward workings of his soul. Seeing his strength so much reduced, I determined to leave him without bidding him farewell. He comprehended the movement, and, just as I was closing the door, gave me this advice,—" Be careful of all Christ's interests, and he will take care of yours."

My happiest years were passed with him and his amiable wife—both of them now removed from earth—not lost but gone before.

Yours in the service of Christ,
R. HUTCHESON.

JOHN McKINLEY.*
1835—1841.

JOHN McKINLEY, a son of John and Abigail (Brannan) McKinley, was born in Philadelphia, July 18, 1815. From his early childhood the love of knowledge seemed to be his ruling passion; and, as his faculties developed, his application to books became so intense as to put his health for some time in serious jeopardy. He was particularly distinguished, even at a very early age, for fine powers of elocution; insomuch that he attracted the attention of some of the most gifted and accomplished men in Philadelphia. At the age of eleven he entered the classical school of the Rev. Dr. Willbank, in his native city, and, after spending three years at that institution, was admitted a member of the University of Pennsylvania. Notwithstanding he was now only fourteen years of age, he maintained a very high standing in his class throughout his whole College course, and graduated with the first honour in 1833.

He seems to have had the Ministry in his eye from early childhood; and, when he graduated at College, his purpose to devote himself to this work was thoroughly matured. Accordingly, he connected himself immediately with the Theological Seminary of the Reformed Presbyterian Church, then under the care of the late Rev. Dr. Samuel B. Wylie. Here he remained a most diligent and successful student for two years or more, and was licensed to preach the Gospel, by the Reformed Presbytery of Philadelphia, in 1835. As he had not, at this time, reached his majority, his father, who was a member of the Presbytery that licensed him, consented, not without great reluctance, to his being licensed at so early an age; and it was only on the express condition that he should remain for some time in Philadelphia that he was persuaded to give his consent at all. He filled several appointments in the West, and preached, for some time, with great acceptance, in the city of Cincinnati. Subsequently, he was called to the Reformed Presbyterian Congregation in Milton, Northumberland County, Pa., where he was ordained and installed in the year 1838. Here he laboured with great acceptance and success until his declining health compelled him to resign his charge,—which he did in the year 1841. He did not long survive his resignation: he died on the 5th of October of the same year; and all who knew him recognized in his death the extinction of one of the bright lights of the Church.

Mr. McKinley was married, April 29, 1839, to Frances Wells Lanphear, of Cincinnati, O. His only child, a daughter, is now (1864) the wife of the Rev. Robert McMillan, Pastor of the Reformed Presbyterian Church in New Castle, Pa.

Mr. McKinley's only publication is a series of articles on the Slave Trade, which appeared in the Miltonian, a weekly paper issued in Milton, Pa.

FROM THE HON. JAMES POLLOCK, LL.D.,
EX-GOVERNOR OF PENNSYLVANIA.

PHILADELPHIA, December 28, 1863.

Dear Sir: I have felt some hesitation about complying with your request for my recollections of the Rev. John McKinley—it has arisen, however, solely from a consciousness of my inability to do justice to the memory of one whose ministry, though brief, was brilliant, and whose whole life beautifully illustra-

---
* Obituary by Dr. S. B. Wylie.—MS. from Dr. T. W. J. Wylie.

ted the doctrines he taught, and presented an example of the highest style of Man,—the Christian Gentleman.

My first acquaintance with Mr. McKinley was in the year 1838, when he visited Milton, then my residence, and preached as a supply to the Reformed Presbyterian Church of that place. The impression made, at that time, by his preaching, on that congregation, was so favourable that he was soon after unanimously called to the pastorate of the Churches in Milton and McEwensville. The call was accepted, and he at once entered upon the performance of the duties thus devolved upon him. The relation, thus formed between Pastor and people, was characterized by mutual and constantly increasing confidence and love.

At the time of his Installation Mr. McKinley had just reached his legal majority—young in years, but of full stature in wisdom and grace. Wisdom supplied age, and grace gave him strength to assume and perform the duties of his sacred office.

He was a man of cultivated intellect, of sound and discriminating judgment, of generous sympathies and noble impulses and fervent piety. His physical organization was delicate—his stature below the medium—of a thin, spare habit, and indicating, by his general appearance, that the most insidious of all diseases had marked him for its victim. His phrenological developments indicated a mind of no ordinary character. His head was well formed; his eye clear and bright; and his face full of intelligence and kindness. These qualities shone in his daily life; won every heart, and made all regard him as their friend.

In his social intercourse he was pleasant and affable. His social and pastoral visits were occasions of pleasure and profit. With a mind well filled with classic lore and the best of the current literature of his day, and with conversational powers of a high order, he delighted and instructed those around him; but, however varied and interesting the subjects of conversation, Christ and his salvation were never excluded. Religion sanctified his learning, and gave both impress and character to his conversation. The young and the old revered and loved him.

His pulpit exercises were of a superior order. His sermons were carefully and well prepared, evidently "the beaten oil of the sanctuary," and full of the blessings of the Gospel of peace. They were seldom written in full, and never read in the pulpit. His notes were copious, and these he usually had with him during the delivery of his sermon, but scarcely ever referred to them. The arrangement of his discourses was natural, perspicuous, logical. His exegesis of the Scriptures was clear, comprehensive and learned, without affectation or pedantry; bringing out, in simple and admirable order, the truths contained in the text. Although his sermons were delivered without having been committed to memory, or even written, yet his command of language was so great that, had they been accurately reported, they might have been given to the press without putting in jeopardy his reputation as a scholar. I never heard him deliver what would be called, in common parlance, "a poor sermon." On the contrary, his sermons were all finished productions; and, whilst they pleased by their elegant and graceful diction, they appealed to the hearts and consciences of his hearers with a power that was often irresistible. His gesticulation was graceful and natural, and his general style of delivery attractive, forcible, and often impassioned.

His weekly lectures were highly interesting and instructive. His exposition of the Scriptures on these occasions was luminous, simple, and in a high degree satisfactory. The prayer-meeting and the Bible class, together with the Sabbath school, shared his labours and his love. He was eminently a man of God; intent on doing his will; "instant in season and out of season." He felt that his time was short, and he laboured the more earnestly to do the work to which he had been called. He realized personally, in all the solemnity of its import, the injunction,—" Work while it is called to-day." He had much to do, but little time—he did it all, and did it well.

He was no bigot. His views on all subjects connected with the Church of Christ, in its organization and doctrines, were liberal and enlightened. Attached to his own denomination, he recognized as brethren all the followers of Jesus,—his and their Saviour. Christ was the name, and Christian the character, he loved above all others.

He died in the midst of his usefulness and with his harness on. He died in his youth—not too early for himself, but too early for his family and friends, for his congregation and the Church of God. What was loss to earth, in his death, was gain to Heaven. Yours very sincerely,

JAMES POLLOCK.

FROM THE REV. T. W. J. WYLIE, D.D.

PHILADELPHIA, January 6, 1864.

Rev. and dear Sir: The Rev. John McKinley, concerning whom you inquire, was a companion of my boyhood, and a dear friend as long as he lived. I desire to record with gratitude the benefit which I derived myself from his wise and kind counsels, and I am sure that there are many others who would acknowledge similar obligations.

Mr. McKinley was early and thoroughly instructed in the truths of religion. It might be said of him that, "from a child, he knew the Holy Scriptures;" and he was perfectly familiar with the "form of sound words" contained in the Assembly's Catechism. Such was his pre-eminence in my father's catechetical class that he was presented as a model to all the other pupils. From a very early age he was ardently desirous to become a Minister of the Gospel; and having been told that *eating sugar* might injure his teeth, and impair his power of speaking distinctly, he refused to use it, and continued to abstain from it as long as he lived. His mother, a person of eminent piety and most amiable disposition, died while he was quite young; but the influence of her example and instruction was increased and hallowed by her early death. He possessed great oratorical powers, and both in composition and elocution he was regarded as remarkable. In the University he stood in the foremost rank in all his studies. Having entered at once, after his graduation, upon the study of Theology, he made the same rapid progress here as he had done in his collegiate course. As a Preacher, he was solemn, earnest and instructive. His words were fitly spoken; and he united two qualities not often found combined,—namely, he was never at a loss for *a* word, and never at a loss for *the* word. Few possessed greater power to arrest and retain the attention of an audience. Out of the pulpit, he was still the minister of Christ, and, in the social circle as well as by his correspondence, he endeavoured to "do good as he had opportunity." In argument he was logical, candid, courteous. His "speech was always with grace, seasoned with salt;" and he seemed to "know how to answer every man." Although his health was very delicate, he was unsparing in his labours, and his exposure and exertion in attending night meetings, if it did not occasion, certainly hastened, his premature death. His ministerial career was short, and, after a pastorate of about three years, he returned to Philadelphia to die. I had not the privilege of being present with him during his last illness, but those who attended upon him were deeply impressed with the steadfastness of his faith, his calm resignation to the will of God, and his ripeness for the Heavenly world. His influence for good has survived his earthly life, and his memory is still gratefully cherished by the people of his charge, as well as by many others who had the privilege of his acquaintance.

With great regard I am affectionately yours,

T. W. J. WYLIE.

ALPHABETICAL INDEX.

NAMES OF THE SUBJECTS.

	PAGE.		PAGE.
Black, John D.D.	28	McKinney, James	1
Blackwood, James	77	McLeod, Alexander, D.D.	9
Cannon, John	68	McMaster, Gilbert D.D.	46
Donnelly, Thomas	25	Reily, John	60
Gibson, Robert	71	Roney Moses	79
Gibson, William	6	Walkinshaw, Hugh	83
Kell, John	62	Wallace, Robert	66
Madden, Campbell	75	Willson, James Renwick, D.D.	30
McKinley, John	87	Wylie, Samuel Brown, D.D.	34

NAMES OF THOSE WHO HAVE FURNISHED ORIGINAL LETTERS.

	PAGE.		PAGE.
Black, John D.D.	22	Moffat, James C., D.D.	59
Forsyth, John, D.D.	37, 44	Pollock, Hon. James, LL.D.	87
How, Samuel B., D.D.	35	Reed, Hon. William B.	36
Houston, Thomas, D.D.	73	Scott, Rev. David	72
Hutcheson, Rev. R.	85	Sloane, Rev. William	8
James, William, D.D.	56	Sproull, Thomas, D.D.	67, 69, 78, 83
McLeod, John N., D.D.	28	Willson, James M., D.D.	42
MacMaster, Erasmus D., D.D.	51	Wylie, Samuel B., D.D.	5, 21
McMaster, Gilbert, D.D.	1, 18	Wylie, Rev. Samuel	60, 65
McMillan, Rev. Gavin	26, 63	Wylie, Rev. Samuel O	81
McMillan, Hugh, D.D.	75	Wylie, T. W. J,, D.D.	54, 89
Miller, Samuel, D.D.	23		

NAMES INCIDENTALLY INTRODUCED IN THE TEXT OR THE NOTES.

	PAGE.		PAGE.
Black, Andrew Wylie	33	King, William	25
Black, John	33	MacMaster, Erasmus D., D.D.	48
Black, Robert John	33, 34	Milligan, James	48, 49

www.ingramcontent.com/pod-product-compliance
Lightning Source LLC
Chambersburg PA
CBHW051726300426
44115CB00007B/488